Bedeah

BARB

NTRY

King Tom's towns

Nyaro

Cavally River

Taboo is 20 miles from
Cavally R. on the Co
Rockbooka

Mouth of Cavally R. 1 mile wide

Rice farm

Slave-town

Watta

Kabluh

GRAND CAVALIS
or Kabluh-kah

Cavally R. station

HALF CAVALLY
or
Bwehteh

kah O

Cavally station

Bweh deh

T R

GRAWAY
or
Blegeh

Rice

Graway station

Cassada
Farms

Blegeh

Yah

Graway Point

MAP OF THE
GREBO COUNTRY,
CAPE PALMAS
WEST AFRICA.
1841.

◻ Mission Stations.
○ Native Towns.

ON AFRIC'S SHORE

A History of Maryland in Liberia

1834–1857

RICHARD L. HALL

BALTIMORE
MARYLAND HISTORICAL SOCIETY

Library of Congress Cataloging-in-Publication Data

Hall, Richard L., 1961–
    On Afric's shore : a history of Maryland in Liberia, 1834–1857 /
Richard L. Hall.
        p. cm.
    Includes bibliographical references (p.) and index.
    ISBN 0-938420-86-0 (alk. paper)
        1. African Americans—Colonization—Liberia. 2. Maryland
State Colonization Society. 3. Liberia—History—To 1847.
4. Liberia—History—1847–1944. 5. African Americans—
Maryland—History—19th century.
I. Maryland Historical Society. II. Title.

DT633.H35 2003
346.82'086—dc21

                                                2003048786

Manufactured in Canada.
The paper used in this publication meets the minimum
requirements of the American National Standard for Information
Sciences Permanence of Paper or Printed Library Materials
ANSI Z39.48-1984.

For Wendy and Daniel

Contents

ANNOTATED ROLL OF SETTLERS IN
MARYLAND IN LIBERIA, 1820–1854
433

Illustrations

Preface and Acknowledgments

I have always been amazed at the way in which small events and seemingly random circumstances can change a life. The present book began innocently enough in 1982 as an undergraduate term paper at the Johns Hopkins University. Among many things, I was interested in African history, and particularly in agriculture, issues of development, and the interaction of cultures. The Department of History in those days had a very strong emphasis along these lines, shared with the Department of Anthropolgy in the Atlantic Seminar, which treated the whole Atlantic world as one great interrelated theatre of history.

I had encountered references to Maryland in Liberia in my studies. Bell Wiley's posthumous book, *Slaves No More,* caught my imagination. This was a compilation of letters from freed slaves in Liberia to their former masters—among them a few from Cape Palmas. Though the book stated that these were all that could be found, I hoped there might be more. It occurred to me that I could examine agricultural efforts by settlers at Cape Palmas in the nineteenth century in the context of later ventures in the colonial and post-colonial periods. The efforts of Americans then presaged projects still undertaken today. Off I went to the Maryland Historical Society, expecting to find a small archive which I could examine and interpret in a few pages. My mind was changed immediately, for I found some sixty boxes filled with letters and accounts. Opening at random, I found Commodore Perry and the United States Navy, with letters from individuals who could hardly write their names, expressing themselves frankly and in remarkably sophisticated terms. I found not only a rich record of agricultural development but an extensive and compelling document of the life of a community with a compelling story.

I found myself generating paper after paper on different aspects of this place and finished my undergraduate days with a concurrent B.A./ M.A. in 1984. This was followed with a grant from the State of Maryland, which permitted me to transcribe the entire African correspondence of the Maryland State Colonization Society, during which time I continued as a Fellow in the Department of History. The following year I was able to continue with a fellowship in the Writing Seminars of Johns Hopkins, during which I wrote the first few chapters and mapped out the rest. Clearly, this book would not exist had it not been for the scholarly environment in which I was immersed at Hopkins.

More than twenty years have passed since I first discovered Maryland in Liberia, and circumstances have led me away from the life of a professional historian, but all along I have maintained an interest in the subject and kept at it. It is a hard thing to explain to those who have not felt it the historian's sense of acquaintance and trusteeship to the people he studies. One comes to know them and their lives in a very personal way and feels an obligation to tell the story. They become one's company in what is often a lonely avocation.

I have many people to thank for their guidance and other assistance along the way. As I have said, the intellectual environment in which I worked and learned at Johns Hopkins was invaluable. Professors in several departments were generous with their time and knowledge, applied across disciplines. In particular, I benefited from the wisdom of Philip D. Curtin, David Cohen, Ronald Walters, John Russell-Wood, Stewart Leslie, Sidney Mintz, Jack P. Greene, David Harvey, John Cady, and Horace F. Judson. Christopher Steiner, whose interests paralleled mine, was a great help. A number of individuals have read all or part of the work in progress. Their opinions and critiques, sometimes painful, have shaped this. Among them I would like to thank Eugene Genovese, Christopher Phillips, and T. Stephen Whitman. I extend a special thank-you to Robert Cottom, publisher of the Press at the Maryland Historical Society, for his patient guidance and close editing of a large and sometimes rambling manuscript. Finally, and probably most difficult to express, my family, who have been with me through this, for what few words can express their wonderful and sustaining devotion? I will say simply thank you, and they may rely on my gratitude.

Richard L. Hall
College Park, Maryland

"Two Warring Ideals"

HERE FOLLOWS A STORY OF AFRICA AND AMERICA, OF PHILANTHROPY and prejudice, of the struggle of a people to define and main tain their cultural identity, and of their legacy. Since 1619, when a Dutch slaver deposited her miserable cargo for sale at Jamestown, Africa has played a critical role in the history of race in North America. Often, white America has used Africa to identify and ascribe negative characteristics to black Americans, who, in turn, have used Africa for their own purposes, often as a symbol of freedom. The image of Americans of African descent returning to the land of their ancestors, with its Biblical parallels, has been a particularly powerful symbol.[1]

In the first half of the nineteenth century, symbol was turned into fact, as white organizations colonized black Americans in Africa. White men told black men that there was no hope for them in America, and that their only home was Africa. The vast majority of black people virulently resented the suggestion, but a few accepted the offer of freedom, a few acres of land, and the opportunity to start a new life. In Africa, they adapted to a radically different physical and cultural environment than they had known, and in the process created distinctive cultural enclaves. One of these was Maryland in Liberia, which the Maryland State Colonization Society established in 1834 at Cape Palmas, near Liberia's present border with Cote d'Ivoire. Today, Maryland in Liberia scarcely exists: climate, economic change, and civil war having wiped away almost all trace of the bustling American expatriate community which existed there in the mid-nineteenth century.[2]

The State of Maryland supported the venture with a liberal grant, continued for more than twenty-five years. The funding was explicitly unconstitutional, but legislators were more interested in an expedient way around racial problems than niceties of law. The active supporters of the Maryland State Colonization Society were, overall, moderate white men, engaged in learned professions and civic-minded. They reacted against the ambiguous goals of the American Colonization Society with regard to slavery, proclaiming their intent to "extirpate" slavery in Maryland. They believed that black people could not compete in a white-dominated, prejudiced society; therefore the only reasonable course for their elevation was to remove them to Africa, where they could develop freely. Rather patronizingly, they thought that black Americans needed social, economic, and political training. To secure this end, they designed a government and policies on utopian, even quixotic, principles. They had an "Ethiopian" vision: that one day their Christian, agrarian commonwealth would spread across the African continent, and "stretch forth its hands unto God." The image was distorted and self-serving, yet its Biblical root and parallels were obvious and appealing.[3]

Others saw a terrible danger in the idea. The great majority of black people, in Maryland and in the United States as a whole, emphatically refused to migrate to Africa. In the 1830s, most Americans of African descent had generations of forebears in the New World. Probably, many had mixed European and African ancestry, and personal memory of Africa was rare. African captives were gathered in desperate circumstances and traumatized in their passage through the markets and across the Atlantic to a life of servitude. The memory of Africa was often unpleasant, and American popular culture fostered the image of the homeland as a region of deserts, serpents, horrid diseases, and savages, in part to quash any desire to run away. With no other source of geographic knowledge, black Americans of the day typically echoed the negative stereotype.[4]

On one level, an ongoing intellectual argument raged against colonization, namely, that people of color in America had sweated and struggled and died thanklessly for generations to make the United States a prosperous country. Their culture was American, and they demanded nothing less than equal citizenship with white Americans. On another level, the argument against colonization was more visceral and xenophobic: the image of burning sands and cannibals having their influence. When colonization agents traveled the Maryland countryside to enlist emigrants, they spoke glowingly of the beauty of Africa and the potential of black people for greatness there. Abolitionists opposed to colonization quietly followed them. They could not tell slaves that they must demand equal citizenship, rather they filled them with horror of the unknown. "The Blacks have been told that I disign to sell them as slaves," wrote one frustrated agent from the Eastern Shore in 1836, "that on their arrival in Baltimore they will be put in irons — that on their passage to Africa they will have nothing to eat. Consequently many of them will die with hunger, that those who so die will be *pickled like pork*, to be eaten by those who survive, that on their arrival at Africa they will be stripped naked, and turned loose on the shore to perish."[5]

Still, some eleven hundred black Americans—men, women, and children; some slave, some freedmen, some freeborn; most from Maryland—did emigrate to Cape Palmas between 1833 and 1856. The immediate circumstances of departure varied. The society insisted upon voluntary emigration, although some slaves were freed on condition they go to Cape Palmas, or face the auction block. These settlers were not empty shells, ready to contain whatever culture the society chose. In fact they were decidedly American in their social and cultural values. They felt the sting of rejection by white society all the more strongly because of it, for what is the cruelty of a jailer compared with the repudiation of a brother?[6]

Perhaps no one has stated more eloquently the critical ambiguity of African American identity than W. E. B. DuBois, who was himself an intellectual heir to such men as Alexander Crummell and Edward Wilmot Blyden, whose ideologies matured on African soil. "After the Egyptian and Indian, the Greek and Roman, the Teuton and Mongolian," he wrote in his classic, *The Souls of Black Folk*,

> the Negro is a sort of seventh son, born with a veil, and gifted with
> second-sight in this American world, a world which yields him no
> true self-consciousness, but only lets him see himself through the
> revelation of the other world. It is a peculiar sensation, this double-
> consciousness, this sense of always looking at one's self through the
> eyes of others, of measuring one's soul by the tape of a world that
> looks on in amused contempt and pity. One ever feels his two-ness,
> an American, a Negro; two souls, two thoughts, two unreconciled
> strivings; two warring ideals in one dark body, whose dogged strength
> alone keeps it from being torn asunder.

DuBois asserted that the history of black people in America was fundamentally the story of their search for a place in American society as a
people with distinct gifts and a valuable contribution to make: "This,
then, is the end of his striving: to be a co-worker in the kingdom of
culture, to escape both death and isolation, to husband and use his best
powers and his latent genius." He recalled the tragic waste of talent that
shadowed the history of black people: "Throughout history, the powers of single black men flash here and there like falling stars, and die
sometimes before the world has rightly gauged their brightness." The
paralysis and apparent weakness of black people he attributed to the
conflict between American black culture and the dominant white culture. As he expressed it, "This waste of double aims, this seeking to
satisfy two unreconciled ideals, has wrought sad havoc with the courage and faith and deeds of ten thousand thousand people, — has sent
them often wooing false gods and invoking false means of salvation,
and at times has even seemed to make them ashamed of themselves." In
this context, colonization was one of those false means of salvation,
and places like Maryland in Liberia offered emigrants the chance, "to
be both a Negro and an American, without being cursed and spit upon
by his fellows, without having the doors of Opportunity closed roughly
in his face."[7]

Although some of the emigrants to Maryland in Liberia were not
up to the rigors of frontier life or lacked any particular ideological
motivation, the majority were hardy souls. They went to Africa for
precisely the same reasons that inspired the westward movement of

European settlers across North America: cheap or free land, economic opportunity, the chance to live, think, and worship in freedom, and the prospect that succeeding generations would have better lives. Moreover, settlers of Maryland in Liberia had a sense that they must prove a point to the rest of the world—that they could live and prosper as well as any other community. *On Afric's Shore* records their efforts to do just that.

The colonization movement has always been something of an illegitimate child of American historiography. It has functioned in the literature as a foil, against which the abolition movement is more clearly understood. This treatment derives from the ambiguous, sometimes hypocritical intentions of colonizationists, combined with the fact that their goal of removing the black population from the United States failed. And because the white promoters of the scheme were suspect, the influence of their ideas, particularly upon black Americans, has been discounted or overlooked. Yet the very vehemence of the debate between colonizationists and abolitionists evidences the power of the colonization ideology, right or wrong.

The leaders of the Maryland State Colonization Society were conscious of the paradoxes that underpinned the national organization. Twenty-five years before the Civil War, they formulated an ideology of black Christian nationality that would persist in the Pan-African and other nationalist movements for generations to come. Settlers shared their enthusiasm. There is an immense web of connections between the Maryland State Colonization Society, its settlers, and the leaders of black intellectual and political life in the second half of the nineteenth century. Alexander Crummell, Edward Wilmot Blyden, and Martin Delany, for instance, all have Maryland links. The Prophet Harris, founder of a Christian sect widespread in West Africa, and William V. S. Tubman, president of Liberia for many years this century, were also products of the former Maryland colony. In the records of Maryland, one often encounters individuals scarcely able to write their name arguing points of law and civil rights in a manner impossible in the old country. Many of these settlers had continuing contacts with family and friends in America. The society sustained an extensive propaganda in favor of black nationalism in Africa that may have failed to spur emigration but still sparked debate and thought.

Relentless adversity made the American community at Cape Palmas a cultural and intellectual hothouse. Confronted with an ecological and social challenge, the American enclave was forced to act cooperatively and with a strong sense of purpose. The present work explores issues of land tenure and environmental change as they affected the community's development. It also examines the problematic dialectic between settlers and the Africans among whom they settled. It is not intended to accuse but to illustrate the complex set of relationships that shaped the history of Maryland in Liberia.

The literature on African American culture and its relationship to African culture is massive. The scholarship is conclusive enough that aspects of African culture survived in America here and there.[8] However, at Cape Palmas, the question is turned on its ear. There, Americans of African descent came face to face with Africans. Their experience challenges the significance of African components in black American culture. While scholars of African American history emphasize the points that differentiate black culture from white culture, West African historiography treats settlers of the Liberian colonies as interlopers, in the same category as Europeans. Moreover, Africans typically referred to settlers as "white" regardless of the color of their skin—culture being the determinant of race. Settlers regarded themselves as Americans sojourning in Africa, and nothing insulted them more than to be regarded as Africans.

Generations later, many black Americans have come to identify ever more closely with Africa. In the antebellum period, black people looked to the day when slavery would end as the day of salvation, when a new era of equality and peace would dawn. The failure of that dream, for a thousand reasons, has led many since that time to idealize a lost motherland and to adopt signs and symbols of that affection.[9]

Scholars have, for the most part, overlooked Maryland in Liberia. One encounters sweeping conclusions without evidence. With the exception of the casual memoirs of a founder of the society and a Johns Hopkins doctoral dissertation of 1892, the place was forgotten until the mid-1960s when two graduate students studied it. The better work is Jane Jackson Martin's, "The Dual Legacy: Government Authority and Mission Influence Among the Glebo of Eastern Liberia, 1834–1910," submitted to the faculty of Boston University in 1968 but never published. An effort in historical anthropology, the work concerned the impact of foreign contact, particularly of the large Episcopal Mission, on the indigenous inhabitants of Maryland County. The author's principle source of information is the archive of the Episcopal Church, and because the mission was often at odds with settlers and their government, the colony does not get a very favorable account. Penelope Campbell published her dissertation, *Maryland in Africa: The Maryland State Colonization Society, 1831–1857,* at the University of Illinois Press in 1971. The author concerns herself with the society's ideology and domestic operations, reduced to a dry recounting of chronic financial shortfall. The African side of the story is not elaborated to any great degree. Moreover, the author writes with the conviction that most settlers were whining complainers, concluding,

> Given every advantage money could buy, that spark of industry and enterprise necessary for greatness could not be kindled. Most colonists resisted all efforts to create a flourishing settlement of which their benefactors could be proud. The tendency of the ex-American slaves to look down upon the Africans and to enslave them was indicative of their slovenly ways and haughty spirit.

Such inaccurate and unfair assertions, peppered through the work, seem almost to argue that settlers ought to have remained in bondage.

The most recent book dealing with Maryland in Liberia is Mary H. Moran's *Civilized Women: Gender and Prestige in Southeastern Liberia,* published by the Cornell University Press in 1990. This is an anthropological study of women in contemporary Maryland County, which deals with historical questions in passing. Similarly, a flurry of articles concerning the ethnic identity of transplanted Grebo and Kru seafarers in Monrovia appeared in the 1970s and 1980s.[10] This debate is only marginally relevant to the early history of Maryland in Liberia. It would also have benefited from a fuller historical understanding. Clearly, the complex criteria defining ethnicity in the region have changed in the course of a century and a half. The ethnic map of southeastern Liberia in 1834 was radically different from the contemporary picture, though current scholarship does not seem to appreciate the point.

There are a number of interesting books on Liberia, a tradition beginning with propagandists and travelers in the nineteenth century and continuing today. The bulk of the current work has scholarly trappings, though the quality varies considerably. Most of these mention Maryland, but they dismiss the place, having little source material and assuming that its history was identical to that of Liberia proper. Richard West's *Back to Africa: A History of Sierra Leone and Liberia* (New York: Holt, Rhinehart, and Winston, 1971) is a far-ranging, chatty discourse, rather fun to read but out of print for some time. Tom W. Schick's *Behold the Promised Land: A History of Afro-American Settler Society in Nineteenth-Century Liberia* (Baltimore: The Johns Hopkins University Press, 1987) is an interesting and well-researched book, which is topical in character. The author scarcely mentions Maryland, but his observations of Liberia are valuable. Likewise, James Wesley Smith's *Sojourners in Search of Freedom: The Settlement of Liberia by Black Americans* (Lanham, Md.: University Press of America, 1987) provides considerable biographical detail of Liberian settlers, sometimes poorly digested, but valuable even so. Charles S. Johnson's *Bitter Canaan: The Story of the Negro Republic* (New Brunswick, N.J.: Transaction Books, 1987) deals with Liberia proper, with an unpersuasive polemic edge. Amos J. Beyan's *The American Colonization Society and the Creation of the Liberian State: A Historical Perspective, 1822–1900* (Lanham, Md.: University Press of America, 1991) has only incidental relevance to Maryland.

The present work must therefore survey historical territory only hastily mapped heretofore. Fortunately, the primary sources for the project are voluminous. The officers of the Maryland State Colonization Society were thoughtful and intelligent men. They believed that their endeavor was truly historic. Accordingly, they preserved all of the correspondence, accounts, and other documents of their activities. When, in 1847, these same men met in the colonization offices to found the Maryland Historical Society, they did not hesitate to include the colonization archives in the new repository. These papers reveal the life of the community at Cape Palmas over a span of more than twenty-five years with a level of detail perhaps unmatched in the annals of any other African American community of the period.[11] This broad corpus is expanded in the archives of Episcopal, Congregational, Roman Catholic, Methodist, and Baptist missionary societies, which all had operations in Maryland. Further detail comes from the accounts of travelers, traders, and officers of the United States Navy, all of whom played their part in the colony's history. These sources, with secondary materials allow the careful reconstruction of the history of a unique and vivacious community, one with a hitherto unrecognized importance in the history of West Africa and the United States and one that speaks to our age about the meaning of race and culture.

Overleaf: A Map of Cape Palmas or the Territory of Maryland in Liberia and Vicinity, 1839. (Maryland Historical Society)

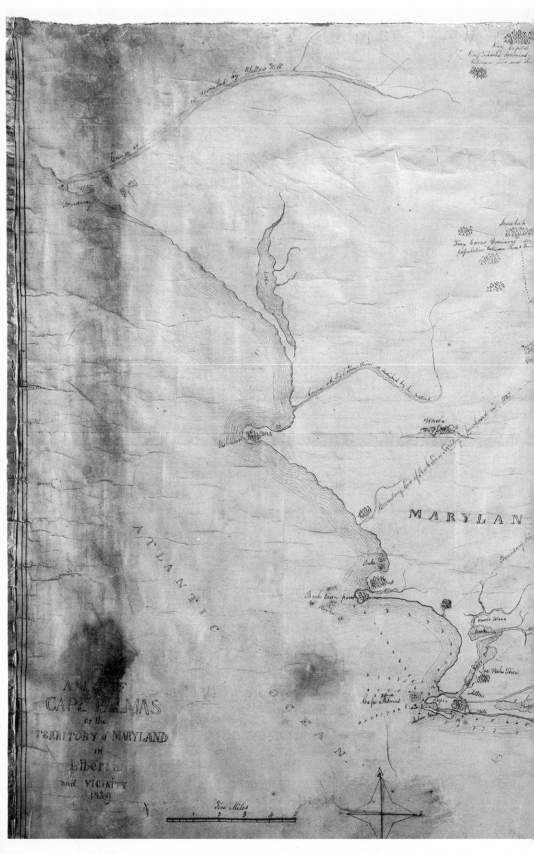

A MAP of
CAPE PALMAS
OR THE
TERRITORY of MARYLAND
IN
Liberia
and VICINITY
1839

MARYLAN

ATLANTIC

OCEAN

Five Miles

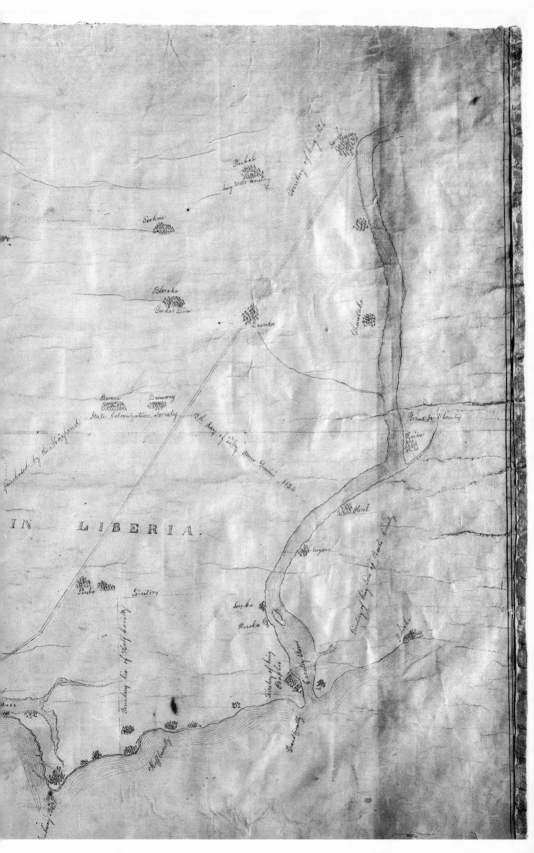

ON AFRIC'S SHORE

I.

"They Foundation Stone of a Nation"

A RAW, RAINY MORNING, THE TWENTY-SEVENTH OF NOVEMBER, 1833, would normally have kept people indoors. Nevertheless, a crowd gathered on a wharf in Fells Point, the deep-water port at Baltimore's east end, to witness a ship's departure. The brig *Ann*, of 160 tons, Captain William C. Langdon, was moored alongside. Ships left port every day with more or less fanfare, but this voyage was out of the ordinary to even the most jaded old seamen and lounge-abouts. Those who could remained in their carriages. Others crowded under the awnings of the ship chandlers and other shops that fronted the wharf: simple brick buildings with steep peaked roofs. Others less fortunate stood out on the cobblestones.

A new banner hung heavily in the rigging, bearing the red and white stripes of the American flag, but a cross in place of stars on the blue field. After a brief speech and benediction, those who had gathered to bid farewell sang a hymn composed especially for the occasion. The romantic lyrics of the first verse embodied the hopeful, naive ideals of the participants:

> For Africa, For Africa, our way lies o'er the deep
> We'll ride the crests of Briny waves and down their vallies sweep

We leave behind the white seagulls at limit of their flight
Until around Cape Palmas, again we'll greet their sight,
As if the feathered things had flown to welcome us, when we
Shall tread, — as stride we Afric's shore — the footsteps of the
free.

The final verse must have spoken very deeply to the gathering:

For Africa, For Africa! — oh who would stay behind
The anchor hangs upon the bow, the sails swell in the wind
Our fatherland, the love within our heart now reigns
Then bid thy wanderers welcome through all thy bound up plains
Yield, from thy bountiful bosom a harvest to our toil
And give us when our life is o'er, our graves within thy soil.[1]

In an odd twist—even the antithesis of the "Middle Passage" of the slave trade, the cruel journey which brought their ancestors to the New World—the Maryland State Colonization Society had chartered the *Ann* to carry twenty-two black American emigrants to West Africa. The ship would call first at Monrovia, Liberia, where more were expected to join the expedition, and then sail to Cape Palmas, 250 miles to the southeast, where the society intended to purchase enough land to settle all of Maryland's free black population. A large stock of trade goods and provisions were tightly stowed below decks.

As the ceremonies concluded, these pioneers, dressed in their best clothes, marched in a body across the gangway. The applause and congratulations of their friends scarcely drowned out the jeers and taunts of others who told them they were fools to think there could be a new life for them in Africa. Men carried Dr. James Hall, the leader of the expedition, aboard on a stretcher. A long-disabled knee and relapse of the fever he had contracted during a former residence in Africa rendered him an invalid, all hoped only temporarily. Everyone must have wondered what the end of this journey would be, whether indeed they might find early graves in Africa.[2]

Although more passengers could have squeezed on board, the living quarters below decks were cramped. Captain Langdon shared his cabin with Dr. Hall and three other white passengers. John Hersey, a

Methodist missionary who expected to die a martyr to the coast fever, was Hall's lieutenant. The doctor later described him as "a man not more distinguished for his piety than his eccentricities, a veritable John the Baptist in food and clothing."[3] Two other missionaries, John Leighton Wilson and Edward Wynkoop, of the American Board of Commissioners for Foreign Missions, a Congregationalist institution, completed the group.

The black passengers quartered amidships. The group comprised three families and three single men. From Baltimore came Joshua Stewart, his wife and infant son, his brother, and a sister-in-law. Joshua Stewart was a jack-of-all-trades: a barber, tailor, and cooper. His wife was a seamstress. Another free black man from Baltimore, William Cassell, was a saddler and barber. He brought his wife and two-year-old son. From the low mountains near Frederick, in Western Maryland, came Charles Gross, head of a family of slave farmers. He, his wife, and five young children were freed especially to go to Africa. Nicholas Thompson, a single man, was a slave who had worked independently as a brickmaker in Baltimore. Eden Nelson was a rough house-carpenter, a freeborn resident of Baltimore. Like the Gross family, Jonathan Jones, a boatman from Washington, D.C., was freed to go to Africa. The emigrants, whether slave or free, had enjoyed advantages denied most black Americans. Most of the adults were literate, and most were artisans or skilled workmen. They were religious people. Though the society would have them portrayed as repatriated Africans, as the hymn suggests, their motives were similar to those of white Americans and Europeans who left Baltimore every day for the western frontier. In Africa, they hoped to have religious and political freedom; they hoped to acquire land and the means to make a comfortable living; they hoped to educate their children and leave them in better circumstances than their own; and they hoped to convert Africans, whom they regarded as savage heathens, to their way of life.[4]

At length, the *Ann* weighed anchor and eased away from the wharf. In the outer harbor, tenders loaded gunpowder. At nine the next morning, November 28, the brig ran down the Patapsco River into Chesapeake Bay. Time was critical: the rainy season at Cape Palmas would begin in late March. If they could not reach the place by mid-February, a distance of some 3,500 miles, buying land and constructing shelters would be difficult, and farming would be impossible until the following year. The odds were against them, in no small part because of the decrepit vessel, which was the only one available for the voyage. She had no copper sheathing: a ragged crust of inch-long barnacles instead covered the wooden hull. "Despair took the place of irritation in the first hour of departure," Hall later recalled, "The Ann fairly *rolled* down the river, it could scarcely be called *sailing*."[5]

Hersey prayed for wind, and a stiff breeze presently gratified him. An overnight run to the Virginia Capes preceded several days' delay due to inclement weather and adverse winds. Life aboard ship was normally tedious, but under these conditions, the wait was especially galling. Tempers quickened among excited, apprehensive, and frustrated passengers. A fire in the vessel's kitchen threatened to wreck the ship before it ever got to sea.[6]

With nothing better to do, the captain, whom Hall described as "a regular dram drinker," settled down for a bout with his liquor, much to the horror of the teetotal Hersey. "On all occasions he (the Captain) would pour out his oaths and blasphemies against heaven and earth," he complained bitterly from shipboard. "In the midnight hour he would rave and swear, and belch out horrid, on the most vulgar blasphemies — He would curse religion, and all concerned in its delusions. He would beat his cook in the most cruel manner, cursing him almost every time he appeared in his presence." Hersey could not imagine such outrageous conduct.[7]

The *Ann* left Chesapeake Bay in mid-December. The voyage was miserable, particularly for Hersey, whom Hall left to do the thankless work of managing the uneasy emigrants. They, after all, were in limbo, having abandoned their old homes, uncomfortable though they may have been, for an uncertain future. Seasickness added to the irritability of the landsmen. Langdon delighted in annoying Hersey, and the two were constantly at odds. Continuing his lamentations, Hersey wrote:

"Soon after we left the capes, the Captain became enraged in the cabbin, and poured out a dreadful volley of oaths and blasphemies, expressed in the most vulgar and uncouth manner. As soon as the storm abated in a degree I observed that it was exceedingly unpleasant to some of us who were his passengers and confined to his cabbin to hear such oaths and bitter imprecations — that we would esteem it a peculiar favour if he would refrain from such excesses." Surprising only Hersey, Langdon "imediately flew into a more violent rage and cursed us all (and me in particular) in the most vulgar and outrageous manner." The minister stood in indignant, impotent silence.[8]

On Christmas Day, the two nearly came to blows. The sinner had the audacity to bring out a fiddle on so solemn an occasion to have a "powerful dance." Hersey got wind of the plan and went to complain. In another letter composed at sea, he wrote, "I peremptorily objected [to the captain]; by saying that I should at least enter my most serious protest against such a course. I also beged him as a favour to forbid the cook from mixing with the emigrants except when he was compelled to go among them to transact his business; and informed him that the day before, I heard him turning religion into ridicule, and using most un-becoming language before the emigrants." The result was predictable, though the poor preacher was caught quite off his guard. He contin-ued, "He sprang out of bed in a most violent rage, and for the first time, spoke well of his cook and most violently and vulgarly abused us all, (the missionaries but particularly myself). He called us every thing but gentlemen. Said the colonists considered us all (but me in particular) hypocrites, etc. Since that time we have not exchanged words, but he continues to swear, and rage, and defy heaven and earth by night and day. He strives to turn the emigrants against me, and has to a consider-able extent succeeded." Hersey found himself trapped "in Jeremiah's dungeon where there is no water but mire." He considered resigning but came to no firm conclusion.[9]

On the open ocean, the *Ann*'s progress was uninterrupted but frus-tratingly slow. The captain navigated by dead reckoning, having nei-ther instruments nor tables to calculate the ship's position. Fearing a wreck, Hall decided to avoid a provisioning stop at the Cape Verde Islands, as was usual for ships cruising to Africa. He also had in mind the steady passing of days, each one lost reducing the chance of the expedition's success. He must reach Monrovia by the end of January.

On January 22 the *Ann* lay near the St. Ann Shoals, one hundred miles off the coast and three or four hundred miles from Monrovia, the captain surmised. A slight breeze blew, but the clumsy *Ann* made scant headway, "without other movement than a dead, heavy roll in the swells of the sea, literally *in the doldrums*." The heat was insufferable. "No awning or deck-house," Hall wrote. "The sun pouring down upon the deck, the pitch frying out of the seams, all felt that the voyage must end there, and we suffer the fate of sundry cockroaches, brought occasionally on deck with fire wood and ship stores, who failing to reach shadow or shelter, would keel over and die."[10] Desperate, he had a lateen-rigged longboat lowered over the side of the ship and had it loaded with a cask of water, a barrel of bread, and a few other provisions. With a seaman from the brig's crew, two of the emigrant men, and John Wilson, Hall left the *Ann* at nine o'clock on the night of the twenty-second, the moon shining brightly overhead. The little craft pulled steadily into darkness, making for the distant coast.

The *Ann*'s mission across the Atlantic had its origins deep in the history of America. Since the sixteenth century, slave labor had made possible the development of a prosperous agricultural economy based on large-scale plantations. This was especially true of South America and the West Indies, where production of sugar demanded intensive labor at little or no wage.

At first, Spaniards forced Native Americans into servitude, but when disease and ill treatment drastically reduced their numbers, merchants supplied huge numbers of captive Africans to do work that free men would not. In North America, planters imported many Africans to Maryland, Virginia, and the Carolinas to grow tobacco and rice. Without so valuable a staple as sugar, however, these colonies remained on the periphery of the full-blown plantation societies of the Caribbean and South America. In the northern colonies, slavery never became widespread.[11]

The geography of slavery changed in the late eighteenth century. British colonies on the North American mainland rebelled and assumed independence as a nation that embraced liberal ideals of freedom and equality. The new nation's economy underwent dramatic changes, too. By the close of the century, slaveholding had ceased in some areas, and in others it became less profitable. At the same time, new frontiers in the South and West offered favorable conditions for the expansion of slave-based agriculture. The century's end also witnessed an increasing awareness and anxiety among slaveowners and other Americans that the institution was morally indefensible. Yet if the consciences of such men were sometimes pained, the feeling was far from universal, and most Americans, whether slave or free, were resigned to a bitter fact of life.

In the first years of the nineteenth century, the scattered voices for and against slavery grew more numerous, and their arguments more clearly defined, with the formation of two irreconcilable camps. Even so, many white Americans still managed to maintain an indifferent stance on the issue. They recognized the moral and economic contradictions of slavery, yet they were unwilling to support abolition, fearing the consequences of freeing a potentially violent underclass, which they believed had no chance of participating fully in American life. Social theory then commonly accepted asserted that peoples of differing races should not mix, that in fact they could not. Indeed, history could provide no examples (they mistakenly thought) of such a thing ever having happened.[12]

It occurred to some that the only way around these sorts of difficulties was the segregation of one people from another. They argued that black people could not compete in a white society. Removed, and settled in homes with their own government and laws, they could develop unfettered. Some looked to the West Indies or Canada, but most thought of Africa as the best place for relocation. It seemed an inspired solution. Everyone would benefit: in a nation with no racial differences. Simply, there could be no race problem. Proponents of colonization in Africa found support for their position in the poor living conditions of black people. The great mass were slaves, most of them uneducated agricultural workers, refused most legal rights accorded whites, forbidden formal marriages, and subject to punishment or sale at the whim of a master. Colonizationists mistook the results of slavery's degradation—poverty, ignorance, and demoralization—as signs that blacks were naturally unfit to participate in civil society. Rather than purge society of the injustices that had put black people in such straits, they chose rather to remove them. Colonization allowed them to sidestep the moral issue of slavery.

The idea of repatriating black people in Africa preceded the American Revolution. In 1773, Samuel Hopkins and Ezra Stiles, both ministers in Providence, Rhode Island, educated several free black men, intending to send them to Africa as missionaries. They hoped that these men would be the vanguard of a black exodus, but the war cut short their plans. In 1777, Thomas Jefferson headed a committee of the Virginia legislature that recommended gradual emancipation coupled with resettlement in the West Indies or Africa. In 1800, James Monroe, governor of Virginia, sought federal aid to deport to Africa a group of free blacks convicted of plotting rebellion in association with Gabriel Prosser in Richmond. The proposal languished.

Englishmen, not Americans, made the first consequential steps toward colonization. In 1787 the Sierra Leone Company purchased land at Fourah Bay, thought to be the best harbor on the West African coast. There it established a colony for London's "Black Poor." The "Province of Freedom," as idealistic sponsors named the place, soon became home for black Americans who fled across British lines during the War of Independence. The Sierra Leone venture, with its explicit objective of ending slavery in the British colonies by a bold, utopian social experiment, appealed to American radicals as well. Between 1787 and 1817, Dr. William Thornton, a close friend of George Washington, corresponded with Granville Sharp and other London promoters of Sierra Leone. President Jefferson also inquired about the possibility of black Americans settling there. In 1815, Paul Cuffe, a black sea captain and merchant of New Bedford, actually sent a small party of emigrants there at his own expense.[13]

In 1815, Robert S. Finley, a Methodist minister, became interested in colonization and launched a campaign from his pulpit at Basking Ridge, New Jersey. Almost simultaneously, Charles Fenton Mercer in Virginia, Francis Scott Key in Baltimore, and Finley's brother-in-law, Dr. E. B. Caldwell, in Washington, D.C., revived the fitful interest of earlier years in colonization. The scattered concern finally reached the intensity of a political movement by the end of 1816. At Christmas, the leading advocates of the cause convened in Washington. In the chambers of the House of Representatives, Finley, Caldwell, Key, and their political allies, Henry Clay, Bushrod Washington, John Randolph, Robert Goodloe Harper, and several others met to delineate a coherent plan of action. They formed the American Society for Colonizing the Free People of Colour of the United States, soon known more simply as the American Colonization Society.

The new organization took no clear position on the question of slavery. Its manifesto hinted vaguely that the nation would be a better place without slaves or blacks generally. As the original name suggests, the founders were more interested in halting the growth of the free black population than in ending chattel slavery. If they could entice slaveholders to send their people to Africa, so much the better. The ambiguous social standing of free blacks was a matter of disproportionate concern. Slaveholders regarded them as a threat to the stability of the enslaved community. Government used every means available to keep black people powerless. In fact, free blacks faced desperate choices. Generally unskilled, they occupied the lowest ranks of the employed and were the first workers fired in hard times. Moreover, the laws of most states assumed their natural servitude. Neither statutes nor the white community had yet adjusted to the reality of a sizable free black population. Freedom was therefore paradoxical, for their condition was in many cases even worse than that of slaves.[14] Colonizationists seized upon the problem, arguing to slaveholders that free blacks were indeed a menace, and to free blacks that their best hope was to flee a land where they could only be oppressed. Interests conjoined: the despair of some black Americans found an outlet in the cynical scheme of the colonization society.

The American Colonization Society patterned their colony after the Sierra Leone venture thirty years before. They obtained land in West Africa for a colony and designed a set of laws which they believed suited the abilities of emigrants. White governors under authority of the society administered a commonwealth in which settlers filled the lower offices by appointment and popular election. They were influenced by the eighteenth-century French physiocrats, who held that all wealth was based upon husbandry and agriculture. They also shared the Jeffersonian ideal of a republic of freeholding farmers as the political arrangement most conducive to human happiness. The foundation of their African commonwealth was agriculture—an agrarian society being the best training ground for newly freed slaves. They shared the physiocratic aversion to commerce, which they termed "traffic" and thought would discourage settlers from business. Yet they advertised their colony's potential for opening new markets to American merchants.[15]

Europeans and Americans of the early nineteenth century, with their industrial and technological advances, regarded the rest of the world as a magnificent project, theirs to take, exploit, and civilize. This was an age of utopian social thought, whose leaders had a naive sense of their power to manipulate and reorganize society to eliminate all sorts of troubles. Advocates of African colonization believed that they could engineer a new society that would one day spread across the continent.[16] The existence of civilized, armed settlers would obstruct slave traders and in time put an end to that evil business. Missionaries, they hoped, would find the colony a perfect base from which to Christianize Africa, to rid it of heathenism.[17]

In 1818 the American Colonization Society sent the brig *Elizabeth* with eighty-five black passengers to Africa. They landed at Sherbro Island, a few miles southeast of Sierra Leone. After only two months malaria, yellow fever, and famine had killed the leaders and scattered the rest. In 1821, a U.S. Navy relief expedition rescued the survivors and carried them 250 miles farther down the coast to Cape Mesurado. At gunpoint, they purchased the territory from its overlord, King Peter. Peter's soldiers nearly wiped out the new settlement, but tenacious settlers under the leadership of such men as Jehudi Ashmun and Elijah Johnson, with the benefit of superior arms, preserved the outpost. Life in the colony was precarious, but by the late 1820s the foothold was permanent.

In 1826 the settlement was named Liberia, "the land of the free," and the main town styled Monrovia, after James Monroe, who as president had aided the cause. By the close of 1830, nineteen ships had carried more than fourteen hundred black Americans to Africa. Most of them had been free for a time before emigrating; many could read and had some employable skill. Virginia and North Carolina had supplied nearly a thousand, and Maryland sent two hundred.[18] In March 1830, John Hanson, a former Baltimore slave, wrote proudly that he had helped to lay "they foundation stone of a nation." He encouraged black people who remained in Maryland:

> If any of them thinks proper to come out we as benevolent fathers are willing to share a part of in heritance with them and protect them from any dred of the surrounding nations that might disturve them while cultivating their land. This is the place where we can look across the forestical country and say it is ours. Our governments is organized as a republican government and the people is become the sovereign. Our civil officers and Military officers is respected, as all like officers in all other governments.[19]

Colonizationists, in Maryland and nationally, acted in an atmosphere of increasing social and political ferment. Through the 1820s the polarization of opinion grew more extreme, as slavery became a pervasive issue. Even so the lines of debate were not yet clearly defined. In the late 1820s radical abolitionism was just coming into its own, and colonizationists had not yet been identified by abolitionists as a pro-slavery faction. William Lloyd Garrison, for example, the master propagandist against slavery, was in Baltimore writing for the *Genius of Universal Emancipation*, an abolitionist newspaper that was nevertheless sympathetic to colonization. Frederick Douglass, with another name, was a slave employed as a caulker in a Baltimore shipyard, just learning to read and think of escape.[20]

In August 1831, a slave uprising near Norfolk, in Southampton County, Virginia, irreversibly changed all of this. Nat Turner, a slave preacher who claimed the direct inspiration of God, set out to overthrow the oppressors of black people. In a few days, he and his followers killed about sixty whites. In the panic that followed, vigilantes killed more than one hundred blacks. Popular opinion in favor of colonization reached a peak. Barely a month after the rebellion's suppression, more than three hundred blacks were packed aboard the *James Perkins* and hurried off to Liberia. Hundreds more followed during the next few months, more or less voluntarily.[21]

Maryland played a major role in the colonization movement, a fact not surprising in view of the state's geographic and economic position. The state straddled the boundary between North and South, exhibiting characteristics of both regions. Slavery and plantation agriculture, typical of the South, coexisted with an expanding industrial economy associated with the North. Slavers had gradually ceased to carry cargoes to Maryland ports about the middle of the eighteenth century. Even then, the economic footings of slavery in the area were eroding. Tobacco, the mainspring of the old colonial economy, began a long decline, leaving as a legacy a degraded landscape of worn-out fields and abandoned plantations. The Revolution, Napoleonic Wars, and the War of 1812 in succession choked off European markets. Economic instability affecting the entire nation left Maryland farmers short of cash.

Wheat, which needed only a fraction of the labor required for tobacco, became the principal crop. Fifty years after the Revolution, Marylanders still owned large numbers of slaves, particularly in the old tobacco-growing regions, in the state's southern counties. Slaveholding was less profitable though, and slaves found opportunities to earn money and purchase themselves. Manumissions by will for reasons of conscience also increased. Growing urban centers, with jobs, attracted the newly free. Baltimore had the largest free black population in the country, nearly fifteen thousand in 1830, and free blacks outnumbered slaves there four to one.[22]

As early as 1818 the American Colonization Society had an auxiliary in Baltimore. General Robert Goodloe Harper, a hero of the Revolution, sometime congressman from South Carolina, and later a prominent Baltimore lawyer, was its head. His associates included Dr. Eli Ayres, one of the purchasers of Cape Mesurado; Moses Sheppard, a Quaker flour merchant; Solomon Etting, a Jewish shipper and banker; Charles Howard, another lawyer; and John Latrobe, a talented apprentice in Harper's office.[23]

John Hazlehurst Boneval Latrobe was the son of Benjamin Henry Latrobe, who was once Architect of the National Capitol and a prominent figure in Washington society. John Latrobe grew up in the acquaintance of Harper and other influential men of the early republic. He entered West Point, where he studied military engineering, hoping to follow in his father's profession. In the spring of 1822, however, Benjamin Latrobe died of yellow fever in New Orleans, just weeks before John was to graduate. The young man resigned his commission, came to Baltimore to support his mother, and went to work for Harper. The old general quickly drew him into the colonization society. He became a tireless advocate of the cause. Using skills acquired at the military academy, he drafted the first map of the new settlement and dubbed the colony "Liberia" and its capital "Monrovia" with Harper's approval.[24]

The Maryland Auxiliary Colonization Society was an ephemeral club composed of Harper's close friends and existed principally to raise funds for the national organization. In 1827, however, they persuaded two prominent black citizens, George R. McGill and Remus Harvey, to emigrate to Liberia. Both had been teachers at the Sharp Street Methodist Church. McGill was among the most prosperous black men in Baltimore, a property owner and proprietor of an oyster cellar at the city's center, from which he operated an "intelligence office," or employment agency.[25]

In January 1828, the American Colonization Society convened its eleventh annual meeting in the hall of the House of Representatives in Washington. Henry Clay presided. Among many orators, Latrobe spoke in favor of acquiring new territories along the African coast, mentioning particularly Cape Palmas, the southernmost point of West Africa. He knew nothing of the place, only that its location was strategic. The society's funds were dangerously overextended, though, and delegates took no action on the proposal.[26]

About the same time, Latrobe initiated correspondence with citizens of Liberia, particularly McGill and Harvey, who had been in Africa above a year. In the spring of 1831 he wrote McGill to ascertain popular opinion about a new settlement for Marylanders. "As quick as I mentioned the letter that I receved of you," McGill responded on September 2, "it flashed like litening from one end of the settlement to the other, and a grate nomber came runing to me to have their names set down."[27] McGill believed that he could get fifty volunteers with ease. The consensus in Liberia was that Bulama Island, not far from Sherbro, where the first American settlers had landed, would be the best site. The Liberians were seemingly unaware of a British attempt to plant a colony there fifty years earlier. Like Sherbro, Bulama was scarcely more than a sandbar, and disease and malnutrition had wiped out the colony in short order.

―――＊――

Nat Turner's revolt electrified Maryland. The bloody events took place just a day's steamboat excursion from Baltimore, and Marylanders feared similar eruptions. The Maryland Auxiliary Colonization Society received scores of letters on the subject. Many promised donations; some even offered slaves for deportation.

In November 1831 the society used the money to charter the schooner *Orion* to carry thirty-one emigrants to Monrovia. All of them were free residents of Baltimore, except one man from Dorchester County on the Eastern Shore. At the head of the company was a white man, Dr. James Hall, who, strange to say, hoped that a visit to Africa, then popularly known as "the white man's grave," would improve his health.[28]

Hall was born in Windsor County, Vermont, in 1802. In 1822 he graduated with the second medical class of Bowdoin College in Brunswick, Maine. He married soon after and in short order had a boy and a girl to care for. Practicing medicine in the White Mountains of Vermont was arduous and proved more than he could handle. He developed "a severe and painful affection of the knee joint and a general debility of the system."[29] His wife's death in 1828 left him yet more despondent. After arranging for the care of his children he departed for the West Indies, believing than an ocean voyage and the warm air of the tropics would improve his health. A year in Cuba was succeeded by another in Haiti, during which time his spirits improved, though his knee remained painful and stiff, forcing him to go about on crutches.

Dr. Hall returned to the United States early in the summer of 1831, landing at Baltimore, then a center of West Indian trade. The University of Maryland had one of the better hospitals in the country at that time, and Hall consulted with three professors, who advised him to undergo "antiphlogistic therapy," which involved irritating one area of the body to reduce inflammation in another. He remained in the school's infirmary for five months, enduring excruciating treatment, during which his weight declined drastically. Near death, he resolved to go to sea once again.

Hall's first plan was to find a ship for China, but by chance he learned of the *Orion*'s imminent sailing. He had known the captain in Port-au-Prince. Thereupon, he decided that Africa would be as good a place as any to visit or in which to die, and he applied for passage, which was granted sight unseen. The officers of the auxiliary were shocked when they met their volunteer, bedridden in a boarding house, unable even to dress himself. They had little faith that he could survive the carriage ride to the wharf, much less a voyage. Hall himself did not realize how ghastly was his appearance. "It was only when I attempted to get up," he later wrote, and "saw myself in the glass, that the utter helplessness, even hopelessness of my condition came upon me. I fell back upon my bed, half inclined to give up and end the long struggle here where I had suffered. But rallying, I was gotten into my clothes, 'a world too wide for my shrunk carcass.'" To travel from Baltimore to Fells Point, where the *Orion* waited, his friends put the doctor "into a common hack, well pillowed up." He continued: "On the way, we were stopped by some fire machinery across the street, and a crowd gathered to see the 'living skeleton.'" Outside a ship chandlery in Fells Point he spied a scale, and his friends urged him to weight himself. "I brought down 91 pounds, with all my heavy clothing, boots, overshoes, and overcoat — somewhere near 75 or 80 pounds net weight." He recovered a little in the following week under the care of an innkeeper's kind wife, and to the surprise of some, survived the transfer to shipboard. His health and spirits improved on the passage across the Atlantic. During a month at sea, he gained thirty-one pounds.[30]

Dr. Hall came to Monrovia in December 1831, amidst the first wave of migration following the Southampton Massacre. The town was then about ten years old, numbering less than one thousand inhabitants. The view from shipboard was unimpressive, the rocky promontory of Cape Mesurado, covered in bush and tall trees, and the adjacent shoreline backed by marsh and mangrove swamp as far as the eye could see. "As we lay well in shore," Hall recalled, "we could plainly see the thatched haycock cottages of the fishermen, and myriads of naked children rolling in the surf and sand." One or two shingled roofs evidenced the American-style town that lay on the cape's landward flank.[31]

More striking was the oppressive humidity and the smell of vegetation rotting on shore. Two Philadelphia brigs lay at anchor near the *Orion*, black hulks, shrouded in decomposing rigging, and half their crews carried away by disease. They had limped into port after forays into Rio Pongas or Rio Nunez, northwest of Sierra Leone. Survivors were on shore to receive what little care the colony could afford them. A cabin boy was too ill to go ashore. His captain asked Hall to treat the youth. Many years later, Hall recalled the horror he encountered as he set foot on the decrepit brig:

> The cook, just able to crawl about, convalescant from fever, and the cabin boy, only, remained on board. On going below, I heard a dull deep moaning from one of the berths, and tried to elicit from the stupid cook and quite as stupid and more brutal Captain a history of the case, before examining the patient. I could learn nothing but that the boy had lain so for a day or two, utterly unconscious, giving no indications of the seat of his sufferings except an occasional raising, of one hand to the back of his head. I ordered him to be turned over for examination; in the dim light of the berth, the back of his neck seemed very black. Placing my hand upon it, to my horror, I found it covered with a mass of black ants. We managed to get him out of his berth on to the transom, when I found the skin, superficial muscles and cellular substance so eaten away that the carniverous devils were nested deep amongst the large muscles, nerves and blood vessels of the neck; the most shocking sight I ever witnessed.

The doctor extracted something like a half pint of the insects. Nothing could be done but to relieve pain, and the boy died the following morning.[32]

The *Orion* cast anchor on a Saturday evening, and the sabbath was occupied with the call on the Philadelphia merchant. On Monday morning, the doctor went ashore for the first time, carried to the Government House on the back of an African porter. Governor Mechlin was taken aback by Hall's emaciated appearance but quickly recovered himself and extended his hospitality. The doctor took up residence in Mechlin's house, along with John Russwurm, another Bowdoin graduate (the first black college graduate in the United States in fact), who was the governor's private secretary. The only jackass in the colony was requisitioned, and "the Doctor and his ass," otherwise known as "the man with two sticks, on him bullock," became a common sight about Monrovia.

Hall had ample opportunity to observe the colony as it entered its tenth year. "Monrovia could not be called a town, village or city; the term *settlement* only, being applicable," he wrote later.

> There were streets, houses, shops and people, but to say the least, not well arranged. The streets had the appearance of a young forest of second growth. It should be borne in mind that there were no carriages or beasts of pleasure or burthen, or likely to be on this rocky cape; and yet, the streets east and west, from a half to a mile in length, were from sixty to one hundred feet wide, and nothing but zig-zag foot-paths traversing them from side to side or from house to house. . . . The founders of Liberia anticipated, in fact, the American "Forest City."[33]

Most settlers in the town lived in small cottages constructed after American models. Nearly all houses were of a single story, sided with weatherboards and roofed with wooden shingles obtained in the surrounding swamps by farmers-turned-sawyers. Many were erected on stone pilings raised high enough off the ground to make storerooms. Medical theory asserted that this would protect the occupants from the ground-clinging night air, or miasma, that was thought to cause fevers.

Monrovia was an administrative and commercial center. Its residents worked for the colonial government, in merchant houses, or practiced various skilled trades. The colony also included two outlying agricultural settlements. The older of these was Caldwell, at the mouth of the St. Paul's River, ten miles north of Monrovia and connected to it by a tidal waterway. Thirty miles farther upriver was Millsburg, recently laid out on land more elevated and better suited to farming.

The American Colonization Society fed and housed new arrivals for a period of six months, during which time they were "acclimated"— subjected to their first attacks of malaria and other diseases endemic to the region. The survivors received ten-acre plots to farm. The society placed the *Orion*'s emigrants at Caldwell. Arrivals by other ships went to Millsburg. Talented, literate individuals often remained in Monrovia, where they found employment. The colonial capital had a thriving community of educated American expatriates.

Liberians maintained a strong American identity, although they already were beginning to think of themselves as an independent people. "I must Emphatically say in the first place that this country is the only Asylum for men whose Epidermis Nature has pencil'd with a dark hue," Remus Harvey, the Methodist lay minister who left Baltimore in 1827, wrote with great feeling in 1829. "Here the man of Sable hue can Rejoice with joy inexpressible arising from the Enjoyment of all those Rights which are guarranteed unto him in common with men of other complexion! Here he can walk abroad on his own Originally native Soil," and contemplate those "mighty Exploits of Virtue and Vallor which were once performed by his ancient Fore Fathers." Notwithstanding his "regret" that these virtues were sometime lost, "yet the memory of them is near to his heart, and Seems to force him to put a more than common worth upon his native soil!"[34] The entire Liberian population did not exceed two thousand, an enclave of radical republicans amidst a much larger African population. A few score miles up or down the coast, slave dealers collected their cargoes for Brazil, the West Indies, and even the United States.

A powerful religious organization shaped and bolstered the emerging Liberian culture and politics. In America, churches had provided many emigrants education and community—in a very real sense, freedom.[35] These attachments were transferred to Africa and even strengthened by the move. The majority of Monrovia's citizens were either Methodists or Baptists, and the town's most impressive buildings were their two barn-like churches. James Hall, who described himself as "born and bred a New Englander in the day of the later Puritans," asserted that Liberian settlers "were the most religious people [he] ever met with." They avoided all profanity. "I never witnessed any game, such as ball, quoits, boat-racing or cards," he later recalled, "nor did I ever hear any musical instrument, unless the rub-a-dub of a little red-coated drummer could be so designated. Never a dance or ball heard of." Public worship was a principal mode of sociability. Some preachers and missionaries, through their pulpits, obtained large followings and wielded formidable political power. Further, the Bible provided language for political discourse in many instances, and settlers often expressed themselves in letters to America with biblical language and imagery.

Liberians relied on imported goods—food, cloth, tools, hardware, and weapons—to supply many of their daily needs. The extravagance of settler society in Monrovia especially impressed Captain William Hardie, who carried settlers to Liberia early in 1833. Upon his return to Baltimore, he stated that "they indulged in sideboards, decanters etc. instead of being thrifty," and went on to say that the "Big Bugs" liked to show off. James Hall had a similar sense, observing in his memoirs, "Fortunately, perhaps, the roads admitted of no outlay in horses and carriages, nor had tailors, mantua-makers and milliners entered the little settlement, but they found ways and means of expenditure, if not of creating capital."[36]

Visitors to Monrovia also noted the number of Africans residing in the town and their subservient role. Captain Hardie, for instance, stated that Africans performed most manual labor, that settlers "would call upon the natives to pick up their handkerchiefs even and to do every menial office for them." James Hall wrote that nearly every household had an African servant. "The consequence of this arrangement was an imperious deportment on the part of the master or mistress and an obsequious subservancy on the part of the servant. One of the lessons taught the colonists or many of them, in this country, was that of control, command, and even *gentle chastisement* on the part of their masters. The most ignorant and worthless imitated only, what they could comprehend, what was beat into them, and they now practiced the same on their inferiors; and apt scholars they proved themselves." African servants could quit if their homes were nearby, but otherwise difficulty of travel trapped them. Alluding to *Uncle Tom's Cabin*, Hall continued, "I have too often seen the cuff, kick or blow, to my indignation. . . . I may add, that this was not practiced except by the lower class of colonists — the 'Legrees.'"[37]

The emergent society of Liberia in 1831 was volatile. Each new company of emigrants, with new talents and characters, changed the small established community. The few educated emigrants competed intensely for the favor of the American Colonization Society, whose funds fueled the economy. The rise and fall of fortunes could be meteoric. Virtually all colonial officers and settlers were chronically ill. Heavy doses of opium and calomel (a drug derived from mercury) relieved pain and some symptoms, but many in authority were subject to confusion or outright delusion. Death was a constant threat. Between 1829 and 1836, Liberia had six governors. Further, Liberians were dependent upon the Africans around them for their food, and shortfalls were common. Salt meat and other provisions, tools, and the sundries of everyday life were imported from the United States or Europe. Deprivation was a constant source of complaint and political unrest.

Divisions in the tiny community mirrored the sectional animosity in the United States. Before 1831 only one or two hundred individuals per year emigrated to Liberia. Most of these settlers had been free and had some amount of education and skill, but by the late 1820s an increasing proportion of emigrants were former field slaves, ill-prepared to start an independent life. In many cases, they were a burden on the colonial government. In the eighteen months following Nat Turner's Rebellion, Liberia's population almost doubled, and the government was unable to cope.

Shortly after the *Orion* put to sea, the ship *James Perkins* left Norfolk packed with 338 emigrants. Colonial officials had neither staff or space for so many new arrivals. Some of their provisions were stolen; medical care was deficient; and they didn't get their land as quickly as promised. The *Orion's* emigrants complained of favoritism and sectional prejudices, too. "There are few that are doing much in the advancement of life but a great number are going back," George McGill bluntly informed Latrobe in a letter of July 12, 1832, continuing,

> One grand reason of this is, that this place above all others is about the poorest, that you can name on the Coast of Africa. In Monrovia

it is an unfurtile, Red Gravelly Mountain, nearly surrounded by an unbounded mangrove swamp, as noixous as death itself to a stranger, and renders us solely dependent for a subsistence; there is no Trade in our vicinity, many speaks of the St. Pauls River; it is a fine river, but it abounds with but little comerce or inhabitants; the natives about us are a lazy, Idol people, and how our Agents do to spout about it to such a degree, I cannot find out unless it is to perpetuate their salaries they have got a number of the new Emigrants, here now heaped upon each other starving to death, the Agent takes no pains to set them to work for a livelihood they take the fevour and a number of them half perish to death with hunger.[38]

McGill, as Latrobe's other correspondents, urged a new Maryland settlement. They changed their opinion about the best site, now preferring Cape Palmas, the spot mentioned by Latrobe in 1828.

Liberia faced famine in the middle of 1832. The previous year's rice crop had failed, and the flood of new settlers outstripped local food reserves. The society's ship, *Margaret Mercer*, with James Hall acting as supercargo, sailed down the coast in a fruitless search for rice. They could not even find enough to feed the crew until they reached Cape Palmas, whose trademen brought out two hundred bushels in two days. During an hour of boredom, Dr. Hall had found and read the society's annual report for 1828, which contained Latrobe's speech concerning Cape Palmas. Curious, he went ashore himself to see what the place had to offer. Soon after, he wrote Dr. Eli Ayres, once governor of Liberia, then agent of the Maryland Auxiliary, that Cape Palmas rice was feeding a large portion of the Liberian settlement. He added, "The face of the Country is entirely different from that around Monrovia. As far as the eye can reach it is open and in a great degree cultivated; and no part is covered with that dense impenetrable undergrowth so prejudicial to agriculture and extensive inland communication, as with us (at Monrovia)." Latrobe and his associates read the letter with the highest interest.[39]

Nat Turner's Rebellion had contradictory effects on the colonization movement, at once raising it to a new height of popularity and demanding ruinous financial commitments. Suddenly, hundreds of slaves and free black people were presented for deportation to Africa, and expenses increased proportionally. Almost simultaneously, William Lloyd Garrison and other abolitionists initiated a withering attack on the society and its principles. Funds dried up, and the society gradually split into factions, culminating in a disastrous annual meeting in January 1833. In Maryland, however, the auxiliary colonization society gained a strong financial base and broad public support. The people of Maryland—a slave state, with the highest number of free black people in the nation—were shocked by the massacre, which took place so near their own borders. Though Turner and his supporters were mostly slaves, popular opinion blamed free blacks for the insurrection. When the Maryland General Assembly convened for the winter session of 1831–32, the first since the uprising, alarmed legislators were eager to prevent similar events in their state. They enacted repressive laws against free blacks that, among other things, forbade them to remain in the state without special permission from a magistrate, and provided for their removal overseas. Although the state's treasury suffered critical embarrassment at the time, the legislature appropriated the generous sum of $200,000 for colonization, to be disbursed in twenty annual installments of $10,000. The Maryland State Colonization Society was reconstituted as a semi-public corporation, chartered by the state and accountable to the General Assembly. The act established a Board of Managers composed of members of the colonization society, which was charged to maintain a registry of all slaves emancipated in the state; to send to Africa any black people who wished to go, and if necessary, to purchase land there for a new colony. The State of Maryland of course had no constitutional right to found colonies overseas, but lawmakers were more concerned with the most expedient way to remove free blacks than such inconvenient questions.[40]

Public and legislative sentiment notwithstanding, members of the local auxiliary embarked upon their new responsibility with minimal enthusiasm. They were not formally independent of the American Colonization Society and had no distinct policy. The national organization had borne the burden of setting the ideological agenda, and they were afraid to incur the tremendous intellectual and financial responsibility of independent action. Robert Goodloe Harper was now dead. Except for John Latrobe and Moses Sheppard, members of the society were part-time enthusiasts. The abolitionists' invective had a chilling effect, making things even more difficult.[41]

Despite bad reports from the *Orion* emigrants, the new Board of Managers decided to send a second company to Liberia. They had little choice, for the society was under great public pressure to begin its work of exporting the black population. Money and names of potential emigrants came from all quarters, but the good will might not last. Failure to accomplish anything with the state's money could well cancel the appropriation. Accordingly, the board chartered the brig *Lafayette* in December 1832 to carry 144 passengers to Liberia. Most of the company came from the Eastern Shore, particularly Somerset County.[42]

The results were predictable. Colonial officials were unable to take care of the new arrivals. They were dumped at Caldwell, on swampy, malarial land near the mouth of the St. Paul's River. The government mishandled and misappropriated their provisions. Medical treatment was inadequate and mortality high. Twenty-six died in the first year. Calls from Liberia for redress grew more numerous and impassioned.[43]

In January 1833, while the *Lafayette* was on her way to Liberia, the American Colonization Society held its sixteenth annual meeting. The organization had run up an enormous debt, and the atmosphere was tense. "At that meeting, it became apparent that Colonization had two sets of friends, who supported it from motives diametrically opposed to each other," Latrobe wrote another colonizationist a few months later.

The north looked to Colonization as the means of *extirpating* sla-

very. — The south as the means of *perpetuating* it, because the removal of the *free* blacks alone, which the South contended for, by
making slaves more valuable, necessarily tended to perpetuate the
institution of slavery. The Colonization Society had attempted to
conciliate for years, between these parties, and so long as it could
keep the question of *principle* from being publicly mooted, it was
partially successful. But the explosion came at last. The discussions
of the last winter in Washington led, as a necessary consequence, to
the fair and distinct development of opposing parties.[44]

Latrobe later noted in his diary that the American Colonization Society "was not a business concern — it was deeply involved in debt. It was
distracted within itself — it had no defined system of procedure. From
this Board Mr. Sheppard and I agreed there was no hope of ameliora-
tion of the condition of things in Africa for some time. Everybody's
intentions were good but that was all."[45]

The Maryland State Colonization Society held a meeting on February 4, 1833, while the parent organization was still sitting at Washington. After much discussion, the Board of Managers resolved to adopt
a conciliatory stance with regard to the schism. They passed a resolution deploring the division as one "calculated to greatly retard if not
utterly destroy the hopes of consummating the great and philanthropic
objects" of colonization. Further, the Maryland State Colonization
Society was "of the opinion that it is neither politic nor expedient, nor
within the limits of their chartered powers as a separate and independent society to interfere in the disputes which may arise out of conflicting principles in that Board."[46] The auxiliary was now moving decisively towards autonomy.

The Board of Managers met again on the evening of April 30.
Latrobe suggested that the society should establish its own colony, rec-
ommending Cape Palmas, to unanimous approval. Latrobe expected
the board to take immediate action, but it still hesitated. Members had
no distinct principle or firm plan of action on which to form the new
settlement, and the task before them was daunting. Reminiscing in his
diary later that year, Latrobe wrote, "I set to work therefore and prepared another set of Resolutions."[47] Latrobe's plan closely paralleled

that originally set forth by the parent society, but with alterations to correct perceived deficiencies. The Marylanders hoped that their colony would regain the true path to an African American civilization which would one day evangelize the continent: a virtuous commonwealth of teetotaling freeholders, an heir to the agrarian ideal espoused by Jefferson. Not long after, a spokesman for the society rhapsodized on the importance of agriculture, "not only as placing the means of their own sustenance in the hands of the colonists, and rendering them independent of remote places or the native inhabitants for food; but because nine-tenths, if not a far greater proportion, of the emigrants from this country would make better farmers than traders: — besides which, instead of having all their bad feelings brought into play by the artifices of a petty native traffic, engendering vicious habits by the intervals of idleness that it afforded, the emigrants, finding employment, in agricultural pursuits, . . . would have their minds in the best state to receive and preserve those sentiments of religion and morality, which it was the wish of the state society should form the character of the population."[48] In a corollary, they maintained that the "division of land into small tracts in the first establishment of civil states, seems to be necessary as a foundation of true liberty."[49] Accordingly, their plan was to grant each head of household five acres, on condition that the land be cleared and farmed. The American Colonization Society gave its settlers ten acres per family, but the Marylanders judged this wasteful, as experience had shown that they were unable to maintain so much. As a result, farmsteads were isolated by tangles of heavy bush. Under the mistaken impression that the lushness of African vegetation indicated extraordinary soil fertility, they reasoned that relatively little space was necessary for subsistence.[51]

The Marylanders firmly believed that liquor was a principal cause of degradation and misery among the lower classes. Black people, like Native Americans, were especially vulnerable to its insidious effects. Indeed, "ardent spirits" had been the downfall of many Liberian settlers. The colonizationists therefore adopted a policy of prohibition: "temperance will find, in a nation founded on its principles, an illustration that must be forever conclusive as to its political benefits and an example powerful in its influences." All emigrants to the projected Maryland colony must swear to abstain from alcohol, except for medicinal reasons.[52]

Latrobe's Liberian correspondents and others had suggested various individuals to lead an expedition to found the new settlement, but decisions on the matter were postponed. In June 1833, James Hall, whose name had figured prominently, returned to the United States to recover his health after a long struggle with malaria and other parasites.[53] On his way to Washington to settle accounts with the American Colonization Society, he paused in Baltimore to visit a doctor. Having but little time, and wishing to meet Latrobe, who had been away when the *Orion* sailed, Hall sent a messenger to bring Latrobe over to the doctor's office. The lawyer put down his work and walked over. Dr. Hall, "an attenuated, feeble looking man," but with a lively personality, introduced himself. "I well remember," Latrobe wrote fifty years later, "that he had no sooner told me that he had just arrived from Africa, than, without waiting to learn the particulars of the visit to Washington, I asked if he was ready to go back at once, and found a settlement at Cape Palmas." Hall said yes immediately but then hesitated. He must first visit his children, whom he had left in Clarement, New Hampshire, almost four years before. He would need a few weeks, but would then be ready.[54]

Over the summer of 1833 the society had no formal meetings, despite the massive project underway. Latrobe was busy with his expanding legal practice. He commuted daily to Baltimore from Elkridge, on the line of his principal client, the fledgling Baltimore and Ohio Railroad. He helped arrange an aeronautical exhibition, in which a hot air balloon rose over the city for the first time. He was also president of a horticultural society. In August he set aside a few days to travel to New England to enlist support for the Maryland State Colonization Society, hoping to take advantage of disarray in the national organization to gather financial assistance for a new venture. He met prominent men in New York, Boston, Andover, and Hartford before returning home. Though many professed support for his ideas and wished him good luck, no one offered money.[55]

The society met on September 6. Latrobe offered several resolutions to give form to the project. He confided in his diary, "I am disappointed in the luke-warmness of many of those with whom I am acting." Three days later, he presented a plan to finance the first expedition. Specifically, he asked the board to contribute thirty dollars of the state's appropriation toward the expenses of each emigrant, and further for an advance payment of $8,000 to cover the expenses of establishing a colony in West Africa. At thirty dollars per emigrant, the advance would be repaid by sending 267 to the colony. The Board of Managers agreed. "This was not done without much discussion," Latrobe wrote, "but in the end I accomplished it, and so brought to a practical scheme the design of years since." The society's local agent, John Kennard, was ordered to present a list of candidates from those who had applied to emigrate. They instructed him "to admit no one to his list of Emigrants who is not of an unexceptionable moral character — and to give the preference to those, who, other qualifications equal, are distinguished for piety and knowledge."

The society had no regular meeting for another month, but in the interval Latrobe and others worked constantly on the project. They had to buy and store everything that the new colony might need, for resupply might not be possible for several months. From the outset, the colony would need large stocks of even the most common items: trade goods (such as cloth, iron, crockery, gunpowder, and tobacco), weapons, provisions, clothing, house frames, tools for farming and carpentry, furniture, medicines, seeds, and many other sundries. They could take nothing for granted.

On September 23, John Leighton Wilson, a Presbyterian minister originally from South Carolina, visited Latrobe with a letter of introduction from the American Board of Commissioners for Foreign Missions. He wished to accompany the expedition to assess the prospects for a mission at Cape Palmas. That afternoon Latrobe met with Wilson and Benjamin Anderson, the head of the A.B.C.F.M. After some discussion, he consented to their proposal, hoping this alliance with a leading missionary society would enhance the whole project.

On September 30, Latrobe enlisted several of his lawyer friends to draft a code of laws for the new settlement. Among them was Hugh Davey Evans, an authority on the Constitution and on Maryland common law. Latrobe reserved for himself the constitution and "form of government" of the colony. The laws were drawn from several sources, but he distilled their substance from the charter that Cromwell's Parliament granted Rhode Island in 1663 and from the Northwest Ordinance of 1787, which provided the framework for civil government and the establishment of new states on the western frontier. Together, the laws for the projected colony provided for a representative government, headed by a governor who was appointed by the society, but whose other officers were selected in Africa, either by appointment or election. The laws ensured settlers' rights of property and inheritance, public education, and freedom of religion. They emphasized the right and duty of citizens to bear arms for the defense of their community. A clause strictly prohibited the importation, sale, or use (except by prescription of a physician) of all distilled spirits. A final clause promised that when the population should reach five thousand, the Maryland State Colonization Society would grant the colony independence.[56]

On September 30, also, Latrobe met with Hall, Anderson, and Charles Howard to discuss a problem that Hall, speaking from his African experience, brought to their attention. The Maryland State Colonization Society had publicly committed itself to temperance. Hall warned that rum was absolutely necessary to the success of any negotiation in Africa. How would it look if the temperance colony were purchased with rum, or, equally bad, if the expedition failed because it did not have the drink? On October 9 the board met to decide. After an emotional discussion, someone proposed that rum be taken aboard the expedition vessel, to use in the last resort. The debate was heated, for the participants were men of high principle, and much was at stake. At length the board took its first and only roll-call vote. Four men, including the Quaker Moses Sheppard, rejected the proposal. Eight voted to allow Hall to purchase as much rum as he might need. Liquor was quietly ordered.[57]

The pace of preparations now quickened. The sailing date was set for the middle of November. On October 16 a General Committee was appointed to meet every day, except the sabbath. On the seventeenth, the committee engaged a builder to make a frame for the Agency House. On the twenty-first, they discussed a name for the new settlement. "New Maryland" was suggested, the first town to be called "Carthage," after the ancient African city that had once rivaled Rome. About the same time James Hall went by steamboat to Norfolk, where the ship *Jupiter* was about to sail for Monrovia. He hoped to persuade Joseph Jenkins Roberts, a prominent citizen of Monrovia who had just completed a visit to his old home in Richmond, to join the Maryland expedition. Roberts declined, but he promised to help the expedition in any way he could when it called at Monrovia.

On November 7, the Board of Managers met and approved a charter negotiated with Captain William C. Langdon, master of the brig *Ann*. The cost of the vessel would be $700 per month for a round trip; $750 if it was decided in Africa to retain the vessel for extra services; or $800 per month, $500 of it in gold, if the ship were discharged at Monrovia. The next day, local newspapers carried an advertisement for the sailing of the *Ann*, soliciting passengers for Africa. Sailing was now set for November 20. During the next two weeks, the equipment and baggage was stowed on board, slowly at first, then with increasing energy as Solomon Etting, a retired merchant, took charge of the business. The proposed day of departure came and went. Cannons ordered from New York did not arrive on time, and then bad weather intervened. A week later than planned, the *Ann* was ready to sail.

II.

"Close on the Promised Land"

HAVING LEFT THE *ANN* BECALMED AT SEA ON THE NIGHT OF JANUARY 22, 1834, Dr. Hall directed the longboat toward the African coast. He hoped to make landfall somewhere above the Gallinas River and then to run southeasterly to Cape Mesurado, the site of Monrovia. On the morning of the third day, they caught sight of Sherbro Island, scene of the unfortunate first settlement of 1818. At dawn the following day they passed almost within sight of Gallinas, where Pedro Blanco and his associate, Theophile Canot, operated a thriving slave depot. Nearby, they crossed the path of a large brig, which they feared might be a slaver. Prepared for the worst, they were relieved to recognize her as the *Mary* of Philadelphia, whose master sent them a pot of coffee rather than a cannonball. The next morning, January 26, they reached Monrovia. As luck would have it, winds had picked up shortly after the longboat set off, and Langdon reached port just a day behind.[1]

To Hall, the green eminence of Cape Mesurado, with squalid Monrovia on its landward side must have been a welcome sight. The nine months since his departure had witnessed few if any improvements. Monrovia lay mouldering, increased only in the number of paupers. Governor Mechlin had resigned on account of sickness. Jacob

Pinney, a Methodist preacher and one of Hall's friends, had taken charge of government.

"The day after my arrival," Hall informed the board on January 29, "I addressed a note to Mr Pinney with a copy of the general address, requesting his permission that a limited number might be permitted to leave this settlement for Cape Palmas; to which he gave his unqualified consent by letter." Marylanders were enthusiastic about the venture. Twenty volunteered at Monrovia and seven more at Caldwell at the first news. Many of them had families to support, so Hall landed provisions to furnish them until their pioneer husbands and fathers could make homes. George McGill had charge of the supplies. He would have liked to bring McGill with him to Cape Palmas, but the old man was reluctant to leave his trading house in other hands.

Despite the initial positive reaction, powerful Monrovians objected to the new settlement. Within a week of the *Ann*'s arrival, they had fomented a strong reaction. Debts, personal obligations, and even threats forced many prospective volunteers to change their minds.[2] John Russwurm, Hall's old friend and housemate, still Colonial Secretary and editor of the *Liberia Herald*, watched indignantly. He informed Latrobe at the end of February, after the *Ann* had sailed, that "Impossibilities and improbabilities were thrown out by those opposed to the new settlement to deter volunteers from joining the expedition. . . . It appeared strange to me that Virginians should be opposed to Northern people forming the expedition as they have always wished us out of their way, but such was the fact." Merchants and government officials did not want to suffer any reduction in their tiny community, otherwise they might have encouraged the exodus, Russwurm implied.[3]

The temperance principle, so proudly advocated in Baltimore, was at first warmly supported, to Hall's surprise, but it too became a subject of discussion and concern. "The Traders and Colonists consider this matter of purchase without rum as absolutely out of the question." A Grebo man from Cape Palmas had eagerly awaited the *Ann*'s arrival, but word that the vessel was dry took him by surprise. "He assures me that his countrymen are anxious we should come and settle with them, but says 'King no put he mouth to that palaver pose he no hab rum,'" Hall reported.[4] After all, rum was an important article of trade and an essential aid to business negotiations in Africa. Wilson was credibly informed that of the fifty American vessels then trading on the coast only two did not stock liquor. Detractors criticized the expedition on the grounds that its absence was a sure sign of the impracticality of the endeavor.

At Monrovia, Hersey decided to resign his post. Really, he had little choice, for his convictions were so adamant and eccentric that he could not lead. Emigrants would not respect his authority, and he would not follow the policies of Dr. Hall, who was uncomfortable with public displays of fundamentalist religion. In Hersey's opinion, Hall was no better than an atheist. "Upon mature reflection, I have concluded to *sacrifice* my own feelings, and continue on with the expedition to Cape Palmas," he explained in a letter to William McKenney, the society's home agent. "To do otherwise would be a serious injury to the cause." He expected to remain until the expedition was "settled and secured on the continent," then "work my passage through heathen Africa, and perhaps back to the United States" without asking the society's assistance. "We must pay for our own folly."[5]

Despite the strenuous opposition of Monrovian officials and merchants, Hall enlisted thirty volunteers: nineteen men, four boys, three women, and four small children. The families of several of the men would follow later, provided the venture was a success. Hall at last persuaded George McGill to come along as "Assistant Palaverman." His experience would be invaluable in negotiations with Greboes, who owned the territory at Cape Palmas. He made Joe Wilson, a Grebo employed in McGill's store, his interpreter. He also hired James Thomson, a clerk in Russwurm's store, to serve as his private secretary.[6]

Finding increasing antagonism on shore during the day on February 1, Hall determined to get underway. Concern for interference by English traders also contributed to his decision. Two had sailed to leeward earlier that day. They would rather have the coast trade to themselves, and he worried they might prejudice the Greboes at Cape Palmas.

The *Ann* weighed anchor by three on the morning of February 2, with a favorable breeze and current.[7]

In late morning, she approached Bassa Cove, about sixty miles southeast of Monrovia. A Spanish vessel with a cargo of slaves obtained nearby passed them—one vessel carrying captives to the New World, the other carrying descendents of earlier such prisoners back to their ancestral land. "These slavers are furnished with cargoes by the natives," Wynkoop wrote coolly in his journal,

> The traders deposit goods with them on the promise of being supplied with slaves; or else open a store at the factory ready to make exchanges when the slaves are brought. Slaves are obtained chiefly from the interior tribes. They are, as we were informed, either captives taken in war, or pledges left as security for the payment of debts. A man is liable to be called to a palaver for the commission of specified crimes; and if sufficient proof of guilt be given, to be fined. If unable to make payment, he must remain himself; or give one of his kindred, or a slave; and after a certain time, if the fine be not cancelled, the pledge may be sold to the slave-dealer.[8]

Trade in human beings was here carried on as casually and in much the same manner as that in palm oil or ivory. What must have been the thoughts of the *Ann*'s company as the vessels ran close enough for the sailors to hail each other?

A year before, Americans had established a colony at Bassa Cove, a bare mile or two from this slave factory. Under such peculiar circumstances about fifty families struggled for subsistence. Among them were several families from the *Lafayette* expedition. "They have been sorely disappointed at Bassa as it regards rations they were to receive, and many have suffered severely," Hall reported. He was able to recruit five more volunteers, including James Benson, once a slave in Snow Hill, Maryland, one of Liberia's first settlers, now proprietor of a successful trading house. With thirty-five volunteers, the contingent of settlers now numbered fifty-three.[9]

Late Thursday night, the *Ann* again set sail. Anticipation grew as the vessel drew "close on the promised land." Despite the excitement, settlers were frustrated and tense. They complained about rations, feeling they deserved more at the end of so tedious a voyage. "I addressed them on the subject," Hersey reported, "stating the ruinous consequences that must result from their conduct. I informed them that there should be no *just ground* for complaint where the evils complained of could [not] be remedied or removed." He promised them he would have the rations increased if he could. Hall, though, would make only slight alterations. "Thus my word became as an idle tale — a glaring falsehood, at least in their estimation," he wrote angrily. The stop at Bassa was not without cost, for Hall, already weak, suffered an attack of fever. The ship had to anchor ten miles offshore because of surf and sandbars, and the long ride ashore in an open longboat in bright sunshine was too much for his fragile system. He was hardly able to stir during the next two days.[10]

Beyond Bassa, the *Ann* encountered pleasant weather and favorable winds. Wynkoop described the scene as Friday's dawn revealed the passing shoreline:

> When sufficiently near the land, we could frequently see handsome and cultivated tracts, extending miles before us. Villages too, apparently large, were scattered along at intervals of ten and twenty miles. The people of these villages always have some article of trade; and if nothing more than a fowl, or bunch of plantain, or a goat, they will come out with it six, and even ten miles, to trade with vessels. On some occasions we were surrounded with as many as a dozen canoes. Some had light articles of trade, from fishing-lines up to pine apples; others came, as they expressed it, "to look ship, and hear the news." For their articles of trade they want tobacco and beads; and receive the rum as a compliment for their visit. Of this latter article they could get none from us.[11]

The crescendo of welcome as they proceeded to leeward cheered the nervous emigrants.

On Monday evening, the *Ann* stopped for the night off a village called Garroway. There was an enthusiastic reception, especially when the citizens learned that the Americans intended to settle among their kinsmen at Cape Palmas. "[They] began at once, with all their zeal and eloquence, to persuade us that their town was on the proper cape; that they had 'too much land' to sell, and that their land 'pass all other land,'" Wynkoop wrote. Residents of Cape Palmas had paddled fifteen or twenty miles up the coast to see the rumored foreigners, for news of the expedition's approach had reached the cape well ahead of the slow-sailing brig. To hear the specious claims of Garroway was truly provoking. "It was difficult for them to restrain their anger, when they saw the attempts made to induce us to stop before reaching their town," Wynkoop noted. "Many strong words and fierce gesticulations were made by the different parties." The Cape Palmas men carried their point. Joe Wilson then set off for the cape with official word of the Marylanders' intentions.[12]

"The natives came off by hundreds and entreated us to anchor, go on shore and view their country," Hall recalled as the ship neared Fishtown. "And when the emigrants saw the broad tranquil bay extending inland, the beautiful fields of grass spreading on either hand as far as the eye could reach, covered with flocks of sheep and herds of cattle, and the rows of majestic palms standing in strong relief against the eastern sky: they besought me, with one voice, to go no farther — to stop and try that country — they wanted no other home — here they would gladly live and die." Hall, of course, would not stop, for Cape Palmas was the destination, and he knew that place to be even better suited to the great project now becoming a reality.[13]

At four on the afternoon of February 11, 1834, seventy-seven days from Baltimore, the *Ann* hove to off a broad, funnel-shaped cove protected on its southern shore by the promontory of Cape Palmas, almost a mile long. A few hundred yards away the Cape rose in three gentle hills to a height of nearly one hundred feet, in sharp contrast to the low topography of the mainland. Covered by scrub and stunted palms, the headland broke to the sea in dark, orange-red cliffs. The Cape's north shore, protected from the waves, was less rugged. At its far end, cliffs gave way to a gently sloping bank, where, just visible through the trees were the conical thatched roofs of Grebo houses, part of Gbenelu, or "Big Town." A creek, clogged at its mouth by mud banks, emptied into the east end of the cove. Continuing their gaze to the left, along the cove's north shore, the Americans could see a smooth sandy beach, backed in some places by grassy plots, and in others by palms. Farther from the beach they could glimpse the high tops of trees.[14] Here at last was the fabled Palmas, even more beautiful than the towns just passed, a welcome sight to the sea-weary company on the *Ann*. "The appearance of the country, the bay, and river is exceedingly fine, and no place could be more desirable for a settlement," Hall remarked in his journal that afternoon.[15]

Once at anchor, the *Ann* was practically besieged by men in canoes, all at once gawking at the foreigners, asking for work on the vessel, offering to sell rice and palm oil in exchange for manufactured articles, and begging for dashes—little gifts of rum, tobacco, or other sundries. The men generally wore old European shirts, jackets, or hats, all items in great fashion, over cotton loincloths. Many were able to converse with the Americans in an English pidgin, picked up in recurrent contact with British and American vessels. Greboes were a nation of traders and seamen, with a transatlantic reputation for their skills. Every ship's arrival signaled new opportunities for employment and trade, and Greboes fully exploited their contacts with foreigners. John Wilson in 1856 referred to them as "the coolies of Western Africa" and asserted, "There are comparatively few of them who do not now serve an apprenticeship of several years on board of foreign vessels."[16]

Although Greboes retained a distinctive culture of their own, imported goods were accustomed accessories of daily life long before the *Ann*'s anchoring. Muskets, gunpowder, rum, cloth, beads, pottery, glassware, and occasional pieces of furniture were in general use. When the Niger Exploring Expedition, sent out by the British government, passed Cape Palmas in 1832, R. A. K. Oldfield, its recorder, regretted not being able to land. He had been informed "that many European articles were to be found in the houses of the chief men, with which they are regularly supplied by their countrymen from Sierra Leone."[17] Western goods, especially cloth, tobacco, beads, and metal rods, passed as money, and the adoption of European or American fashions was a mark of prestige.

The sea also yielded salt and fish. These, along with imported manufactured goods, supplied an active inland trade: maritime products for
ivory, dye-woods, palm oil, and especially rice, the staple of Grebo
diet. Wilson and Wynkoop were quick to recognize the fact. "The tribes
on the sea coast are the merchants or factors for those in the interior,"
they reported to the American Board of Commissioners for Foreign
Missions:

> Their knowledge of the principles of trade, and their acquaintance
> with foreign languages, resulting from their intercourse with Euro-
> peans and Americans, render them far superior, in their own estima-
> tion, to their neighbors. Still, however, they are jealous and afraid of
> the very people whom they affect to hold in contempt. Hence most
> of the towns on the beach are strongly barricaded, and a watch is
> constantly kept to prevent surprise. Great pains are taken by the
> people on the coast to prevent any intercourse between foreigners
> and the tribes in the interior, doubtless for the purpose of keeping
> them in ignorance, and of monopolizing the whole of the foreign
> trade.[18]

Other testimony confirms and illustrates this fact, which would
have incalculable importance in the history of the colony at Cape Palmas.
"The inhabitants of the coast look upon the bush (i.e. interior) people
as an inferior race of beings," a colonial official wrote with some humor
in 1836. "[They] act as sort of commission merchants for them, and
receive more than two thirds of the sales, as their recompense. And it is
not very uncommon to see one Bushman, and eight or twelve coast
people following, to sell one chicken worth 12 1/2 cents. There is some
difference however between them and commission merchants as the
trouble of the coast people consists in dividing the money."[19] James Hall
must also have been aware of the peculiar economic niche which Greboes
occupied, although no written note of the fact has come to light.[20]

While the *Ann* still lay off Garroway, Joe Wilson went to Gbenelu
to inform the Grebo leadership of the mission. This was mere formality, as news had already arrived. When the vessel put in at Cape Palmas,

Wilson came back aboard. The agent asked him the news, and what the king had said. Wilson reported,

> "He very glad — say you must come look at the place yourself; if you like it you can sit down there." He also informed us that his townsmen had slept none the last night, which we could easily have inferred from so many of them coming off to us at so early an hour in the morning.[21]

Soon after, Pah Nemah, whom foreigners knew as "King Freeman," sent emissaries aboard ship to welcome the newcomers and invite them ashore. In his ongoing letter home, Hall wrote on the night of February 11: "The natives evince the utmost anxiety that we should stay with them; but many difficulties will doubtless be thrown in the way by other towns who are extremely jealous, however. I shall visit the King tomorrow, and arrange matters as speedily as possible."[22]

Early on the morning of the twelfth, Dr. Hall, John Wilson, and one or two other Americans rode through the surf in a Grebo dugout. The doctor was careful that neither he nor any of his companions wore any military apparel, but the wasted little man on crutches can hardly have cut a martial figure anyway. "An immense number assembled about the place of our landing," Wilson vividly wrote in his journal. "Our boat stranded, and we were carried ashore upon the backs of the natives. Several of the headmen of the town met us at the water side to escort us to the king's palace. As soon as our whole company had landed, we moved forward in a regular procession; each one of us having a staff-man or two to clear the way for us." The newcomers were objects of great novelty, and all the townspeople turned out to have a look and shout a greeting. Wilson wrote that their exclamations, combined "with the dingling of the bells and chains which they wore about their necks and ankles," practically deafened them.

Slowly, they made their way through the maze-like streets of the town to Pah Nemah's compound. "We found his majesty sitting under the roof of one of his houses, on a low stool, with a striped umbrella held over his head," Wilson wrote.

He retained his seat, but shook hands with each one of us. He is a fine looking man, very stout, with a dignified, modest, and sensible appearance. The only clothes he wore was a striped cloth fastened around his loins and extending down to his knees. He had a string of beads around his neck, several iron rings around his wrists, and at least half a dozen coarse iron rings around each ankle. Immediately behind him stood his wives; on his left side sat his interpreter, a small, sprightly, pleasing looking fellow; next stood the king's counsellors. Seats were furnished us around the king, immediately under the vertical rays of the sun. This, together with the number of human beings who wedged up every avenue through which air could pass, made the place almost intolerably warm.[23]

A short interview transpired. Hall stated that he wished to buy Cape Palmas and the adjacent territory on behalf of the Maryland State Colonization Society. King Freeman appeared to favor the proposal and promised to summon kings of neighboring town-states to a palaver the next day—at which they would negotiate the sale of their countries. The whole business was handled rather casually, and Hall spent the afternoon on a tour, conducted by Freeman himself, intended to impress him with the Cape's advantages for settlement.

That night, canoes passed regularly to the *Ann* and back ashore as Hall and Freeman quietly worked out the terms of an agreement. The failure to offer rum in payment posed an obstacle, as Hall and others had feared. Even so, the agent kept secret that he had enough liquor stowed aboard ship to buy half of Africa. At daybreak, the question of rum remained open.

On the morning of February 13, most of the *Ann*'s company came ashore for the first time. They proceeded as a group to the heart of Gbenelu, where they found their hosts gathered in an open area, in the shade of a tall tree. Present were Pah Nemah, or King Freeman of Cape Palmas; Weah Bolio, or King Will of Grahway, neighboring Cape Palmas territory on the east; and Baphro, or King Joe Holland of Grand Cavally, at the mouth of the Cavally River, about twenty miles east. Scores of head-men, trademen, captains of soldiery, and other dignitaries accompanied them, all ready to conduct business.[24]

The Grebo states were very nearly pure democracies. Citizens discussed public issues, shaped policy, and enacted laws in a public assembly, called a *tapanu*, or "palaver" in the pidgin of the coast. Citizens usually "talked" palavers in an open area near the center of a town, although trivial or secret matters might be argued inside the "palaver house" or *takae*. Parleys between towns at war usually occurred outside town gates.

A customary formula governed the proceedings. At an appointed hour, every one interested would gather in a rough circle or square, each person placing his stool in its proper place among his peers. Those directly involved, or who planned to speak, took places nearer the center. "The speaker takes his stand in the center of the circle, with a long staff in his hand, and says 'bateo' (listen)," John Wilson later wrote.

> The people reply, 'bate' (we do listen). He then states the object for which the assembly has been convened, asks their counsel and advice, and then throws down the staff to be used by the speakers in succession, and goes back to his seat. Some one (generally the younger members speak first) rises up, adjusts his cloth, as if he were about to perform an important duty, takes up the long staff and makes a harangue. The staff is turned to good account by tracing on the ground certain marks to indicate the different points in the speech, and great emphasis is imparted to an argument sometimes by bringing it heavily upon the ground. At the conclusion it is thrown down violently on the ground to express strong emotion or fixed determination; but if the speaker should be in a gentler mood, it is quietly handed to the next person ready to take the floor. The use of the staff prevents more than one person from speaking at the same time, and it might add to the decorum of more august bodies if a similar usage were adopted.[25]

Acclamation almost always decided issues, the majority dictating. Such government could be unpredictable in policy and unfair to the rights of minorities.

On the morning of February 13, the parties ranged themselves on opposite sides of a square. On one side sat representatives of three Grebo states, each king flanked by his subordinates, behind them a mass of soldiers sitting, their muskets held upright between their knees. Across from this imposing body, Hall and nearly fifty Americans took their places. A few wicker seats had been set out for their convenience—in fact, Hall could not have stood for very long at all. He took one chair and was joined by Hersey, McGill, Thomson (who recorded the proceedings), Wilson, and Wynkoop. The rest of the Americans stood or sat in the rear. Most of the inhabitants of Gbenelu, probably, turned out to watch.

The palaver began in the usual manner. Simleh Ballah, King Freeman's interpreter, stood up and cried "Bateo" three times, with the audience responding "bate" each time. As Ballah spoke quietly with King Freeman, "There was no floor on which to hear a pin drop, but silence reigned," Hall recalled later. The interpreter then turned to Hall, saying, "King say, what you come for? King want your full, true word."[26]

Hall answered directly, and in short sentences, so that his meaning would be clear.[27] He stated that the Maryland State Colonization Society had sent him to buy land to make home for black people from America and expounded at length the advantages that a settlement of foreigners would bring, mentioning in turn trade, education, and defense.

Freeman, speaking for the others, expressed his belief that an American settlement would make his country rich. He refused to give up his town or his people's right to farm and go to sea as they always had. To Hall, this seemed only just. "We no want your town, you shall keep all, nor the land you cut for farm," he answered. "You keep your canoes, fish, trade with vessels as before. But when a ship comes, it comes to the Governor and no captain must land goods except to the port officer."[28]

Then followed the crucial question. "Very well, you say you buy country — what you go pay for it?"

Hall told them to name a price. "A consultation of the trademen ensues. They find little difficulty making out an inventory of all the trade goods they ever heard of, but in quantity, their knowledge of arithmetical numeration failed to come up to their greed."[29] On the evening following the palaver, Hall listed the goods initially demanded: "20 Puncheons Rum, 20 Cases Guns, 20 1/2 barrels Powder, 20 bales of Cloth, 20 Neptunes, 20 Brass Kettles, 20 Boxes Hats (2 dozen each), 20 boxes Cutlasses, 20 boxes Beads, 100 Iron pots, 20 Cases looking glasses, 100 Dozen Red caps, 200 Iron Bars, 20 gross trade Knives, 20 Crates Wash Basins, 20 hogsheads Tobacco, 1 Box Umbrellas, 100 Boxes pipes, 20 Kegs Flints, 2 Boxes large copper wire or rod, 2 gross Spoons, 3 gross forks, 100 Tumblers, 100 Wines, 20 Boxes Soap, 10,000 Fish hooks, 100 Tin Pails, 100 stone jugs, 20 Demijohns, 20 Cases snuff Boxes, 20 Boxes Candles, 2 Cases Bells, 20 suits Cloths, 3 Beds and Bedsteads, 6 Boxes Cloths, 3 Cock'd Hats, 6 Epaulettes, 3 Dozen Flags."[30]

The agent, adept at the time-honored art of bargaining, laughed contemptuously as the interpreter recited the list aloud, even causing him to pause in embarrassment. When it was his turn to speak, Hall informed the Grebo kings first, "My master sent me to buy land without rum." Thomson then read a previously prepared list of goods the society was willing to offer for the territory. The secretary had hardly begun reading when, "a howl of derision from the mass of trademen broke up the *dignity and order* of the palaver."[31]

Negotiations ceased for nearly an hour as excited discussions passed through the assembly. At length, with the sun low in the sky, calm returned. Simleh Ballah voiced the Grebo consensus: it was bad enough to do without rum, but Hall's offer was scarcely enough to pay for a prime elephant's tusk. Freeman would consider a better offer. Believing that Greboes would make almost any concession to have Americans live with them, the agent held firm. He said quietly, "I can make no other offer, no more, no less. My master gave me these things to buy a home for these people; if you will take them, good! If not, I go my way."[32]

The Grebo kings and headmen now discussed the offer among themselves, eventually asking Thomson to repeat the list. This time they listened silently, more carefully: "4 Cases Muskets, 20 Kegs Powder 110 pieces of Cloth, 10 Neptunes, 10 Brass Kettles 20 Hats 100 Cutlasses 200 lbs Beads 1500 lbs of Iron Pots, 6 doz looking Glasses, 4 framed ditto, 24 Iron bars, 100 trade knives, 100 wash basins, 3 Hogds. Tobacco 10 Boxes pipes, 2 Kegs Flints 6 doz locks 24 Decanters, 50 Tumblers, 50 Wine Glasses, 24 Stone Jugs 10 Demijohns 3 Suits of Cloths, 3 cocked hats, 25 Razors in Cases, 50 Pitchers, 50 Mugs, 50 Bowls, 3 pr. Brass barreled pistols 1000 Fish hooks, 50 pr Scissors."[33] Hall recalled, "They seemed to count and calculate how it could be divided between the three general kings; begging for some addition to supply special lacks."[34] The total value of goods was about $1,200. To make up for deficiencies, Hall added fifty Spanish silver dollars, which they readily accepted. The palaver was now "set."

That night, Hall wrote his superiors in Baltimore that he had successfully negotiated the purchase of Cape Palmas, encompassing a territory, he thought, "generally penetrating about twenty miles in the interior and to the same extent of sea board." He continued exultantly, "This purchase is all that we could possibly desire, and far, far more than we had reason to expect, and the compensation therefor much less than any one acquainted with the African character could have anticipated. And I will venture to say that no treaty of the Kind was ever effected, or a palaver of this magnitude set with the natives of this country in so short a time."[35]

Early on February 14, Marylanders and Greboes met again to ratify and sign the deed of cession, which Hall had composed overnight. The deed gave the Americans, at first sight, extensive rights in the Grebo territories. The kings agreed to "grant and sell" a tract of land of which they were then "lawfully seized by right of possession and descent" to the Maryland State Colonization Society. The territory was alleged to include some four hundred square miles, including twenty miles of beach front, extending in an irregular quadrangle twenty miles inland. Greboes would retain "so much of the said territory as is now under cultivation by the inhabitants thereof, or such places as are occupied . . . as towns and villages." James Hall promised Greboes that "neither themselves or property shall be trespassed upon or molested in any manner whatever, and no lands under cultivation, or towns or Villages shall be taken from them, except by special contract; paying the desired remuneration Therefor." For this, they received an assortment of trade goods, some practical, others frivolous, which were relatively valuable on the coast. Hall also promised "that free schools shall be established for the benefit of the Children in each of the . . . Towns." Hall and the interpreters read and explained the document in laborious detail, but the business was concluded by midday with remarkably little wrangling.[36]

In signing the deed of cession, Hall and the Grebo kings committed their people to an arduous competition. Greboes must now share their territory with strangers who had radically different ideas about how to use it. Land is a resource of immeasurable importance, for all economic and most cultural activities have some spatial dimension. It provides the basis for subsistence and supports material aspects of culture. Moreover, land is almost never used by an individual in isolation from others, formal arrangements arise to regulate and ensure the rights of each user. Of course, land tenure is not the only determinant of economy or culture, but it is nonetheless a significant factor. Where land is scarce, or when peoples with differing attitudes toward it meet, land takes on a critical importance in the life of a community.

In all cases of colonial expansion, settlers must struggle to understand the conditions of their new environment and then to control all or part of the landscape: to grow food, construct shelters, and participate in the life of the community, all according to value systems carried with them from their old homes. Black Americans seeking a new home in Africa were no different. Neither culture, place, or epoch of settlement alters a process of adjustment. Intimately bound up in this is the confrontation with land tenures of indigenous communities: settlement is also a struggle between people. The history of Maryland in Liberia relates the unfolding of precisely these sorts of conflicts.[37]

Though Greboes had continuing contact with the western world through trade with merchant ships and slavers, and many had visited foreign ports, Grebo culture was distinctly autonomous, having a strong internal coherence and momentum. Men went to sea, sojourned in strange lands, and returned home to resume their old way of life, remaining suspicious of innovation. A language of trade and widespread use of imported goods, especially among the privileged, were the principle results of generations of contact. A subtle and important paradox arose from this ambivalence toward western cultures. Greboes were eager to have the Marylanders reside amongst them so that they could have unlimited access to western goods, yet they wanted these things on their own terms: a particular color and weave of cloth; tobacco of specific leaf size, color, and flavor; rum of a certain clarity and taste, and so on. They had no interest in goods that did not meet a highly precise set of standards. Thus Greboes welcomed the settlers, but on certain conditions which the latter did not fully understand and many of which they would not accept. Adding to the complexity of the issue, each side seems to have misjudged the intentions of the other. Greboes apparently thought that the colony would remain a trading post, while the Americans envisioned a huge immigration of free black farmers from the United States. The history of Cape Palmas in this regard is that of the struggle between Americans who thought they had secured extensive privileges and Africans who sought to limit encroachments on their territory.

Relatively speaking, the Grebo deed of cession was remarkably open and fair. The deed specifically guaranteed autonomy to the Grebo states and secured them in their property rights. Both Greboes and Americans would be "members" of the colony of Maryland in Liberia. In this respect, the deed differs substantively from treaties with American Indians, who almost always agreed to desert the whole of their territories or settled for a tiny fraction or "reservation." Americans purchased Monrovia in the Western style. With a gun literally at his head and a cask of rum, King Peter saw the light and agreed to abandon his lands to the Americans.[38]

Contrary to appearances, the deed of cession rested upon paradoxes that rendered it almost preposterous. Because it took nothing away from Grebo sovereignty, two states—or four, if the autonomous Grebo towns are counted separately—ruled the same territory. No constitution defined their jurisdictions or harmonized political or legal practice. Even more important, the meaning of "lands under cultivation" was ambiguous. Greboes sold only the land that they were not using for towns or farms. This meant something very different to Greboes than Americans. Greboes used fields briefly then left them to a long fallow. Thus lands in use in an extended cycle would appear vacant to strangers accustomed to fencing and permanent, intensive cultivation. Both parties either failed to notice or ignored the contradiction. The fact is, both Greboes and Americans were eager to make a deal, even if that involved misunderstanding and deception.[39]

The society and its settlers imagined that Africa was a vacant wilderness, most of it covered with lush, dense vegetation. Certainly, people were there, but they, like Indians in the American wilds, had underused the land and therefore could lay little claim to it. Luxurious tropical plant life seemed to indicate that soils were extremely fertile, and they were confident of practicing agriculture as they had in Maryland, or at least in the manner of Southern plantation agriculture. Their faith was firm: to make this as productive a region as any other in the world, all that was necessary was regular cultivation with the tools of western agriculture.[40]

Unfortunately, the newcomers based their high hopes on incomplete and mistaken information. Cape Palmas presented the *Ann's* emigrants an environment radically different from anything in Maryland, different in physical geography, climate, vegetation, and human ecology. They had left a land of diverse geology and topography—some from mountains, others from tidewater, still others from cities—but, a land of temperate climate, and an ethical and economic culture rooted in the Christian European tradition. They found a low-lying coastline hemmed by tropical rainforest, where the old seasonal pattern of spring, summer, fall, and winter was replaced by nearly constant temperatures and alternating wet and dry seasons. Moreover, a populous African community, the Greboes, had made the landscape their own by means of fire, axe, and livestock over the course of generations. They had adapted to the constraints of land quality and availability, health, and economic opportunity. This was tropical Africa: no amount of wishful thinking, money, or hard work could recreate a North American landscape here.

The Marylanders encountered a community whose attitudes toward property differed markedly from their own. Land belonged to the town as a whole. Individual families might acquire rights to certain tracts or to particular trees, but these privileges could be revoked whenever popular will demanded. Moreover, competition for productive tracts was keen, and boundaries a common source of dispute. Land was not free: the cultivator owed a share of everything he harvested to town officials, to his age-grade, and to his clan.

Greboes were unfamiliar with the concept of exclusive ownership of land by individuals. John L. Wilson, who was an eyewitness to the deal, later noted this as a general cultural feature along the coast. "The Kru people have no idea of the appropriation of land by individuals except for temporary purposes. It is regarded as common property, and any man can use as much of it as he chooses, but he cannot sell any. The only exclusive right which any one has is that of occupancy."[41] It was, he thought, a concept foreigners seldom comprehended. When Greboes "sold" a tract of land, they did not have "a correct apprehension of the nature of the transaction, whatever pains may have been taken to make them understand it; and they never do comprehend it fully until the contract is carried into execution, in connection with their own observation and experience."[42]

The Grebo kings undoubtedly had a conception of sale that differed from the Marylanders'. Wilson's description, though pertinent to the sale of Cape Palmas, raises difficult questions about the common sense or gullibility of the Greboes. Certainly, they were not fools. Their shrewdness in dealing with foreigners was legendary. Wilson himself wrote from long experience of the "skill and cunning with which they can 'drive a bargain;' and the perfect adroitness with which they practice upon the unsuspecting credulity of white men." He added, "Such is the closeness of observation of these people, that they will ordinarily find out more about the general character and disposition of a white man in a few hours, than he will of them in as many months or years."[43] The majority of Greboes probably knew very little about American laws or attitudes about land use. Still, some must have understood what the Marylanders intended to do. Examples of foreign settlement at Sierra Leone and Monrovia were in plain view. James Hall made no attempt to hide his object, nor could he have done so conveniently, landing, as he did, with a shipload of supplies and a contingent of some fifty settlers. What is more, the Grebo kings were sober when they talked the land palaver, a point of considerable significance. Why then did they give in so easily to James Hall's terms, allowing their sovereignty to be compromised by a foreigner, with no more serious discussion than how many bolts of cloth, fish hooks, and other trinkets they would receive?

The principal reason was that disease and the remoteness of Cape Palmas were effective barriers to any substantial or permanent European settlement. Therefore, Greboes, like other African coastal peoples, felt they could afford to make extravagant concessions, confident that nothing would come from them. In 1820, for instance, George Alexander Robertson, an official of the British colony at Sierra Leone, sailed down the coast collecting deeds for territory. With one treaty, he acquired all of the coastline between Bedoo, an obscure village, and Cape Palmas, a distance of as much as two hundred miles. The African dignitaries who signed the document gave up "all their right and title of sovereignty and Royalty" in favor of his "Brittanick Majesty." No price was mentioned, but liberal dashes of rum and satin stripes probably smoothed the deal. The treaty was a dead letter as soon as Robertson departed, though, and Parliament was quick to repudiate his pretended acquisitions.[44] Oliver Holmes, who succeeded Hall as governor briefly in 1836, was not overly cynical in asserting, "I think I could for a Cask of Rum buy and get a Deed from any of the Coast Tribes of the whole continent of Africa, and then if I at some future time should want to occupy a farm in the Country of these same people, I would have to buy the same for five times as much, provided that they had not sold the same to some person else in the mean time."[45]

The Grebo kings negotiated with Dr. James Hall. In their eyes, settlers belonged to him, and his death or removal signaled the end of the contract. Most likely, Greboes regarded the American settlement as a supplier of manufactured goods, discounting the idea that very many foreigners would come to live among them. "It would be difficult to convey to you an idea of the exact relation which these people conceive they bear towards the Colony," Hall wrote J. H. B. Latrobe in May 1836. "They have a vague and indefinite hope that they shall be benefitted by their connexion with it, and the grounds of this hope are as various as are the characters of the different people." The Greboes "have deeded their land, believing that we shall never require any part thereof, or as they express it, from a conviction that we 'can't fit it,' . . . The sole good which a large majority of them expect from the connexion, is the advantage of free trade."[46]

Such an interpretation is supported from a variety of sources, not least in the smattering of messages from Greboes. For instance, King Freeman of Cape Palmas, sent his interpreter, Simleh Ballah, to the United States in 1836. He was a guest at Latrobe's house for several weeks, and every effort was made to impress him with American civilization. At a meeting of the board, he spoke about the benefits Greboes expected from the Maryland colony:

> Long time past, slave man come we country. He do we bad too much, he make slave, he tief plenty man for sell. By and by all slave man knock off. This time we no sell slave, no man come for tief him. All man glad this palaver done sit. Beside that we have plenty trouble. All man have to go for ship to get him ting, iron, cloth, tobacco, guns, powder, and plenty, plenty little ting. Some time canoe capsize, man lose all him money. Some time he die, plenty water kill him; he can't come up. This hurt we too much, and make we heart sorry. By and by one white man come we country. He bring plenty black America man. Him buy we country, we give him land for sit down. Him say he come for do country good. Him build house — put all

him money shore — make farm — make road — make all country fine. This time all good ting live shore — no more go ship. Ebery man can buy that ting him want. No money lose, no man lose. This make all men heart glad — make King's heart glad. King tell me, "Bally, go that country: see how this ting be. Tell them people all we heart say. Thank him for that good ting them do for we country. Beg him for send more man, for make house, make farm — for bring money, and for make all little childs sava read book, all same America men."[47]

From the Grebo point of view, Americans made life safer and more convenient. They supplied inexpensive imported goods and also promised to educate Grebo children, thus making them especially employable on ships. In addition to trade, the Americans promised union: mutual defense, mediation of disputes, and unhindered travel.

James Hall, however, was Agent of the Maryland State Colonization Society, whose mission was not commerce but the resettlement of a large population in a utopian agricultural community. He negotiated an outright purchase of territory and claimed the right to distribute land as he saw fit, to make settlers proprietors of the soil. The Americans would insist upon the contract as they interpreted it, with military force if necessary.[48]

Dr. Hall was careful to leave the boundaries of the purchase vaguely delimited, just in case valuable resources might turn up, or traders might try to claim land too close by.[49] Even so, Hall seems to have misunderstood egregiously the geographical extent of the purchase and the political divisions within the Grebo nation. In the negotiations, the Grebo kings encouraged Hall in the belief that they owned vast expanses of land, when in fact they controlled miniscule territories. A year and a half later, he knew better. "Kings Freeman Bolio and Baphro did not act in good faith in deeding territory to me," he told Latrobe, but though he suspected as much any delay while he investigated would have been "exceedingly dangerous to the whole undertaking."[50]

Greboes inhabited a strip of coastline about forty miles long, from Fishtown on the west to the Cavally River on the east, extending no more than five or six miles inland. This territory was broken into six loosely associated states. The actions of one were not binding on the others. Thus Hall acquired paper rights to some four hundred square miles, when King Freeman and his two colleagues had less than one hundred to sell.

To understand this more fully, it is necessary to review Grebo history, at least as Greboes themselves explained it.[51] According to oral traditions, ancestral Greboes had inhabited the grasslands north of the rainforest in what is now Cote d'Ivoire. Overpopulation or slave raiders seem to have forced a small group, comprising six extended families, from their homes at some uncertain time in the late seventeenth century. They moved southeast first, but their advance was halted when they met powerful states in the Gold Coast hinterland. They then turned southwest, eventually reaching the coast near Beriby, thirty miles east of the Cavally River. They lingered among the Bolobo there for a few years and learned to manage boats and fish. Still discontented, they resolved to move again.

Sometime about the year 1700 they stole canoes from their hosts and left. Grebo informants in the early 1850s told the missionary John Payne that this event was the source of the name, "Grebo."[52] Moving westward, the refugees scattered but then regrouped at Cape Palmas, called by them "Gbenelu," literally, "the hill on which all the various families assembled." The Bolobo pursued them, and they were forced to flee twenty miles farther up the coast to Garroway, or Yuabo. After the war with the Bolobo ended, they made a new town, called Rocktown or Taake, a few miles east. The group split about 1704, evidently because of overcrowding. With mutual assurance of friendship, a group moved to Cape Palmas. Later that year, these same people, now distinguished as the Nyomowe, "the people of Nyomo (Hoffman's) River," were at war with Rocktown, whose people were called Kudemowe, after the Kude River there. Tensions persisted ever after.

In subsequent years, Greboes spread from these two towns over the adjacent coastline. A disaffected Nyomowe faction moved ten miles east of Cape Palmas to establish Bleje, later called Grahway, for Glei, a famous sailor who once lived there. (It should be noted that Grebo orthography often interchanges r and l. Thus, the Marylanders at first called Baphro, "Pahfleur"; again, "Glebo" is an alternate spelling for Grebo.) Another party from Cape Palmas settled Wodoke, "the place of rest," on the banks of the Cavally River. Shortly afterward, a small group from Grahway built Kablake, "the place of running crabs." Both towns were ferrying points. People from Rocktown settled several towns to the west of Cape Palmas, including Middletown (Lede), and Fishtown (Wah). A faction of Rocktown people also settled at Half Cavally (Gbede), east of the Cape. The origins of these towns and their order of settlement had a continuing influence on the internal politics of the Grebo people, and later on, the way they dealt with the American settlement.

In 1834, the Greboes were divided into two chiefdoms: the Kudemowe, centered at Rocktown, and the Nyomowe, centered at Cape Palmas. The unity of each chiefdom effectively consisted of a promise of alliance in wartime. The chiefdoms in turn were composed of seven small, autonomous towns, practically states in their own right. Allied with Rocktown were Garroway, Fishtown, and Half Cavally. Allied with Cape Palmas were Grahway and Grand Cavally. Each of these states had a main town, perhaps one or two small villages in addition, and a patch of coast-hugging territory, extending a few miles inland.

The sum of the matter was this: Freeman invited the two subordinate kings of the Nyomowe confederacy to come and hear the palaver talked. The Kudemowe took no part in the deal, as might be expected, since Freeman had no intention of giving his rivals any of the benefits of an American settlement. On the other hand, Freeman was happy to leave Hall with the impression that he spoke for all the Grebo people, as that would tend to enhance the value of the cession.

III.

"A Field for the Farmer"

THE LAND PALAVER SETTLED, OBSTACLES CONFRONTING THE PIONEERS did not diminish but transformed in character and even magnified. Now they had to put into practice plans made in Baltimore, at least some of which were idle speculation based upon improbabilities. Settlers could waste no time establishing their foothold either. They came ashore on February 14 with machetes and grubbing hoes in hand. As soon as the deed was signed, they set to work.

The following week, according to Hall, "Cape Palmas resembled an ant hill for industry." The Americans and their Grebo employees cleared away brush from the summit of the Cape to lay out roads and lots for a town. McGill conducted the survey. Writing on the fifteenth, he described the place to Latrobe as "a delightful . . . Country, a field for the Farmer."[1] In a subsequent letter, he elaborated on its advantages. "The Situation of the Cape, makes it one of the most desirable spots on the Western Coast of Africa it is high and receives the Sea breeze, and runs westward from the main land about 3/4 mile into the Sea on which our town is located, and all around the Cape abounds with Fish and Oysters, the largest I ever saw. . . . The Country around it is not infested with Swamps and Mangrove like it is about" Monrovia. Cape Palmas presented "a beautiful view, raising gradually from the Sea board, and may be seen for twenty miles in every direction, and a beautiful place for a farmer."[2] Hersey supervised the grading of a rolling road from the landing up the steep hill to the village site. "The agent's business was on shipboard," Hall later wrote, "first to deliver the consideration for the purchase; a matter requiring no little address and management. The next thing, lumber must be landed for erecting a rough board shanty for the agents, and effects necessary for immediate use. The natives in the meantime hastily putting up wattled and thatched tenements for the new families now on board."[3] Construction of houses, a warehouse, and even a rough chapel went along quickly.

Within two or three days of arrival, the agent decided that the Cape itself was the best place to focus settlement. Its level summit could accommodate some sixty lots, each of one-eighth acre. Medical knowledge of the time suggested that the elevation of Cape Palmas and its regular exposure to sea breezes rendered the spot healthier than the low-lying mainland. The cove on its northern shore was the safest anchorage for miles up and down the coast. Most importantly, the Cape was easy to defend. A small garrison at its eastern end could threaten Gbenelu, one hundred yards to the east, and also protect the harbor. Nonetheless, the agent understood that settling on the Cape would incur "many inconveniences," principally, that settlers could not farm there. Lots were too small, and the soil was thin and rocky, polluted by salt spray. Hall found himself in the awkward position of offering land to settlers in fragments, not in five-acre parcels as the society intended. Suitable farmland lay a mile or two to the northeast, on high ground north of the marshy lagoon soon dubbed "Lake Sheppard." Few settlers could afford to build both a town house and a farm house, and so had to choose to live in one place or the other. Virtually all preferred the Cape, with its fine view, sociability, and sense of security. Agriculture, the intended mainstay of the colonial economy, took second place.[4]

Despite the society's plans and Hall's desperate attempts to expedite the voyage, the *Ann* arrived two or three months too late for settlers to begin farming. February was planting season indeed, but settlers were too busy making homes and often too sick with malaria to clear land and plant crops. Agriculture had to be postponed for a year.

In the meantime, the colony would have to subsist on food purchased from Africans. Making matters worse, the previous year's rice crop had been meager, and Greboes could supply but little. Provisions and trade goods were running short. Many emigrants were unprepared for the arduous work of homesteading, and morale was low. "There is not the least particle of public spirit or patriotism in them, and it is with utmost effort that I can produce unanimity of feeling sufficient to enable them to mess together," Hall informed the board on February 15. They complained, he said, "like the children of Israel" for the want of such simple luxuries as coffee and sugar. He advised the society to send a supply ship as soon as possible.[5]

"On the memorable 22d, formal possession was taken of the Cape, with due religious ceremonies, and the first night on shore followed, much to the relief of the women and children, who had rolled for some three months in the old tub *Ann*," Hall later recalled.[6] Settlers would celebrate this date as their national holiday. Yet, Maryland in Liberia was a mere foothold. Houses that Grebo workers built for the Americans had leaky roofs and muddy floors.[7] Settlers were not only vulnerable to the weather but also their Grebo neighbors, to whom all things American were treasures. "At present clustered as we are on this little cape with a constant night guard of two men something is missing every night and in many instances great boldness is manifested," wrote the doctor. "They have slipped their hands thru the watling of the houses and stripped the bed clothes from the sick. Yet 'tis impossible to seize them, owing to the darkness of the nights during the rains." Latrobe had instructed Hall to build a timber block-house of the type found on America's western frontier, but the agent quickly realized that this was impractical. He and the settlers had too much else to do before they could start so ambitious a project. To close the matter, the local timber was inadequate. Grebo farmers had long since cut out big trees to make rice fields.[8]

The colony therefore had to rely on Hall's policy of tact and conciliation for its security. As a more tangible assurance of peaceful relations, he persuaded his three liege kings to send one son each to America for schooling.[9] In a dispatch of February 23, Hall noted to Latrobe that Greboes "will not attack us while we have possession of the Kings' sons." "This measure cost me much trouble and coaxing," he explained. "I wrung them one by one, and promised them in the most solemn manner that they should be well-treated and taught to read and write." The step was unauthorized, but he hoped the board would see its value and fulfill his promise.[10]

In so vulnerable a situation, Hall was convinced of the folly of landing the *Ann*'s cargo without first having a safe place to keep it. Violent thunderstorms, called "tornadoes" on the coast, had for several days warned of the approaching rainy season. What the rains wouldn't ruin he felt sure Greboes or settlers would steal. He resolved therefore to send the *Ann* back to Monrovia, out of harm's way. There, she could get supplies and pick up families left behind by some of the volunteers. He was also glad to be rid of the cantankerous captain for a little while.[11]

The *Ann* weighed anchor on the twenty-third and beat to windward. George McGill returned home aboard her. Wilson and Wynkoop, the missionaries, also sailed with a report for their sponsors in Boston. They believed that Cape Palmas was an excellent site for a mission, and Wilson was particularly eager to establish it. The three boys who would be wards of the society in Baltimore were under Wilson's care. Hall got King Freeman's consent only on the day of sailing, "and was followed by him, boy and mother to the beach, all howling." The *Ann* reached Monrovia by March 6, and there waited.[12]

The colonists at Cape Palmas lost no time preparing for their ship's return. Hersey continued to work on the frame of the Agency House, with much confusion and frustration. The second story was too tall and had to be cut down to size, and several key pieces were misnumbered. Even so, he and his workers succeeded in erecting the first American house at the Cape. Hall supervised construction of a warehouse and longhouse for new emigrants, both thatched by Greboes.[13]

These African workers were of invaluable assistance in these first weeks, providing a day's hard labor for hardly more than a piece of cloth and a clay pipeful of tobacco. Relations between Greboes and Americans nevertheless were tense. Hersey was particularly critical. "On our arrival at Cape Palmas the emigrants discovered not only an indisposition to work, but they manifested an unkind and hostile feeling towards the natives, and a wrangling spirit among themselves," he reported. To illustrate, he related the case of a Grebo workman who went into the cookhouse one afternoon for a drink of water. A settler found him there and insisted that he leave, still thirsty. They began to argue, "a scuffle ensued," and the settler had his face bloodied. "This event threw the colony into a complete ferment — they threatened to kill all the natives — to exterminate them from the land, and burn down their town, accompanied with the most horrid imprecations." The crowd eventually calmed, and the palaver was set peacefully.[14] Such fights were probably daily occurrences, though they did not normally get so far out of hand. These settlers on a foreign shore, beset by neighbors whose language and culture they did not understand, facing constant intimidation and theft, and in some cases quite unwell, cannot help but have been violently jealous of any intrusion.

Hall was in poor health during March. Intermittent attacks of fever confined him to bed many days, and he was delirious at least some of the time. Hersey's condition was hardly better. Settlers, however, remained remarkably fit. The society had reasoned that Monrovian volunteers, proven survivors, would be able to work from the time of landing, when newcomers might be prostrated. The disease environment was harsh. New arrivals on the coast underwent a period of "acclimation"—an initial exposure to malaria, yellow fever, parasites, and other maladies endemic to the region. The death toll among foreigners in Africa was staggering, a fact that discouraged many potential emigrants from undertaking the voyage. If the victim survived the shock of the first attack, however, he might live for many years, though in a weakened state. Children and old people suffered the worst.[15]

In a letter of early June, Hall stated with some qualifications that Cape Palmas was a "far more healthy place than Cape Mesurado." He observed, "quite a number of our colonists were extremely weak and sickly when they embarked from that place and every one will bear testimony *personal* that their health is quite restored." New emigrants got just as sick at Cape Palmas as those in old Liberia, Hall thought, but mortality was lower for reasons he could not explain.[16] In retrospect, it is apparent that settlers in Maryland fared better because they had more attentive medical care. Moreover, Dr. Hall treated fever with Peruvian barks and their extract, quinine—exactly the right medicine— at a time when conventional medical practice recommended bleeding, heavy doses of mercury and opium, and assorted purgatives. Hall some- times used these, too, but having been a victim of cruel medical treat- ment, he was careful not to continue detrimental regimens.[17]

The success of Dr. Hall's treatment led many settlers to underesti- mate the risk. Joshua Stewart, for instance, one of the emigrants from Baltimore, wrote a doctor there, before he had suffered himself, that "The disease is similar to the ague and fever that which predominates in America. It is more severe, the fever when it comes on those persons it reigns to that degree that they become delirious in the head, and at the expiration of this fever, he or her has a very slight chill, which they are able to go about, this disease lasts on some persons ten or fifteen days, and again some thirty days or two months, it keeps them continually in this way but a great many recover from it there is very few die with it."[18] A few weeks later, he and his family were all sick. Stewart then wanted nothing more than to return home, even if he had to sell himself into slavery to pay for the passage. On June 10, his infant son died of dysen- tery, the first death in the colony.[19]

The *Ann* returned to Cape Palmas at the end of March. The agent, though sick, made the unsettling trip through the breakers to hasten the discharge. "The Captain evinced no disposition to forward mat- ters," he complained to Latrobe, "throughout the whole he has done every thing to retard the expedition and not to infringe upon or forfeit the charter." Dr. Hall also wished to witness the destruction of the rum, lest it be sold somewhere on the coast. Reserving a few casks for the apothecary, he stood at the rails as sailors brought up the rest from the hold, a cask at a time, and poured the intoxicating contents to the sharks. They were not yet finished when a signal went up on shore for Hall to return at once. Ten kegs of gunpowder and other goods had disappeared almost as soon as they were landed. "We were very nigh having an engagement," he wrote Latrobe, but he managed to smooth things over. Hall suspected that Freeman and his headmen had instigated the thefts, but he could prove nothing.[20]

Anticipating Hersey's departure, the governor organized an election of civil officers at the end of March. Hersey labeled the winners, "the most ignorant and exceptionable class."[21] Whether this was true or not, Hall did not trust them either. "'Tis hardly to be hoped that they will elect a man at once intelligent and honest," he wrote Latrobe the following June almost prophetically of events two decades off. Even if the elected officer "does not commit any open flagrant dishonest act, still you can hardly expect them to elect a man who is not in some way interested in trade, and then all of the Agencies funds must pass through his hands as merchant." All contract labor would be "paid off at his or friends shop and the Agency charged not over a hundred persent upon an average. . . . It is but reasonable to suppose that a man whom you should see fit to appoint as Agent would make a more judicious selection, than the *canaille* which does and ever will constitute a majority of our Colony."[22] Hall continued almost single-handedly, assisted principally by James Thomson.

The *Ann* sailed at last on April 4, carrying off John Hersey in shamed defeat. Hall felt a combination of relief and disappointment. Although Hersey was eccentric and disagreeable, he was an energetic worker, and competent help of any sort was badly needed.

From the landing day, trade and the management of commodities dominated Hall's activities. Without utmost care, settlers might well have starved, and the colony fallen into war with its African hosts. On any day, Hall once wrote Latrobe, "some important work is going on, some good trade is offered, some native and colonists palavers are to be sett or some one is very sick, and sometimes all come together and sick myself into the bargain."[23] As the colonial factor, Hall advanced cloth, gunpowder, and sundry items to Grebo brokers, called trade men, who used them to purchase rice, palm oil, and other African produce. Such deals were sealed with the dash of a clay pipe and tobacco or some other little consideration to the broker. Every day, practically, some new deal was made, creating an accountant's nightmare. Hall and his secretary, Thomson, kept written records of the advances, when either was well enough, but often they went unrecorded. Grebo trade men kept accounts in their memories, and disagreements between the agent and his African factors were common.[24]

On April 15, Hall participated in a palaver concerning protocols of trade and prices, which had sharply risen over the past few weeks. "Knowing our necessity to purchase rice," Hall commented, "they are determined to charge at least twice the amount paid by all trading vessels on the coast, so that our food will come higher than at Cape Mesurado." Prices were fixed, and for nearly a month after remained stable. The two communities lived peacefully, and Hall even recovered some stolen goods at Grahway.[25]

"Our present standing with the natives is such that I have little . . . to apprehend from them," the doctor wrote optimistically at the end of April.[26] In fact, the partnership of Greboes and Americans was unstable and, to him, unpredictable. In retrospect, the availability of rice seems to have played a crucial role. The Americans arrived inadequately provisioned, too late to plant their own crops, and in a year when rice was scarce. In the middle of May, Hall estimated that he had less than a month's supply of food on hand.[27] He began to trade with more distant towns, particularly Rocktown, the long-standing rival of Gbenelu. Jealous, and sensing their advantage, Freeman and his headmen imposed an embargo sometime about May 10. No Greboes of any town were to sell the Americans provisions or work for them until they agreed to pay sharply increased prices for produce. On the morning that the edict went into effect, Cape Palmas men drove Rocktown factors from the agency store, even as they measured out rice.

Hall knew that the survival of the settlement depended upon a firm stance against the embargo, and he reacted accordingly. Infuriated by the incident at the store, he got himself and crutches aboard his donkey and trotted alone into Gbenelu to give Freeman a piece of his mind. He found the king in council with headmen, and disregarding etiquette, berated them. At first they ignored him. "They did not pretend to reason," Hall told Latrobe, "but only said they would do as they pleased right or wrong." The agent was beside himself. He told Freeman that unless they permitted the Rock Town people to bring rice "we must starve, that we were as ready to meet death one way as another, that as yet we never had done them any wrong or ever threatened violence when they were sensible that they had deserved it." The Greboes had "broken the contract they had but lately made, to allow free trade with all tribes." He had but one thing to say, Hall seethed. "If they attempted to stop by force any trade coming to me or intercepted any trade goods which I should send for rice, . . . war would begin and it should not end while one American lived at the Cape or until I had destroyed every native town within gun shot of our fort."[28]

Such warlike words mortified the council. Unexpectedly, the insidious game played since February involved a real threat of war. Although settlers were few in number, their technological and strategic advantages over Gbenelu were obvious. Besides, few wished to lose so valuable an asset as the American settlement, so recently acquired.[29] The assembly broke into heated discussion on all sides, and Hall for the first time realized that he was alone and defenseless. In characteristic understatement, he told Latrobe, "I thought best to make good my way home."

The agent slipped through the uproar and reached Harper safely. He called all forty-five members of the militia to arms. They spent a sleepless night, muskets loaded and primed, but the expected assault never came. Early next morning, Simleh Ballah, Freeman's spokesman, and a head man came to see Hall. They apologized on the king's behalf and announced the embargo's revocation. Hall accepted, but sternly warned them that the next time Greboes imposed such strictures, he would shoot rather than negotiate.

Thus ended the most serious attempt to date to force the Americans to serve Grebo economic and political interests. During the first three months of Maryland's existence, a distinct pattern of interaction had developed. The newcomers intended to take control of the land. Independence and liberty were their dearest ideals, yet in fact they were in a most dependent and vulnerable situation. Greboes, too, were a sovereign and proud people. On paper they had conceded privileges to the Americans, for which they hoped to gain specific advantages. Chief among these was a ready supply of manufactured goods at low markups, on which they themselves depended for food, by trade with interior states. Greboes wanted Americans to live with them, but on their own terms. Control of the rice supply was the tool with which they hoped to force the colony into submission. Yet Greboes also suffered when rice was scarce, and this made the struggle between the two peoples all the more desperate.[30]

Greboes resorted to theft and intimidation to control the Americans. The tactics were simple and crude but effective. For Greboes, whose property was largely communal, stealing was not the same criminal act that it was to Americans. As freed men, settlers valued most highly the things denied them as slaves—foremost among them private property. Greboes took from settlers, partly, perhaps, from covetousness, or the belief that the objects were common property, or genuine need. Very often, however, theft seems to have been a tool for demoralization.

Freeman and his headmen apparently encouraged stealing, and Hall claimed to have good evidence that the king retained a professional thief. Many letters comment upon the boldness of thefts, and the risk—a musket ball—was plain. The material returns were small: a scrap of cloth or handful of tobacco in many cases. What end could the snatching of bedclothes from a sick man have had, but to depress him and his comrades? Examples of intimidation are also common, the embargo being merely the biggest of a series of incidents. Hall consistently responded with bluster and bravado equal to the challenge.

Greboes made every effort to confine the American settlement to Cape Palmas. They had a geographical advantage, for Gbenelu, King Freeman's main town, was situated between Harper and the mainland, obstructing free passage. Even so, Marylanders steadily learned more about the country, making forays along the coast and inland. They generated good will with surrounding African states, often to the dismay of their jealous hosts at Gbenelu.

Cape Palmas is the seaward end of a chain of diorite hills stretching in a northeasterly course across the coastal plain, contrasting sharply with its low-lying marine topography. The contrast is especially evident at the Cape, whose flat-topped promontory met the sea with rocky orange-red cliffs. "This bold headland of red argillaceous earth, based upon a black micaceous granite" along with the "tilted-up strata in the amorphous trap formation" visible at Russwurm's Island, just south of the Cape, impressed the far-ranging English traveler, Richard Burton. The springs on Cape Palmas had an established reputation for soft water of the best quality available anywhere on the coast.[31]

The accounts and maps of nineteenth-century travelers, colonial officials, and settlers, combined with modern soil surveys of comparable areas, give some idea of the soils about Cape Palmas and their agricultural potential.[32] Taken together, these sources indicate that soil types and productivity varied greatly over relatively short distances, even of a few score yards. The soils around Cape Palmas are of great age and have been subject for thousands of years to intense leaching by heavy rains. The sandy marine soils of the coastal lowlands are the least fertile. Those on hilltops, where mineral nutrients are closer to the surface, or in stream beds, where rich alluvium is deposited, would be the most productive. Many tropical soils are damaged by prolonged cultivation. Exposing certain soils to the air can result in erosion and the rapid leaching of nutrients. Exposure also compacts the soil's structure, making it more difficult to work. Lateritic soils, which would be common around the Cape, have high concentrations of iron and aluminum and are especially vulnerable, as exposure hardens them like brick. A long phase of rest or fallow, between brief periods of cultivation in a system of shifting cultivation such as Greboes used, minimizes degradation.[33]

At Cape Palmas, as anywhere else in the world, climate has had a tremendous impact on the landscape and ecology, and consequently on the way that people have lived there. The region is subject to a humid tropical weather pattern, characterized by high rainfall, concentrated in wet seasons alternating with dry ones, and uniform temperatures, with daily highs about eighty degrees Fahrenheit. The wet and dry seasons result from the interplay over the course of the year of the dry high-pressure system covering the Sahara and the moist low-pressure air mass that lies over the equatorial Atlantic Ocean. Two rainy seasons, one from March to June, the other from August to November, pour more than one hundred inches of rain annually onto the countryside around Cape Palmas. To the windward, rainfall is higher, but it declines steadily to the east along the leeward coast. Timing and intensity of wet and dry periods can vary greatly from year to year, and although the total precipitation may be high, exceptional dry periods or excessive rains often ruin crops like rice. The alternation of wet and dry periods tends to increase the rate and destructiveness of erosion, especially on land that is sparse in vegetation or over-cultivated.[34]

In April and May, the agent grew familiar with the environs of the Cape. He spent a day along the Nyomo or Hoffman's River, which meets the ocean at Cape Palmas. Once past the muddy sand bar at the stream's mouth, Hall found a crescent-shaped lagoon extending about a mile and a half inland.[35] Canoes could navigate the stream for a distance of six miles, he informed the board, but logs and other debris blocked further travel. "From its immense breadth and shortness," he added, "you will of course conclude that it is little more than a creek, subject like the sea to a full flow and ebb of the tide and salt nearly to its source, except in the rains. The land on either side of the river is sufficiently elevated, the soil rich and (what is of great importance in this country) easily cultivated."[36] Another jaunt along a bush path took

Hall ten miles inland to the northeast. "The whole is well wooded and watered with few or no fens or swamps so common on the sea coast," he informed Latrobe, "the surface generally slightly undulating and covered in some parts with a second growth of timber: at intervals however spreading into most luxuriant and extensive savannahs equaling in richness and beauty the far famed plains of Leogane in the Island of Haiti."[37]

The Americans quickly learned that the soils away from the beach were of better quality. Hall would have liked to begin farming there, but he thought it better to secure the coast than to extend settlement too fast. The soils covering the hills associated with Cape Palmas and the higher land in the interior naturally support a broadleaf evergreen rainforest, but most of this was subject to periodic clearing for farms. Only a fraction of the primeval forest remained in 1834. The land was instead covered by sterile grasslands, bush, and secondary forest in various stages of regrowth.[38]

Hardly a week after he had threatened all-out war, peace was secure enough for the agent to visit the leeward towns of Grahway, Half Cavally, and Grand Cavally.[39] Early on May 18, Dr. Hall, a Grebo head man called Yellow Will, and two settlers set out in canoes from the western end of a salty lagoon that runs for several miles parallel to the beach. Settlers called this Lake Sheppard, after Moses Sheppard, a leading supporter of the settlement. This is the westernmost of a series of lagoons that extends eastward with only a few interruptions all the way to the mouth of the Niger River. Greboes used it as a canal, as it was safer than negotiating the surf. The travelers floated past thickets of coarse grasses and palms on their right, fronting the beach, while marshes and mangrove swamps fronted the mainland.

Mangroves thrive in brackish water, where they form impenetrable tangles as immersed branches themselves take root. They proved a bane to settlers of Liberia, who in some cases were given mangrove swamps to farm. In 1833, a group of the *Lafayette*'s emigrants residing at Caldwell complained to the Board of Managers that, "The land is good, but overrun with this deadly poison mangrove which stinks so when you begin to dig amongst it that it lays you up with the Fever."[40] In fact, the swamps were breeding grounds for mosquitoes, carriers of malaria and other parasites, of which medical science of the day understood but little. In 1837, for instance, Dr. Thomas S. Savage, an Episcopal missionary and trained doctor, overlooked what today is obvious, in describing the swamps near Cape Palmas:

> Within the dark recesses . . . crocodiles and other aquatic animals find a lurking place. It is from these mangrove forests, these hiding places of water serpents and other reptiles, proceed those *nameless things* which seem to have their origin and place in the theory only of some medical authors — the tales of travellers and the Peter Parley's of the day. They are represented as coming forth in millionary numbers, and with the blight of their wings spreading far and wide the seeds of disease and death in the atmosphere of Africa! These invisible, infinitesimal creatures or principles, I need not say, I have been unable to see or detect.[41]

Sixty years would pass before Walter Reed proved that mosquitoes transmit malaria. But Dr. Hall was far ahead of his time in using lima barks and their extract, sulfate of quinine, as a preventative of disease. The remedy had no scientific proof at the time, only the recommendation of folk wisdom and Hall's personal experience. Cape Palmas settlers would remain remarkably fit compared with others, including foreigners and Africans, living on the unhealthy coast.[42]

Two hours' travel on Lake Sheppard brought Hall and his party to a village at the eastern end, near Grahway, where they had breakfast of fish and rice in piquant "palaver sauce." Several Grahway headmen joined the party when they got underway again. Hall was quite feeble and the night before had sent his donkey to Grahway. He now mounted the animal, and the others walked alongside. Shortly after clearing the town, they encountered a grassy stretch that seemed almost like a park, "one of the most beautiful meadows I ever beheld," Hall told Latrobe. The swath of grassland was from one to two miles wide and extended over five miles, from Grahway Point to Half Cavally. "It was literally covered with fine fat cattle, sheep and goats belonging to the neighboring towns."[43] Such savannahs were a prominent feature of the coastal landscape—broad expanses of grassland, dotted with palm trees, bushes, and grass. Just as their English predecessors in the Chesapeake had two centuries earlier, the American settlers saw in such lands great potential for farming and raising livestock. In this they were more or less in error, for the savannahs were the result of land degradation, not careful husbandry. Grebo farmers had in generations past systematically cut the original forest for firewood and rice farms. When the fields were abandoned, depleted soils could no longer support new forest. Only grasses and hardy trees able to withstand frequent burning grew there. These "old fields" (as settlers called them, recalling a distinctive feature of the tobacco-worn Chesapeake Tidewater) and swamps were of little value for cultivation, but the land had other uses. Greboes annually burned the scrub grasses to provide fresh pasture for their livestock. Among the few trees that thrived on the savannah, the oil palm (*Elais guineensis*) was a rich source of food. Later, as the industrial market for palm oil developed, palms would become an important cash crop.[44]

The next town along the beach was Half Cavally, whose territory yet remained outside of Maryland's jurisdiction. The town had had relatively little contact with the Americans, since they, like their cousins, the Rock Town people, were on bad terms with Gbenelu. The agent's arrival with Nyomowe dignitaries was a momentous event in this, a Kudemowe town. "Within a mile or so of Half Cavally we were met by not less than a thousand men women and children in whose countenances and gestures nothing but wonder and astonishment were visible. . . . Their hair bound their heads like a well hoop'd cask or they would have burst from the tremendous screaming which issued sans intermission from every throat," said an overwhelmed Dr. Hall of the thunderous reception they received. "'Twas enough to see their Kings rigged out in the clothes I gave them, but a white man and a jack ass to boot, was too much."[45] Even fifty years later, Hall recalled a joke connected with his reception:

The donkey stopped and refused to move. For explanation of the scene, I turned to Yellow Will, but found him, stolid and grim [?] as he usually was, lying in the sand convulsed with laughter. After some delay and much scolding, I brought him to order. "You want to know what make dem people act so?" "Yes, that's just what I do want." "I most fear to tell you, but it be dis: — all dem peoples tink you and donkey be one — one Gubnoo — dey laugh so, cause one face look so he be sorry, go cry, and t'other face laugh, all same *man!*"[46]

The governor took refuge from the clamor in the house of one of the town's trade men, Prince, who had lived in England about twelve years, where he learned English habits. Upon his return to his home town, he built a two-story frame house with clapboard siding and a thatch roof. The ground floor was a storehouse, and the second floor comprised "sleeping and drawing rooms." Hall napped there, "on a hair mattress laid upon a high port field bedstead." He added that he "was favoured the while by [his] host with Paddy Carey and sundry other popular airs upon a fine toned chamber organ. The room was ornamented with many good english engravings, a large looking glass, and contained the common useful articles of chairs and tables etc."[47] Because of the antipathy between the Nyomowe members of his party and the people of Half Cavally, Hall had to cut his visit short. Taking a friendly leave, he set off again.

Now they turned to the northeast along a bush path to meet the Cavally River two or three miles above its mouth. Extensive savannahs covered the land between Grahway and Half Cavally, but on moving inland, Hall was struck by fields newly cleared and planted with rice and cassava. "To an enthusiastic admirer of nature, nothing could have been more charming than a stroll along the border of these beautiful fields." Natural beauty abounded "among almost impervious clusters of young palm trees whose spreading branches exclude every ray of the scorching sun: there opening suddenly upon an immense rice field of the most delicate fragrance. Skirted by the beautiful broad leaved plantain and bannana, literally groaning under the immense masses of their golden fruit." "This jaunt would have been delightful," he groaned, "but to me *ill at ease* upon my ass, winding along a narrow native path, my feet mauled by every stump of the fallow bush, my clothes seized upon by every projecting thorn of the palm, my hat displaced whenever I made an attempt at the perpendicular; laugh'd at by the natives and hooted by the monkeys sporting overhead; it was quite otherwise."[48]

After some hard going, they reached the Cavally River. Before them was a broad sheet of water, hemmed right to its edge with tall trees and undergrowth. "This is a most splendid river," Hall wrote, "near a mile in width, running with great velocity into the sea, perfectly fresh even to its mouth." Hall apparently did not realize that sandbars blocked the river's mouth, and that the dammed water backed up several miles inland, making the river appear very substantial. His imagination immediately seized upon its commercial potential, and the idea would persist in his thought. "I was exceedingly anxious to ascend it and half gave orders a number of times to get ready, but prudence forbid," he admitted.[49]

Proceeding downstream, the travelers reached Grand Cavally, at the river's mouth, by two in the afternoon. The agent was pleased to "perceive our Colonial flag floating on the barricade encircling the Kings houses," a sign of his allegiance. Despite its impressive name, Grand Cavally numbered only a thousand inhabitants, the least of the Grebo states in area, but influential because it controlled the river's mouth. The town subsisted on its trade with the interior.[50]

Baphro, otherwise known as King Joe Holland, a man well over six feet tall, welcomed the visitors, "in his usual frank rough manner." Hall lodged in Baphro's house, one similar to Prince's at Half Cavally. The king ordered a bullock slaughtered for his guests' use—which was, Hall wrote, "much to the satisfaction of my travelling country friends, who had little inducement other than this to undertake the jaunt." At three the following afternoon, Hall left, reaching Cape Palmas by nine that night.[51]

James Hall's health improved in June 1834. On the tenth, he was off his crutches and commented wryly to Latrobe that he was "likely in time to become a real biped."[52] With his health, the fortunes of the colony improved. Disputes lessened in frequency and gravity, partly indeed because many Greboes were encamped at their rice fields, a few miles inland. Construction progressed, as did the vital work of surveying farm lots around the western end of Lake Sheppard. Hall did most of this himself, leading him to complain to Latrobe that he had "already been obliged to ride through bush and brier until clothes and skin are nearly stripped from my lower extremities." He was forced to do so much alone because he was short-handed. James Benson had returned to Bassa Cove to rescue his foundering business. He would never return, though his son would one day play a significant role in the colony's affairs. James Thomson had gone to Monrovia to settle accounts and bring his wife and young son back to Cape Palmas. Hall asked the society to let him hire a more permanent assistant. He had his eye on Charles Snetter, formerly of Charleston, South Carolina, a patriotic and able citizen of Monrovia.[53] Three or more months would elapse before the agent would get a response from Baltimore, and the matter rested.

At the end of June, the agent reviewed the colony's progress. "Every town lot with one exception is cleared, fenced and planted." He had built "a large kitchen and rice house" largely of African materials "except the flooring plank and doors," a stockade fort, and jail, a large "native house for emigrants" and two others that he would take down and relocate later. The colonists had a dozen framed houses, and two substantial "rock houses" were under construction, one of them two stories high.[54]

Important obstacles remained. Members of the *Ann's* original company were still too weak to do much for themselves. Everyone depended upon the agency store for food. Seven weeks more would end the six-month ration period, and the need to extend the term of support was obvious. Settlers borrowed goods and money to buy building materials and hire Grebo laborers. Hall defended his seeming generosity, stating, "It encourages *them*, and will stimulate the new comers, and gain the colony a good name, as every house tells ten miles at sea."[55]

The agent proclaimed the Fourth of July a day of thanksgiving, following a popular New England custom. In a public notice two weeks in advance, he recounted to the pious pioneers of Maryland in Liberia the apparent instances of God's providence during the past few months.[56] On the appointed day, a Friday, all settlers refrained from work and attended a public religious service. They afterwards gathered for a picnic on the Cape, congratulating and toasting their prospects with a rare draft of porter.

———•———

When dispatches from the African coast at last reached Baltimore, the society was thrilled. Dr. Hall's urgent request for assistance was not lost, and they forthwith chartered a schooner, the *Sarah and Priscilla*, to carry supplies to Cape Palmas, which she reached on August 9, 1834. Ironically, her arrival left Hall a little disappointed, for he had managed to buy the materials he needed from passing merchantmen. What he wanted was emigrants. "I cannot say whether I rejoiced or sorrowed the most," he wrote Latrobe on August 17, "to receive your greetings and *money* was extremely gratifying, but then, that an expedition should come to our relief and bring no people was a source of extreme mortification: inasmuch as I had given the natives to understand that I daily expected one hundred at least."[57]

In fact, the *Sarah and Priscilla*'s arrival precipitated a crisis.[58] The agent was already angry with Freeman. Several days before, he had requested the king to locate some stolen lumber, presumably taken by men from Grahway. A day or two later, Freeman reported that Weah Bolio had made a diligent search on his behalf, but could find no trace. This was a lie, for Hall had communicated with Bolio himself in the meantime and learned that Freeman had never mentioned a word of the matter to him. The agent would deal with Freeman, and the *Sarah and Priscilla* provided the opportunity. Her cargo included dashes for Freeman, Bolio, and Baphro. When the vessel's contents were secure in the warehouse, the agent directly summoned each king to come and receive his gifts. Normally, he would have done this through Freeman, as a mark of respect, and the king was indignant when he learned of the slight. The agent was prepared for his complaint. He told him that he could not trust him to deliver messages, that he was aware of the double dealing with regard to the stolen lumber, and that he "could not respect him as a king unless he acted like one and punished thievery instead of fostering it."

Freeman responded predictably, for his prestige was as much at risk as Hall's. Harper posed enormous political challenges to the Grebo states. Conservative and progressive factions struggled to control policy. Freeman himself seems to have supported a liberal stance toward the Americans, but his opposition was entrenched. "All business respecting our colony being new to them they have to act without precedent," Hall explained to Latrobe in an April dispatch. "The more intelligent" Greboes were cognizant of the fact that their country "will ultimately be much benefitted by our settling in it." But there were other influential men in Gbenelu "who know very little of the customs and habits of Europeans and 'tis next to impossible to convince them that we have any good object in view, and so jealous are they respecting us that when you speak of the subject of schooling their children and teaching them our mechanical arts they shake their heads and will not believe one word of the matter." In as much as all "palavers and matters of business" had to come before this "Sanhedrine" it was "almost impossible to affect any thing with them."[59] Any betrayal of weakness in so tense a political environment could mean overthrow or even death. Freeman's predecessor had met his end this way, his body tossed unceremoniously into the bush.[60]

Thus Freeman, his authority flagrantly insulted, was obliged to make an exaction of Hall. He forbade his subordinate kings from accepting any gifts from the agent and ordered them to have no contact with him. He doubled the price of rice and other goods. Then he demanded one-half of the *Sarah and Priscilla*'s cargo because the Americans had not paid nearly enough for his country. Finally, he insisted that the agent provide him with a steady supply of rum.[61]

Hall also had to tread a narrow line, giving in to Grebo demands where he could without sacrificing the long-term interests of his own people. The survival of the tiny colony depended largely on settlers' solidarity with their leaders. In the midst of the crisis, he complained to Latrobe that he was, "blamed on the one hand by colonists for being partial to [Greboes] in all difficulties which have occurred between both parties and on the other hand by the natives for the same reason."[62] A deadlock persisted over the next three weeks. Trade ceased, and Grebo workers stayed away. The *Sarah and Priscilla* went down the coast to buy rice from neutral towns. Hall talked belligerently, made a show of his militia, and cut rations in half. He and the settlers were willing to wait out the embargo, confident of a favorable, peaceful end. "To succomb and grant the unreasonable demands *I never will*," he told Latrobe. "I believe the majority of the colonists generally possess the *virtue of obstinacy* to the same extent."[63] A victory at this stage of the struggle could be decisive. As each tense day of the embargo passed, pressure on Freeman mounted, while the Americans benefited. That is, each day demonstrated more forcefully the Grebo inability to manage the colony. Conversely, each day the colony continued its defiance made the Americans appear even stronger.

The standoff ended early in September, when a settler was caught digging cassava from a Grebo garden, to Hall's "extreme overwhelming mortification." Freeman immediately sent a messenger to ask why he was stealing from Greboes, "that if his boys stole from me I accused him of countenancing it, that he had a right to suppose the same of me." The agent could no longer claim the moral high ground. "The tables were turned and we had nothing to do but back out." It did not matter that Hall had offered to surrender the thief to Freeman. The colonists were "branded as thieves and put on a level with them, and the ground that I had taken to make the King responsible for thefts was by this movement rendered untenable. I could in justice do no less than acknowledge it."[64] The chance detection of a hungry forager had enabled the king to extricate himself from his predicament.

His honor restored, Freeman allowed trade to resume as before, and African workers returned to their employments. Hall set a new date to give out the society's dashes. The gifts included settees, beads, military uniforms, and other items specified in the deed. Freeman was not satisfied and asserted again that the Americans owed much more for his land. Hall reported to Latrobe afterward, "They well knew that this was the last time that they would have the like advantage and they were determined to improve it." He recounted the solution: "I affected at last to believe that the interpreter had misunderstood me at the time of purchase and compromised matters by giving them about 800 lbs. of Tobacco which was so bad that I could never trade it off, and 214 yds cloth, together with what properly belonged to them." Hall admitted to Latrobe that he had "*put it into them* pretty well" at the first purchase.[65]

Relations improved over the next few weeks. Hall bought several hundred bushels of new rice, in fact more than he could securely store. The palaver over the stolen lumber, which had caused so much trouble, was at last settled. William Davis, one of Freeman's many brothers, returned from a long sojourn at Sierra Leone. He personally searched Gbenelu and returned "hoes, axes, hatchets, crows, etc. etc."[66]

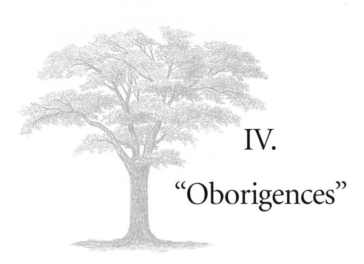

IV.

"Oborigences"

MARYLAND IN LIBERIA QUICKLY SHIFTED FROM A UTOPIAN FOLLY and mark on a deed into a physical and geographic fact. Americans laid out roads and property lines; erected houses, churches, and public buildings; and settlers began to express their cultural identity. They also became increasingly aware of their African neighbors, "Oborigences" in the words of a petition, by whom they were "thickly surrounded and in many respects unavoidably associated."[1] Points of conflict and misunderstanding between the two peoples were innumerable.

The most apparent differences between Greboes and American settlers were material. Dress, architecture, diet, and patterns of land use served as constant reminders of their contrasting ways of life. Social organization and religious beliefs divided the people even more profoundly.

No information has come to light concerning an indigenous Grebo craft of weaving, if there was one. Clearly, at the time of James Hall's arrival, foreign cloth was in common use throughout the area. Greboes, like other people, did not want just any cloth, but demanded certain patterns and qualities. Different fabrics, by the "piece," a unit of variable meaning, came to have set values. At Cape Palmas, satin stripes, blue bafts, and osnaburgs, all with blue and white dominant colors, were in particular demand. "Penitentiary Handkerchiefs," woven in the Baltimore prison, were popular items of trade.[2] Grebo men prized articles of Western clothing that they sometimes acquired while working aboard ships. Women generally wore a piece of cloth wrapped around their waists as a skirt, without a top. Children generally went naked until puberty. To settlers, this general casualness about dress, in their eyes amounting to nudity, was shocking. They associated clothing with civilization and Christianity. Nakedness violated their standards of decency.[3]

James Hall laid out the settlement according to American rural patterns.[4] The colony was designed to spread out across the land. It had a capital, Harper, which would comprise its administrative and commercial center, the home of civil servants and the commercial elite. Most settlers, however, were expected to occupy rectilinear, five-acre plots, divided at regular intervals by straight roads. Citizens were conscious of being land owners and of belonging to a particular neighborhood.[5] Greboes lived concentrated in towns and villages, most of which were on the beach. Their farms were generally located two or three miles in the bush, and they camped at them for periods during planting and harvest. Town plans reflected the democratic political organization of their inhabitants. "The houses are huddled together without order or arrangement, and so closely, that the projection of one roof frequently overlaps the other," John Wilson, the missionary of the A.B.C.F.M., wrote in 1856.[6] People built where they found room, and roads were often mere interstices between houses. Westerners, with their geometric aesthetic, usually found these towns chaotic and unpleasant. Other travelers, seeing the same thing, were impressed by the communal aspect of the town's layout. Captain William F. Lynch, an officer of the U.S. Navy in the 1840s, remarked that towns were arranged as if of one large family.[7]

The only public building in a Grebo town was the *takae*, a rectangular wooden structure which custom dictated must be built in a day. It usually stood in an open area somewhere near a town's center. This was the residence of the *bodio* and his wife, the *jide* (who had priestly duties) and the repository of trophies and protective charms. The *takae* was occasionally used for secret palavers.[8]

Greboes lived in round thatched houses. "They have no windows, but generally two Sometimes three doors — which are not as large as our windows," Dr. Thomas Ramsay Steele, an Episcopal missionary, noted in 1854. He continued,

> In order to get into the house, you have to stoop almost to a kneeling posture. They are Generally very warm, though sometimes when the doors face the sea there is a pleasant air passing through them. The floor is simply the Earth which has become very hard and dry by the fire they keep *almost* constantly burning to cook their food.
>
> It's remarkable how smooth and dry these floors are — they look almost like smooth brick. In a great many huts the utmost neatness prevails. A mat constitutes the only bed, a few stools the chairs, and perhaps there may be a chest in one corner, not for clothes, for of these they have *but little*, but for keeping rice perhaps or some other article of food. Then the few cooking utensils are arranged with great order around the hut on nails.
>
> Some times you will see a half dozen or more *white wash basins* hung around the walls. Out of which they eat their rice and palm oil. This is the *only* purpose for which they are used.[9]

Houses had no chimneys. Smoke trapped in the rafters preserved rice, salt, and perishable belongings hung there. Large houses were sometimes partitioned for privacy, but more often the residents slept in the open.

To build a house, Grebo workers drew a rough circle on the ground, between twelve and thirty feet across, depending on the wealth and needs of the occupants. They then dug a shallow trench, throwing the dirt to the inside. More clay was piled within the circle, so that, spread out and beaten down, the floor would stand about a foot above the surrounding ground level. The builders then set tall, upright stakes in the trench, leaving from five to six feet of each stake above ground. They then wove thin branches around the uprights and applied thick coats of clay on either side. Inside, they stamped the clay on the floor, and in the center planted three large rocks to make a hearth. A conical thatched roof, extending two or three feet over the wall, capped the house. Artisans constructed the roof separately then lifted it into place. Such houses could stand for years, but the warm humid climate was extremely destructive to most building materials. American-style frame structures were temporary at best, if for no other reason, because of termites. Grebo houses had the advantage of being cheap and relatively easy to put up.[10]

Food was perhaps the most significant element in the interaction of Greboes with Marylanders. Settlers brought to Africa the dietary customs of their homes, which varied according to regional origins and social status. The diet of many would have consisted of corn meal, preserved meats, especially pork, and garden produce: greens, squash, potatoes, and dried beans.[11] In Africa, settlers had to adopt many components of Grebo diet. Rice and cassava were the Grebo staples, one or the other consumed at almost every meal. Rice was favored, and a fair portion of every woman's day was spent in pounding rice from its husks and cooking it. Cassava was not especially palatable, and no matter how much might be available, a shortage of rice was cause for worry, as American acounts show. "Palm Butter" was a favorite complement to rice. It was made by boiling the whole fruit of the oil palm and then pounding it in a mortar with water. Oil would rise to the surface. This was skimmed and saved, and the pulverized fruit strained out. The remaining orange-red fluid was then boiled and strongly seasoned with red peppers or malaguetta. If it could be procured, meat was added to make a stew. Meat was a minor component of diet. Fresh or dried fish, meat from livestock or game, or even carrion, were rare and expensive commodities.[12]

Greboes had altered the landscape dramatically from what their ancestors had encountered when they first arrived at Cape Palmas. Over generations, they developed a system of land use adapted to the constraints of land quality and availability, health, and economic opportunity. Newcomers, no matter how grand their plans, could not easily sweep them aside. Outsiders commonly thought that Africans had no concept of property. They were mistaken, for land tenure was vested in the city-state rather than individuals. Competition for productive tracts of land was keen, and the location of boundaries separating farm lands was a common source of dispute. Moreover, the use of land was not free: the cultivator owed a share of everything he harvested to town officials, to his age-grade, and to his extended family.[13]

The coastal environment did not permit the keeping of large numbers of livestock, so the small indigenous breed of cattle was especially prized. Various kinds of poultry, including chickens, guinea fowl, and Muscovy ducks were raised for meat. The ducks were originally introduced by Portuguese traders and remained long after their trading posts had disappeared. In the nineteenth century, vessels occasionally managed to buy them, and the bird had an established value of one bar, a quarter-dollar. (The Maryland State Colonization Society pictured one on its twenty-five cent note and two on its fifty cent note in 1837.)[14]

Lake Sheppard provided an abundant supply of fish, which Greboes harvested by periodic draining. "At the narrowest place," Hall wrote of the operation, "the natives once or twice a year dig a trench level with the surface of the lake and it soon discharges its water into the sea, leaving an immense quantity of fish of all kinds which are gathered up by all the tribes in the vicinity and smoked in great numbers. The sea very soon fills up the breach thus made and the lake is again replenished by the rains and small creeks."[15]

In the near bush, women often kept small fenced gardens. The vegetables and fruits grown in them added variety to meals. They raised in such plots oil palms, plantains, various fruit trees, and vegetables, some brought from America. This intensive agriculture resembled what the American settlers would practice, with the exception that the African system involved the mixing of crops, with little disturbance of the soil. American farmers would be continually frustrated that they could not use plows and draft animals to create neat, furrowed fields.[16]

Cassava, or manioc, which American settlers in Liberia almost always called "cassada," was often grown near the beach as a convenience, though it was better raised on new plots each year. Farmers sometimes put it in as a second crop in the rice fields. It was easy to raise and required relatively little cultivation. Farmers simply buried pieces of the stalk in hills worked up with a hoe. It was resistant to drought, and tubers could be harvested as needed in times of scarcity. While many varieties of cassava contain prussic acid, which must be removed before eating, the one in common use around Cape Palmas was sweet and could be eaten straight from the ground.[17]

Greboes grew rice, their principle crop, in a shifting field system, in which tracts of about twenty acres were cultivated for one or at most two years, then abandoned to grow up in bush for some years before reclearing. Contrary to practice in the Far East, Africans typically grow rice on dry uplands.[18] Grebo rice fields were almost all located two or three miles from the beach, where the land was higher and free of salt spray. Farmers walked out to their fields each day along meandering paths. John L. Wilson, the missionary, often watched Greboes at work in their fields. "The mode of cultivating the rice is very simple," he wrote in 1856:

> A piece of fresh land is selected, and, about one month or six weeks before the commencement of the periodical rains, the trees, under-brush, and grass are cut down, and permitted to remain on the ground until they become perfectly dry. At the first intimation of a coming shower, fire is set to this superincumbent mass of dried vegetation, and in the course of one or two hours every thing, except a few of the larger trunks, is reduced to ashes, presenting the appearance of a fall of snow. The ground is scarcely allowed to cool before the seed is deposited in the soil, which is done by simply scratching the surface of the ground with a little iron instrument, and depositing the seed without covering it up. It sprouts immediately after the first shower of rain, and grows so rapidly that it ordinarily needs very little weeding. When it is necessary to remove the grass, it is always pulled out with the hand. As soon as the rice begins to head it is assailed by rice-birds, and must be guarded with utmost care for several weeks, or it would be completely destroyed. This is done by stationing boys in different parts of the field, who keep up a constant screaming, throw stones, shake dry bushes, beat old brass pans, and employ every thing they can think of to frighten away these perti-naceous intruders. Sometimes they have a kind of net-work of cords

extending over the field, by which they can shake dry bushes or little bells at a dozen or more points.[19]

The technique of raising rice must have varied to some degree. John Payne, an Episcopal missionary, also had many opportunities to observe Grebo farming. His account differs materially from Wilson's:

> With a piece of flat iron, called a bill-hook, they cut out all the grass and undergrowth. The larger trees are then felled, either by the small axes of the natives, or by fire. The whole is then suffered to remain until perfectly dry, when fire is communicated, presenting scenes of the most sublime and awful character. The labor of *planting* the farms is principally performed by women. It is a slow and tedious process. Instead of sowing the rice broadcast, they make small holes in the ground with a pointed iron, and deposite a few grains in each, drawing the earth over them with the foot. This is done in April, immediately before the rainy season, which commences in May, and the harvest is reaped in August.[20]

Wilson described the harvest:

> In four months from the time of planting the rice is ready to be harvested. The only reaping instrument used is a small blade, not larger than that of a pocket-knife, with which they cut each head of rice separately. It is tied up in snug, neat bundles, of about a hundred pounds, and carried home on their heads. It is a singular and very pleasant sight to see a long train of one or two hundred men trotting home, single file, with these large bundles of rice on their heads, screaming and shouting as they go. The party always become highly excited, and are on a full run by the time they reach the village, screaming and yelling at the very top of their voices.[21]

The harvest continued during August and September. For a few months afterwards, food was in good supply. If the crop was poor, or if wars cut off inland trade, supplies would begin to run short after the new year. A season of scarcity would follow one of plenty, with an attendant rise of social unrest.

A complex hierarchic framework divided Grebo society, but a network of allegiances balanced the forces of division. Greboes shared the tale of their migration. Men shared in the government of their town and owed a loyalty to it; age-grades unified generations, in part countervailing the set of loyalties claimed by ancestral lineages. The extended family entailed its own obligations. For the most part, property was communal, and wealth shared. Yet these mechanisms of social unity could also conflict and cause divisions within a community. The Americans shook Grebo society to its foundation when they settled among them.[22]

Male members of the community were organized in age-based groups or cohorts. Age was a principal determinant of social rank and function. The least significant of the age-grades was the *chiehnbo*, composed of boys between six and eleven years old, which had minor duties around the town. Older boys up to the age of eighteen belonged to the *kinibo*, which trained them in the responsibilities of adulthood. The *sedibo*, composed of men up to about forty-five years, was the most influential, comprising the soldiery and half the work force. Members had to pay regular dues, and the *sedibo* had the authority to impose fines for misdemeanors. "In times of war they lay their hands upon any man's property that comes within their reach, and if any one has the temerity to complain or remonstrate, he is charged with insolence, and suffers four-fold in consequence," Wilson observed. "Being a member of the body does not shield any one from their rapacity, for when they have nobody else to plunder, they prey upon the members of their own order; and there are but few individuals in the community, whether belonging to the *sedibo* or not, who have not had their entire property confiscated once or more in their lives, and, in the great majority of cases, upon no other charge than that of being insolent."[23] The *sedibo* could accumulate great wealth, which principally took the form of a large stock of cattle. Two leading officers, the *yibadiah* and *tibawah* took active roles in times of war, one leading the column of soldiers, the other bringing up its rear. In peacetime, they had ritual functions only.

A member of the *sedibo* oversaw the *chiehnbo* and safeguarded its treasury. Past the age of forty-five, men entered the *gnekbade*, the senior age grade, which functioned as a senate in the town's government.

The *bodio* and *wodoba*, the two leading officers in a town, were drawn from the *gnekbade*. The *bodio* was primarily a religious officer, but his closeness with the supernatural gave him political influence. He could overturn any decision made in a palaver, could interpose to end any argument, and could offer sanctuary. His powers, though, were balanced. If he was not careful to assess the general will before exercising his privileges, he would have to face the consequences of an irate public. The *wodoba* was a loosely hereditary office, generally occupied by the oldest or most influential head man of a town, selected from those who were lineally descended from their town's founder. The *wodoba* received a share of meat whenever a bullock was slaughtered and was entitled to many other such honors. In time of war, he could assume dictatorial power, but ordinarily, his rank was about the same as other head men of his age. Europeans unfamiliar with Grebo political organization usually termed the *wodoba* "king." Freeman's rank was probably *wodoba*, but this is not made clear in any of the records. Real authority did not rest with the *wodoba*, however, and the misperception often caused serious problems in relations between the two cultures. The Marylanders looked to Freeman and other "kings" to exercise authority where they had none.[24]

Grebo society was further divided into lineages. The legendary group who migrated to the coast had consisted of six families. A seventh joined the group before the move to Cape Palmas. By the middle of the nineteenth century, there were twelve principal lineages, representatives of each in almost every town. In each town, the senior male member of a lineage was the head man of that family. A town's headmen constituted the *wodokai*, a council of elders, who advised the *wodoba* and *bodio*. The head man was the spokesman for the interests of his lineage and controlled its collective wealth. He could stand trial and pay fines for the indiscretions of others, except in capital cases. In return, he was entitled to a share of the wealth of his kinsmen.

Children kept their mother's family name as a prefix to their given name. Even so, a child belonged to his father's lineage, and no man could take a wife from either of his parents' lineages. Individuals owed primary loyalty to their own lineage, and the differentiation among clans was an important factor in the politics of a town and between towns. The bonds of kinship transcended those of citizenship, giving the Grebo people a kind of national identity. Yet kinship could be divisive, as clans would feud, sometimes for generations, as a result of petty insults that may well have originated in other towns.

Grebo men were polygamous. Families usually lived in fenced compounds containing a small house for each wife and her children. In the nineteenth century Grebo men commonly undertook voyages on foreign ships to earn the money to buy a wife. Since the number of wives was a sure gauge of wealth and status, some men would embark on journey after journey to acquire women. Many households were thus without an adult male resident for months or even years at a time. Women, for their part, considered it a disgrace to be married to a man who could afford but one wife. The customs attending courtship and marriage were intricate and of great cultural significance. "Some of the natives have a half dozen or more wives," clucked Episcopal missionary Thomas R. Steele. "He is called a rich man, who has a good many women." The majority, who had but one wife, did so not from choice but "because they are *too poor* to buy them." Steele learned that a man's first wife was often "a free gift of the parents to the man," but for subsequent wives "a *large price* has to be paid. . . . one or two *oxen*, a certain quantity of *rice, tobacco,* and some cotton cloth, all of which is equal to about $20 of our money." Moreover, one "mustn't suppose that these are grown women that are purchased thus. No, they are girls from 4 to 10 years of age who are sold by their father . . . for this sum, and they are taken home to the house of their future lord and supported by him until they attain to womanhood, when they become his wives."[25] Wives were servants, and the more women a man had, the better were the prospects for a comfortable old age.

A woman's primary loyalty remained with her father's family rather than her husband's. In wartime, women were suspect on this account, since they often came from other towns than their husbands and always came from other lineages. As outsiders, women sometimes assumed the role of intermediaries in diplomacy between towns. Women had the prerogative of forbidding a battle, but often they were as eager as their husbands for the glory of victory. A beaten town sent its women to the victor to beg for peace. On the other hand, men fought battles and actually concluded peace. When a man died, his brothers or some other near kin usually inherited his wives and children. A woman could flee her husband's household, but divorce was uncommon, since the wife's family had to refund double the original brideprice to the husband's family.

Children of both sexes experienced similarly divided loyalties. They customarily owed their allegiance to the father's family. This created tensions within the household, however, since the father often divided his attention between more than one wife and was often absent anyway. Children's loyalties naturally rested with their mothers, who raised them, were the providers of food, and were their allies in conflicts with half-brothers and sisters.

In the household, men arbitrated disputes between wives and between children. They were not responsible, however, for any part of the housework beyond erecting and repairing houses. Men performed heavy work in the fields, cutting and burning trees, and carrying home the harvest. They hunted and fished, bringing home meat, a scarce article of food. As noted, many men worked as sailors and stevedores aboard ships. They also conducted trade with interior states and with foreigners.

Women were responsible for many of the tasks of subsistence, performing most of the work to make their husbands' lives comfortable. In a husband's absence, the head wife managed the household. Women had the work of planting and tending the rice fields and of maintaining vegetable gardens. A portion of every day was spent pounding, winnowing, and cooking rice. Women had also to maintain the stock of firewood and keep the house clean. Grebo women later supplied the Maryland colonial market with rice and produce from their gardens.

Greboes were animists. That is, they believed that the material world was closely linked to a supernatural realm of good and evil spirits, who had a pervasive influence. Although the Grebo cosmology included a supreme god, they thought that he was too far away to hear them. On the other hand, people could contact and even manipulate spirits through the objects they inhabited: trees, rocks, animals, and any number of other things. In the absence of a codified dogma, a complex and immensely varied set of beliefs and customs arose, by which individuals and communities dealt with the supernatural.[26]

Greboes attributed extraordinary powers to certain rock outcrops. One on the beach near Grahway, where the legendary discoverer of Cape Palmas rested on his return to his people, was a favorite site for sacrifices of rice and palm oil. By far, the most important of these places was near Haidee, on the far side of the Cavally River, in the Bulyemah country, about twenty miles from the sea. A sort of priesthood watched over the stony oracle there, whose pronouncements had a reputation reported to extend as far as the Fantee states, some three hundred miles to the east, on the Gold Coast.[27]

The "Grand Devil" of Bulyemah was the source of authority for the *kwi iru*, which acted as a moral police force. John Payne, an Episcopal missionary and careful student of Grebo culture, could relate very little about the society even after fifteen years residence:

> There is a curious secret association or society to be found in every Grebo community, styled *Kwi-iru*, or "children of departed spirits." Although it is attempted to keep everything connected with this association concealed, it is known to be composed of persons of almost all ages in the community, except children. They have a "father," as he is called, but he is never visible or known, except to members of the society. When as is rarely the case, the *"Kwi-iru"* appear in the day, the "father" is always so masked as to be perfectly disguised.

The society usually held its ceremonies at night, when members patrolled their town in search of witches and evil spirits. As they passed among the houses, their characteristic wail—"as if their object was to frighten man from the earth," wrote Payne—warned women, children, and odd men to run and hide. Offenders were subject to beating or even the accusation of witchcraft.[28]

The *bodio*, already mentioned, was perhaps the most influential official in a Grebo town, a sort of *pontifex maximus*, holding both spiritual and political power. He was not envied, though, because of the strictures entailed upon the office. The oldest male member of the *bodio* family who could be caught after an old *bodio* died inherited the title. The *bodio* had a uniform consisting of a black robe, an iron ring on his left ankle, and a line of chalk drawn down the center of his face. He carried a special staff and a monkey skin at all times. His wife, the *jide*, dressed similarly. Both of them claimed the deference of their townsmen, who supplied all of their wants. The couple resided in the *takae*, where they cared for the town's charms and fetishes. Among other duties, they sacrificed rice and palm oil to the spirits every two months. Taboos surrounded the office: the *bodio* could not leave his town; he must eat his meals in daylight; he could not look at a corpse. Elaborate rules of behavior, diet, and accountability often shortened the *bodio*'s life. The *bodio* and *jide* were responsible for a town's good fortune. If anything went wrong, if the rains were late, or if ships didn't call for trade, citizens might accuse them of negligence or malignance and have them punished.[29]

Apart from the *bodio* and *jide*, the chief religious functionaries were the *deyabo*, known as "doctors" or "devil men" in the local English. They had the ability to make charms and detect witches, and some built reputations that extended scores of miles. A *deya* lived an ascetic life and submitted to numerous rules of dress and behavior. Shortly after his arrival, John L. Wilson met such a man and described his uncouth rival in his journal:

> The dress of his head consisted of a kind of cue, made of a [monkey] skin, with long hair tapering from his forehead and reaching some distance down his shoulders. The front part of the skin, which extended over a considerable portion of his forehead, was decorated

with shells. Around his neck he had not less than half a dozen strings of different kinds of beads. Around each wrist and ankle he had several coarse, iron chains, and rings of iron. The weight of iron on one ankle, I supposed not to be less than three or four pounds. On each finger he had several steel rings. Under his left arm was suspended a war horn. But the most ludicrous part of this parade of ornaments was a *tail* suspended down his back having a small bell attached to the extremity, which made a loud dingling at every step he took. All this parade of ornaments was rendered still more ridiculous by the circumstance that he had not a particle of clothing with them except a narrow strip of cloth around his loins. . . . He carried a long iron spear in his hand, which he struck upon the ground as he walked, with much emphasis.[30]

The *deyabo* were thought to have a special ability, drawn ultimately from the oracle at Bulyemah, to communicate with the supernatural. "They suppose themselves possessed of a 'ku,' demon or spirit, under whose inspiration they act, and give their responses," John Payne wrote. Under the influence of this spirit, they were prone to fits, during which, "they appear dead, while they utter strange, unearthly sounds." Signs of possession could come at any age, and to members of either sex, but usually to adolescent males. According to Payne, when an individual first manifested signs of possession, he was "at once placed with an old '*Deya,*' to be instructed in the arts and mysteries of the profession." His "novitiate" lasted from one to three years, during which time he was not permitted to wear any covering "other . . . than some grass tied with a cord around his loins." He did not wash or see his wife or family, but "sleeps apart, sits apart, etc." When the *deya* was satisfied with his "proficiency," the candidate's family "get a bullock ready to pay for his education," and a day is appointed for "inducting him into office."[31]

The initiation was an elaborate ceremony, often witnessed by a whole town. The most striking part of the rite was the demonstration of divining powers. A favorite means was to sacrifice a chicken before the crowd and cast its head into the bush. The initiate, blinded with the fowl's blood, would then have to find the member, much to the merriment of onlookers. If he succeeded, he could then bathe and cut his dredlocks.[32]

The primary occupation of the *deya* was fabricating charms for all sorts of purposes. The price was adjusted to the strength of the magic and the buyer's wealth. Almost every Grebo man wore a charm, called a *greegree* in the coastal pidgin. These varied in form, but they were most often pieces of horn or small leather pouches, stuffed with clay or some other substance. A leather thong secured the charm to the body.[33] Every house also had a charm. The missionary Payne described one as "a wooden bowl filled with mud, and surmounted by horns and feathers."[34] Freeman had a charm of suitable power, which Dr. Thomas Savage, another Episcopal missionary, related was, "a small stick about five feet in height, and an inch in diameter, standing at the entrance of his hut. . . . The charm consists in having a few fibers of the inner bark of some tree dyed black, suspended from the top. Here, night and day, this charm exerts its wondrous power, as it performs a thousand mysterious motions, waved to and fro by the four winds of heaven."[35] Towns also had a special shrine, apart from the images in the *takae*. Barrakah's, a few miles inland from Cape Palmas, was a basket anchored in the ground and filled with beach sand. That of Grahway, the town neighboring Gbenelu on the east, consisted of "two bee-hives decorated with feathers, goat horns, grass, etc." When Dr. Savage asked what the charm was good for, a Grahwayan informant answered, "Great deal; the people be bad people — the devil get among them, and bewitched 'em so they kill one another, and some be sick — sick head — sick leg, and ebery ting bad — bad too much — we send for devil man (doctor) — he come, he put up greegree, he cure 'em all — no sick now — all ting go on fine — be good people, and *dat de good they do*."[36]

Once in a while, the *deya* was called upon to make a specially potent charm. In cases of war, according to Payne, "Hostilities having been resolved upon, a doctor or deya, distinguished for making war *greegrees* is sent for. Often weeks are spent in preparing charms to make the soldiers invulnerable, or the town impregnable to the enemy." Payne recounted another remarkable incident that occurred at Grahway in 1838, when a house was struck by lightning. The lightning passed through the top of the house and down into the dirt floor, "tearing up the earth in its passage." This alarmed the town, which thought the "thunder" had lodged itself under the floor. The town would be in "imminent danger as long as it remained there, as it would attract constantly other 'thunder.'" No one was able to locate the hidden thunder but one man who lived in a distant town. A messenger was sent to obtain this "doctor," who, "after a great deal of . . . mummery," began digging in the floor. "At length . . . under the little mound of earth, on which fire was made, he found the 'thunder!' It consisted of an animal very common in this country, somewhat resembling the lizard, with a piece of iron near its head. Such was this fearful 'thunder!'" According to Payne's informant, "when the doctor touched the magic thing 'he died three hours;' nor could he be induced to move until he was forcibly taken up and compelled to take nourishment!"[37]

Death, because it released the spirit of a man, was an object of special concern among Greboes. They believed in a netherworld, where souls remained for an indefinite period before rebirth. Yet if a soul was not properly sent off, it would remain to terrorize the living. Funerals were therefore the focus of elaborate rituals to demonstrate communal sorrow, proportional to the importance of the man who had died, to appease his spirit. Unlike men, women were disposed of shortly after death, and without much ceremony.[38]

When an important man died, his body was rubbed with soot and placed in a canoe, then carried to the plaza at the town's center. Hunting and war trophies of former days, imported cloths, crockery, and guns were piled nearby. At an appointed hour, ceremonies began with beating drums and musketfire. "It is customary on such occasions," Samuel F. McGill (George's son) wrote with some humor, "to collect as large a variety of noisy instruments as possible, drums, horns, and cowbells, and in one instance a miserable creaking hand organ was brought into play, and the performer most vigorously ground away at yankee doodle, with very awful and solemn effect."[39] Family and friends gathered around the body, wives took hold of his hands and feet. Elsewhere, a goat or bullock was slaughtered and roasted for the mourners to eat. After some time, the dead man's brothers painted his face with red and white clay. They then adorned the corpse with strings of beads and wrapped it with fine cloths, each one held up for the crowd to admire, to appreciate the wealth and importance of the deceased. Finally, bearers would raise the canoe with the body in it and carry it to the place of burial. "On lifting the body, the bearers experience a formidable obstacle to their movements from the objections raised by the deceased one to being removed from his home endeared by so many fond recollections," Samuel McGill related.

> An attractive power seems to exist between the body and dwelling: the bearers make violent efforts to bear it away, but it is impossible, the burden is swayed from side to side on their heads, they move a few paces, perform a slight evolution and return again to the spot whence they started. The bearers pull against each other, and wildly run about the town, rearing and plunging "as if mad," and sweating from every pore at the violence of their exertions. The town after many efforts is completely encircled, the bearers previously tutored, stop before the door of some unfortunate wretch, who has now for the first time to learn that he is thought to be the destroyer of the deceased.[40]

The body finally relinquished its grasp on the living and allowed itself to be carried to its final resting place. Greboes of Gbenelu deposited their dead on a barren island south of the Cape, which they referred to as "hell," but the Americans called "Auburn Island." The body headed a procession of men firing muskets, followed by others carrying, in succession, the uneaten remains of the bullock, crockery and cloth, rice, and musical instruments. Survivors of the departed man brought up the rear. Once on the island, the body was laid on the ground and the canoe set upside down above it. Crockery and other goods the spirit might need on its journey to the netherworld were smashed on the ground. Finally, rice was set out for the dead man to eat.[41]

Greboes firmly believed in the malignant agency of ghosts, and many lived in terror of necromancy. Furthermore, they held as an article of faith, that witchcraft caused most deaths. John Payne, who is consistently the best authority on nineteenth-century Grebo customs, never saw a witch at work, but he was reliably informed that they did in fact exist and that they were "particularly active in practising their arts at night." He continued, "They strip themselves naked, and go to the houses of those whose lives they seek; and especially is it their delight to visit and dance on the graves of those whom they have succeeded in killing by their enchantments."[42] Samuel McGill related in a letter of 1840 that, "men have gone to the houses of sick persons, knocked at the doors, and informed them in a feigned voice, that they were the originators of the disease. This fills the inmates with dread, and none are so bold as to come forth and detect the prowler, lest they themselves may be exposed to their necromancy. Not long since, an instance of the kind occurred, but the wizard 'caught a tartar,' a friend to the sick man was in the house at the time, and instead of coming out, poked his gun through a crevice, and lodged its contents in the fellow's back."[43] Townsmen found the wounded man the next day and punished him as a witch.

When evidence indicated witchcraft, a *deya* was hired to seek out the perpetrator, who very often proved to be some enemy of the deceased. The *kwi iru* often had a hand in finding the witch, hinting to the doctor who should be the culprit. The accused witch might flee, or confess and pay a huge fine, or try to prove his innocence by submitting to an ordeal. Occasionally, this involved dipping the hand into boiling water (quick healing demonstrating innocence), but the most common method of testing guilt was *gidu*, called "sassy wood palaver" in pidgin. In such trials, the accused was made to drink a narcotic potion infused from the bark of a tree of the mimosa family. If the poison killed the subject, then a witch received justice. If, on the other hand, he survived, his innocence was proven. Such trials were public, and settlers often witnessed them. "On the day appointed," Samuel McGill wrote of one such trial, "the culprit was led to a remote spot from the colony, and witnessed the preparation of the bark," as a pound of it was stripped from the tree, cut into small pieces, pounded in a mortar, and added to two gallons of water. "After the water was suitably tinged, it was poured off and the individual required to drink, which he did without any reluctance." Having drunk "nearly the whole, he started on his return to town, and accomplished the walk of nearly a mile with ease. After his arrival in town he was kept constantly walking, in order to allow the poison its full operation. Short periods were occasionally allowed him to expel the contents of his stomach." While he walked, the victim constantly muttered, "If I am guilty of the crime alleged against me, may I be seized with cramps! may my breath be cut short, and may my body be transferred to hell." After five hours' walking, regularly interrupted with spells of vomiting, the poison had worn off. The man was now free to return home, his innocence manifest.[44]

Quite often, the accused was not so fortunate, and the ordeal could drag on for hours more before a fatal end. In notorious cases, sometimes, whole populations would come out to watch and perhaps hasten the end. Scenes like this took on a special significance in relations between Greboes and Marylanders, for they often took place within the confines of the colony.[45]

Greboes genuinely believed in the reality of sorcery. Even so, magic and the sassy wood palaver became tools in the struggle between innovative and conservative elements in the Grebo community. Writing for *Maryland Colonization Journal* in 1840, James Hall explained that many Greboes resisted technological change. Colonists using their axes could fell a tree in a matter of minutes, whereas Greboes needed hours, but whenever approached with an offer of superior tools they would reply, "'my country fash; no sabby, be devil palaver;' that is, they prefer their own fashion, they do not understand ours, and think there is witchcraft in it. If a native was to attempt an innovation of this kind, he would be tried for witchcraft, and no doubt lose his life."[46]

Four or five incidents of *gidu* took place in Gbenelu during the nine months following the Marylanders' landing, two with fatal outcome. Hall guessed that an equal number of trials had taken place at each of the towns up and down the coast. The colonial government was powerless to stop the practice, except in individual cases.[47]

James Hall intervened for the first time in October 1834. The accused was one Popo, a head man of Gbenelu, who "was arraigned and found guilty of bewitching sundry members of the family of one of his rivals." Hall was particularly interested because Popo had been a consistent ally of the settlement. The sassy wood concoction was duly administered, and although the poison worked hard with him, he survived. This was not enough for Popo's enemies, who succeeded in getting a retrial. Before the ordeal began the next morning, Hall went to plead for the condemned man's life, unsuccessfully. "They appeared to owe him a deep grudge," Hall said, "which nothing but his death could appease." Freeman had also tried but failed to save Popo from a second trial. Frustrated, the agent went back to his office to attend other business. There, a Grebo informed him that he could indeed save the man. "Any friend of superior rank or standing can clear him by taking him by the hand when the potion is about to be administered, but the one so doing takes upon himself the responsibility and is liable either to supply his place or pay heavy damages."

Hall got his crutches and went immediately to the beach near Gbenelu, where Popo was taken to drink the poison. Falling down the rocky hillside in his hurry, he reached the scene and pushed through the crowd. "I arrived just as they were driving off his wives and children who had been taking their last farewell." About five hundred people had assembled into a hollow square, "in the midst of which was his Satanic majesty in full panoply, just raising a huge two gallon pot filled to the brim with the poisonous decoction to the lips of the wretched Popo." Popo was still reeling from the effects of the previous day's poisoning, and "his countenance was despair itself." Hall stood forth and took hold of the victim, announcing that he would take responsibility for any crimes that could be proven against the man. He then led Popo away, "amid the mingled shouts and execrations of his friends and persecutors."[48]

V.

"Better Than Mere Eating"

JOHN LEIGHTON WILSON AND EDWARD WYNKOOP ARRIVED IN BOSTON EARLY
in the summer of 1834. They reported to their sponsors, the American Board of Commissioners for Foreign Missions, that Cape
Palmas was an ideal site for a mission. The climate was pleasant and
seemed healthy. The Maryland State Colonization Society favored their
project and promised to reserve land for them. Moreover, settlers living near the mission would certainly defend it. The local Africans were
heathens subject to various vices, but the travelers judged them better
than others. Moreover, Greboes had made clear their eagerness to learn
American customs. In response, the A.B.C.F.M. resolved to send two
ordained ministers and several teachers to staff a mission at Cape Palmas.
Wynkoop returned to seminary, and Wilson prepared himself for the
arduous task of founding a mission.[1]

The newly ordained and newly married Wilson returned to Cape
Palmas on Christmas Eve, 1834, aboard the schooner *Edgar*. "I was carried ashore in the largest canoe about the cape," he wrote, "rowed by
twelve or fifteen native men, who sung and rowed with great spirit,
from the time we left the vessel till we reached the shore. The king was
among the first to pay his respects, and has been particularly kind and
friendly ever since. . . . The natives generally pretend to feel interested
in our object, and claim me as their man, in distinction from the colony."[2]

The agent had constructed a house of imported American lumber for the mission. It stood between Gbenelu and the western end of Lake Sheppard, fairly removed from Harper. "I know not that I have seen any place where the beauty and grandeur of nature are more harmoniously united," Wilson continued in his letter of January 10. "On the south side the sea rolls on the beach with tremendous and majestic power. On the east we have a beautiful, calm salt lake. The north presents a plain of the richest verdure, through which winds a beautiful fresh water stream, that we can trace to a great distance with the eye from our piazza. On the west we see at one view three native towns and the colonial settlements."[3] On December 27, Wilson observed that more than five hundred Greboes had gathered around his house, simply to have a look at him.

The brig *Bourne* left Baltimore on December 14, 1834, with supplies and a company of fifty-nine emigrants. Forty-eight came from Calvert and Anne Arundel Counties in Southern Maryland. Eleven others were from Allegany County in the state's mountainous west. R. B. F. Gould, a Methodist lay minister well-known among the black population of the Eastern Shore, had charge of the company. A chronic throat irritation had ruined his voice, his livelihood, and like Dr. Hall before him he undertook an ocean voyage to improve his health. Two of the three Grebo boys earlier sent to Baltimore were also aboard. Charles, Bolio's son, had died, despite the society's utmost care. Fearing retribution from the Grebo kings, they returned the other two to testify to their good treatment.[4]

Many of the passengers were seasick during the voyage. A pregnant woman fell and went into labor. She bore a child, but both died soon after. Their burial at sea was "a horrid seene," wrote James Scribner, an emigrant.[5] Nevertheless, he and most others were enthusiastic. "Without an exception from a deliberate Judgement there was no manifestd wish to look back," Gould wrote of them. When they came in sight of

Cape Mount, "all attempt to discribe our fealings would fall so far short and so *awfully* meager and beggar the subject that I mus ask the privaledge simply to remarke that after fealings ware able to resolve themselvs in to words the unanimus declaration from the Captain down to the last that was able to speake was, this is the prettyes prespect that aver fell unde my sight." The *Bourne* paused two days at Monrovia. Gould ventured ashore to meet his fellow Methodist clergy and have a quick look. The accounts of the captain and crew of the schooner *Edgar*, which had left Harper less than a month before, were so favorable that he almost doubted their truthfulness.[6]

The *Bourne* met a grand welcome at Cape Palmas on January 24, 1835. "The Govener I find to be a man of bisiness and well Calculated to Conduct the affairs of the Colony — and I have every promis of pasing a *verry* agreeable visit at this place," Gould wrote four days later. Harper, he thought, was admirably situated, and the rank vegetation was a sure indication of the region's agricultural potential. "The staple Commodity of the Contry is not possitively Know, but so far as observation will bear us out, I think we may place it upon Cotton and rice, which can without dout, be raised in the greatest abundance." He advised the society to send out a net so that settlers could take advantage of the abundant fish. The woods were full of game, "and many good things that amerricans Knows nothing about." His great point: "This is the Colored Mans home, one that will offer him more Comforts than amerrica."[7]

Despite Gould's enthusiastic comments about Hall's abilities, the agent was sick in bed, and had been for nearly a month, his usual fever compounded with dysentery. Hall had expected the *Bourne* to bring out a capable man to relieve him of his responsibilities, so that he could at least take a voyage, that reliable cure for his ailments, or perhaps return to the United States. "I had hoped inasmuch as the understanding with Mr. Gould, that he was to succeed me if dead, or run away, that he might be induced to tarry and let me have the only chance of a perfect recovery by returning to America, but notwithstanding all my negotiating, he absolutely declines," Hall complained. On March 1, he warned the board, "recovery from so long an illness is not to be effected thoroughly, nor even partially in a twinkling." He looked but could find no candidate at Cape Palmas to succeed him. Wilson refused, on the grounds that running the agency conflicted with the interests of his mission. Hall was convinced that the society must appoint a "spirited intelligent, patriotic coloured man" to act as agent. James Thomson, agent by default during his illnesses, was too mild-mannered to lead the colony alone. With this in mind, Hall offered the post of assistant agent to Charles Snetter, a citizen of Monrovia. When he finally replied, the response was negative.[8]

In March, Wilson fell dangerously ill, a victim of his own zeal, having neglected to rest a body exhausted by malaria. "I have never known a case that was so many days absolutely hopeless recover," a feverish Hall remarked. The doctor left his own bed to help the missionary, whose life he probably saved.[9] It was fortunate for the colonial interest that he did, for Wilson's death would have staggered the will of the A.B.C.F.M. to continue a mission in so unhealthy a place. Merchants, slavers, and common seamen died on the coast all the time, and still, more came. Though many asserted the importance of missions, resolve to face the sacrifice involved was weak.

While Hall was sick, Gould looked after the *Bourne*'s emigrants. Joshua Stewart, who was not competent for the job, ran the apothecary. Five children died, partly as a result, though Dr. Hall blamed the emigrants themselves. "No adult of the new expedition has died as yet and 'tis a miracle that they have not for they are no more observant of my reiterated [orders] than Cattle," he groused on April 1, under a heavy dose of morphine.[10]

Gould had a fine sense of propaganda, and he encouraged several of the *Bourne* company to write. These letters offer a fascinating glimpse of the emigrants' thoughts. They often told more than Gould realized or may have wished. Settlers faced privations in their new home, and rarely could they avoid touching on some. Even so, they reveal aspirations for better things to come.

John Harris wrote to William McKenney on March 2. He was thirty-one, recently freed by Capt. John Wood, of Anne Arundel County, to go to Africa. His wife, Jane, twenty-five, was freed with the couple's two children by Benjamin Sheppard, of the same county. A sister or elder daughter of John, age twelve, freed by Alfred Weeks, accompanied them. Harris announced his safe arrival in Africa and expressed concern for his son, Ephraim, whom McKenney had apparently agreed to look after. "[I] hop that you will take Care of him as Long as you Have him, and use evry Efort to make Him a Smart man, I would not wish for him to be Sent out here until he becam a man." He then asked for some woodworking tools and cloth for trade, complaining of the high prices at the agency store. For his wife, he asked a bonnet. In a second letter to McKenney, dated March 11, he added, "thou theare can be mad in affrica accorden to my oppinion and menney other that com out with me think the sam as i dow that a desnt and respectable living can be maid out here if we had teemes and horses or oxen here."[11]

James Scribner sent a letter to McKenney on March 4. He was thirty-six, a free sawyer and farmer from Anne Arundel County. He came to Africa with his free wife, Rachel, eleven years his junior, and two infants. He informed McKenney that he and his family had arrived safely, though all had been sick after landing. His daughter, Susan, age three, had died on February 20. He went on to say that the land promised well, that he had planted corn and beans, but that the colony couldn't be self-sufficient for at least two more years. In the meantime, settlers needed various items: provisions, cloth, tools, and so forth. He was in need of shoes, carpenter's tools, and trade cloth, all of which he asked to have sent out to him.[12]

Alexander Hance, a former free farmer from Anne Arundel County, was much more critical of the situation in a letter penned on March 14. He opened wishing McKenney good health, but noted his own indisposition. He was disappointed to find no plows or teams in the colony. Moreover, he was homesick and missed his children, who remained slaves in southern Maryland. Cape Palmas was a good place to live, he wrote, but he wanted draft animals, proper farming implements, and his children. "If you will by my children and send them to me, and if I can get team to assist me," he stated, he would be happy. "I will pay the Board whatever Expences they go to for me, for I Canot bear the ideas of Staying heare without them, for if it is ten or twelve Years to com I Will go Back again to them. But if I can get them out heare I dont think I Ever shall return again thare to Live." He requested various common household items—treasures in remote Cape Palmas—such as a mirror and tea kettle, padlocks, a bed tick, and some muslin for clothing. In closing, he sent greetings to old friends: "I feel destinated to meat them on the banks of deliverence wheare parting will be no more and all those that wants to come out must come as I did Especily those that have Children and [wants] them to be any thing thay bett[er] Come out heare."[13]

William Hawkins, a thirty-five-year-old free farmer and sawyer from Anne Arundel County, left a wife in America. On March 15, he wrote McKenney that he was pleased with Africa. Even so, he wanted cloth, and above all, chewing tobacco, "for here we cant get it her as with the leefe to bacco and that we cant get as yet. Theare is a great destress for it among peple."[14]

"I feel but too certain that this climate is seriously undermining my constitution and if I continue here until I am completely *used up*, the time will be but short," Hall wrote Latrobe on June 1. His health had improved a little toward the end of March when Gould left, but then declined again. Besides malarial attacks, he suffered from "a troublesome and incessant" cough which exhausted and worried him. Opium, calomel, quinine, and other self-administered medicines altered his perceptions and mood, rendering him impatient and sometimes irrational. When a captain invited him to visit England for a few months, he was unwilling to leave the colony in the hands of settlers. Charles

Snetter refused the offer of a job, so Hall asked John Revey, superintendent of the Junk River settlement to the northwest. At the start of June he still had no answer. Hall informed Latrobe bluntly, "I cannot continue to act as a permanent resident agent in this Colony either with advantage to its best interests or with safety to myself. Should you see fit to appoint a new Agent this fall and send him out, I will render him all the assistance in my power . . . until he shall become in some degree acclimated and . . . learn something of the manner of communication with the natives."[15] The board, satisfied with Hall's performance, delayed selecting a successor.

Many settlers were unhappy with Hall's ill temper and the slow pace of development. On the evening of June 24, 1835, there was a public meeting at Harper to air grievances. Settlers regarded such meetings seriously, as they were largely forbidden them in America. From the outset, these meetings reflected the democratic sensibilities of the community. They followed a protocol that included naming officers to conduct proceedings, a statement of the issue at hand, comments in order from the floor, and often nomination of a committee to write a report, to be presented at a later date. This time, Benjamin Johnson took the chair and William Polk acted as secretary. Ten settlers spoke of their concerns. The colonization society and James Hall, its agent, had promised free land to all emigrants, as specified in the colony's constitution. In many cases, the promise remained unfulfilled, for the agent withheld deeds from debtors. Since virtually all settlers owed the store, they were thus effectively denied ownership of land. Several expressed their resentment at having to depend on the agency for employment and provisions. The governor, said one, forbade citizens to trade with foreigners or Africans and forced them to purchase from the store at outrageous prices. Another stated that he had worked steadily for the agency for seven or eight months but was still in debt. He suspected Hall of some dishonesty and claimed, "The Agent makes his boasts to the natives that he pays the colonists such money as he pleases, and even the natives pronounce us the Agents Slaves." Henry Duncan added another story. "A Captain sent a ham of bacon ashore for vegetables, the Agent took the ham and kept it, and sent a small piece of pork about the town to buy vegetables and when the Capt came ashore he asked the Agent how he came to keep him so late for his dinner and that the Agent told him that the Colonists were so damned lazy that he could not drive them to make vegetables as he was but one white man among so many —." Alexander Hance captured the sense of the meeting, saying that he would like Hall to prove that, "we are not slaves according to our treatment." The meeting called on the governor to answer their queries. His response, if he condescended to make any, was not recorded.[16]

Settlers, systematically denied rights in America, were acutely conscious of any infringement of them in their new home. Henry Dennis discussed this point along with other causes of settler discontent in a letter to Dr. John Martin of Snow Hill, Maryland, dated July 23, 1835. Dennis was once a slave there. Martin and others helped him buy his freedom, and under their influence he was converted to Methodism and learned to read and write. He married a free woman, seven years younger, apparently before gaining his liberty, and with her had at least eight children before 1830. In 1832 he and his family went to Africa on the *Lafayette,* then were dumped in the swamps of Caldwell. There, Dennis buried his youngest son. When the *Ann* called in 1834, he needed little persuasion to volunteer. At Cape Palmas, he enjoyed the reputation of being a solid citizen (one of the few who made a real attempt to farm) and clear-thinking man. Dennis informed Martin that his wife had died a few months earlier and the care of seven children had fallen on his shoulders. "I cannot say that I have that abundance and plenty which I enjoyed in the United states," he wrote, adding that the move from Messurado and ill health had added to his difficulties. "Still I have enough to make me grateful . . . and you know I looked forward to something higher and better than *mere eating* when I left America — the enjoyment of liberty, freedom of conscience, the privilege of educating my children, and the hope of doing something for the ignorant natives of this land. . . . And although I have forfeited many of the comforts of life, . . . I trust, that by the grace of God, I shall never regret

that I have pursued the course I have." Gardens, he wrote, were producing well, but actual farming had hardly commenced, and the pro-
ductiveness of the soil remained to be seen. He commented that draft
animals would be a great help, but they were unavailable and of little
use until roads could be improved. He went on to discuss the kinds of
settlers wanted in the colony and what they should know about Africa.
A prospective emigrant must be in good health, should have a little
capital, and should be prepared for hard work. "Let him come prepared to make sacrifices if necessary," he wrote. "Let him be actuated by
a desire of Civil and Religious Liberty — let his soul be inspired by a
desire to improve the condition of these benighted heathens, and we
will welcome such an one with all our heart." He warned Martin and
others eager to convince black people of Africa's advantages not to
exaggerate. "My coloured brethren . . . come here expecting the earth
to yield them an abundant supply of every thing good to eat — they
expect to heap up wealth without labour — they dream about their
future greatness whilst they are wafted on the ocean's bosom." But life
in Africa offered hard work. "What is their disappointment when they
are told that they must eat bread by the sweat of their brow? They
become disheartened and are seldom happy afterwards."[17]

Through June and July, the agent was well one week, on death's bed the
next. At the end of July, however, he felt well enough to visit the leeward
towns, if possible to explore the Cavally River. This project had long
been on his mind. Natural curiosity aside, he recognized the economic
importance of the river, which was the region's principal avenue of
trade. The towns that controlled the river's lower reaches and mouth
jealously guarded their interests, but Hall hoped that friendly visits
and handsome dashes could insinuate a share for the colony.[18]

He set off triumphantly on the morning of July 22 with a party of
four settlers and a dozen Greboes. He had already communicated his
intentions to Baphro and asked him to ready a canoe for the journey

upriver. Coming to Grahway, however, they found unexpected opposition. Bolio and all his headmen met them and earnestly asked them to return home. After an inconclusive palaver, Hall resolved to go forward. The travelers waded through the crowd that blocked their way and walked on to Half Cavally. The town was nearly deserted, as most of the inhabitants were in the bush to protect their ripening fields, and those who remained seemed oblivious. They found Jim Wilson's house, where they had been so cordially entertained the year before. Wilson was trading in the bush, but Hall went in anyway to rest.

Word of the Americans' boldness quickly spread to the bush farms. The headmen soon came to him and insisted that he return home. Hall asserted his right to go where he pleased, broke up the palaver, and ordered his men to get underway again. "The whole Town was ready for a fight, arms, drums, and war bells," he wrote soon after. Stepping onto the front porch, he found it was obviously impossible to go further. The house was perfectly hemmed in by the town's *sedibo*. Hall stalked inside and put up a brave front, demanding dinner, which was due him by the common hospitality of the country. He waited hours, however, before any arrived. The whole while, the crowd kept up a tremendous noise. Amidst the tumult, men took the baggage from the storeroom downstairs.

Hall had now to prevent physical harm and maintain as much of his dignity as possible. With harsh language and open threats he secured the return of his property and cleared out. As dusk fell, the party walked into Grahway, where they were kindly received and spent the night. The next morning, a march through a miserable drizzle brought them home.

On July 28, Hall convened his liege kings to decide some action against Half Cavally. Though war might result, he felt compelled to fight, for the risks of keeping peace after such an indignity were unacceptable. Besides, he reasoned, a war with Half Cavally could well result in its conquest, or at least a negotiated cession to Maryland in Liberia. The town must either submit or become an ally. Cool heads, with a realistic idea of the colony's military strength, prevailed. Hall decided to wait for a chance to even the balance peacefully.

Expansive projects and diplomacy were incidental to important developments in relations between Gbenelu and settlers. In the middle of August, Hall took advantage of his friendly alliance with King Freeman to address the problem of thefts. He outlined a draconian policy: henceforth, he would seize Grebo property to the value of anything taken from settlers. He emphasized that the confiscations would be indiscriminate, believing that this would force honest Greboes to detect and suppress thieves. Freeman and his headmen listened quietly and went away to confer. Five hours later, they returned to argue the plan's injustice. Politely, they acknowledged crime's demoralizing effect, but they balked at Hall's solution. "What I had proposed was new to them," Hall recounted to Latrobe. They could not understand, even those who had visited "white man's country," how such a law could be made, that "as we were one people and under one flag, I had no right to make one class more than another suffer for all the thefts." Had the colonists and Greboes been "two different tribes having no political connexion, and could prove that their people had injured our persons or property, they would be bound as a people to make restitution." The Greboes "demanded that same course should be pursued with them as with our own people. That a constable should be appointed and a court held in like manner as if an American Colonist was to be tried for the like offence."

Hall told them that he was willing to give a constabulary a fair trial, with one reservation: if the system was not working smoothly after six months, his policy would take effect. Accordingly, he appointed six Grebo constables and six justices of the peace, instructing each in his duty. If a constable found evidence of a crime, he must report to one of the justices, who would issue a warrant if the evidence was sufficient. Any indictment issued by a Grebo justice of the peace would be under jurisdiction of the Court of Monthly Sessions, with the addition of two Grebo justices, to sit on the bench with the governor.[19]

The schooner *Harmony* dropped anchor off Cape Palmas on August 23, having left Baltimore on June 28. The little vessel carried twenty-eight emigrants. Among them was the Gibson family, free black people from Talbot County, consisting of six brothers and sisters and a niece. Joseph Gibson, then age twelve and the oldest child, would grow to be an important figure in the community. Shadrack Smith, a free man from Prince George's County, was fortunate to have his wife and five young children freed to accompany him to Africa. One month before departure, his wife bore him a son, his first free child. Two masters in Charles County, George Parnham and Henry Goodwin, freed seven related slaves to allow the family to emigrate undivided. A Dr. Hammond of Talbot County, gave William Scott, age twenty-one, the choice of moving to Africa or facing resale. He and his freeborn wife, Caroline, preferred the former.[20] James Hall paid the new arrivals special attention. He had already surveyed their lots, which he thought were the colony's best and with which the newcomers "appear to be extremely well pleased. . . . I have little doubt but they will be an important acquisition to the Colony." One white woman, Margaret McAllister, was among the passengers. Little biographical information has come to light, but she was apparently a young enthusiast, affected with the religious spirit of the revival. The Ladies' Society for Education in Africa had hired her to teach and evangelize settler children in a projected academy.[21]

Jacob Gibson soon after wrote Latrobe and McKenney of the pleasant voyage and his satisfaction at finding everything as he had imagined. He planned to join Wilson's church and send his children to the mission school. He expressed sadness, though, for those left behind: "I will be ten thousand times obliged to you if you will make an effort to get my children freed and sent out to me. Neither of you, perhaps, know the pain which a father feels at being seperated from his own offspring." He went on to ask for a whip saw and large nails for house-building. "I hope you will go on in the work of colonization," he concluded, "I look upon it as the cause of God and the hope of benighted Africa."[22]

Not all the new arrivals were so delighted as Jacob Gibson. One, who could not write, had a letter penned for him to William McKenney. "You are well aware of the Views you held up to Me in Emigrating to this Countrey and had Such Inducements Been fulfilled I should feel Satisfied," he began. But the clothing they were to have received "is a Deade Letter," and the tools and materials to build housing "Cannot be had wothout the Means of paying for them." Some of the farm implements they had been given in Baltimore were now "withheld." "You are well aware of our poverty and Destitute Sittuation when we Left Baltimore and of the assurance Given us that Sufficient Stores Should Be given us for a certain Period but as Such is not the fact."

McKenney was mortified at the suggestion that he had lied. In his own defense he wrote on the letter that he had only repeated what he had read and heard from visitors to Cape Palmas. He suggested that the society should allocate a little more for new arrivals. Obviously, the adjustment to the new country would be difficult: starting with nothing, as most settlers did, made matters worse.[23]

After Hall's misadventure at Half Cavally, at the end of July he and his liege kings agreed that the best revenge was to break that town's commercial influence. Half Cavally did not control the mouth of the river, but she was more populous than her neighbors, had more farmable territory, controlled convenient river landings a mile or two from the sea, and had a safer beach landing than the choppy waters nearer the river's mouth afforded. Thus, a better market for produce, advantages in trading with foreigners, and a jealous protection of mercantile interests made Half Cavally a powerful force among the Grebo states. Hall decided that the best plan was to open a road from Cape Palmas to Denah, a town on the Cavally River some ten miles above its mouth, to pre-empt Half Cavally's trading posts. The project involved more than merely clearing a path, for Hall had to negotiate rights-of-way through several small states. A balance of power was at issue, and Half Cavally strenuously opposed the project. Hall sent messages to each of the states, and a few came in or sent envoys, but nothing concrete was established.[24]

Two months later, Hall found an unexpected chance to pursue the plan. In the middle of October, King Tom, or Barrah Keaby, of Robookah, four miles east of the Cavally's mouth, sent word that he wished to unite with Maryland. He did so for his own reasons, to counter opposition from his liege kings, but Hall was quick to seize the opportunity. On October 16 he set out with a small company of settlers and Greboes for Robookah, which they reached the same day. During the next two days, Barrah Keaby ceded his territory to Maryland in Liberia for little more than assurances of schools, trading privileges, and mutual defense. The rebellious liege kings would not condescend to attend the palaver at Robookah, and James Hall therefore visited them in their towns, obtaining perfunctory ratifications of the deed of cession. Overcoming Half Cavally's machinations, Hall and his party continued upstream for nearly a week, visiting towns that no Westerner had ever before seen, as far north as the Cavally's fall line. During the trip, he met and negotiated with the King of Denah and won tentative approval to extend his road to the town. Hall was filled with a vision of a future African republic, of which this area would be the breadbasket.

The exploration of the Cavally ushered a period of optimism and good will. Days after his return, the governor sent an envoy to confront Half Cavally for various insolent acts against the colony. They speciously blamed Barrah Keaby for having urged them to this course and then betraying them, begging forgiveness. They even agreed to accept whatever terms the governor would dictate. On November 25, they ceded their territory to the colony. Half Cavally was exceedingly eager to complete the arrangement, and the headmen pressed James Thomson, who carried it to them, to let them sign it, even foregoing the requisite dash. The borders of Maryland in Liberia were now consolidated, and a permanent peace seemed firmly established.[25]

VI.
"Infirmities of Our Comon Nature"

WE CONTINUE TO PROSPER," HALL REPORTED IN A LETTER OF DEcember 10, 1835. "I believe we may truly say that every month of our existence witnesses an increase of energy, industry and contentment among the fine inhabitants of our little settlement."[1] William Polk illustrated this optimism on November 29, in a message to a former benefactor in his home town, Salisbury, Maryland. "I want to tell you that I am now living at the Maryland settlement with fu others that came out with me," he wrote, "We are Going on Farming and building." Give his old friends a message, he asked. "I would not Exchange homes with them on no Condition unlyse thay could make me as the white man, we have every thing hear that is meant by the word liberty both Civil, temporal, and spiritual Oh what a faint hearted set of people must Dwell amongst you. Arise out of your slumber and sleep no more! I want you to Enjoy some of this lifes happyness."[2]

The new year arrived in peace, and for several weeks after remained so. Hall proclaimed February 22, the settlement's second anniversary, a day of thanksgiving. By apparent miracle, Maryland had survived and even prospered in a modest way, Hall reminded settlers:

But two years have elapsed since you the first founders of this colony were floating on the bosom of the mighty ocean without home or country, seeking among the heathens and barbarians that liberty which the land of your birth had denied. No Combination of circumstances could tend more deeply to depress the mind of man than those in which you were then placed. Behind, you had left a land of light and freedom, a people intoxicated with the element which you, and you alone were not permitted to taste.

Before you, all was darkness, doubt and uncertainty; scarce a ray of worldly hope pierced the gloom in which you were enveloped. Nothing under such circumstances could serve to [revive] and animate the drooping spirit, but a firm and unshaken confidence in the special protection of Divine Providence. Such confidence I believe to have been your support: and that it was not misplaced, subsequent events have most clearly verified.

In Africa, they had made a home. Here was a productive and beautiful land, together with a government suited to their needs. In justice and true piety, Hall exhorted them, they could do nothing less than offer thanksgiving.[3]

At the end of January, James M. Thomson, colonial secretary and storekeeper, received an appointment from the Episcopal Board for Foreign Missions to set up a new station with a school for African children. Thomson eagerly accepted the honor, unprecedented for a black man, for evangelization had originally led him to Africa. Besides, he had become extremely unpopular as storekeeper (and therefore, tracker of debts). The news disappointed Hall, for Thomson was his most capable assistant. He granted the mission ten acres of prime land: a hilltop just beyond the edge of the settlement, overlooking the newly opened Maryland Avenue, with a distant view of the sea. He then chose William Polk to serve as secretary temporarily.[4]

The brig *Fortune*, Captain F. W. Perry, hailed Cape Palmas on February 4, 1836, with thirty-nine emigrants and Oliver Holmes, Jr., a young Baltimore dentist sent out to relieve James Hall as agent. The

Fortune had left Baltimore on Christmas eve, a nasty season to sail.
Perry's strong recommendations proved misleading. In port he behaved decently, but once beyond public eye, his demeanor transformed.
"He is the most profane immoral, and passionate man I ever knew,"
Holmes reported, advising Latrobe not to hire him again. By all accounts, he acted the tyrant, abusing the crew as well as emigrants. At
sea, an inventory revealed that two barrels of the passengers' store of
beef were missing. Perry refused to let Holmes search the hold to locate
them. Rations of meat for the emigrants ran short. More, Perry was
particularly jealous of his water. Enough was stowed to allow the forty-
two passengers forty gallons a day, but the captain at first gave out only
fifteen. Upon complaint, he raised the amount to twenty, still scarcely
enough for drinking, let alone washing. When pressed further, Holmes
later wrote, he "threatened (not to give them enough) but to give them
all that was on board for them and let them waste it, and then he said
'he could live on as little as any of us. We should all then be on an
allowance.'" Perry divided the able-bodied men into gangs and forced
them to do regular watches, all over Holmes's protests. Several seasick
passengers were whipped when they refused to work. "He was in the
habit on the voyage of useing the most indecent language to the females, and this was his chief delight," Holmes complained. "He was
cursing and swearing from morning until night, and . . . he spent the
sabbath when not otherwise employed in the buisness of the vessl, in
playing Checkers, and all the sabbath evenings during the voyage was
spent in this way, . . . he had floged all his men at least once and some
more, and . . . this had been done with his fists a part of the time whilst
the men was *at the helm*." When emigrants tried to air damp, stinking
bedding on deck, the captain ordered the articles thrown into the sea.[5]
"Such Starvation I never experienced before," Luke Walker, an educated and enterprising free sawyer, remembered. "My Little Boy at the
rise of four years old I saw him my self one day in the cabin Picking up
the crumbs of the deck eating of them. Then My Very Soul were Grieved
for taking advices and Plunging my whole family in to sufferance and
Affliction."[6]

Holmes's arrival aboard the *Fortune* was a huge relief to Dr. Hall. He resolved to sail to Monrovia aboard the vessel when she should leave in a few days. There, he hoped to replace Thomson and buy trade goods for the agency before returning to America. Over the previous few months, he and Thomson had distributed large amounts of merchandise to Grebo factors for rice. With the palm oil season coming on, he must have more to satisfy his contracts.[7]

Dr. Hall left Holmes to learn for himself the wrangling business culture of the coast. On February 10, Captain Perry entered the office and handed Holmes a bill for his passage to Africa, demanding a draft on the society then and there. Holmes had had every reason to believe that his employers had taken care of this before the *Fortune* set sail, and he refused. Hall was also in the room, occupied with his own business. He watched silently as the two quarreled over the bill, Holmes determined not to pay and the captain intent upon extorting whatever he could. At last Holmes offered to give Perry a draft with a conditional clause, stating that the note was void if the passage had already been paid. Perry violently objected, affecting insult at the implication of dishonesty. They argued awhile, but Holmes kept his money. He resented the fact that Hall had not taken his side, but it is evident that the outgoing agent wanted to see how his successor would handle such confrontations, which were part of everyday business.[8]

On February 11, Holmes signed a receipt for the society's property in Africa as agent and governor. Hall rode out to the *Fortune* immediately. In his hurry, he neglected to bid farewell to Freeman and his headmen. At the time, nothing was said, but the slight was consequential. The colonization society was a vague and shadowy entity to Greboes. Dr. Hall was the society in their opinion. Now he had left a new man, barely known to them, in charge. Naturally, they doubted Holmes's legitimacy.[9]

Soon after Hall had left, a settler discovered a Grebo woman digging cassava roots from his farm. He bound her and with some friends took her off to the jail, a log house on the Public Farm. To get there, they had to walk through Gbenelu, where the woman lived. Her friends turned out to stop them, and Freeman then set her at liberty. The settlers returned to Harper and complained. Holmes immediately called Freeman to account. The king claimed that the woman was innocent. Holmes produced evidence to the contrary, and Freeman had to concede. The discussion turned on the right of American officers to enforce the law on Africans as well as Americans. Holmes asserted that the American laws provided for an impartial trial of facts, whereas Grebo procedure was less fair. Moreover, declared Holmes, he must judge such cases because he was governor. "This last," he later wrote Latrobe, "was an argument they could not get over." The woman was subsequently yielded up to the Americans, found guilty at trial, and fined five times the amount of the cassava she had dug.[10]

Shortly after Hall's departure, Holmes fell ill, joining the rest of the *Fortune*'s company in the usual "acclimating fever." In fact, he was bedridden for twelve of the eighteen days following February 11. Nevertheless, at the start of March he was recovering a little and expected (rather optimistically) to conduct his business with a minimum inconvenience.[11]

James Hall returned to Cape Palmas unexpectedly on March 2. At Monrovia, he had succeeded in replacing Thomson with George McGill's spirited and brilliant young son, Samuel. The young man, known familiarly as Ford, had accompanied his father to Africa in 1827. Hall took him away from a clerk's desk in the firm of Russwurm & Daily, which required little persuasion, as McGill rather disliked Daily. Hall failed to find a ready passage home. Rather than sit idle, he returned to leeward with McGill. A large purchase of supplies and trade goods would follow shortly in a chartered colonial schooner.[12]

James Hall's reappearance disturbed Greboes, who were unsure just who was in charge. They had a score to settle with him, for he had insulted them when he left the month before. By way of retribution, therefore, Greboes pillaged the farms of several of the hardest working settlers and shot several hogs that strayed into Gbenelu. They did not destroy houses or injure anyone, but food and months of labor were wiped out. Grebo sources informed Holmes of the reason for the dep-

redations, but Hall believed that they were merely a ploy to evade fulfillment of rice and palm oil contracts. That the best farms were singled out
suggests something more. In retrospect, it is evident that the raids were a
deliberate blow against the settler community, which was then expanding rapidly and beginning to show signs of self-sufficiency.[13]

During a sojourn at Cape Palmas of about three weeks, Hall tried
to instruct Holmes. Both were unwell: at the least, dosed with calomel
and opium. One must wonder whether Hall was as bad a teacher as
Holmes would have been a student. The new agent would probably
have been better off left alone. Thrust into immense responsibility with
scarcely any training, he had staggered through and even established
himself. Hall, however, had little respect for the younger man and considered himself agent as long as he remained at the Cape. Indeed, he
kept control of the account books until the day he left again. Holmes's
authority was thereby measurably reduced. Adding insult, Hall scheduled an election of militia officers without bothering to tell Holmes.
Early on election day, Holmes found officers waiting at his office to
appeal the action. James Thomson, acting commander of militia, informed Holmes that Hall had ordered the election, giving no reason.
Holmes closed the polls, for the officers had performed satisfactorily
and the military code specified no term of office. When Hall returned
from a foray to buy rice, Holmes confronted him. "I am not to consult
you," the old agent icily replied. "Truly, whilst he remained, it was hard
to tell when he was governor and when he was not," Holmes fumed in a
letter home.[14]

The schooner *R. R. Gurley*, named for the secretary of the American Colonization Society, arrived at Cape Palmas on March 15, laden
with goods purchased at Monrovia. Hall worked frantically in heavy
rain and surf to get her unloaded and return to Monrovia on her. In his
frenzy, he risked the cargo. Salt water damaged several barrels of rice,
intended as payment for the goods from Monrovia. The sodden contents were sent back on shore. Several hogs died after eating the spoiled
grain, which settlers bought at a discount.[15]

Hall prepared to leave at last on March 18. Perhaps aware that he had neglected Holmes, he wrote up some advice, which he sent ashore the next evening with a note explaining that the instructions were meant as suggestions. Indeed, Hall's advice was cursory and obvious, detailing policies and promises of which Holmes was already aware. He regarded the letter as self-serving and indicative of Hall's lack of respect. For two more days, the *Gurley* rode just offshore. Hall ventured to the wharf only briefly, as the vessel was likely to sail with the first favorable breeze, which made up on the twenty-first.[16]

On March 25, the *Gurley* hailed Monrovia. There, Hall learned that George McGill's friends in Baltimore had arranged for young Ford to attend medical school. Happy for him, Hall was yet unsure who could replace him at Harper. Unable to consult Holmes, he took upon himself the duty of replacing McGill. He got Charles Snetter, whom he had tried to lure to Harper for more than a year past. The cost was high—a handsome salary of $400 per annum, payable in drafts or goods from the store at a mere 25 percent over cost. (The standard mark-up was 100 percent, and even more for some items.) Moreover, Snetter had the privilege of living in the Agency House, as had McGill, until he could build a house for himself. Hall noted to his superiors that Snetter was not "bred a mercantile man," but he was confident that the South Carolinian was the best man in Africa to take charge if anything happened to the agent. Hall reiterated former praises: "He is possessed of sterling honesty, cool and undaunted courage, profound sagacity, and the warmest Patriotism." Snetter provided for his wife and son and boarded the next vessel to leeward. He arrived at Cape Palmas in April, without warning, and moved into the cramped Agency House with Holmes and McGill.[17]

On the day of Hall's departure, Freeman and his interpreter, Simleh Ballah, called on Holmes expecting pleasantries and a dash. The new agent instead scheduled for the next day a palaver to settle the damage to the plundered farms. Holmes's forthrightness caught Freeman by surprise. He meekly acceded to the demand. Holmes was aware that Greboes would watch his first acts in office carefully. His conduct would determine his future success.[18] Moreover, he wished to suppress thievery, which "had a tendency to depress still more, the minds of the Colonists." Informers had singled out the instigators of the raids, and Holmes resolved to make them pay, even if that meant war. Nevertheless, he had to be careful, Despite his confidence that the colonists would easily win any conflict, the likely possibility remained that the Greboes, "if driven to the bush . . . would always be upon our frontier and as an opportunity offered would murder our Colonists. I also knew, that in case of war unless an example was made of them they would excite the neighboring tribes to hostility against us." Knowing the futility of protracted warfare, and with the best interests of the society in mind, he "determined to act with forbearance, and rather to persuade than to threaten."

On the morning of March 22, 1836, Freeman and forty-nine of his headmen came to talk the thief palaver. Holmes canted the history of the settlers and the benefits Greboes received from their presence. He told them that the robberies must stop. In turn, Freeman submitted a long list of grievances against the colony: principally, that the price of rice and palm oil had declined since the Americans' arrival (which was not true), and that settlers had killed some Grebo bullocks. Neither side would compromise, and after an hour's inconclusive discussion, the meeting was at an impasse. Suddenly, and to Holmes's complete surprise, Freeman expressed a grievance which seemed unrelated to the subject at hand. He told Holmes that the palaver could not be set because, as the agent reported, "I gave to Mr. Thomson for farm [meaning the land transferred to him for missionary purposes] and plenty land to new America man [meaning the land given to the Emigrants who came in the brig *Fortune*] and that this land was not sold first time when Dr Hall bought tother land."

Apparently, Holmes had not yet heard of the trouble that the ongoing expansion of the settlement had aroused. The Episcopal mission was in possession of ten acres of prime land, which Hall assumed was vacant but was actually a fallow rice field. Thomson had devoted the past two months to clearing the hilltop where he would build a house and school. The *Fortune* emigrants were just now claiming some sixty more acres of land along Maryland Avenue, and Greboes threatened to pull down houses as fast as they went up. The land in contention was subject to periodic cutting for rice fields. To Greboes, it was in current use and therefore guaranteed them by the deed of 1834. Holmes understood the matter differently and refused to recognize the African practice of rotating farm fields. He referred to the deed and read Freeman the relevant passage. Freeman countered, "All land, that they made into farm land before the Americans settled upon it was theirs forever: that Dr. Hall had told them so, and because they did not understand book, he had made fools of them. They said that country man made new farm every year, and he keep old farm for another time."

The talks then broke down as the headmen began to argue among themselves. Some, who were more sympathetic to the Americans, objected to Freeman's claim of ignorance of the deed's terms. The animated debate subsided after a few minutes, when Freeman's opponents left the Agency House. The clock had now advanced past four, the dispute nowhere near resolution, and the agent lost patience. "I told them," he wrote, "if what they had said was true they were cheats and had cheated Dr Hall, as this country, about Cape Palmas, had all been rice farms for them many years before, with few exceptions." Surely, he remonstrated, the Greboes sold something to the Americans. "I told them this land palaver had been brought up, either for fear that we wanted to make a road to the Bush for trade or to balance the [thief] palaver, but I was not to be made a fool of by any such nonsense." The opponents were deadlocked. Freeman forbade any further expansion, nor was Holmes in a position to admit any Grebo claims, for the repurchase of land would set a dangerous precedent. He was determined to put up the boldest possible face.

During the next week there were a few fruitless private meetings. On March 29, Holmes posted a proclamation, claiming that "whereas there appears to be little hopes of the said natives settling the dispute amicably," and "to preserve the peace and welfare of the Colony, and to let them see we are not to be intimidated by the threats they are openly making," all trade with Greboes would cease after March 30, and the colony would assume a military footing. On hearing "two guns in quick succession," colonists were to muster at the Agency House with their weapons.

The agent intended his notice to outline a common ground for defence. He had heard that there was dissension within the militia and even that a mutiny was possible. Ten acres of the land in dispute was assigned to the Episcopal Church, under the stewardship of James M. Thomson, who was despised for his association with the colonial store. Many settlers grumbled that they would not risk their lives and property to protect him.

As the sun rose the following morning, Holmes and his troops began to carry out the ultimatum. Captain Anthony Wood and a detachment of twelve men hauled a cannon out to the Public Farm from the Cape, an act either of amazing boldness or naivete, as they wheeled the piece right by Gbenelu. At the same time, Thomas Jackson approached Holmes and earnestly told him, "many of the men would have nothing to do in this buisness, because, they thought Mr. Thomson should give up his land." The governor rebuked him and sent him back to the ranks.

Everything was now at the ready. The heavy field piece was set up on the Public Farm, about nine hundred yards north and east of Gbenelu. Two smaller cannons formed a battery on the summit of the Cape. From these emplacements, the Americans could well have leveled Gbenelu and its satellites. Freeman was aware of the danger, so he stalled for time and requested a last palaver to avoid war, exactly what the agent had hoped for. He, Ford McGill, and a young settler conversant in Grebo, went into Gbenelu, unarmed, but with the militia ready to open fire at first signal. "After wandering about among their huts for some time," Holmes related, "we at last found the King and head men assembled under the 'palaver tree.' As soon as the King saw me, he arose from his chair (all were seated some upon native chairs and others upon the ground) and advanced to me holding out his hand, to shake hands." Holmes kept up a bold air, returning the coolest of greetings, "to let him know at once I had not come to be trifled with." Like Quakers, they sat silently for fifteen minutes. Simleh Ballah then announced for the king that the palaver must be set. Holmes believed that Freeman was tired of the contest and would give it up if he could save face. He chose to push his point, however, stating that he would make no concession. The headmen began to argue. Seah, head of the *sedibo*, was ready to fight, asserting "He never would give up the land without war." Freeman answered, "You talk like a fool, there is war already; have they not sent a big gun to the Bush?" "The debate now waxed warm," Holmes wrote, "and at last I began to think, that the whole of the head men would be engaged in a regular row, although to the credit of the people who were spectators, they did not open their mouths or move from their places." The hurly-burly continued for about an hour, while Holmes and his companions watched in silence.

At length Simleh Ballah announced that the palaver was resolved. The agent could only ask what the outcome was. He was told that Thomson and the others could clear their land and no one would interfere, to which the agent retorted he could allot land to whomever he pleased without regard to Grebo authorities. Holmes added that they must sign a release for the land in question and settle the thief palaver in a week. They agreed, promising to come to the Agency House after the midday meal. While Holmes had his dinner, a dash was prepared for Freeman and his head men. After eating, he composed a document for Freeman's signature that relinquished to the colonists "all claim that the people of the native towns of Cape Palmas think they have to a certain tract of land known as the old rice farms, situated upon the Maryland Avenue."

Freeman and his men came according to appointment, and Holmes had the document laid out on the table for them to sign. He read it aloud, endeavoring to explain it fully as he did so. When he had finished, Freeman declined to sign it, protesting, "That was old book, he no be a new fine book; he be the same book, old gubnor fool king first time." He insisted that Holmes write the deed again. The agent complied, with the king looking over his shoulder, quietly hoping for a chance to alter the document, without knowing what Holmes was writing or how to ask him to alter it. Freeman was in an embarrassing situation, for he wanted some of the land reserved to himself, but he was afraid or ashamed to say so in front of so many. He sat down again and sulked, only reluctantly informing Holmes of his wishes. Furious, the agent threw down his pen and stalked about the room. When he had calmed himself, he warned the king not to make a fool of him, that he should return home if he was not ready to make peace. Indeed he did wish to go, Freeman responded, let him sign the book and be done with it. The marks were quickly placed upon the sheet. The agent shook hands all around and distributed the dash, a welcome present at the close of a difficult day.

The victory pleased Holmes, but he was probably unaware of its full significance. If he had yielded, Greboes would have effectively confined the colony to Cape Palmas, to remain a trading post or garrison. His success signaled a material weakening of Grebo constraint of the American community. Similar conflicts would continue, but the Americans had won the right to expand their settlement as needed.

The next week was calm. Freeman was relieved to have escaped his predicament, for the young dentist at Harper had quite unexpectedly proven himself a match for the old king. But if Freeman imagined the matter settled, he was mistaken, for Holmes still insisted upon restitution for the settler farms ruined the month before. April 7, the deadline, passed without a word. The next morning, Holmes cut off trade and sent all the agency's African workers home. He had plenty of rice on hand and could hold out for some time. Greboes, though, depended on their trade and labor at the agency and had more to lose in the short run. At the end of the day, Freeman and some of his head men visited Holmes to find out why he had cut them off. Freeman complained that Dr. Hall had condemned him for halting trade, but now Holmes was using the same tactic. Holmes responded that Freeman was free to forbid his own people from trading or working for the Americans, but he had no right to otherwise interfere with the colony. Freeman realized there was no alternative but to settle the original palaver. He admitted that he knew who the thieves were, then stated his willingness to pay whatever damages Holmes demanded. The agent imposed a fine of two fat bullocks, one for the gardens and the other for the lost hogs. Freeman assented and went home.

Next morning, loud voices in the Agency House yard awakened the agent. Only partly dressed, he went down to claim the two bullocks from Freeman and the headmen. Immediately, everyone crowded around him, asking for goods in advance for the purchase of rice. Holmes refused, since distributing advances among so many factors would never work. This new palaver dragged on through the morning, and hard words passed yet again. Holmes angrily informed the king that he would not be bullied. If Greboes wanted the store, they could try to take it, but it would be in the face of the militia's guns. Freeman backed down with the comment, "It was true, one White man spose he be Pickaniny he was pass all countryman for War side." That is, even though Holmes was just a child, he was more warlike than any African. Everyone went home. Later in the afternoon, Freeman returned quietly with three of his headmen to ask the privilege of buying rice for the agency on trust. Holmes now advanced them goods, and these factors were scrupulous to fulfill the bargain.

In fact, Greboes seem to have adopted a conciliatory policy after their brush with the colony's irascible new leader. Soon after the palaver was laid to rest, the son of a Half Cavally headman was caught stealing two handkerchiefs from the store. He was thrown in jail and kept there until his father could pay the fine, a bullock and a sheep. Once the Americans had freed the young man, the *sedibo* arrested him again and forced the father to pay a second penalty of two bullocks. With this, they warned neighboring states not to spoil the honest reputation of Gbenelu.

Though settlers were intimately involved in the colony's relations with neighboring African states, the concerns of daily life were usually of greater moment. They had to build and maintain shelter; plant and weed farms; secure food and clothing; and nurture communal, family, and spiritual life. While the letters of colonial officials often concern business and intercultural relations, settler letters typically reflect such personal issues.

At the close of May, 1836, Henry Dennis wrote another of his old benefactors in Snow Hill, Dr. John Martin, to report his progress and ask for help. He assured the doctor of his continued religious devotion, "thru many trials and dificulties." Homesick, he lamented that he would never see his American friends again, yet he hoped to meet them in Heaven. "I pray for you," he wrote, "tho the Atlantic rolls between it will sever my body but not my affection from my dear friends in America." Dennis was an industrious farmer, and with ten acres was perhaps the largest private landowner in the colony. At the time of writing, he had six acres either being cleared or under cultivation. His corn had risen so far six inches above ground. Could the doctor, he asked, send him some black-eyed peas and Irish potatoes? All he needed to be self-sufficient, he believed, was a team of oxen or mules. He asked if a collection could be made on his behalf, stating that they would cost fifteen dollars a pair if the required trade goods were purchased in America, twice as much if purchased with goods from the colonial store. "I have not come here to sit down and calculate on my friends for support," he apologized. "I have worked harder here than I ever did in America and still feel willing to persevere, but I need assistance."

Dennis, like almost every other settler, was dependent on the store and constantly burdened with debt. He had no choice but to buy manufactured goods there, since it was the only commercial outlet in the colony. The society usually priced goods at 100 percent over first cost, to cover the expenses of shipping and losses due to climate and theft. Settlers had no cash and had to pay for goods by labor. Having once gotten into debt, many never recovered their finances. Hall, and Holmes after him, took advantage of this for the society's gain. The agency paid laborers a maximum of seventy-five cents per day—the daily wage in America—but half that in real value at Cape Palmas. In a situation the opposite of the classical economic model, labor on this frontier was cheap, because it was at the mercy of a monopolistic employer. To extricate themselves, settlers had either to become totally self-sufficient—an unlikely possibility, but what the society hoped they would do—or to develop their ties with Greboes, which many were loath to do. Greboes could supply a limited inventory of food, but the agency discouraged settlers from trading with them, on the principal that such traffic was inimical to the interests of an agrarian community (not to mention that competition threatened the agency's trade). Settlers were inexperienced traders and occasionally got into trouble, drawing in the agency to bail them out. In fact, settlers had very little on their own that Greboes wanted to trade for, and what they had was reduced in value by high prices, hard bargaining, and theft. Of this, Dennis wrote, "I find we never will be able to get rid of this extravagant price for stock untill we begin to raise them the natives will have their price for every thing that we do not raise as soon as we can make a start they will fall as they have done for other things." As a community, settlers would work out a niche between Greboes and the agency, but they would remain unhappy with the situation.[19]

By the beginning of April, 1836, the *Fortune*'s company were at last settling on their lands. The first few months in Africa had scarcely been more comfortable than the voyage. Several families lost their baggage at sea, and they arrived with only the clothing on their backs, entirely dependent on the society's dole. The longhouse that Dr. Hall had constructed a few months before proved inadequate. Built directly on the ground and inexpertly thatched, the occupants suffered from exposure. "The Fortune Emigrants was particular Miss Fortuned in this respect as well as some others," Holmes wrote the board in July, "as soon as the rains commenced the *sick, dying* and *dead* was drenched, and when it happened to rain at night and whilst it rained those that could (without exception) rolled their beds, and bed clothing up and endeavoured to find a dry place to stow it." He added that insects and lizards infested the roof and constantly fell onto the inhabitants below.[20]

Inadequate medical care made the situation far worse, and the attention that some settlers received did more harm than good. Holmes was usually too sick or too busy to treat them. Dr. Hall might have helped, but he was preoccupied with trade and escape from Cape Palmas. Their treatment therefore fell to Joshua Stewart, a vain and ignorant man who had come out aboard the *Ann*. In Baltimore he had made a living as a saddler and barber. He was tolerably well educated for a black man in that day, but he was in no way qualified for medical practice. Old settlers and newcomers alike suffered at his hands.[21]

John Harris's wife, Jane, delivered a baby with the aid of a midwife shortly after landing. Within five days, she was on her feet. Even so, Stewart thought fit to administer "necessary medicine" in such doses that the woman fell dangerously ill; nor did he bother to mention the case to Holmes until she was almost dead. She failed to recover, and the neglected infant died soon after. With calomel, a mercurial compound, Stewart overdosed Margaret McAllister, the teacher of the Ladies' School, "without knowing how much was a dose," wrote Holmes, "or consulting me, the consequence was, (she not knowing she was taking it) [she] was dreadfully salivated." Other patients were underdosed, for Stewart was too proud to follow instructions. James Spriggs died of the notorious African fever. Rebecca Delaney was a victim of dysentery. Eventually, Holmes dismissed Stewart.

Charles and Lilly Croney, freed by separate masters in Prince George's County to settle in Africa, died scandalously of drug and alcohol abuse. In America, reportedly, they had been heavy drinkers. They smuggled a supply of liquor aboard the *Fortune*, Holmes asserted, and were drunk during much of the voyage. Once ashore, they suffered severely from malaria. Since Holmes's remedy included rum, they made frequent calls on him for treatment. One day Charles Croney asked Holmes for "some Snakeroot and a little Rum . . . to make some bitters for his wife, as her chills had returned." Holmes gave him both, only to learn that Croney drank the rum on the way home. The next day, he drank a bottle of Snakeroot bitters intended for his wife, "then went to bed and remained insensible for three days when he died." Mrs. Croney died a few days later, apparently under similar circumstances.

—◦—

At the end of April, Charles Snetter landed at Harper with a commission from James Hall. Holmes had no warning, but he was bound to make room in the already-crowded Agency House. Holmes regarded this as yet another instance of Hall's disrespect. Holmes and Snetter did not get along from the first, but their private animosity took a month or more to break into open dispute.[22] The precipitating cause is uncertain, but Snetter was as arrogant and stubborn as Holmes. Other factors certainly contributed to the feud, not least among them, Snetter's poor education. He was not so good a bookkeeper as Hall had supposed. A shambled, phonetically spelled inventory of the agency store in Snetter's hand indicates his inability to handle his duties. In early September, James Thomson had to apologize to Latrobe for the disorganization of the accounts (they were in fact scarcely more than a pile of drafts and receipts) hinting that Snetter had not kept them properly.[23] A year later, Snetter mentioned the accusations against him in a letter to the board: "As to the society Books I had never seen them although I do not Know what I might have done with (as is reported) them," implying that he had actually lost the records.[24]

Snetter was the sort of man who thrived on public attention, and he did not hesitate to make his grievances known at large. The case soon divided the settlement. Rev. John Wilson took Snetter's side and informed the board that Holmes was to blame, that his hatred for his lieutenant sprang from "an unreasonable, unhallowed prejudice." Holmes was so irritated that he refused to feed Snetter anything more than sea rations. "He fed me on Coffe and navy bread during the time I remained at the agancy house," Snetter wrote, "and when I wanted to tast animal I realy had to go to the Revd Mr Wilson and he was Kind enought to let me dine at his house." Snetter in turn did his best to make Holmes's life miserable.[25]

In the middle of 1836, the prospect for African education and evangelization seemed promising. In a letter of June 25, John Wilson reported that education had suddenly increased in popularity, "since our boys begin to read and particularly that one of them has acquired the mysterious art of committing his thoughts to writing, their feelings have materially changed and we have been put to the painful task of refusing a good many who have recently been brought to us." Wilson's wife instructed twenty African children. Kate Strobel, a settler employed by the mission, taught forty American children. The demand was far greater than the capacity of the teachers.[26]

When the thief and land palaver was settled at the start of April, James Thomson had redoubled his efforts to erect buildings for the new Episcopal mission. He left his wife in Harper and lived in a temporary shelter on the construction site. In June he was ready to gather students for his mission school. He could easily have filled his class with Greboes from Nyomowe towns but chose to get his students from farther afield. This tended to broaden the territory under the influence of the mission. Also, children from distant towns could not run away as easily, nor could their parents impose on teachers. Wilson had found this troublesome: if he didn't regularly dash parents, they would take their children home. Girls posed special problems. At thirteen they were marriageable and might be seized at any time by parents or a stranger-husband. Wilson found it necessary to pay bride-price for his girls—in effect to purchase them for his own use—and Thomson followed suit.

In June, Thomson went to Robookah to recruit scholars. In the coastal pidgin he asked King Tom for girls to take back with him, trying unsuccessfully to explain his reason for doing so. At night he retired and took a dose of opium to ease his sleep. Presently, one of Tom's wives entered the house and "prostrated herself" beside him. Whether they had sexual relations or not is unrecorded, but the incident nevertheless had scandalous potential.[27]

All of this remained a secret burden on the missionary's conscience, added to the unabated grudge of settlers, who blamed him for their store debts. They were only too happy to pass on nasty rumors. Wilson warned Latrobe of these in a letter of July 22, stating that gossips were calling Thomson a drunk. "He has at my instigation challenged prosecution," Wilson wrote, "and as yet no prosecutor has appeared, and he ought of course to be held guiltless until proof is established." This curtailed some of the talk, but did nothing to lessen the ill will.[28]

Ford McGill remained at Cape Palmas at the end of July, no opportunity having offered to return to Baltimore. Then, unexpectedly, the *Fortune* appeared once again off the Cape. The vessel had never left the coast. Captain Perry had died, and the first mate was now master. The vessel's supercargo, now in command, took aboard a few parcels free of charge and accepted McGill as a passenger.[29]

Several months earlier, Moses Sheppard, wealthy Quaker philanthropist and avid colonizationist, had persuaded the Young Men's Colonization Society of Maryland to sponsor McGill, promising to pay $250 per year for his tuition and living expenses. The society approached Washington Medical College, a proprietary school in Baltimore, whose trustees included several colonization advocates. They reminded the Dean of Faculty, "that a very large portion of the most intelligent people in this community are deeply interested in the success of this enterprise and by obliging, . . . you will gratify many of our most influential citizens." Samuel McGill, they said, would be willing "to perform any services" that did not interfere with his studies.[30] The faculty accepted McGill for instruction. "We trust that such an arrangement may be made in regard to this matter that Mr. McGill's attending the lectures at Washington Medical College may be compensated by Service to the institution." Despite their magnanimity, they conceded to popular opinion by stipulating that the new student should pretend to be a servant.[31]

James Hall knew of these plans, but he evidently doubted their chance of working, and therefore he made other arrangements. In the months following his return from Harper, he had settled in Baltimore and set up a trading concern in association with George McGill. Hall shipped provisions, cloth, and tools, which McGill traded for palm oil, camwood, and ivory. Knowing George's desire to see his son a doctor, he corresponded with Dr. E. E. Phelps, an old friend and member of the medical faculty at Vermont College, in Windsor, Vermont. Phelps informed Hall in a letter of November 4, 1836, that he would be happy to take McGill under private instruction with the same curriculum provided by Vermont College, one much more thorough than that of Washington Medical College. He added that he would arrange to get "a degree for him whenever he may be deserving of one from our University." Hall would have to send up anatomical specimens, he added, and he "would prefer that they be coloured ones, having always used such here in consequence of the disturbances which are occasionally made in this quarter, by grave marauders."[32]

If they were aware of Phelps's generous offer, the Young Men's Colonization Society still was determined to send McGill to Washington Medical College. Baltimore winters were milder, and they could shield McGill from abolitionists, who might turn him against colonization. But if the sharpness of New England's climate or abolitionist invective might have overwhelmed McGill, the racial attitudes of southern whites were just as menacing. Baltimore, after all, had a tradition of political and racial violence that had earned it the nickname, "Mobtown." Before McGill returned to the United States, Moses Sheppard warned the young man of what he would encounter: "You must not expect to hear the term Mr. McGill from a white man. In the College you must appear as a servant; there is not a medical school in the U. States into which you could be admitted in any other character, but you will have all the means of improvement and the same instruction as the other students, and in proportion as you waive the claim of equality it will be conceded to you, in proportion as you claim it, it will be denied."[33] The idea of sending a black man to a white school, let alone a medical school, as an equal of the white students was incendiary.

A half-dozen Baltimore doctors ran Washington Medical College for profit. They lectured in a small building across from City Hall. Very few institutions of the day offered formal training in medicine, and theirs was probably about average for those that did. In 1838 the school was prosperous enough to build a magnificent new hospital on a hilltop at the edge of the city. Instruction was typical for the time. Students paid to attend two four-month semesters of lectures covering anatomy and physiology, with the basics of medical practice. At the end of the second semester, students had to submit a thesis on any relevant topic that interested them. On graduation, they received a certificate that legally qualified them as doctors. By 1838, eleven years after the school's establishment, more than one hundred students, whose intellect, breadth of education, and competence varied widely, had graduated.[34]

In contrast, Vermont College was one of a handful of schools that offered a systematic and rigorous course of instruction. In a letter to the society, Dr. Phelps explained that his school's curriculum, "differs essentially from the course pursued in other medical schools, inasmuch as it is progressive, the different branches of the science being taught in a definite order, and the student not allowed to pass from one branch to another until he has mastered the preceding." At Vermont, a student was expected to complete his studies in four years, though he might take five or three, depending on his abilities. Apart from the scientific training, the program put emphasis on what Phelps termed "Medical Philosophy."[35]

McGill enrolled at Washington Medical College at the start of December 1836. From the outset he refused to pretend he was a servant, but behaved as any other student, to the mortification of his classmates. On December 12 students met in the lecture hall to draft a set of resolutions against McGill. They noted that a report had gone through the city that the professors had admitted "a Negro Boy into the Institution as a student." Such rumors must have been spread by "some malicious, designing, and prejudicial persons having nothing in view but the opression and injury of the College," for it was a certainty that "any persons who possess any degree of self-esteem cannot conceive that the faculty would consent that Students of fair complexion should mingle with those of dark skin." Continuing their remonstrance: "We conceive, that this Boy has gone far beyond the limited space granted him, and has encroached as far upon the privilege enjoyed by the students, as to wound their feelings, disgust them by his actions, and has called for their immediate and determined action." They demanded McGill's removal from the college.[36] In a cover letter to Dr. Samuel K. Jennings, dean of faculty, they warned that a black student might arouse a mob. Moreover, they worried about the "blighting influence" a black classmate "would undoubtedly exert upon our future professional prospects."[37]

The Young Men's Colonization Society met on December 15 to respond to the students. They decided to withdraw McGill and then negotiate his readmission. Ira Easter addressed an obsequious letter on their behalf, which he sent with their resolutions. "It was never the wish of the Board of Managers that Saml. F. McGill should be esteemed an equal," he wrote, "or as claiming privileges at all comparable with the Students but that in the capacity of a Servant, he might, thro the mere magnanimity of both the Professors and Students, be gratuitously instructed in the Science of Medicine." He asked for a meeting with students to explain McGill's case more fully.[38]

Students gathered again on Christmas Eve to consider the society's request. On a traditional day for charity, they assumed a self-righteous stance and flattered themselves of their own fair judgement. They wrote, "Our conduct in this unhappy affair has been the result of an unbiased deliberation, in which the views and wishes of your society as well as our own feelings of philanthropy possessed ample influence. It would be illusory then to entertain hopes of reconciliation or rather the readmission of Saml. F. McGill, since he has overstepped that line of conduct which prudence and public opinion demanded of him." They stood firm against McGill and refused to meet with colonizationists. Nor would the faculty intervene, for fear of losing their whole student body. The battle was lost; McGill prepared to return to Africa.[39]

—•◆•—

Life at Cape Palmas was contentious, but during Hall's tenure, politi-cal life remained fairly free of faction or coteries. Snetter's fight with Holmes put an end to this. By the beginning of September, the dispute reached a climax: on the sixth, the agent announced his departure.[40] The *Financier*, just arrived, carried word from the board that they had appointed John Browne Russwurm to succeed him. Holmes's initial reaction is unclear. His enemies accused him of racial prejudice: he was "terribly mortified at the appoint," Snetter later wrote.[41] Yet indica-tions are that Holmes got along well with Russwurm, and he went to Monrovia to speed the transfer of authority. James Thomson wrote the society on September 6 of Holmes's trials: "The manner of men he has had to deal with is enough to dampen the zeal and perseverance of any youth of his experience and years. . . . Mr. Snetter is not exactly the man that Dr. Hall, as well as myself, expected to find him."[42] John Wilson was as quick to defend Snetter as he had been a short time before to speak for Thomson against slanders. Adding yet another letter to the bundle destined for Baltimore, he compared Snetter, who was one of his parishioners, to a "lamb" amongst "devouring wolves." Holmes, he asserted, was "influenced wholly by an unreasonable, unhallowed preju-dice," against Snetter. If their characters were compared, Snetter would surpass the agent. He accused Holmes of distilling liquor from rum and molasses and distributing it to Grebo laborers. "I have remon-strated very seriously with him about it, but without effect. He calls the mixture *wine* and the natives received it as such; but whether it is an infraction of your laws or no you are to decide for yourself."

The missionary affected righteousness, denying any wish to defame the agent: he had all along been motivated by the concern of a brother. Holmes, he wrote, bordered on insanity. "His mind at times has been much and alarmingly affected by the fever. Sometimes I have dreaded in his case entire derangement. And after his mind becomes more calm and composed, as I think it will be after he leaves, he will either bitterly regret things he has done here or will not rem[em]ber them at all."[43]

Thomas Jackson, voicing the probable sentiment of most settlers, wrote, "Under Existing circumstances I feel Sorry. I only repeat I feel sorry."[44]

On September 7, Oliver Holmes left Cape Palmas, placing James Thomson in charge, in the capacity of principal factor and bookeeper. Strangely, he named Snetter second factor. Thomas Jackson would serve as third factor and take over the management of the store as soon as William Polk stepped down. "God knows what will become of us," Thomson commented in a letter home, "but as I consider myself one of the founders of the Colony, and still as much solicitous as ever for its welfare, I will use the utmost of my exertions to keep things straight, and to prevent the Colony from sinking."[45]

VII.

"Liberty and Equality"

IN THE MID-1830S, SCIENCE AND POPULAR OPINION HELD THAT PEOPLE OF color were naturally inferior to whites and incapable of self-government—the darker the skin, the less ability. These putative racial differences rationalized and justified a system of slavery that contradicted the national ideals of liberty and justice. Such notions influenced the most liberal of white people, and even black people were susceptible to them, taking for granted, despite themselves, the assumptions of the ruling class about race. The Maryland State Colonization Society's choice of a black man, John Browne Russwurm, was therefore momentous, though it was tempered by some cynical considerations. James Hall argued persuasively (though mistakenly) that a black agent could survive the tropical climate better than a white man. Politics also influenced the board. The Episcopal Church had just hired James M. Thomson to establish their first African mission. A black governor, the colonizationists reasoned, would draw attention and demonstrate a commitment to colonial independence absent in Liberia proper. Paradoxically, John Russwurm existed between two worlds: a black man in America, but white in Africa.

He was born the first of October, 1799, at Port Antonio on the rainy northeast coast of Jamaica. The town was then a backwater. It had enjoyed some prosperity several decades before as a British naval depot. By the late 1780s, according to Edward Long, the exhaustive commentator of Jamaica and its society, it had declined to a mere "fifteen or twenty straggling houses about the harbour."[1] The boy was born amidst rain and mud and rotting houses. The area had none of the big sugar plantations that were the basis of the island's wealth. Nevertheless, Port Antonio did draw a few entrepreneurs who saw advantage in the town's proximity to Haiti.

Russwurm's father was of the sort who came to Jamaica, as another observer said, "with one invariable view — that of making or mending their fortunes."[2] There he ran a store. As adventurers in the region often did, he sojourned with a local woman, a quadroon, who became his mistress.[3] The storekeeper disregarded his octoroon son at first. When the boy was four, he was given the name John Browne, in honor of a local physician and friend of the father. Fifteen years were to pass before he added his father's surname. Yet, the elder Russwurm's attachment to his son grew. In 1807 he left Jamaica and took John with him. He placed the boy in school in Quebec, where he studied for ten years.[4]

The elder Russwurm did not stay long in Canada but moved to North Yarmouth, Maine, a small seaside town. There, he married a widow who had three children. During their years together, Russwurm told his wife that he was supporting a black child in Quebec, but not that the boy was his son. He told his secret only on what seemed his death-bed. Heedless of the stigma of acknowledging an illegitimate child, much more, one who was black, Mrs. Russwurm immediately sent for the boy. Her husband recovered a little, and lived to see John Browne welcomed as a member of the family. At his stepmother's insistence, he took his just surname.

The elder Russwurm died a few months after, leaving what should have been enough money to complete his son's education, but complications in settling the estate reduced the patrimony to a trivial amount. For two years, John Russwurm lived with his adoptive family, dividing his time between school and whatever work he could find. Mrs. Russwurm later wrote, "It was difficult at that time to get a colored boy into a good school where he would receive an equal share of attention with white boys, and this I was very particular should be the case."

The young Russwurm was extremely self-conscious. Though he was treated well, the feeling that he was an outsider, at best an honored guest, stung him. He hated to be treated as a curiosity and patronized. About 1819 he decided to return to Jamaica, where he hoped to persuade his father's old friends to finance his education. On the docks of Portland, his stepmother offered to take him back home. "No; that will not better my color," he responded with characteristic resignation. "If I was a white boy, I would never leave your family, but I think it is best for me to go." The trip proved a terrible disappointment, for the old man's friends declined to help him. He took the first berth back to New England.

John Russwurm landed at Portsmouth, New Hampshire, feeling quite defeated. He ran into an acquaintance from North Yarmouth who informed him that his stepmother had remarried during his absence. In effect, his only anchor was cut loose. Expecting insult and ejection from the house of an unknown stepfather, he resolved to scuffle for a living in anonymous back alleys until he could find a better situation. He drifted up to Portland, where as it turned out things were not so bad. Mrs. Russwurm had bound her new husband to accept John as a member of the family, and the couple were eager to have him return to them. After some time, a friend in Portland notified them that John was there, "looking very much cast down." They sent for him the same day and had him brought home.

With help from Charles Stockbridge, a local politician and philanthropist, Russwurm went to school for another year.[5] When money again ran out, he became a school teacher. He worked for about two years, first in Philadelphia, then in New York City, both of which had large free black populations. In 1821, he settled in Boston. There, for three years, he taught at the Smith School, the first municipally supported school for black students in the nation.[6]

In 1824 his adoptive family urged him to go to Liberia, but he chose instead to attend Bowdoin College, in Brunswick, Maine. No black man had ever attended the school, in fact, there was only one other black person in the United States enrolled in a college. Russwurm pursued a liberal course of studies, comprising a broad range of arts and sciences. At one time he planned to study medicine and even attended anatomy lectures, but he did not pursue it. Bowdoin had two literary societies. Russwurm belonged to the more progressive one, which counted among its members Nathaniel Hawthorne. His other schoolmates included Henry Wadsworth Longfellow, Franklin Pierce, five future Senators, a future paymaster general of the U.S. Navy, and others who became noted preachers, lawyers, and businessmen. Russwurm earned his degree in only two years and graduated with honors in 1826.[7]

As the school's only black student, Russwurm was the object of intense curiosity, which he countered with equal reticence, living apart and scarcely speaking to anyone. "He was exceedingly sensitive, amounting even to jealousy, and having once lost confidence in a person, he seldom, if ever, re-acquired it," James Hall recalled years later.

> He was usually very distant and reserved to strangers, never opening himself until he was satisfied he had no evil to apprehend from so doing. He was exceedingly jealous of any allusion to his position in society as a colored man, and it required the greatest delicacy in the choice of words to render even praise acceptable to him, when coming from a white man. Few, probably, have suffered so much from causes of this nature as Mr. Russwurm.[8]

Horatio Bridge, one class ahead at Bowdoin, recalled that Russwurm lived with a carpenter on the edge of the village of Brunswick, where he kept entirely to himself. On more than one occasion, Bridge and his close friend, Hawthorne, tried to visit him but were disappointed. Russwurm would hide from them, Bridge recalled. "His sensitiveness on account of his color prevented him from returning the calls." More than fifteen years later, when Russwurm was the respected governor of Maryland in Liberia, and Bridge was an officer in the U.S. Navy's anti-slavery patrol, the two met and became friends.[9]

At his Bowdoin commencement ceremony, Russwurm delivered a valedictory. In a singular expression of his political views he spoke in praise of the revolutionary republic of Haiti, established in 1795 after a bloody uprising of slaves overthrew the cruel French colonial society.

Russwurm held up the country's achievements, real and mythical, as an example of what black people could do in the quest of liberty. He defended the violence as an unfortunate but necessary consequence of the slaves' struggle for liberation. "It is the irresistable course of events," he told his listeners, "that all men who have been deprived of their liberty, shall recover this precious portion of their indefeasable inheritance. It is vain to stem the current: degraded man will rise in his native majesty and claim his rights. They may be withheld from him now, but the day will arrive, when they must be surrendered." The correspondent for Portland's *Eastern Argus* who recorded the speech reported that Russwurm intended to settle in Haiti.[10]

John Russwurm was uneasy in the United States. He spent his first eighteen years in Jamaica and Quebec and probably felt little connection with black Americans, either slave or free. Except for his three years' teaching, he would have had almost no contact with free black people, much less with southern plantation slavery. In fact, it is likely that he never saw an American field slave at work. A man one-eighth black, of light complexion, his African ancestry most evident in his hair, in West Africa he was considered white. In the United States, by contrast, he was a member of a proscribed caste, and ashamed of it. He yearned for a home where he would be judged upon his character and accomplishments, unqualified by race.

Both colonizationists and abolitionists courted Russwurm to advocate their cause. As a college graduate he was a symbol of the potential attainments of black people. Moreover, he was a talented writer. Taking the advice of friends, particularly his benefactor, Stockbridge, he chose to work for abolition. In light of his private desire to emigrate, this might seem an inconsistent choice. Among abolitionists, the principles of colonization were suspect, and the name Liberia—"the land of the free"—a mockery of the true ideal of freedom. Russwurm seems to have set aside his own feelings to better the condition of black people in his adoptive country. In New York he accepted the junior editorship of a projected newspaper, the first ever to be published by and for the free black community.[11]

Freedom's Journal first appeared March 16, 1827. During the following six months the essays of Samuel Cornish, the senior editor, earned the paper national attention. In September, Cornish relinquished his post to give full attention to New York's Free African Schools. Russwurm was too reserved to maintain Cornish's outspoken, radical standard. What is more, he grew increasingly sympathetic to colonization. As these convictions developed, he moderated the paper's tone. Criticisms from readers, and especially from Cornish, increased. At last, in the issue of March 7, 1829, Russwurm published his views. His assertion that the black man's "rightful place is in Africa" shocked his readers, most of whom opposed colonization. A mob burned Russwurm in effigy on a New York street. On March 28, he resigned.[12]

Russwurm stayed in the United States for a few months. Some sources have him returning to Bowdoin.[13] The American Colonization Society offered him the post of superintendent of public schools in Liberia, at the modest salary of four hundred fifty dollars a year. He left New York for Africa late in 1829 aboard the brig *Susan*, one of a handful of emigrants who went at personal expense.[14] At Monrovia, Russwurm's education qualified him for more than school administration, and he quickly took on the additional responsibilities of colonial secretary and colonial printer. He joined James R. Daily to run a commission merchant house. In 1834, Russwurm married Sarah E. McGill, a daughter of George McGill, who had recently stepped down as vice-agent, the highest elective office in the colony. Russwurm was commonly regarded as the most capable man in Liberia. Even so, his life at Monrovia had difficulties and discontents, and these mounted.

Dr. Joseph Mechlin became governor of Liberia in 1829, following the protracted illness and death of Dr. Richard Randall. He governed for three and a half years before returning home. Rev. Jacob Pinney, a Methodist minister, succeeded Mechlin. Russwurm prospered under Mechlin's and Pinney's patronage, but he was unable to protest policies which he believed were ruinous. In a confidential, critical letter of 1833, Russwurm warned John Latrobe of an impending crisis and told him that his name must not be mentioned as a source. Quietly, Russwurm's reports helped the Marylanders to formulate their resettlement scheme.[15]

In April 1834, Liberia was embroiled in a constitutional crisis which had at its heart the issue of colonial autonomy. Jacob Pinney set up a "High Court of Appeals," even though the American Colonization Society had not authorized the move and the constitution made no provision for one. Pinney's proclamation on the matter, with the order to "stay the execution of inferior writs where appeals had been made," met with open rebellion from many citizens. On April 15, Vice-Agent Colin Teague published a declaration in support of Pinney, accusing citizens of disloyalty and sedition. Pinney was sick and unable to cope with the stress. He resigned, and Monrovia was in an uproar.[16]

Russwurm's printing press, the only one in the colony, was taken apart by a mob. Some said Russwurm co-operated with the rioters, a charge he denied. In a letter of October 5, 1835, to Ralph Gurley, the secretary of the American Colonization Society, he explained that he was "present at the Court House when the sitting of the Quarterly Court of Appeals was interrupted and the authority of Mr Pinney publicly contemned." "Publicly and freely" he had advised Pinney to "adjourn and await the decision of the Board respecting the constitutionality of the law, " while privately he argued with Teague against declaring the colonists to be in a state of insurrection. "I predicted that the people would allow no such proclamation to be printed." After it was printed, and the sheriff had notified him that "the mob were about to destroy the printing press and types," he went out into the night and "persuaded them that the press etc. were mere machines which had cost a good deal of money in America, and the removal of two or three pieces would effect all the objects which they had in view. Accordingly they spared the press . . . and merely carried away the springs which were deposited nearly opposite in the same street."[17]

Russwurm and Daily opposed the administration. In the violent political atmosphere, made even more tense by the near extermination of the Quaker settlement at Bassa Cove a month later, their opponents labeled them "Nulli-fyers." Daily was slandered as "Mr. Garrison's deciple."[18] Their enemies accused them of associating with slavers.[19]

The American Colonization Society appointed a missionary, Dr. Ezekiel Skinner, to replace Nathaniel Brander, the settler who had temporarily assumed the post of governor. Skinner took office in June 1835, and restored order. Believing that Russwurm had been an instigator of the colonists' rebellion, helping them to shut down the press and circumvent the government's authority, he refused to allow Russwurm any responsibility in the government. Russwurm thereupon stood for the office of vice-agent in an election held that month. He won more votes than either of the other two candidates but failed to get an absolute majority. Skinner then obtusely interpreted the colonial statutes and voided the election. Russwurm was beaten in a subsequent run-off. To Ralph Gurley in Washington Russwurm complained that "great injustice has been exercised towards me by Mr Pinney through the instigation of my enemies the Teagues and Prout; but . . . I can . . . in silence with a clear conscience" endure it. "But is there to be no end to these things? Is Mr Pinneys successor to throw himself and all the influence of Government into the same hands? One would hardly believe it, but such is the fact, nevertheless: and the Governor of Liberia, at this moment is the nominal *head* of a party in *politics and religion.*"[20] He hung on at Monrovia, editing the *Herald* and continuing on a modest basis with Daily, but he was bitter and eager for an opportunity to leave. His appointment by the Maryland colonizationists was just the opening he sought.

―――――

Oliver Holmes arrived at Monrovia in the middle of September, 1836, and conferred with Russwurm during the rest of the month. The agent-designate tried to wind up his business with Daily, without success. He hired his irrepressible father-in-law, George McGill, to serve as assistant agent. Holmes balked at the idea of returning to Harper, but Russwurm persuaded him to do so, promising that he would soon follow and relieve him of his burden. Holmes landed at Cape Palmas early in October. The acrimonious dispute with Snetter had not subsided, though, and Holmes's authority counted for nothing against his adversary. Finding his situation untenable, he retreated again to Monrovia, leaving Maryland in the hands of settlers again.[21]

Opportunities for passage were unpredictable, and Russwurm was forced to wait two or three weeks until a suitable vessel called. Late in October, the brig *Saint George* of London, in service of the British West India Company, hailed Monrovia. William Hutton, supercargo of the vessel, befriended Russwurm and agreed to carry him, George McGill, and Dr. Holmes to Cape Palmas free of charge. They sailed on October 28. Russwurm's wife and children would come to Harper a few weeks later.[22]

The passengers of the *Saint George* landed at the Agency Wharf on November 11, 1836. As their longboat approached shore, a team of settler militiamen primed a rusty field piece, with which they planned to salute the new governor. The result was disastrous—the cannon exploded. The blast took with it William Norris's arm and killed William Duncan. Despite the bad omen, Russwurm took control of Maryland solemnly and without challenge from Charles Snetter.[23]

Soon after his arrival, Russwurm set about reorganizing the government. James Hall had been a vigorous manager but a poor accountant. Holmes was little better, and had incompetent assistants to boot. Consequently, Russwurm began the books anew, something his years in business at Monrovia enabled him to do quickly. His explicit accounts, accurate to every penny and leaf of tobacco, would continue uninterrupted for above twenty years.[24]

The civil service also underwent a change of personnel. Thomson resigned his post to devote full attention to the Episcopal mission. He was anxious that accommodations should be ready before the daily expected arrival of ordained ministers. Russwurm offered Snetter the less responsible office of storekeeper, which he refused, feeling insulted (and perhaps also unwilling to be subjected to the same bad will that Thomson had suffered).[25] John Wilson then hired Snetter to teach settler children, at a reduction of pay and benefits, and criticized Russwurm in a letter to Latrobe. Snetter had been "deeply wounded by the officers of the Colony," he wrote, and "my enticing him away, . . . was with me a matter of serious regret, for I felt that he was the *only man* upon whom your society could rely in case of war with the surrounding tribes." Russwurm's removing Snetter as secretary "has in my estimation and Dr Hall's too, disarmed the Colony or at least rendered its military very inefficient."[26]

Yet Russwurm could not very easily have continued Snetter. Although a capable military man, Snetter had proven himself ambitious, manipulative, and too strong-willed to serve the interests of the society. Russwurm, an extremely sensitive, retiring man, could not have dealt well with Snetter's outspoken, reckless style. He had suffered enough at the hands of such men at Monrovia. He asked John Revey, a mild-mannered, capable Marylander, then superintendent of the Junk River settlement, to take the job of colonial secretary.[27]

During Holmes's absences from Maryland, Greboes had mounted a campaign to rob the store. They took small things at first. A guard was stationed in the warehouse at night in response, but the conspirators were clever. With keys of their own making, they continued to pillage, growing bolder each time. Russwurm straightaway barred the windows and added locks to the door. The burglars flouted his precautions. Early one evening, they stole some five hundred yards of cloth, all the tobacco, and sundry other items.

Russwurm complained to King Freeman, who merely shrugged and promised to do something if the new governor could name the thief. (Russwurm had reliable evidence that Freeman himself was one of the conspirators.) Reluctantly, he referred the case to the Grebo constables, though he had little faith in them. They investigated, and to his surprise, returned in a few days with a sizable portion of the stolen merchandise. Moreover, they named one of the culprits, a young man who lived in a satellite village of Gbenelu. Colonial officers got a warrant and checked the house where the stolen goods were discovered, but they found nothing more, and the thief had fled into the bush. They next searched his father's house in Gbenelu. There they found some more loot, which they confiscated. The old man was a head man, a relative of Freeman's, and an influential figure in his community. The officers did not pursue him when he also ran off. His freedom was short-lived though, for the next morning the constables returned to arrest him. This involved some struggle, but they secured him and marched him to jail. There it was intended he should remain a pawn pending the son's surrender. Whether Russwurm authorized this strategy is unclear. Certainly, the plan was rash, as Greboes resented such an insult to the dignity of one of their leaders. The situation was explosive, but Russwurm seems to have been unaware of the danger.

In the middle of December, while this was unfolding, the U.S. Frigate *Potomac* cast anchor off Cape Palmas. The visit was significant, for it marked the start of a continuing American military commitment to the Maryland colony. Russwurm addressed the secretary of the navy on December 27 to thank him for his support of the colony. "Hitherto many of the native Kings have been quite incredulous about the Americans owning any large vessels of war," he wrote, "but the sight of this noble vessel will dispel all such ideas for the future." The commerce of Africa as yet was "in its infancy," he continued, and if "those benevolent individuals . . . laboring to plant colonies along this coast and . . . civilize the natives," managed to succeed, the world might see "vast markets" opening to supply the interior with "American fabrics of every description."[28] The officers and men of the warship showed settlers every kindness. By the simple act of buying produce and having their laundry done on shore, they infused needed cash into the economy. George McGill even received the supreme honor of sleeping in the officers' cabin one night. "The unighted states and English comodors Captains agents are only my Eaquals when they come here," he wrote in typical style, "and as such they treat me, as a proof when the purtomac Friget was here I slep on Board one night in the cabins with Capt Nicolson of Baltimore I slepd Breakfasted and dined with him in his Cabbin, such is the case of a collered gentleman in Liberia." Far from being pleased, he felt "sory, and ashamed that I have Kinfolkes and acquaintences in Baltimore that are capable of higher honres then I and yet they stick by their disgracefull dens like dogs and Fetters to the Hands. Here I am poor and hapy, all I know about distinction, is when I read about some runaway Negro, or black man hired as a servent stole a coat and a pare of Boots, and went of, 5 Dollars reward will be guiving if apprehended."[29]

Freeman and many of his headmen visited the ship. The king even measured the vessel with fishing line to demonstrate to those on shore. Russwurm, amused at Freeman's reaction, quoted his comment that "she is bigger bigger pass all Englishman and Frenchman." Freeman was "fairly in raptures with every thing he saw," he went on, "and the cold sweat stood on his brow when he was describing the 'big guns.' The marines who were ordered out to drill excited much wonderment in the old man's mind. He seemed to think that after this it would be all folly for them to fight America man." To bolster the impression and fact of colonial strength, Captain Nicholson sent weapons and ammunition ashore. He also advised the agent on improving defenses.[30] Maryland was pathetically vulnerable in fact, and even as the *Potomac* set sail, any accident could have sparked a war. Freeman's awe of American naval power ebbed as soon as the vessel departed. Russwurm was yet new in office, and Greboes were intent upon testing his mettle, just as they had done with Hall and Holmes.[31]

A spark was not long in coming. James Thomson caught a Grebo boy stealing from the mission grounds and sent him before Anthony Wood, justice of the peace. The magistrate sentenced the youth to a fine and whipping. Russwurm rescinded the judgement before it could be carried out, ordering Wood to set the boy free. He instructed all magistrates to use the utmost reserve. Wood either failed to understand this or simply defied the order, for he sent the boy to prison. Thirty or forty men gathered to escort the convict to the jail, a log structure on the Public Farm, about half a mile east of Harper. The road ran directly through Gbenelu, and settlers reasonably expected resistance. They had hard work passing through town, but with pushes and threats they lodged the prisoner.

The Grebo populace was outraged. Four or five hundred armed men turned out at once to break up the jail and take revenge on the arresting officers. When the Americans started back to Harper they came upon a furious mob. In an instant they turned and ran for the mission at Fair Hope, a few hundred yards to the south, the mass of Greboes in pursuit. Settlers hopped the fence and rushed into the house, shattering its peace. Their haven was safe, however, for the pursuers would not cross the fence out of respect for Wilson.

The moment called for the coolest of action, and the missionary acted the part admirably. Once the refugees had calmed a little in the house and the situation was clear, he strode purposefully to the gate and addressed the angry crowd. Speaking quietly, he soothed them to the point that they accepted his request to wait peacefully until he had a chance to present their grievances to Russwurm. Wilson then walked off to Harper, leaving Greboes surrounding the mission and two or three dozen Americans trapped inside the house.

In the meantime, another party of Greboes liberated the boy and head man from the jail. Emboldened, a large number proceeded toward Harper, intending to attack. Just east of town they met Freeman, Russwurm, and Wilson, who assured them that the old man's freedom was safe, that Russwurm had agreed to place him in Freeman's custody. They promised to hold a palaver the next day to settle differences. This appeased the crowd somewhat, and they went home.

Once in Gbenelu, however, their bellicose spirit rose again. The *sedibo* blockaded Maryland Avenue, determined to stop the passage of any Americans through town. Some of them made threatening motions toward Harper, which was defended by a mere six or eight armed men. About one-third of the colony's able-bodied men sat in Fair Hope, unarmed, some of the more agitated ones locked up by Mrs. Wilson to keep them out of trouble. The rest of the settlers were at work on their farms or cutting timber. They were mostly unarmed, and none were aware of the dangerous situation at the Cape. As evening drew on, they walked home, only to find themselves cut off. They went to Fair Hope and Thomson's new station for shelter. In such a predicament, the colony might well have been massacred. The gun emplacement on the Cape could have leveled Gbenelu, but with minimal permanent damage or loss of life, and it could not have withstood an onslaught. Unarmed settlers at the missions or in the bush would be easy prey. War drums pounded all night, but fortunately, neither side fired on the other.

Early the next morning the opposing sides convened near Gbenelu to talk a war palaver. Freeman and his headmen waited with the *sedibo* arrayed in full battle dress. Wilson and many of the settlers who the night before had been kept away from their homes came up on one side. Russwurm's arrival from the other direction with a number of the settlement's women and children initiated a happy reunion. The menacing countenances of the Grebo soldiers cooled the rejoicing. Wilson opened with a brief conciliatory message. Freeman then spoke, purposely ignoring Russwurm as he recounted his people's grievances in exaggerated detail. He summed up with a broad criticism of the new agent and George McGill, who had failed to honor him properly with dashes, and so forth.

Russwurm was hardly able to gain the floor to rebut the accusations, but at length he was allowed to speak. He called on Simleh Ballah "to testify that I came not to reside among them because I was a poor fellow or wanted chop — that it was well Known to Simlah when in America that the great men there had appointed me to be their representative at Cape Palmas." Greboes held settlers in contempt because of their status as slaves in America, though they regarded white people with great respect. Russwurm assumed this lay at the heart of their challenge to him. In this, he was probably a little wrong-headed, for as far as Freeman was concerned, Russwurm was white. He had a light complexion, and more importantly, he could read and write. In any event, Russwurm's speech accomplished little. Freeman resumed his recital of grievances, and the meeting broke off.

The palaver resumed about 4 o'clock. This time, the king and his retainers were unarmed. A change of mood was apparent. Now that the Americans had reunited, the Grebo advantage was lost. Besides, they were aware that war would gain them nothing.[32] Russwurm had prepared a grand oration but was unable to speak a word of it. Freeman recited his grievances once again and finally announced that the palaver was set. Like Holmes before him, the governor could only ask, how. Nevertheless, he put on a bold face, and acquiesced in the peace. The next morning, Freeman dashed him a bullock in apology for the hard words the previous day. Thereafter, they got along better.

Settlers celebrated Christmas, 1836, with a profound sense of thanksgiving. The *Potomac* had put a fair amount of cash in circulation. Russwurm's and Wilson's courage and tact had averted a disastrous war. On Christmas day, moreover, a new company of emigrants arrived aboard the brig *Niobe*, completing the passage in less than two months. The vessel, under James Hall's command, carried supplies, thirty-two emigrants, and a group of missionaries.[33]

One of them was Dr. Thomas S. Savage, appointed by the Episcopal Church to take charge of the mission begun by James Thomson. Savage's background is uncertain, but he is recorded as having earned a medical degree at Yale College, then attending seminary. He went to Cape Palmas convinced that he would die a martyr for "the regeneration of bleeding Africa." To the church, he was an ideal candidate. His education and race lent a legitimacy that Thomson, who was black and unordained, could not give the venture. On December 28, Savage informed his superiors of his safe arrival. His praise of Thomson and his wife was unreserved. Since the end of March, Thomson had cleared three acres of ground and planted a thorn hedge around the perimeter of the property. He had dug a well, broken the first pair of African bullocks in the colony, and built a plentiful stock of cattle and fowls. He had erected a small thatched house for his own use and a schoolhouse, at which he taught and boarded eleven African children. Savage described how Thompson and his wife had denied themselves, living at times upon "rice and palm-oil," that his little house "might be made ready in time for our reception." On Sunday his school was "assembled in his house" in "prayer and thanksgiving." Savage was overwhelmed with feeling. "I once more joyfully vowed to live in His service, upon these bleeding, benighted shores. My dear Sir, I am sincere when I say, that I had rather been on Sunday last and now, James M. Thomson, the colored teacher of the benighted African, in the service of the Protestant Episcopal Church of America, than the hero of the world."[34]

Within a few days of landing, the *Niobe*'s passengers experienced their first bouts of fever. George McGill and Josh Stewart grudgingly made way as Savage confidently assumed care of the sick, although he had no experience with tropical disease. His self-assurance evaporated as fevers worsened despite his medicines. Then he too fell ill. On January 17, with seventeen of the emigrants sick, seven near death, he called for assistance. McGill and Stewart succeeded in reviving six of the worst-off patients, but Peter Redmond, a tanner, died that night. During the next week, David White and his wife, new Congregational missionaries, also died. Savage was nearly lost as well, but he recovered after a hard struggle. "Practice and experience in this contry's acclimting Fevour, is worth more then all the Theory about it in america," McGill wrote soon after. He felt vindicated, but still resented the reverend doctor.[35]

February 22, 1837, was set apart according to custom as a day of thanks and celebration of the colony's third anniversary. Three blasts of a cannon heralded sunrise, and at ten o'clock the militia mustered in front of the Agency House. With all the pomp they could affect, they formed a column to lead colonial officers, clergymen, and distinguished visitors to the Methodist meeting house, where most settlers worshiped. Their preacher, Rev. Francis Burns, addressed the assembly, to general approval. He was followed by a more powerful speaker, Squire Chase, a noted Methodist preacher then visiting Africa to assess the prospects of evangelism. Though Chase suffered debilitation from malaria, he stirred his audience with reflections upon their good fortune thus far, exhorting them to demonstrate their worthiness of such blessings by being good citizens. John Revey, the newly arrived colonial secretary, recorded the spirit of the day. "Here live a plain, moral, industrious and in many respects a happy people, the descendants of those whome avarice dragged from Africa now in the possession of the blessings of liberty and equality."

Even as Squire Chase spoke, the *Niobe* coasted to anchor in the roads, and James Hall fired a salute before coming ashore. Festivities continued with a picnic at the Agency House and an afternoon of sociability, punctuated with thirteen cannon blasts at noon (for the original American states) and one more at sundown.[36]

Russwurm used the election of March 6 to consolidate his authority. Settler dissatisfaction in the aftermath of the jailbreak helped him, and new men were voted into almost every office. Russwurm appointed new magistrates and an auctioneer, collector of customs, measurer of lumber and inspector of shingles, and constable. Intending to make the colonial government more democratic, he initiated regular meetings of the Colonial Council, hitherto inactive. Significantly, the first sessions of this little legislature concerned the militia. Recent events had demonstrated the settlement's vulnerability. On March 4, the first recorded meeting, they appointed Charles Scotland commissary. On March 18 they formally constituted the militia. Henceforth, every able-bodied man in the colony must serve either in the artillery or infantry, ready to fight "at a moment's warning." To ensure preparedness, the militia companies were to muster on alternate Saturdays for three or four hours' drill. The statute called for a quarterly parade of the whole militia. Failure to attend parade on time and with working weapons entailed a stiff fine of from one to three weeks' wages. A court-martial would hear all such cases and impose penalties.[37]

On June 6, 1837, the agent and council met to review the appeal of John Bowen, whom a court-martial had condemned for missing parade. Bowen was a former Virginia slave who went to Liberia aboard the *Jupiter* shortly after the Southampton Massacre. He left Caldwell for Cape Palmas in 1834, probably as a volunteer with the *Ann.* In the census of 1837 he appears as a sawyer with a wife and young step-son.[38] Bowen also engaged in petty trade, as did many others who wished to improve their condition. In the militia, he had held the rank of orderly sergeant, until a parade day when he was absent trading in the bush. The commanding officer reduced him to the rank of private for the offence, which was very likely not his first. When he later appeared before the court-martial to answer for the absence, the court fined him $1.25, the standard penalty for an officer. Bowen appealed to the agent on the ground that his fine should be that stipulated for a private, seventy-five cents, if the fine was justified at all, since he had suffered a full loss of rank. The agent and council agreed with him and remitted the money. Even so, they resented the fact that Bowen was competing with the agency store, and they resolved as follows: "From and after this date it shall not be lawful for any Colonist to go into the Country, at the distance of five miles from the sea coast for the purpose of *trade* without a permit from under the hand of the Colonial Agent, under the penalty of *Ten Dollars*, for each offence." They went further, "that it shall not be lawful for any colonist to give more than the *current rates* at the Agency Store for any articles of the produce of the country under the penalty of Ten Dollars; which said fines shall be recoverable before any Justice of the peace, One half to go to the informer, and the other half into the Colonial Treasury."[39] Bowen and other settlers continued to trade, but they were hindered by this and subsequent acts.

On April 17 a broken-down topsail schooner flying Portuguese colors and scarcely afloat hove to off Harper.[40] The captain addressed a note to the agent in an awkward mix of Spanish and Portuguese explaining that he was on the coast buying rice and asking permission to anchor in the harbor to repair storm damage.[41]

The captain's illiterate request was polite and innocent on its face, but the true nature of the vessel was more sinister. A few days before, word had reached the Cape that the British had broken up Pedro Blanco's factory on Bonny River in the Niger delta some weeks earlier. Refugees were reportedly on their way up the coast to Gallinas River, Blanco's stronghold. Brazil and Cuba were then principal markets for human merchandise. Spanish and Portuguese nationals were the most avid participants in the trade. They favored the fleet Baltimore-built schooners for the work of darting in and out of the rivers where the barracoons lay, faster than warships could chase them. No one on shore with a bit of sense could have doubted that the wretched *Constanza* was in some way involved in the traffic. The obvious conclusion was that this was the very vessel from Bonny River. Russwurm might have refused any assistance and forced her from the harbor with cannon fire, thereby condemning the crew to shipwreck and death. Otherwise, he could grant their request and move them on their way as quickly as possible. The agent was not very scrupulous about slavers; the firm of Russwurm and Daily had even done business with Pedro Blanco. It was enough for him that the boat was not actually transporting slaves.

When the captain came ashore, Russwurm questioned him closely. The Portuguese explained that British cruisers had seized the *Constanza* when they raided the Bonny River factory. Pedro's employees had then purchased the vessel and loaded it with their belongings, including a few servants. As they passed to windward, they purchased what rice they could, knowing the food would be useful at Gallinas. The Royal Navy had twice halted them and each time allowed them to proceed. Russwurm permitted the ship to remain until repairs were finished.[42]

Predictably, the governor's decision was controversial. Three or more days elapsed before John Wilson was aware of the *Constanza*'s presence. As soon as he got the news, though, he went to see Russwurm. He left the meeting uneasy and resolved to send the governor a note outlining his concerns, with a request for a written explanation. This offended Russwurm, but he did Wilson the honor of writing a response. In it, he assured the missionary that the schooner had no captive Africans aboard. Moreover, he maintained that the colony had no effective means of excluding ships from the harbor, and there was little choice but to comply with the captain's request. These rationalizations were unconvincing, and when the two next met, the missionary rebuked the agent. He also penned a long complaint to Latrobe. "I do deplore in the bottom of my heart so serious a digression from the course, which I suppose your Board and the world expected of him," he wrote, and continued:

> I never concieved it his duty or the duty of the people of Liberia to commence offensive measure against slavers — to this their means are inadequate and by so doing they would involve themselves in great straights. But to have them come into the harbor by permission, trade with the Americans, take lodgings in their houses, transact buisness through the public store and have the citizens do work for them, is giving the affair quite a different aspect. Mr. Russwurm is still more reprehensible in this affair in as much as at the time these spaniards came here they were permitted to buy rice at double the usual rate and the American citizens are [in] distressing want of it.[43]

In Monrovia, Russwurm had suffered at the hands of missionaries who meddled in secular politics. Wilson seemed cut out of the same cloth as Ezekiel Skinner and the rest of the white religious establishment in Liberia. Wilson could not alter Russwurm's decision, and the incident started a lasting rift. Their animosity increased by stages over the next four years.

Wilson was still fuming over Russwurm's concessions to the *Constanza* when yet another issue presented itself. Word had gotten around that the agent was considering various restrictions on trade, among them that a colonial factor would broker all trade to vessels offshore. This would compromise the economic independence of the missions, whose storerooms rivaled the agency for variety and value. The missionaries began to see Russwurm as an opponent and worried what he might do next.[44]

A question also arose concerning the status of the teachers of the mission schools: Were they resident foreigners or citizens of Maryland? The answer had great implications. The missions had hired several well-educated emigrants almost as soon as they landed, leading Russwurm to complain that missions were draining the colony of its potential lights. If the mission teachers were citizens of the colony, and the reasons for regarding them as such were plain, they should enjoy the privileges but also the responsibilities of citizenship. Here the missionaries balked, for the colonial administration depended on unpaid settler participation in public works and the militia. Since 1834 a sea change had taken place in American public opinion with regard to colonization. Within evangelical and abolitionist circles, particularly, the American colonies were a disgrace in both principal and practice. Focusing missionary activities in Liberia seemed blunderous to many. They, and Wilson among them, wished to disassociate themselves as much as possible from the American enclaves, even though they benefited from their protection. Two Saturdays per month, all male settlers had to turn out for parade, or pay a stiff fine. The missionaries' purpose was pacific, and they could not reconcile military service with evangelism. Russwurm refused even to consider their point, and after each parade day he fined the missions. He did not demand payment, but he kept a tally anyway, which augmented his grudge.[45]

The *Niobe* left Cape Palmas on June 10, 1837, on her way to Baltimore via Monrovia. Oliver Holmes was at last on his way home, with a large collection of curios gathered during his peripatetic sojourn on the ship. Luke Walker and his family also returned home. He had come out on the *Fortune* with the hope of setting up a saw mill but was unable to do so. Having had some wealth in America, he was dissatisfied at the material shortages so common in Liberia. Moreover, he resented his inability to have a drink when he wanted. John Russwurm took temporary leave of his post, placing George McGill in charge of the agency, so that he could settle his accounts with J. R. Daily. He would be absent from the colony for several eventful weeks.[46]

VIII.

"The Dismal Fountain of Vice"

A T THE EPISCOPAL STATION, NOW CALLED MT. VAUGHAN IN HONOR OF a former head of the church's missions, construction progressed slowly. Dr. Savage moved there from Harper on March 4, 1837, into a house "barely sufficient to protect us from the weather," reminding his superiors that Thomson had not completed his assignment in time. Writing on April 8, he continued in a similar vein, "Even at this period, an elapse of time of more than four weeks, our culinary operations are conducted beneath a booth or thatch of palm leaves."[1] In the course of a few months his original enthusiasm gave way to a more critical opinion. More or less subtly, the doctor pushed Thomson into the background. Subsequent events indicate that their relations were uneasy at best.

"Easter was the day selected," wrote Savage, "upon which to *open fully our Missionary* operations." Since this was the first holiday celebrated by an ordained minister, the occasion was solemn. Only a handful were eligible for the Eucharist, and James Thomson was conspicuously absent. After the service, Savage sought him for an explanation. In a painful exchange, Thomson would say only that he was unworthy to receive the sacrament. The conversation ended, but Savage suspected something more in Thomson's diffidence than pious humility. In soil watered with jealousy, the seed of mistrust germinated.[2] Whispers passed within the mission and through the colony. Settlers generally disliked Thomson, the former storekeeper, and they easily credited dark stories about encounters with young girls in the mission.[3]

Rumors of scandal at Mt. Vaughan circulated for several weeks after Easter. Toward the close of May, a female student complained to Savage that Henry Harmon, a sixteen-year-old orphan employed by the mission, had tried to seduce her. Collared by Savage, Harmon tried to excuse himself with the claim that Thomson had set a bad example. He elaborated in lurid detail, how Thomson had molested several mission girls and seduced the head man Jack's wife.[4]

Harmon's accusations naturally disturbed Savage, but they were so outrageous he scarcely credited them. He took Thomson aside and asked him to investigate. Of course, each of the children whom Thomson questioned denied spreading stories about him, and he reported to Savage that they had said nothing. Yet his conscience was pricked by the exercise, and soon after, Thomson resolved to confess. "This I did, lunatic-like," he later wrote Holmes, "(the discovery having unstuck every nerve) in writing, in the form of a long confession, which I deemed to be the duty of a member to his pastor." He handed Savage an account of his involvement with a young mulatto orphan named Sally, who had been living in his house, before his appointment by the church. The incident reportedly occurred in their shared bedroom. While Elizabeth Thomson, who was pregnant, slept, James crept over to Sally's bed, uncovered her, and rested his hand upon her. It is not certain whether anything more happened—Thomson and the girl both asserted that that was all.[5] Clearly a transgression had taken place, one absolutely shocking in this conservative community. Thomson should have resigned on the spot, but he did not. Instead, he became a pawn in a controversy that had less to do with sexual conduct than with power relations in the colonial community.

After meeting with Savage, Thomson went upstairs and locked himself in his bedroom, as he said, to pray. Savage considered the situation, then wrote Thomson a pained, diffuse note. "I hardly know what to say under the embarrassment beneath which I labour. . . . You may confide

in me. . . . I must earnestly beg you to confess to me all that you may
have done, if you have not already." He hinted that he was sympathetic.
"Another man besides Harmon has said something about this, and
some other things, I have not yet been able to ferret it out. He told me
the one who professed to know something about it to suppress it, for it
would hang you. This escaped my mind last night." After more lines
urging Thomson to confess, Savage offered hope. "If it lie in my power,
the whole affair shall be conducted in such a manner as shall result to
the smallest injury of your unfortunate family."[6]

The doctor's allusion to capital punishment terrified Thomson,
the absence of laws providing for such a penalty notwithstanding. In a
guilty panic, he accepted Savage's ambiguous promise of secrecy. As
asked, he added to his confession an account of his night at Robookah,
almost a year before, when King Tom had sent one of his wives to share
his bed. This failed to satisfy the doctor, indeed, it even whetted his
suspicion. His thoughts turned from sex to money, and he wondered
whether Thomson was a thief as well. He addressed yet another note to
Thomson, who remained locked in his room. This was more insistent
and offered a clearer promise of secrecy. "Mr. Thomson," he wrote, "I
need not say that my heart bleeds at what I've heard. What a prospect
now does our mission assume! Christ my Saviour, *your* Saviour wounded
in the house of his friends! Be careful that your sorrow *be not* that
which arises from fear of detection and exposure. O poor degraded
human nature — not afraid of the heart searching God, but *more vastly*
afraid of this wicked, weak, dying world!" He went on to tell Thomson
that his post in the mission was forfeit, and that he must render an
account of all the money he had handled. He must then confess the
truth to his wife and leave Maryland in Liberia. Savage promised that
the mission would look after his family, "so far as they shall sustain a
good character." In closing he asked Thomson to make a new copy of
the confession, this time in ink, and signed. In a postscript, he detailed
what he wanted Thomson to write:

> You cannot lose anything by confessing all. I wish to have your
> solemn declaration that your conduct has either been, or not been

exceptionable towards the girls in this house, or not. Write all you have done and sign your name to it, addressed to me. *It shall be sacred.* If you have committed murder (which of course I do not think) *confess that only to God.* Any thing else affecting the Mission, *I desire you to confess* if you be truly penitent you will not hesitate to do it. . . . I wish you to give me a paper stating the instances of crime that I may send it to the Board. It of course will be sacred with them.[7]

Sobered a little, Thomson did not respond to the request. He had expected forgiveness and support from Savage, who was in no position to comply. "Alas! It was a woful confession," he later wrote Oliver Holmes, "such an one as I shall never make again to mortal man, while I have my senses about me."[8] His confessor was no "meek, Christian-spirited minister," he decided. Another hour elapsed, and Savage wrote an order for Thomson to come downstairs and go about his business as usual, to prevent rumors. He advised Thomson again to leave Maryland, perhaps for the West Indies. If he could reform himself, then he might one day reunite with his family.[9]

Thomson opened his door as instructed and tried to behave normally. He remained in the mission house for about ten days. During this time, Savage was outwardly friendly and affected concern for his future. Privately, Savage repeatedly referred to the "painful case," Thomson related to Holmes, "so as to tantalize me, and excite my feelings; using the information he had received from me as a cudgel wherewith to crack my head were I to make any objection to his proposals." Thomson bore Savage's calculated barbs patiently at first, but at length he could stand them no longer, and he lashed out at the doctor. Savage immediately threw him out of the house, then went to Wilson with the story. Over the next few days, news of the affair, embroidered with increasing detail, circulated among settlers.[10]

Public fury was intense at the end of June, when civil authorities became involved. Russwurm might have handled the case quietly, but he was at Monrovia. Thomas Jackson, the justice of the peace who had nearly sparked a war the previous December, initiated a public inquest on June 28. He called Dr. Savage to appear before the court. The missionary complied reluctantly, undoubtedly aware that he should not have made details of the case public and fearing the furor the case had aroused. On the stand, he insisted that Jackson establish the date of the society's acquisition of Robookah before answering any questions about Thomson's actions there. Jackson could not say whether Robookah was under the society's jurisdiction at the time, and he had to abandon the subject. When asked about improprieties in the mission, Savage answered that the reports were merely the wild stories of children. The court adjourned. Thomson remained free, though the community was not satisfied.[11]

The next day, Jackson was making pilings for a new house at Fair Hope. John Wilson, who was sick in bed, called him upstairs to have an account of what had happened at the hearing. The report so upset him that he got up from bed and rode over to see Savage. Returning later in the day, Wilson assured Jackson that Savage would co-operate if questioned again. Jackson hesitated, believing it was beyond his duty to discuss the case with the minister outside the courtroom. The matter rested for a few days.[12]

In the time intervening, the community was further agitated by a large accession of emigrants, as well as a painful reminder of the time of bondage. The brig *Baltimore* cast anchor off Cape Palmas on July 4, 1837. She carried supplies, three missionaries, and a company of fifty-five emigrants. Seven of them were Marylanders. Two others were Virginians freed to go to Africa. The rest had shortly before been the property of Mrs. Elizabeth Tubman of Augusta, Georgia. As her husband, lord of a huge plantation, lay dying, he felt the sting of conscience and told his wife to free all their slaves, and to send those who wished back to Africa. No one else heard his request, and his will said nothing of it, so she might well have ignored him and protected her inheritance. But she did as her husband wished, and more. Over one hundred slaves were freed and told of their choice. She hired a man to teach them to read and to live on their own. About half of the slaves chose to emigrate, and when the time came she accompanied them to Baltimore and paid the Maryland State Colonization Society fifty dollars apiece for their passage and resettlement. Before boarding, each of the emigrants gave his name to a clerk—twenty-four in a row with the surname "Tubman." The clerk looked up in frustration at so many men and women without clear family ties or specific knowledge of age and told them they could not all be Tubmans. Therefore, the next twenty-one gave their names as "Cummings." (In Africa, all of the Cummings later took the name Tubman.) Maryland emigrants normally made their family relations clear, by contrast, and gave their age as near as they could tell. The society was pleased to have these Georgians, because they were experienced cotton farmers. If anyone could make a success of the crop, they would.[13]

Shortly after leaving port, crewmen discovered a black boy about fourteen years old hiding in the hold. It was then too late to return him to shore, so the captain had no choice but to carry him to Africa and back. The boy said that he was free but had no papers to prove it, and Maryland law was clear on the point that the captain of any vessel carrying a runaway slave to freedom was liable to suit for the master's loss and criminal prosecution. A healthy young man was worth four hundred dollars at least, and the captain was determined to bring him back to Baltimore to settle the truth of the matter.

While the *Baltimore* rode at anchor off Harper, settlers came and went. One young settler befriended the detainee, who had free run of the vessel, and the two plotted an escape. In the first hours of Sunday, July 8, they took one of the ship's boats. They landed at the Agency Wharf and went to the settler's house. The stowaway's absence was noticed at daybreak, and the captain and some seamen came ashore to apprehend him. They first called on George McGill to explain their mission, He gave them the go-ahead and a guide.[14]

Charles Snetter was up early and observed the men as they began the hunt. He sounded an alarm and a crowd of settlers gathered around him. Soon after, sailors returned with the boy, a bound captive. Snetter remonstrated with the captain on the wharf. The captain stated that he must take the boy back to Baltimore or risk having to pay for him. Snetter appealed to George McGill, but was rebuffed. The acting agent mocked him and told him to mind his own business. Snetter stood and wept before agitated settlers as the boy was carried back to the ship. "Never," he wrote Latrobe the next day, "did I se a captive Runaway in Custody since I left america untill I seen it in this Colony." He went on, "I ask you whom must Know, wether slavery did not exist at the time the little prisoner was in custody was he not taken as a slave from the cost of africa to be carried to the united states?"[15] Most settlers sympathized with Snetter, but the authorities did not. Even Wilson, his usual defender, mentioned to Latrobe that, "It is very mortifying to my feelings to acknowledge that Charles Snetter was conspicuous in the affair. . . . I assure you that no one for the future in my employ shall ever take part in a similar affair."[16]

Public pressure to bring Thomson to trial continued unabated after the first inquiry. The selectmen took up the case on July 13. They called upon Savage to divulge his evidence against Thomson, which he now did more willingly. They indicted Thomson and entered the case on the docket for the next Court of Monthly Sessions. So hated was Thomson that he could not walk in public for fear of assault by vengeful settlers. Overwhelmed with a sense of his vulnerability, he wrote an apology to Savage and begged for forgiveness. The doctor affected concern and pity in his response, but the case had clearly become a political matter.[17] He assured Thomson that he had long since forgiven him and that his public actions in the case should prove that he "loved *justice, truth and mercy.*" "But you have it seems broken the laws of the Colony," he continued pedantically. "You therefore deserve and inevitably receive the punishment due to the crime." He urged Thomson to confess everything to the Court, promising him that if truly penitent he would find mercy. Yet Savage was clearly worried about his own conduct. "In confessing before the court you'd better include my course towards you. If I have dealt by you *justly* — state it to the court. If I had no disposition to conceal your transgression of the laws of the Colony state so." Savage might then remain advantageously silent. "I then shall not find it necessary to say a word, and shall be relieved from saying what will do you no credit, and what will give me much pain."

Christ himself was again betrayed by Thomson's sins, Savage wrote, and only full repentance could save him. Savage added a postscript the next day to convince Thomson that he had made no promise of secrecy:

> If you make any confessions before the Court I shd like to have you expressly testify that I never promised to conceal your crime, otherwise I shall have to state it. You know that, what I said in relation to such a point was said under the idea that it was committed beyond the limits of the Colony's *jurisdiction*, and that such being the case I would try to aid you, should you prove penitent, in living a life of usefulness to you fellow men by giving your wife employment in the Mission till you could establish a character for piety and sobriety. But when you resolved to settle down on the Cape and not go off to the West Indies or elsewhere I saw your penitence to be insincere, told you that all I had said in regard to your wife and self could have no force.

The missionary would never have written such a thing unless he realized that he had compromised himself.[18]

John Russwurm returned to Harper in the first week of August. At Monrovia, he had made some progress with Daily but was unable finally to close accounts with him.[19] The uproar within the settler community soon made him forget these troubles. Rice supplies were dwindling, and a month of torrential rains had nearly destroyed the crop in the fields. Settlers were in a state of moral outrage, goaded by worry and the inflammatory statements of missionaries and demagogic settlers.[20]

Early on Monday, August 7, 1837, the Court of Monthly Sessions sat to hear its docket. The bench consisted of three men: John Russwurm, the chief, Thomas Jackson, and Joshua Stewart, both of the latter respectable and patriotic citizens, appointed the previous March. John Revey was secretary. Thomson's was the first case. He pleaded not guilty. Dr. Savage then testified, basing his account on Thomson's confessions. When asked to produce them, he could not, for he had sent them home to his superiors with a report of the case. Instead, he pulled from his pocket a tattered transcription in his own handwriting. Such scraps of course were not admitted as evidence, and when the doctor was asked for further proof of his assertions, he had none. Savage remained on the stand for a few minutes while the judges conferred. He twice asked if he could make a statement, and each time was asked if what he had to say was evidence, to which he could only answer no. His testimony stymied, he left the courtroom in disgust. Other witnesses testified, but all traced their information to Savage. This put to rest the question of crimes committed at Robookah, but adultery within the mission remained at issue. The orphan Sally had once before opposed James Thomson in a lawsuit, whose exact nature has not come to light, though it may be inferred that Thomson won the case. The girl now told the court scandalous particulars of their relationship. Other witnesses then testified that Sally had told several other versions of the story. Even though Thomson was unquestionably involved in some irregularities, the court discounted Sally's testimony as unreliable. The judges adjourned after hearing two other minor cases, to reconvene privately in the evening.[21]

During the day, Thomson visited George McGill. He brought the letters he had received from Dr. Savage. After McGill took some time to go through them, Thomson asked him somewhat anxiously if he thought they would have a bearing on the trial. McGill asked him if he wished to be free of the charge. Thomson answered, certainly, to which McGill responded that these letters should do just that. He asked Thomson to let him take them to the judges at their meeting that evening. The accused man was wary, however, and he took the documents away, only to return with them late in the afternoon.[22]

At first candle light, Russwurm met Jackson and Stewart at the Agency House to review Thomson's case. The issue was thorny, for

Thomson was clearly guilty of grave moral lapses. Yet there was no hard evidence, and what remained was colored by Savage's prejudice and the extreme malignancy of the community. In point of law, his conviction was doubtful. The agent was feeling for a solution that would cause the least political damage. As he tried to reach a consensus with the other two judges, George McGill delivered Thomson's letters. The judges read them, paying special attention to Savage's promises of secrecy. They consulted Blackstone's *Commentaries*, which condemn "hasty unguarded confessions" made under duress.[23] The appropriate conclusion was clear: Savage had extorted confessions from Thomson with false promises of secrecy and had then tried to coerce him to lie under oath. McGill gathered up the letters and went home. The judges adjourned until sunrise the next day.[24]

The court resumed before a large audience of settlers despite the early hour. Thomson, who had gotten the letters back from McGill the night before, approached the bench to offer them as evidence. The judges looked them over as if for the first time and conferred among themselves a little. Russwurm then discoursed on the requirements of law for conviction as they were set out in Blackstone, hoping vainly that he could soften public opinion. He and each of the judges then delivered their verdict. Unanimously, they found Thomson not guilty.[25]

Dr. Savage stalked off in indignation. Settlers soon dispersed to trade stories and speculate. A man so clearly guilty must be punished, regardless of technicalities in the law, they reasoned. The following day, a group met in the public school to protest the court's decision. By popular assent, William Dulaney took the chair and Ambrose Simpson acted as secretary. Dulaney suggested the appointment of five "Judicious persons" to investigate and compose a remonstrance for the Board of Managers in Baltimore. Charles Snetter, William Reynolds, Jacob Gross, Steven Smith, and John Banks were duly assigned the task. The meeting adjourned until they might finish, at which time settlers were "earnestly requested to meet as the reputation of this our little infant is at stake."[26]

The next day, the committee interviewed Thomas Savage at Mt.

Vaughan. He received them warmly and offered to answer any questions. Of course, he presented the case entirely to his own advantage, and to individuals predisposed to condemn Thomson. He gave them his transcript of Thomson's confession, which confirmed the opinion "that there is not the least shaddow of doubt of the guilt of that poor man." Savage then reassured the committee that he had never had any intention of hiding Thomson's crimes. He castigated the Court of Monthly Sessions, particularly that they had not allowed him to introduce his evidence. William Reynolds, who was in some measure familiar with the case, caught Savage in some inaccuracy at this point and questioned him. The missionary responded angrily at the implication that he was a liar, and the committee, cowed at the rebuke, left him.

Subsequently, they obtained a transcript of the correspondence within the mission house. They concluded that the missionary may indeed have compromised himself in gaining a confession from Thomson. They asked Savage for a written clarification of several points. He responded with a terse note asking them what points they wished him to address, and also, significantly, who might read his statement. The committee apparently answered these queries satisfactorily, for on September 15, Savage composed a long narrative of the events of the previous few months.

The committee then produced a rambling document incorporating the correspondence of Thomson and Savage, between Savage and themselves, and minutes of their meetings. Having presented their evidence, they addressed the board directly, apologizing for having to bring such facts before them but with hope that the board would pay more attention to the colony's moral development. They asked rhetorically, "Will these documents say that prejudice led us to this step? (We think we hear you say no) is it the love of vice that led us to this? No sirs, the Fear of its consequences among us an Ignorant People." How shameful, they argued, that their children should have such an example of immorality, and that he should go free, while the victims were humiliated by a prejudiced court.

> Shall we Individualy drink at that dismal fountain of Vice one after
> the other untill we all drown Collectively to the disgrace of your
> highest Philanthrophy? If the heads of our community begins this
> awful pull towards our downfall. What must we say who have no
> inclination to Honesty, no Force of Character. Down with the Colony?
> no sirs We *Humbly* hail to you across the Atlantic and declare in
> bahalf of the majority of this Colony a *solomn Protest* against the
> proceedings of James M Thomson. We also pray that the Honble.
> Board will take some steps in this matter as we suppose it to be
> noised abroad before this time.

In conclusion, the committee acknowledged Savage's helpfulness
in preparing the report. In fact, it was rumored that the missionary
had even written a first draft, but the truth of this cannot be verified.
On December 2 all citizens were invited to a public meeting to hear the
committee's report. Once read, all but three of the audience approved
the findings and resolved to send them to the Board of Managers. Fifty
men then signed or marked the document, which was mailed to Baltimore at the next opportunity.

Thomson remained in the colony, a broken man. Savage, though
defeated in law, could still take satisfaction in having ruined his opponent.

Charles Snetter's participation in the affair confirmed him as a
leader of public opinion. A populist of the Jacksonian school, his rough,
spirited eloquence captured the mood of the community. He spoke for
a faithful remnant, self-styled Children of Israel in the wilderness, besieged in a hostile environment by heathen Africans and betrayed by a
weak and hypocritical government. He and his adherents yearned for
freedom. Yet their ambition was imperial, for they hoped to drive away
their African competitors, then to establish some ideal republic. Snetter
envisioned himself a new Toussaint, and but little would have launched
him on an armed crusade. Russwurm saw him for a demagogue and
awaited his chance to put him down.

IX.

"A Prey Unto Themselves"

RUSSWURM WAS, AS HE SAID, BARELY OVER SEASICKNESS AFTER HIS return from Monrovia, when he had to face an unprecedented palaver brought by the Grebo states in unison. They had met during his absence to discuss trade. Stores of rice had run low in April, which was nothing unusual. Greboes had long since accustomed themselves to shortage as the previous year's crop was consumed and the new one matured. The harvest of 1836 had been poor, though, and the shortfall was unusually severe. Settlers depended on African farmers for rice, their staple, but Greboes would feed themselves first.[1]

Freeman dictated new prices for rice and palm oil, about double what they had been, speciously justified as an attempt to improve the lot of impoverished bush states. Russwurm knew too well that inland towns would receive no benefit from the increase. He was inclined to resist but considered the power arrayed against him. "The prices demanded were most unreasonable, but as we had not 10 croos Rice on hand, with the new emigrants and all the sick who were entirely dependent on the Agent, I saw no way by which I could surmount the difficulty than by partially agreeing to pay it until I could do better." John Wilson argued on behalf of the colony, but Greboes were unmoved. "They knew we had no rice on hand, or cassadas or potatoes to any extent in the ground: we must therefore either give their prices or starve."

169

Russwurm asked for a small vessel for trade outside Grebo territories. He hoped, vainly, that the higher prices might force settlers to raise more food on their farms.[2]

Prices would normally have fallen off again as the harvest was gathered in October and November, but the crop of 1837 was even worse than the previous year's. Greboes and Americans alike contemplated the possibility of famine.

———◆———

During the summer of 1837, the settler Alexander Hance traveled through his old neighborhood in southern Maryland with the Rev. John Kennard, the society's traveling agent. Hance had been a prosperous free farmer in Calvert County before emigrating to Cape Palmas on the *Bourne*, which left Baltimore in December 1834. When he reappeared, a citizen of Liberia, in equal standing with his white fellow traveler, both of them speaking in religious meetings of a glorious new life waiting in Africa, the appeal was powerful. Many volunteered, and Hance was able to return with eighty-one old friends and neighbors aboard the *Niobe*, which cast anchor off Cape Palmas on January 12, 1838. This was the largest group yet sent to the colony, and twice the number carried on the *Niobe*'s first trip.

Any addition to the populace would normally have been welcome, but the *Niobe*'s arrival caused some difficulty. Russwurm could scarcely provide for those already on shore, much less supply full rations for the newcomers. He complained of the high proportion of women and children in the group, fearing they would be a burden. The emigrants suffered their fevers in the society's shabby housing with little more than personal attention.[3] Hance they thought had tricked them into coming to this ramshackle, hungry place, though he shared their chagrin. "I with many others am deceived as you promised that Emigrants should be furnished with every thing necessary." He old Kennard to have emigrants bring all they have to Africa, "for every thing is wanted here." He reported the scanty supplies given settlers: "C. Gross, 5 Plates only for seven in family the others got from 2 to 3 plates only no Knives forks nor any thing Else."[4]

The new settlers brought him before the Methodist elders for lying, and he was hard pressed to defend himself. In letters home, he begged Kennard to publish the journal of their travels to prove he had told the truth.

On February 22, 1838, Maryland in Liberia celebrated its fourth anniversary. John Revey gave an address at the Methodist Church, and settlers enjoyed a modest picnic at the Agency House. The following morning, Russwurm left to retrace Hall's trip up the Cavally River. Denah's King Neh, who had once hosted Hall, had continued to invite the Marylanders to establish a base near his town. Now, with rice scarce and the beach towns exerting pressure on the settlement, Russwurm hoped to expand his sources of food. He took with him King Freeman, Anthony Wood, and twelve Grebo men. Though Freeman was sometimes an adversary, Russwurm thought his presence would enhance the mission's prestige. Gbenelu was also hungry, and a successful venture would certainly promote peace.[5]

The party encountered some delays on the beach, but they got to Grand Cavally about eight at night. A canoe had delivered their baggage earlier in the day. Baphro was hospitable, and they tarried for two days, giving time for news of their expedition to ascend the river. While at Grand Cavally, delegates from Half Cavally earnestly urged Russwurm not to go any farther. They used all sorts of arguments, but they were transparently jealous of the interior trade. Baphro advised Russwurm to ignore them, and they left.

Early Monday, the travelers set out in a large dugout canoe. As they passed up the lagoon, Russwurm relaxed and took in the lush fields and forests on its banks. The Grebo boatmen, accustomed to the ocean, kept a swift pace against the sluggish current. Soon they approached Ploroh, where Hall had encountered some trouble during his exploration. Opposite the first of the satellite villages, a musketeer fired at them. Immediately they heard the deep pounding of war drums in other villages, and at once forty or more canoes, each with three men armed with machetes or muskets, filled the river. They quickly moved around the dugout, which was helpless against them.

The travelers braced themselves, perhaps to die, or at least to suffer a beating. The brief calm ended when someone snatched a prize. A free-for-all ensued. Freeman, Russwurm, and Wood were all thrown in the water. Wood was severely beaten and almost drowned. King Freeman received similar treatment until his oarsmen could save him. Russwurm, whom Greboes accorded special rank as a white man, fared a little better. Three men pulled him from the water, only to confiscate his clothing, but otherwise they left him unharmed. Somehow, everyone reached shore, deprived of all but a few threads of clothing. They walked up to Ploroh to complain to Toureh, whose subjects had robbed them. He listened politely but pretended that he had no knowledge of the incident and could do nothing about it. He provided a boat to carry them back to Grand Cavally that afternoon.

Baphro received them with apparent sympathy, giving them food and dry clothes. He sent word to Cape Palmas, and called a general palaver for the next day. Freeman and Russwurm remained overnight, hoping to get redress. At the palaver, Grand Cavally and Robookah blamed Toureh for the whole thing. Freeman would rather have believed the story, but Russwurm did not. He thought that Half Cavally and Grand Cavally must have conspired with Toureh to keep the Americans from interloping on the river trade. He regretted giving Baphro opportunity to divert responsibility. In any case, the palaver was inconclusive. Freeman and Russwurm went home and found their constituents united in outrage against Toureh. Many advocated an immediate campaign, but the two leaders successfully opposed so rash a plan. They chose instead to await an opportunity for revenge.[6]

Resentment persisted between Russwurm and the missionaries months after Thomson's acquittal. The governor looked upon them as meddlesome rivals, but he conciliated and eventually won from Savage a qualified apology. Savage even restored Thomson to a modest position in the mission.[7] Russwurm's strained relationship with John Wilson worsened. To Wilson, seeing the unfaithful Thomson in Russwurm's confidence and back in Savage's employment was intolerable. The governor, he believed, had abused the powers of office for the sake of his friends, out of blind and misplaced loyalty. He was too willing to sacrifice principle for expedience, as the repair of the *Constanza* had demonstrated. Worst of all, the agent seemed determined to make the missions subordinate to the colonization society, even if that impeded the spread of the Gospel.

The missions were communities carefully designed to support themselves in unfriendly lands. Their purpose was to teach Christian principles and make converts. Conversion was more than a matter of belief; it entailed a complete adoption of Western culture. The Protestant missionaries of all sects maintained that their way of life—"civilization"—was alone compatible with the Gospel. So long as vestiges of African culture remained in an individual, true faith was impossible. Each of the missions had a church and residence for ministers, of course, but their program also called for a school, residences for students, a separate village for converts, and a working farm. Consequently, construction, trade, a large staff, and payrolls followed. The principal attraction of Cape Palmas to the missionary societies was the proximity of the American colony, a ready supplier of labor, an exemplary enclave of Christian society, and guardian should danger threaten. In practice, however, the interests of the colony and missions were not always in harmony, and their proximity could be uncomfortable.

The society had looked to the Congregational and then the Episcopal mission to open schools for American children. They were disappointed, for missionaries saw their duty to the heathen children of

Africa more clearly, though with a romantic conceit. To them, the mass of settlers, ragged ex-slaves, were more objects of contempt than souls worth saving. Ethiopia called loudly, but Americans could fend for themselves. The society and settlers strongly disagreed. Literacy set them apart from Africans, for whom to "sabby book" was a skill held in awe. So long as Africans remained ignorant, Americans held an advantage. To the more cynical of the colonizationists then, Grebo education materially weakened the settler community, increasing the economic and cultural struggle between them. In a letter of January 1838, John Wilson scolded Latrobe for Friend Moses Sheppard's opinions published in the *Maryland Colonization Journal* some months earlier. "Christian people will see discrepancy," he wrote, "between your pretensions of philanthrophy and the sentiments embraced in that letter. Mr. Sheppard certainly fixes the value of native education at a very low point and would lead the world to think that the good and improvement of the natives of Africa was no part of your scheme."[8]

Making matters worse, the missions employed some of the most talented settlers as teachers and prejudiced them against the colony. Russwurm magnified the loss in bitter dispatches home. The status of these teachers was controversial. The governor maintained that they were citizens of Maryland and therefore must serve in the militia. The missionaries, believing that the military was antithetical to their calling, countered that the teachers were in fact resident foreigners. Neither side would compromise.

The issue had first arisen in 1837, when Russwurm formally organized the militia. Then, he had decided to ignore the teachers' absences from parade so long as they stayed at home. The dispute erupted again in April 1838, when John Banks, an A.B.C.F.M. teacher, appeared in Harper on a parade day. Banks was a freeborn Baltimorean who had emigrated to Liberia in 1831. He joined the *Ann* in 1834, as Dr. Hall's house servant and assistant. When Wilson arrived at Cape Palmas a few months later, Hall sent Banks to him to work as servant and interpreter. Wilson taught Banks to read and write, eventually promoting him to the post of teacher. The settler was not especially religious, and he had no scruples concerning war, but Wilson forbade his participation in the militia. The sight of Banks, walking casually about Harper, incensed officers and men. When the court-martial met the next Monday, Captain Anthony Wood fined him $1.25, the usual penalty for unexcused absence.[9]

Banks appealed to Wilson, who immediately sent an inquiry to Russwurm. The agent questioned Wood, and the two agreed that though Banks had not been fined in the past, if he showed himself publicly on parade day they must penalize him. On April 15, Russwurm sent John Revey, his secretary, to explain the government's position to Wilson. The interview was polite, but the minister heard only what he wanted to, that Banks had not been fined in the past and would not be in the future. What was his dismay then when Sheriff William Reynolds appeared at his door the next day to collect $1.25. They exchanged angry words, and a volley of notes passed between agent and preacher.[10]

Mad as a hornet, Wilson complained of "a more serious insult than I shall ever be disposed to receive again from an officer of your Colony." He and Hall had had an understanding that teachers should be exempt from the military, he asserted. Banks had never signed the emigrant roll and now resigned the title to his farm—the deed was enclosed. He stated bluntly that Fair Hope was outside colonial jurisdiction, warning Russwurm not to trespass upon an American's liberty or property.

The defiant letter angered Russwurm, but he retained his composure in a response sent later the same day. Addressing Wilson in the third person, he reiterated his determination to have Banks perform the duties of a citizen or pay the penalty. He reminded Wilson of his earlier promise to pay if sustained by higher authorities. Was Wilson bold enough to challenge the testimony of the whole militia and vice agent, who had seen Banks in Harper on parade day? "I conceive it out of your line of duty to question the legality of any fines imposed by one of our Court Martials; or to use such language towards the Colonial Agent in the regular discharge of his duty, as you have in your note." The society had deeded Fair Hope to the A.B.C.F.M. for missionary purposes, not as a refuge from the laws of the colony. "I have ordered the officer to collect the fines," he concluded, "and I prewarn all persons against interrupting him in the regular discharge of his duty. There is force enough in the Colony to carry into effect the judgement of the Court."

Wilson castigated Russwurm the next day for his threats and unclear policy. Revey, the colonial secretary, had assured him that Banks would not be fined. "Had you acted as an honourable man and stated the results of your investigations, the fine would have been paid and no necessity would have existed for the course which I felt myself compelled to adopt." The mission was not a refuge for felons, as Russwurm suggested, but indeed had sheltered settlers at times of danger. He informed Russwurm that he had referred the matter to his superiors at home and it would be resolved soon enough. The exchange of notes here ceased, but the question remained open. Missionary and agent nursed their grudges.

The quarrel between Russwurm and Wilson took place in an atmosphere of general irritability and contentiousness as food supplies steadily dwindled. Greboes and Americans alike faced starvation. Had Russwurm's venture up the Cavally River been successful, rice might have been forthcoming from Denah. Garroway, a few miles to windward, provided some, but factional strife there, bordering on civil war, combined with difficulty of transport, limited the relief. The agent went to Garroway and declared peace, but trade improved scarcely at all. At Cape Palmas, rice and other African produce again doubled in price. Tobacco, the principal colonial currency, declined in value. So much had been paid out for provisions that Greboes had little interest in accepting more.[11]

John Wilson blamed everything on Russwurm. On April 26, on the heels of the dispute over Banks, he wrote his brother-in-law in Columbia, South Carolina: "Since the election of a Colored man to the office of Governor of this Colony, and another for Liberia proper, the progress of Colonization has been a rapid and fearful decline; and I look upon it, at this moment, as on the verge of a ruinous precipice." He promised to publish an exposé that would show that, "Colonization as conducted at present, is little less than a system of iniquity and oppression." He added, "The Colonists of this place have become idle, vicious and turbulent in the highest degree: and must starve to death unless they commence a career of plunder and robery of the property and persons of the native inhabitants: and this latter event is by no means improbable, unless the natives of the Country, should combine and overwhelm them."[12]

More moderate members of the community believed that the failure of settlers to raise their own food had caused the present difficulties. After more than four years of hard work, the record of settler agriculture was one long disappointment.[13] Many settlers regarded farming as slaves' work, beneath their status as free men. Moreover, their efforts to raise crops often failed miserably. Most settlers, therefore, had to find other employment. Many cut lumber, though they knew the activity was unhealthy and dangerous. Others engaged in petty trade or practiced crafts learned in America. "We have been too negligent about our farms," Oliver Chambers, master of the public school, wrote Ira Easter in a letter of July 10, voicing a popular opinion. "Yes Sir, we have shamefully thrown our Farms A way and Greedily Grasped the hammer and Saw and declare ourselves Carpenters for the sake of a little currency because it is An immediate reward, and depend upon the Natives for our food But we begin to discover that our Natives are not fools, if we buy of them we have to pay *well* for the Article or starve."[14] He hoped that his fellow citizens would learn a lesson from their adversity.

Colonial officials frequently criticized the aversion to agriculture, which they blamed on laziness or improper ideas of liberty, but the causes were deeper. The society tried to recreate agriculture as practiced in Maryland or on southern plantations. They assigned fixed plots of land for intensive cultivation. Many crops that the agency promoted would not thrive at the Cape, or individual settlers could not grow

them in sufficient quantity to repay their efforts. Settlers, who did not
know better, also tried to farm according to their experience, in a manner inappropriate for conditions at Cape Palmas. Cotton required just
the right soil and weather to flourish, with extraordinary labor—and
for all that, weevils destroyed most of the bolls. Cape Palmas tobacco
was inferior. Coffee flourished, and young plants or seeds were available to any settler who applied. Few asked for any quantity, though,
because several years were required before a harvest was possible. The
oil palm was also plentiful. Greboes gathered enough for domestic use
and usually had a surplus to sell to the agency. Russwurm and Hall
both advocated its cultivation, but settlers again resisted. The international market for palm oil was just developing, and settlers would not
plant and cultivate trees when they could collect the fruit all around
them. Until they could identify a crop that would grow without extravagant amounts of labor and money and could find a consistent
foreign market, settlers were unlikely to devote more than marginal
attention to their farms. This was only common sense.[15]

The failure of colonial agriculture was essentially the result of ecological conditions. Greboes also faced difficulties that few Americans
seemed to recognize. Launcelot Minor, an Episcopal missionary, addressed a letter on the subject to Latrobe in 1838, noting that acquaintances had "entered into a series of calculations to prove that this country is incapable of supporting more than the native population." He
apparently accepted the contention, but he thought that improved
technology and more suitable crops would alleviate scarcity and permit higher population densities.[16]

Americans found Greboes in possession of a country that seemed
to be fertile and underused. Yet now, with the addition of only about
four hundred individuals, chronic food shortages were developing.
Geography and the ecology of food production help to explain what
was happening. A successful agricultural system must produce enough
to meet the needs of a community consistently over years and generations. These needs are related to the size of a population, its dietary
preferences, and its economic habits. Overpopulation is a relative term,

having ecological significance primarily in terms of land degradation, which occurs by any of a number of processes in which the physical structure or chemical composition of the soil is altered, resulting in destruction of the numbers and variety of living things or in reduction of productive capacity of the soil. For example, the coastal savannahs are a product of degradation: where once had been forest, agriculture had worn out the soils and left barren scrub.[17]

Scholars have argued that precolonial Africa was generally under-populated, and that the land could have supported larger populations but did not largely because of the slave trade.[18] This may have been the case in many areas that were devastated by slave-raiding campaigns, but the historical record for Cape Palmas indicates overpopulation instead.[19] The beaches offered economic advantages that tended to draw larger concentrations of people. At the same time, the salt air and poor marine soils made them less productive than areas farther inland. This is reflected in the keen struggle for land among the Grebo towns, and seasonal hunger. The Grebo states were sparsely populated, but their system of agriculture could not have supported many more people than it did when the Americans landed in 1834.

Using nineteenth-century estimates of Grebo population and of the extent of their territory, in combination with modern information on nutritional requirements and the production of upland rice under shifting cultivation, some crude calculations, perhaps along the lines of those mentioned by Lancelot Minor, are possible. Sources estimate the Grebo population between twenty and twenty-four thousand, tending toward the latter figure.[20] The total area occupied by the several Grebo states was about ninety square miles—about twenty-three miles along the coast from Fishtown to Cavally River, with a boundary about four miles inland.[21]

Grebo farmers grew rice and other crops in a system of bush fallow rotation, which required extensive tracts of land but also maintained sustained yields. Their farming achieved an ecological equilibrium, nevertheless, yields were probably not very high. Horatio Bridge, who visited Cape Palmas in 1843, learned that Grebo farmers planted about

two bushels of rice per acre, hoping to harvest thirty. Greboes generally planted their rice on hillsides and riverbanks rather than swamps
and marshes, despite the fact that upland rice produces substantially
less than lowland varieties. Lowland rice typically produces forty or
fifty bushels for every two planted, though disease and parasites associated with the lowlands make their cultivation less attractive. Only a
fraction of the Grebo territories were suitable for rice, for the seacoast
soils were less fertile. Grebo farmers concentrated their activities two
or three miles inland, along the northern edges of their states, or on
isolated hilltops closer to the coast.[22]

The principal goal of shifting cultivators is to grow enough to feed
themselves, with a surplus to offset a poor harvest or to sell for goods
that cannot be made in the household. Agronomists estimate that one-
third hectare planted in upland rice will sustain an adult for a year, and
further that for every five adults an extra one-third hectare must be
planted: that is, two hectares are necessary to support five adults.[23]
Greboes of the nineteenth century probably planted similar proportions. If we take the lower population figure of twenty thousand, then
eight thousand hectares of upland rice would produce the necessary
subsistence and a small surplus. Shifting cultivation demands territory. With a fallow period of ten years, ten times more land would be
needed to support a population over the long run than would be needed
to feed it for one year. Eight thousand hectares annually in an area of
ninety square miles would allow field rotation in a period of between
six and seven years. This is fairly fast. Agronomists agree that eight to
ten years of fallow is generally necessary to avoid degradation in a
tropical rainforest environment. What is more, the actual area suitable for growing rice would have been much less than ninety square
miles. As noted, Greboes confined rice cultivation to the northern
fringes of their territories, where soils were better and the salt spray not
so damaging. Perhaps only forty-five square miles were actually available. If this was the case, then fields would have to be reused every three
to four years, an unsustainable rate.[24]

Gbenelu was the largest of the Grebo states, comprising about thirty-five square miles, with the highest proportion of interior land. A population of about four thousand was concentrated in three towns. Taking the ratio of two hectares for every five adults, then sixteen hundred hectares would be cultivated every year. If all of Gbenelu territory could be farmed, then farmers would reuse fields every twelve to thirteen years. Deduct one-third as unsuitable, and the cycle must have been closer to eight years, which is still reasonable. On the other hand, if the other Grebo states are taken in aggregate, then fifty-five square miles, much of it close to the beach, would have had to support sixteen thousand people. Thus, 6,400 hectares cultivated every year, and fields recleared every four or five years, at best, or, allowing for unsuitable land, perhaps every two or three years.

These are rough estimates, but they demonstrate that the Grebo states could not have produced all the rice they needed, though Gbenelu may have made enough for bare subsistence. The beach towns sacrificed an easy food supply, and perhaps less hazardous disease environments, for the economic benefits of access to the sea. The Grebo people were not starving. Cassava, bananas, and other crops would make up a large part of their food deficit. Fish, game, and livestock provided more food. Trade with neighbor states in the interior accounted for the rest. For this reason, Greboes were extremely protective of their interests in the bush.[25]

Despite hard times, Russwurm encountered little trouble with Greboes. He and Freeman shared an interest in vengeance upon King Toureh and the Barboes of Cavally River. Lulled by a sense of friendship, Russwurm broached the topic of moving Big Town, which straddled Maryland Avenue between Harper and the village of Latrobe. So many bumptious, heathen Africans upset the sensibilities of straight-laced settlers.[26] The agent thought that a physical separation of the two peoples was a reasonable means of ensuring peace, but he misjudged the issue's sensitivity. "The natives are becoming exceedingly uneasy at the amount of land appropriated by colonists," John Wilson warned Latrobe. "They are apprehensive that they will be crowded out of their reservations." They had asked him repeatedly whether the society would send out an agent to investigate the situation and protect them. Settlers were experiencing the effects of this unrest. Thefts, with their political overtones, increased as the supply of food dwindled. Greboes continually taunted settlers as "slaves" and took advantage where they could.[27]

They picked out some settlers for particular bullying. One was Eben Parker, a freed slave from Queen Anne's County, on Maryland's Eastern Shore. He had emigrated to Maryland early in 1836 with his wife and five young daughters. In Africa, he had toiled and suffered, crippled with arthritis. Two of his children died.[28] In spite of hardship, Parker was one of the few settlers committed to farming. His neatly cleared, fenced lot on Maryland Avenue, opposite Mt. Vaughan, was a model. Early in 1838, he chose to grow rice for himself rather than buy it. This was too much for Greboes, who regarded the lot as one of their former rice fields, reluctantly ceded in their confrontation with Holmes in 1836. If Parker could make a success of rice, others might follow and measurably reduce their dependence on African produce. The *sedibo* decreed that no African could work for Parker, a blow, but the old man made due with the help of his wife and girls. He carried a stool with him, which he put down whenever he needed rest, and weeded whatever lay within arm's reach.

Greboes systematically badgered Parker and his family. They stole whatever they could, and when he resisted, they resorted to the colonial courts, repeatedly calling him to answer petty charges. Once, a Grebo woman accosted Mrs. Parker and a child on Maryland Avenue as they returned from visiting a neighbor. The woman menaced them with a billhook, cutting the little girl's arm, then threw the mother into a ditch alongside the road. Eben Parker saw the scuffle, hobbled out, and wrestled with the woman while his family escaped. She went straight to Harper to file a complaint, and Parker was fined for assault. Nor was this the end of his troubles. On another occasion, a Grebo broke into his house and stole a gun. Mrs. Parker followed the thief, satisfying herself of his identity and residence. She went to Thomas Jackson, justice of the peace, to complain. He was sympathetic and went with her to recover the weapon, but the thief was not prosecuted for fear of raising a palaver.[29]

On June 16, the agent and council discussed the growing incidence of thefts. They urged settlers to be more vigilant—empty advice to a community that did not lock doors. More pragmatically, they posted night watchmen throughout the settlement, with instructions to shoot any suspect disobeying orders to halt. Early in July, some palaver among the Grebo states shut off the supply of cassava for a few days, and the prospect of famine grew more vivid.[30]

The schooner *Columbia* anchored off Cape Palmas on July 2, with thirty-six slaves from Savannah, Georgia, the property of Mrs. John Wilson and her brother, Nicholas Bayard. When their opinion of Maryland in Liberia had been more favorable, the Wilsons had arranged to settle them at Harper. Bayard delayed their departure while he rented the slaves to Savannah for public works, but finally he sent them to Baltimore to emigrate.[31] Wilson wrote Bayard in April to dissuade him from the plan, but the letter arrived too late. These new emigrants arrived at the worst possible time. Wilson and Russwurm were hardly on speaking terms, though the missionary had to rely on the agent. There were scarcely any provisions on hand, settlers were daily begging for food, and even this small accession was more than the agency could provide for. To his credit, Russwurm did all he could for Wilson's people, and they did not fare too badly. Wilson could only cast blame, however, condemning Russwurm as "short-sighted and improvident." His policies and incompetence had rendered the colony dependent upon African produce. "If the natives should demand *two* dollars this year for a croo of rice instead of one it will not surprise me — and they may make it *five* unless the colonists will render themselves independent by their own industry," he added. "The time was when rice could be shipped from the place, but the demand now exceeds the amount produced."[32]

About the middle of July, a Grebo man broke into a house and stole various articles, including a good hunting gun. Grebo constables detected and jailed him to await trial. The following Sunday afternoon, July 22, Russwurm heard of a plot to free the prisoner. He called the militia to arms and declared martial law for the next three days. He was determined not to be humiliated as in the summer before. War seemed imminent, but settlers were braced for whatever might come. Greboes did not hazard an assault.[33]

On Tuesday morning, the twenty-fourth, a man from a bush town, Barrakah, walked along Maryland Avenue with a sheep and other articles to trade at Harper. Eben Parker stopped him and bought the sheep, then continued his chores with little thought about the transaction. He was surprised late that afternoon to see the Barrawe at his front gate. The African wanted his sheep back, claiming that the price was not enough. Parker argued, but to no end. The bushman was determined to take his animal home again. Parker went into the cabin for his musket, and the Barrawe man walked off with the sheep. When Parker came to the door, they were out the gate. He took aim and fired. The heavy lead slug caught the bushman in the shoulder, throwing him down, seriously but not mortally wounded.

The gun's echoing report attracted Africans and settlers in the vicinity. Greboes carried the wounded man to Harper. Settlers retrieved the sheep and stood in the yard to sympathize with Parker, who was nearly in a frenzy. He declared that he would shoot any officer who might try to arrest him. They shared his sense of abandonment. If the law would not protect them, they were resolved to take care of themselves. At the Agency House, the noisy entry of the wounded man with an outraged entourage disturbed Russwurm and Freeman in a palaver concerning the threatened jailbreak. The agent ordered Parker's arrest, then resumed his conversation with the king.

Sheriff William Hawkins received the warrant early in the evening, but it was too late in the day to act. He was aware that Parker was armed and prepared to defend himself. The next morning, July 25, men of Gbenelu carried the Barrawe man back to his town, where he told an angry story of having been assaulted for no good reason, and without redress. His bearers corroborated the story and embroidered the details, using the chance to raise even more trouble for Parker. Barrakah's *sedibo*, consumed in a flash of rage, quickly decided to send a war party to set the palaver.

An accident that same evening fostered their object. Somewhere in the labyrinthine streets of Gbenelu, a neglected cooking fire spread sparks into a house thatch. In moments, a spectacular blaze, visible miles away, consumed the major part of the town. Few if any lives were lost, though the general panic and destruction of property was immense. Normally, looting would have followed such a misfortune, but agent and king were both anxious to prevent it. The militia mustered once again, to spend yet another wakeful night at their guns—now to protect those whom a few hours before they were prepared to fight.[34]

At dawn on July 26, a troop of some fifty Barrawe men approached the drowsy garrison at Mt. Tubman on Maryland Avenue. They carried clubs and machetes (many of the latter received by trade with the agency), and the united movement of so many men toward Cape Palmas should have aroused suspicion. When the chief officer questioned them, they indicated that they had come to see the damage at Gbenelu and commiserate. This satisfied him, and the pickets let them pass. The settlement was just then rising to the new day. At Mt. Vaughan, John Payne observed them trotting along the thorn fence in front of the mission. Across the road, Eben Parker also watched, sensing danger, but unwilling and unable to do other than face it. He called a warning to his wife and children, telling them to stay inside the house. The Barrawe soldiers entered the yard. One hit Parker with a club, and another slashed him with a cutlass, and then the rest took turns at his body. Some others went after Parker's wife and daughters. Mrs. Parker climbed out a back window and fled with her youngest in her arms. She managed to escape, though she was wounded. Two other girls were cut down as they ran, one killed and the other left as dead. The Africans rifled the house and set fire to it, then rushed into the bush behind Mt. Vaughan. A column of black smoke marked the ghastly site, a contrast to the lush, vivid green rice field, gray with dew, that grew behind the homestead.

In moments, word passed the length of the settlement, "murder" and "African rebellion" on everyone's lips. The Greboes' terror of the previous night now fell upon settlers. Naturally, the report grew more confused and extreme with repetition, and the news that reached the main garrison at Latrobe was absolutely horrid. The moment he heard the report, without knowing precisely what had occurred, Charles Snetter picked a small detachment of his men and hastened to Parker's farm. As they approached the spot, they intercepted a group of Grebo men and boys. At least one of them had a musket. They were very likely suspects, in Snetter's opinion, though in fact they were innocent, merely returning from their farms to survey their losses in the previous night's fire. Snetter questioned them but got no satisfactory answer. He ordered them to turn and walk ahead of his men, who carried muskets with fixed bayonets, toward Parker's farm.

Other settlers came up, pointing at the Greboes and identifying them as killers. The captives had good reason to fear that the growing crowd might lynch them. They walked a short distance, but as they reached a cross street, they saw another troop of militia coming toward them from Parker's. In an instant, they darted from their captors and scrambled for the bush. Captain Snetter ordered his men to fire, though he was too late: a volley of musket balls was already leveled at the fleeing Greboes. Three of the escapees were hit in the back. One fell dead, and two wounded, one mortally. The rest got away in the underbrush.

The crackle of gunfire jarred the whole neighborhood. Within minutes, armed settlers and Greboes gathered at the scene, prepared for a pitched battle. For a few moments, war seemed inevitable. Only the concerted efforts of Russwurm and Freeman to calm the crowd averted disaster.

For the next few weeks, the militia was on full alert. The pressure would have been taxing under any circumstances. On the verge of starvation, with no relief likely for another two or three months, the settlers' uncertainty and stress were near intolerable. On two occasions in the first week of August, men of the night watch at Mt. Tubman, under command of Charles Snetter, slaughtered Grebo bullocks. Freeman immediately protested, for livestock were money to Greboes. Russwurm investigated. Some of the Tubmans informed him that Snetter had dined with them—tasting only rice, they said—while the rest feasted on beef-steaks. When questioned, Snetter claimed to know nothing of the affair. The officer left Russwurm and straightaway met a group of sympathetic settlers. He read from the eighth chapter of Joshua, which described the Israelites' destruction of a Canaanite town and the taking of booty and cattle, "for a prey unto themselves."[35]

Charles Snetter was a clever, energetic fellow, and a stirring speaker with an attractive South Carolina lilt. Freely employing biblical language and analogy, he articulated the anxiety of many settlers who believed that their government capitulated to Grebo demands too easily. Russwurm, who never responded gracefully to criticism, rather disliked Snetter. In his opinion, the man was an ignorant fraud—one who pretended to accomplishments of which he was incapable. He saw Snetter as a demagogue, whose intention was to mislead and manipulate public opinion for his own benefit, amply demonstrated in the persecution of James Thomson. Snetter rose to shrill extremes of rhetoric, urging settlers to exterminate their heathen neighbors, just as God had ordered the Israelites to overrun Canaan.[36]

On the morning of Parker's murder, settlers hailed Snetter as a hero. Even Russwurm had to excuse his actions, though mistaken, under the circumstances. In the next two weeks he changed his mind. As those involved in the shooting discussed the incident, a more sinister story emerged. Some speculated that Snetter ordered his men to fire even though he knew that his prisoners were innocent, possibly even before they began to run. Russwurm was predisposed to think the worst of Snetter and grew more disgusted with each report. He suspected Snetter of countenancing the thefts of bullocks but could prove nothing. On August 8, he and the council met to repudiate the shooting and the thefts. It was resolved that any violation of military discipline must be treated with utmost severity.[37] Russwurm appointed a "Court of Inquiry," though the colony's constitution provided for no such thing.

A court-martial would normally hear such a case, but the agent apparently believed that no military court would convict so high and popular an officer. He therefore resorted to means outside the normal process of law.

Early on August 18, a Saturday, the court convened. There were ten judges: Russwurm at the head, associated with James Thomson, Alexander Hance, Benjamin Alleyne, John Revey, and other loyal citizens. They first questioned Launcelot Minor, the Episcopal missionary, who had spoken with the party of Greboes just before Snetter's men intercepted them. The soldiers from Snetter's detachment testified with small differences of detail. They all agreed, however, that Snetter had given the order to fire after the captives had begun to run. Snetter did not testify. Meeting privately on Monday, the court concluded that Snetter had no right to order the shooting of his prisoners. They criticized all such actions on "the spur of the moment" but acknowledged that the excitement and confusion then prevailing mitigated the case. The court then deferred the case to Russwurm for disposition.

The tables had turned completely, and Snetter was now at the mercy of his enemy, Russwurm, delivered by the agent's hand-picked judges, among whom was James Thomson, whom Snetter had nearly destroyed less than a year before. Questions of legal technicality were irrelevant, for Russwurm and the court were determined to ruin Snetter. The agent held the court's resolutions until August 26, when he sent a copy of them to Snetter. He enclosed them in a letter informing the captain that his civil duties were terminated and that he had thirty days to settle his business in the colony. At the end of that period, he must take up residence in Harper and leave Maryland at the first opportunity.[38] The man who had before endeavored to have Thomson banished now found himself under the same sentence.

The proceedings were patently unfair, and settlers reacted angrily. Snetter augmented the fervor, walking the length of the colony to tell his story. In a community in which everyone knew everyone else's business, he was the principal subject of conversation. Early in September, citizens convened at the militia's central station, in the township of

Latrobe. Snetter was absent at first, but a group of settlers went to get him. In the meantime, citizens took turns voicing concerns for their personal safety and the future of their country. When Snetter arrived, the crowd received him warmly and listened attentively as he read Russwurm's letter and commented upon it. In response, they nominated five men "to draw up a remonstrance Such and one as their weak abbility will allow to show that a large majorrity of citizens took task at that movement as a high handed measure and Consider it the first move to give the lives of our wives and Children into the hands of the Savages around us who thirsts for our Blood."[39]

The committee set about its task vigorously. None of them were fully literate—at least three could not sign their names—and the document they produced was awkward. Even so, they demonstrated a clear understanding of the colonial constitution and their rights as citizens. They cited, by article and clause, the provisions they believed the agent had violated in Snetter's case. They argued that the law guaranteed citizens due process in prosecution; that citizens were entitled to bear and use arms for their own and their country's defense; that military offences must be tried in a court-martial; and that only a court, not the governor alone, could impose a sentence of banishment.

Their petition expanded from a defense of Snetter to a critique of Russwurm's administration. They asserted that he had overstayed his term of office, contrary to law and complained that the governor treated citizens with contempt and showed too much favor to Africans. Though they shared Russwurm's anger over the robbery on the Cavally River, they were more upset that one of their own, Anthony Wood, was nearly killed than for the agent's humiliation. They believed that Greboes had plotted the incident and condemned Russwurm for relying on them to assist his revenge. As an instance, they related that shortly after Parker's murder, the agent sent John Bowen with guides supplied by Freeman to offer King Neh of Denah money to kidnap some of Toureh's people on the Cavally River. On the first evening, the party halted at a town, which Bowen presently suspected was Barrakah. Fearing for his life, he fled back to the Cape. Finally, the committee accused Russwurm of catering to Freeman's whims, namely to sacrifice Snetter, the best military man in the colony. "To oblige this savage who sirround us we are to be deprived of our Right Eye and then to lay down and die. We the undersigned say that we solomnly protest in the name of the Maryland State Society as well as the welfare of this colony (an do plainly say that he is not for us is against us) against Capt Chas Snetters leaving at all under that decree and otherwise untill we are better settled with our affairs." The men presented their report on September 12. Fifty-six attached their names. They handed a copy to Russwurm, posted another publicly, and mailed a third to the board of managers in Baltimore.[40]

Indeed, Russwurm had acted outside of strict accordance with the law, partially to take revenge for Snetter's persecution of James Thomson, but also because the man was a hothead, a dangerous individual in a tenuous community which emotional manipulation could sway. The agent was much more sensitive to the real power of Greboes than were most citizens, who entertained naive ideas of sweeping them away. He had little affection for Grebo culture, yet he realized that settlers must live with it or be destroyed. He therefore did what was necessary to preserve peace without conceding too much.

The turbulence hurt Russwurm's feelings, though there was truth in the settlers' criticisms. He reacted with characteristic choler, adding more enemies to his list. When someone informed Freeman that Russwurm was unqualified to be governor—because he was not really a white man—and the king challenged him, Russwurm reached his limit. He informed the board that he intended to resign as soon as they could find a replacement.[41]

During the months following his conviction, Snetter wandered the colony, offering apocalyptic visions to a receptive audience. At night meetings he was known to pray for the agent's salvation, and when agitated to shout, "Fire, fire! Fire! Fire from heaven!" as he moved on his knees from chair to chair. Major Anthony Wood made a similar campaign, though with less verve. At length, they went too far, and more sober members of the community rejected their extremism. Wilson expelled Snetter from his congregation, so he joined the Methodists. Francis Burns, their new preacher, took up the case and even preached a sermon portraying Snetter as a martyr for the cause of righteousness.[42] In late January, Snetter at last sailed for Monrovia, leaving debts and an unhappy memory.[43]

X.

"Suitable Locations for Man"

THE CONFLAGRATION OF GBENELU WAS A DISASTER FOR GREBOES BUT A blessing for the agency. In the months before, Greboes had acquired more goods than they could conveniently use. Pottery, mirrors, gunpowder, cloth, and countless other imports filled their homes. They had more tobacco than they could smoke or trade away. African produce rose steadily in price, the trend exacerbated by the scarcity of rice. Economies with durable, compact currencies can absorb an oversupply of money for some time before inflation comes into play. On the other hand, when the medium of exchange is a mixture of goods, whose value may vary according to fashion or changing demand, an individual can easily acquire too much. Bulky items are difficult to store, and they may spoil before they can be used or traded—crucial considerations in a humid tropical climate. The agent was constantly writing off dampened barrels of gunpowder, moldy tobacco, and bug-infested flour from the store accounts. Greboes got around this in part by buying livestock or wives with perishable goods, but the exchange took time to accomplish. In a few moments, though, flames consumed a glut that might have taken years to eliminate. The storekeeper encountered renewed demand for items not salable a day before. Prices fell across the board, though rice remained scarce until harvest, in late September.[1]

Fortunately, the growing season of 1838 was favorable, and the yield, no record, was still sufficient. Hunger had driven many settlers to work their farms, and the coming year promised more extensive efforts. Colonial officers did all they could to encourage them. The agent collected useful plants and tested them on the Public Farm. About the middle of 1838 he received a new variety of sweet potato from Monrovia. They were popular, and a few months later, settlers competed to grow the biggest. One weighed several pounds, even after rats had consumed part of it in the field. Other crops were less successful. Corn produced scarcely anything at all. Cabbage never formed heads because temperatures were too warm. Russwurm begged the board for draft animals, but they were too expensive, and their chances of survival in Africa were known to be slim. Greboes raised a small breed of cow, but they were also costly, and settlers generally wore them out prematurely in hauling logs from the swamps, and then made dinner of them.[2]

Late in October 1838, Baphro of Cavally convened a grand palaver to settle a number of disputes that lately had choked off interior trade. The attack on Russwurm and Freeman near Ploroh was on the agenda, so both sailed there to take part. King Tom of Robookah attended, but his treacherous liege, Toureh, the Barbo king, refused at the last moment, fearing a plot against him. Two minor dignitaries came in his place. Russwurm blamed Baphro for wasting his time. "He is on our side as he pretends," he reported, "while he is all the time consulting the Barboes and secretly throwing every obstacle in the way: he is an arch rogue, and for double dealing and low cunning I have never found his equal." In fact, Baphro was protecting his economic interests on the river. The agent was naive to expect full cooperation, notwithstanding treaties and dashes over the years. Russwurm and Freeman went back home disappointed. Toureh finally came to the beach to talk the palaver. He admitted his responsibility for the attack and agreed to pay a fine. Russwurm was skeptical. He continued to plan armed retaliation if Toureh did not comply with his promises, but in fact there was very little he could do.[3]

———•⊷•———

After the Parkers' deaths and the ensuing unrest, Russwurm fortified Mt. Tubman, where the militia had had a post for some time past. Laborers dug a ditch around the summit, throwing the dirt inwards, and erected a heavy palisade. With a field piece and arsenal of small weapons, the fort could withstand any African onslaught. George McGill and Governor Russwurm laid out a second public farm on the hillside. The site had better soil and less salt spray than the first farm near Cape Palmas. Russwurm hoped that experiments with cash crops might now be more successful.[4] McGill was losing his health and worried about the financial security of his family. His older sons continued the trading business he had begun in Monrovia in 1831. His son Ford remained in America.[5]

At Christmas, 1836, Samuel Ford McGill's prospects had been bleak. The students of Washington Medical College had petitioned to have him expelled, and his backers had capitulated abjectly. It seemed that the young Liberian would have to return home. As a last resort, Ira Easter wrote Dr. Edward Phelps in Windsor, Vermont, of McGill's troubles and asked whether the offer of instruction was still good. On January 9, 1837, Dr. Phelps wrote that it was, even offering lodging in his house. "Africa ought not always to be dependant upon America for knowledge of medical science," he wrote. "It is our duty now to send them a scion of knowledge, and just as much our duty to send them genuine stock." With this in mind, he would have McGill follow the curriculum of Vermont College. This consisted of four years' study: first, logic, mathematics, and natural sciences; second, anatomy; third, "the history, nature, and treatment of diseases, purely medical"; fourth, "Surgery and Medical Philosophy." He hoped that McGill would have some knowledge of Latin and Greek before he began. Phelps would make him recite his lessons daily. If he worked hard, he might complete the course in three years. Phelps promised to have Vermont College grant a diploma at the appropriate time.[6]

The society immediately arranged to send McGill to Vermont. They worried that abolitionists might corrupt their protégé, and they lectured him sternly concerning his obligations. Ira Easter penned a long letter to make sure there would be no misunderstanding. McGill must always exhibit a sterling, religious character, and keep careful track of all the money he used. Moreover, he must devote himself to acquiring "such knowledge as may be rather useful than ornamental." Easter continued, "In regard to your general deportment to all classes of society your residence both in Africa and in this country, cannot fail to have taught you, that prudence and circumspection are particularly needed in the present excited state of the public mind, in regard to the African race. You must not forget for a moment, that you are an *African in America*; and in that relation, whatever may be your sense of equality with your fellow men, remember, it will be dangerous to show it."[7]

Ford McGill met Dr. Phelps in Windsor, Vermont, on February 15, 1837. The doctor gave him a room in his house and contracted with a black family in town to give McGill his meals and clean his laundry. Study began immediately with anatomy. McGill showed zeal and talent, but he needed a cadaver. He requested his patrons to send him two, repeating Phelps's caution that they must be black, to eliminate any question of grave-robbing.[8]

McGill worked tirelessly through the spring and made good progress, and he could not help but take an interest in politics and society. His regular letters to Moses Sheppard and other sponsors reveal an immense curiosity. A typical letter, to Ira Easter, dated June 29, noted his academic progress and the decline of his finances. He then discussed various articles he had read in the Baltimore papers, including a flood near Baltimore. He had heard that Oliver Holmes was on his way home, bitter about his experiences in Liberia. "I do not believe that his enmity can injure the Colony," he wrote, "he acts too much from the impulse of a moment," and most people would recognize Holmes's "disappointed ambition." He also enclosed a local paper, to which he had contributed an article on Liberia.[9]

At the end of the spring semester of 1837, Dr. Phelps resigned from the faculty of Vermont College to enter private practice. This posed problems for McGill, who needed to hear two series of lectures, but without Phelps's authority, he might have trouble gaining admittance. The doctor decided to transfer McGill to Dartmouth College, just a few miles away in Hanover, New Hampshire. Classes would begin on August 1 and continue for fourteen weeks. Two semesters, combined with rigorous private study, would qualify him as a physician, Phelps believed. McGill liked the idea of attending Dartmouth. The surgeon's craft appealed to him, he wrote Easter on July 17, but he needed a proper set of instruments. He anticipated higher expenses in his new circumstances and asked for an allowance. He would forego it if necessary, however, "until I become nearly as much reduced as the farmer's horse, when he attempted to reduce him to one straw per diem."[10]

McGill was in Hanover for the start of lectures. In Windsor, Phelps had shielded him from curious townspeople, whom he was afraid would waste the young man's time or mock him. Now McGill found himself in the midst of the very people the colonization society had wanted him to avoid. As it turned out he had no trouble. "I was introduced as a Native African and I believe the deception carried the point," he wrote. "A general inquiry was made as to the place I learnt to speak English so fluently; but easily satisfied them. . . . Foreigners of any colour are respected."[11] McGill enjoyed himself and made friends at school. The student body included American Indians and black Americans. Among them was a young man from Boston who had been an apprentice printer for Garrison's *Liberator*. The two engaged in long debates, which McGill loved, but he was not swayed to the abolitionist cause. "I frequently meet with individuals, calling themselves abolitionist, but possessing but a small share of the true Thompsonian spirit, — which I believe calls for amalgamation as one of its principal doctrines," he wrote in January 1838. Now he pretended to agree with those who professed lofty and philanthropic ideals, politely hinting "what a blessing it would be" to achieve full racial equality. "It never fails in producing such a degree of nausea, that I am generally amused." Relating an incident that must have horrified his sponsors in Baltimore, he told how he had met one young abolitionist at Hanover, and after "constant importunities" from the young man "concerning the benefits of Abolition" McGill "was induced . . . to make a rather serious proposal for the hand of his sister. I need hardly say that it effectively silenced him, and altho' I was often in his company afterward, I never found him anxious to harp on the subject of abolition."[12]

In fact, McGill had little time to socialize. He attended lectures and studied diligently at home, making remarkable progress. His closest friends were a year ahead of him in their studies, and he determined to catch up to them. He spent the summer of 1838 under Phelps's constant instruction. In August, he passed tests which credited him with nearly three years' study. Soon after, he earned his diploma, whereupon he returned to Baltimore.

Dartmouth did not include clinical training in its curriculum. Though McGill had once written quite confidently about surgery, he was now less certain of himself. He asked to stay in Baltimore for a few months, to practice his newly acquired knowledge (and to pursue a difficult courtship). The society would hear nothing of it; their man should attend the needs of settlers. They still feared abolitionists might persuade him to stay in America permanently. Recognizing his need for practical experience, they hired Dr. Robert MacDowell to assist McGill during his first few months at Cape Palmas. MacDowell was a black West Indian with a Glasgow education and experience in the tropics, an ideal instructor.[13]

The two doctors left Baltimore on the *Oberon* on November 22, 1838, with a company of fifty-three emigrants, thirty-one of whom were less than eighteen years old, and most of them girls.[14] They reached the Liberian coast in February, and news flew ahead that the young doctor was coming home. No sooner was anchor cast than kroomen brought him ashore in a launch. Old George and a joyous gathering of family and friends met him on the Agency Wharf. They led him up to a church service, since it was Sunday morning, and a thanksgiving indeed. Though Africa was his adopted home, whose people he loathed, Ford McGill was inspired by a vision of a future civilized black republic.

Many changes had taken place since 1836. He had left a straggling village, a mere toe-hold established with the simplest tools, perseverance, and courage. Food was now so abundant that potatoes rotted in the ground. The landscape was transformed. "A half miles travel on the Avenue," he wrote, "brought me to the nearest farms. Where I had left a dreary wild I now saw well cultivated fields — the sturdy trees of the forest had been thrown down, and converted into materials for building — the favourite haunts of the fierce leopard had been invaded to furnish suitable locations for man. Nature even seemed to clothe herself in a new aspect." On the road, he now passed an oxcart and watched men plowing fields, both unheard of when he left. Mt. Vaughan, which reminded him of the tidy farms he had seen in New England, was entirely new. Maryland Avenue, where it passed the mission, had been a morass—"the favourite haunts of the formidable *boa constrictor* which at a single gulp could swallow a man"—but now was raised on a solid causeway. The swamp on either side was ditched and drained, and the spot where Parker had lost his life remained covered in rice. Beyond Mt. Vaughan, where once was a ford across a stream, was now a stone bridge. When he had left, all was bush, but now ahead of him rose the steep hill-fortress, Mt. Tubman, where his father, the vice-agent, resided. Six acres on the landward side were planted in vegetables and sugar cane, which seemed to promise a future income to the colony. At the summit of the hill, McGill could look across the neat frame houses and farms of the Tubmans, seeming to fulfill the most sanguine hopes of colonizationists.[15]

Early in 1839, it was rumored that John Wilson planned to move his mission from Maryland. He had visited Fishtown, a few miles to windward, outside colonial jurisdiction, and was said to have negotiated with the local headmen and the English expatriate, Spence, who ran a trading post there. Afterward, he sailed to leeward, inspecting harbors as far as Cape Coast Castle. Wilson made no public statement, though, and Russwurm doubted his seriousness.[16]

The rice harvest of 1839 was the best in recent memory. Russwurm bought all he could, until he ran out of storage space, even until the joists in his warehouse failed.[17] Having faced starvation, many settlers had cleared their land for vegetable gardens. Russwurm offered rewards of $30 and $20 to the two best farms in the colony as of New Year's Day, 1840. Even the pauper Catherine Ross, a single woman with small children, busied herself clearing and planting her lot with corn and potatoes. In a letter home, she asked for cabbage and turnip seeds, but she complained of the lack of flour and meat, reminding the society that she must have something to eat while her crops matured. She asked also for a few chairs, tin cans, knives, and forks, and hoped that the society could get more of her family to come out.[18]

Other disappointments tempered joy at the revival of agriculture. During 1839, as the colony became better established and more populous, concern with law and order increased, for disintegrative forces were at work. Immorality was more evident. Single women gave birth at an alarming rate. Two such cases occurred in the first half of 1839. The government prosecuted one of these women, but she was acquitted despite the evidence against her. Provoked, Russwurm ordered a new trial, warning the board of dire consequences were the evil not stopped. He firmly believed that single female emigrants were a drain on the colony. The nightmarish fear, only implied, was that they might drift into the African community and subvert the civilized character of the settlement. By contrast, married couples were much more likely to work for the good of the community. Cattle thefts by settlers were also on the rise. Mt. Vaughan, the Public Farm, and a Grebo man were all recent victims, and in one case the thieves had gotten away undetected and probably would strike again. Russwurm suggested a stricter, more dignified application of justice. He asked the board to appropriate money for a stone courthouse to replace the spare room in the Agency House that had served the purpose. The jail too was inadequate, a log structure ten feet on a side, that could hold only four individuals. He asked for a stone edifice with male and female wards and a regular jailer.[19]

At the close of 1839, the colony's relations with Greboes were more peaceful than at any time before, largely because the abundant rice harvest reduced competition for food. Russwurm thought he perceived a fundamental change taking place within the African community. Individuals now owned canoes, and remarkably, other Greboes respected them as private property. A movement was afoot to put an end to trials by ordeal, but the *sedibo* was strongly opposed. The agent had no illusions that change would be swift, but he hoped that contact with the American community would eventually result in abolition of the custom.[20]

Although peace prevailed on the beach, the bush states suffered great unrest. Barrakah, the colony's enemy, fell on hard times after the Parkers' murder. Their trade with the beach ceased. Then, for uncertain reasons, Barrakah went to war with its neighbor Saurekah. Several battles, whose musketry echoed at Cape Palmas, resulted in about twenty deaths, the Barrawes receiving the worst. The agent made a good trade with Saurekah of castoff muskets for rice. The whole population of Cape Palmas enjoyed the savor of revenge as the proud Barrawe people were reduced to poverty.[21]

The Maryland State Colonization Society, chronically short of money, found itself in desperate financial difficulties late in 1839. The board dismissed several staff members and consolidated the duties of those who remained. With what scant funds they could muster, they chartered the brig *Boxer* to carry thirty-two emigrants to Cape Palmas, with word that no more would come for several months at least. The news pained Russwurm. His requests for material assistance (particularly donkeys) were a dead letter, but he resolved to make the best of what he had. Luckily, food would be plentiful for the next few months, and his trade was largely self-sustaining, though he regretted not being able to make enough profit to relieve the society's distress.[22]

Dr. MacDowell handed charge of the colony's medical practice to

McGill on November 20, 1839. He briefly visited Monrovia, where he had once lived, then returned to Baltimore on the *Boxer*. McGill soon faced an outbreak of dysentery among settlers. Thirteen fell ill at once, but to his relief, none died. Gbenelu was losing one or two every day to the same disease, with a corresponding increase of deaths by *gidu*. Except for two children, the *Boxer* company passed through the fever without incident. Many of the emigrants were unhappy with Cape Palmas, though. Several complained that the society offered free passage to Africa but not to return home.[23]

The farming season of 1840 began auspiciously, as the previous year's enthusiasm persisted, but it did not remain so. In April or May, a distemper killed forty or fifty swine, despite great efforts to save them. Sugar cane, which had shot up with great promise the year before on the slopes of Mt. Tubman, had since mysteriously withered. A few settlers experimented with cotton, but few expected success any time soon. Others set out a few coffee trees. Men racked their brains to think of a crop suitable for export.[24]

In May, following six weeks of almost constant rain, a drought set in. By the end of July, the rice crop began to suffer. At the close of September, no rain had fallen for nearly four months, and the rice crop was expected to fall one-third short of the previous year's level. The governor was not particularly worried by the prospect, for he had plenty of last year's rice still on hand. In fact, harmony prevailed, and all hoped that a lasting peace had settled in.[25]

Captain Isaac Spence, an English factor many years resident at Fishtown, died during the first half of 1840, leaving an estate of boats and other equipment. James Hall, who was on the coast on business, was aware of Russwurm's need for a vessel. He purchased a ketch, which the agency would pay for with rice. The boat was too small for long voyages, but she could carry up to sixteen barrels of palm oil short distances. Russwurm had plenty of rice to pay the bill, though he encountered some trouble delivering payment because of heavy surf.[26]

With clear skies and calm seas, the ketch went right to work in the palm oil trade. The early rains were good for the palms, and the crop was so plentiful the agency could not store all it bought.[27] Observing the rapid growth of the oil trade, Russwurm urged the society to hire Dr. Hall to develop a profitable business in it. Promising as the venture might seem, the board was in no position to make such an investment, and declined.[28]

———

In January 1841, the Maryland State Colonization Society remained crippled with debt. Russwurm even had the embarrassment of having a draft for tobacco and other supplies protested and returned. Fortunately, the note was drawn in favor of an old customer and friend, and he was able to make good on it with a quantity of palm oil. The oil season of 1840 had been very productive, and the agency traded some 13,000 gallons at an average of thirty-seven cents per gallon. The upcoming season gave every sign of being as good, but Russwurm worried about a market fluctuation. He expected a record number of ships searching the coast for it this season. A large portion might go home empty handed or with cargoes obtained too expensively. The next season, oil production might well increase, but fewer vessels would venture to the coast and prices would then tumble. He doubted the prudence of a full-scale venture by the society until the market stabilized. Time bore out his prediction. At the height of the season in 1841, more than forty English vessels were reported waiting off Bonny River and Calabar, recently slave markets, paying prices that the market at home would not bear. More than half were expected to leave with short cargoes. This bid fair to the agency's short-term interests, since it had oil to sell, but next year there might be no demand at all by comparison.[29]

The previous year's dry weather, which was good for oil, reduced the rice crop. Grebo farmers therefore planted earlier and in larger tracts than usual in 1841, to make up the shortfall. Farmers from Cape Palmas and Rocktown both laid claim to a piece of land on their border. The two states were traditional rivals, and the dispute over ownership of the land drove them to the verge of war once again. In an unusual display of co-operation, Russwurm and John Wilson mediated the palaver, with a favorable outcome. Russwurm believed that neither side really wanted to fight, but each felt bound by tradition and honor to continue the feud.[30]

About the same time, the agent initiated a program to expand the camwood trade. He sent envoys with dashes to distant bush towns. They returned with qualified approval of the project, but the movement was delayed in April, as Grebo farmers migrated to their rice farms to protect them from birds and other predators.[31]

Russwurm urged the society to let him purchase Spence's concession at Fishtown. British interest in African trade was manifest, and Maryland ought to get control of as much coastline as possible before they interloped. Wilson had just established a mission post there, but the town wanted a new factory. He thought he could buy Spence's deed for one or two hundred dollars, which would give the society a toehold.[32]

Russwurm purchased a schooner of forty tons burthen from Captain Spence's estate early in 1841. The vessel could carry eighteen puncheons and a number of barrels on coastal voyages. She had sailed from Sierra Leone before Spence bought her and was now showing signs of age. Even so, Russwurm believed that minor repairs would render the vessel serviceable. He sent her to Monrovia under command of John Revey with five hundred croos of rice to cover the cost. To forestall criticism of his investment, he renamed the vessel *Latrobe*.[33]

Shipwrights at Monrovia took advantage of Revey's mild manner and ran up charges. What Russwurm had estimated at two hundred dollars cost instead five hundred, all the while their delays deprived the agency of her use. The *Latrobe* did not return to Harper until the beginning of April. Russwurm immediately boarded for a cruise to leeward to contract for rice and oil and to discuss opening new factories. During the trip, the vessel began to leak. Russwurm brought her into Hoffman's River and had her careened. Carpenters with inadequate tools then performed the tedious work of lifting the copper sheets from the hull and replacing bad planks that Monrovian shipwrights had ignored. The agent had to beg the board for copper sheets to replace the ones too corroded to nail back.[34] While the *Latrobe* was under repair, Spence's ketch, now called *Doctor*, was doing a brisk business carrying palm oil from factories up and down the coast. In a few months of service she had paid for herself and turned a good profit. Despite Russwurm's best efforts, however, the agency was losing money, and the board instructed him to cut back. He apologized to Latrobe for having purchased the vessels and drawing on the society's depleted reserves.[35] Moreover, he abandoned the new Public Farm at Mt. Tubman, except for the cane field. On the society's advice, he also reduced the number of indigents employed on the old farm, leaving them to fend for themselves.[36]

Russwurm thought again of resigning his post. In June he asked the board to select a successor by year's end. A recurrence of his old feud with John Wilson over the question of militia duty for mission teachers also influenced his decision. Wilson employed educated Africans from Cape Coast and Sierra Leone as "Assistant Missionaries," and he claimed for them the same exemption granted to emigrant teachers. Russwurm objected, but he agreed to lay the matter before the board. He asked Wilson to state in writing that he would abide by the arbitration and pay any fines that might be imposed for missed parades. Wilson refused, in a bitter and sarcastic letter. He then made his defiance clear in public statements as well, causing some excitement among settlers.[37]

Most citizens shared Russwurm's sense of insult at the mission's arrogant disrespect. For example, Henry Hannon, Master of Public School No. 1, wrote the board concerning the state of the colony in September 1841. "Never have I seen more Pleasur in all my life, than I have seen in this Place," he said. "Here I enjoy my freedom, as much so, as are white man that walks the streets of Baltimore — I can set down to own table and drink Pam wine, and eat free bread," he said proudly, then added with self-evident pride, "Com on, com on, you black facies and take your hand out of those white mens Pockets we can com out with white brest like soldiers for the armey." He noted that the militia had not yet seen action, but that missionaries disturbed the peace of the colony. He defended the colony's right to make its own laws. If the missions resented it, they should leave, just as they threatened to do.[38]

Public meetings condemned Wilson and the missions in general. Settlers were less concerned with the question of civic duty than with the missions' fiscal policies. If they claimed exemption from military duty because of their evangelical character, neither were they entitled to act as merchants, they believed. Often, Wilson and Savage competed with the agency in trade, in ways that tended to drive up prices. The missions, large-scale employers, treated workers unfairly, paying them with trade goods, whose values they set arbitrarily, in many instances higher than those at the agency store. Settlers knew that the missions regularly received chests of coins from home. They wished to be paid with them so they might purchase where they wished. Settlers were also aware of a law recently passed at Monrovia that restricted trade to settlers. They asked the agent to enact the same law at Harper.[39]

Responding to the settlers' complaints, the agent and council passed the desired ordinance on July 31, 1841. The act began: "Hereafter, no person or persons other than Citizens of the Colony shall Carry on trade or do business in buying and selling or Exchanging articles by way of trade or for labor, directly or indirectly as a merchant within this colony." The new law specifically stated that the missions could buy food or other items for their own use or their employees, but that they could not sell food, cloth, or other items to settlers or Africans simply to make a profit. On August 7, Savage and Minor wrote the governor for a clarification of the meaning and enforcement of the new law. Russwurm answered them coldly, confirming some of their worst fears: that they could no longer pay American workers with goods, though they could pay Grebo workers as before. Moreover, a point not obvious in the act, Russwurm forbade them to hire a settler to carry on trade under their auspices.[40]

The more independent and patriotic settlers resented the missions' apparent prejudice in favor of Africans. They dreaded a day when Africans would be better educated than settlers, and thus gain a commercial edge.[41] Many parents neglected to send their children to school regularly. It was education enough, in their opinion, if a child could sound out the Bible and slowly write down his name. Ford McGill had much to say relative to this point in a letter to Latrobe of June 1840. He was "fearful that ere we could be supplied with a teacher the natives would become our equals and even surpass our youth in literary acquirements." For him, civilizing "the heathen" was secondary to building the colony. Education was "the only superiority we possess over these natives and for us to suffer or approve to equality in the [education of Africans] unaccompanied by the restraining moral influence of Christianity, would be to give them weapons for our destruction." Were they Christians, he would see it otherwise, but as things currently stood, "I am inclined to the opinions of the residents of the Southern States in relation to their blacks — they had better remain in a happy state of ignorance."[42] Such statements provided the missions with good reason to suspect the motives of colonizationists and settlers.

"The missionaries acted like men, who were dealing with beings of an inferior order, and by their speeches only tended to widen the breach," Russwurm told Latrobe in September. "Invidious comparisons were drawn between the standing of both parties in the United States," he continued. The missionaries pointed out to the natives that "they had rich societies to back them while the Maryland Colonization Society was known to be poor." Moreover, the missionaries told the Greboes "that the colonists wished the missionaries away, so that they might drive King Freeman and his people off the beach." The inflammatory language worsened the situation needlessly.[43]

Wilson's behavior was so controversial that even members of his own mission questioned his stance. An anonymous clergyman who visited Harper at the time of the dispute wrote the editor of the *New England Puritan* that Wilson himself was largely to blame for the animosity. "Is there not in that language an offence to the governor, as great as well could be given, and was it not calculated to stir up the spirits of any one, not a poor crushed slave, to resistance." Wilson's open defiance of Russwurm's authority was out of line. "The coloured governor found a white man denying his authority — bidding defiance to his officers with legal process, and assuming in an arrogant tone principles which, if assumed by others, would have been seditious. Was not this calculated to excite his jealousy, and if he had the soul of a freeman — lead him carefully to maintain his authority?"[44] Having created a tempest, Wilson and his wife took passage to leeward, avowedly to find a site to relocate the mission.[45]

The agency's recent cut-backs and restrictions on missions hurt many settlers. One such was Benjamin Bostick, an old man who had never gotten established on his farm. He wrote John Kennard in early September to plead for help. "I am so far advanced in years that I am not able to do for myself as I could if I was a young man if I was in the prime of life I should be ashamed to ask of your pecuniary aid but as it is out of my power to help the advance of old age." He asked for a hoe and shovel and for the society to intercede with Russwurm to get him a job with the agency. Complaining of the statutes against the missions, he wrote, "What we poor colonest will do that have depended on them for work to cloth ourselves and family God only knows. If the missionary and colony can not live together peacefully one or the other must be bad with which the fault is you that are wise must judge!"[46]

Finding an angry and strident voice in the mission controversy, settlers expressed more openly their resentment of Africans. In a letter of October, Russwurm noted the "strong prejudice and hatred of the natives" exhibited by many citizens. Even the most ignorant were well versed in their rights under the colonial constitution, but in their opinion such rights did not extend to Africans. Sometime in September, a settler was caught stealing rice from a Grebo farm. He was brought before the court, fined, and thrown into jail until the debt was paid. On the night of October 10, a group of his friends went out and robbed another Grebo farm to raise the funds. They were detected, and the case immediately went before a magistrate, who convicted the settlers but imposed only a small fine. The Grebo victims appealed the case to Russwurm and Freeman, who agreed and raised the fine, but many citizens vehemently opposed the decision. They got up a petition which asserted that no citizen should face a suit brought by Africans except before a jury of twelve settlers. They also sought to deny Africans the right to testify against settlers, just as black people's testimony was refused in North American courts.[47]

As 1841 passed, the oil trade was not as lucrative as Russwurm had hoped, quantity and prices falling short of the previous year. Oil was abundant, but the weather was too strong for the little ketch, *Doctor*. Russwurm sold her to John Bowen and Jonathan Jones, two enterprising settlers, for 1,140 gallons of palm oil, a little more than he paid for her. At the end of September, the *Latrobe* was also up for sale. She had been an albatross from the beginning. When finally she was seaworthy, Russwurm hired a Monrovian to manage her. He was incompetent, losing several anchors, each time jeopardizing the vessel. To make matters worse, he stabbed and killed two Kru sailors from the windward town of Woppie one evening while the vessel lay off the Cape. The captain claimed they had tried to rob him and that he had acted in self-defense. Russwurm did not believe the story. He fired the captain and paid the king of Woppie a large fine for fear the palaver would result in retaliation against some luckless American vessel.[48]

At the end of September, Russwurm remained at his post, impatiently waiting for the society to allow him to retire to a more peaceful private life. In a letter of September 24, George McGill observed that the governor faced many difficulties, not the least of which was neglect by the society. "Save him if you can," he advised, "I tremble at the thoughts of his leaving, it is not my opinion that you will ever get his equal here (to supply his place) — he is a man of unequaled furbearance."[49] In fact, the board was satisfied with their agent, and they were not prepared to replace him. They therefore let his resignation remain on the table, in hopes that he might relent.

XI.

"Muskets Are Too Light"

ATE IN 1841, THE SOCIETY'S FINANCES RECOVERED ENOUGH TO RE-
sume normal activity. The brig *Harriet* left Baltimore on December 20, just over two years since the previous expedition.
The company was small, numbering only twenty-four, five of them
from Petersburg, Virginia. Still, any expedition was something of a
victory in the face of growing abolitionist opposition and public indifference. The vessel also carried a party of Roman Catholic missionaries. The bishops of New York and Philadelphia had jointly proposed
the venture to the American Colonization Society, but that body would
have nothing to do with Catholics. The effort then fell to Rev. John
Kelly, born in County Tyrone in 1802, sometime pastor of a church in
Albany, New York, and in 1840 posted at St. Mary's College in Baltimore. He had suggested Maryland in Liberia as an alternative site and
wrote John Latrobe on the subject in September. Latrobe was a devout
Catholic (his father had designed the first Catholic cathedral in the
United States), and he referred the letter to the board. A Catholic mission posed no threat to the state society, for Catholics had founded
Maryland, and old Catholic families maintained social prominence
unusual in the United States. Latrobe wrote Kelly that the society would
offer every encouragement to missionaries, and the Church immediately made the arrangements. Dr. Edward Barron, an Irishman edu-

cated in Rome—in 1841, pastor of St. Mary's Church, Philadelphia—
would lead the mission. John Kelly volunteered to assist him. Dionysius
Pindar, a black lay catechist from Baltimore, completed the group.[1]

The missionaries landed at Cape Palmas on January 30, 1842. They
said their first public mass on February 6 in the presence of a dozen
Catholic settlers, the governor and other colonial officials, and a few
Greboes. The priests then held a retreat for three days, reappearing
again on the third, Ash Wednesday, in their finest vestments. They
walked behind a crucifer into Big Town, reciting the Litany. At Freeman's
house, they held their first missionary service. Dr. Barron preached, as
Father Kelly reported, "the object of the mission — its regularity —
authorized by the representative of Christ the head of the Christian
World." A crowd pressed around to hear these new words, "yet many,
as is their custom when hearing anything strange or hard to credit,
laughed at the doctrine of the Trinity and the eternal punishment of the
unbeliever and unbaptized." After service, the priests dashed Freeman
a colorful silk robe and turban, as if he were some oriental prince, and
gave him tobacco and cloth for his subordinates. Freeman seemed to
like the newcomers, at least he hoped to make them his own. His half-
brother, Bill Davis, formerly John Wilson's interpreter, went to work
for them.[2]

The priests expected to be reviled, and even though they were received with civility, withal some curiosity, they were quick to perceive
prejudice. They were aware of a bitter feud between the Methodist
mission and Liberian government. At Cape Palmas they found a similar situation and determined to stay on the agency's side. Kelly learned
that Bill Davis had been a communicant in good standing with Wilson,
even though he kept four wives. Only when he took a fifth did Wilson
expel him from the congregation. "Well may such men abuse *the Pope*
who never allowed such an 'Indulgence' even to emperors," Kelly wrote.
"Kings have in vain sought it by menaces and by gold." On interviewing
teenage students of the Protestant mission schools, he was shocked to
find that none of them had been baptized, the missionaries insisting
that they have a "new heart" before administering the first sacrament.

The Catholic standard was more liberal, founded on the belief that only baptism could save a soul from perdition. They conducted classes illustrated with colorful biblical pictures, preparing the way for mass baptisms, they hoped. John Wilson spied on them and tried to sabotage their efforts, but his influence was waning, and the Catholics went about their business.[3]

The next few months were filled with hardship and frustration. Dr. Barron was sick almost the whole time. Kelly and Pindar fell ill also, more sharply, but for briefer spells. McGill prescribed a regimen that included quinine, Peruvian barks, morphine, calomel, and regular sips of brandy. "The *vis vita* needs help," Kelly noted after a fit, "found in the valuable inestimable febrifuge quinine, bark, and proper food — cleanliness, etc." On April 8, Barron left Cape Palmas for Europe, where he hoped to get more support from the Church. In his absence, Kelly and Pindar oversaw the erection of a church and schoolhouse and taught. Since they had money to spend, settlers and Greboes alike charged exorbitant prices for services. The missionaries lived with Joshua Stewart, who charged them forty-six dollars per month for room and board, as much as he might have expected from six weeks' hard labor. Nurses charged one dollar per night, but often neglected their duty. Kelly grew irritable, his temper worsened by morphine, emetics, and a constant ringing in his ears attributed to quinine. At the end of April, he argued with Paul Sansay, a parishioner with whom he had contracted to build the schoolhouse. "Resolved henceforth to trust neither Catholic nor Yankee," he wrote acerbically in his diary.[4]

In a letter sent by the *Harriet*, the board praised Russwurm's service and urged him to continue as agent. Their flattering language persuaded him to stay until the following October. In answering them, Russwurm upbraided the board on several counts. They did not seem to understand their colony very well, he wrote. Too often, their orders had little relevance to conditions at Cape Palmas. He cited their often-repeated, naive idea of using tobacco or cotton as currency. "I am aware of the Tobacco currency of Maryland, but those are 'bygone days,' and the poor man now looks for more comfort than the rich of Ad 1632. The poor slave now parades your streets arrayed in finer cloth than kings and courtiers of olden time." He proposed instead that the society send out cash to pay his employees.[5]

The board also ordered Russwurm to refund the fines collected from the Episcopal and Congregational missions for absence from drills, which amounted to sixty-four dollars. He flatly refused to give Wilson the satisfaction. On February 12 he addressed a blunt letter to Latrobe. The laws of the colony were clear enough to settle the dispute, he declared, but a vacillating policy in the home office had made the matter intractable. The colonial courts and a special committee in Baltimore had both concurred with his position. Moreover, the board had upheld the authority of the colonial courts in the cases of James Thomson and Charles Snetter, despite the bitter objection of settlers. Now, having changed its mind for political reasons, the board would embarrass their agent and subvert the colony's authority and dignity. Russwurm asked Latrobe to refund the fines from the home office, if he felt he must.[6]

On February 6, the booming of cannons to leeward startled Harper. A few days later, news came that a French man-o'-war had bought Garroway and fired its guns in celebration. Black Will, a Garroway headman, reported that they would build a fortress there in about six months. European powers had not yet partitioned Africa, though Liberians had long feared it. Now the axe seemed about to fall, and Russwurm urged the society to consolidate its territory.[7]

To that end, he renewed efforts to acquire Fishtown, which lay between Garroway and the Maryland territory of Rocktown. Russwurm had long coveted the spot, but Captain Spence had an exclusive right. After the old man died in 1841, he had tried to buy Spence's deed, but the captain's heirs refused. John Wilson secretly negotiated with Fishtown late in 1841 and got a new concession. He wasted no time building a station, which he made his base of operations early in 1842. Fair Hope was reduced to a subsidiary post, under charge of Benjamin Griswold, an irascible young preacher who held the colony, its citizens, and Greboes in utter contempt. In the heat of some discussion, Griswold let slip that Wilson had actually obtained territorial rights to Fishtown. Russwurm was incredulous but quietly sent an emissary to investigate. The headmen produced a deed written out by Wilson, which they could not read. When the Marylander explained the terms, they were outraged at the rights they had signed away and swore to a man that the missionary had tricked them. Russwurm asked the society to take up the matter with the American board, but he could do little else.[8]

On April 24, 1842, a tragedy occurred at Half Beriby, beyond the Cavally River on the Ivory Coast, that might have gone unnoticed but for the presence of the Episcopal missionary, Launcelot Minor, at Tabou, thirty miles west.[9] Rich merchant cargoes often tempted those on shore to petty robbery, and sometimes more. Such was the fate of the schooner *Mary Carver* of Boston, on the coast to buy camwood. Some time before, the vessel's captain, Eben Farwell, had left goods with Ben Krakow, Half Beriby's titular king. On his return, Farwell found that Krakow had fallen short of the contract by several hundred pounds. He accepted a canoe in part payment and went ashore to negotiate for the balance. His dealings with Krakow had been friendly. "The Captain, apprehending no danger, was enticed on shore," Minor wrote the secretary of the navy the next day,

> While amused with a pretence of trade, his boat and several canoes, all loaded with camwood, were sent to the schooner. The mate, suspecting no harm, allowed all hands to come on board, and while engaged in weighing the wood, was suddenly set upon. He, one seaman, and the cook were the first who fell. One seaman, a very old

man, was thrown overboard, and the only remaining hand, having taken refuge in the rigging, was induced by fair promises, to surrender, and instantly butchered. At a preconcerted signal, the captain, till then unconscious of what had been going on, was seized, bound hand and foot, and cruelly beaten. The women struck him so severely with their rice-pestles that his skull was fractured just above the eye, causing it to protrude from the socket in a manner horrible to behold. He begged for time to pray. It was refused. He was then taken out to sea in a canoe, and thrown overboard, bound as he was. Still, the unhappy man struggled for his life with all the energy of desperation, and succeeded in tearing, with his teeth, the cords with which his hands were bound, and even seized a paddle with which to defend himself, but a blow on the head sent him to the bottom.[10]

Ben Krakow's henchmen hauled the schooner close to shore, then looted and scuttled her.

The missionary was livid. The seamen were innocent, honest men, slaughtered for the sake of avarice. The inhabitants of Half Beriby and the neighboring towns, who shared in the plunder, boasted of their crime. Minor implored Abel Upshur, secretary of the navy, to order the sternest retaliation to prevent similar incidents. "There is, in the minds of many in America, and more especially in England," he commented, "an over-wrought sensibility with regard to the African race, which leads them to reprehend, in the strongest manner, the infliction of any punishment, however well deserved. Believe me sir, this is a mistaken kindness." Unless a demonstration approaching extermination be inflicted upon these pirates, he argued, others would certainly take the cue, and no legitimate traders would be safe. Russwurm echoed Minor's call for a quick, violent punishment.

Early in 1842, Reverend John Wilson shifted the base of A.B.C.F.M. operations to Fishtown, where he built a new station on territory ceded him by the town's leaders. (His stay there would be brief, for Russwurm succeeded in showing the headmen that Wilson had dealt unfairly with them. Soon after, Wilson and most of the mission's staff sailed for Gabon

River, where they established a new mission.) While at Fishtown, Wilson placed Reverend Benjamin Griswold, newly arrived in Africa, in charge of operations at Fair Hope. Griswold had heard nothing but malice toward the colony and its officers, and when Russwurm shunned him he was confirmed in his hatred. He kept to himself, nursing a bitter grudge for injuries he never received.[11]

In August, Grebo thieves plundered Fair Hope. They took trade goods and a human skeleton that Griswold had purchased in the United States and brought to Cape Palmas for some obscure reason. He took his loss quietly, making no complaint to authorities. Even so, word quickly spread, and several urged the missionary to ask for help. He bluntly refused, telling John Banks, for example, "If the natives was to steel all that I have I never would go to your Govnor to get them for me and I ask no favers from aney one of you." Instead, he waited for some other opportunity to take revenge. Griswold investigated and suspected that Freeman was himself involved. His efforts to confront the king were fruitless, for he would never admit complicity. Griswold threatened retribution when an American warship next called.

During the summer of 1842, the United States Ship *Vandalia* cruised the African coast in search of slavers. Her captain, William Ramsay, learned of the *Mary Carver* piracy at Monrovia soon after the incident, and he immediately decided to retaliate. On September 2, the warship cast anchor two or three miles off the Cape. Her identity was something of a mystery, for no flags were visible in the rigging, but Greboes knew exactly what she was about. The same morning, King Freeman sacrificed a goat at a shrine in the bush, in the vain hope that it might keep the palaver off him. Captain Ramsay was too sick to come ashore, but he invited Russwurm and Launcelot Minor (who had returned to Mt. Vaughan from Tabou) to meet him aboard ship. The next day was stormy, but the two men braved the danger and rode out. They were disappointed to find that Ramsay had already fixed upon a stratagem. Apprehensive that a man-o'-war would scare the culprits away, he would use a decoy to catch them unaware. The captain of the *Atalanta*, which also lay off the Cape, was a willing volunteer. At Sinoe a few days before, he had been beaten in an argument over trade, and he was in a mood for revenge. Ramsay intended to send *Atalanta* ahead to Half Beriby with a squad of marines. With luck, they would draw some of the townsmen aboard and seize them as hostages, to force a palaver when the warship came up.

The *Vandalia* remained at Cape Palmas for a few days. Settlers revictualed her, and junior officers ventured on shore to satisfy their curiosity and get washing done. A naturalist gathered data on local flora and fauna. Their visits were friendly, and on September 5 and 6, several officers dined at the Agency House. Even so, their impressions of the colony were not entirely favorable. Griswold was particularly vocal, telling of his sufferings and emphasizing the failure of the colonial government to intervene on his behalf, which of course was only a half-truth. Officers were naturally sympathetic and relayed the story to Captain Ramsay, who offered to assist.

On Saturday morning, September 8, Lieutenant Ring and an orderly came ashore. They went straight to Fair Hope to meet Griswold, who called Minor and Savage from Mt. Vaughan. They then summoned Freeman to appear before them. At first, the king refused, as he was fearful of the missionary's threats. He asked the missionaries and officers to talk the palaver at Gbenelu, as befitted a man of his dignity. When they refused, he reluctantly went to Fair Hope with a few of his headmen. The palaver was a one-sided affair. Ring told Freeman he must give Griswold two bullocks for the skeleton and several hundred croos of rice for the other stolen items. Freeman argued that only Russwurm could make such a palaver with him, to no avail. At length, he promised to comply with the dictate. The officer told Freeman that he would return to make sure he upheld the settlement.

Captain Ramsay's principal concern, however, was Half Beriby, and his crew prepared for a show of force. Marines transferred to the *Atalanta*, and at dawn, September 11, the merchant hauled sail, taking a long lead on the *Vandalia*. The scheme might well have worked, but fortune was against them. The two vessels were separated, and Ramsay suffered the embarrassment of drifting by Half Beriby without recognizing the place. Several days' search yielded neither town nor *Atalanta*. He returned to Cape Palmas on September 19, fearing the worst. Russwurm offered him the services of Yellow Will, a competent pilot, and arranged to resupply the vessel with firewood and water.

While the *Vandalia* was away, Freeman had delivered two bullocks for Griswold's skeleton, together with six more bullocks and some rice to make up for the rest. Griswold rejected them, insisting on nothing less than the return of the stolen goods. When the warship returned, Griswold informed the captain that Greboes had not made restitution. Ramsay, frustrated by his failure, was ready to fight. He trusted Griswold and cheerfully agreed to send troops ashore.

Lieutenant Ring and a group of marines landed on September 23. Russwurm protested their trespass on colonial sovereignty, but they insisted. At a palaver, Freeman produced the goods he had offered Griswold a week before, but Ring was unmoved. He now demanded five hundred croos of rice to settle the matter. Freeman was indignant at the arbitrary ruling. He flatly refused to pay, whereupon Ring threatened to destroy Gbenelu. Freeman walked out of the meeting with his headmen. Two of the chief krumen of Gbenelu, one of whom was Freeman's half-brother, were taken hostage later that day as they delivered supplies to the *Vandalia*.

For two or three days both sides stood ready for war, Russwurm placed in the awkward necessity of having to defend Greboes against his own countrymen. On September 24, he sent Ramsay a copy of the colonial constitution and code of laws in an attempt to demonstrate the viability of his government and his right to settle the palaver without outside interference. Ramsay missed the point and returned the documents with a condescending note. He was determined to protect the mission, even if that jeopardized the government and lives of other Americans on shore.

On Sunday, the twenty-fifth, Freeman attended Roman Catholic services, contrary to his custom, rather than sit with the Protestants. After mass, Father Kelly offered him some money to help pay the debt. Freeman thanked him but declined the offer, saying, as Kelly recorded,

Suppose man-of-war go burn town well he may do that — all man glad to see it — suppose they come — all man must fight — if they be killed that be small thing. Because if they go pay this Palaver now *then it be law* — all time — then if two men choose steal, King must pay — if one Spoon be thieved then Missionary say pay or never mind it to that time man-of-war come — then we must pay two, three bullocks. Suppose man-of-war take them two men — they can do it — Mr. Griswold say, first time he came to do good — well he say come for God now it be not so — he accuse King — say King be thief.

Griswold, he concluded, would have to settle the dispute himself.

Lieutenant Ring came ashore a third time the next morning, in a pouring rain. He brought a party of marines with him, and it was reported that weapons were stowed in the boats in case the palaver was not set. In the event, Ring and Freeman negotiated more favorable terms, namely six bullocks and three hundred croos of rice, to be paid at an unspecified time. Although Gbenelu was terrified as long as the warship rode in the offing, the crisis was passed.

Savage and Minor were widely blamed for inciting Griswold to his uncompromising course. "Muskets are too light for such gentlemen," Ambrose Simpson, a carpenter, commented penetratingly in a conversation with Father Kelly. "They seem to prefer the cannon. They hate the colored man and show it more here than in America." The missionaries' inconsistency was remarkable, at once refusing to let their employees perform military service and appealing to a warship to smash the very people they wanted to convert.

—◦—

Ford McGill sailed for the United States at the end of May, 1842. He hoped to pursue a romance begun in Baltimore in 1838. The young girl's parents were then firmly opposed to their daughter moving to the wild shores of Africa and forbade the marriage. Letters from Baltimore now indicated that they had relented.[12]

In Baltimore, McGill was an ardent advocate of colonization. In private conversations, public meetings, and letters to newspaper editors, he advanced a radical and new African American identity gathered from diverse strands of personal experience, colonization and missionary rhetoric, acquaintances, and the personal philosophy of his father, all synthesized through his own genius. He voiced a Pan-African ideology fully twenty-five years before Alexander Crummell, Edward W. Blyden, Martin Delany, and others made it the center of black intellectual activity. Indeed, McGill later had contacts with all three men and cannot have failed to influence them. He loved controversy and would express himself as a free man in whatever circumstances he felt moved.[13]

When he arrived in Baltimore, McGill found the society in an acrimonious argument with the A.B.C.F.M. Having received unfavorable reports from John Wilson, the Congregationalists corresponded with the Maryland Colonization Society. The colonizationists tried to conciliate, but they found that their concessions only exacerbated difficulties in the colony. The missionary society appointed a panel, chaired by Chancellor R. H. Walworth, an outstanding New York jurist, to consider the situation. Their report reviewed the dispute at Cape Palmas, questioning the intentions of the colonization society and settlers. The committee stated that it could overlook the colonial insistence on military service, and also the restrictions on trade, but the problems ran deeper. The different aims of colonists and missionaries, though each was natural and justified, were incapable of being ameliorated. It was "perfectly natural" that the colony's government would concern itself with the settlers' temporal needs, just as the missionaries devoted themselves to the spiritual. The panel concluded that "The result of such a conflict of interests and of duties, between the colonists and missionaries, has been, in this case, to render the colonists hostile, both to the native inhabitants of the coast and to the missionaries who are labouring for the spiritual welfare of such natives; and thus to render a removal of the mission necessary as well as expedient."

The A.B.C.F.M. accepted the recommendation and resolved to withdraw from Maryland at the first opportunity. The matter would have ended there, buried in private annals, a subject of bitter memory at Harper, but the report of Walworth's committee appeared in *The New England Puritan* on September 22, 1842, eliciting strident protests from Baltimore and Harper.[14]

Doctor McGill defended his fellow citizens in a caustic letter to the *Puritan's* editor. "I am aware," he wrote, "that the bare assertions of an humble colored man, banished by a cruel prejudice from his native land, and who has sought a home in barbarous Africa, can have but little weight when thrown in the balance against the dicta of the congregated learning and piety of the most intelligent body of Christians in the United States." He then challenged the veracity of Walworth's report, asserting the colonial view. The root of the problem, he said, was "the extreme aversion on the part of the white missionary to be subject to the authority of a colored man." Certainly, settlers concerned with survival could not work at evangelization to the same degree as clergymen, yet they were not opposed to missions. Moreover, as a community, they achieved more by example and worked more good toward Africans than all the missions together.[15]

While Samuel McGill offered an intellectual rationale for colonization in Baltimore, three other citizens of Cape Palmas who had accompanied him to America visited their old neighborhoods with even greater effect. Stephen Smith, Joshua Cornish, and John Bordely were simple men. They bore testimony that colonization was not a trick to sell them into slavery in the Deep South, that Africa was not a land of snakes, burning sands, and cannibals; and that black Americans might make an independent life there. To their old friends and acquaintances, most of them ignorant agricultural workers with limited geographical knowledge, they provided more convincing proof than all the other propaganda combined. The bark *Globe*, which left Baltimore on December 23, 1842, carried 110 emigrants, the largest company yet to sail to Cape Palmas. The society hoped that this marked the beginning of a growing exodus.[16]

Stephen Smith, formerly a free blacksmith, was particularly successful in St. Mary's County, where he persuaded James Lauder to emi-

grate. Lauder, patriarch of an extensive family, had very little education, but with hard work and an honest reputation he had acquired
considerable property, including boats that ferried the broad Potomac
River. He had wished to go to Africa for some time, but his wife was too
much attached to her home. Stephen Smith answered each of her objections, and the family packed up. Twenty-eight relatives boarded the
ship with Thomas Lauder. Lauder also loaned Smith three hundred
dollars to buy one of his children from bondage.

Bernard Dean, a slaveholding farmer from Anne Arundel County,
sent out ten of his people. He had offered all the rest the same opportunity, but they refused. For those who chose to leave, he stripped his
house of furniture, tools, clothing, and other items that he thought
they might want. Though an old man, who had not spent a night away
from home for years, he accompanied his former property to Baltimore and stayed with them until the vessel sailed. Reportedly, they all
shed tears at parting.

The voyage of the *Globe* was horrible. The captain did what he
could to alleviate conditions, but with little effect. During the first two
weeks, the bark made good progress, but then the weather turned.
Water had been shipped in dirty whale-oil casks, and emigrants could
hardly use it. Living quarters were cramped and perpetually damp.
Seasick, listless passengers were unable to keep them clean. Mumps,
measles, and whooping cough then broke out. Moses Ashton, a man in
his forties, died of pleurisy. Then Margaret Lauder, in an advanced
stage of pregnancy, progressed from seasickness to constipation, mis-
carriage, peritonitis, and death. Her husband, James Lauder, pierced
his foot on an old nail. The wound seemed to heal, but infection developed, followed by gangrene and death shortly after landfall. At
Monrovia, one of Lauder's nieces, a girl of fourteen, fell through a
hatchway while playing on deck. She struck her head on the rim of a
barrel. Although she would recover, her skull was fractured, and she
remained helpless the rest of her life.[17]

The emigrants' ordeal did not end at landfall. Russwurm was unprepared for so many. The frame receptacles built in 1834 were de-

signed to hold seventy at most, and years of rain and insects had almost ruined them. The overflow were placed in scattered houses, which made it hard to provide everyone with rations and medical attention. Dempsey Fletcher, McGill's assistant, fell dangerously ill and was of little help. Moreover, McGill had to fire several nurses for disobedience. As a result, some of the company died needlessly. At the end of June, twelve of 110 had died. Sally Brooks, age thirty-eight, died three days after delivering a daughter, of complications including her first bout of malaria. Cornelia Denton died of fever that would not respond to treatment. Her infant son followed a week later. Two other children died with severe intestinal parasite infestations, complicated by misdiagnosis. On arrival at Harper, McGill administered anthelmintics. They expelled so many worms, he assumed they were cured. The boys played outside together one day, then fell sick that night. McGill treated them for heat stroke, with fatal results. Autopsies revealed the actual cause, and McGill advised the society to clear children of worms before the voyage. A lightning bolt took James Watts, one of the ill-fated Lauder clan, just a few days after landing. McGill dispensed unusually large amounts of quinine, so much in fact that he ran low and then did without it for the last third of the year.[18]

Russwurm placed most of the new emigrants on disused lots within the settlement. Since 1834 many settlers had failed to make use of their land, and working farmers complained of the rough appearance so much wilderness gave the settlement. Everyone agreed that a compact settlement was necessary for defensive reasons, even if the society in Baltimore wished to have a broader area surveyed as farms. "We are in a land of savages," Russwurm wrote, "and your infant colony must not be jeopardized by overhastiness on the part of your Agent." Suggestions were made at home and in the colony to reorder the settlement into compact villages at strategic locations, the farm plots radiating from these hubs, but in fact it was too late to do so.[19]

In January 1843, George McGill secretly married Lucinda Stephens, a woman many years younger than himself, who had earned a scandalous reputation during her first years at Cape Palmas. The old man believed that she had been led astray. "Her reform was evident to me," he wrote James Hall later, "beside she being one of the handiest weamen in liberia." The *Globe* carried the proud son, Ford, to Harper with his beautiful young wife, Lydia. "He wished all the Famley to Fall down and worship, her and him," George complained. When Ford learned what the old man had done, he was seized with jealousy. "He told me that I was an infurnal old Fool," George wrote, "ordering me to kick my wife out of doors and carried on to such a rate untill I could not bare it any longer and to take my cane and foot, to him."

Ford made his grievance public, spawning much gossip. George McGill then retired from public life and occupied himself with trade. His wife conceived soon after and bore him a son on November 21. Though he did well enough to support his new family, he was embittered by his loss of prestige. "I attribute the whole to Dr. Sam he has got to be such a big learned carrecter that it has made him a fool." He remained steadfast in his choice of wife. Ford remained estranged, though he was afterward a little ashamed of his impiety.[20]

Ford McGill suffered the extreme disappointment of losing his new wife on July 12, 1843, concluding a lingering illness that had defied his best efforts. The board was informed of her death, but McGill did not write of it for several more months. When he received the society's condolences, he thanked them for their sympathy, though it revived the grief that he had begun to put away. He had wrestled with remorse for having brought his love to a place where he knew she would fall ill and perhaps die prematurely, and yet he "could not have acted otherwise. I could not or rather would not have resided in the United States nor could I have left one of my race there for whom affection was entertained. I would have sacrificed much very much to have averted danger, but my liberty would have been a sacrifice entirely too great." Indeed, liberty was his consuming passion, and he was too much his own man to sacrifice that, whether to his wife or father.[21]

———•———

Among the board's dispatches by the *Globe*, Russwurm received strong praise for his handling of the crisis with the *Vandalia*. Latrobe promised to take up the matter with the A.B.C.F.M. and to set things straight with the United States Navy. The agent responded that American officers should not intervene on shore unless authorities asked them to do so. He wrote, "None can be more sensible than I am, that the most friendly feelings should be cultivated between the colonial Governments and the officers commanding the different vessels. The interests of the colonies require it: and the best of every thing that could be procured, has ever been placed at their service." The success of the antislavery patrols depended on cooperation with those on shore, and Ramsay's high-handed activities served no good end.[22]

Even though the A.B.C.F.M. had resolved in 1842 to cease activity at Cape Palmas, they maintained a presence well into 1843. In a letter of June 24, Ford McGill reported that they were finally leaving. He regretted that things had gone so far, but he was resigned to it, writing, "It is necessary that the Colonial Government in Maryland in Liberia should exercise the supremacy, as far as accords with our Constitution, and when the exercise of this supremacy becomes offensive to those who reside within our Colonial Jurisdiction, *they must* evacuate the premises." He hoped that the whole experience would be a lesson, and that good relations would be maintained with missions henceforth. Russwurm was quite relieved at the news that the A.B.C.F.M. would soon be only a bad memory. He asked the board not to offer their station to any other missionary society. Harper was expanding, and settlers could better use the six-acre site, prime real estate near the beach. "Let [their lands] form part of our township, as they already do naturally," he wrote, "and the name of '*Fair Hope*' die." [23]

XII.

"Powder and Ball Diplomacy"

IN JULY 1843, THE GREBO STATES HELD A GRAND PALAVER AT HALF CAVALLY, at which the host town urged united action to raise the price of rice and other produce. The effort failed, largely because Gbenelu would not support it. Afterward, Russwurm fined Half Cavally for disloyalty, failing to recognize that the movement was something new and posed a serious threat. "Recent events teach them that they will be held to a more strict accountability as the colony increases in strength," he confidently told Latrobe. He asserted that the colony's progress was a model for Africa. "If this is a continent ever to be civilized," he wrote, "God has decreed, that the work is to be accomplished by Colored men, who are to be the pioneers in planting colonies and schools in all quarters — and doing all of the efficient labor towards carrying forward this great end. The mere teaching of letters, without a knowledge of some mechanical art, will never civilize a savage — he must also be taught to support himself as a civilized Being — in which state, he has a hundred more wants, for all of which he must be able to provide." Instead of growing jealous, Africans should adopt new habits, he reasoned. Greboes, of course, thought differently. Half Cavally regarded the agent's fine as insolent—no foreigner would dictate their policy— and they worried that his influence was growing too much.[1]

King Freeman assembled the governments of the several Grebo

states at Gbenelu early in November, 1843. Since July's congress, the king had concluded that they must do something to contain American influence. The Grebo monopoly of inland trade had eroded steadily over the past few years, to the benefit of Americans. Moreover, the supply and quality of trade goods was so high that interior markets were saturated; consequently, prices had slipped. All Greboes had a stake in the question of trade, but none so much as Gbenelu, at the epicenter of American activity. Hence the second congress at Cape Palmas, which for the first time united the Grebo people in one purpose.[2]

For four weeks, delegates publicly talked various palavers and privately discussed ways to restore the old balance of trade. Some settlers speculated that the outcome of these talks would be war or some other adversity, but Russwurm relied on his friend Freeman's word, that trade was not in contention. He believed that July's failure at Half Cavally would discourage any attempt at union. Russwurm even hoped to use the palaver to expand camwood trade. This was the very root of the problem, however, and the mere mention of free trade with the bush fanned flames of jealousy and resentment.

On Saturday, December 2, Greboes invited Russwurm to address the convention. He declined, having much to do in the office and thinking that little would transpire that day. He was mistaken, for the critical question of how to restrain the colony was broached. The next day, a delegation called on him while he and McGill were engaged in some business. Freeman was conspicuously absent. He dared not show his face when Russwurm realized the mendacity. The Greboes enumerated new prices, two to three times higher across the board. That these strangers should interrupt his work and dictate to him made Russwurm furious. He told them he "would sooner eat grass" than pay, then threw them out of the office.

The Grebo congress reacted angrily when they heard how the governor had responded. If he wanted a fight, they blustered, they were ready to give him one. They approved a list of harsh restrictions, illustrative of the interdependence of the two peoples. Henceforth, natives would be prohibited from performing any sort of labor for the colonists, and all children and laborers should retire to their homes. No native would be permitted to carry messages to or from colonists and missionaries, nor could they board vessels or land cargo. Anyone caught breaking these rules would be steeply fined on the first offense, and on the second expelled from the Grebo tribe. Every Grebo "shall do all in his, her, or their power" to prevent colonists and missionaries from procuring wood and water, "and to starve them into an agreement with the demands of the Tribe." The same night, the delegates dispersed, hoping to distance themselves from a palaver that might well end in violence. Freeman, secretly responsible for the price increases, was left with the burden of having to enforce them. Though he had promises of military assistance from all the beach towns, he knew that he could not count on them.

The embargo was evident to settlers the next day. Grebo workers did not appear at their usual jobs, and traders ceased to bring in produce for sale. Russwurm alerted the militia and placed extra guards at the Agency Store, as he had done often enough before, expecting that a little sabre-rattling was all that was wanted. Rice and other staples were in good supply. The colony could hold out for some time. Later in the morning, the governor met Freeman and demanded the new laws' repeal. If Freeman would not comply, he threatened, Greboes must leave Gbenelu, for they and Americans could no longer live together. Freeman made no substantive answer and went home. Women and children quickly evacuated Gbenelu, leaving the *sedibo* to prepare a defense. The situation continued thus for three or four tense days. Any accident might have initiated hostilities. Freeman called for reinforcements from other towns, but as he had suspected, none arrived, which was fortunate for the cause of peace.[3]

Meanwhile, the colony had help on the way, for the U.S. Navy's African Squadron, under command of Commodore Matthew C. Perry, was nearing Cape Palmas. In 1840 the United States and Great Britain had nearly gone to war, primarily because of disagreements over the Canadian border. America's role in the slave trade was also at issue. Britain was expending huge sums patrolling the African coast while the United States, which had equated the slave trade with piracy in 1807, still did nothing, even winking at surreptitious cargoes that arrived on the Gulf Coast. Americans had a deep-seated resentment of British warships stopping and searching their vessels for contraband. In negotiations, Daniel Webster conceded to Lord Ashburton that Americans should make a more effective stand against the trade. Specifically, the United States agreed to devote several warships with a total of eighty or more guns to hunt for slavers.[4]

April 1843 found Commodore Perry at the Brooklyn Navy Yard outfitting the newly formed African Squadron. The assignment was a back-handed punishment, for his Democratic politics did not sit well with the Whig administration of John Tyler. Even so, Perry had a personal interest in Liberia, having participated in the original purchase of Cape Mesurado some twenty years before. A confirmed enemy of slavery, he resolutely undertook the task.

The squadron consisted of four vessels. The largest was the sloop *Macedonian*, Captain Mayo, of thirty-six guns, which the *Constitution* had captured in a famous engagement during the War of 1812. Next in size was the sloop-of-war *Saratoga*, Captain Tatnall, of twenty-two guns. The sloop *Decatur*, Commander Abbot, rated sixteen guns. The lightly armed brig *Porpoise*, Lieutenant Commander Lewis, was a supply ship. She was the first to leave for the African coast. On June 5, 1843, Perry boarded the *Saratoga*, which immediately hoisted sail, the *Decatur* close in her wake. The *Macedonian* would follow as soon as ready. In July the squadron made Porto Praya in the Cape de Verde Islands their base, then sailed for the coast.[5]

At Monrovia early in August, Perry met with Governor Roberts and others to discuss commerce, the slave trade, and retaliation for various acts of piracy, including the attack on the *Mary Carver*.[6] Perry concluded that immediate action in any of these cases was impractical, not least because of the oncoming rainy season, with its dangerous surf. The commodore was not one to waste time. Since the rest of the squadron had assembled, he ordered his command to leeward on patrol. He sent the *Decatur*, fastest of the vessels, to Fernando Poo. The *Macedonian*, *Saratoga*, and *Porpoise* would move together at a slower pace to call at various points along the Liberian shore. They hove to off Cape Palmas on August 10 and stayed two days to collect information about Half Beriby and the crime there. Perry was inclined to assist the colony, and Russwurm gave him a tour with long discourses on Maryland's military and economic situation.[7] The *Macedonian*'s purser, Horatio Bridge, had been one of Russwurm's classmates at Bowdoin, and they struck up a friendship that the reclusive Jamaican had evaded seventeen years before. On August 12 the three warships returned to windward. Perry argued with Captain Tatnall during the cruise, and soon after, the commodore made the *Macedonian* his flagship.

The vessels returned to Porto Praya for supplies. At Praya the squadron suffered the loss of the supply ship *Renown*, which foundered in the harbor.[8] A fair breeze on the night of October 12 carried the *Macedonian* and *Decatur* toward the coast once again. They planned to rendezvous with the rest of the squadron at Monrovia in mid-November, but light winds and opposing currents delayed their arrival until the twenty-second. The time had now come to set palavers all along the coast. Governor Roberts and other prominent Liberians boarded the *Macedonian* for the cruise.[9]

On November 28, the three warships rode off Sinoe, a slave market just a few years before. Three parties now contested the ownership and trade of the spot. A handful of Americans occupied Greenville. Bassas, more numerous, inhabited several towns along the beach nearby. Fishmen, former brokers of the slave trade, held two or three other towns. Settlers and Bassas wanted the Fishmen chastised (or rather, driven off) on the pretext of a recent attack on an American merchant ship, *Edward Burley*.[10] Perry was of a different opinion. "The natives have been as much sinned against as sinning," he wrote the secretary of the navy on September 5. "The Government at home hear but one side of the story. It is not known there that the Masters of trading vessels often maltreat the Natives, it is in proof that Towns and fishing boats have been fired into, and lives destroyed, and that the Natives of one tribe at war with another, have been carried and delivered up to their enemies."[11] He was determined to have a fair hearing of the case. Colonial officials and a number of witnesses were called from Greenville to provide what information they could. At sunrise, November 29, the commodore reviewed the case with his senior officers, who also had heard the testimony. With one exception, they felt that the *Burley*'s captain had provoked the incident, but that the resulting deaths were uncalled for. Perry requested their opinions in writing.[12]

The commodore arranged to hold a palaver on shore that morning, confident that the affair could be settled without bloodshed. "We left our ships with thirteen boats, flags flying, muskets glistening, and the oarsmen pulling the short, regular man-of-war's stroke," Horatio Bridge, the purser, wrote. "Having landed, an escort of seventy-five marines, with the band playing, proceeded Commodore Perry, Governor Roberts and several other officers . . . to the Methodist Church where the palaver was held." The proud martial display went largely unnoticed, for most of the Fishmen had fled to the bush in fear of an attack. In the church, the officers found settlers, Bassas, and Fishmen. The Fishmen were outnumbered and outvoiced. One, called Prince John Smith, was accused before the assembly of having instigated the fight. He bolted but was seized, and chances for an easy settlement of the palaver diminished.[13]

Perry held another palaver on November 30, but no Fishman dared present himself. Their towns were deserted. Bassas proposed an alliance to drive the Fishmen from the coast altogether. Perry reluctantly decided that expulsion was the only solution, and the next day he formalized plans. On December 1, his men burned the Fishmen villages and warned that any attempt to rebuild them would meet with violence. Governor Roberts reported to the American Colonization Society: "The colonists appeared really overjoyed to be rid of the Fishmen, said they would now have some chance of raising live stock and cultivating their farms with some degree of success and not run the risk of being robbed of every thing they could raise." Still, the outcome irked Perry. It was contrary to his expectations and violated his instructions not to interfere in colonial politics.[14]

The squadron left Sinoe on the morning of December 2 and reached Settra Kroo about noon. They found the place in mourning for a missionary who had died from a heat stroke the day before. "The flags of the ships were at half-mast during the funeral ceremony," wrote Roberts, "and the officers of the squadron paid every attention to their afflicted country woman." Dr. J. Lawrence Day, a Methodist missionary seeking a respite from the commotion of Monrovian politics, chose to remain for a season to help run the school.[15]

On December 4, the squadron remained at Settra Kroo to seek restitution for the beating of Captain Brown of the *Atalanta* in 1842. The Kru headmen were eager to make a quick settlement, as they knew that their reputation had caused trade to suffer. The threat of such awesome military force as stood offshore was also persuasive. At a palaver that morning, the commodore warned the assembled kings and headmen that the United States would not tolerate violence toward American citizens or their property. America was prepared to defend them, no matter how far from home. The Kru chiefs answered that the attack was indeed unprovoked. They would have punished the perpetrator, but he had run away. Perry demanded a written apology to the American government and a personal apology to Captain Brown on his next visit to the town. He further demanded ten bullocks, five goats, and four sheep for the squadron's use. Their cash value would be paid to Brown as an indemnity. All was quickly agreed, papers drawn up and signed, and the livestock tendered. Before the palaver broke up, Governor Roberts offered to purchase Settra Kroo. This met with a lukewarm reception, and when he admitted that he had no money or goods with him, they rejected the proposal. They promised to offer Liberia the option to buy their country, if they should ever choose to sell. Perry and his officers stayed out of the discussion.[16]

The squadron left Settra Kroo for Cape Palmas, unaware of the dangerous state of affairs there. About noon on December 6, the

Macedonian hailed the Cape. An inexpertly managed canoe approached them from shore. The Reverend Mr. Hazlehurst, an Episcopal missionary, came aboard with an excited narrative, confirmed by a gloomy letter from Russwurm. The *Decatur* was flagged on to Half Cavally before anchoring, and Perry prepared his command for action. The day was too far advanced for a landing—the commodore refused to allow his men on shore in the evening because of increased risk of fever. Instead, he sent a reassuring message to Russwurm in the hands of Governor Roberts, who had no qualms about being on shore. All hands prepared for a palaver and possible fight in the morning.[17]

Some months before, the Episcopal mission had moved its headquarters from Mt. Vaughan to Half Cavally to distance itself from the colony. Mr. Hazlehurst remained at the old station to maintain the church and school. Dr. Savage took charge of the former A.B.C.F.M. post at Fishtown. John Payne supervised these stations and outlying schools and chapels from Half Cavally. Despite reorganization, the mission was an integral element of politics on the beach, and the congress at Gbenelu had serious repercussions. The *Mary Carver* massacre would have gone unknown but for the proximity of Launcelot Minor, who had since died. The pirates threatened the mission directly, and the missionaries demanded colonial or American military intervention on their behalf.[18]

While they waited for retaliation, the missionaries at Cavalla Station went about their usual work. Their letters home, usually hopeful, swelled with enthusiasm as the harvest of 1843 approached. Occasionally they hinted that not all was well. Early in October, Liverpool, one of the head trademen of the town and a friend of the mission, died. "There has never been such a display of wealth at any burial," Mrs. Payne commented in a letter, adding that his death would increase political tensions. "A great deal of gidu will no doubt be given." On October 25, Payne wrote happily, "There is now seldom any loud talking or laughing during religious service, as formerly." Two weeks later, though, he noted a marked reduction in attendance, which he attributed to house-thatching season. Such sabbath-breaking was a common disappointment of his work. Sunday, November 12, his congregation evaporated for more serious reasons. The day before, an English merchant commenced trade, offering desirable goods quite cheaply. When he learned of the mission on shore, he sent a package of newspapers as a present. Payne responded with a note of thanks and an invitation to dinner the next day. At daybreak, trade resumed, but the Briton offered poorer goods—totally unacceptable to the Grebo trademen, who knew that better materials were at hand. They returned to shore blaming Payne and ordered that no one should hear the God palaver that day. Gnebui, Payne's interpreter and the bearer of the offending correspondence, was also punished with the prodigious fine of $100, beyond the means of even the richest Grebo. After a tedious palaver at which Payne and the captain both pleaded for the man, they settled for the whole of his possessions, valued at six dollars.

The matter did not end with that. Next morning, as the mission family sat at breakfast, a mob of men and boys brandishing machetes entered the mission grounds to drive away the students and African workers. The missionaries coolly finished their meal, prepared to wait out the palaver. By Tuesday, November 14, a few of the children and workers had stolen back, and the imminent threat subsided. Payne complained to the *gnekbade*, the town's senate, who were preparing to leave for the congress at Gbenelu. He had been persecuted with no opportunity to hear or answer the charges against him. The *sedibo* must not interfere with his students or employees, for they were entitled to sanctuary by custom. As for female students, he had paid the bride-price for each one, and they were his to govern with all the privileges of a husband. The *sedibo* had no more right to force off his students than they had to divide families. The *gnekbade* sympathized with him and restored the girls to the mission, though they could do nothing to get the boys back. Payne refused to set the palaver until they returned, too.

The *sedibo* rejected the decision of the *gnekbade* and resented Payne's appeal over their heads. To retaliate, they raised the pitch of the confrontation. At 8 o'clock on the evening of November 15, they adjourned a meeting in town and rushed the mission gate in an intimidating demonstration. There they decreed a series of injunctions. No Americans could preach in their towns, and Christian meetings of all sorts were banned. They declared mission property off limits to all the boys of Half Cavally. Boys were no longer permitted to wear western clothing but instead must go naked, or dressed as others their age. Finally, books and reading were outlawed. Thursday, all of the schoolbooks in Half Cavally were confiscated and dropped at the mission gate.

For nearly three weeks, the *sedibo* and missionaries at Half Cavally remained in a standoff, while the Grebo nation held its congress. Payne busied himself with little jobs and preached to his colleagues and the few brave girls and boys who had sneaked back. The finale of the palaver at Cape Palmas precipitated a crisis. United behind Freeman to restrain the growth of American power, and as well to raise the price of rice and other produce, the *sedibo* imposed more weightily on the mission. On the afternoon of Thursday, December 5, they entered the premises once again to drive away the boys and workers. No argument could soften their position, and Payne was promised only that the girls could remain. Within minutes, though, this was a dead letter, for a mob rushed the mission house and dragged out the girls. Two who had hidden under their beds were later sent out to prevent another onslaught.

Friday began quietly, and the beleaguered missionaries took stock of their situation. "We find ourselves located in a tribe which has determined to break up all our schools — refused to hear us preach — to interpret for us — to sell us any thing," Payne wrote in his journal. The palaver was obviously calculated to achieve economic ends, like many others, but the current one seemed more dangerous than any before. Greboes had abandoned their usual respect for the missions. They were for the first time united under one leader. They had entirely deserted the American settlement, a sure portent of war. Payne continued, "It is reported that the Colony and natives at Cape Palmas are on the eve of engaging in war. In this event shall we not be necessarily involved? Under these circumstances had we not better move? But then how can we? Mrs. Payne cannot walk to Cape Palmas, the natives will not take her, and she has no conveyance thither."

After breakfast, Payne and the Reverend Mr. Smith, whose school at Cavally River Greboes had broken up the day before, discussed their options. They decided that Smith should take Payne's horse and make for Cape Palmas. Payne would stay to defend the mission and quietly prepare to evacuate if he found opportunity. Smith left on his errand soon after. He rode up the beach unmolested, though the staff at Cavalla Station could not know whether he was safe or not. They packed their belongings and prayed for relief. Encouragement came early in the afternoon with news that the African Squadron was approaching Cape Palmas—help would surely come the next day.

When Smith reached the settlement, he went directly to Hazlehurst at Mt. Vaughan. His excited statement of affairs at Cavalla so agitated Hazlehurst that as soon as the warships' sails were sighted he set out to meet them. No African would help him with the boat, so three settlers paddled him across the surf to meet the *Macedonian* even as she cast anchor. Hazlehurst impressed Perry with his vivid description of the perilous situation at Half Cavally. The commodore signaled the *Decatur*, which had not yet come to anchor, to go to the rescue.[19] "We were not a little surprized," Payne related, "as we stood upon our piazza, and were looking out by a beautiful moonlight upon the sea, to observe a large vessel moving down majestically from the windward, and presently come to anchor off our house." Certain the ship belonged to the squadron, Payne was preparing for bed when at 10:30 he was startled by a loud rap at the front door. On opening it he found "four kroomen . . . in man-of-war dress," who delivered two letters, one from Hazlehurst, and the other from Captain Abbot of the *Decatur*, who offered any assistance Payne thought warranted. The missionary asked for an armed force to land in the morning, as there could very well be a confrontation.

At 9 o'clock in the morning on December 7, Captain Abbot came ashore with marines and hired African seamen (krumen) in four of the ship's large boats and two smaller craft. Payne pushed through a throng to welcome his rescuers. They returned to the mission for breakfast and to plan a strategy. Later, they called the town's leaders to the school-house for a palaver. Abbot argued Payne's case, but to no avail. Nothing remained but to withdraw the mission. The Americans emerged to gather their baggage. Payne believed that the whole of the town's population of four thousand was on the beach to watch. They did so in amazement as soldiers carried boxes and trunks from the buildings and stowed them in the boats. A few broke from the crowd to beg the missionaries to stay. The king himself, called Yellow Will, promised Mrs. Payne that no harm would come, that the palaver would be set the next day at Cape Palmas. His assurances were worthless, and the Americans were determined to leave. Gnebui, the interpreter, who had fallen gravely ill during the previous week and was near death, was brought up in a hammock by his family just as the boats were about to pull from the beach. Payne took him aboard, and the boats plunged through the breakers. The next morning, the *Decatur* anchored off Cape Palmas, the missionaries glad to land and have the protection they had once shunned.[20]

Early on December 7, the *Macedonian*'s Lieutenant Poor went to Harper to schedule a palaver for 10 A.M. Russwurm approved, but Freeman protested that the other Grebo kings should also be present. He suggested postponing the palaver to the next day. The officer returned to his ship to report and Perry agreed to schedule the meeting for the same time on the morrow. Later in the day, Perry came ashore with a force of marines. Leaving sailors at the wharf to look after their nine boats, the troops marched with their officers to the Agency House, where they performed an impressive drill, complete with musket salutes. The colonial militia, not to be outdone, also paraded, with musketry.[21]

Perry, Russwurm, and others then went inside to talk. The agent had suffered tremendous strain during the confrontation, and he unburdened himself to Perry. He stated that Harper and Gbenelu could no longer be neighbors, and he asked Perry's help to force Freeman to move his towns to the other side of Hoffman's River. Perry, however, would not be used as Roberts had used him at Sinoe, to intervene in local disputes. He assured Russwurm that his squadron would protect the colony but flatly refused to be involved in the private goals of the colonization society.

The governor labored with him, but after a few minutes, Perry's mind wandered. He absorbed the view from the Agency House window—American clapboard houses and thatched African ones along Maryland Avenue; the backdrop of lush green hills; the still, shining waters of Lake Sheppard, on its shore a crowd of Greboes; the surf pounding on the beach; and his warships a short distance offshore—but what were all those people doing there by the lake, he suddenly asked, interrupting Russwurm's harangue. McGill told him that a headman of one of the smaller Cape Palmas villages, one who was sympathetic to the colony, was suffering *gidu* for a rival's death. Russwurm was hardened to such occurrences, but Perry immediately rose to do something about it. He gathered his officers and men, who were eager for action. With McGill, they ran to the scene, undaunted by news that the man was nearly dead. Greboes had enough warning to put their victim in a canoe and paddle into the lake. Perry argued with the chief persecutor, and in frustration grabbed him by the neck. Marines seized one or two more, whereupon the dying man was surrendered. McGill and two ship's doctors forced him to vomit, which saved his life. Perry and his men returned to Harper roused by the adventure.[22]

Meanwhile, six militiamen stood guard at Mt. Tubman, the rest having gone to their farms for provisions to sell to the squadron. As they watched, about ten Barrawe men, all in war dress and armed, emerged from the woods and asked permission to go to Gbenelu to attend the funeral of Tom Freeman, the king's brother, who had died the previous week. The guards were suspicious, remembering how

Barrawe soldiers had slipped by them and murdered Eben Parker in 1838. They also knew that Tom Freeman's funeral had been held a day or two earlier. They demanded that the men lay down their arms if they wished to pass. The Africans refused and backed away, guns raised. As they did so, guards on the palisade spied a larger force, later estimated at about fifty men, moving in the bush. An attack seemed certain. Three of the guards leveled their muskets and fired. Three men fell dead. The Barrawe soldiers fled so quickly that they were out of range before a cannon could be trained on them. Used to warfare with their neighbors, they were unprepared for their American opponents to target them rather than fire randomly.

The day had now advanced to mid-afternoon. Back at Harper, Russwurm had ordered a fine luncheon, and tables were set as Perry and his men returned from Lake Sheppard. Before they could fairly seat themselves, a messenger ran in from Mt. Tubman, breathless with news that an attack was underway, skirmishers advancing on the frontier. Everyone jumped at once, and in a moment they were on the march to the east end of the settlement. Horatio Bridge reported with lively detail:

> Passing by the foot of Mt. Vaughan, we came to Mt. Tubman, ascended a steep conical hill, perhaps 100 feet high and found ourselves on a level space of 100 yards in diameter. In the center stood a solitary house, and surrounding the plain was a strong picket fence, not more than five feet high, 15 or 16 men were on the *qui vive* and the piazzo was crowded with women and children. Within the dwelling were some 20 or 25 children, ignorant of danger and in high glee. A blind old man sat apart by the wall, silently grasping his staff with feeble hand, and near him was a sick woman who had been brought in from a farm in the vicinity. The first alarm had driven the whole population to shelter within the stockade. On the side opposite the cape a steep path rose abruptly to the gate. Down this, some 20 yards, lay a native, dead, with an ugly hole in his skull; and in a small path to the right lay another, who had died where he fell, from a bullet wound in the center of his forehead. The ball had cut the ligature which bound his "gregree" of shells around his head, and the faithless charm was on the ground near him. The flies were already clustering about the dead man's mouth, and I was not unwilling to leave the spot.[23]

Afterward, Barrakah maintained that their purpose had been pacific, but the whole colony believed that the bushmen had heard the salutes fired when the marines landed that morning and presumed that war had begun, that they had come to the beach to assist their Grebo allies in the fight or participate in the plunder. The marines inspected the battlefield, but little remained for them to do, for the militia was in control. Evening approached, and Perry ordered his men to the boats.

Before leaving, Perry reminded King Freeman of their conversation three months before. Then, Freeman had wholeheartedly professed his affection for Americans. Now he was at the point of war with them. The king protested the charge of duplicity, claiming that the whole Grebo confederation was responsible for the laws, and that he opposed them. He promised to try to have them repealed. There the matter stood for the night.

A palaver convened the next morning, as appointed. The incident at Mt. Tubman the day before, combined with the presence of well-armed marines, intimidated Freeman and his colleagues. Russwurm also felt a little restrained, for he knew that Perry would not support a bid to force the removal of Gbenelu. Though the outcome was largely determined in advance, each side recited grievances, legitimate and otherwise, in tiresome detail.[24] Perry listened quietly to the proceedings. When his turn came, he lectured as if to children, ordering Greboes to restore free trade at the old prices and to shake hands and be friends with their American neighbors. Greboes appeared to agree, asserting that the price increases were merely a misunderstanding. Perry then admonished the Africans to treat missionaries fairly and closed the palaver. No one, with the exception of Perry and his officers, believed that such momentous questions could be settled by fiat. Both sides remained at arms for several days.[25]

Russwurm and Ford McGill, his brother-in-law and advisor, had opposite ideas how to proceed. The previous few weeks had exhausted the agent, and he was glad for peace under any circumstances. He believed that the palaver was mostly bluff and would be given up, like so many others, if met with equal bravado. "The arrival of the United

States Squadron on this coast is a new era to us — it has instilled new vigor into every heart and I trust the result will show an improved state of things," he commented in a letter of January 12. Ford McGill, by contrast, wanted to thrash Freeman for his insolence. He was even sorry that the squadron had arrived when it did. "I was and am yet of the opinion that if any fighting *must* be done, we should do it ourselves, as we cannot always have the assistance of an American vessel of war. But for the arrival of the squadron our position was such that we must have driven off these Natives, or have been broken up. I know not how a war with them would terminate, but judge from the bold fronts displayed by our men that we might, nay *certainly would* whip them."

The squadron now prepared to make a demonstration upon Half Beriby. Perry asked Russwurm to come along, but he declined, urging McGill to take his place. "I could not exactly tell what was the best course to pursue," the doctor wrote Latrobe shortly after, "it was then likely that we would have fighting enough at home on our own hook. Russwurm and myself debated the question. I urged him to go and he insisted on my going, he afraid that a row would be kicked up during his absence, for the want of forbearance, and I afraid that nothing could go right in the event of war during my absence, consequently both of us remained at home." In the event, peace prevailed at Cape Palmas, while the commodore, whom McGill criticized for "his milk and water expressions . . . in relation towards the 'pure unsophisticated African,'" engaged in a pitched battle.[26]

The "chastisement" of Half Beriby for the destruction of the *Mary Carver* was among the squadron's explicit assignments. The facts of the case were clear, but the navy left the manner of punishment at the commodore's discretion. Reverend Launcelot Minor, who first published the incident, had advocated nothing less than extermination. Russwurm called for actions but a little less stern. "Should you be fortunate enough to secure any people from Little or Half Beriby, no ransom ought to redeem them but a halter; they were all concerned in the murder — men, women, and children," he told Perry. Further, the village was so poor, having "wasted and destroyed all the property" of the *Mary Carver* and another Portuguese schooner that remuneration was out of the question. "They are a bloodthirsty set, who have lived for the last few years by piratical acts, and some little trade in camwood and ivory. Their custom has ever been to rob the poor wayfaring man cast on their shores, foreign and native."[27] Yet the *Vandalia* fiasco demonstrated the inadequacy of sea power for such purposes. Moreover, every town along a sixty-mile stretch had a share of the plunder. The squadron could not very well destroy all of them and maintain credibility as a neutral arbiter.

On the afternoon of December 9, Perry and his captains, Governors Russwurm and Roberts, and others met aboard the *Macedonian* to plan the campaign. The usual strategy in such a case—to capture as many kroomen from Half Beriby and neighboring towns as possible and use them as pawns to force a palaver—was dropped. Although the *Porpoise* had succeeded in taking some men from Half Beriby, no one felt that this would be enough to bring Ben Krakow to the table. They agreed to use a quieter approach, to visit the towns concerned and seek their cooperation in apprehending and punishing the murderers. Then Beriby and the other towns directly involved in the crime might be forced to make restitution to the vessel's owners and her crew's families. As the squadron sailed to leeward the next day, Perry met with his officers again, to refine the plan and decide what they would do if those on shore failed to comply. "Severe measures" should not be undertaken, they agreed, against the towns along the coast without stronger than they now had before them. Perry thought "they were all implicated in the murder, but the proof of guilt was not sufficient to justify reprisals" and that, because their actions would be considered those of the U.S. government, they first needed "strong proof." Perry decided that "it would be more easy to decide what amount of chastisement should be inflicted upon them after visiting the scene of outrage and murder." All present concurred with him, though they expected a fight.[28]

The squadron rode off Robookah the afternoon of December 10. The *Macedonian*'s head krooman went ashore in one of the longboats. He met with King Tom, or Barrah Keaby, and scheduled a palaver for ten the next morning. At early daylight, the commodore and ships' officers, Governor Roberts, and a force of two hundred marines boarded thirteen boats and made for shore. Violent surf forced a transfer to dugout canoes for a wild ride through the waves. Some of the canoes foundered, but everyone got ashore safely, if drenched. A long line of five hundred or more men, three or four deep, armed with muskets, cutlasses, spears, and any number of improvised weapons, met them on the beach. The chiefs of the *sedibo* ran up and down the line, ringing bells and exhorting the men to valor. Although its motions were warlike, the phalanx was meant to frighten rather than assault the landing party. Even so, Perry signaled Captain Mayo to send ashore the troops held in reserve. The sailors and marines on shore quickly formed and marched directly into town, which was almost empty for fear of attack. The few guards at the gates gave way peacefully, and marines took over. Seeing this, the *sedibo* made feints of attack, but Roberts warned a headman that marines did not fight the way Africans did, that they would shoot to kill.[29]

King Tom remained on the beach with his soldiers. He refused to talk the palaver unless he could bring an armed guard with him. After some discussion, this was agreed, and the king entered his town. Seated under a huge tree, marines on one side, *sedibo* on the other, the palaver quickly got under way. Perry stated the facts implicating Robookah in the piracy. Tom admitted that a headman of Half Beriby had been in town at the time of the incident (because he was sick and hoped to stay out of reach of witchcraft) but that he had no advance knowledge of the plot. Ben Krakow had sent a few pieces of cloth, but this was all the plunder that came to Robookah. Perry asked the king to demonstrate his innocence by accompanying the squadron to confront Half Beriby. Tom balked at first but then changed his mind. By three in the afternoon, he and a few of his headmen were safely on board the *Macedonian*. On shore, messengers ran down the beach with word that the day of reckoning was at hand, and each town must explain its role in the piracy or suffer retribution.[30]

The squadron was again underway. Next morning, December 12, they stopped at Bassa and picked up King George, who also denied any role. Like Tom, he blamed Ben Krakow. Dawn of the thirteenth found the warships anchored off Half Beriby. At 8:30, the officers held a council of war. They now had little doubt that all five towns clustered about Half Beriby had participated in the destruction of the *Mary Carver* and a Portuguese vessel shortly before that. "Unless some exculpatory evidence should be educed at the palaver," they resolved, "the five towns in question should be destroyed, after first ascertaining that the women and children had left them."[32]

Perry and his officers worried that their approach might have driven Krakow and his subjects to safe havens in the bush, though a flag (which later proved to be a relic of the ill-fated Portuguese schooner) flying over the town gave evidence that Krakow remained at home. The American forces pulled for the beach. Their landing was again rough, and a fair amount of ammunition was spoiled, but the marines quickly formed ranks on shore. Some of them set up a tent with tarpaulins and oars in which to hold a palaver. The *Mary Carver's* rotting hulk lay just to windward, Half Beriby a short distance the other way. Perry walked with other officers to meet Ben Krakow, who stood outside the town. The king received the strangers without emotion. Purser Bridge and others casually toured Half Beriby, where they observed men preparing for battle, whereupon they returned safely to their lines.[32]

The Americans took seats within the tent to await Krakow. Marines guarded the side of the shelter closest to town. The king presently strode under the awning, accompanied by several of his headmen and an interpreter. His soldiers arrayed themselves opposite the marines. Perry wasted no time with diplomatic niceties. He demanded to hear what Krakow had to say concerning the *Mary Carver*, whose timbers lay in plain view. Krakow answered with an elaborate, specious story, that Farwell had indeed been killed, but for murdering two kroomen from the town, and that the vessel had then drifted and foundered with a total loss of cargo. When asked what had become of the crew, the interpreter was at a loss. Perry stood up and walked menacingly toward the king, telling him that he would hear no further lies. Ben Krakow did not understand much English, but he comprehended clearly that he could not invent a story to extricate himself. He stood up as the commodore faced him, and all of his men followed, heading for the open air.[33]

Accounts of what happened next differ materially. Apparently, Perry seized Ben Krakow's calico robes. These tore, and the king broke free. The commodore grabbed at him again, but Krakow had the better hand. He now held Perry and dragged him from the tent, receiving several bayonet jabs as he did. Outside, Perry, a big man, lost his footing and fell in the soft, hot sand. Krakow was suddenly unshielded, whereupon a marine put a pistol to his neck and fired. The force of the ball threw Krakow to the ground, mortally wounded.[34]

As soon as fighting erupted, muskets crackled among the palm trees and tall grass facing the beach, but with almost no effect on the struggle around the tent. Krakow's interpreter got out from under the canvas and was running for the woods when Captain Tatnall felled him with his rifle. Within moments, panic seized the Half Beriby *sedibo*. They ran from the beach in terror as the Americans fell in formation and pursued them. The soldiers who crouched behind little dunes at the edge of the woods, natural breastworks, were braver, but the marines made a determined charge upon their positions and drove them away too. Then without orders, someone fired flares to signal a general bombardment of the bush from the ships. "Such a roar of artillery for a time was deafening," one witness wrote, "the shells exploding in the forest made it terrible, and the screams of women and children who fled there when the battle began was heart-rending."[35]

The town of Half Beriby was quickly secured, since no one remained to defend it. Marines made a quick search of houses, rounding up stragglers, and snatching chickens for dinner later. They recovered navigational instruments, the *Mary Carver*'s log, and Farwell's letter box in one house. When all was clear, the town and four satellite villages were torched.[36]

Random ineffectual gunfire continued from the tree line while the towns burned. Their work done, Perry ordered his men back to the ships. The hostage kings of Robookah and Bassa had kept out of danger's way during the fight and were now happy to retreat to safety. Soldiers stood around Ben Krakow, who lay where he had fallen, covered with blood and sand, still breathing. "Put the poor fellow out of his misery," Captain Mayo ordered his aide. The officer hesitated, feeling some scruples about shooting a helpless man. In anger, Mayo drew his own pistol, but as he aimed, Krakow moved with desperate strength and grabbed him by the knees. The two men wrestled briefly before marines could separate them, the captain's bright white uniform sodden with blood. Other officers intervened, and Krakow was carried out to the *Macedonian*, where he lingered a couple of days before succumbing. He was given a common sailor's burial.[37]

The next day, the squadron moved to leeward. Aboard the *Macedonian*, Perry met with the kings and principals of Robookah and Grand Bassa. He praised them for their manifest loyalty in the previous day's fight and absolved them of culpability in the *Mary Carver*'s destruction. Notwithstanding, he insisted that they sign a declaration of friendship to all Americans, with a pledge to respect their property. They agreed without debate. In light of the terrifying display of weaponry they had witnessed, they would have signed whatever terms Perry dictated.[38]

On December 15, the squadron anchored off a cluster of villages belonging to the Krakow clan, whose inhabitants were also involved in the massacre. Marines landed in the morning. Under sporadic gunfire, they marched down the beach, burning villages as they went. Casualties were light on both sides: no Americans were killed, and a small, unrecorded number of Africans.[39]

The following day, the squadron lay off Grand Beriby, whose king was quick to disassociate himself from Ben Krakow's crimes. He added his signature to the declaration of friendship as a sign of good faith. At Tabou on December 19, King Karple also signed the document. Perry now considered his task complete and ordered his command to windward.[40]

The African Squadron intimidated Freeman, but its intervention did not solve the issues that gave rise to the conflict. Consequently, both sides remained at arms after Perry had left. The first day, Americans and Africans rested. The second day, each party had settled on a course of action. Russwurm informed Freeman that he must sell Gbenelu or return the money and goods paid for Cape Palmas in 1834. He threatened, unrealistically, to withdraw the colony if the king did not comply. That night, settlers fired a rocket given them by the squadron. The new weapon, fired harmlessly, startled the *sedibo*, which had never seen such a thing. Ford McGill, who commanded the garrison on the Cape, made matters worse, telling Greboes that the rockets would not be used against them without "just cause," but that if a fight broke out, "the rockets most certainly would be used."

The *sedibo* responded with a show of force. They assembled at the edge of Gbenelu in full war dress, drums beating and bells ringing. Several times they feigned attacks on the company of twenty-five men at Harper, but each time they retreated before advancing more than a few yards. The militia held its fire, though under such threatening circumstances some one might well have lost control. As darkness fell, the African soldiers retreated into their town. The war drum pounded all night and the next day, but the crisis had passed. By ten on the night of the fourth day, both sides were utterly exhausted. Russwurm sent word to Freeman either to stop the bluster and racket or come out and fight. The drums soon ceased their rhythms, and with them failed the king's strategy to control the colony and raise his revenue.[41]

XIII.

"Liberty Without Bread"

COMMODORE PERRY'S DEMONSTRATION OF FORCE, IN COMBINATION with the militia's sharp defense of Mt. Tubman, chastened King Freeman and his bellicose *sedibo*. The king endeavored to restore good relations, knowing that he might not escape another such palaver so easily. A tremendous amount was at stake, not merely in economic terms, but in cultural ones, for daily contact with the Marylanders profoundly influenced the citizens of Gbenelu. The enticements of the new culture conflicted with their traditional way of life. If there had been any doubt, it was now clear that the Americans were a permanent presence, and Greboes must either accommodate them or move away.

Though outwardly smooth, the agent's relationship with King Freeman was tense during the first months of 1844. When Father Kelly left for America, the king took him aside and asked him to tell the board, "that when he sold the land to Dr. Hall it was with the reservation of that part of it occupied by the natives who were not to be disturbed. But that Gov Russwurm spoke now differently. He had encroached upon the native rice farms." Holmes, he said, had "declared that the Americans should have the whole land, and that this was governor Russwurms idea also, — that the colonists had at times taken the agricultural implements from the natives." Freeman sought peace, but "america man was for war, and . . . the King desired to know whether the Society countenanced such conduct." The society intended settlers to live in peace but knew there must be challenges. It relied on Russwurm's good judgement and diplomacy in dealing with Freeman, who had proven himself, to say the least, duplicitous.[1]

The settler community resumed its peaceful aspect quite quickly. It might seem strange that a people poised for war one week could trade muskets and cannons for hoes and saws the next, but life at Cape Palmas was replete with paradoxes that could foster such behavior. Here on the shore of tropical Africa, where slavers still lurked, existed an expatriate community that tried with all its strength to live up to the agrarian, republican, Christian ideals of its native land—in Africa, because that is where prejudice dictated people of their color *ought* to be— living in the midst of an indigenous population with mutual contempt, suspicion, and fear. That two governments should control the same territory and live in peace at all is remarkable. Settlers quickly grew used to the bullying and posturing that characterized day-to-day life with Greboes, and they took occasional interruptions in stride. Life was demanding, and few could afford to sit and ponder or mourn adversity.

The bark *Latrobe* struck sail off Cape Palmas about January 10, 1844. She carried emigrants, supplies, and new commercial laws that would cause much unrest. The Board of Managers apprehended a dangerous slide toward commerce in the colony, and they designed the statute to stifle this and nurture a utopian commonwealth of small farmers. They also wanted to put the colony on a better financial footing, to ease the burden on themselves.[2] In summary, the law established a customs house and collector, who had the responsibility of meeting every ship that anchored off Cape Palmas. The collector was required to impose a lighthouse fee, at a rate of eight cents per ton, then to oversee the landing of any cargo at the Agency Wharf. Merchandise was to be taxed at 10 percent of the value declared on the vessel's bill of lading. Violators were subject to high fines and the seizure and auction of contraband. The law stipulated an annual fee of one hundred dollars for an importer's license, designed to prevent settlers from conducting trade. Owners of retail stores must pay twenty-five dollars per year for a license as well, the only exception extended to women with inventories worth less than a hundred dollars.

Russwurm strongly disagreed with the board's new ordinance and the rationale that had spawned it. "We feel, that our colonists are too poor; and the foreign and domestic trade too trifling, to have any obstacles . . . thrown in the way," he argued.[3] To support his contention, he convened the council on February 12. They recommended a sales tax of 1 percent on foreign goods in place of the tariff. They also reduced the commission merchant's license fee to twenty-one dollars, and the retailer's license to $10.50, both payable in specie each February. The agent sent the resolutions home, knowing that they defied the board's instructions but with the request that they reconsider.[4]

The *Latrobe* also carried orders for Russwurm to buy Fishtown, to preempt English or French encroachment. He had already done so on his own initiative. Maryland in Liberia now spanned more than forty miles of coast, more land than settlers would ever occupy. Fishtown had a deep water harbor in which large ships could safely anchor. The agent and others urged Perry to make the spot a base of operations, and he gave the proposal serious consideration.[5]

On February 6, Russwurm, George McGill, and others went to Fishtown to meet the warship *Porpoise*, sent there to survey the harbor. Captain Craven was pleased with the place. The water was deep enough to anchor the *Macedonian*, the squadron's largest ship. On shore, Russwurm negotiated the use of a spring—touchy business, as the spot was sacred to the "Country Devil," who was not inclined to share his domains. A dash was prepared for the divinity, and the doctors of the neighborhood conducted an elaborate ceremony to inform him that they had not violated the site, and that Americans took responsibility for appropriating the water. At the end of the palaver, Russwurm told the Fishtown king and headmen, "in our opinion, the Devil had no water in his domains; and that our hearts always gave God, who created all things, thanks whenever we discovered so fine spring as this." The Africans smiled politely at his bumptious ignorance, but the agent believed that he had taken a great step toward bringing civilization to them.[6]

The Roman Catholic mission withdrew from Maryland in 1844. Because they sided with the colony against other missions and because they paid workers generously with cash, they had once been popular, but the good feelings did not last. Bishop Barron left Father Kelly in charge when he departed for Europe. Kelly grew more irritable and stubborn as time passed, opium and calomel having their effects on his character. In 1843, Paul Sansay, a Catholic settler, contracted with Kelly to saw a quantity of lumber. On delivery, the priest found faults and refused to pay. The dispute dragged on. Russwurm declined to arbitrate, and George McGill's mediation was unsuccessful. In December 1843, threatened with a suit for back wages from his employees, Sansay sued the mission. Kelly had the case postponed to January, but the delay gained him nothing, for the court found in Sansay's favor. The priest appealed, producing a contract that he had tricked the barely literate settler into signing. The judges rejected the new evidence, and Kelly was obliged to pay. Soon after, he sailed for the United States, leaving about seven French novices and their servants, who had arrived in December.[7]

Bishop Edward Barron again visited Cape Palmas briefly in March, soon after Kelly had deserted the place. He found a shambles, with a sick and dying remnant of Frenchmen, who were unable to speak with settlers. He took them with him to Assinee, on the Ivory Coast, where he would start a new mission. Barron urged the colony's Roman Catholics to follow him to leeward as soon as they could. On April 18 he wrote Russwurm from Assinee, having changed his mind. "I now find that the resources of this place do not present hopes to colonists of their being able to provide comfortably for themselves and families, and accordingly beg of you to discourage them in every possible way from leaving Cape Palmas."[8] The agent happily sent this vindication back to Baltimore.

Evangelists remained hard at work in Maryland. The Episcopal ministers became more friendly with Russwurm. The Methodist Church, the church of most settlers, also began to expand its efforts toward the education and conversion of Africans. Reverend John Seys, head of the Methodists at Monrovia, sojourned at Harper for a few weeks in 1844 to attend to church business and escape angry politics at home. Maryland's order and peacefulness impressed him deeply.[9]

Seys desired to visit the schools that members of the congregation had recently established at bush towns. The governor had his own reasons to go inland, and the two men resolved to go together. Reverend Amos Herring, who led the congregation at Harper, John Banks and Alexander Hance, brothers in good standing, and a retinue of porters composed the expedition. Banks acted as interpreter. He had once worked for John Wilson and was well-versed in bush dialects and customs, which were somewhat different from those on the beach. Alexander Hance, whom Greboes nicknamed "Sunday" for his piety, was a popular figure in the bush. His presence emphasized the good will intended by the jaunt. Early one June morning, the party was paddled up Hoffman's River. At the head of navigation, they met an advance party, which had brought up jackasses and baggage. Russwurm offered Amos Herring one of the jacks, but he preferred the "Missionary Carriage" that he had designed and made himself. This was a sedan chair, with the addition of a single wheel near the center and a seat supported on springs, which relieved the bearers of a considerable burden. On it, the zealous preacher could cover thirty miles a day in comfort, at a cost of fifty cents for the two porters. They started for Gilliboh, about eight miles north. They passed first through fields of young rice, which had grown up about eight inches. Seys noted the neatness of the clearings, compared with those in the vicinity of Monrovia. Travel was more difficult as they moved from beach territory into old fields covered with rank, wet grass, interspersed with the rotting trunks of fallen trees. Once, when his jack balked, Russwurm was thrown to the ground, but he landed uninjured.

Gilliboh's leaders welcomed them early in the afternoon. The travelers ate dinner, annoyed the whole while by a crowd of onlookers. Many of them had never seen white men before, and their curiosity knew no bounds. Everyone wondered at Seys's and Russwurm's slightest movement or sound. The little boys of the new school took turns holding Seys's hands, though the cautious missionary looked for every opportunity he could afterward to wash them, for fear of "cutaneous diseases." The settler Frederick Lewis had erected a thatched frame church and schoolhouse there two or three months before.

The ministers held a service in the new chapel. Seys described the event with some humor to the Liberian readers of his *Luminary*. During evening services, "the people behaved exceedingly disorderly. They were little accustomed to religious worship, and talked, and laughed, and acted the uncouth savage to the life." As soon as Seys explained what they were doing, called for the first hymn, and began to sing, "why they thought they must sing too, and such another yelling I never heard. It required some time, much perseverance, and yet more patience, to make them understand that this was a part of the God palaver which we did not expect them to join in." With order tentatively restored, Seys finished the service, "with but little faith I must confess as to much good being the result."

The meeting closed with more solemnity than it began. The church and school would have their influence, though its initiation was more comic theatre than pious liturgy. The visitors went to bed early, but they were kept awake much of the night by mosquitoes, of whose injuries Seys was unaware and whose effects could not be washed away. The visitors examined the students the next day, then continued to Saurekah and Barrakah before returning to Harper.

The palaver of December 1843 had a profound impact on Grebo politics, though some consequences did not manifest themselves for months. About June 1844, some sixty households moved from Gbenelu to a site across Hoffman's River. Cragh, King Freeman's younger brother, led the migration. Yellow Will, who had worked for the colonial government since 1834, went with them, declaring himself an enemy of the Americans. In December, Yellow Will had ceased to work as Russwurm's interpreter, unable to fight his own people. Afterward, he concluded that the two communities could not coexist in peace but must separate. Yellow Will's defection surprised and offended Russwurm. Soon after, when Barrakah made peace and opened trade, he concluded that Will had been a spy and saboteur. He blamed Will and Cragh for having distorted Eben Parker's violent actions and the colonial attitude toward Africans, then inciting Barrakah's *sedibo* to a hasty revenge.[10]

The colony's growing influence in the bush also seems to have precipitated the movement to a new town site. Recently, Saurekah had threatened war against Gbenelu after several of their people were robbed as they carried produce to Harper. Russwurm took Saurekah's side, contrary to Freeman's expectations. Just before moving, Cragh met privately with Samuel McGill to explain himself. Cragh apologized for the unfriendliness of a certain element of his people. He had always opposed them, he said, but now he felt betrayed, because Russwurm regarded him as an enemy. Now that war with Saurekah was imminent, he expected the governor to try to avert it, but no help was coming. He wanted nothing more than fulfillment of the terms of the original compact between his people and James Hall, which called for mutual defense. McGill translated for him. "I am often led to reflect," Cragh began, "on the great inconveniences we labored under previous to the establishment of the Colony" for the want of tobacco, iron tools, and clothing, all of which they now procured "with ease and abundance." He had "never in my life been engaged in any altercation with Americans," and although he was younger than Freeman and less influential, he was nevertheless, "opposed to the lawless confusion, and the irregularities, which my Brother suffers to go unpunished." Now, "disgusted with this inefficiency or disinclination to suppress them, and seeing that their continuance must eventually turn to strife between us and the Americans," he had "determined on removing to a greater distance from you, so that in the event of a war I may remain a neutral spectator." Colonial authorities welcomed this new development, hoping that it might begin an even greater migration, parallel to the removal of Indians before the advance of American civilization.

In August, Dr. McGill voiced the common opinion that Grebo culture was too slow to adopt American customs. "Up to the present we regret no effect of this kind can be discovered, they are to a man polygamist, they murder each other constantly, and they scruple not at any act of dishonesty. There has been effected by Missionaries and others some slight improvement in the young, but the bad influences exercised by their intimacy with the parents must exclude the hope of its permanency." Missionaries discouraged their converts from joining the settler community. Civilized—meaning converted—Greboes lived in a sort of exile in segregated villages, accepted by neither their own people or the Americans, "a mongril tribe of half civilized loafers." Better not to teach them anything at all than to leave them thus, McGill and others believed.[11]

As Russwurm had expected, the Board of Managers did not appreciate his rejection of their revenue laws. Several months intervened in the controversy because of distance, and when the board's rebuke reached Russwurm in August, he was ready to counter. He wrote Latrobe on the twenty-fourth that the resolutions of the agent and council were clearly worded as "recommendations." "You are well aware," he wrote curtly, "that your Agent, however willing, is unable of himself to enforce laws against the views of the whole community, and in the present case, it was deemed most prudent by himself and Council to make a fair representation of the matter, and recommend such a Tariff as would suit the circumstances of your people. Our trade *now* is so *inconsiderable* that it needs every encouragement to extend it into the interior, and to invite Trading vessels to stop on their routes down the coast." The board's system of tariffs was unlikely to work because merchants almost always falsified manifests to understate the value of their cargo. Settlers knew that any imposts would be passed on to them in the form of higher prices. Moreover, the colony did not have the means to enforce the laws.[12]

The society's restrictive commercial policy frustrated and angered settlers. A community of transplants, many contemplated moving away. In October 1844, G. R. Butts, an agent of the British colony, Demerara, on the Caribbean coast of South America, visited Harper. Laborers were needed for Guiana's sugar plantations, and he offered free passage to anyone who wanted to work there. He held forth glowing stories about the wonders of Guiana, its abundant good food, and easy living. By contrast, Cape Palmas seemed a very poor place indeed.[13]

On October 24, a group of citizens met at Emanuel Davenport's house. Several respectable settlers, including Jacob Gross and Stephen Hall, were named to conduct the meeting. Having reviewed some general causes of discontent, they opened the floor. Settlers complained that agriculture was not viable: "We have tried to the best of our ability poor as we are. . . . All that we can raise on our farms is not sufficient to feed and clothe a mans family leaving out of the Question the vast expences yearly by repairing our houses." Another said, "You recommend us to go to our farms and we can say with confidence that the soil is poor and we have tried it — its true the 1st or the 2nd crop of Potatoes will produce tolerable good and after that we might as well plant them on the sand beach without manure." Moreover, the colony had no exportable crop, and the agency had drastically reduced its payroll, depriving many settlers of their only chance to earn a living. One man asked pointedly, "What is liberty without bread or something in place of it?" Another was even more strident, asserting that the society owed settlers a debt,

It is impossible for us to live and except our Society does something to immelorate our sufferings it will place us in a great deal worse of situation and we where in the land from whence we came and what would be the state of your flourishing country to day if it hadnt been for the labor of the colored man, now you have said to us we are going to better your Condition by sending us to the land of our forefathers. Here we are brought here and settle amidst of parcel of savage heathens and they are amongst us continually and will not come under our Government and under these considerations we are greatly agrieved, themselves and their stock destroys nearly one half of what we raised on our farms and we can get no redresses.

Another expressed frustration that his struggle in Africa was equated with the experience of Europeans settling in America, where conditions had been much more favorable. Knowing that white citizens of his native country, who had banished him to so harsh a land, criticized him for lack of success in his exile, was more than he could bear. Settlers complained bitterly that they had no cash but the agency shinplasters, which were only good at the store and were steadily losing value. The assembly unanimously implored the society to help them. Stephen Hall and Emanuel Davenport volunteered to visit South America with Butts and report back to Cape Palmas.[14]

Governor Russwurm viewed all of this with unusual sympathy, for the complaint corroborated his assertion that the society must do more to foster the colony. He sent a copy of the proceedings to James Hall, explaining the circumstances in a separate letter. In it, he confirmed the lack of employment and inadequate currency. He proposed redeeming five or six hundred dollars of it in the next six months, which would remove the bulk from circulation. He was not particularly worried about a migration to Demerara. A native Jamaican, he knew well the conditions of labor in the cane fields.[15]

In September 1845, the Grebo and American delegates who had gone to Guiana returned to Cape Palmas. Butts and his associates had done their best to show the advantages of making sugar for British planters, yet the visitors agreed that South America was no better a place for a black man than Liberia. When they reported this to a public meeting, some refused to believe them. They had decided in advance than Guiana must be the promised land. They made quixotic plans to emigrate, but good sense prevailed. When Butts called at Cape Palmas in October to pick up volunteers, he went away without one.[16]

The *Chipola* rode off Cape Palmas about the middle of January, 1845. Besides some seventy settlers and stores, she delivered a revised revenue code, which Russwurm was bound to enforce. Settlers scoffed at the idea that their government could support itself on the duties gotten from the unpredictable visits of merchant vessels. The Episcopal Mission closed its school for American children in protest. Most citizens were resigned to the taxes, however. Fortunately, trade was brisk. Sources of supply were expanding, and demand in Britain and America for African products growing. Trade was also getting more competitive. Dr. Hall was slow to respond to changes in the market, despite advice from Africa. Russwurm was disappointed that Hall did not send English goods on the *Chipola*. They had become necessary to maintain trade. Some settler merchants now had better stores than ever, and the agency had to adapt to the changing circumstances, since it could not suppress them.[17]

The health of settlers remained a major concern of the Maryland Colonization Society. Fear of persistent disease and death discouraged many prospective emigrants, but it is to the society's credit that mortality among their settlers was far lower than foreigners experienced anywhere else in tropical Africa. The *Chipola* brought an order for Dempsey Rollo Fletcher to come home for medical training. Fletcher was a native of North Carolina, born "a 'few miles beyond the court-house,' (and probably, less distance from the whipping-post,)" according to James Hall, who knew him well. He had been taken to Liberia when he was seven. There he was orphaned, and from an early age, he fended for himself. As a boy, Fletcher could write phonetically, so he found employment with Ben Johnson, a small-time trader. He moved with Johnson to Cape Palmas during Hall's administration. The doctor recognized talent in the youth and hired him to work in the Agency Store. At the same time, he began to instruct Fletcher in science and medicine. Soon, he was given charge of the apothecary. When Samuel McGill returned to Cape Palmas, early in 1839, he began to share some of his knowledge with Fletcher. Their personalities clashed, and Fletcher chafed at the low wages and hard work, worsened by the condescension of Dr. McGill. In 1844 he had even threatened to quit if the society did not soon fulfill its promise of a proper medical education.

Russwurm tried to get Fletcher a passage aboard the *Chipola*, but the captain asked for a hundred dollars, quite a high sum. The bark *Palestine*, bound for Boston, offered the next opportunity. Fletcher made his passage uneventfully and took the train from Boston to Baltimore, where he arrived in March 1845. The society had immediate plans to use him to recruit emigrants for Cape Palmas, then to send him to Dr. Phelps at Dartmouth.[18]

Barely a year after their attempt at confederation failed, the Grebo states were embroiled in civil war, the sides forming according to traditional loyalties of the Kudemowe and Nyomowe chiefdoms. Control of trade lay at the heart of the troubles. Russwurm had recently opened a new path to Denah, and Half Cavally insisted on its right to use it to the exclusion of Grahway and Grand Cavally. The issue simmered for several weeks, scarcely noted at Harper. The spark that exploded into war was more mundane. Grand Cavally and Half Cavally had long disputed ownership of certain fields near the river. This year, it happened that the contested fields were prime for growing rice. Each town sent parties to clear the fallow bush. Control of the land shifted back and forth in fistfights with little bloodshed, though hostages were taken, and the matter threatened to grow worse.[19]

Late in January, Grand Cavally soldiers killed three Half Cavally men in a skirmish. At the beginning of February, Payne persuaded Russwurm to go to Half Cavally to avert war. The governor told the leaders of the contending towns that they must lay their palaver aside until after the rice harvest, six or more months away. Hostages on each side were given up unharmed, and the heads of each army spewed water and tasted human liver according to the country's custom of making peace. Russwurm left, satisfied that his dictatorial diplomacy had ended the matter.

Within two or three days, however, reports reached him that the Half Cavally *sedibo* was preparing to attack Grand Cavally. The governor consulted with Captain Bruce of the man-o'-war *Truxton*, and both agreed that only more fighting would settle the dispute. Russwurm was angry at the defiance of his fiat and at the duplicity of the war-men, particularly of Half Cavally. He hoped that Commodore Perry's successor, who was expected to arrive on the coast soon, would assist him in punishing the town.

Later in February, men of Half Cavally and Grand Cavally met each other in canoes on a tributary of the Cavally. Half Cavally had anticipated the engagement and sent out a large force, but in a brutal fight with clubs and machetes, the tenacious river people beat them and seized nine prisoners. When the victors discovered the bludgeoned body of one of their comrades, they beheaded all of their captives. In the meantime, the *sedibo* of Grahway, having plotted with their river cousins, took advantage of the defenseless position of Half Cavally, which was guarded only by old men and boys. They rushed the town, beating two or three to death and taking two more prisoner, but they failed to burn it down. Later, they also beheaded their prisoners. Such uncommon ferocity heightened the stakes of the combat.

When he heard the news, Russwurm conferred with Freeman, and they went to Half Cavally to mediate. Half Cavally was willing to make peace with Grand Cavally, but peace with Grahway, who had played them a dirty trick, was impossible. The Cape Palmas delegation returned home disappointed.

On February 22, the Half Cavally *sedibo* marched three miles up the beach to Grahway, which they reached about eleven in the morning. Grahway expected a fight, and eighty men issued to meet their enemy. The two armies sat down in formation on the beach, about twenty yards opposite each other. Their leaders talked the palaver for two tense hours, interrupted twice when the soldiers of each side stood and leveled their muskets at each other, only to sit down again. A third time, Half Cavally stood to fire, but the Grahway men sat still. The Half Cavally soldiers let off a volley, killing nearly a score and wounding almost half of the rest. They then charged and routed their opponents, setting Grahway ablaze before heading home.

That same day, Maryland in Liberia celebrated its eleventh anniversary, giving thanks for continued peace, though war raged all around. Even as citizens conducted their patriotic festivities, they heard musketry. Soon afterward, a great cloud of smoke arose to leeward. Samuel McGill excused himself and put together a medical kit. He walked to Lake Sheppard with two other Americans and boarded a canoe for Grahway at the other end. As they paddled down the lagoon, they soon saw women and children fleeing the other way along the strand and in boats. A short distance further, they encountered wounded refugees drifting about in canoes. They beached their craft at a small village adjacent to Grahway. There, the doctor found twenty-five wounded men. He helped them hurriedly, then went to the main town to see the damage. Grahway and two satellite villages were smoldering ruins. Twenty-two headless bodies lay in the sand on the far side of town, where they had died. The danger had passed for the time being, for Half Cavally withdrew immediately after setting the fires. McGill and his comrades walked on to Half Cavally, where they saw the captured heads prominently displayed on pikes. In the battle, Grahway lost twenty-two men killed and some forty wounded (several mortally) while Half Cavally suffered five deaths and ten wounded. Grahway must now have revenge, and all expected another engagement.

On March 31, Half Cavally weathered the combined assault of the Grand Cavally and Grahway *sedibos*. The day ended with the burning of the Grand Cavally town, Kablake, "with great loss of life," Payne related soon after. He continued, "The war has been characterized by more courage and a greater loss of life than I ever expected to witness amongst Greboes. It was designed I think to root out these people [i.e., Half Cavally], against whom you know Grahway and the River Cavalla towns have ever cherished the most bitter hatred." The Grebo armies now seemed to have taken lessons in warfare from the colonial militia and men-o'-war. After so much carnage, Baphro of Grand Cavally called more strongly for peace. Payne thought that Grahway would also like to set the palaver, but needed a chance to save face. Russwurm and McGill both suspected that Freeman secretly encouraged the hostilities. Rumors said he had promised to send soldiers against Half Cavally after harvest. Such an action would bring the entire Grebo nation into war. Gbenelu would likely be a battleground, and at the very least, trade would cease. The agent was therefore determined to mediate peace as soon as possible.[20]

A year after the chastisement of Half Beriby, Captain Charles W. Skinner relieved Matthew Perry of command of the African Squadron. On April 13, 1845, the new commodore arrived off Cape Palmas, on his first cruise down the coast. Russwurm met him aboard his flagship, the *Jamestown*. They had a friendly conversation, during which the agent recounted the war to leeward, emphasizing that the Episcopal mission at Half Cavally was in the midst of the war zone. He asked the squadron's aid in setting the palaver, and Skinner agreed. The *Jamestown* sailed to leeward on the seventeenth and anchored off Half Cavally that evening. Skinner asked John Payne for an assessment, to which the missionary replied that further hostilities were possible but that the mission was in no danger. The next morning, Russwurm and Freeman reached the town by land. Half Cavally was willing to talk peace, but Grahway stubbornly refused, determined to restore its honor on the battlefield. Skinner regarded the matter as an internal dispute, and he had clear instructions not to involve himself in such. He took a polite leave and sailed on.[21]

Russwurm was left to sort things out on his own. Early in June, he won an armistice. The two towns remained uneasy for quite some time, and citizens hesitated to go to near the other for fear of witchcraft. Trade was curtailed, and food would be scarce, because the conflict had prevented them from planting and tending their farms. Unfavorable weather worsened the situation.[22]

Despite the shortage of foodstuffs, traders brought increasing amounts of palm oil and camwood from the distant bush.[23] The interior was unexplored territory, unknown even to Greboes, whose travel was hindered by parochial boundaries. Russwurm reveled in rumors of a rich country far inland, the territory of the Pahs. During the second half of 1845, these stories became more concrete. Russwurm wrote Hall on September 18 that he had seen a sample of native cotton, "called *Pandarrah*," woven by the Pahs, and it was a "fine specimen of their ingenuity." Pah country was also rich in ivory. As the Pahs were described as "numerous and powerful" but "peacable," he concluded that "if we could once win our way to their country, the advantages of an intercourse with the colony would be apparent to them, and they would adopt measures to keep the path open for trade." Their nearest tribe was reputed to be only three or four days' walk from Cavally, and although "the beach people say the intervening tribes are Cannibals who thirst after human flesh," Russwurm was inclined to "distrust our beach neighbors very much, as they are not overanxious to have us penetrate into the interior."[24] Near the end of September, a Pah trader visited Cape Palmas. No Grebo could recall a time when someone from so far in the bush had gotten to the beach. They loaded him with dashes and sent him home with a grand story to tell.[25]

On October 9, Josh Stewart, John Banks, and Charles McIntosh set out with five Africans for the Pah country. Among the Africans was one Pobe, a resident of the upper reaches of the Cavally River, who had actually visited the Pah country. Russwurm dashed him handsomely in advance of the journey, giving him a bright robe, top hat, and umbrella. The party reached Barrakah after two or three hours' tramp and stopped for the night. The town's headmen could scarcely contain their jealousy of Pobe's fine raiment and privilege as a guide. They

John Hazlehurst Boneval Latrobe, photographed by Mathew Brady Studios, circa 1855, an informal portrait of leader of the Maryland colonization movement about the time he assumed the presidency of the American Colonization Society. The son of the great architect Benjamin Henry Latrobe, he attended but did not graduate from West Point, then studied law in Baltimore. An inventor, active in a great many civic projects, Latrobe believed that in the Maryland colony he was creating a utopian nation that would one day spread across Africa. (Library of Congress)

Dr. James Hall, circa 1855. A medical doctor turned propagandist and businessman, he was genuinely committed to improving the condition of blacks in both the United States and Africa. He became the first governor of Maryland in Liberia and subsequently the leading ideologue and business manager of the Maryland State Colonization Society. (Maryland Historical Society)

"Fishtown Station," wood engraving, circa 1855: a settler-constructed farmstead near Cape Palmas, showing typical domestic architecture. (From Anna M. Scott, Day-Dawn in Africa, 1858)

John Browne Russwurm, wood engraving from a daguerreotype, circa 1850. A Jamaican octoroon whose white father transplanted him to Maine, Russwurm graduated from Bowdoin, the first black man to graduate from a four-year program in an American college. He edited the first African American newspaper in the United States, Freedom's Journal, *then traveled on his own to Liberia, where he became the colonial secretary and editor of the* Liberia Herald. *James Hall recruited him for the governorship of Maryland in Liberia, a post he held from 1836 to 1851. This is how he would have appeared when he returned to America and visited Baltimore in 1849. (Bowdoin College Library)*

JOHN B. RUSSWURM.

"Rocktown," wood engraving, circa 1840. The neighbor and rival of Gbenelu occupied a strategic point of land about five miles west of Cape Palmas. (Missionary Herald, *37 [1841]: 354)*

"Fair Hope," wood engraving, circa 1840, showing the mission station in a panoramic landscape with Latrobe township and Sheppard Lake, from the west. (The Missionary Herald, *Vol. 37, 1841*)

"Mount Vaughan," wood engraving, from a letter posted from Cape Palmas on September 23, 1842. The mission station is seen from across Maryland Avenue, with a settler homestead in the countryside to the right. (Brune-Randall Papers, Maryland Historical Society)

EPISCOPAL MISSION, NEAR CAPE PALMAS, W. AFRICA.

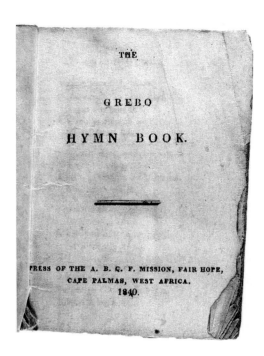

Title page from a small book published at Cape Palmas in 1840. The Episcopal and Congregational missions each printed Grebo and English language tracts, devotional works, and even a magazine. These circulated widely, though few have survived. (Maryland Historical Society)

The following year, missionaries complained, "we have still to deplore the apathy and indifference of the people to the subject of religion, and sometimes feel exceedingly discouraged. If their loss of interest in their greegrees, and their want of confidence in their doctors were balanced by a corresponding interest in the overtures of mercy which are tendered to them, it would be the source of much encouragement. But such is not the case." (The Missionary Herald, Vol. 37, 1841)

18   **GREBO HYMNS.**

Swĕh yidĭ, keḍidă yidi
Eh năh diḍe teḍĕh nĕnu.

3 Gnono nede Gnïsuah mâh,
Oh năh yi blidi dĭ, nĕmä
Oh plĕ mi blemu ti biye,
Kâri oh tih Gnïsuah mâh.

4 Bă nu Gnïsuah winh tĕtinu,
Bă ko ne, ă mi nâ yimu;
Ne ă miwă nâ mâh nemu,
Ne ă plĕ mi blemu băka.

HYMN 16. C. M.
Judgement.

1 Yisu Kraisĭ wodă kună,
Â munä â buh blih;
Â ne Gnïsuah didăh sonh mâh;
Â boăh ne băka.

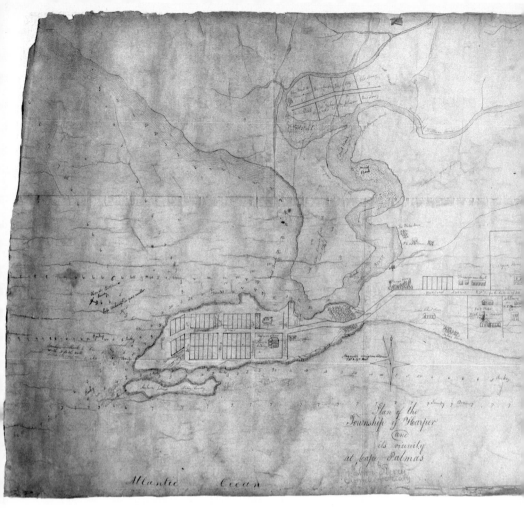

Plan of the
Township of Harper
and
its vicinity
at Cape Palmas

Atlantic Ocean

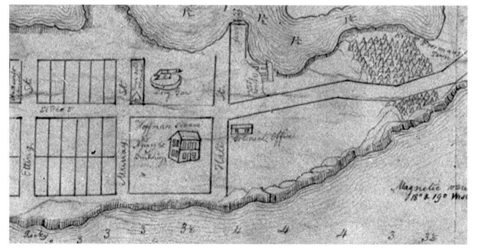

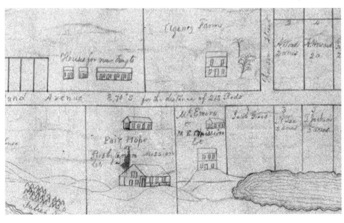

Map of the settlement at Cape Palmas drawn by settler John Revey in 1839. Detail of Harper (left), showing the principal Agency buildings and Gbenelu. Detail of Latrobe (right), showing housing for new emigrants, the Public Farm, Fair Hope mission, etc. (Maryland Historical Society)

"African town," watercolor, circa 1850. Characteristic Grebo house construction with the straight roofline of the "takae" or "palaver house" visible in the background. (Library of Congress)

"Sassa Wood Palaver," wood engraving, circa 1855. A dramatic interpretation of a missionary's intervention in a case of gidu, or trial by ordeal of a suspected witch. (From Anna M. Scott, Day-Dawn in Africa, 1858)

regarded him as a bumpkin whom the Americans had unduly honored and would have stopped them there. After a long palaver, however, they permitted the Americans to go on. They walked to Denah the next day, where they had a similar reception. Bush towns saw no advantage in letting strangers explore the interior, as they could only upset the status quo. Still, handsome dashes and outright bribes had their effect, and the explorers prepared to travel up the Cavally. They loaded their baggage into canoes and paddled upstream as James Hall had done in 1835, to Faye, in Paleah country, which was Pobe's home. The town's headmen welcomed the strangers, who promised the benefits of a more direct trade with the beach. A few dashes satisfied them, and they gave their assent for the journey to continue.[26]

From Faye, the party traveled partly on foot and partly by canoe up the course of the Cavally. Several villages stopped them, ostensibly out of jealousy for the guide but with a deeper-lying xenophobia. Dashes and bravado kept them on their course. At Wattah, they paused to prepare an overland journey into Half Pah Country. On October 24, they reached the town of Newbayeah and spent the night there. Emissaries from Pah and other towns visited them. Each insisted that the strangers must visit his town first. The Americans, who were used to obstructions, were at a loss how to proceed when welcomed. John Banks fell ill, and his mind settled on the idea of how far he was from home. He could think of nothing but returning to the beach. He and Josh Stewart argued publicly about whether to continue. The Americans stayed where they were for a week, which caused some bad feelings. At length, Banks felt better, and Stewart persuaded him to press a bit further. On October 31, they marched ten miles to Mattaw, on the edge of Pah territory. They stayed there until November 3, when they turned back to Harper. Retracing their steps, they were home by the middle of the month, laden with curiosities and wonderful tales. The Americans encouraged Pahs to visit the colony. A group of them began the journey, but soldiers of Katuboh, who had opposed the American foray, turned them back. "The intervening tribes can never keep the Pahs from the Colony," Russwurm commented on December 30, "now 'our ships' as they termed their visitors have anchored in their waters. They now trade with Tabou, Bassa, and Grand Berriby, and it is said, they will find their way wherever there is money to be made." A tremendous amount was at stake—if a secure line of trade with the far interior could be established, Harper could quickly become the principal city on the coast.[27]

XIV.

"The True Yankee Enterprise"

MAJOR ANTHONY WOOD, A RESIDENT OF AFRICA FOR SEVENTEEN years and of Cape Palmas since 1834, returned to America early in 1845. The old man intended to visit his old home, to see friends once again, and to encourage emigration to his adopted home. The society could not have found a more sincere witness to their activities in Africa. Though he had not always agreed with their policies, he was a loyal citizen, chief militia officer, and active participant in the community.[1]

Anthony Wood was born in the West Indies about 1794. In 1808, while a boy, his master brought him to Baltimore, then sold him to one Howard Mitchell of Harford County, in the northeast part of the state. Technically, Wood had been imported and sold in violation of the ban on the overseas slave trade, but he continued a slave for ten more years, becoming a skilled blacksmith. In 1817, Elisha Tyson, an influential Quaker miller of Baltimore, won a lawsuit to free Wood. Though nominally free, inferior status and lower earnings for the same work as white smiths frustrated Wood. In 1819, he went with George McGill and other free black Baltimoreans to Haiti. They landed in Port-au-Prince, in the midst of a bloody civil war. Conditions there were worse than anything he had experienced in Maryland, and he returned home. In 1824 a

Haitian envoy passed through town and persuaded him to give the black republic a second try. He took his family, but prospects were scarcely better, and they soon sailed for New York. He decided to try his luck there, but life in a northern city was no easier. Once again, he returned to Baltimore. Finally, in the winter of 1827, he took his wife and infant son to Liberia aboard the brig *Doris*.

Life in Africa was also difficult. He lost his wife and child to fever in 1828. Still, he persevered. He carried on his trade, pausing in his labor only on Sunday, when he attended Methodist meetings. As time passed, he became active in politics, consistently supporting the "Radical" faction, which advocated Liberian self-government, and therefore drew the enmity of the establishment. He and his friend George McGill thought again of moving. Both communicated with the colonizationists in Baltimore and encouraged the creation of a new settlement. They offered to help in any way possible in such a venture.

When the *Ann* appeared, Wood instantly volunteered, then recruited others. Hall named him captain of the projected militia. At Cape Palmas, Wood had charge of the work party that began clearing the land the day the deed was signed. He had the distinction of cutting down the first bush. Moreover, within three days he had set up his forge and was hammering out mounts for the cannons.

Anthony Wood was a man of strong temper, whose self-confidence had grown as a free man in Africa. In his exile, he recollected America with some fondness, and he celebrated his return. His pleasure did not survive long in Baltimore. "On he comes," James Hall commented in the *Maryland Colonization Journal* at the time, "flushed with the most delightful anticipations; but alas, poor man! He has not yet set foot on this sacred soil of freedom ere he awakes to the sad realities of his condition; he finds that he is not a *man* but a *nigger.*" Expressions of "kindness and good feeling on part of those who would be his friends, . . . cause a shudder, to the sensitive mind of a Liberian," accustomed to liberty and equality in Africa. "Every thing is strained and unnatural, the *effort* necessary for even the ordinary salutation is always apparent. But among the thousands with whom he comes in contact, few, very few are even disposed to make this *effort*: he is generally treated with indignity and contempt, or, at best, with indifference."

Even something as trivial as asking a white person for directions on the street subjected him to insult. Yet, white people were not his only problem. He found himself alienated from the great mass of black people as well. "Not one of ten have the least conception of the causes of his grievances. Nothing short of personal violence or restraint, a knock, kick, cuff or lock-up in jail would be to them a source of annoyance." The remainder better "comprehend the perplexities of his situation," but they "look upon him with suspicion and distrust, as the pet of the white colonizationist. They rebuke him as being an enemy of his race, in not remaining in this country and making common cause with them, in claiming their *rights*, viz: those of absolute social and political equality with the whites. He is derided by one party for presuming that he has claims to the privileges of a freeman, and hated by the other for having taken the only available steps to secure these privileges."

Major Wood traveled with John Seys through every county of the Eastern Shore, talking about Africa and soliciting emigrants with very little success. Whatever Wood said about Liberia, Hall reported bitterly, some "plantation lawyer" countered with tales of big snakes, burning sands, and fevers, preying on the ignorance and xenophobia of rural black people. "The conceit and insolence of these men," he wrote, "proved entirely too much for the patience and equanimity of Major Wood, and he declares, as has every other Liberian who has visited America, that no circumstances could induce him ever again to urge the coloured people of Maryland to emigrate." The next expedition for Africa was scheduled to sail November 1, and Wood could scarcely wait to go back to his adopted home.

Although Anthony Wood returned to Harper disgusted and frustrated, his visit was not in vain. He spent considerable time with Garrison Draper, an old acquaintance. Draper was a free black tobacconist, who kept a shop in Govanstown, a village just north of Baltimore, where gossip and politics were stock in trade. With Wood's encouragement, Draper established a "Committee of Enquiry" to weigh the advantages of colonization. He gave new life to an idea long advocated by the society, of forming a company to trade between Baltimore and Liberia, to take advantage of markets opening there. The society had once raised money for the purpose, but in insufficient amount to get the scheme off the ground. Draper suggested that black people should own and operate the company. James Hall seized upon the idea, and with the society's support won a charter from the General Assembly for a joint-stock company, in which any white shareholder was bound to sell his interest to any black investor on demand. James Hall named himself business manager, agreeing to use his experience and contacts for the company's benefit. The Maryland and American Colonization Societies each pledged to ship all of their cargoes to Liberia on the line at market rates. The company proposed to build a clipper ship large enough to carry 2,500 or 3,000 barrels, with specially designed quarters for one hundred or more passengers and their baggage. They hoped that such a vessel could make at least two voyages to Liberia each year. In April the society announced in the *Maryland Colonization Journal* that the capitalization of the Chesapeake and Liberia Trading Company was nearly complete and that a contract to build a ship would soon be negotiated.[2]

———

The new year, 1846, opened auspiciously with the arrival of the brig *Kent,* carrying fourteen emigrants, an Episcopal missionary, and supplies. The most notable of the emigrants was Major Bolon, a free black man from Dorchester County, who had spent the past several years in a Baltimore shipyard, at full pay despite his race. The society hired Bolon to build a rake-masted topsail schooner, popularly known as a "Baltimore clipper," as well as a smaller boat, both for local trade. Bolon's old boss contributed an exact builder's model of a schooner of fifty tons, and the society loaded the *Kent* with tools, hardware, and lumber for the undertaking. Unfortunately much of this material was lost in a storm at sea during which the vessel pitched so perilously that the master ordered his men to cut loose whatever was lashed to the deck.[3]

Bolon's arrival caught Russwurm by surprise and caused some financial embarrassment. The previous July, he had ordered a schooner from a shipwright in Providence, Rhode Island, to be paid for in palm oil, at a cost of $472.50. Russwurm was expecting delivery when the *Kent* arrived. In fact, the *Roderick Dhu* cast anchor off the Cape on March 7, carrying the boat piggy-back. Bolon and other carpenters immediately set to work laying on the deck, using what was left of the *Kent*'s lumber, and applying copper sheathing. Russwurm had to order an extra 2,500 feet of two-inch yellow pine plank from Providence to deck the vessels Bolon was to build, since suitable wood could not be obtained locally. The expense was hard on the treasury, for Maryland still owed Fishtown a large dash for having united with them.[4]

Shipbuilding was a sure sign of industry and progress, a symbol of economic independence and even national prestige. "I belive that the people ar doing Now better than ever thay did sence we settle at palmas," Anthony Wood wrote James Hall, expressing the community's enthusiasm.[5] Bolon was caught up in the excitement, too. In a letter penned for him on January 21, he informed Hall of the difficult voyage and loss of materials. "Thus far I am highly pleases with every thing I have seen here," he continued.

> I think all that is wanted is a few smart enterprizing men to take the lead, and set the people an example, and show them what can be done by industry and enterprize. After I have finished our schooner I hope to return in her once more to the United States, and then come back and spend the remainder of my life in Africa. If I should return in command of the vessel would there be any difficulty in receiving me into port, provided I had on board a white man for mate? If so I should be glad if you would inform me.[6]

Of course, the society saw no good at all in risking the vessel in a transatlantic voyage of dubious value for propaganda.

The decision to construct boats in Maryland in Liberia is evidence of the society's realization that commerce must comprise an integral part of the colonial economy. James Hall and Russwurm after him had called for boats, if for no other reason than to make it easier to find rice to feed settlers, who could not grow enough food themselves. Now, the market for other African produce, notably palm oil, was growing, and the agency was well placed to compete and make money in it. The increase of trade was accompanied by conflict.

Settlers had traded in one form or another since the first landing in 1834. After a decade, a few were quite successful, but none so much as the McGills, who had warehouses at Harper and Monrovia and relationships with American and English merchant houses. George McGill died on April 26, 1844, of acute laryngitis. The old man left behind an active business, with money laid out in merchandise, boats, and real estate, encumbered with heavy debts. Liquidation of the company's assets would not yield enough to pay obligations. Therefore, Ford McGill chose to keep the concern going, to support his newly enlarged family, which included George's widow and infant daughter, and his three brothers.[7]

The *Kent*'s arrival provided Samuel McGill, now probably the richest citizen of Maryland in Liberia, an opportunity to write Latrobe a long, flattering letter. "Could you be on the spot," he wrote, "and witness the gradual yet continuous improvement of the Colony particularly within the past year, it would satisfy you that with the same judicious management, the ultimate results of Colonization would no longer remain a matter of doubt, for even the most skeptical could not but admit that we are in the way of realizing all that was ever promised by the originators of the scheme." A stone jail and court house were under construction, and Russwurm had grand plans. "The Governor displays the true Yankee enterprise," he said. "When an idea is formed it becomes with him his hobby His last one was 'Pah Country and Ivory Trade' now it is 'Sheppard Lake and River Cavalla Canal' as it was also with the 'Camwood trade' until his perseverance overcame the obstacles opposed to its reception. The fact is we can discover that our advancement is commensurate with the amount of labour and energy exerted by the principle men in community. We possess the materials for allmost any enterprise it only requires the will and exertion to make them serviceable."[8] Despite his rosy expressions, there were problems, and the doctor would soon find himself at the center of controversy.

At the beginning of 1846, Russwurm had fired the collector of customs, D. C. MacFarland, for negligence. The man's records were a shambles, and there was suspicion that he had accepted bribes. In any event, the accounts did not balance, and it was clear that the agency was losing revenue. On February 13, the agent and council voted to replace MacFarland with Joshua H. Stewart and William A. Prout. Stewart was scarcely literate, but motivated by a strong principle of civic duty. Prout took charge of the store, advanced from the status of clerk.[9]

The new officers began their duties under the agent's close supervision. Among the first vessels to call was the schooner *Janey* of Sierra Leone. McGill purchased merchandise from her and instructed Stewart to calculate the duties as he and John Bowen had persuaded MacFarland to do: namely, that he should charge 2½ percent on the gross purchase price and thereby arrive at an amount equivalent to the 5 percent on invoice cost stipulated by the law, assuming a uniform mark-up of 100 percent. In the colony's earliest days, the agency and merchant ships consistently priced their goods for resale at twice their cost. By 1846, however, competition had increased. The margin was often lower, but it varied considerably, depending on desirability and ease of transport. The result of McGill's method of calculation was a reduction in the amount collected. Stewart knew no better and complied. In actual terms, the sum lost was small, but the treasury needed every penny, and principle was at issue.[10]

When Russwurm checked the accounts a few days later, he noticed the irregularity and questioned Stewart, who explained what McGill had told him. The agent was furious that his own brother-in-law had preyed on Stewart's ignorance. Soon after, he handed McGill a bill for the uncollected duties. The doctor protested strenuously that he had acted within the law. He argued speciously that Russwurm could not reinterpret the law without consent of the council, and other mer-

chants took the same stance. They viewed Russwurm's policy as nothing less than an attack on their livelihood. Russwurm openly accused
them of conspiracy to defraud the government.[11] He commented, "Seditious remarks have been made by men connected with the society
and government of the colony altogether out of the way — on account
of a few cents duty on a piece of Satin Stripe and 100 lbs. Powder."[12]
Other settlers jumped into the debate, and soon the agent faced organized opposition.

On May 14, Dr. McGill asked the agent and council to exempt from
duty miscellaneous merchandise shipped to him on the *Kent*. They refused, presumably on grounds that the doctor intended to use the material for trade. It is somewhat surprising that McGill should have
asked for such a favor, since he had led the other merchants in subvert-
ing the law and stridently opposed the agent's attempts to reform it.
The council met again on May 15 to take up the problems exposed in
the garbled accounts of D. C. MacFarland. They resolved that henceforth, the collector must record all his receipts in a substantial ledger.
He must enter anchorage and lighthouse duties on a separate account
and store the money separately. At a session the next day they went
further, repealing the 5 percent duty on the declared value of goods
landed, replacing it with fixed rates for about fifty of the most common
trade goods.[13]

The controversy opened a deep rift between Russwurm and McGill.
The doctor seems to have known that he was wrong, but rather than
admit error he blamed the governor. Moreover, he lied to outsiders
about his role in the affair. On July 12 he wrote Latrobe that political
life in the colony was harmonious, barely hinting that there had been
any dispute, though he blandly mentioned that news to that effect might
have reached Baltimore. He acknowledged that fixed charges on imports probably did increase the colonial revenue, but he would have
preferred that Russwurm "persevere" in charging duties the way they
had been before. The laws were obeyed, though complained of, the
only seizure being of some samples, valued less than a dollar, that were
sent ashore without duties. Again, in a letter of September 6, he admit-

ted to Latrobe that he was one of Russwurm's opponents. "By frankly stating to him in private wherein his proceedings were generally considered illegal and unjust," he wrote self-servingly, "I have had the misfortune to incur his displeasure, so that now any farther approach to friendly and confidential intercourse is out of the question; he is not moved by generous impulses such as often influence others." Portraying Russwurm as a tyrant, he claimed to act in the cause of liberty against "arbitrary encroachments."[14]

At the July sitting of the Court of Quarterly Sessions, the governor had the unpleasant duty of prosecuting two settler merchants on three charges of "dealing in ardent spirits." George Hardy was fined seventy-five dollars for his first offense, the details of which are not on record. John Bowen was convicted of two counts of retailing rum through a factor at Half Cavally. McGill defended Bowen in court, increasing Russwurm's fury. "I did so because on my refusing at first, [Bowen] charged me and others as being determined to convict him, as a reason for the refusal," McGill wrote Latrobe shortly after. "Upon reflection I thought that my doing so, and doing it energetically might serve a good purpose, by tending to satisfy the sympathetic feelings of those who are his followers, (as he is a regular political demagogue, and disturber) I do not regret that I done so, altho' our Governor seemed a little 'riled' in consequence." He added that if Russwurm "cannot appreciate the motives that influenced me it is no fault of mine." He pretended to be glad that Bowen lost and was punished. Although he may have persuaded himself that his motives were pure, his own livelihood sprang from trade, and having once betrayed his brother-in-law (at least so far as Russwurm was concerned), he had little to lose by continuing an open opposition.[15]

Having purchased Fishtown after much expense and palaver, the agent was unable to take advantage of the acquisition. He expended most of his available funds on lumber for a house but was left with no funds to pay builders. Moreover, he could find no settlers willing to move to so remote a spot. In 1843, Dr. Savage had occupied the old A.B.C.F.M. station, which consisted of a cluster of tiny frame houses with high-pitched, shingled roofs. The Episcopal mission's purpose had been to operate out of the colony's reach, and they would not assist in any colonial expansion there. Russwurm consoled himself with the knowledge that the French too had failed to fulfill plans for a coaling station for their man-o'-war steamers at Garroway. The deed could remain dormant with no harm, available for future expansion.

For the time being, Russwurm was interested in expanding colonial influence to leeward. At the end of 1845, Tabou and Bassa were reportedly eager to align themselves with Maryland, or, if necessary, the English or French, to improve their trade. Russwurm wanted to be first with an offer, to forestall foreign encroachment, which he felt was imminent. "The mania for acquiring territory in Africa is quite the rage," he informed Latrobe, "and every point of note to Windward and Leeward of us, favorable for trade has been seized upon, and books, dashes and flags given to the poor untutored natives." The colony wanted Tabou, Bassa, Little and Grand Berriby to the leeward, and Garroway and Grand Sess to windward, "but here our pathway is blocked up by the French who claim Garroway and half the coast of Africa." Lately, British captains had told him that the French had asserted claims to Cape Lahou, "on account of some palaver with the natives for taking possession of the goods of a vessel which was cast away on this coast."[16]

An opportunity arose in the middle of February, 1846, when Tabou, Bassa, and the Beribys sent word that they wished to discuss union. They had recently rebuffed a French offer to buy their towns. Now, they feared some retribution, and the standing offer of association with Harper became more inviting. The governor, Freeman, and other Grebo dignitaries immediately boarded the *Palestine*, a fine brig and auspice of the advantage of union. On February 23, the ship anchored off Bassa, where representatives of the four states had convened a grand palaver. The talks over two days were uncomplicated, considering what was at stake. With assurances of mutual protection, free trade, and schools, Russwurm annexed a fair portion of the Ivory Coast. The Marylanders walked up the strand to Harper, an uninterrupted stretch of colonial territory some sixty miles long.[17] On March 3, 1846, Governor Russwurm proclaimed the accession of Tabou, Bassa, and Grand Beriby. From this time forward, citizens of the colony must, "Honor the said Kings and headmen of the aforesaid countries with all due respect, as the true and lawful rulers thereof — to receive the subjects of said Kings as citizens of our common country, and not as strangers; and further, it is enjoined on all Magistrates and civil officers to have Justice fairly meted out to them in all palavers; and that they have free passage through our common country without hinderance."[18] Later in March, delegates from Half Beriby came to Harper to join their cousins in association with Maryland.

Russwurm also made overtures to Grand Sess, to the windward of Cape Palmas. A delegation went there to discuss annexation. When they arrived, they found the king and headmen drunk beyond comprehension, an English trader having left a good supply of rum there two or three days earlier. The embassy returned home to await a more favorable opportunity.[19]

The dry season during March and April, 1846, was much warmer than usual, averaging eighty-six degrees, with scarcely a drop of rain. Grebo farmers, experienced in the portents of weather, anticipated an adverse season and selected low-lying lands for their crops. Teams from Gbenelu cleared the swampy tract between Maryland Avenue and Hoffman's River, which they cut in a swath nearly three miles long, extending (by permission) onto unused portions of colonial farms. To Americans, who identified progress with the clearing of forests, the sight of gently undulating land covered with bright green blades of sweet-smelling young rice was quite cheering. Yet, the results were devastating for reasons then poorly understood, which McGill referred to as "exhalations" and "miasmatic effluvia." A distemper, probably borne by mosquitoes, soon broke out, killing most of Maryland's livestock. Disease also ravaged human communities, striking most severely areas adjacent to the newly cleared fields along Hance Road and in Tubmantown, where most deaths occurred. Residents of Harper went virtually unscathed.[20]

The doctor had some 130 patients under his care and lost fourteen. "Diseases hitherto simple," he noted, "mild in their character and uniform in their course, assuming complicated, severe, irregular and malignant features shortly after attack." He was hard pressed to attend to so many. To make matters worse, his own young wife fell ill and soon died, leaving him with a daughter just ten weeks old. He hoped that Dempsey Fletcher would soon return to relieve him of some responsibility.[21]

By September the weather had resumed its normal patterns, and the health of settlers improved. The previous few months were unparalleled for mortality. By the end of October, thirty-three citizens had died, twenty-six of them adults. A hunting accident, in which a party of settlers recklessly shot a Grebo man whom they mistook for a deer, raised some difficulty, but the palaver was settled amicably. At the visit of the U.S.S. *United States*, the Latrobe Artillery Company fired a salute with one of their rusty field pieces. On preparing a second charge, the cannon exploded, blowing a hand off each of the men ramming it. The ship's surgeons treated them, and both survived. Their prospects were bleak. One of them, whose wife had also lost a hand, had seven children to support. Officers collected $141 for their benefit.[22]

Major Bolon suffered considerably from his first attacks of malaria. "I had the fever very Bad," he wrote Hall on May 25, "But thanks B to god that I have got well of it." For some time after, he had a severe tremor in his hands. Construction began in earnest halfway through March. At month's end, workmen had laid the keel and cut out some ribs for the larger boat. Bolon was pleased with the quality of the African timber, especially the tortured trunks grown in forests subject to periodic cutting, so suitable for fashioning knees and other bent-grain pieces. He planned to finish by the first of September. "Dokter Send the word and i will Bring her to Baltimore," he wrote, "for if you never trost a Colard man you never now what he Can Do." He promised that he would return to Africa after a brief visit. John Lewis, a caulker sent out as Bolon's assistant, worried that his family was suffering in Baltimore and so was unhappy. Russwurm appeased him by promising to have fifty dollars delivered to his wife, and he wrote Hall to make sure his word was fulfilled.[23]

McGill had a somewhat different impression of the shipwrights. He commented about the same time that Bolon had talked before of returning to the United States, but now he seemed determined to stay at Cape Palmas. Having been master in Africa, a return to the Baltimore shipyards would be difficult to bear. Lewis, the caulker, he labeled "soulless," saying that he was much too complacent, "contented under any and every thing."[24] In reality, McGill seems to have cultivated Bolon as an ally, and so blinded himself. Bolon was in fact eager to return to Baltimore, contrary to the doctor's assertion.[25]

On December 17, Major Bolon tried to launch the larger schooner, christened *Cavally*. The railway was defective, and the vessel rolled off on her side in shallow water. The next three or four days the builders worked frantically to push her through the mud into the channel of Hoffman's River. She was larger and heavier than Russwurm had realized, rating nearly fifty-nine tons and drawing seven feet of water unloaded. In order to get her over the bar, as it was dry season, workers made up a raft of oil casks and careened the vessel over it to raise the keel. This was successful, and everyone was proud of the result of so much hard work. In January she cruised to leeward, proving herself an excellent sailor. Russwurm believed that with a full complement of sails she could outrun any other Liberian vessel. The four canvases that she had were adequate for the time being, but he urged the society to send the rest without delay.[26]

As soon as Bolon finished his assignment, Russwurm cashiered him. In the first intimation of trouble, late in January, Russwurm wrote

Latrobe that Bolon was a good craftsman but an overbearing spend-thrift. "Backed by certain men of standing here," he reported, "he fairly got beside himself, and instead of economising in the building of the vessel, put the society to every possible expense: the least expostulation from me, threw him into a passion, and such language — such cursings I never heard before (for the latter he has been fined twice.) Desirous to second your views, the workmen under Bolon and myself bore until toward the last, the fellow fairly forgot himself, and set my authority at defiance." From his erratic behavior, the governor speculated that Bolon was an alcoholic, in any case unfit for a good citizen. He thought much better of John Lewis, the caulker, and hoped that he would return to Cape Palmas with his family, as he planned.[27]

Concurrent with the ship-building activity in Africa, the Chesapeake and Liberia Trading Company was building its *Liberia Packet*, which left Baltimore on her maiden voyage on December 3, 1846. At 10 A.M., white and black citizens gathered on the wharf for religious services and speeches. At their conclusion, they cheered as the passengers—thirteen for Cape Palmas and twenty-six for Monrovia—and their belongings were loaded onto a boat to carry them out to the *Packet*, which lay farther out in the harbor. Other small craft came along, but the departing visits were kept short. With a brisk northwest breeze smacking of oncoming winter, the new vessel hauled anchor and quickly made way into the bay.[28]

James Hall, speaking for the society in the *Maryland Colonization Journal*, lamented that so few black people had invested in the project or volunteered to emigrate on the first voyage. Nonetheless, he hoped that this vessel would awaken black Americans to new economic and national opportunities. "The passing of this shuttle between the Chesapeake and Liberia," he exclaimed, "will weave a bond of union between the coloured man in America and his *free* Liberian brother that shall never be severed." He went on,

We have long since declared, and we were the first to declare it effectively, that if Liberia was ever to be free, and to be well governed, that
government must be administered by a coloured man; and we now
as firmly believe, that if the cause of colonization is to prosper — if
the colonies are to receive large and valuable accessions of emigrants
from this country, it must be through the agency and action of the
coloured people themselves, — it must be in vessels of their own, and
under their own direction; and we view this one barque, this "Liberia
Packet," of which we have said so much, for which we have felt so
much and laboured so hard, as but the *small* beginning of an extensive system of operations to be by them prosecuted and perfected.

Here Hall, a white propagandist, formulated ideas of black self-
sufficiency and nationalism, decrying at the same time the lack of support from the black community itself. In the same issue of the *Journal*,
he reported that a black Bible society had sent a few books to Harper,
the first such act he had ever heard of, and he hoped, a sign of better
things to come.[29]

XV.

"A Clap of Thunder"

A SPIRIT OF OPTIMISM PERVADED MARYLAND AT THE BEGINNING OF 1847. For a moment, everything seemed to portend a bright future. A ship of settlers' own making was in the water, business was good, and planting season was about to begin. Relations between the colony and its African neighbors were peaceful. The chronic palaver between Grahway and Half Cavally eased, so much so that citizens of Grahway felt secure enough to rebuild their town, though each side feared sorcery and kept aloof from the other. The governor's influence increased. "If I demand it, I might almost dictate in their palavers, but this would be going to needless trouble and expense; and unless requested never interfere," he wrote Latrobe at the end of January. Pahs were reportedly trying to reach Cape Palmas but were turned back by threats and violence. He could do nothing but wait for them, faithful that they would at last make their way to the beach.[1]

The *Liberia Packet* sighted Cape Palmas on January 22, 1847, completing her maiden voyage in fifty days, including layovers. Besides settlers and supplies, she carried the board's resolution to amend the tariff law, confirming the fixed rates set in a meeting of the council some months before. "All good citizens and lovers of peace" were happy with the board's action, Russwurm wrote, thanking Latrobe.[2]

Dempsey Fletcher returned to Africa aboard the *Packet*, having completed a course of medical instruction under Dr. Phelps in New Hampshire. The new doctor was a disappointment when compared with Samuel F. McGill. He was no scholar and lacked polish and self-confidence, for which he compensated with the superciliousness of a house servant. Consequently, society officers did not treat him very well. They granted him a salary considerably lower than McGill's and then made his post more onerous. The colonial physician had heretofore treated settlers without charge. Dr. Fletcher was instructed to make them pay some share of the cost of visits and medicines, according to their ability. The fees were not very high—approximately ten cents per dose and medical visits from five to seventy-five cents, depending on the case and wealth of the patient—but citizens were unanimously opposed to the idea. They blamed Fletcher for creating the new policy. Anthony Wood and Paul Sansay got up a petition in protest. "Our people have been made children of so long, that they are really spoiled," Russwurm wrote contemptuously. From the end of January to the beginning of March, Fletcher had receipts of twenty-five cents, though he had continuous work.[3] In a letter of October 5, Fletcher admitted that he had originally supported the plan of making settlers pay for care, but now he asserted that they were genuinely too poor to pay. "It is a pity for them to die for want of such," he wrote. He paid for medicines out of his own pocket, "without the least expectation of any compensation."[4]

Fletcher was not fully prepared for his new responsibilities. The practice required more effort than medical school, and much of what he had learned in America was irrelevant to the maladies he encountered. He had no generous, learned counselor like Dr. MacDowell, for McGill ignored him. In fact, McGill sailed to America on the *Packet* and would be absent for eight months. On his return, he laid down the tiresome duties of physician, confining his practice to family and friends, though he continued to draw full salary from the society.[5]

The *Packet* set off for home once again early in March, entering Baltimore harbor on April 6, a remarkably quick passage. She was a fleet sailer, and was reported to have beaten even pilot boats under full sail. In addition to Dr. McGill, she carried home Mrs. Russwurm, her daughter, a servant, the shipwrights Bolon and Lewis, settlers Jackson and Wilson, and other passengers. At the Cape De Verdes, she picked up a number of men sent home from duty on the African Squadron. The Chesapeake and Liberia Trading Company's plan was to make two or more voyages to Africa each year, but the prospects for emigrants were so bleak upon her return, Hall had her loaded with freight for a voyage to Le Havre, France. He hoped that things would improve by her return.[6]

At the start of June, Russwurm fell dangerously ill. The episode began with excessive salivation, often a sign of too much calomel. It is quite possible that the inexperienced Dr. Fletcher overmedicated him. Soon after, he developed a persistent cough and fever that confined him to his bed. Colonial officers kept the government on an even course while he was incapacitated.[7]

Russwurm's principal assistant during his illness was William A. Prout, a young man born a slave about 1820 and sometime resident of Baltimore, who had spent most of his life in Africa. Prout, for all of his good qualities, had a weakness for alcohol—scandalous in a community sworn to temperance. Like James Thomson, he seems to have had a meek temperament, too easily swayed by circumstance. Though Russwurm liked and trusted Prout, his family detested him. Mrs. Russwurm would scarcely speak to him because of his moral lapses. Ford McGill was jealous of Prout's growing influence over his brother-in-law.[8]

On the night of June 1, the small schooner, *King Freeman*, sent from America at great expense, ran aground near Garroway in a gale. The crew came ashore safely and were treated courteously. The headmen of the nearest hamlet promised to look after the wreck, and the crew went up to Garroway for dinner. When they came back the next morning, the villagers had stripped the boat and sawn up her timbers. The crew reclaimed the sails and most of the cargo, but their vessel was gone. Not long after, Russwurm talked the palaver with the king of Garroway. He won four hundred croos of oil as damage, but he hardly expected to get the full amount unless a man-o'-war would support him, which he knew was improbable. The alternative was to take some Garroway people hostage, but since he traded regularly there, he would rather absorb the loss than suffer a long-term feud.[9]

The schooner *Cavally* continued in constant motion, delivering trade goods to various factories and collecting palm oil and other African produce. On August 1 she loaded a cargo of a thousand gallons of oil at Garroway. Captain Oliver, whom Russwurm had recruited at Monrovia, stowed the puncheons toward the bows rather than distribute them evenly in the hold. The vessel left Garroway under full sail with a brisk breeze, expecting to make a quick run home. The arrangement was obviously dangerous to the krumen of Garroway, fearless sailors, who saw her list sharply in the gusts. At noon, the sun shining and the wind a little variable, the schooner approached the Cape. The captain went into the cabin to write up his accounts. Then the helmsman went below to get his dinner, giving the wheel to an inexperienced hand. The first mate was in the bow preparing to cast anchor. He called to the helmsman to turn the vessel into the breeze, "hard to luff," but the man did just the opposite. Broadside to the wind, the *Cavally* rolled over. Her crew jumped into the water, and all made it safely ashore.[10]

Russwurm was sick in bed at the time, and when told what had happened supposed he must be delirious. For three days the vessel bobbed, almost stationary, despite efforts to tow her to shore. Sails still spread beneath the waves, a current then caught and carried her to leeward. She snagged a reef and remained for a day or two between Cape Palmas and Grahway. She then drifted toward Grahway Reef and foundered again, soon to break up. A German vessel large enough to have towed the hulk arrived a few days later, but by then all trace had disappeared, except for some sails that washed ashore. The agent hoped that the board had insured the vessel. "This unforeseen calamity has come upon me like a clap of thunder," he wrote, "all my arrangements are frustrated about trade to Leeward." He had fifty puncheons of oil on hand that he could send home immediately, and in three months he could have as much again. The season was coming on though, and bills for trade goods were falling due.[11]

Soon after the wreck of the *Cavally*, and perhaps because of the stress, the governor was struck with a severe headache that continued unabated for more than two months. About the first of September he suffered a nosebleed that persisted for three hours despite Fletcher's close attendance. Russwurm, a veteran of illness, was frightened for his life. At the beginning of October, he was still too feeble to do very much and was very low in spirits. He missed his wife terribly and longed for her to return to him soon.[12]

Early in November, the agency was left with no boats at all when Major Bolon's little schooner ran aground. Russwurm believed that there must be something wrong with the design of the vessels. He encouraged the society to send a shipwright again, only someone other than Bolon, whom he dreaded might come out under contract from McGill and Bowen.[13] The *Liberia Packet* was already late, and the thought that she too may have been lost at sea weighed heavily upon him.

Money was to be made, but unless he had a serviceable boat, others would assume the agency's business.[14] The agent saw a crisis of sorts at hand: "Our region of country is flooded with trust money: the spirit and desire to monopolise has induced some of our traders to trust almost every body who called for credit. Where all this oil is to come in, is a great question." Greboes never refused an advance of goods, whether or not they could fulfil their bargain—let the foreigner try to catch them if they failed. Russwurm himself had advanced a considerable amount, but he did not expect to recover a quarter of it, having lost the *Cavally*. If he was not able to pick up the oil soon after it was gathered at the factories, Grebo trademen would sell it to the first ship that passed.[15]

With hard work and luck, things turned out better than hoped. When the *Packet* finally did arrive, about the middle of December, the agency was free of debt with a good supply of trade goods on hand. Russwurm had sixty casks of palm oil to send home for the society's benefit. He would have had even more, but the long wait for an opportunity to ship it had resulted in a loss of 10 percent from leakage and other accidents. Rice was scarce, but he had been lucky enough to purchase a supply of corn meal, which would serve the new emigrants well.[16]

The *Liberia Packet* delivered forty-one emigrants, Dr. McGill, Mrs. Russwurm, and other passengers to Cape Palmas. The voyage was almost twice as long as normal, ninety-six days from Baltimore to Cape Palmas. Provisions ran low. Captain Goodmanson's frustration increased as the days drew out. He fought with his crew and George Hall, the supercargo, which made the passage even more unpleasant. McGill excused the captain under the trying circumstances. Goodmanson had faults, the doctor admitted, but he still considered him the best man for the job. The first mate, a black man named Haley, was doing well in his apprenticeship. After another voyage he should be able to take command of the vessel, McGill thought.[17]

Ford McGill returned ready to fight with his brother-in-law. They met at the wharf but had no opportunity to speak, as Sarah Russwurm fainted while the longboat tossed in the breakers. She required nearly three hours of attention before she revived. McGill found much to criticize. During his absence, the governor had been so sick that he thought he must die. He turned desperately to Prout, whom he had earlier dismissed for intemperance. McGill loathed Prout and hoped that Russwurm would fire him at the soonest opportunity. He also condemned the continuation of Thomas Jackson in office, stating that Russwurm was Jackson's only ally in the colony, that the judge was so unpopular that Russwurm only hurt himself by keeping him on.[18] "Russwurm must now be convinced of one fact," McGill wrote Hall, "I have never striven to render these people disaffected toward his administration. I find the people openly complaining against him and his measures. My cause will be as it ever has been to use every effort in my power to restore tranquility: this I shall do until he classes me among the disaffected, and then I shall attend to my own business and leave him to settle matters without my aid or assistance."

McGill's critique of the colonial government was certainly biased. The agency was his rival in trade, and his interest was not the good of Maryland in Liberia but his own coffers. He had long since given up medicine in favor of business and politics. His father's company had prospered under his direction. McGill, Brothers had branches at Cape

Palmas (operated with his brother, Roszell) and Monrovia (managed by brother James, who was active in politics there). Brother Urias was a sea captain. The firm was closely linked with the Chesapeake and Liberia Trading Company in Baltimore under the titular head of George Hall, closely watched by his father.[19] Thinking his relationship with Hall cozy, McGill asked him to arrange the gift or sale of the landing place to leeward of Russwurm's Island, where Fair Hope had once been. He now leased the site from the agency and had built a warehouse there, but he would prefer to own it. Hall seems to have ignored the request.[20]

On May 5, the governor asked the board for guidance, complaining angrily that McGill, Brothers were running rum from Cape Palmas to Grand Sess aboard the sloop *Star* to trade for malaguetta pepper. Samuel McGill did not consider this illegal, since Grand Sess was outside the limits of the colony and the sloop was registered at Monrovia to Urias McGill. Even so, she had sailed from Harper for the previous year, her crew was composed of Marylanders, and Roszell McGill, her supercargo, was a resident of Harper, though he was a citizen of Liberia. Liquor was handled in Maryland, and Maryland merchants profited. Moreover, traders who obeyed the law stood no chance against vessels offering rum. McGill was determined to follow his own interests and the law be damned.[21]

John Russwurm left Cape Palmas on February 7, 1848, aboard a merchant ship whose captain intended to coast down to Fernando Poo and back. McGill advised him to do so, as he was too weak to work, and a release from the strain of duty ought to do him good. Trade was dull, and the community was at peace, so the governor felt free to go. Nicholas Jackson, vice-agent, had formal charge of government, but McGill, whom the board had appointed assistant agent, had the stronger personality and actually governed. A major part of the burden fell to Prout, who conducted trade.[22]

Within days of Russwurm's departure, the Kudemowe and Nyomowe towns to leeward of Cape Palmas resumed their war. On March 15, Half Cavally took and burned two Grand Cavally villages, killing eight and wounding fifteen others. Two more engagements quickly followed, Half Cavally the victor in each. By the end of March, twenty-five men and an uncertain number of women and children had been killed in fighting that was remarkably cruel. "Quarter is never given," McGill wrote disgustedly, "they decapitate men, women and children." He predicted that there would be no peace until one or the other of the opposing sides was driven off the beach or exterminated.[23]

Gbenelu was eager to join the fight against Half Cavally but was afraid of drawing in Rocktown and Fishtown. "We are of course neutral," McGill wrote home, adding that he had done all he could to maintain peace. "As we could not prevent the war I am truly glad that they are now being pummelled for their blustering obstinacy," he remarked of Grahway and Grand Cavally. "Should our Cape Palmas natives aid in the contest and bring upon themselves an attack," he continued, "we shall only stipulate with their assailants to leave us unmolested (and be prepared to repel any encroachments) and let them lay on — should they be vanquished and driven from our immediate neighborhood it will be a blessing, and I very much question whether we could ever agree to their return." As long as Russwurm was away, McGill chose to let them murder one another rather than waste time trying to impose an armistice.[24]

Rice was already in short supply, and none of the leeward towns would be able to plant this season. In all likelihood, the windward Greboes and bush towns would sell to their warring cousins before the Marylanders. McGill foresaw hardship and even famine if supplies did not arrive soon. Moreover, with Russwurm away, no one was authorized to make a large purchase of provisions if the opportunity offered. He complained that settlers knew that rice might run out but still neglected to plant their gardens. The few industrious farmers in the community risked losing their crops to Grebo and settler pilferers. He hoped vainly that hard times would teach a lesson in self-sufficiency. The supply of palm oil also dwindled, because noncombatant Grebo farmers devoted their attention to their rice farms. McGill guessed that no appreciable amounts would be offered before the middle of May.[25]

On the last day of March, the brig *Amazon*, chartered by the Chesapeake and Liberia Trading Company, hailed Cape Palmas. Her arrival
was cheering, not so much for the new arrivals as the food that accompanied them. There was not enough in the ground, McGill estimated,
to last the settlement ten days. Roszell McGill had cruised to leeward to
buy rice, but at last report he had passed Beriby and beyond the limits
of Maryland with little success.[26]

Russwurm returned to Harper in time to see the *Amazon* sail, still
weak, but in improved health. In nine weeks, he had traveled as far east
as the Portuguese island of Sao Thome, which recently had been a key
post in the slave trade to Brazil. He landed at various points as the ship
went about its business, promoting the Maryland settlement to whomever would listen. He also gathered breadfruit and other useful plants
to try on the Public Farm.[27]

———⋅✦⋅———

William Cassell was one of three emigrants aboard the *Amazon*. He had
been one of the *Ann*'s company, but he left Harper after a brief stay,
made bitter by the death of his wife. He resumed his profession of barber in Baltimore, determined to make the best of things under the slave
power. He married again and started a new family. Yet Liberia haunted
him, and he kept in touch with James Hall and other colonizationists,
who appreciated his honesty and intelligence. They apprenticed him to
Hugh Davey Evans, a principal architect of the colony's constitution and
civil code. Cassell learned quickly, and his sponsors planned a career for
him in the colonial courts. At the end of his instruction, Evans issued a
certificate stating that Cassell was qualified to practice law in Maryland,
his race only preventing him from doing so.[28] The new lawyer was nowhere more enthusiastically received than in the home of his former
brother-in-law, Joshua Stewart, who rejoiced that a man like him, with
no formal education in childhood, could become a lawyer. His children
would "live to Se capepalmos Rise," Stewart exulted, "Like the Sun Shooting from behind the Eastering Harason, Giving Light to the world."[29]

Russwurm was also glad to see Cassell in Harper. He gave him the post of storekeeper to provide him with a living wage. The agency's trade had grown so much lately, despite the temporary abatement, that Cassell would have plenty to occupy himself. Russwurm was disappointed that the lawyer did not carry a judge's commission, for the administration of laws was onerous to him.[30] Nicholas Jackson, vice-agent, was nominally one grade below the agent on the bench, but he was too ignorant to be effective. The justices of the peace appointed to hear petty cases were inadequate and added to his troubles. One of them, Thomas Jackson, was despised by most everyone, but he had continued in office for years. McGill labeled Jackson "mischievous and tyrannical," but Russwurm remembered that Jackson had supported him in acquitting James Thomson back in 1837, and he would not betray him.[31]

The *Amazon* carried an invitation to Russwurm to come to Baltimore by the next return of the *Liberia Packet*. He immediately arranged for an extended leave. Prout had conducted the agency's trade satisfactorily during his voyage to leeward, and he was confident of the young man's ability to manage affairs during a longer period. Cassell would support him as storekeeper, and Ford McGill would resume charge of government. McGill would rather not have had the duty, as times were likely to be difficult and settlers hated him as much as he did them. Nevertheless, he promised the agent and the board that he would protect the agency's resources as best he could—something like leaving the wolf to guard the sheep.[32]

In fact, many settlers were discontented, though not many had the ability or courage to complain to the board. Joshua Stewart was an exception. "In this little Republic, the sam Administration have Existed too Longe," he wrote James Hall on June 12. "This longe Administration have been detrimental to the Intrest of this Republic and it have been a question here, wether the Board of Manejer have determined to keep this Colony under the administration of one Man for Life." Citizens were aware that Russwurm was competent for the job, but twelve years in office was enough. "Where a Man have lived in Ofice So longue, having Great Power Guaranteed to him, he in time looses all Sympathy for thouse he govenes, and becums a petty Tyrant." They wondered whether the precedent was good for an infant state. What was worse, a rumor was current that Ford McGill would be acting governor during Russwurm's absence. Stewart could hardly believe the report, but if it were true he hoped that the board would reconsider. "Well But if it take Wel with them, it Whant take Well with ous," he wrote, "Becaus he is too young, the Next place he is too Near in famely connection and Monopoly is his Object."[33]

With Russwurm about to depart for America, Freeman took the opportunity to ask for a consideration from the society. He hired a scribe to remind Latrobe that his people had lived in peace with the Americans for fourteen years with scarcely an interruption. In 1834, Dr. Hall had promised him an annual dash and dinner every Saturday. He had held his peace when these promises were discontinued by his successors in office. To make up for the slight, he asked for "1 Case Muskets 1 Crate wash Basins 5 Furred Hats 2 Brass Kettles 1 Box Brass Rods one over Coat 5 — 20 lb. Kegs Powder 5 ps. Satin Stripe 1 Box Cutlasses." Moreover, he wanted a frame house. "I am tired of living in my native made huts," he explained. Bill Williams, alias Simleh Ballah, would appreciate a hat, a coat, and a large pitcher like a treasured gift left in Baltimore in 1837.[34]

The *Liberia Packet* made Cape Palmas about the middle of June, having collected a cargo of oil and other produce. Within two or three days, she was ready to sail to windward. On the seventeenth, Russwurm addressed instructions to McGill, careful not to patronize one who already knew the governor's duties and the needs of settlers. His advice was therefore fairly specific.[35] McGill received the letter courteously but with considerable regret, for with the economy so weak much of it was moot. Rice and palm oil were almost unavailable. Medicine and other supplies were also running out. The future seemed barren, and he was at a loss how to make matters any better.[36]

The *Liberia Packet* returned to Baltimore on August 10, having left Monrovia twenty-eight days before. The passage was very nearly the shortest on record and made up for the terribly slow one of the previous year. Russwurm was visiting the city for the first time, to see the place where his wife grew up and meet the men who had had so great an impact on his life. He also planned to visit his adoptive family in Maine. Bowdoin College would hold its commencement exercises about the same time, and he wanted to attend.

The Russwurms' welcome to Baltimore was more humble than they might have expected, for Latrobe and many other officers of the society were out of town on vacations when the *Packet* came into port. Only James Hall—an old friend certainly—was there to greet them, and he was caught unprepared. The doctor sent notices to his colleagues and suggested that the Russwurms take the train to New England. They went directly to North Yarmouth, where they had a pleasant reunion. At Bowdoin, Russwurm was reportedly offered the presidency of a projected black college, but he declined the opportunity.[37]

At the beginning of September, the Russwurms came back to Baltimore for a brief visit until the *Packet* should be ready to sail again. Their reception now was far more cordial than they expected. The society and many of its friends gathered to meet and fete their agent. None except Hall and old Moses Sheppard had ever met the man who had served their cause so long and faithfully. James Dorsey threw a banquet for him at the elegant Exchange Hotel, where the society congratulated itself for having chosen so able a man. The astonished Irish waiters crowded around the doors to see a black man so honored. Competent doctors examined him and recommended treatment that improved him perceptibly. Russwurm even sat for a daguerreotype. The governor boarded the *Packet* once again on September 6 to return to Africa, leaving his wife behind for a more extended visit.[38]

━━

Russwurm was away during some of the hardest times the settlement at Cape Palmas had ever witnessed. The war between Half Cavally and her neighbors dragged on. In July, McGill traveled to Grand Cavally to mediate a cease-fire, but he was rejected with such threats that he dared not spend the night. He believed that he had been in grave peril in the episode, and he blamed Freeman for having deceived him about the risks of the undertaking. He determined to have revenge at the earliest opportunity.[39]

Gbenelu wanted to send soldiers to aid Grahway but feared that that would bring Rocktown into the fight. Freeman knew that McGill would defend settlers against any harm, and also that he would happily stand aside and let Gbenelu burn to the ground if Rocktown attacked. "I cannot perceive any course," McGill wrote, "whereby I can check or arrest the disasters that threaten our territory by this general warlike feeling, and can only promise to keep our Colony from any participation in it. We cannot force them to make peace yet we can withhold aid and support even from Cape Palmas people if they bring war upon themselves by an unjustifiable interference with others." As it turned out, relations between settlers and the Gbenelu remained exceptionally calm.[40]

Neutral traders were restricted from the beach, which hindered the mercantile operations of the agency. The leeward towns were also unable to plant rice for themselves. McGill had reports that inhabitants of Half Cavally were dying of starvation. The crop in the fields looked like it would be a good one, but most of it was destined to feed the towns at war, rather than Americans. As a consequence, what rice there was was ten times more expensive than it had been the year before. McGill was encouraged to see that settlers had more vegetables growing than at any time in their history, but nothing would be ready for harvest for another two or three months. All of the potatoes, ripe or not, had been stolen from the Public Farm. McGill ordered more planted and also planted cassava on the public lands around Mt.

Tubman. Food was at least as scarce as it had been in 1838, he reported, but settlers would not starve.[41] During the first week of August, McGill sent the agency's sloop to Monrovia for provisions. This was against his instructions, but he thought he had no alternative.[42]

In early November, McGill wrote Latrobe that settlers were living on palm cabbage and potato leaves. They were paying five or six dollars per bushel for green rice, "in the straw." The Public Farm was again stripped of unripe potatoes and anything else that might fill pinching stomachs. The inevitable result of such a diet was an increase in disease and mortality. Still, Greboes suffered even more severely than settlers. McGill estimated that their mortality was proportionally three times greater than that of Americans. At Grand Cavally, many had starved. The two agency boats were now continually employed getting rice, but they were getting scarcely enough to meet daily needs. Not surprisingly, traffic in palm oil almost ceased. McGill asserted that the previous five months' receipts had not equaled those of five weeks in the previous year. Malaguetta pepper was the only thing plentiful, but there was currently no foreign market for it.[43]

The fourth voyage of the *Liberia Packet* to Cape Palmas was as remarkable for slowness as the previous one in the opposite direction had been for speed. On October 25, fifty days from Baltimore, she hailed Monrovia. During the passage, she had sprung a leak, which was patched, but not before much of the cargo was damaged by seawater and bilge. Almost two weeks were spent off Cape Mount, each day's progress lost at night to opposing currents. Provisions ran low, leading Russwurm to complain that a cabin ticket that cost one hundred dollars ought to include better fare. She finally reached Cape Palmas on November 17. In a letter to Latrobe upon his return, Russwurm wrote that his health had continued to improve at sea, the tedious passage notwithstanding. The treatment he had received in Baltimore had been so beneficial that he believed ten or fifteen years had been added to his life.[44]

Greboes and settlers alike welcomed Russwurm back to Harper. They looked to him to set things straight. With guests to entertain and many loose ends, he found himself quite busy indeed. At three in the morning on November 22, he composed a letter to Hall. He joked about William Prout, who was busy building a house and looking for a wife. The young man was badly disappointed that he had not brought a bride back from America with him, but Russwurm had no intention of taking on the burden of match-maker. He was pleased to find that Prout was completely temperate now, declining even ale.[45]

⚬⚬⚬

The Grebo states finally declared an armistice early in 1849. Serious fighting had ended months before, but bad feelings persisted, trade was interrupted, and the danger of a flare-up continued until the spewing of water, the traditional gesture of peace. Each side had played dirty tricks on the other. Moreover, Gbenelu had successfully fostered distrust among the leeward towns, to its own advantage. King Freeman delayed the palaver as long as he could and then tried to sabotage it, as he had when McGill attempted to end the war in July. Russwurm visited Half Cavally with Freeman beforehand to select delegates. The king suggested two who might serve well, but in fact they were the most detestable men who could have been found. The two Half Cavally men walked to Grahway with the governor, king, and their retinue. As soon as the Half Cavally men were recognized, Grahway soldiers rushed to kill them. Russwurm stepped between them, at risk to his own life to prevent it. He was furious at Freeman, and some time passed before he could even bring himself to speak to him. In retaliation he forbade all trade in guns and powder with Gbenelu. "They don't like it," he commented laconically, "we don't care."[46]

The missionary John Payne recorded an episode at Half Cavally connected with the end of the war that illustrates the depth of the social disturbance it had caused. On Saturday, November 10, 1848, the townspeople had slaughtered fourteen bullocks to the spirits of those killed in the war and to commemorate the close of that "glorious struggle." A *deya* then made a greegree "to cause general prosperity in the country, and especially to ensure a good supply of fish," but a few days later, while the town awaited the charm's effects, a crocodile unexpectedly appeared in the center of the village. "This creature, although if taken in ordinary circumstances, would have been killed and eaten, a most acceptable food, yet when found in so unnatural a situation, was at once declared to bode evil of no ordinary magnitude."

The townspeople immediately fetched the *deya,* who interpreted the omen and named the witch, a woman who had been born at Grahway. She was seized, Payne continued, and "very soon made a partial confession of her crime, saying that *she* did not take the crocodile into town but that she knew who did." The woman was hustled off to undergo *gidu,* as she had done once before, and, as then, she was given only a punishing dose and survived. She was then put under charge of a *deya,* who by some means elicited a confession. The woman was brought before the town to admit her guilt, but now she added details that implicated some of the most respectable citizens of Half Cavally. Her accusations mortified the people, and the *deya* had hard work interpreting them to prevent the delivery of a round of *gidu* to all of those she named. He gave new meaning to the crocodile that exonerated all except the poor woman. The deya "declared that she *was* a witch, and one of the worst kind; that she was in league with her relatives the Grahwayans, and visited them constantly at night to get 'we' (witchcraft,) in order to destroy this place and people, and as they valued their own safety, at once to kill the woman, before she had time to carry her plans into effect."

The victim was immediately taken to drink the poison, which worked hard with her. She fell unconscious and was dragged onto the beach, where she lay all day in the hot sun, visited only by individuals whose purpose was to torment her. Payne was warned from making any attempt to intervene, as the townspeople were intent upon killing her. At nightfall she was placed in a hut, and surprisingly, she was still breathing the next morning. The *sedibo* were done with her, and they turned her over to the *kedibo,* the boys' society, to finish the job. When Payne woke up that morning, he continued in his journal, "I saw these merciless executioners dragging the miserable victim, tied by her hands and feet, towards the spot where she was shortly to close her wretched existence. The poison, when taken, soon produced its effect. In an hour she was beyond the reach of her enemies, and in another, we saw her body tied on two poles, and borne on the heads of two relatives, towards the witches burying-place."[47]

XVI.

"A Threat at Nationality"

I N THE SECOND HALF OF 1847, LIBERIA GAINED FORMAL INDEPENDENCE
from the American Colonization Society. The colony had been
autonomous almost since its foundation, because of distance and
the brief life expectancies of its agents. Citizens of the new republic
elected former governor Joseph Jenkins Roberts president. Senators
and representatives of the various settlements, now established as counties, took their seats in Monrovia, as befitted a new nation. This development caught the Marylanders a little off guard. "The Monrovians
are making great calculations," Russwurm commented skeptically to
Hall on November 8, "Some only look at one side of the question: time
will show. Our people here generally dissent. The flag has been changed
to one star instead of the cross — rather impolitic I think."[1]

The move for independence was indeed a perilous one. No one
could tell whether other nations would honor Liberia's independence
or gobble up the helpless state. Great Britain and France soon established diplomatic relations. Although the United States refused to follow suit, the fact of Liberia's existence and thriving community was
apparent to black Americans. For those who considered emigration,
the republic was much more inviting than Maryland. To keep pace, the
society styled Maryland a "Commonwealth" and declared that henceforth, the colony must pay for its own public works. The society ex-

pected settlers to embrace their new dignity, but instead they objected loudly. The reason was plain enough: the colonial economy was simply too feeble to maintain the system of public charity on which they depended. Nominal independence meant nothing, because the society still insisted upon a restrictive commercial policy designed to promote an idealistic agrarian society that was demonstrably impractical on the coast of tropical Africa.

News of the colony's new status reached Harper late in 1848. Russwurm did not like the changes, but he was bound to follow them. Lately he had spent a considerable sum building a new stone jail and a treasury, paying workers with drafts on the store amounting to some four hundred dollars. He recorded the drafts as debts to the society. When McGill learned of it, he initiated a general protest. Russwurm laid the matter before the council. Vice-agent John Bowen argued that the debt might be called in at once. Russwurm countered that the society would not willingly bring on a financial crisis, but Bowen was unconvinced. In any event, his was the lone dissent, and the rest overruled him. Settlers who shared the vice-agent's opinion accused him and the rest of caving in to Russwurm's pressure. Joshua Stewart led a campaign against the incumbents in elections held the first Monday in March. Voters swept them from office and elected Stewart vice-agent.[2]

On April 7, 1849, citizens gathered to discuss the issues. The meeting named as a committee to petition the society for relief Rev. Boston Jenkins Drayton, Joshua Stewart, Reverend Francis Burns, Samuel Blackstone, Joseph T. Gibson, James B. Dennis, and W. C. Cornish. Most were longtime citizens of Maryland, but Boston Drayton was a newcomer from South Carolina, placed in Maryland with a vague commission from the Southern Baptist Missionary Society. The committee was instructed to deliver its remonstrance to a meeting one week later.[3]

Their report expressed a deep sense of grievance. As in other such documents, the writers were careful to assure their loyalty and patriotic intent. "In Petitioning to your Honerable Body," they wrote, "we are moved by natural, patriotic, and christian feelings, to pray for the removal of certain objects, which we earnestly beleive long since, have been, are now, impediments in rendering us comfortable. To set aside the sad and unpleasant feelings of despondency, which under existing circumstances nessarily arises, and according to the virtue of the priviledge; which, the '*Law*' *guarantees* we as sufferers, are not timid to make known, emphatically, yet respectfully our need." They declared that laws are the crown of civilization if they suit the condition of those whom they govern, but if not, they are society's curse. "It is clear there fore, that what we now testify against, tends to destroy the sinews of government, nor is it difficult to discern its tendency, to sap the foundations of our hoped for comforts; which we expect in this our 'Adopted Country' dear to us, because we anticipate while being here, through the kind Providence of God, to enjoy 'Sweet Liberty' in all its various branches, According to Law and Gospel." The poor citizens of Cape Palmas had borne meekly with inappropriate laws for some time, but the committee hoped the board would now pay heed to their peaceful dissent. They complained that the new arrangement would impoverish the colony and reduce its autonomy. Colonial revenues were too small to pay for the public works and charity on which the community depended. By themselves, Russwurm's recent building projects were more than settlers could ever reasonably pay back to the society.

The second complaint concerned mercantile licenses, which they felt were entirely too expensive. Most settlers had no chance of making a living by farming alone, and trade was a natural occupation for many to pursue. The law, however, prevented most from doing so. The result was monopoly—trade controlled by the agency and a few settlers with capital. Moreover, the cost of licenses was passed directly to settlers by merchants, raising the price of produce. In the third instance, petitioners argued that their paper currency should be based upon something more substantial than goods at the Colonial Store. The society's shinplasters, first issued in 1837, were worth but a fraction of their face value. Citizens worked hard for their living and ought to be paid with something of real value, like palm oil, camwood, or ivory. If the board was not willing or able to improve the currency, they should withdraw it. "There is an intimate connection between, Liberty and comforts," they wrote, both moves together in concert, one are dependent on the other, for Vitality, if one is taken Away the other must suffer. If one comforts are taken away, or such things be put in the way, as shall presumptuously hinder its influx. Then, Liberty which we are seeking after will be disregarded. The dignity of soul which is necessary, for a Man or Men to have as free-men, Must sink, for the want of a proper system. It is natural when wants becomes ones Companion, real happiness takes wings and fly Away, in this state, the mind is left to suggest and devise, All manner of evils, and if not quickly remedied, the result will be *Awful hence* we beg for a better system of things, for fear, such a Catastrophe will enevitably befall us. We desire it not! it is hoped, the time will never come to pass, to be said, We have no *Souls*, such are our *love for Freedom*, and our "Country" before it be said of us, we would prefer risking our Bark, upon the Sea of Nationality, and trust the "God of Nations" for the final result.

As appointed, citizens met again on April 14. Boston Drayton read the petition, largely his composition, with his most stirring oratory. When he had finished, there was some discussion of the facts. The document was then approved as written and signed by the five committee members and some sixty settlers. The signers included William Cassell, J. B. Bowen, Jacob Gross, Anthony Wood, many of the Tubmans, and other old settlers.

Russwurm was sympathetic to the complaint but doubted it would have much effect. He commented to the board that cutting duties was imprudent, given the impoverished state of the treasury. He did agree that licenses cost too much, but he was resigned to letting the board set its own policy. As for the paper money, he knew its shortcomings perfectly well. At first, he thought it was better to preserve it, though inadequate, but when he had seen the petition, he urged the society to withdraw it from circulation. The governor perceived a nascent movement to unite Maryland with Liberia, which disturbed him. Some of the principal men behind the petition supported union, and Russwurm suspected that they might turn their constituents toward the same position.[4] He particularly resented the newcomer, Drayton, who had taken so visible a role in the matter. The governor wished that Drayton's sponsors would give him some instructions about the duties of a missionary.[5]

While all of this political activity was developing in Maryland in Liberia, the society was just receiving dissenting letters and documents composed late in 1848. "This, although unpleasant to hear of, we rather like upon the whole," Hall wrote in *Maryland Colonization Journal*. "It proves, that, if any thing is wrong, which they can right, they will ultimately make it right."[6] Privately, James Hall resented the criticism. Unaware of the petition and other letters soon to arrive in Baltimore, he returned a scolding letter to Russwurm on the *Liberia Packet*, which was towed through the ice of Baltimore harbor on February 24, 1849. She experienced a slow and uncomfortable passage and did not reach Cape Palmas until the second half of April.

When he received the letter, Russwurm was already quite upset, frustrated that he could do so little to improve matters without the society's cooperation. Russwurm therefore appealed to Latrobe with a revealing explanation of the difficulties that he and the others faced. Settlers relied too much on the Agency Store he admitted. The society might do better to close it altogether, since it was the object of so much complaint. At least the store should stock goods of greater variety and quality. The society instructed him to buy supplies from the *Packet*, he complained, only to fault him for buying too much. "I am aware," he fumed, "that a considerable amount of goods is shipped yearly to the colony, but is your agent here to blame, if they are unsaleable"? The society was effectively glutting the market with too many goods of the same type, so that some things, even powder, could hardly be given away. "The blame lies somewhere," Russwurm asserted, "but not on us who have to sell the goods." "Of penitentiary handkerchiefs, furniture checks and blue prints, the colonists (as well as your agent) are heartily sick," he reported, not the less "because we think, that the same amount might as easily be expended in other goods." To emphasize his point, he put five bales of penitentiary handkerchiefs and three cases of furniture checks, just landed from the *Packet*, as well as three puncheons of handkerchiefs and checks from earlier cargoes, back aboard ship, informing

Latrobe that they would be easier to dispose of in Baltimore. The society should buy an assortment of other prints, in any colors but blue. If they would only adapt a little to changing fashions, he promised that there would be many fewer complaints from settlers. The last two shipments of powder were nearly ruined in transit, forcing him to the unpleasant and dangerous task of repacking kegs of bad powder mixed with good. Priced at two-thirds the going price, he could sometimes dispose of it at remoter ports, but no self-respecting Grebo would accept such trash in trade. In fact, the stuff was barely passable as a dash. If the society was content to see emigrants suffer and even starve, he concluded angrily, he would follow their policy.[7]

—•—

Early in August 1849, Maryland acquired Garroway, about fifteen miles to the northwest. The French never followed through with their plans to build a base there. Now, with wars raging in the bush and new threats from Nifou, her neighbor to the northwest, the town sought American protection. Russwurm returned to Cape Palmas without making peace, but he planned to send a commissioner for the purpose. Nifou and Garroway had feuded for generations, but Garroway was now tired of fighting. An outsider acting as intermediary could provide a face-saving way out, he believed.[8]

At Garroway, Russwurm slept in an open, drafty approximation of an American frame house. This, with exposure on the *Curlew*, the agency's small ketch, brought on an attack of rheumatic fever. The disease resembled gout, and soon he was unable to walk because of inflammation in his ankles. His illness, or possibly the drugs he received to combat it, deranged him intermittently. Dr. Fletcher prescribed the usual remedies, with no improvement. At a loss how to proceed, he reluctantly consulted Dr. McGill, who had always treated him with contempt. Though he was currently fighting with Russwurm, McGill overcame his pride and stepped in to help. Russwurm feared that he might soon die, and he turned over the government to McGill, who was his designated successor as assistant agent. Under McGill's care, Russwurm slowly got better. Ulcers appeared on his ankles and drained, with a reduction in swelling. Soon after, he felt well enough to write letters and perform other duties from his bedroom. Circumstances forced Russwurm and McGill to cooperate with each other, and they even managed to recover a degree of their former friendship.[9]

The *Liberia Packet* returned to Baltimore in August, 1849. She was at sea again by the first of September with missionaries, Mrs. Russwurm, several prominent Monrovians, and twenty-one emigrants. Ten were from Maryland, the balance were South Carolinians bound for Monrovia. The society was disappointed once again at so low a number for their own settlement, for the initial prospects had been quite fair. James Hammond, an old settler, had traveled through southern Maryland and had met a friendly reception in several places. A good number said they would emigrate, but when the traveling agent returned, nearly every one had an excuse not to go. The ties of family and neighborhood were strong, and candidates for Africa were often lobbied by their friends and (the society believed) abolition agents to stay.[10]

The *Packet* carried a response from the Board of Managers to the settlers' petition of the previous April. The letter politely explained in detail the reasons for maintaining the currency and other points of policy. It was intended to form part of a discourse, and Russwurm had separate instructions to put the question of currency and license fees to a vote.[11] Settlers, though, interpreted the board's letter as a rebuke. Many who had signed the petition now disavowed it. "The blockheads seem to imagine that they have acted criminally in signing it," McGill observed contemptuously, because they had not stood behind their beliefs.[12] Settlers also feared that the society might soon grant them independence, which would deprive them of considerable financial and material assistance. Henry Hannon, for example, wrote Hall at the time that he was glad that the board had cowed the petitioners. "The

Currency of this Colony has fed and Clothed me Ever since I have been here," he noted. The prospect of its elimination was hardly attractive.[13]

Thomas Jackson wrote to Latrobe after reading the letter. He regretted that citizens had made such a complaint in the first place. By way of parable, he suggested that his fellow citizens had gone too far, though they intended no disrespect or harm. The matter portended something deeper, he thought—a move toward independence. "I hope it will be like the Boy that undertook to Scare his father, hid himself Behind a bush when his father came Riding by his Son Jumped out and said Boof And the Horse throw the old man on the Ground the old man Said Son you boofed me too hard that time. The Sea of nationality I Cant Say much about, tho I have Been on the Ocine of time for a number of years I have Seen Some of the nation of the earth upon that Sea, and Experience teaches me that my Son John will not Be able to Ride that Sea as I would wish as I am Placed Like Mordeci who Set in the Kings Gate."[14]

Several weeks passed before citizens found courage to answer the board's letter collectively. A group gathered on December 29, 1849, to discuss it and appointed a committee to put their thoughts into words. William A. Prout, Anthony Wood, and Henry Hannon wrote that the petition's origin lay in the machinations of a few influential men— especially McGill and Bowen—who objected to the enforcement of tariffs and favored union with the Republic of Liberia. They conspired to create a general opposition to the society, which resulted in the remonstrance. Although it may not have been obvious to the board, the committee asserted, the petition contained a "threat at nationality." Now, however, most signers had reconsidered. Of some sixty, scarcely ten would now advocate independence. On the contrary, the majority of settlers were quite sensible of, and grateful for, the society's continuing assistance. They promised to comply with the board's economic policies. At a second public meeting, in 1850, the document was read aloud, and ninety-five settlers signed.[15]

The governor wrote Latrobe on January 4, 1850, that he had been very sick recently, suffering in part from a persistent crippling ulcer on his foot. At the time of writing, he could get about on crutches, but really he could do little more than sit at his desk. He wrote that he was improving, but the letter was full of uncharacteristic misspellings and ungrammatical lapses, which suggest impairment. Fortunately, the next few months were relatively uneventful. Rice was abundant. The palm oil season promised to be a good one, partly because more bush towns were beginning to export it. There were few American vessels on the coast, however, which Russwurm attributed to the Gold Rush in California, to which African trade was marginal.[16]

In March, Baphro, king of Grand Cavally and one of the original parties to the deed of 1834, died suddenly. There was no successor, and the town was consequently in a state of anarchy. The agent had advanced money to the trademen there, but he had little prospect of having his contracts filled. Without a ruler to enforce them, the townsmen considered themselves exempt from debt.[17]

XVII.

"A Microscope"

THE MARYLAND GENERAL ASSEMBLY'S UNPRECEDENTED, UNCONSTI-tutional grant to create and support a colony in Africa would expire at the close of 1851. Twelve months in advance, no one could tell whether the legislature would renew it, for twenty years' effort had achieved very little. Almost all black Marylanders rejected exile in Africa, despite the grand claims of its promoters. Little wonder, Ford McGill wrote James Hall in September. Who would willingly risk emigration, to settle in a colony rather than a free republic? "Only think of it A Negro Republic! a Negro President, Negro Senators and Representatives, and Negro Laws!!! is there any thing under Heaven more likely to cause the Negro race to rush by thousands on board the 'Ebony line of steamers' bound for this Negro land!!!" He recalled his own boyhood, his father's tales of the Republic of Haiti and the prom-ise it held for black independence. Many others had been raised with such stories, yearning for a free black country. Maryland had failed to fulfill this dream, if than for no other reason she was too small to exist as a free nation.[1]

Making Maryland a "commonwealth" had only impoverished set-tlers. Trade was dull, and settlers hardly farmed at all. The board con-cluded that their colony must either unite with the republic or declare independence. They outlined their position in a dispatch that reached

Russwurm on February 10, 1851, and which he announced immediately. Settlers responded energetically at public meetings, which resulted in a letter to the board. In it, they complained of economic stagnation, manifested to many in their inability to find and buy provisions, clothing, tools, and other material adjuncts of their American culture. They perceived the cause of this in their isolation on the remote shores of Africa, neglected by their patrons in Baltimore, surrounded by heathen Africans, ruled by a man who had been in office too long.[2]

Russwurm favored free discussion of the colony's future, but the extreme opinions of a few who desired union with Liberia and their distortion of facts offended him. He criticized them for "leaving their business undone and running from one end of the colony to the other, unsettling the minds of the poorer class, and giving them only one side of the picture." Russwurm thought that union was inevitable. "I am not opposed to annexation on fair terms, whenever the Board deem it expedient," he added. "We ought to join as a sovereign state, and I believe this will be the difficulty in the way. It would improve our coasting trade by keeping off foreigners from putting factories on shore, unless permits had been granted and duties paid on the same: but I hardly think it would improve the situation of the discontented ones." He was encouraged to see settlers take so much interest in determining their futures and felt that good sense would prevail.[3]

Greboes were also disappointed with colonization. The headmen of the Nyomowe towns met for a general palaver at Grand Cavally in October 1850. Relations with the Americans, specifically in matters of trade, were a principal concern, as they informed their "Dear friend," Dr. Hall:

> Our hearts are very much trouble for this same thing we have been told you, for when these Colony first come to this country, they told us that they were sent here by the head men in the united state, and

told us that we all should be one, the American man and the native man should be friend to each other, and love one another. They told us that they would teach us and our children to learn books and learn how to trade, and lived as they themselfes. This is the same thing which the missionary who living here told us to know and about God. So we took our children and gave them to the missionary, and now they are in the School. Some of them could read and write, so the white man who living here are trying to do us good. But the colney who came to settle at Cape Palmas, does not treat us kindly, but treat us as if we were their Slave, . . . My friends the reason why we write this to you is this: We wants you to write to these colony that they [should do what they] Promise to do. They once with us that they shoud be friend and kind to us or treat us friendly and teach us. They promised to make the same trade as themselves.

This letter written from Fish town, Rock town Cape Palmas, Cavally people, all head men of these towns.[4]

Greboes had expected a vast improvement in their standard of living, but this had not happened.

Early in 1851, Maryland and Gbenelu nearly went to war. Russwurm had lately been so sick that others had to perform his duties, and the more subtle indications of trouble may have gone unnoticed. An altercation between a Grebo and settler provided an excuse to the *sedibo*. Sixty soldiers in full war dress—bodies painted, draped with wild animal pelts and charms—marched into Harper the same afternoon. They came upon McGill and a few others who were on Baltimore Street going about their business, defenseless except for two or three hunting guns. The doctor stood closest to the soldiers as they formed a line and raised their muskets. He and his comrades picked up what weapons they had to make a stand. At that instant, Sarah Russwurm rushed from the Agency House, through the *sedibo's* ranks shrieking. McGill and his friends lowered their guns, as did the Greboes, and there was an opportunity to speak. Cooler heads took charge, though tensions remained high for several days.[5]

During the first months of 1851, Russwurm was confined to bed. William Prout, his confidant, and other settlers quietly performed most of the duties of government.[6] Dr. McGill, assistant agent, did little, though he was designated successor to Russwurm. He despised Cape Palmas, its citizens, and its laws, which were an inconvenience to his business interests, nor was he comfortable with his role of heir-apparent. "We are at a dead stand still here — in a state of complete torpidity," he told James Hall in a letter of September 15, 1850, adding with contempt and striking immodesty, "Our people are not fit to plan and carry out any scheme of their own, and I will not furnish one lest all responsibility for the future might fall on my shoulders. I am convinced of one fact," he added ruefully, "which is that I made a blunder when I settled here, this can't be remedied. I must hold on and watch events and in the meantime try and make money." He lied that he was about to give up his medical practice in favor of business; he had long since done so.[7]

McGill seemed to sense that momentous changes would soon overtake Harper, and he thought of escape. In April 1851 he left Cape Palmas to visit Monrovia and to give his son, who had been sick for two months, the benefit of a cruise, sea air being a tonic of proven effectiveness. The journey had the desired effect on the little boy. Also, it had a profound, inspiring impact on his father. Monrovia was all business, and he reveled in the industry and virtue he found in her leading citizens. Even Sinoe, which had been a straggling village when he had seen it four years earlier, now seemed to surpass Harper. His brother James, who ran the family business in Monrovia, was sickly, and Ford determined at once to move up to take charge. He bought a large house, ordered furniture from Baltimore, and reorganized McGill, Brothers. Roszell would have charge of the business at Cape Palmas. For the time being, he planned to return to Harper to set everything straight, then move to Monrovia in December.[8]

The *Liberia Packet* cast anchor off Harper at the end of May, completing her eighth trip to Africa. She brought a continuation of the

correspondence initiated the last time out. Russwurm's response then
to the suggestion of independence or amalgamation with the republic
had been encouraging. The board now sent Russwurm a proclamation
to read to citizens. It informed them that Maryland's appropriation to
the colonization society would expire on the last day of 1851. The society was lobbying for an extension, but the vote of the General Assembly was uncertain. If more money was given, it might have to be devoted to collecting and shipping emigrants, rather than supporting
them in Africa. Therefore, settlers should plan for their future, whether
it be union with Liberia or independence. The board expected the
former, but settlers could choose their course.[9] Russwurm was too ill to
make a public address, and the proclamation remained on his desk.[10]

Dr. McGill returned to Harper aboard the *Packet*. He made no
secret of his plans to move away. Most settlers were glad to see him go.
Dempsey Fletcher was a little jealous. "He says that his practice and
business will be more lucrative," he wrote. "I don't know how his practice will be more so then it was here unless he does more there then
here." The fact that McGill received pay as Colonial Physician, even
though he had given up medical practice four years before, galled
Fletcher, who had scarcely enough money to live on, let alone buy a
horse or jack to carry him on his daily rounds. He would leave too, if he
did not feel an obligation to his community and the board.[11]

As events unfolded, McGill was unable to leave Harper, for
Russwurm's condition suddenly deteriorated. He did not experience
any particular pain, and he retained his faculties, stoically performing
as many duties as he was able from his bed. His decline was more evident to his wife and Dr. McGill, but they kept the fact a secret from him
and from citizens. When William Prout, the agent's protégé and friend,
tried to see him, Mrs. Russwurm coldly turned him away. He later
regretted that he did not insist, but he had not known how grave the
situation was. Near midnight on June 9, 1851, John Browne Russwurm
died, unaware until his last hour that death was near. He left no final
instructions, at least none that were made public.[12]

The unexpected news threw the entire community into anxiety-laden mourning. "Even the heathens in these parts ex claims — We have lost a friend and father!" Boston Jenkins Drayton proclaimed in a eulogy written a few weeks later. "His character since my acquaintance with him stands unimpeached." Forgetting their occasional resentment of Russwurm, most of the settlers apparently agreed that "Persecution and trials he had, but the worth of a man is never appreciated by some while he is [alive]. So with the majority in Cape Palmas." Russwurm's name, Drayton continued, "shall ever live, as a monument of Liberian glory. The first coloured governor, lived virtuous, steady and determined, yes, extraordinary successfully; and died in office an honourable patriot. Peace with his neighbor and his God. I hope that yourself and the Board may be able to stand the shock, and take this as a microscope to view the turning of providence."[13] The only leader the great majority had known was gone. Everyone knew that this was the time for decision.

Dr. McGill assumed the governorship on Russwurm's death. The transition was business-like. Prout inventoried the Agency Store and property, balanced the ledgers, and turned them over to McGill, prepared to resign all of his duties, which he expected because the acting agent disliked him so much. McGill needed Prout's services, though, and retained him. He also advanced William Cassell. "Mr. Prout is undoubtedly the best qualified as an accountant and correspondent," McGill faithlessly wrote Latrobe on July 11. "With Cassell you are well acquainted, for straight forward upright honest manly abilities he is incomparably the superior of Prout. With Mr. Cassell as Agent, Prout as Secretary, and the appointment of the next best man in the Colony as Assistant Agent we might trust that in time every thing would work right."[14]

Cassell seems to have gained McGill's genuine respect. He is a puzzling character, for his simple letters do not reveal much of his personality or beliefs. Apparently, he was mild-mannered, with a dignified and polite demeanor, graced by obvious intelligence, though something short of genius. Prout in contrast was clearly brilliant, and by all accounts an alcoholic. Russwurm was patient with him, but his family loathed him. Prout, displeased at the way things had worked out, found there was little that he could do.[15]

Most settlers opposed McGill's succession. John Bowen, Anthony Wood, and Joshua Stewart led a quiet campaign against him. They blamed McGill for Maryland's political unrest. On his return from Monrovia, the doctor had resigned his offices in the colony and insulted the good citizens of Maryland. Then, when the governor lapsed into his final illness, his wife (who was Ford's sister) kept the matter secret, with the doctor's approval, "till, he was Speachless." No one knew what Russwurm's wishes were, therefore, and McGill illegally took charge. "A wrong Sperit of Ambition have arrive on him," Joshua Stewart speculated a few months later, "too eager for power, Though unlawfully usurped, yet it will never do him eny good, the Stinge of concions; he must feale, and cant helpe him Self. Ambition for power is good, when it is Rightly Obtained, and Simpatha observed at the Same tim to thouse and over thouse whome on have the power to act."[16]

Bowen and Stewart reportedly went to King Freeman a day or two after Russwurm's death to persuade him to withhold support from the new agent. The king refused. Soon after, he told McGill flatteringly, "I and my people have for several years past, known that McGill was Assistant Agent, he has always been present and assisted in 'setting palavers,' and during the temporary absence of Govr. Russwurm has allways acted in his place and the Colonist obeyed him." Mixing honesty with diplomacy he added, "Now altho' we are not all satisfied with his being so yet we recognize him as being Governor of the Colony, and respect him as such. We are determined to await a hearing from Mr. Latrobe when if his appointment is made permanent we will be satisfied."[17]

A number of citizens gathered at the new stone jail on June 18. Although everyone mourned Russwurm's death, they were preoccupied with questions of their own lives. The acting governor, who did not attend, heard that the speakers complained about both the old administration and him. He regarded their dissent as ingratitude. Those present at the meeting appointed Reverend Francis Burns, Reverend Boston J. Drayton, William Prout, Anthony Wood, and Joshua Stewart to compose a letter to the Board of Managers to request a replacement for McGill, preferably a man who was new to the colony. When these men met to draft their letter, they found that they could not agree on important points. Anthony Wood and Joshua Stewart believed that Maryland needed a white governor to keep Greboes and settlers in line, with the ultimate goal of removing Gbenelu, an obstacle to progress.[18] Burns, Drayton, and Prout withdrew from the committee because they would not support the return of a white governor.

Two weeks after Russwurm's death, the acting governor shocked citizens with the publication of the board's message on independence. When the letter arrived in May, the governor had been too weak to call a meeting, and he had died without making it public. McGill, the only person who knew of it, kept it to himself, except to taunt settlers with hints that the society would soon cut them off. He told them that Maryland must beg for the protection of Monrovia. Thus, when McGill convened the citizens, they reacted with great skepticism. They thought the address must be a trick to make them appear disloyal, coming as it did from the hands of an enemy so long after the *Packet* had left.[19]

The proclamation included instructions for Russwurm to visit Monrovia to discuss the question of union. McGill suggested that a delegation of citizens take his place. Prout, at the prodding of his fellow citizens, met privately with McGill soon after. The doctor read the society's letter aloud, and Prout concluded that only the agent could make the trip to Monrovia. He told the doctor what he thought, but McGill argued that he would be a very poor advocate. His opinion of his fellow citizens was a matter of common indignation. Besides, he knew already what response the republic would make. Prout countered that he had only to answer to the society, regardless of what citizens thought. Prout left the office unconvinced and publicly argued against an embassy of citizens on the grounds that it was unconstitutional: the governor was empowered to conduct foreign affairs, but citizens had no such authority. He was probably mistaken, as the board intended a fact-finding mission, and the delegation would not have to make any agreements. Prout blamed McGill for distorting the meaning of Latrobe's letter to Russwurm in order to win quick annexation as a county. Settlers wanted instructions from the board in light of Russwurm's passing, and this stalled any change. Months must pass before word could be received from Baltimore.[20]

Settlers were active during the interval. Discussions in public meetings, in private homes, in churches, and on the streets, soon led to the formation of parties. Many settlers were frightened at the prospect of independence. Nearly everyone was beholden to the agency to some degree. In July, Prout told Latrobe, "The people, generally, are not entirely in want of a spirit of independence, but any attempt at national pride or republican liberty, is often overuled by their utter dependency on the Society's Agent. They are in want of decision of character, and the little spark that flickers in their breast from time to time, and might with a little encouragement, prompt them to manly action, soon disappears upon consideration of their total destitution."[21] A few wished to maintain the status quo. Others advocated union as a county, as Liberia's constitution provided. Another small group advocated outright independence. The majority was determined to seek union with Liberia as a sovereign state, under terms similar to the United States under the Articles of Confederation.

The party supporting annexation to Liberia as a county was disproportionately powerful, as it counted most of the richest and best educated citizens. Dr. McGill was their most articulate proponent. Maryland had everything to gain by annexation, he argued. United with Liberia, Harper would enjoy true independence, recognized by the European powers, if not the United States. Settlers would once again land on the wharf, and businessmen from the windward would expand their operations to take advantage of Maryland's resources. Liberia also offered a significant military force. "We require strength and numbers to control, and if necessary subdue our Native population. This will be the first work for Liberia to assist in, and well enough they know it. Should we undertake it alone, it would be likely to involve the destruction of more than half the improvements in the Colony," he told Latrobe early in 1852. "But with the force, that the Liberians are able and willing when required to take the field we could easily subdue all around us if necessary. When our strength became known, we could easily interfere and prevent the wars existing around us constantly and which are so detrimental to the interests of our Colony."[22] Many settlers were jealous and resentful of the annexation-ists, not merely for their ideas but for who they were. Anthony Wood, for instance, wrote that the principals of the Annexation Club were all ministers from southern states, "engaged in striveing to Bring about confusion in the colony insted of preaching the gospal as thay was sent to do." With McGill at their head, their plan was automatically suspect.[23]

Feelings ran high. In July, annexationists planned to celebrate the republic's fourth Independence Day. About a week beforehand, they posted a notice in Harper resolving "That we beleive the time has come wherein we Should begin to think, speak, and Act upon the important and desirable subject of we being *Annexed* to the Republic of Liberia, and as freemen in common with them Shall use every honourable exer-tion, to be united to them with credit to ourselves and posterity." The annexationists also intended to celebrate July 26, 1851, "it being the Anniversary of the Republic of Liberia." Nine men attached their names to the document.[24]

Almost as soon as the notice was nailed up, other settlers objected. McGill and Drayton provoked them with assertions that they were citizens of the republic as well as Maryland. A rumor spread that the Liberian flag would be raised at the picnic, a brazen act of subversion. Annexationists denied any such plans, but many settlers were prepared to use force against even a symbolic infringement of their sovereignty.

On July 26, the Annexation Club gathered with families and guests to mark the day. Two-thirds of the remaining male citizens also met nearby, McGill wrote, "the first bent on eating their dinner, and the latter on interrupting them." The acting governor had anticipated a fight and had ordered the sheriff and an unnamed captain of militia to muster some volunteers. The show of force worked. The annexationists refrained from raising the Liberian flag, and their opponents contented themselves with shouting abuse.[25]

"Never has there been so much disturbance in Cape Palmas before, never has there been a time when the people was so near shedding each others blood," settlers complained to the agent and council in a petition in August. They blamed the outbreak on irresponsible clergymen, naming Francis Burns, Boston J. Drayton, and Joseph Thomson (leaving out McGill and merchants). They asked for a statute to forbid preachers from using their pulpits for political agitation, and another to outlaw the display of other nations' flags.[26]

During the next few weeks, citizens increasingly realized that union with the Republic of Liberia on satisfactory terms would be difficult. Some doomsayers even predicted that a forced union would result in bloodshed. "It is . . . apparent," the acting governor informed Latrobe, "that nothing short of impending ruin will ever reconcile the Colonists here to the idea of uniting with the Republic as a County; how to reconcile such wide and conflicting difference is a question."[27] Settlers began to consider independence.

Such eventful times inspired settlers to exert more effort on their own behalf. Expressing the feelings of many in the community, Joshua Stewart wrote Latrobe in July that Russwurm had given out too much charity, which fostered stagnation. For his part, he asserted (only half-truthfully), he had never relied on handouts. "Indulgenc I Know it not," he wrote proudly, "[except] when I have confered it on my Self, lent not by other, who had it in their power, by a croo of Rice, a quart of oil, a pound of Suger or flower to Soften down my ambition to take advantage of me, this way are Some Other, that I may become, Like unto a dog walking with his tail down."[28] At the end of the year, McGill noted that settlers had planted fully one-third more than at any previous time. For once, he seemed pleased. He asked Latrobe whether a machine existed for hulling coffee beans. With so many now busy on their own land, the acting governor began to curtail the aid given out to paupers. This was unpopular with those who depended on it, but McGill believed that the measure was necessary. He assured Latrobe that he would assist people in "real distress," but settlers must exert themselves. Some angry and cynical settlers would charge that McGill, Brothers picked up the slack to make a handsome profit.[29]

Citizens of Maryland knew that they must soon be a sovereign state, but few had any idea how to accomplish it. Answers came from an unexpected quarter. On November 10, William Prout outlined a plan to a group of citizens in the hearing room of the Quarterly Court.[30] "Mr. Chairman and fellow Citizens," he began, "by a proclamation issued from the Acting Governor of this Colony, we learn, it is the pleasure of the Board of Managers of the Maryland State Colonization Society, that we should accustom ourselves to the consideration of an independent government, shortly to be organized." He apologized for his own weak abilities, emphasizing the gravity of the challenge facing the community and contended that agricuture, manufacturing, and commerce were "the three grand essentials which give support and permanence to independent governments." As "a people in your infancy," he argued, "I think your case naturally preponderates in favour of agriculture." He discoursed at length on the state of agriculture in Maryland. "What have we done to sustain our little barque now about launching on the sea of freedom and independence," he asked. "Have we improved the heritage which the Author of goodness has suffered us to possess, or is it now lying in wild and dreary wastes throughout various sections of the Colony! — If I have correctly observed the state of agricultural improvements in the Colony, I must assert, that, in my opinion, they are not as they should be, if we wish to maintain the pride of freemen." He asserted confidently that the land about Cape Palmas could produce enough for subsistence and for international trade, if only settlers would apply themselves to the task. "An attention to the culture of these things, will give you ease of the turmoils incident to the busy scenes of other occupations, will invigorate your bodily and mental powers by enabling you to conquer the now difficult task of accomodating the soil to the growth of rare plants, and will abundantly recompense your labors by spreading comfort and plenty around your homesteads." He pointed to the prosperity of the United States, the result of the hard work of settlers applied to a similar wealth of resources.

"Of manufacture, I can say nothing," Prout went on, "except that the total want of this important matter" was the result of defects in the colony's agricultural economy. Manufacturing was "common" in countries "where agriculture is prized and encouraged," and if Maryland desired the ability to manufacture goods, "the importance of agriculture must be felt and attended to with constant and untiring will-go-a-head principles." It would require "anxious and unflinching toil," but the result would be "that, the things which now seem beyond our ability of attainment, will be raised and procured for the support and honor of our individual Selves, and the glory and eventual success of our independence as a people." Indeed, Maryland participated in the lucrative foreign trade of palm oil, but Africans produced it. He warned citizens that they must develop their own products, or forever remain dependent.

Prout then turned to the question of trade, noting that the colonial economy lacked vitality and that new sources must be found to replace the largess of the colonization society. Wealth, he claimed, must come from the land. "If we were an agricultural people, we would be a [commercial] one, . . . Cotton would then be prized for its usefulness — Coffee, for its value. These two grand matters would then open the gate (now partially closed to Cape Palmas) for commerce, and the benefits resulting would be surprisingly great." Refined agricultural products "would arrest the course of many vessels which now pass our Colony, and cause them to be put into our port to be laden with useful commodities." Relations with "foreign commercial houses" would "spring up" and give "stability and influence to our commercial position" and increase government revenue.

Prout explained that the independent government of Maryland must be compatible with the constitution of Liberia. "In view of the union which is to be effected between this and the government of Liberia," he observed, "I am strongly impressed in favor of organizing ours on the plan of some of the States in America — especially so far as the executive or chief officer is concerned." He had "no example for this in any Sovereign Government not confederated" but believed that "the period is not far distant when these several peoples on this Western

Coast, planted by different Societies in America, and having for their objects the same end, will conclude an union between themselves for the giving of power and strength to the governments of the oppressed sons of the colored race, driven out from the place of their nativity, and compelled to seek shelter on these shores." Citizens must work out the details of this government themselves. He proposed a republic, headed by a governor, with a congress composed of senate and general assembly, an independent judiciary, and various civil offices, modeled closely on the Maryland state constitution.[31]

Prout urged citizens to unite for the common interest and to formulate laws to enhance civil harmony. He recommended fair and courteous treatment of African peoples and of foreigners. The fledgling country would need whatever goodwill it could earn. Moreover, he advised citizens to cultivate the best possible relations with the Maryland State Colonization Society. "As a people the relations in which we have stood for years to the Society, must give place to new ones." Support of the government would "devolve on ourselves — as men, we are to front all political disadvantages, and have the storm of wintery days. We are to put our shoulders to the wheel, and peradventure a gleam of light may burst from some unexpected quarter, and dispose the dense atmosphere which darkens our vision and checks our onward march."

Prout warned his audience not to take for granted the society's property. They might have to negotiate for land, public buildings, weapons and ammunition, medical services, schools, and debts settlers might owe the society at the time of separation. Moreover, citizens of the new government would face all sorts of expenses. He suggested a possible budget, including salaries of public officers (amounting to $2,635.00), diplomacy, government printing, internal improvement, and so on, to which he affixed no estimate.

The next point logically, was how to pay for all of this. Prout offered a series of recommendations with glosses on the reasons for them. He summarized them as follows:

1st. 20 cents duty per gallon on Spiritous liquor,
   estimating the quantity imported at 5000
   gallons annually   1000.00

2nd. 8 per cent duty on the sales of foreign
   merchandize, estimating the imports at
   25000$ annually   2000.00

3rd. Tax on the estimated value of all real Estate,
   probable amount of which 35000$ at .90
   per hundred dollars   315.00

4th. Specifick tax on uncultivated lands,
   probable number of acres 500 at .75   375.00

5th. Direct capitation tax on non-freeholders
   numbering 43 at 2.00   86.00

6th. Annual tax of 3$ on all Coasting vessels   15.00

7th. The probable profits resulting from Commission,
   wholesale and retail business   1000.00

8th. The probable gains resulting from trade in
   African productions, allowing a man of steady
   business habits, with means to procure in one
   year 27000 gallons = 9000$, which will give
   clear gains 33/100   3000.00

9th. Wholesale and Retail Licenses   200.00
                                                   _____

                                                      7991.00

These were sums beyond the comprehension of most present, so Prout was careful to explain that the revenue might only be barely sufficient to cover expenses.

Some of Prout's taxes were aimed at improving society. For instance, the tax on uncultivated lands was designed to stimulate farming. He commented that such waste land was "pernicious to the labors of the more enterprising of the Community, injurious to the measures in progress for our prosperity, and detrimental to the impressions which we are anxious to excite with foreign visitors to our State." Others were pragmatic and controversial, particularly the question of allowing trade in ardent spirits. Maryland had a strict temperance code, and despite the fact that rum was a principal article of trade on the coast, few citizens wanted it in their community, no matter how much money it might bring in. Prout's emphasis on trade was also controversial. He believed that the new state should assume the agency's mercantile role, explaining that "A regular business of whole sale and retail dealing [should] be opened for and on account of government, to be conducted in a warehouse to be denominated 'Government Store,'" under the secretary of the treasury. The government would oversee the importation of foreign manufactures, wholesale and retail trade practices, and traffic with the natives in the interior. In connection with this, he proposed that the government should negotiate an annual loan of five thousand dollars from the society to provide capital for the venture and which would be repaid in semi-annual installments. To conclude, Prout stressed the importance of communicating with the society to ensure that there would be no misunderstandings, particularly with regard to sovereignty over outlying African states. He finished without a flourish and resumed his chair.[32]

The audience was delighted to hear the matter of independence treated so thoroughly. They named a committee of nine individuals, including William Cassell, Josh Stewart, Phillip Gross, and Anthony Wood, patriotic old citizens, to review Prout's plan and revise it where needed. They found little to do, so complete did the young man's reasoning seem. The committee read its letter aloud at a public meeting on November 24. On motion, citizens approved it as written and sent it to Baltimore with Prout's address.

McGill watched the proceedings bitterly. "I need hardly assure you that Mr. Prout has neither my sanction, support, nor approval in what I consider schemes for his personal aggrandisement," he wrote to James Hall early the following January, his first opportunity in months to send a letter home. Prout was motivated by a desire to secure a job, he asserted, having "appropriated to himself" the office of treasury secretary in the projected government. In fact, Prout's ambitions were modest, and his abilities were unmistakable. McGill even admitted to visiting American officers that Prout was "the only man fit for the office here," though in the same breath he called Prout a drunkard.[33]

McGill's opinions were certainly biased. In fact, he had only himself to blame for the ill will of his fellow citizens, but he was too proud to recognize the fact or do anything about it. "Thare was a time," John Bowen, a fellow merchant and former friend, told the board "when Doctor McGill was held in asteem by the pepel At that time he certanly did appear to have all qualetis necessary to a governor and all the Zeal a Man might be expected to have for his country." That was six or seven years ago, and since then McGill was not the same man. "What has wrought so great a change in him I cannot tell perhaps Sirs you may know. It appears he has forsoken us at the Very time when his talent and ability are most needed in our favor."[34]

Evidence indicates that the acting governor used his office for his own financial advantage. Soon after taking office, he purchased the site of his warehouses, which he had formerly leased from the society. These were prime oceanfront lots, where the old A.B.C.F.M. mission, Fair Hope, had once stood. The society had kept them until they might be needed for public purposes. Prout remarked to Latrobe early in 1852, "It seems as though the present Acting Agent from a sense of honor, thought it would not look well to use the power as an occupant of the executive office, to deed to himself certain water lots intended on terms of lease, and on which he had built. One of the members of the Council being a lessee on the same principles, the subject was laid before that Body for action and speedily disposed of by way of authorizing the sale of these lands at a trifling price."[35] McGill bought the property for forty dollars, which he tendered in devalued colonial currency. John Bowen, vice-agent, purchased his store lot for twenty dollars. Major Anthony Wood was offered the land on which his smithy stood for a mere ten dollars but refused to pay in the belief that the transaction was illegal. He later wrote Latrobe to ask permission to buy the parcel for what-ever price he would name.[36] McGill even offered Prout a lot, to buy him off. Prout too refused, believing the action was against the law. In mentioning this to Latrobe, he quoted Madison to the effect that good government required its leaders to have the people's interest at heart. "All are for self-interest and what conduces to it, leaving the government and its dependencies to take care of themselves."[37]

Nor was this all. "There has been a grog-shop," Prout wrote Latrobe in January, "regularly kept up with supplies for over eight months, in the native town [Gbenelu], where the colonists can purchase as much liquor as they please." There too many colonists spent all their hard-earned cash. "Nor does the sale of liquor stop at the native town; I learn it is now being sent out into the interior by jugsfull." He identified the proprietor of the shop only as "a gentleman of note, and of whose name you would blush, were I to inform you."[38] Evidence points to McGill, Brothers, the principal business in the colony, which actively traded rum elsewhere. Certainly, Governor McGill would not have allowed a rival to deprive him of trade by illegal means. He had the whole authority of government to protect his interest, though he may have granted himself such a concession. It is easy to imagine that Prout hesitated to accuse him directly.

"We are on the most friendly terms with all of the Native tribes around us, and they are all warring with each other," McGill wrote James Hall on December 15, 1851. Grand Cavally was at war with Robookah, her neighbor across the river; Garroway with the Po River Fishmen; Sadika with Worebo in the bush. On a positive note, Half Cavally and Grahway had recently settled their differences, but these former enemies now threatened Gbenelu, which was then suffering considerable internal unrest. A faction opposed to King Freeman had recently strengthened. Before the Americans had settled at the Cape, Freeman had led a similar opposition to King Wah, his predecessor. On some pretext, Freeman's party forced Wah to undergo *gidu*, with fatal results. Having proven a witch, old Wah's body was cast in the "Devil Bush," the sacred grove of sassy wood, to rot. Now, after twenty or more years, Freeman's enemies gathered the bones and gave them a funeral with great show of mourning, to show that Freeman's reign had brought misfortune. If he failed to improve things soon, he might also face trial for "making witch." "I have advised Freeman in case he is threatened to throw himself on us for protection," McGill wrote Hall. This might involve the

colony in conflict, but he felt it was necessary "for the cause of humanity." He went on, "We cannot bear the idea of having the old scamp
murdered, as there is some good traits in his character."[39]

For the time being, Americans were immune to the strife, though
many feared it. As a matter of precaution, McGill strengthened the
militia, satisfying himself that his men could whip any African force
foolish enough to hazard an assault. He had a new stockade erected at
Mount Tubman late in 1851, and another was planned for East Harper
in 1852. He also built a second battery on Cape Palmas, as Fort Hall
seemed too vulnerable. The blacksmith cast one thousand pounds of
lead into musket balls.[40]

With so much unrest, trade dropped off. McGill was not inclined
to do more than keep the agency solvent, since any agency profits were
at McGill, Brothers' expense. Settlers found McGill's laissez-faire policy
particularly frustrating. McGill was a rich man, with access to whatever he desired. They, on the other hand suffered immensely because of
the interruption of trade. "We realy are depending on the native for
their Rice," Joshua Stewart complained to Latrobe, "Which dependency
mus Continue for a longe period yet, before we will be able to Remove
them by Agraculturel persuits."[41]

The governor miscalculated the rice harvest. Early in the season it
was plentiful, but McGill did not buy it since some of last year's crop
still remained in the store. In November his stock ran low, and none
was available. Circumstances forced him to send the agency boats in
search of rice rather than palm oil. What was worse, McGill, Brothers
profited by selling food to hungry citizens.[42] Though much of the responsibility for the well-being of the colony was his, McGill laid the
blame elsewhere. "This Colony has increased its numbers only since
you governed it but I really cannot discover any material increase in
intelligence respectability or self dependence," he told James Hall. "The
Governor still must originate every enterprise, must instruct every one,
and perform every thing, there are none from whom he can seek reliable council or advice; if he is successful, he gets no thanks, if he fails
through inadequate means or assistance he is d——d — ignorance

ingratitude, and malevolence meet him at every point and renders his life miserable." As McGill saw it, settlers seemed content to live on the society's charity, "from the cradle to the grave." With a little more understanding, he noted that this had its origins in the systematic degradation settlers experienced in America. "These same people are now snatched suddenly from the plantations and uninstructed and unimproved are expected by the simple passage across five thousand miles of ocean to be fit to fulfill the functions and duties of free and enlightened citizens."[43]

By the second half of 1851, the *Liberia Packet* had proven herself an unpredictable sailor. James Hall decided to purchase a second vessel for the Chesapeake and Liberia Trading Company. He obtained the bark *Morgan Dix*, an old vessel but with more capacity than the *Packet*. On November 1, 1851, the new ship sailed for Liberia laden with supplies and passengers, most of which was on the American Colonization Society's account, to be delivered to Monrovia. Only one emigrant went to Maryland.

The *Liberia Packet* sailed into Baltimore's harbor on December 15, having made a slow voyage of fifty-six days from Monrovia. As much as a fortnight was lost in calms off the African coast. James Hall and his son George rushed to fit her out to leave Baltimore once again on January 1 with emigrants and cargo. Passengers from Virginia and Maryland were to board in Baltimore. The *Packet* was then to call at Savannah, where a large contingent awaited passage to Monrovia. Scarcely any would elect to sail on to the little colony of Maryland.[44]

On the last day of 1851, the Maryland General Assembly's grant to the Maryland State Colonization Society—$10,000 per annum, for twenty years—expired. Surely, the officers of the society had reason to be discouraged, for they had scarcely made a dent in the free black population of Maryland, and emigration had slowed to a trickle. Circumstances had changed substantially since 1831. Sectional feelings had increased steadily. Abolition had formed a clear and influential ideology, which opposed colonization. The great majority of black people rejected the idea of expulsion from their native land. On the other hand, the society could show a colony in Africa, established and maintained on a sound economic footing that might one day blossom into a great republic if circumstances in America should change. In fact, this was a period of tremendous demographic upheaval. The previous three years had witnessed the rush to California and the opening of vast new territories in the West. A series of revolutions and famines in Europe sent waves of Irish and Germans flooding into Baltimore and other Eastern cities. These were people who if necessary sacrificed everything they had to come to America, where they systematically replaced free black laborers. (Frederick Douglass described vividly in his memoirs his fights to keep his job in a Baltimore shipyard in the face of concerted Irish opposition.) What more would it take before black Americans pulled up stakes and moved on, colonizationists and many others wondered. They argued persuasively that their appropriation should be continued for six more years.[45]

XVIII.

"Civilized Modes of Living"

HAT THE QUESTION OF UNION WITH LIBERIA SHOULD STIR SO MUCH anxiety among Maryland's citizens might seem strange, when in fact the two peoples were not very different from one another. Almost everyone recognized a clear and common interest with Liberians, with whom they shared a comparable origin and future. Yet, Maryland was founded partly in response to the shortcomings and failures of the older colony, and many of Maryland's residents were veterans of Liberia. "The people of Cape Palmas, are a people themselves," William Prout explained to Latrobe in April 1852. "I believe . . . that the ultimate object of christianized colored people planted on this coast under the auspices of separate and distinct Societies in the United States, is the same. A union between them is inevitable. Their national importance demands it, and in the course of time it must be accomplished." But though Maryland and Liberia shared similar destinies, "it does not argue that the one part is to sacrifice the prerogative of self rule, and render nugatory its rights and privileges, and the importance consequent in its future growth and improvement, to accomodate itself to the embarrassing conditions fixed and determined by the other."[1] Joshua Stewart had written Latrobe earlier in a similar vein. "We are marylanders, if not Received on these terms we will Remain a Republic Stat Government alone and confederat for each other mutial assistance in case of wars We are determined not to desend to a county annexation before this will take place, Should it ever take place as Such our people would march at the point of the banett and Sword before their would Surrender to Such Termes."[2] Such strong feeling may have been founded in part upon a mistaken fear of the unknown, but citizens thought of themselves as a separate people, whose culture was worth defending. Indeed, they had good reason to do so. Isolated as they were, they had nurtured a way of life consonant with their ideals of liberty and cultural identity, in the face of great hardship.

What was Maryland in Liberia like then? A visitor in 1852 would have seen the coast about Cape Palmas much as those aboard the *Ann* had in 1834. The Cape itself was somewhat altered, with a stone lighthouse at its tip and a collection of frame houses running along its spine. Maryland had two landing places, the Agency Wharf, on the Cape's north shore, and McGill's Landing, on the beach east of Russwurm's Island, where the Congregational mission, "Fair Hope," had once stood. Landing at the Wharf involved crossing the shallow and dangerous bar at the mouth of Hoffman's River, but its solid stones were safer than the beach. There were two or three stone warehouses built hard against the bluff and a steep rolling road to Harper. McGill's landing presented a line of surf at the last moment and perhaps a drenching, but many preferred it to the treacherous bar. At McGill's there was a frame warehouse and other buildings associated with his business; a blacksmith's shop belonging to Anthony Wood; and Bowen's warehouse. Harper lay up the hill, beyond Gbenelu.[3]

The layout of the colony had not changed much since James Hall's tenure. He had followed specific instructions concerning the dimensions of town and farm lots and the arrangement of avenues and cross streets, conceding to the local topography where necessary. Governor Hall and George McGill surveyed the town of Harper on the summit of Cape Palmas and extended a road, Maryland Avenue, inland along a low ridge bounded on the east by Lake Sheppard and on the northwest by the broad, shallow valley of Hoffman's River.

Harper's main thoroughfare, Baltimore Street, extended lengthwise down the Cape, ending close by the lighthouse. Soon, the site would also include a Female Orphan Asylum, run by the Episcopal Church. At Baltimore Street's eastern end stood the Agency House, offices, and a gun emplacement called Fort Hall, which overlooked Gbenelu. Between these two points was a collection of small frame houses. Picket or live thorn fences enclosed most of the lots to protect the occupants' belongings and gardens from pilferers. The spot was a pretty one, with fine views of the ocean and of forested hills, so much so that the visitor might overlook the decrepit condition of many structures. Humid climate and constant salt breezes weathered them quickly.

Baltimore Street met Maryland Avenue just east of Fort Hall. The road ran through a hollow then up a low hill, straight through Gbenelu. The contrast between the settler homesteads along Baltimore Street and the chaotic crowding of round thatched houses in the Grebo town shocked many visitors. They hurried along the avenue, relieved at last to reach open ground beyond. A few minutes' walk farther, and the visitor would have seen on his left the Public Farm, with plots of sweet potatoes, cassava, and various experimental crops neatly laid out. Here was a house for the master of the farm, sheds, and an old log jailhouse. The agent and other colonial officers made a special point to show visitors these facilities, to impress upon them the importance of agriculture in Maryland. Farther along were receptacles that housed new emigrants.

The visitor would next come to East Harper, or Latrobe, a substantial village. Here was St. Mark's Episcopal Church, a neo-Gothic stone and brick structure with a square belfry at one corner; the Methodist Church, a stone and brick structure no less imposing; a stone courthouse and jail; the old Ladies' Academy, now used for civic activities; Free School No. 1, which most of the neighborhood's children attended; and a few houses.

Beyond this point, cross streets intersected Maryland Avenue at regular intervals. Two or three roads ran parallel on either side, dividing the five-acre farm plots. Maryland Avenue, the main road into the interior, was well maintained, built up on a causeway over low areas and adequate for wagon traffic along its whole length. The side streets were all passable, but varied according to the energies of the adjoining landowners, who were required by law to maintain them.

The agency built a house for each newly-arrived head of a household, which the settler would then have to pay for. These structures, modeled on the slave cabins and sheds of the southern mid-Atlantic states, dotted the landscape. They were built of locally sawn timber on rock pilings, with shingle roofs. The standard frame was ten by twelve feet and cost twelve dollars delivered. It included, according to an 1854 letter of instructions, "4 Sills, 4 Plates, 4 Corner Posts; of hewed timber 6 sleepers, 6 Joists: 14 Rafters, 32 Studds of round timber." Pictorial evidence indicates a room below and one above in the eves. One window and the open front door would suffice for light. Houses did not typically have fireplaces, but rather separate booths for cooking. Settlers might alter these structures according to their own needs and means, often with the addition of a porch. Some of the more prosperous houses boasted glass window sashes and a coat of American paint.[4]

In contrast, the visitor would also have found squalid hovels—residences of the old and infirm, or of the poorer wage laborers and traders. Other plots were little more than a tangle of trees and undergrowth, much as it had existed when the first settlers walked over it. The society had given up trying to expand settlement unnecessarily about 1840, when immigration ceased for two years. Soon after becoming governor, McGill commented to Latrobe that the number of new immigrants was too low to justify expansion and moreover that settlers did not want to live in vulnerable spots at the edge of settlement. "There are numbers of unoccupied farm lots on the Avenue which have once been improved sufficiently to secure deeds of possession, the owners, who from different causes have abandoned or neglected them, have suffered them to grow up into 'bush;' such lots widely separate farms that are improved. It has been the policy of your Agent to buy up such lots when practicable and give them to new settlers, this gives greater security to all and to the favourable appearance of the Colony."[5]

Three or four miles' walk up Maryland Avenue, past such varied habitations, stood Mount Vaughan, the original Episcopal outpost, now a high school, neatly fenced and cleared, and richly planted, with two large frame houses and dependencies on the summit of the hill. Just beyond, the road crossed a small bridge and ascended a conical hill with a stockade at its summit, Mount Tubman. Here was a school and a trading post run for the agency by Henry Hannon, once a slave in Baltimore City. On the other side of the hill was Tubman Town, where many of the freed Georgian slaves who arrived in 1837 still resided, now surrounded by a younger generation born in Africa.

Clothing was an obvious and attainable indication of American culture.[6] Though temperature hovered year-round about eighty degrees, damp sea breezes and the chills brought on by chronic fevers required warm clothing. Settlers abhorred nudity, which they associated with savagery. Most dressed according to fashions with which they had grown up. As slaves and poor freemen, they had owned castoff clothing, cheap factory-made pieces, and other items of their own making. In Africa wardrobes were typically limited. In many cases emigrants landed at Cape Palmas with only the ragged clothes on their backs. "Persons arriving entirely destitute of decent wearing apparel or bedding should be furnished with both," Samuel McGill instructed Joseph Gibson, about to assume the office of agent, in a letter of June 1854.[7] Once settled, many continued to receive used clothing from America. Settlers also made some of their own clothing from cloth purchased at the agency or one of the other stores. The census recognized three women skilled enough to be counted seamstresses in 1852.[8] An inventory of the Agency Store taken on June 1, 1854, included

12 pieces and remnants	light colored prints	610 yds
3 do.	blue denims	164
2 do.	pants stuff	151
9 do.	4/4 bleached shirting	320 3/4

41 do.	3/4 bleached shirting	1510
9 do.	furniture check	693 1/2
4 do.	apron check	242
1 Case	American Satin Stripe	1485
1 do.		1465
3 pieces and remnants do.		128 1/2
		3078 1/2

79 pieces and 167 handkerchiefs English romauls
52 do.   American romauls
2 1/3 pieces Turkey red and yellow stripes
46 pieces and 21 3/4 yds blue baft
131 pieces English satin stripe
8 11/15 pieces satin stripe handkerchiefs
1 piece royal check[9]

Greboes favored romauls, bafts, and satin stripes, which were practically currency.

The typical man's costume consisted of a loose-fitting long-sleeved shirt and pants and close-brimmed hat, following American models of the period. The more prosperous men in the community possessed larger wardrobes, including imported jackets, shoes, and hats, more in keeping with American fashions of the time. Women likewise dressed simply, typically in long high-waisted skirts and full blouses, often with a kerchief about the head. Some also possessed full dresses, typically with broad collars of contrasting material. Again, women of more prosperous families had more imported clothing and kept closer to American fashions. Children dressed much as their parents. None but the wealthy had shoes to wear. The colony's cobblers could rarely get suitable leather. Moreover, leather products were vulnerable to decay from humidity, insects, and hard use.[10]

All but the richest households were sparsely furnished. The *Liberia Packet* and other emigrant vessels had little space to stow furniture. Therefore, settlers had to do for themselves. There were no specialized cabinetmakers listed in the emigrant roll or censuses. The more skilled carpenters probably knew enough to fit and nail together some useful items. "Families arriving without them should be furnished with a suitable number of rough bedsteads, a table, and stools or benches," McGill instructed Joseph Gibson in June 1854. These probably followed the American vernacular patterns termed "primitive" and "country Hepplewhite." In the 1840s, the community possessed a skilled turner in the person of Amos Herring, the Methodist preacher. He taught some his craft and probably supplied some pieces to his neighbors.

Other household items were mostly utilitarian. Newly arrived families received a bucket, two mugs, six plates, two pint-size bowls, a covered Dutch oven, an iron pot and skillet, a tea kettle, a tin cup, a basin, and a chamber pot. Settlers acquired more items as they were able.[11]

As one might expect, settlers preferred foods with which they had grown up. New emigrants received rations that included a fair portion of imported foods. A week's ration for an adult included three pounds of salt beef or pork, a half croo (or quarter bushel) of rice, two pounds of flour, half a pound of sugar or a pint of molasses, a quarter pound of coffee or two ounces of tea, a quarter pound of dried soup, and a half pound of tobacco.[12] Thereafter, they had to make due with local produce, supplemented with a little salt fish or pork purchased from the stores. Settlers quickly adopted rice and palm oil as staples, and they depended on Grebo suppliers for them, either directly by trade or indirectly through the stores, to colonial officials' constant frustration. Yet little could be done. Most settler farms were not suited for rice, and Greboes harassed those who tried to raise it. Sweet potatoes and cassava added variety to meals. Settlers grew diverse garden vegetables, whose seeds came from America. Some of these did well—beans for instance—but others, such as corn and cabbage, which were favorite foods, did poorly. Many settlers kept chickens and hogs. Some even acquired Grebo cows. Hunting and fishing rounded out the larder.[13]

Africa was a new country, which presented a radically different economic environment. Many skills and trades settlers had pursued in America were no longer useful there. Nevertheless, they explored and adapted to the new economy. The society had also to adapt its theories to economic conditions of the West African coast. Thus there developed a three-way dialectic involving the colonizationists' actual trade practices, their utopian image of the society they wished to create, and the pragmatic needs of settlers. This interaction was a hugely important factor in the development of the community.

In many respects, Maryland in Liberia was a stereotypical "company town," with a single large employer exercising a paternal influence over a beholden community. Harper's situation as an enclave in the midst of a hostile social and ecological environment exacerbated matters. Backed with money and fifteen years of legislation from Baltimore, with the confirmation of local acts, the agency dominated the local economy. Essentially, its trade fell into two categories. The first and most important financially was the transatlantic trade in "African produce," namely palm oil, dye woods, ivory, and so on, conducted as a profit-making venture. The secondary trade comprised the regional traffic in rice and other foodstuffs, which provided subsistence both to new arrivals and established settlers, given to the former during their first six months in Africa and sold to the latter. The agency conducted both sorts of trade simultaneously.

In 1834, James Hall found Greboes occupying a lucrative economic niche as brokers of international trade. He and his successors had engrossed an increasing share of this business, much to the dismay of Grebo factors. Short of violence, there was little they could do to reverse the tide, though. The agency was better equipped culturally to deal with foreign ships and trading houses. It also had the advantage of capital, of transatlantic sailing ships, and of a superior array of merchandise.[14]

The individual transactions that composed the African trade were immensely varied and complicated. Cash was practically unknown, and goods exchanged directly for produce. Imported trade goods were not interchangable, though the agency continually experimented with substitutions. "You speak of getting suitable iron pots cast for the trade, why not iron-bars, cutlasses, and brass rods?" Russwurm asked Hall in 1847, "I shall send you sample cutlass and brass rod suitable for our trade: they are in very great demand with iron bars. We cannot get along without them. There is no limit hardly to the sale of brass rods for palm oil: they bring it when other goods fail. We pay from 17 to 20 cents per hundred. Our iron bars are 9 or 10 feet and weigh about 10 lbs. These we shall sell for one croo palm oil. Last year I bought 3000 [croos] at 25 cents, but cannot purchase under 35 cents at presen." In a letter of October 1849, Russwurm noted that, "Satin Stripes in close imitation of the English, are now manufactured at Fall River, Massachusetts: they only fail in width which ought to be from 32 to 34 inches, and each piece 18 yards exactly. The Episcopal Mission has a large quantity 34 wide, which trades readily for Rice, but not for Palm Oil." Tobacco, counted as a head with twelve leaves, with a nominal value of one (iron) bar, or twenty-five cents, was more broadly acceptable, especially for dashes.[15]

Units of measure were worked out by precedent, and the society sometimes failed to meet the needs of commerce when it shipped trade goods. Russwurm repeatedly scolded James Hall for errors in this respect. In a January 1847 letter he complained of receiving gunpowder in twenty-five pound kegs rather than the usual twenty-weight. As far as Grebo factors were concerned, a keg was a keg, with a specific value, despite the extra 25 percent in weight.[16]

The value of imported trade goods fluctuated according to taste and supply. Russwurm attempted to keep his American suppliers informed of such changes. "Our native trade has altered very much since when you were on the coast," he advised James Hall in October 1849, "then American Romauls and furniture check were in great demand for Rice or even Palm Oil, but the case is altered now: they demand the best English goods for Rice even, Gun Powder and good tobacco are always in demand however." The agency faced further difficulties in storing trade goods and preventing their spoilage.[17]

The agency usually conducted trade on a credit basis. Greboes designated "trademen" to conduct most transactions. Typically, the agent or one of his factors would contract with an African factor to deliver a specific quantity of some produce on or before a certain date. The African would then receive "trust money"—most of the goods needed for the purchase, plus something extra by way of a dash. Thus, disagreements over terms were frequent, and the agency lost considerable amounts to factors who made off with their advances.[18]

Even so, the agency's trade was substantial and profitable. In 1850, the colonial agency took in 16,877 gallons or 4,219 kroos (each equal to four gallons) of palm oil, valued at just under $6,000. The agency's two boats, *Angelina* and sloop *Curlew*, counted 2,496 kroos between them. Greboes sold 718 kroos more at the store in Harper. The Mount Tubman factory contributed 767 kroos, most probably from trade with bushmen. Settlers sold another 235 kroos at the store in Harper, the result of private traffic with Grebo producers.[19]

On January 1, 1850, the society reported that its trading operations in Africa since 1832 had resulted in a net profit of $59,334.48, just over 20 percent of total income. "Instead of sending money to Africa, which would be spent there in the purchase of goods for native trade, at an advance of from one to two hundred percent," they explained, "the Society buys the goods in this country, and sends them in lieu of money, to the Colony." They counted these as purchases by the agency, which had to be repaid. They were frank in the result of this: "The Society thus is made, in fact, a commercial firm: because the sending of goods requires arrangements for disposing of them at the market rates in Africa; requires accounts to be kept and rendered, and involves the return of palm oil, camwood, &c., to this country to be disposed of on the Society's account." This policy allowed them to get maximum benefit from limited funds. "There are certain articles," they noted by way of illustration, such as prints and iron ware, which are necessary for the African trade, and which can only be obtained in England. To purchase them in [America] would be to pay most dearly for them. They are taken by the English traders to the coast, where they are purchased at low rates with tobacco, which the Englishman requires to complete his cargo, as much as we require the products of England. An hundred dollars worth of a print, in demand for the season, on the coast, may be obtained for the proceeds, (invested in native productions,) of Maryland or Kentucky tobacco, which cost fifty dollars here, whereas, if it were bought in the Baltimore market, it would cost from $150 to $200.[20]

Two years later, on the first day of 1852, the aggregate profit had risen to $76,369.03, a net gain of $17,034.55.[21] This was scarcely enough to fund anything more than the society's foreign operations, as witnessed by the constant vigilance and care required of the agent over the years.

By 1852, international trade had become more regular. When Maryland was established, in 1834, ships of various nations laden with trade goods would arrive on the coast somewhere between the Senegal River and Sierra Leone, then work to leeward, usually within sight of shore. Following business practices evolved over centuries, they made contracts and landed trust money and dashes to African factors who promised to have exchanged the materials for produce before the ship's return. Such voyages were filled with risk, not least from fever and parasites picked up during visits on shore. Yet the profits were substantial enough to draw captains on repeated ventures. American merchants, especially those based in Salem, Massachusetts, dominated this trade.[22] The list of arrivals for 1850 included forty-four vessels of all descriptions, including eighteen English, fourteen American, seven Dutch, four Liberian, and one French. In several cases, these vessels called more than once, as they stopped on their way down and back up the coast.[23] In 1852 independent traders continued to make such voyages, but their numbers were declining. The California Gold Rush in 1849 and subsequent years drew a number of vessels from the African trade. Larger concerns, with capital and more carrying capacity, were entering the field.[24] The formation of the Chesapeake and Liberia Trading Company in 1846 was largely due to the recognition of the potential profit from regular trade to Africa.[25]

The commercial demand for palm oil, subject to some volatility, nevertheless trended upward, and African suppliers along the whole coast responded with higher production. American firms encountered increased competition from Europeans, particularly British and Germans. The Hamburg firm of Epperhausen was a favorite at Harper. "The agents are very accomodating, and keep a supply of English trade goods at fair rates, they stand a good chance of monopolizing 2/3 of our trade," Russwurm wrote in November 1847. All of this presaged a steady encroachment of Europeans on West Africa, culminating three decades later in the imperial seizure of nearly the whole continent.[26]

<hr />

Settler economic activity presents a very different picture. Life in Africa was difficult for Americans, who had to learn to survive and work in an unfamiliar, sometimes dangerous, ecological and cultural environment. The society, though paternalistic in its policies, was paradoxically an obstacle in many respects to the development of a viable settler community.

As mentioned, the society maintained a strong prejudice in favor of agriculture, based upon the Jeffersonian ideal of an agrarian republic. The Board of Managers knew quite well that they could make themselves and the colony rich by promoting trade, but their purpose was to create a virtuous commonwealth of husbandmen, not a querulous, parasitic marketplace. Instead, they wished to have "trade just sufficient to supply the colony as an agricultural people." They commented in the *Maryland Colonization Journal*:

> Not a few of our emigrants have had such a connection with trade in this country, as would perhaps lead them to its pursuit in Africa, and this, added to the natural seductions of a trade carried on between the civilized and the savage, in which a large amount of native produce might be brought into market, to be exchanged for imported

goods at a handsome profit, would tempt many into commerce, whose labour, for the benefit of the colony, would be better bestowed elsewhere. If colonization had for its object the enriching of emigrants that they might return and expend their wealth, or the creation of a trade, the results of which were intended to benefit this country, then it would become us to stimulate to activity in commerce; but seeing that its great purpose is to build up an independent and self-dependent nation, a nation whose interest is in the soil, and whose bread is wrought out of the soil, it rather behooves us to discourage trade, that the industrial force of the people may be directed to pursuits which will bind them and their descendants by the strongest ties to their new home.

These men, most of whom were businessmen and professionals, did not live the rustic life, yet they congratulated themselves for having successfully planted the germ of an agrarian nation, not for personal enrichment but for the good of its citizens.[27]

The society provided food and shelter to settlers during their first six months in Africa, theoretically until they could clear land and raise crops to feed themselves. They were disappointed to find that at the end of the period most settlers were only just gaining enough strength to work regularly. They must continue to borrow from the Agency Store or starve, and after nearly twenty years the situation had scarcely changed. Settlers did not become self-sufficient for a variety of reasons, though the society could see no further than spitefulness or laziness. "I know not what farther steps I can take to infuse into the colonists [more of] an agricultural spirit," Russwurm complained to Latrobe in April 1849. "The colonists could raise rice if they would, but my belief is, that the wrong ideas which they imbibe about 'liberty' is a hindrance to their engaging *vigorously* in any undertaking in which patience or perseverance are necessary."[28]

The few settlers and colonial officials who were financially independent often criticized those less fortunate. "Ninety out of every hundred of our people are paupers, and would be contented as such during their lives if the Society would give," McGill observed on September 18, 1851. "If a child is born the Society must furnish food and raiment. If an adult dies the Society must furnish a shroud and coffin. Thus from the cradle to the grave it is a regular system of pauperism." Apologizing for his rather negative interpretation, he went on to explain his view of the problem. "The greatest pains have been taken for a century or more to degrade the coloured man in the States to the level of brutes. These same people are now snatched suddenly from the plantations and un-instructed and unimproved are expected by the simple passage across five thousand miles of ocean to be fit to fulfill the functions and duties of free and enlightened citizens."[29]

Some of the fault also lay with the shortage of cash in the economy. The society floated some paper currency, redeemable at the Public Store for merchandise, but the scrip had minimal circulation and almost immediately declined from its face value. Trade goods, African pro-duce, or labor took the place of money, preventing the accumulation of capital. Like their Grebo neighbors, settlers found that the local soils could not produce enough to sustain them, and they must also depend on rice and other staples from the interior. Some enterprising fellows engaged in this business on their own account, but the agency aggres-sively opposed them. Most had no alternative therefore but to let the agency do the palaverous work for them and then buy or borrow from the store as needed.[30]

To foster the development of agriculture and help feed destitute settlers, the agency operated the Public Farm, some fifty acres of land, located on the low plain between Hoffman's River and Maryland Av-enue, between Gbenelu and Latrobe Township. The agricultural cen-sus of 1848 indicates 5½ acres under cultivation: 5 in potatoes and cas-sava, and in addition, 445 coffee trees, 475 cotton trees, 4 orange trees, 170 plantains (3/8 acre), 3 coconut trees, 1 breadfruit, 1 cocoa, 2 man-gos, and 28 other fruit trees. The farm served as a nursery, from which settlers could obtain young plants. "It being constantly necessary to give employment to a number of the Colonist," McGill wrote Latrobe in September 1851, "the Public Farm has been kept up for this express purpose." He continued, "From eight to twenty persons receive em-ployment daily at the farm, and twice the number apply whom we cannot receive. Indigent widows, and orphan boys have the preference of employment, as they when unable to procure work invariably apply to your Agent for the means of subsistence." During the months after Russwurm's death, McGill made strenuous efforts to reduce the number of settlers getting such assistance, for every indication was that the society could not continue it very much longer.[31]

Settlers had conflicting feelings about farming. Some resented the society's quixotic insistence on agriculture. Joshua Stewart, always a voluble commentator on colonial affairs, wrote James Hall in April 1849 that

> Our people are down, as low, as they poseble Can be. I dont Know What is to Raise them upe, they are Still Dependent on that Public Store, and What are they to do, to prevent their despondency? It Whant be potatar and Cassava etc. etc. No, Never, they Cant procour Sufucient quantaty of Seed to Plant, So as to make farming an object, What must be done, I Cant Say, our people ar; Without Jesting; Extremely poore they Realy do Sufer for the whant Suiteble Comfort of Life they work it is true, But the moneys they Receive in Returns is Worth nothing.[32]

Others still regarded agriculture as the most worthy of occupations. They tended to blame hard times on neglect of farming.[33] During the dark days of 1838, for instance, the schoolteacher Oliver Chambers wrote, "We have been too negligent about our farms. Yes Sir, We have shamefully thrown our Farms A way and Greedily Grasped the hammer and Saw and declare ourselves Carpenters for the sake of a little currency because it is An immediate reward, and depend upon the Natives for our food But we begin to discover that our Natives are not fools, if we buy of them we have to pay *well* for the Article or starve."[34] Similarly, in 1851, during one of the periodic agrarian revivals, Jonathan Moulton observed, "Agriculture is Now on foot here people finds they can live Better By attending to their farms then they can by all other Business put to Gether. The farmer is all now more or lest clearing and planting their farms in coffee, and adviseing with each-other which is the most prefitable thing to attend to." He concluded hopefully, "Oh that I may See the day when Cape Palmas will Stratch foth her wings and Be an example to the world, but this will never be done if We Give up, and do Nothing for our-Selves."[35]

In fact, settlers were poorly qualified to succeed as subsistence farmers. Many had only minimal agricultural experience, having been house servants or craftsmen. What such people might have known about farming—what they had experienced in the mid-Atlantic states—had little relevance to the rainforest of the West African coast. A good number were single women with small children. Few had enough capital to buy tools and seeds, and so had to make do with the paltry tools and supplies they could get from the agency. The typical inventory included an axe, hatchet, draw-knife, grubbing hoe, weeding hoe, shovel, cutlass, and occasionally, a saw. "You are to judge of the real wants of individuals," McGill counseled Gibson in June 1854. "All will apply for tools, you should supply none but those who are without them, and actually in want, and promises to make good use of them." Experience had shown that discouraged settlers would sell their tools at any price.[36]

The society may have attributed the failure of American style agriculture at Cape Palmas to cultural values or faults of character, but the root cause was ecological. The climate and soils of the coastal rainforest and savannahs simply could not sustain the intensive agricultural systems that the society and settlers had in mind, whether the cultivation of cash crops or subsistence farming. Americans insisted on raising American crops in the old American manner. They were continually frustrated at their inability to till the soil with ploughs and draft animals. Crops did not grow the way they did in America, and insect pests were much more severe.[37] Moreover, soil fertility dropped rapidly under a regime of permanent cultivation.[38] Livestock were vulnerable to all sorts of parasites. Epidemics repeatedly swept away whatever pigs, horses, or other animals settlers managed to husband.[39] The ecological impracticality of agriculture as the society envisioned is clear. Their insistence upon it after so many years of failure appears as folly.

Settlers may not have succeeded as cash-crop or subsistence farmers, but they were still avid horticulturists. In 1848 the agency made an agricultural survey of the colony. It found ninety-five individuals who cultivated about 155 acres altogether, an average of 1.63 acres apiece. The largest farm, 4.5 acres, belonged to John Barnes, who planted almost all of it with sweet potatoes and cassava. Thirty-six farms were of one acre or less; thirty-three more, above one and including two acres, and six above three acres. The size of these farms seems to have depended upon the circumstances of the landholders. The seventy-eight men listed cultivated 141.5 acres (an average of 1.81 each), while the seventeen women worked on 13.5 acres (an average of .79 each). The most important crops were cassava and sweet potatoes, which occupied 89.13 acres, or 58 percent of the land under cultivation. They were commonly grown together, it seems, for the census does not give proportions between them. The balance of farmland was given over to perennial or tree crops. These included nearly six thousand plantains, at least some grown on nearly every farm (eighty-six of the ninety-five); 1,035 coffee trees, grown on 52 farms, the great majority with ten or less, and four farms growing 635 of them; 1,638 "cotton trees," probably perennial bushes, grown on 88 farms, one of the Tubmans tending 436 of them; and a large number of citrus fruit trees. Some settlers were more adventurous, with cocoa and breadfruit trees. Notably, the census did not include any oil palms, which must have existed on some farms, if only wild. Also, the census did not record any vegetables, though they were raised in fairly large quantities.[40]

Settlers knew that subsistence by horticulture alone was impossible. Many turned to trade, despite the obstacles the society put in their way. In times of scarcity, settlers would take their wages in tobacco leaves or other trade goods and walk up the bush paths to meet African traders on their way to the beach. The agent and council legislated against this ineffectually. Settler letters requesting trade goods are common, and it is clear that men, women, and even children pursued the business.[41] There was a market space on the north side of Maryland Avenue, east of Gbenelu, which was formally opened in 1840, under a statute which mandated that all produce be traded within its confines. The law exempted fresh fish, which settlers could sell door-to-door. Other settlers ran informal shops out of their homes.[42] Some were more successful than others in negotiating the intricate and variable terms of African trade, but all asserted their right to make a living to the best of their ability.

The agency had its principal competition from the large independent traders, particularly McGill, Brothers and Bowen. Their business was similar to the agency's, but they had to make their own contacts with suppliers overseas. McGill, with warehouses at Monrovia and Harper, and arrangements with merchants in Britain and the United States, was truly an international house. The firm was able to finance the building of a ship, *George R. McGill*, in Baltimore in 1848, at a cost over $10,000. The same shipwright produced a second vessel, *Moses Sheppard*, which sailed to Liberia on its maiden voyage on November 10, 1856. McGill, Brothers sent $15,000 to Baltimore to pay for the construction and buy a cargo to take to Africa, all without interrupting their English trade.[43] Although the agency felt some ambivalence about carrying on business, settler merchants had no such scruples, and the two therefore were frequently at odds. Import duties and trafficking in rum and other ardent spirits often caused conflict.[44]

The community harbored a strong resentment of the big merchants. In 1849, for instance, an anonymous correspondent complained to the society about the scarcity of pork, beef, and flour. "The Packet comes and goes," he wrote, "and she never has anything to dispose of. Every thing that she has is bought up by a few persons, and sold out for 2 hundred perscent, for beef from 16 to 20 cents a pound, pork .25, and flour 12½ and now I would ask how can the people get along. Some two or three are making themselves rich, while the others are suffering."[45] Such opinions may have had some foundation in frustration and envy, for most settlers, if they had the means, would have done the same.

A majority of settlers engaged in wage labor of some sort, in addition to their horticultural or agricultural activities. They brought various skills from America, and continued them where possible at Cape Palmas. The census of 1852 recorded the most common employment as sailor, with twenty-two men, almost all between the ages of eighteen and thirty. In order of frequency there followed eighteen sawyers, most older men in their thirties; seventeen laborers, of diverse ages from sixteen to fifty-four; eleven carpenters, primarily men in their thirties or older; seven farmers, the youngest forty-three; six teachers, men in their late twenties or early thirties; five storekeepers and assistants, of diverse ages; five lumbermen, all but one over forty; three each of coopers, stonemasons, and gardeners, of various ages; two each of blacksmiths and clerks; and one each of physician, nurse, surveyor, factory clerk, turner, jailer, ditcher, minister, barber, tailor, gunsmith, bricklayer, tobacconist, cook, and trader.[46] Other settlers could not continue their trades for lack of tools, materials, or demand. Thus Russwurm had to beg for tin and tools for an emigrant tinker. Shoemakers had to get leather, and blacksmiths, coal, from Baltimore.[47]

The living of the wage laborer was precarious, for illness, injury, or even bad weather could plunge worker and family into debt or worse. Samuel McGill was not alone in criticizing what he termed a lack of "manly and independent spirit." "Those who engage in sawing and lumber getting are . . . thoughtless and improvident," he wrote in September 1851. "When the weather is unfavourable for this work, the time is spent in idleness which might have been profitably employed in planting; if attacked with sickness (to which they are peculiarly liable from their great exposure in swampy lands) and for a time disabled, having neither money nor produce growing they are forced to beg, starve, or obtain on credit from your Agent the means of procuring food for their families." He concluded, "this pernicious system has existed in this Colony ever since its formation," and predicted that it would persist for many years to come.[48]

Maryland in Liberia was a community of transplants. By 1852 a small group of African-born individuals had accumulated in the population, but the oldest of those born at Cape Palmas could scarcely be eighteen years old, and the majority still children. At the close of the year, the Maryland State Colonization Society had sent 840 individuals to Cape Palmas. Others had come to Harper from settlements in Liberia proper. These included six from the *Orion* and forty-one from the *Lafayette* expeditions. About 125 had come to Liberia under the auspices of the American Colonization Society between the years 1820 and 1842, then moved. Many others appear in the records, whose arrival is otherwise unrecorded. Thus, the aggregate number of settlers arrived at Cape Palmas from 1834 through 1852 must have been close to 1,150.[49]

Of those sent by the Maryland State Colonization Society to Cape Palmas, nearly half, 428, came from the lower counties of the western shore of Maryland. Calvert County supplied 159; St. Mary's, 108; Charles, 63; Anne Arundel and its later offshoot, Howard, 64; and Prince George's, 34. The northern tier of western shore counties, where slavery was less prevalent but which had better-established free black populations, sent 239 of its population to Cape Palmas. These included 117 from Baltimore City and County; 23 from Cecil County; 15 from Harford; 58 from Frederick; 11 from Washington County; and 15 from Allegany. The Eastern Shore was the scene of considerable colonization promotion, but only 121 individuals went from there to Cape Palmas: Queen Anne County sending 26; Caroline, 16; Talbot, 11; Dorchester, 42; Somerset, 13; and Worcester, 13. Fourteen other Marylanders, most of whom went to Africa under the auspices of the American Colonization Society, have unrecorded origins in the state, and another twenty-three have origins altogether untraced. Though Maryland in Liberia was founded by and for Marylanders, settlers did come from other parts of the United States. These included 91 from Virginia; 81 from Georgia; 22 from North Carolina; seven each from South Carolina, New York, and Kentucky; six from Louisiana; five from Tennessee; four from Washington, D.C.; three from Mississippi; and one each from Alabama, Missouri, Maine, and Connecticut.

Significantly, the emigration data points to a large proportion of clearly defined families. This is remarkable considering the disintegrative forces arrayed against black families in Maryland at the time. It appears that colonization had particular appeal for families and that the society made a special effort to coordinate the emigration of related groups, even to the point of securing the release of slaves owned by different individuals. Despite this, emigration frequently resulted in the division of families, and colonial officials regularly complained of single female emigrants and their young children, who had little means of supporting themselves in Africa. The sense of loss is frequently expressed in the letters that settlers sent home to the society and their former masters.[50]

Emigrants sometimes left behind spouses or partners, which posed emotional and legal difficulties. For instance, William Hawkins, a free-born emigrant from Anne Arundel County, who arrived at Cape Palmas on the *Bourne* in 1835, left his slave wife and child in America, then remarried in Africa, raising a legal question of bigamy. He was allowed to remarry, however, and soon had new children.[51] Such family divisions also caused financial stress to the agency. Samuel McGill commented to James Hall in August 1844 that, "All of the widow women (five or six) have been furnished with dwelling-houses at considerable expense to your agent, and it is now to be hoped that (in the event their husbands cannot be rescued from slavery and induced to come out) they may speedily secure to themselves husbands, so as to relieve your agent of all farther trouble on their account."[52]

The census of 1852 recorded a population of 785 individuals divided into 179 discernable households, giving a mean of 4.38 individuals per household. Ninety-one of these households comprised a husband and wife, usually with children and sometimes other adherents (who might include kinfolk, orphans, or African "apprentices," or servants). Eighty-four households were headed by single men or women, again with children or other adherents in many cases. These included fifty-three houses headed by "widows"—some literally such, whose husbands had died in Africa, others who had left husbands behind and not remarried. The majority of them had children to care for. The census notes five female householders as "single," though four of them had children, out of wedlock by implication. Men, whether widowers or unmarried, headed twenty-six entries. Most of them cared for children, and a few had other adherents.[53]

Only eight households appear to have included children and grandchildren. Adult offspring often continued to live with their parents until they were married. There were in addition several households that appear to have comprised relatively large groups of unrelated orphans of indigent youth. One such was the charge of Elizabeth Thomson, who was a teacher for the Episcopal mission. William Prout and Samuel McGill also seem to have had houses filled with cousins and distressed neighbors.[54]

What is striking about the community of Americans at Cape Palmas is how closely their culture remained identified with that of the mother country. In fact, settlers were so conscious of their American identities, that their culture was in some ways a caricature of what they had known. Yet the experience of other colonial societies has been similar: in their quest to maintain stability and order, emigrants distill features of the old country that most represent it. Beyond the self-conscious homesick rhetoric were the everyday habits that made the place so distinctive.

Settlers participated in a vivacious community. They organized institutions after models in their native land. These included mutual aid associations, debating, agricultural, and choral societies, and even a public library.[55] "A spirit to become more enlightened is seemingly at work in the minds of many persons here," William Prout wrote on behalf of the Cape Palmas Lyceum in 1848, thanking a group of Baltimoreans who had shipped a collection of books for the library. Such gifts were indeed appreciated, for they offered a window to the outer world, bringing the community into the "Republic of Letters."[56] Such organizations provided means of sociability, at the same time fostering intellectual and material improvement. They were also criteria by which settlers distinguished their culture from that of Africans around them.

Schools constituted a key component of the community's institutional structure. In 1851, McGill reported that the agency conducted two schools, each with an average attendance of twenty-nine students daily. He wrote that the teachers worked hard at their charges, but that they faced great difficulties, not least their own lack of education. Books were also hard to find.[57]

Settlers were emphatically Christian. All of them at least professed to believe in the divinity of Jesus, to believe in a last judgement with heaven or hell as rewards, and to subscribe to a set of ethics set out in the Bible. Language and examples from the Bible, evident in much settler correspondence with the society, also colored everyday life. Churches were therefore quite active in the community. Each of them held regular Sunday services, along with other services during the week. Their Sunday schools were vital components of the community's culture. Churches were the setting for a high proportion of sociability, where individuals shared their spiritual and temporal concerns. Ministers, because of their higher education and positions of authority, often had tremendous influence over their followers.[58]

The Methodist Church counted the most members in 1852. They had churches at Harper, Mt. Emory in East Harper, and at Mt. Tubman. In 1852 residents of Harper had undertaken the construction of a stone church, a structure fifty-four by thirty-five feet, with a foundation three feet above ground and walls sixteen feet above that, high enough to accommodate a gallery. The materials were gathered, and the foundation laid, but then funds ran low. Much of the masonry was exposed and would be damaged by rains before construction began again.[59]

In 1852 the church ran two Sunday schools, numbering 130 pupils between them, which met on Sunday afternoons. Adults came with their children to learn the catechism and to read the Bible, sharing their precious few books between them. John D. Moore, a lay preacher, conducted the weekday school, in which thirty or more students of various ages studied reading, writing, grammar, arithmetic, and geography. Again, books were in such short supply that learning suffered, as the only text common enough for general reading was the Bible. Every Friday the students recited their catechism, which was also the case in the agency schools. In addition, the church sponsored stations at Barrakah, Saurekah, and other towns in the bush, each consisting of a school and chapel, staffed by intrepid settlers.[60]

The Methodist Church in Maryland had a history of controversy in the late 1840s. Under the energetic guidance of Amos Herring, the church had been quite vital. Herring left Maryland at the end of 1845. Francis Burns, who had headed the congregation for a time in the 1830s, replaced him, taking up the post by February 1846. Reverend Benham, head of the church at Monrovia, visited Maryland the next month. Amos Herring, though popular, had left debts behind. Various settlers approached Benham with bills, but he put them off. They appealed to the governor, who expressed his opinion that the church in Monrovia, having pastoral oversight of that at Cape Palmas, was liable. Benham reluctantly told the claimants that he would have the bills paid when Captain Lawlin, a regular visitor, made his next run down the coast. He returned to Monrovia and consulted the elders, who agreed with him—wrongly and selfishly—that debts contracted at their station in Maryland were not their responsibility. Benham was "no business man and quite incompetent for his station," Russwurm wrote Hall disgustedly early in November 1847, when he learned of the duplicity.[61]

The missionary activities of the church caused additional difficulties. Reverend Herring had established schools and chapels in several bush towns, staffed by lay preachers from the colony. Most of the towns in the interior were eager to have schools. Africans looked at education as power, a means of bolstering pride and gratifying avarice. Soon after his arrival, Burns learned a bitter lesson in the case of the station at Saurekah. Herring had built a substantial schoolhouse there, forty-five by twenty-four feet, on a tract of old field suitable for an experimental farm for the students. The townspeople robbed and drove away James B. Dennis, the teacher, and the station fell to ruin. The new preacher visited Saurekah in March or April with Phillip Gross, his choice to manage the re-opened station, and some carpenters. A pala-ver with the headmen satisfied him that Gross would be treated better than his predecessor. Gross remained with the carpenters, and Burns returned to Harper. The workmen had hardly begun their labors when townspeople began to harass them. They retreated to Harper, but Gross stayed on, as he was not the object of wrath. Burns sent John Banks and a Grebo man separately to find the cause of the palaver. They learned that Saurekah was determined to recover the fines Russwurm had im-posed for the beating of Dennis from any settlers they could catch in their territory. Burns complained to the governor, who renewed the palaver. The Saurekah delegates admitted that they had no complaint against the Methodists. Nevertheless, they refused to guarantee their safety. Russwurm ordered an embargo on the town until they should reconsider. Gross came home and the matter rested.[62] Soon after, Tho-mas Jackson also returned to his home from a failed bush school. On May 14, the agent and council restored his commission as captain in the militia.[63]

The Episcopal Church at Cape Palmas, counted far fewer members among settlers—only twenty-five communicants in 1849. The church had an influence greater than its numbers, though, because its congre-gation comprised much of the colonial elite. After 1844 the mission's adversarial relationship with the colonial government evolved into a more cooperative one. Mrs. Russwurm joined the congregation, and her husband soon followed. Moreover, the church had tremendous financial support from the United States and an extensive missionary operation. There were five schools: Elizabeth Thomson, widow of the unfortunate James Thomson, conducted a day school and a Sunday school; likewise did Joseph Gibson, an American orphan raised in the mission; and James B. Dennis, a settler originally of the *Lafayette*'s com-pany, ran a Sunday school. The day schools counted fifty-five students on average, while the Sunday schools, which probably also included day-school scholars, enrolled eighty-four.[64]

On January 1, 1849, the Episcopal Mission opened a "High School" at the old station on Mt. Vaughan. John Payne intended this as a boarding school for the training of settlers in the ministry, in the belief that they would prove better missionaries than unacclimated white Americans who would have little or no knowledge of African customs when compared with men brought up in Liberia. As an adjunct, he set up a manual labor school for indigent settler children. "The general plan is for the children to support themselves by their labor, while they receive their education gratuitously at the High School," he wrote Latrobe. He believed that the school would help to prevent youths from "trafficking amongst the natives at a time when character is forming" by giving them some means of support while they learned. He worried that, "there is far more licentiousness than in former years amongst the young in the Colony, and I attribute it in a great degree to the fact." Joseph Gibson, a settler orphan raised by the mission, had charge of the school. A few years later, Alexander Crummell, a leading figure in African-American history, would succeed him.[65]

Like the Methodists, the Episcopalians took their beliefs very seriously, and controversies over doctrine and administration were sometimes intense, just as in America. John Russwurm wrote in October 1847 that the church had recently acquired several new members by defection from the Methodists. "Our people are just beginning to see that so much noise and shouting are not religion." In February 1850, Rev. Eli Stokes, arrived at Cape Palmas to serve as Rev. John Payne's assistant in St. Mark's Parish, Latrobe Township. Stokes was a black Marylander but had grown up in Connecticut and Rhode Island. Bishop Whittingham of Maryland had made him a deacon in 1843, and Bishop Brownell of Connecticut ordained him a priest in 1846. The new minister appears in his letters to have been quite literate and competent enough, but he ran into controversy almost immediately, apparently because his views were "high church," which conflicted with the more liberal, individualistic tendencies of most of the congregation. McGill commented that, "Stokes has been rejected by the brethren here, who will not receive the Sacrament at his hands, but he swears he will not leave Africa, but will seek a parish elsewhere. . . . He is truly a smart and intelligent man — but goaded allmost to phrensy by the envy and malignity of his sable brethren — and the hostility of the clergy." He urged Dr. Hall to use his influence to find the minister a new post, fearing that he, like Charles Snetter, might do great harm to the cause of colonization if he returned home disaffected. The dispute raged on, descending to a charge of mishandling money. Eventually, Stokes left Maryland for Liberia, where he established an independent Episcopal Church, amidst even more rancor and suspicion of corruption.[66]

The Baptist Church had a presence in the community, but until the late 1840s very little else. In a report of October 1849, Russwurm noted that the church had 37 communicants, more indeed than the Episcopal church, but with very little social or political clout. The church was without regular clergy until the arrival of Rev. Boston Jenkins Drayton in 1848, sent out by the missionary society of the Southern Baptist Convention. Drayton was South Carolinian by birth, apparently part of the Charleston free black elite. He received a rather substantial education to prepare him for his assignment. The society sent him along with Samuel Crowther to West Africa with high expectations for the work they would accomplish. Drayton settled at Cape Palmas, and Crowther went on to the Niger Delta, where he became a very notable figure. Drayton, on the other hand, was unsure just what he was supposed to do. His duties were not clearly defined, and though the existing church accepted him as their leader, there was no revival of spirituality or increase of membership for some time. In April 1851, Drayton reported that he hoped to expand his missionary activities among Africans, but that caution was necessary. "There are wars, and still rumours of more wars; and I see no way to mitigate this evil some, only by planting the missionary standard at every available spot: and let the blood stained Banner be unfurled to every breeze; so that the numerous Tribes may rally under it, and catch its healing savour." The preacher took a keen interest in politics and soon became an active participant, to the chagrin of Russwurm and other established leaders of the community. He would one day play a central role in Maryland's history.[67]

The militia were also important in the life of the community. Every man and boy capable of bearing arms—generally about 175—belonged to one of three groups: the Latrobe Artillery Company, the Howard Volunteers, or the militia. They held quarterly parades at which officers inspected arms and the men practiced their drills, all the while reaffirming their communal identity and the need for self-defense. When in September 1851 there was a threat of war with Greboes, soldiers were ready at first notice to take up arms and meet at defensive posts. William Howard, a poor settler who identified himself as the former slave of Mrs. Cyril Harper in Anne Arundel County, wrote proudly of the fact to James Hall on the twenty-second. He asked for a cape and suitable cloth to make a uniform, so that he could join the elite Howard Volunteer Company. "In The time of Deferance Beteen us an the natives," he wrote, "I Sopoted Each Station With box Catrdgs for Each Station and 2 Bags of Bugk Shots Each an Then I had to keepe Garde in The Raine for 2 Days at The time befo Relest from My post. . . . An When I Carid to Tubman Town an homs Street. The Cuered Womans Rejoiced Grately." The "frightfwl" war dress of Greboes impressed him deeply. In a report written late in 1849, Russwurm noted that "We have 2 Volunteer and 1 Militia Company and can turn out 175 men and boys capable of bearing arms. My son Frank 10 years of age is quite a marksman — perhaps there are many others not older, equally so."[68]

Henry Hannon provides a good example, stressing his identification of freedom with participation in colonial institutions. He had come to Africa on the *Niobe* in 1837 and shortly after gone to work for Russwurm as schoolteacher and head trademan for the agency at Mt. Tubman. He continued in those posts at the time of writing in October 1844. A former slave, with little formal education, he had endeavored under difficult circumstances to promote the school, having to beg for reading books from the missionaries. Nevertheless, he believed that "*God* will raise up a People here, for himself, and for the good of those natives with which we are surrounded." "What is the matter with the Poor black man, in your Place," he exclaimed,

> Tell them for me, that I am *free* as a man can be, – I hold my sword
> as the Captain for the Howards Volunteer Company of soldiers, of

sixty men, – I hold my office as a Justice of the Peace for this Colony, – I had . . . office as Register for the same, – I keep the Colonial school, – I measure all Lumber for the sawyers, or those Person who get lumber to sell, Myself I enjoy the life of a freeman, in africa, we can set in our own court house, we can have our jurymen of coloured men, – we have our Council to make our buy laws for us.

He asked for news of various white and black people who had been his friends in Baltimore and southern Maryland. He invited everyone to come and join him, "For we can Praise *god* in this Place and no man interferes with us, neither can any man make affread or molest us, while we live under our fig tree."[69]

By 1852 settlers were growing more aware of their own distinctiveness and nationality. In the first place, they were conscious of possessing a beautiful territory, in which they could enjoy liberty. "When I rise in the morning before the sun is up, and view the country, east west north and south, for miles around the forest lookes beautiful and green," wrote Thomas Gross in March 1851. He continued, "We are all free men here, and have the privinledge of makeing our laws, and our children will be free citizens let them go where ever they may go." He predicted that black Americans would all soon "flock to the Shores of africa, where they can enjoy their freedom, and become an independent people."[70]

Additionally, settlers were aware of their isolation from other centers of power and culture. Monrovia was at least a week's travel away, and America was even farther. Ships could make the passage in as little as twenty-eight days, which the *Liberia Packet* achieved on her return from Monrovia in the summer of 1848, but the average was more like forty days, and often could take even longer. Separation by the ocean is a recurrent theme in settler letters home.[71]

Settlers looked back on America with a sense of longing for family, friends, and material things left behind, mingled with bitter frustration that more did not follow them. The Methodist preacher, A. F. Russell, spoke much to this point in a letter to John Seys, penned in July 1852. Russell complained about the resistance of black Americans to emigration. He wrote,

How can it be thought by a colored man, a poor ninety-ninth rate being in America, that he is disgracing himself or blighting his honor, to leave America before all his brethren are free? Where is the honor of hopeless oppression? Where is the honor arising from holding a few self-torturing, feeble, worse than time-wasting anti-slavery meetings in a free State? Telling over to each other what they have experienced a thousand times, and will experience a thousand more, without altering their condition. Why sing to each other, we are degraded, oppressed? We free people choose to be so, because our brethren are just like us — are oppressed! I see heathens every day who choose to be so, because their fathers were. Refuse the boon of liberty because it would please the Colonizationists for me to be free in Africa! And suppose it pleased the devil, would it alter the fact, or thing?

This was incomprehensible to him. Africa beckoned, but America offered no future at all. And what of the future?

How miserable it looks to see a parcel of free blacks inflated by Garretson, Abdy, Kelly and others, with a nonsense that is to fall upon, and is falling upon the blacks only, who are thus made the cats-paw of foul and false mercy, to refuse conviction and fight against the only practicable hope before them — sinking every day and refuse to be saved because a Colonizationist comes to their aid, and comes honestly, without sophistry, or hypocrisy — without a crocodile tear, telling them what I know to be the *truth*, and which they could see if they would. In the United States you are only men in shape — and when slave labor is no longer needed, years hence, you will remain in the United States if you will — holding a position somewhat analogous to the ourang-outang, "an animal," they will say, "something like a man, that used to work with our oxen, plough with our horses, hunt with our dogs," etc. What is the hope of the American black? Is it to be annihilated and lost in the Irish, German and other "streams pouring in?" This would do, were it not that the mark of slavery of himself or his ancestors, was not indelibly impressed upon him in the color of his skin.

Cape Palmas was the prettiest country he had seen in Africa, he concluded. Though it was underdeveloped, there was no limit to the agricultural and mercantile wealth it might one day generate. Moreover, here was freedom.[72]

Samuel McGill wrote along similar lines in March 1845, in response to a letter sent him by Henry Goodwin, a southern Maryland farmer who had freed most of his own slaves and encouraged many others to go to Africa. The *Chipola* had carried two more of his people, Jesse Flanagan and Peggy Simpson, both born before the Revolution, and Goodwin was eager to know how they had fared. The doctor informed him that all of the *Chipola's* company had passed the first attacks of fever and were then moving onto their farms. One young woman had married a settler, and their union had promise of a happy future. He hoped that the wife and children of Jesse Flanagan would soon decide to leave their servitude for freedom in Africa. How, he wondered, could anyone prefer slavery to freedom, the watchspring of his own life. Though he had never been a slave, he found the atmosphere in American insufferable. To his mind, the chances for emancipation were "dark and gloomy"—nearly hopeless in fact. Yet he had an ardent faith that things must get better. Mere emancipation was insufficient. "Suppose for instance slavery abolished: will this necessarily secure to the colored man *social and political* [equality] without which to an intelligent mind there cane be no real freedom. To be free in reality a man must enjoy every blessing in common with others, unless from mental or pecuniary deficiencies he be constrained to foregoe them." Here abolitionists betrayed their hypocrisy, he asserted, because most would not accord black people equal rights with themselves. Freed black Americans must remain an underclass even fifty years after some hypothetical emancipation. Only emigration offered a solution, he believed. "I do assure you," he concluded,

> were the colored man once to imbibe the true spirit of liberty, he could no more content himself under existing circumstances in the United States, than in a bed of thorns. I have myself experienced something of what I write. I have visited the States as a free Liberian under circumstances the most favourable, and even then felt that to be called a free colored man in the States, is synonimous with what we here term slavery, – it is, a kind of freedom which the unwearying kindness and coutesies of our *best and most undoubted Colonization friends* can hardly render agreeable — we never breathe freely again

until the goodly boat conveys us once more to the shores of our . . .
happy home.[73]

Historians of American race relations have duly noted the vehement opposition of the great majority of black Americans to colonization. This opposition was well founded, for Africa had little to offer in terms of easier living, and most settlers endured privations they would not have in America. Even so, settlers went to Africa with a different motive than easy living. They had despaired of American prejudice and caste, but not of an American ideal of freedom and the opportunity to create a better society for succeeding generations. The correspondence from Africa is filled with sentiments similar to those expressed by Russell and McGill—often more homely compositions by men and women who had difficulty writing even their own names. Yet the desire for freedom is a fundamental of human nature, only the ability to express it to posterity limited by literacy. In America, by contrast, such ideas, though shared in many cases with emigrants, would have been subversive and largely inexpressible. The steady stream of letters back from Africa and their publication in colonization periodicals and the general press cannot fail to have had an impact on race relations in the United States.[74]

Settlers in Maryland were conscious of a parallel between themselves and the ancient Jews. This is evident in comments made by Russwurm in an 1845 letter to Latrobe. After reporting some adversities caused by a war among the Grebo states, he continued, "still we manage to get along. We have some croakers in black, who cant see how we poor colonists are to get along by ourselves — the same soothsayers we had 7 years ago — thus, an unseen has fed us 'with manna' by the way 'in our passage through the Red Sea,' and in all our wanderings 'through the Desert': — Infinite Wisdom has decreed, that we are not to know what eveils are to obstruct our paths through life, nor what blessings are to be ours: — our faith is still unshaken in his goodness, mercy and justice."[75]

Confronted with African culture, settlers quite often felt the urge to win surrounding African peoples to their way of life. They were encouraged in this by the apparent eagerness of African parents to have their children learn the magical secrets of the new technology.[76] Joshua Stewart gave remarkable expression to this desire in a letter of March 14, 1844, to Moses Sheppard. "I am doing Nothing in the way of Giting a living," he admitted, "at least ondly doing a little Jobe of Painting an a little Jobe of Sadling wich but Trifling." Stewart had preceded Russwurm into the bush the previous year and was inspired by the experience. He observed that the soils were much better back from the beach, and he saw acres of corn with nine-inch ears and sixteen rows of kernels. Here was a place he could make a living as a farmer. More than this, he crossed territories with populations in the thousands who had never seen a foreigner from across the seas, be he black or white. He was amazed at the eagerness of the populace to learn Western customs, "the Rule of Sivelization." In this he saw an opportunity for himself. "If Siveliz men expect to do Eny thing at farming in this country it must Be from the Sea Board where they will make ther Bread, independent to the Native." He asked Sheppard whether he knew of any society or person in America who might sponsor his efforts to open a school in the bush. "I am one that Stands Ready to go at a word to carry the Word of Truth."

> I see so meny thousand Souls whom are destute of the light and power of Redeeming Love and who Know not God. I have to morne and weep Day an Night for thease dark and benighted Son of Africa. How Grievious it would be to you if 2 or 3 thousand Souls were to Surround you and ask you to Speak Gods Word, and they Never hered it befor, and dont no how to Read, nor Know the first Rule of Civelization, and would Bage you to com and teach School among them.[77]

Settlers attached special meaning to the Old Testament passages concerning the Children of Israel in the land of Canaan when they considered their relations with the surrounding African peoples. Though Greboes and Americans avoided war, squabbling and fistfights

were apparently rather frequent. Should an event like the murder of
Eben Parker and his family have recurred in 1852, the community would
have responded just as they had in 1838, for they were determined that
this was their Promised Land, and that in any event this was where they
must make a stand. Despite daily contact with their neighbors for nearly
twenty years, Greboes and Americans persisted with their own cultural habits. Settlers held Grebo rights in contempt and would move
them away from Cape Palmas if they could. This would not happen
without war, however, and the colony's leadership was steadfastly determined to keep peace.[78]

The letters and reports from Maryland in Liberia sometimes seem
to float free from their African origin and reflect more of North
America. They create a vivid impression: small frame houses with
shingled roofs; garden patches with rows of onions, squash, beans, and
sweet potatoes; churches, stone public buildings, and graded roadways; sailing ships lying in the roads. We see men in denim breeches and
blue check shirts, and women in calico skirts; men and women on their
way to labor; blacksmiths and sawyers at work, women nurturing children and tending their gardens. We hear men and women speaking
English in the old Tidewater lilt: the sermons to Sunday congregations
of several denominations, the public meetings to address political concerns, the evening conversations of neighbors at gateposts; busybodies
and quiet sorts. We can think of any number of rural American communities at the same period and expect to find the same. As in frontier
America, settlers faced a challenge to their culture, not in the presence
of Native Americans, but of Africans, who shared, more or less, skin
color, but whose way of life scarcely corresponded, who spoke different
languages, who had multiple wives instead of one, who farmed a different field every year or two instead of owning and cultivating a single
plot, who believed in sorcery and trial by ordeal, with persisting ritual
killings, even on the public roads. Almost unbelievably, the two peoples
coexisted without serious outbreak, despite mutual suspicion and
animosity.

Through all of this, we gain an impression of the citizens of Maryland in Liberia as a community evolving into something wholly distinct—retaining selected features of the old country, shaped by the bitter experiences of leaving home and family, and in the process of adapting to the new life in Africa. At Cape Palmas, we see clearly defined the difference between ideal and circumstance, a society learning to maintain itself in the face of great adversity, and yet holding forth the hope for something much bigger and better.

XIX.

"The Invaluable Rights of Freemen"

D URING THE FIRST FOUR MONTHS OF 1852, MARYLAND'S CITIZENS lived peacefully, if not in harmony, pursuing their various occupations, their future very much on their minds. When a ship called in April, McGill reported that the war at Garroway was at armistice, but the conflict at the mouth of the Cavally continued. "It fills me with regret that we are not able to command peace," he wrote, "we trust that the early exhaustion of one or the other of the parties, will soon enable us to bring them to terms." Harper seemed at peace with Gbenelu, but McGill doubted that the situation was permanent. He constructed a new stockade at East Harper and planned another for the Cape. The militia continued its Saturday drills and kept the cannons in constant readiness. McGill's and other houses in Harper contained small arsenals, muskets loaded and primed, just in case.[1]

McGill's fears were realized in May, when a settler "of little note, but of reckless daring," came upon a rowdy group of Greboes about to administer sassy water to a young woman accused of sorcery. He rushed in to rescue her, throwing the bowl of poison onto the ground. Her furious persecutors immediately fell upon him. The woman's family came into the fray on his behalf, and a general brawl ensued. Several

Greboes were injured, one quite seriously. The American was mauled too, but the woman's family saved and hid him. Exaggerated reports flew through the settlement, and the militia mustered to rescue their comrade. Gbenelu's *sedibo* met them fully armed, prepared to protect their institutions. Fortunately, restraint prevailed before more blood could be shed.[2]

This custom of trial by ordeal—*gidu*—had always caused tension between Greboes and Americans. The steady execution of innocents on superstitious pretexts, often culminating in bloody beatings on the roadways, confirmed Africans as "savages" and did more than anything else to harm relations between settlers and natives. Greboes lived in dread of witches. They firmly believed in the efficacy of their method of detecting them. Yet *gidu* was sometimes a weapon in feuds between individuals and families, or a means of social control, typically the tool of conservative elements in society. Freeman and other influential Greboes who were more progressive, that is, sympathetic to American culture, had lately begun to oppose the custom because of its cynical uses.[3]

"We have been on the lookout for many years," McGill wrote soon after the incident, "for some favorable moment for effectively declaring our repugnance to witnessing the barbarous murders that are so frequently perpetrated, by the Sassy Bark ordeal, in full sight of our very doors."[4] Freeman had opposed this particular trial and was glad that someone had intervened, though he maintained his belief in sorcery.[5] Negotiations occupied the better part of two days, but at last, they came to terms. Henceforth, the governor and members of a special commission would have sole authority to rescue Greboes subjected to ordeal for witchcraft. When *gidu* was administered as punishment for murder or other capital crimes, these commissioners were not to interfere so long as the trial did not take place on the colony's roads. Freeman pledged his *sedibo* to aid any commissioner in the exercise of his duty. The document was read and duly executed by the king and his headmen. A suitable dash, consisting of "two pieces of Blue Baft, twenty bars Tobacco and two dozen wash Basins," was then distributed among them.[6]

Four days after signing the treaty, McGill appointed four commissioners to enforce it: William Cassell, Joshua Stewart, Dempsey Fletcher, and Roszel McGill. On June 19 he gave each of them a letter of instructions. "It is expected that you will always use persuasive rather than coercive measures," it read, "better indeed that the evil should continue, than that you should suffer injury, or our government be involved in war by our efforts for its suppression." He advised them to be careful not to intervene when the chance of success was doubtful. He cautioned them "against the too frequent exercise of the power conferred on you by treaty." The custom of *gidu* had "existed in Africa for centuries, and however cruel and wicked it may appear to us, the native African has the most implicit faith in its infallibility, as a test of innocence or guilt." So long as "we are not intruded on by them, nor made the unwilling witnesses of their barbarities," it might be best "to wink at occasional administration of the Sassy Bark infusion." It was far better to enforce the treaty occasionally, decisively, than to make a regular but impotent demonstrations. The commissioners would have only limited influence, in fact, and the custom is continued with some frequency to this day.[7]

Soon after, Gee Palm (alias Gik Pameo), one of Freeman's brothers, proposed that his people move to a vacant tract in Bolobo Country, bordering the Cavally River above Denah. Palm went there in early July to negotiate a purchase. King Freeman, Simleh Ballah, and others supported the idea. With the assistance of a Grebo convert, Freeman and Ballah addressed Hall and Latrobe on the subject on July 15. They began by saying that Americans and Greboes had lived peacefully together since 1834. Yet as time passed, their towns had grown into each other, which posed problems. "We are heathens," they wrote,

> It is heard for us to understand Your religion — and hearder still to see the necissity of Civilized modes of living. True they may be best for man kind — but we must learn them. And now; their is that — with our present knowledge to see it with — which makes things impossible and inexplicable Connected with Christianity. Our Children some of them begin to see and love it — but the progress of their insight is slow and they who see fiew Compare with the Great

mass of our people. We too see the day for future, when we and the Americans amongst us will be one Great and united people. Having one law living under one rule, and we hope serving one God. But this is a long future day.

Russwurm was dead, and the older leaders who had worked out coexistence would soon be gone too. It appeared that the younger generation might not be so inclined to peace. Referring to incompatible systems of land tenure, they noted: "The land too according your mode of settling and our mode of Cultivation is getting too Timberless for the Collonist — and too small for us." They concluded that a voluntary separation would maintain peace and also yield other benefits. With a good road through the bush, the two peoples could provide mutual protection and develop a boundless trade.

> We must so settle as to give each other elbow room, without confusion. Which we cannot do, all together, as we are now. We love to dance — and play — and sing — with drums and other music. The americans love to pray God. They have a sabbath — it is sacred. We have none. They do not wish us to use that day as we do others. We too have our sacred days and things, that we do not wish them to handle roughly. They have a law and their mode of settling differences — we have another, that they cannot bear. We do not understand theirs — they say ours is folly, and murder.

They complained that successive governors had treated the several Grebo states with an even hand, even though their most significant relations were with Gbenelu. They had many enemies, and Americans had shielded them from attack. They requested as a condition of removal that the Americans promise to come to their defense in the event of war, and that they send teachers.[8]

King Freeman and Simleh Ballah approached McGill and the colonial council with their plan at its June sitting. McGill was willing to grant their wishes under certain conditions: fifty or sixty families must initiate the move, with a steady emigration for four years afterwards, ending with the purchase of the Gbenelu town site; Greboes in their new territory must not interfere with trade on the Cavally River; and

Harper must arbitrate any conflicts that might arise between the new settlement and its neighbors. Three of the four members of the council approved some form of assistance, in principle, without specific commitments. In a letter of July 12, McGill urged Latrobe to support the project in any way possible short of giving out money. He remarked the change of spirit in Gbenelu. Hitherto, the subject of giving up town sites was so sensitive, that mere mention entailed the risk of war. Now, Greboes had offered a viable plan themselves.[9] Once again the talk went nowhere. Gbenelu remained on its original site, and Greboes and Americans wrangled for elbow room.

Although the Maryland State Colonization Society had little success finding emigrants for its colony, the American Colonization Society enlisted a steady stream for the republic. The Chesapeake and Liberia Trading Company had committed itself to carry whatever freight and passengers the national organization might offer. This had often caused hardship when they had reserved space for emigrants and cargo which then failed to arrive. The *Liberia Packet* was an unpredictable sailer, alternately making record voyages for swiftness and slowness. Hall's original plan for four voyages a year proved unrealistic, two being barely attainable, nor was she big enough to meet her obligations.[10]

In the fall of 1851, while the *Liberia Packet* remained at sea, the American Colonization Society sent to Baltimore a large company of emigrants and baggage, including a steam saw mill. When Hall found he could not charter a vessel large enough, he purchased the bark *Morgan Dix*, of 276 tons burthen, at an advantageous price. She made a successful voyage and returned to Baltimore to prepare for another in late spring, 1852. The *Morgan Dix* was also too small, so the company exchanged her for the *Ralph Cross*, a vessel eight years old, built to carry European immigrants and capable of handling some four thousand barrels of cargo. James Hall had the vessel refitted, inserting deck lights at six-foot intervals on either side to make her berths fresher and brighter.[11]

The *Ralph Cross* left Baltimore on her first voyage to Africa on May 1, 1852. She had on board about 150 emigrants, most of them Virginians bound for Bassa Cove. She anchored off her destination about June 16. The surf there was dangerous, and the crew spent almost three weeks trying to land cargo, with considerable loss. The captain fell ill as well. On July 10, she finally reached Cape Palmas, casting two heavy-chained anchors against a stiff gale and massive swell. The captain went ashore to have his fever treated. During the next week, a large amount of freight was carried ashore and palm oil loaded aboard. The work was complete on the eighteenth and departure set for the next morning when the captain would come on board again. Sometime in the night one of the anchor chains parted, and relentless seas drove the bark toward shore. All efforts to stop the remaining anchor from dragging failed, and the crew went for the lifeboats. One man, a passenger sent to see Liberia on behalf of a black emigration society, perished when he tried to get back aboard ship from the lifeboat. Everyone else made it safely to shore.

The vessel foundered on rocks east of Russwurm's Island, then withstood a battering of forty-two days before breaking up. Greboes customarily regarded shipwrecks as a windfall, but McGill was determined to protect the company's interest. He hired krumen to undertake the risky work of boarding the hulk. With a show of militia, he demonstrated that he would tolerate no looting. The strategy worked, setting a valuable precedent, though only a fraction of the cargo was recovered. The *Ralph Cross* was insured for $10,000, which was $1,500 less than her replacement value. Adding the value of lost cargo and the cost of chartering another vessel for November's expedition to Africa, Hall estimated the loss to the Chesapeake and Liberia Trading Company at close to $6,000.[12]

The *Ralph Cross* brought news that Maryland's General Assembly had extended its annual appropriation for colonization for another six years. Many settlers had feared that the society would cut them off when its funding ceased. They had devoted extraordinary energy to agriculture in response. In the months following, the same difficulties that had retarded agriculture in the past confronted them, and their enthusiasm flagged. With the extension of funding, there was time to arrange for independence calmly and rationally. "Dependence on the society will be endured with the most creditable fortitude and resignation," McGill wrote sarcastically, exposing yet again his frustration and contempt for Maryland.[13]

It is surprising that McGill hung on so long in the face of so much opposition, in a place which he so hated. He informed the society that he would remain at Cape Palmas until September or October 1852, but then he must leave for Monrovia. His own extensive business interests required more attention than he could devote, and he feared a substantial loss. He was well aware that it was unconstitutional for him to maintain a private business in competition with the agency, he told Latrobe defiantly on April 12, 1852, but he would do what he pleased, regardless of the unfavorable opinions of the society or citizens. Though trade had been dull because of wars among African states, he could point to the fact that the agency was solvent and that he would soon ship a quantity of palm oil and produce to Baltimore for the society's benefit.[14] "My time is so thoroughly occupied with my own and government affairs, and my business correspondence is so engrossing," he confided to Moses Sheppard in a letter of April 13, "that I am from shear necessity neglecting my most valued friends. I feel it, but cannot help it, I am suffering from mental and physical exhaustion."[15] September passed, then October, and McGill remained at Harper. His old plan of moving to Monrovia in July 1851 having been foiled, he found he could as well stay where he was.

Old Pah Nemah, King Freeman, died early in 1853. In his last years, he had grown friendlier toward the Americans, and McGill had endeavored to strengthen the bond. The *gidu* agreement of the previous year would have been impossible if not for this.[16] In fact, the sassy-wood commissioners intervened a number of times immediately following the old king's death, interrupting a long-standing tradition. In a movement without precedent, the *wodokai,* or council of elders, approached McGill before Freeman's burial and gave him the privilege of naming a successor, a mark of how completely Gbenelu had come under American influence. The governor selected Yellow Will, or Peroh Neh, to the Greboes' satisfaction.[17]

Yellow Will had been an intermediary between the colony and Grebo leadership since Maryland's inception. Prior to 1834 he had traveled widely as a kruman on merchant ships. At one point he had been a work-gang boss on the then-British island of Fernando Poo. Hall hired him as interpreter soon after the *Ann* arrived off Cape Palmas. He had assisted in the amicable settlement of numerous palavers. Even so, Yellow Will struggled to reconcile conflicting allegiances. "In the time of the greatest excitement," Hall remembered,

> I was never able, in any manner whatever, to shake his fidelity to his people, nor would he ever give the most distant hint of their disposi- tions or designs. His answer to all interrogatories in this respect, was, "I am this countryman, not an American, I work for you to get money, not to betray my own people; when I join the Americans, I shall leave my own people, I can't have a heart for both sides."[18]

Russwurm and Yellow Will had not gotten along very well. Will openly opposed the colony after Perry's intervention late in 1843. Nevertheless, he later moved to Harper, where he built an American-style house and adopted many settler customs. The new king was a good and honest man, respected by his own people and Americans alike, ideally suited to mediate between them. "The King is already making efforts for the introduction of civilized customs and laws among his subjects," McGill remarked at the end of January. "I am forced to admonish him of the dangers that are likely to result from his too rashly, undertaking the immediate work of reform."[19]

Letters and other documents concerning independence received from settlers during 1851 and 1852 thoroughly impressed the society. They regarded them as clear evidence of the effect of liberty on individuals freed of oppression, and therefore as an indication of the benefits of colonization. A committee reviewed the various papers and concluded that the question of independence should be put to a popular vote. A proclamation to that effect, with explicit instructions to McGill for its execution were sent aboard the chartered ship, *Shirley*, which anchored off Harper on January 25, 1853.[20]

These new instructions relieved Governor McGill of considerable difficulty. Having been encouraged to consider their future, the settlers had lately grown impatient and initiated proceedings for independence. On January 4 citizens petitioned McGill to let them convene a constitutional convention. McGill thought that the society must first authorize such a measure. At his instance, the council had tabled the troublesome proposal until its February session. The *Shirley*'s dispatches gave citizens what they wanted. Remembering the criticism he had suffered for delaying earlier, he read the society's message to a public meeting. Settlers were thrilled. They scheduled a plebiscite on the next Monday, January 30. The acting governor saw no need to delay the matter, for independence had dominated colonial politics for the past eighteen months.[21]

At six o'clock on the morning of January 30, the polls opened for twelve hours. In the interval, the adult men of the community cast 122 ballots, every one for independence. The vote inspired considerable enthusiasm, as exemplified by Nicholas Jackson, who was moved to write John Latrobe on February 4:

> As we is about to float on the Sea of nationality, Say to the a pressed Sons of Ham, this is their Place, this is their home, and this the time, come on, when Cape palmas must Stand alone and walk, like, the nations of the Earth, come forward and help to ratify and lay the foundation of this Colony as a nation, — fun damental and Share

that when we are gon, our Children will not look at there ancesters with Shame and Confusion, but may Share the honour of a good foundation that we have left behind, we now call for you men, of intelligents, and men of ability, with that Evangelick Spirit. Pressing forward with vigour and undaunted Courage to the Summit.[22]

Samuel McGill looked upon the whole thing with considerable trepidation. At the end of 1852 he had come to realize that he would be stuck at Cape Palmas for some time to come. His inability to leave Harper when he had planned the previous June had damaged his business. Now it made sense to stay in Harper for another year and rebuild. The *Shirley* carried an appointment for William Cassell to assume the duties of governor, leaving McGill the option to resign if he wished. Having changed his mind about leaving, the governor filed the appointment and told Cassell nothing of it. "You may rest assured that I shall use every effort in my power to give effect to the suggestions we have received from the Board," he told James Hall on election day. "It's clear that this people *must* declare their Independence there's no help for them otherwise. Should the affair assume at last the form of County annexation I shall do all in my power to promote it, with the full conviction that it will be the means of saving this Colony from Calamities such as I tremble to contemplate." McGill could not "shake off the trouble and inquietude arising from thoughts of the Independence question." "Never before in my life," he complained, "have I been so hopelessly at a stand still, incapable of having some plan for the occasion." He was "positively sick from my anxiety on this subject — every thing works opposite to my ideas of what is right and proper. I can't control events, things must take their course, and I hope all will end well."[23] He hoped the convention would be finished by May. Then envoys would sail to Baltimore to work out the details of separation.

Having voted for independence unanimously, settlers needed little spurring to take the next step, organizing a constitutional convention. At a public meeting on February 8, citizens named nine men: William Prout, William Cassell, Joseph Gibson, Boston J. Drayton, John Bowen, Anthony Wood, Ambrose Simpson, John Moulton, and Thomas Mason. Prout, Cassell, Drayton, and Stewart stood for the office of commissioner for the embassy to Baltimore, two of whom would go. On February 15, citizens elected the nine delegates as nominated. Prout and Cassell were chosen by large margins for the trip to Baltimore, an outcome McGill had tried to prevent, partly from jealousy, partly because their absence would leave him shorthanded.[24] "The result of the Election has been just what was anticipated when Prout and Cassell suffered themselves to be nominated as candidates," the governor wrote angrily. "I have been informed that each of these Gentlemen look for the continuance of their official salaries during their absence. I shall take care to inform them, that upon their relinquishment of the duties of their respective offices, their pay will cease; leaving it optional with the Board to reverse or confirm my decision."[25] McGill could easily replace Cassell in the store, but he would have to sit as judge of the court and assume all of Prout's commercial and secretarial duties.

The constitutional convention began deliberations on Thursday, February 16, and met almost daily thereafter. In March, William Prout presented a draft "Declaration of Rights" and "Constitution." The lengthy pair of documents were modeled on the constitutions of the United States and the State of Maryland, adapted to the legal history and conditions of Maryland in Liberia. Together, they constituted a workable plan for a republican government.[26]

The constitution divided the government into three branches—executive, legislative, and judicial—as did the U.S. Constitution. The executive, who would be called governor, would serve a term of two years. He would oversee foreign and African relations. He was commander-in-chief of the militia, but could not act as general in the field unless authorized by the legislature. He also had the right to veto acts of the legislature. A lieutenant governor was to be elected simultaneously, to assist the governor, and succeed him if necessary. The governor was to appoint a collector of customs, a secretary, judges, and justices of the peace, with the advice and consent of the legislature. The legislature would consist of a senate and house of delegates, which together constituted the General Assembly, as in the State of Maryland.

The legislature was proportional to the population and therefore at the outset would number only two senators and three delegates, to be augmented as the state grew. The judiciary included a supreme court, which would handle all disputes that involved foreigners, as well as appeals. Lower courts would hear other cases in monthly sessions. Prout was determined to ensure the continuity of law and made explicit provisions for doing so.

The Declaration of Rights began: "We, the people of the Commonwealth of Maryland in Liberia, acknowledging with devout gratitude the goodness of Almighty God, for having safely conducted our infant colony in peace for nineteen years, under the auspices of the Maryland State Colonization Society; and for having made us the instruments, *in diffusing the* blessings of *civilization* and *Evangelical truth* among a heathen people; taking into consideration the best means for securing our civil and religious liberty, and the establishment of a good Constitution in this Commonwealth for the sure foundation and permanence thereof, declare: . . ." There followed a series of thirty-eight articles that were statements of principle on a variety of situations in which the government might have a role. The first article read: "That all government of right originates from the people, is founded in compact only, and is instituted for the people's good; and they have at all times agreeably to this Constitution the indefeasible right to change, reform or abolish their form of government, in such manner as they may deem proper." Succeeding propositions conformed in format and tenor: Citizens of a country have the right to regulate themselves. They are entitled to carry into their new government all laws and precedents that are not explicitly superceded. All citizens have the right and duty to participate in government. No one may suppress legitimate political discourse. Every citizen must pay taxes to support the government. All courts must be public, and everyone should have the right to seek redress in them. All defendants have the right to call witnesses on their behalf, to have their charges written down for them, to face their accusers in court, and to be judged by a jury, "of the neighborhood, county, or district." A militia is necessary to protect the community, but standing armies are dangerous to liberty, therefore, only the legislature can authorize a permanent force, which must always be strictly subordinate to civil authority. All citizens are at liberty to practice religion according to their own consciences, so long as they hurt no one. No religious test may be required for public office. Article XXX stated that: "the free communication of thoughts and opinions is one of the invaluable rights of freemen; wherefore every man may freely speak, write, and print on any subject, being responsible for every abuse of that liberty." The government ought to take every reasonable measure to encourage literature, arts, and science, and make special effort to instruct and protect Africans. Article XXXII was understandably eloquent:

> That in all ages, bondage, wherever it has existed, having proved itself a bane to the true principles of civil society, and a violation of the indubitable rights of man, wherefore neither slavery nor involuntary servitude shall be tolerated in this Commonwealth, except for the punishment of crimes, of which the party shall have been duly convicted; nor shall any male person, arrived at the age of 21 years, nor female person arrived at the age of eighteen years, be held to serve any person, as a servant, under indenture, or otherwise, unless such person, while in a state of perfect freedom, shall enter into such indenture and on condition of a consideration, in good faith received, or to be received for their services, except as before excepted.

By April the convention had finished, and the commissioners prepared for the trip to Baltimore. Maddeningly, no passing ship was bound directly for the United States.

About this time, a British labor contractor visited Harper. He met McGill and proposed to open an office to recruit Grebo laborers for the West Indies. The scheme involved signing on volunteers for three-year terms with part of the wages advanced and free transportation in both directions. The Briton claimed that recruits could work for whomever they wished once landed in the Caribbean. He made the proposal as palatable as possible, yet the thing smacked of slavery. McGill did not think the scheme would get far, but conditions led him to give tentative consent. "From motives of policy," he explained to Latrobe, he was inclined to permit the Briton to go about his business, "as he is disposed to make the authorities cognizant of all of his transactions with the Natives, and to hold himself amenable to our laws." Were he not so disposed, he might "have it in his power to operate against our interests far more effectually." Besides, "his presence among us will add to the Revenue" by the duties he had to pay on the advanced wages. "Now, regarding the matter in its bearing upon the natives," McGill added cynically, "he will take from this, from one, to two hundred, efficient and able bodied heathen annually (diminishing by so many the number of those we shall bye and bye have to contend with)" and place them where "they must imbibe something of civilization, and acquire knowledge of modes of husbandry that will be of use in Africa, and besides afford us time to gain by immigration the strength and numbers we so much need to maintain our position amidst an over-whelming disproportion of heathen neighbors." Withal, he assured Latrobe that he had only listened to the proposal and made no commitments. He expected advice from Baltimore on the matter.[27] There is no record of the office having been opened, but other recruitment offices operated successfully at Monrovia and other points on the coast. Maryland would one day become the center of an international scandal because of precisely the same practices.[28]

In the spring of 1853, all signs indicated a large emigration from Maryland and Virginia. In March, Hall had received one hundred applications from Baltimore, and the American Colonization Society had lined up 150 more to board at Hampton Roads. The Chesapeake and Liberia Trading Company chartered the ship *Banshee*, a Baltimore clipper of the largest class, over five hundred tons burthen. She hoisted sail on April 25, and though little notice was given outside of colonization circles, a surprising crowd turned out on Brown's Wharf in Fells Point to see her off. Hymns were sung, the chorus aboard the ship mingling with that on shore "with overwhelming effect," Hall wrote. Colonizationists hoped this was a sign of renewed interest in their cause.[29]

The *Banshee* arrived at Cape Palmas with twenty-nine emigrants at the end of June. Her arrival was particularly welcome, as the store had begun to run out of sundry supplies, which she replaced. The captain intended to sail to Rio de Janeiro before returning to the United States. It was therefore impractical to send Prout and Cassell home by her. Another ship was known to be in the offing, and they would have to wait for her.[30]

In dispatches sent home on the *Banshee*, McGill noted regretfully that Yellow Will showed signs of leprosy, which had killed a younger brother about two years before. "The disease has not yet fully developed itself," he wrote, "but he has every appearance of one threatened." At Will's request, McGill sent him aboard the agency boat *Curlew* to Nifou, where there was a *deya* noted for his skill in treating the malady. The governor respected the king, and he could think of no one who could fill his shoes if he should pass away.[31]

The *Shirley*, on her second voyage for the Chesapeake and Liberia Trading Company, reached Cape Palmas at the close of August, completing a long and tedious voyage. She landed emigrants and supplies as usual, and by the second of September was preparing to sail back to Baltimore. Governor McGill wrote a perfunctory letter of introduction for Prout and Cassell, confirming that they had been chosen by the citizens of Cape Palmas to negotiate with the society. A ceremony was held on shore to wish them good luck. Dignitaries delivered speeches, and one of the Gibson brothers recited a clumsy poem of his own composition. The delegates boarded a canoe to cross the surf. The next day, the vessel was on her way.[32]

Since assuming office, McGill had done little more than maintain the agency's trade at a level sufficient for the support of new arrivals and the indigent. Why, after all, should he make the agency a profit-making venture in competition with his own business? He had also declined to play peacemaker in a number of conflicts. By the middle of 1853, therefore, the colony was on very good terms with Gbenelu, but wars had broken out all around.

One conflict involved Grand Cavally and Robookah, at the mouth of the Cavally River. Grand Cavally was a populous country of small territory. In better times, Robookah had permitted Grand Cavally farmers to plant on a tract of their land on the east side of the river. Two years before, Robookah had demanded the land for themselves but found their tenants determined to stay. Skirmishes followed, and a full-scale war seemed inevitable. McGill's half-hearted diplomacy had no effect. At the time of Russwurm's death, the agency had done considerable business at the mouth of the Cavally River, but the strife, combined with the competition of English traders who used rum to great advantage, reduced the business to nothing.[33]

When agency boats repeatedly returned from leeward with empty holds, McGill began to send them to Garroway. The Pedees, who lived there, were friendly and had plenty to sell. In the second half of 1853, however, Fishmen from Nifou, or Poh River, next to Garroway, could not contain their jealousy of the rising prosperity of their neighbor, with whom they had often feuded.[34] In August, these Fishmen attacked and overran Garroway. The conquest troubled McGill, not only because of his trade there, but also because Russwurm had purchased the town in 1850. The deed of cession called for the Marylanders to defend Garroway against invaders, but McGill could not afford to do anything, nor did he wish to involve Harper in a war on the eve of independence. He was constrained to sit and utter threats, but no more.[35]

Though he could do nothing for Garroway, McGill was able to help end the war at the Cavally's mouth.[36] When the *Constitution* called at Cape Palmas at the end of August, he persuaded Captain Mayo, a veteran of Perry's African Squadron, to lend assistance. The *Constitution* cast anchor off the mouth of the Cavally River on September 4. Two longboats then pulled for shore, one for Grand Cavally, the other for Robookah. The king of Grand Cavally was disposed to make peace and sent back word that he would abide by Captain Mayo's arbitration. By contrast, Robookah's King George refused the warship's dash and declared that he had no interest in setting the palaver until his neighbors across the river should vacate the disputed lands. They sent the longboat back to the *Constitution* with a threat of violence if anyone else came ashore with a similar insolent proposal.

The next morning, Mayo had five longboats fitted with arms and men. They waited outside the surf with a flag of truce while one boat carried in the messenger, Ben Coffee. The kruman was rebuffed as he had been the previous day, and all of the boats returned to ship. Mayo then ordered his men "to commence firing signal rockets over the town by way of intimidating the inhabitants, and bringing them to a sense of what was proper." This had no effect, so he ordered a gun crew into action. The big twelve-pound gun sent twenty-four shells over and around the town at relentless, steady intervals, which left no doubt about the Americans' willingness and ability to destroy it. A white flag presently rose over Robookah. Ben Coffee went ashore a third time, at last to meet the king in person. George now professed a change of heart and agreed to put an end to the war.

On September 6, representatives of the warring towns rode out to the *Constitution*. Robookah's ambassador tried to renege on some of the promises made the previous day. Mayo would hear nothing of it, and the Barbo capitulated. The opposing parties then drew mouthfuls of water and spit them out, according to the peacemaking custom of the country.[37] They returned home with handsome dashes and mutual assurances of friendship. The palaver soon flared again, for Mayo had insisted merely on a cessation of hostilities, doing nothing about the root of the dispute. Captain Page and the brig *Perry* had better luck with this at the end of the month.[38]

In November 1853 the Royal Navy bombarded and destroyed all of the villages east of Robookah as far as Bassa in retaliation for the destruction of the London schooner *Heroine* earlier in the year at Grand Taboo. Reportedly, no one was killed in the attacks. In early January the officers planned to land an expeditionary force against Grand Taboo. These towns were within Maryland's jurisdiction, and McGill should probably have taken a more active role in the affair. Instead, he was content to let the British do as they wished, without making any attempt to exert the colony's authority to set the palaver before blood was shed. The territory on the far side of the Cavally River had always been somewhat peripheral to colonial interests. Nevertheless, the acting governor's lack of energy in the matter set the stage for future European encroachment on Liberian borders.[39]

XX.

"The Poisenest Licquid"

WILLIAM A. PROUT AND WILLIAM CASSELL, THE COMMISSIONERS elected to negotiate independence, finally left Harper aboard the *Shirley* in the first week of September, 1853. The vessel called briefly at the bustling port of Monrovia—long enough to inspire hopes of a similar future for Harper. Having put to sea again, two weeks of adverse winds kept them close to the coast. On November 12, the *Shirley* was cruising the open sea with a strong southerly breeze, carrying only her light topsails, when a violent shift of wind took away her main and mizzen masts. The captain made for the Danish Virgin Islands, the closest haven, but two days later the ship suffered another gale. "We had to nail down all our companion ways and lash ourselves to the stumps of the masts to save us from being swept away by the waves, which almost constantly broke over the Bark," the captain reported soon afterward. On December 1 the ship limped into St. Thomas. Prout and Cassell sojourned for two or three weeks, hoping for a passage to Baltimore. At length, they boarded a vessel bound for Boston. A fierce storm drove them off course to Newport, where they landed. Late in January, they finally arrived in Baltimore.[1]

The two men delivered the proposed Constitution and Bill of Rights, along with a list of questions concerning the division of the society's property and the role the society would take, particularly with regard to charity, in the new state. The Board of Managers considered these carefully and in a series of meetings with Prout and Cassell composed "Articles of Agreement" closely modeled on those made between the American Colonization Society and Liberia in 1847. In summary, the society would transfer all of its territory to the new government with the understanding that Maryland must always allow free land to the society for the purpose of settling emigrants. The parties agreed further that the society's activities in connection with settlement would be exempt from taxation; that African captives recovered on the high seas could be settled in Maryland; that the society would cede all of its buildings and other tangible property not used for resettlement to the new state; that all new emigrants be entitled to the same rights as earlier settlers; and that any successor to the Maryland State Colonization Society have the same rights in Maryland. On February 22, 1854, the twentieth anniversary of Maryland's founding, all met for a signing ceremony.[2]

The whole business was completed in a whirlwind. The two delegates would have liked to stay for a while. This was Prout's first visit to Baltimore in more than twenty years, and he found tremendous changes. "I have been struck by the amount of intelligence and ability of so large a number of persons of my color," he noted to Hall, "Among whom, there are men, whose qualifications entitle them to rank and station, but who cannot find their positions. . . . it is such men as these, from whom much might be expected." They were just the men Maryland in Liberia needed. "If a goodly number of them could be induced to emigrate to the Maryland Colony, they would doubtless be called to fill such offices as the government in its new organization could offer. Some of them, sensible that they can never employ their talents here, think of removing to California; but this change of place can ultimately work nothing in their favor as freemen."[3] Though Prout and Cassell may have wanted to persuade some such men to try Africa, they had more important business. James Hall rushed to return to Harper. They sailed from Baltimore on the *Linda Stewart* on February 27, 1854, and were safely home in April.[4]

By early May settlers had met and selected delegates to a second constitutional convention to ratify the agreement. That convention met for the first time on May 11. McGill, anxious for them to finish the business, imposed a deadline of June 10, whereupon he would leave, whether or not settlers were prepared. He complained to Hall of their "hanging back," noting that Prout was absent from the first sessions. Prout claimed that he was sick. "The fact is he has indulged rather too freely in liquor since his return and is yet stupified," McGill wrote acidly. "His best friends despair of his ever becoming a sober man."[5]

Undoubtedly, McGill's opinion of Prout was distorted by prejudice and jealousy, so much so that Prout's alcoholism is called into question. It is hard to believe that a hopeless drunkard could so consistently compose sophisticated political discourses, each of them written in a disciplined, miniscule hand. In fact, McGill did what he could to obstruct and embarrass Prout. During Prout's absence, McGill relieved him of his duties as colonial secretary, pretending that the society had instructed him to do so. He refused to restore him to office and denied him any salary for the time he was away, though he was engaged in public business. Prout wrote Hall on May 18, a time when McGill asserted he was too drunk to be seen in public, to complain. Not only was McGill's malice personally painful, it hurt the whole community. The acting governor had told officers of the American warship *Dale*, Prout wrote, "that I was the only man in the place fit for the office of Governor; but that I was a confirmed drunkard." Prout countered that he had no ambition to become governor, had said so in Baltimore, and expected Cassell to fill the office. Let alone the personal insult, such statements to foreigners could have a lasting effect on the new state.[6]

With momentous changes underway, Gbenelu worried about what might be in store for them. On May 12, Simleh Ballah wrote the board on behalf of King Yellow Will and his headmen:

> Sirs, we the Native of Cape Palmas, has all agreed together to Write this note to our maryland Friend. Sirs we please you to answer we this time to our own Question we agreed with Docter Hall who Came here first to buy our land on the side were your Colonies are.

We made a treaty with the white man who Came over there to buy our land. we told them we wanted know war, we wish to make friend with them now the Colonies wants to take away our own Ground on which we build our houses by force, but it is not Good to force men away from his home. We have Give all rest o land, yet they wants our Town we do not like to Gave up our Town. we think you tell them to drive us away by force therefore we wants to know the truth.[7]

Paradoxically, Samuel McGill reported on May 13 that the colony was at peace with its neighbors and should remain so through independence. Though he discounted any problems that the change might cause, McGill hoped that the new state would abide by former agreements and treaties. He was sensitive to the fact that the several subject states might not accept a self-ruling state formed over them. Without their recognition, Maryland stood no chance of viability and would probably end up at war. After so many years, Greboes still looked to "Ho" and "Latoba"—Hall and Latrobe—as the true rulers of Maryland, belittling the colonial government and citizens. In previous letters, McGill had advised the board to send out a proclamation to the Grebo kings to reassure them. Now he went further and suggested that the proclamation conceal the fact that the society's influence would be materially reduced. "Establish the idea that your rights are in no way effected by the change of government, and that any invasion of those rights will certainly be resisted through the agency of the American Naval Commanders on this Coast. The natives should also be led to believe that they have it in their power to appeal to the Society (Mr Latrobe) whenever they fail in obtaining redress for their grievances here." The acting governor also decided to make a handsome dash to the Greboes as part of the independence ceremonies. He worried however that this might cause some difficulties with the society, as the expense was considerable and unauthorized.[8] In a letter to Hall of May 17, he suggested "800 lbs. Tobacco, 2 or 3 Bbls. of Inferior Gunpowder, 12 ps. Assorted Cloths, 1 Box Pipes, Crockery and other small articles." He was so sure of its necessity, he was willing to risk censure for providing the goods to the new government.[9]

During May, the constitutional convention worked with a strong sense of responsibility. The delegates considered point by point the agreement with the colonization society, the articles of their proposed constitution, and their declaration of rights. They warmly argued the question of ardent spirits and at length agreed to continue the prohibition. They also debated the property qualifications for officeholders stated in the constitution. The most obvious candidate for governor was William Cassell, who lived modestly in Harper, without enough money or property to hold the office as stipulated. A motion was offered to make an exception or alter the clause, but it was rejected. Against his expectations and wishes, William Prout found himself the candidate for governor. He had thought all along that he would hold some quiet appointive position, and when his name was placed in nomination his first impulse was to refuse. Yet after some reflection, he consented to stand for the office.[10]

On June 6, 1854, the citizens of Maryland in Liberia unanimously elected Prout governor. Boston Jenkins Drayton was named lieutenant governor; Joseph T. Gibson, Anthony Wood, John B. Bowen, and Thomas Fuller, senators; Daniel F. Wilson, John E. Moulton, Henry Pinkett, Charles H. Harmon, and John W. Cooper, representatives. With the encouragement of a united vote in his favor, Prout rose to his duty. June 8 was set for the transfer of authority.[11]

Citizens gathered for a ceremony in the morning. Receipts were signed, and the newly elected government took charge. Prout then delivered a lengthy, and in some ways prescient address, that began with a discourse on two opposed qualities of human nature—ambition, and modesty. "Fellow Citizens," he began, "there are many persons whose bosoms would swell with gladness on account of being thus distinguished by their fellow Citizens. Mine heaves, but not from joy." The responsibility of office was a heavy burden. He called for the support and understanding of his fellow citizens. The events of these first few months and years would be without precedent, and unity and public virtue would be essential for the state's survival. He promised to do his best to act consistently with the new constitution for the community's development. Citizens must support the new government, not only with their personal wisdom, but also with their diligent application to farming and other economic activity. "The independence of your State, will be feebly supported without exertion and labor," he insisted. Moreover, the new government "takes the comparative place of an exhibit paper, posted at some corner for all men to read, and admire or condemn. . . . Your dignity as a nation, is not to be supported by mere show . . . but in having a competency . . . which will enable you to [exert] an influence, that State of dependence could not, over the heathen of your neighborhood, and on foreigners who would seek your market for the surplus commodity consequent upon such a state of things."

Maryland had never gone to war against its African neighbors, Prout noted proudly. He promised, "My policy is peace," adding that he would never resort to arms except when "absolutely necessary to protect and secure the rights of the people, and defend their Constitution." Maryland would make every effort to open routes into the interior, to open up vast markets even a half-day's travel inland which heretofore had been inaccessible. He called for the establishment of good relations with the Republic of Liberia, advising citizens to put aside any bad feelings. The interests of the two states were too closely linked to permit animosity.

Independence brought with it great opportunity for growth and prosperity, Prout concluded. "Every thing is now in your own hands — make yourselves worthy of the stand you have taken, by something firmer than mere words. Let it be deeds. And by and by should you succeed well, you will be able to look back and contemplate the germ of a nation, planted, nurtured and fostered by the State Society, until able to stand alone, and wonder at the change."[12] As Prout spoke, a torrential rain began to fall, and every one retired for the afternoon. Late in the day, the downpour ceased, and citizens gathered again to celebrate.[13]

On June 9, Samuel McGill presented his successor to Yellow Will and his headmen. The question of a dash had posed a problem, because

the society had not given permission for the expenditure. McGill prepared a selection of merchandise, which Prout examined and reduced,
fearing that the society might charge the new government with the
expense: "15 Kegs or 3 Bbls Gun Powder; 600 poinds Tobacco 6 pieces
Blue Baft; 6 pieces Satin Stripe; 1 piece Romal; 2 doz [illegible]; 2 Boxes
Pipes; 6 doz Plates." Yellow Will and his headmen received the gift gra-
ciously. McGill was relieved to think that the new government had
gotten off on the right foot. He left Harper with his wife and children
on June 14 and was on shore at Monrovia by the seventeenth.[14]

The General Assembly held its first session on July 5. When the
meeting was called to order, William Prout outlined the condition of
their country and set a legislative agenda. He enjoined upon legislators
their great responsibility. Nothing was more important than establishing the government's revenue, he told them. He suggested various
means by which they could accomplish this, leaving them to decide the
most effective and beneficial ones. He promised to have a complete
statement of the government's finances drawn up within a few days. He
urged legislators to consider ways of fostering trade, which must be the
foundation of the state's prosperity. "I once thought differently," Prout
admitted, "but many years experience, watching the various turns it
has taken, assures me of this fact. Agriculture is by no means to be
despised. But the very absence of utilities necessary to its operation,
increases the doubt of its becoming very great until men of substance
take it in hand, and develope those rich plants whose fruits etc., will
offer commodities differing from the natural ones now in market to
freight ships of foreign nations." This was a radical statement, because
the society had always held, almost as an article of faith, the physiocratic
principle that all wealth comes from agriculture. Prout suggested a
reduction of trader's license fees.

Prout reported that he had called in all of the kings and headmen
of towns west of the Cavally River. He informed them of the change of
government, warning them that American warships would continue
to protect those on shore, then offering dashes to ensure cooperation.
John Bowen visited the Maryland territories east of the Cavally and

delivered a similar message. An ambassador would soon visit the bush states. Maryland was at peace with her neighbors, with the single exception of Garroway, which Fishmen from Poh River had recently conquered. The Pedees were now refugees, and Harper was obligated by treaty to help them.

In closing, Prout urged the legislators to make the ratification of the agreement between the colony and the Maryland State Colonization Society their first order of business. This would enhance the legitimacy of the new government. As soon as this was accomplished, commissioners should visit Monrovia to apply for recognition as a sovereign state.[15]

On July 11, Governor Prout published his list of appointed officers. He named Thomas Mason secretary of state and William Cassell chief justice. Thomas Dent was appointed treasurer, assessor of public taxation, and inspector of lumber. Henry Hannon continued as justice of the peace and public surveyor. Frederick Lewis was named justice of the peace, jailer, and Special Magistrate for Native Palavers. Familiar names appeared throughout the list: Dempsey Fletcher, William Hawkins, and N. Jackson Jr. as justices of the peace; Paul Sansay, Register and Measurer of Buildings, the latter office with J. B. Dennis, who was also Collector of Imposts; Major Anthony Wood, Inspector of Ammunition and Munitions; and so on. It is evident that the colony assumed the status of state with scarcely an interruption. Many individuals simply continued in appointive offices they had held under the colonial government. The community at large settled down to take care of itself.[16]

The new status of the settler government caused some uneasiness in Gbenelu. Sometime about July 7 a faction moved to the opposite bank of Hoffman's River, to a spot that had served tentatively as a town site more than once but had failed each time. Lately, a Grebo convert named Harris had begun a school there, and a permanent village had taken hold. As the movement began, Prout was uncertain how many households would cross the creek, but informants told him that three towns were projected. In a letter of July 13, Prout asked Hall whether the society could provide some assistance for the purchase of the town site of Gbenelu, to make the removal permanent. "I think with a few hundred dollars to back it, the subject may be laid before them without, as formerly, hazarding the peace of our people, and with effect." Tremendous obstacles presented themselves. The bulk of the Grebo populace would remain where they were unless violent circumstances forced them to go.[17]

Scarcely any note remains of the life of the newly independent people of Maryland in Liberia for the rest of the year. Governor Prout performed his duties ably. Little ruffled the tranquility of the community.[18] Prout wrote James Hall on March 6, 1855, that the state's relations with Greboes were peaceful, although he had encountered a few difficulties. In one instance, a citizen had accidentally shot a Grebo from Gbenelu while hunting, but the resulting palaver was set amicably. The idea of buying Gbenelu was shelved for the time being because of its continued sensitivity. The previous July or August, when the idea of moving across Hoffman's River had risen again, he had extended a few "feelers," but Yellow Will had rejected them. Since that time, there had been no opportunities to broach the subject. "It would be barbarous under the circumstances," he wrote, ". . . to insist upon their selling their towns at present." They had lived so long "under the wing of the Americans" that they had lost confidence in themselves and felt menaced by "other tribes whose effects in being brought to our market have suffered material deduction, and in some cases actual plunder, makes them stick closer to their old home."[19]

Complicating matters, Yellow Will was in poor health. Soon after McGill had named him king, he had begun to show signs of leprosy, a disease of which a brother had indeed died years before. McGill treated him unsuccessfully, and Will went to a traditional doctor at Nifou. After a year he was no better and returned to Cape Palmas in time to see McGill leave. Dempsey Fletcher wrote Hall on March 14 to say that Yellow Will had "not had the attention justly due to him from the time you left until Dr McGill filled the office of Governor," and in fact had been badly served by the colonists. "Every thing that has been brought against Yellow Will to show his infidelity towards the Americans had it been justly dealt with would have amounted to nothing: he has better feeling toward the Americans then any one of them I know of, and I sincerely hope that he may be benefitted by the means I am using." Fletcher managed to control the sloughing, but he was certain he could not cure the malady.[20]

Further afield, and more significantly, in February, Commodore Mayo and the *Constitution* helped Prout set a palaver between Grahway and Half Cavally, another episode in their long-standing feud, which threatened to escalate to war once again. During McGill's administration, Half Cavally had taken the false position that they had never sold their territory, rather they had agreed only to a treaty of friendship. McGill had failed to enforce the colony's authority, and Prout had no influence except with the presence of the venerable man of war. Afterward, Prout asked Hall to direct a letter to the headmen of Half Cavally to remind them of their obligations.[21]

Sometime in May 1855, a storm drove the British cutter *Earl of Liverpool* ashore near Garroway. The crew was saved, and the men made their way to Harper. Poh River Fishmen took all the cargo they could lay hands on, according to the custom of the country. The headmen had promised the master of the boat that they would give him back the chronometer and other navigational instruments if they recovered them. When they did they realized they had a valuable prize. Henry Gross, captain of a small boat owned by John Bowen, called at Garroway soon after. He purchased the instruments with cash. News of what had happened quickly reached J. M. Harriott, agent for the English owners, Hatton and Cookson.[22] Harriott, then at Grand Sess, sent a letter on the subject to the British consul, J. G. C. L. Newnham, at Monrovia. The consul then addressed an inquiry to Governor Prout on June 18.[23]

Prout was already aware of the matter. He was eager to demonstrate to the British and Monrovians that his government was determined and able to pursue a just course. Bowen made no secret that he had gotten the instruments, and the captain of the *Earl of Liverpool*, George Harris, complained to Prout. Bowen flatly refused to relinquish the property, arguing erroneously that they were purchased beyond Maryland's borders. The government sued Bowen at the July sitting of the court of monthly sessions. The judge agreed with the state's contention that citizens, "are responsible to their government for Acts of wrong and injustice wherever committed; and that the property in dispute being obtained by plunder, the purchaser, with a knowledge of that fact, had no right to retain it." Prout took possession of the instruments.[24]

Captain Harris then asked to have them, but Prout refused. He acknowledged Harris's right, but he also knew that Messrs. Hatton and Cookson had an agent on the coast with a stronger claim. Harris had given every indication of his intention to return to England by the first opportunity, and the governor suspected that he would take and keep them for himself. Harris went to Monrovia feeling wronged. As soon as he got there, he complained to Newnham. The consul wrote an angry letter to Prout in the middle of July, asking why he presumed to withhold the stolen property. Prout was mortified, as he wanted nothing more than to create a good impression. In a letter he assured the consul that the items in question were safe and that they would be forwarded to Monrovia by the first reliable carrier.[25] It seemed that Prout could please no one. In his zeal to do things correctly, he had offended the British consul and made bitter enemies of Bowen and others.

At the beginning of July, another issue disturbed the community. James Payne, superintendent of the Methodist mission at Cape Palmas, was building a seminary at Harper. No one doubted the project's benefits to the community at large, and Prout was eager to foster it, even calling the General Assembly's attention to it in his initial address to them. Lumber and other construction materials were delivered at the end of 1854. Then the question arose of whether these goods, intended for the benefit of the entire community, should be subject to import duties. The wording of the statute on the subject was ambiguous. The clause exempted all school materials and charitable donations—items not intended for resale—from import duties. Building materials for schools were not mentioned, but the spirit of the law would surely have included them, Prout thought. Since Payne was about to visit Monrovia, Prout agreed to lay the matter over until his return. The minister gave a written bond to the collector to pay the duties if the law required them, and the supplies were released so that building could continue.

Reverend Payne reported the situation to his superiors in the United States in terms that gave the impression that there was real difficulty. In light of former disagreements between missions and the colonial administration, the missionary society reacted with great consternation. A flurry of correspondence passed between the colonization society and the missionary society. Prout had word of what had happened by the bark *Cora* early in July. Again embarrassed, he hastened to show how insignificant the problem really was. He got written statements from James Payne and Charles Harmon, the collector, and sent them home with a letter to James Hall to vindicate the regularity of his government. "Now, dear Sir, can you see any cause for troubling the good people in the States, and exciting them to alarm at the fearful turn matters are taking in our poor, little isolated State?" he asked. "Knowing the difficulties, by reason of misunderstanding, which frequently occurred here, between Missionaries and the government," in the past, he was keeping a close eye on "the movement of things in order to save the place . . . from falling into fruitless jars."[26] Prout was doing everything in his power to establish the viability of his country, but the obstacles were formidable. He faced considerable opposition from abroad and increasingly at home. Trade was dull, and independence did not bring with it immediate benefits. In many respects life got harder.

The old annexation party formed the nucleus of opposition to the administration. The leaders were close to Prout: Lieutenant Governor Boston Jenkins Drayton and, surprisingly, William Cassell, whom Prout described as a "good kind of soul, but with very little sense about matters of a high and grave nature."[27] The group now drew into its ranks individuals who had previously opposed them. Joshua Stewart, once an ardent supporter of independence, gave evidence of such a change of feeling in a letter to James Hall. Stewart wrote that he had never expected to see the colony, of which he had been a founding member, achieve independence. The advance thrilled him, and now he looked forward to the day when Liberia would expand across the whole African continent and Maryland would be a component state. Yet competent men were hard to find, and until they appeared the community must suffer. "I feale that there is Wisdom in the Colony," he wrote,

> if it is ownly Rightly applyed, and Citizen act Consistantly with that which is Right and that we will be of use to them, that is, put such men in office who will act Justly, walk up Rightly and keep Sober and not let Rum be their great Hoby horse, as is the case now though Sorrow that I have to mention it here, but it is a fact. theire is Some amoungst us that are at the head of affairs like [too] much of the poisenest licquid preferes the Bottle of Rum and In one hand and a Glass in the Other Rather than the pen.

Citizens were poor and ignorant. They needed a model of behavior, a leader with their interests at heart, to inspire them to develop their potential. "I am awfully affraid we will never have a Nother Russwurm at the head of affairs," he concluded ironically, for he had often criticized Russwurm's administration, but discontent often casts a golden glow on the past.[28]

In June and July, Prout's opponents found a more strident voice. In a series of public meetings they scrounged up a list of grievances. Some were as absurd as the destruction of public property: because a hole was cut in the secretary's office door so the cat could get in at night to chase rats, which "were running riot with everything," according to Prout. When the remonstrance was published most citizens saw its foolishness and shunned Drayton and his party for a time.[29]

Governor Prout had a base of loyal supporters. One was Thomas Fuller, a recent emigrant from the Eastern Shore of Maryland. He wrote John Seys, the society's traveling agent, on July 23 to say that he was now settled at Cape Palmas and "happy as a lord. . . . Here I am a *free man*; here I enjoy the rights of a freeman and citizen; here I have the right not only to say what laws I will be governed by, but the privilege of aiding in making those laws, for you must know that I am one of that honorable body, *a Senator to be sure*." Since his arrival, Maryland had advanced from colony to independent state, "quietly and in good order; another witness added to the last, that the colored man is capable of self-government."

The government ran smoothly with William Prout at its head. "It is true, that we have had a few slight jostles," said Fuller, "but none to hurt." The government officers discharged their duties "with fidelity and credit to themselves," and the people "seem to take delight in obeying the laws." For a time it seemed they had been put "as we thought at first, to our trumps, to find men capable of filling the many offices created in our new Government," but those selected "were found equal in some good degree to the task, so that all is well on that score." He had gone into business as a storekeeper in the township of Latrobe. He had made some mistakes, as he had been a barber in America, but he was now more knowledgeable and would do better. Settlers worked industriously on their farms and the community's prosperity grew steadily, he reported. Maryland, he thought, boasted the finest public buildings in Liberia. A literary society was popular and church services well attended. "I am told that our ladies used to appear at church in your day in calico, but now they appear in silks, muslins, lawns, etc."[30]

Though Prout was optimistic about his little country's prospects, the situation was really quite foreboding. Independence had sparked strife among the African states within and all around its borders. Half Cavally was very nearly in open rebellion. The Poh River people defiantly occupied Garroway. The people of Gbenelu worried that the government might take some forceful action to move them to a new town site. Political disturbances and wars in the bush choked trade. The government's greatest failure was diplomatic. A delegation ought to have visited

Monrovia immediately after ratification of the constitution, as Prout had suggested, to receive recognition as a sovereign state. The task would not have been too difficult. In the case of the *Earl of Liverpool*, the British consul at Monrovia regarded Prout as a chief of state. The governor did what he could to live up to the role, but the delay in recovering the stolen goods and sending them to their rightful owners can only have created an impression of impotence and incompetence. These circumstances were not Prout's fault, but they made his situation difficult.

Prout addressed the legislature at the commencement of its second annual session on August 7, 1855, well aware of the menacing change of feeling toward his administration.[31] The previous year had been one of trial and experiment, he said. It had taught the importance of a uniform policy and strict economy. Maryland ought to follow the United States' example of a conservative foreign policy, avoiding as far as possible all external conflicts, so that "Liberia, now but a germ, will soon become a great tree whose branches will give shelter to all the suffering descendants of Ham; and whose wants will be abundantly supplied with cherishing resources." Prout then reviewed events of the past year, the current situation, and looming problems. He also discussed questions of social policy, finance, and relations with the African states. The latter occupied most of his attention, as several palavers and wars had broken out. Maryland had not yet been involved in any fighting, but there was a distinct possibility that the coming year might see some. Russwurm had promised to defend the Pedees at Garroway when he bought their country. In McGill's tenure, the Fishmen of Poh River had driven them from their homes. The conquest spawned wars in the bush, which cut off trade from that quarter. Closer to home, the state encountered difficulties with Half Cavally, whose elders still repudiated their treaty of cession made in 1835. The age-old feud between Half Cavally and Grahway erupted again in February when Grahway began to clear disputed land for fields. Prout had prevented an outright war with Commodore Mayo's help. Half Cavally resented the threat of force and retaliated by fanning animosities in the bush. The Krebo and

Barrakah paths were both shut off for a time, which reduced trade. The governor hinted that military action might be necessary to counter such machinations. He also laid some blame on citizens, who relied too much on Africans for their food. He urged the General Assembly to consider ways to foster agriculture, perhaps by offering premiums for the best farms or taxing uncultivated land.

In his address, the governor pointedly noted his correspondence with the British consul at Monrovia concerning navigational instruments salvaged from the *Earl of Liverpool* at Poh River. "Setting up claims as a christian and civilized people to independence," he said sternly, "of course, the government could not tolerate the citizens of this Commonwealth in the act of purchasing property which of right belonged to British subjects, and the captain of the wreck at the same time trying to recover it from the plunderors for the benefit of his owners. The judicial tribunal before which the matter was laid for adjudication, decided the purchase to be illegal and willfully wrong, and therefore the purchaser had no right to retain the property in question."

At the sitting of the court of quarterly sessions, on the first Monday in August, John Bowen appealed the decision of the lower court, which had deprived him of the navigational instruments. The judges rejected Bowen's plea, a defeat for Drayton and his followers. Prout asserted boldly on August 14, "I am no 'gentleman tender heart,' and will do my duty." He went on, "Had Bowen been allowed to keep these articles, I know not what would have been the consequences. A petty independent State authorizing and licensing its citizens to become accomplices in plundering and stripping distressed foreigners, and turn them off with abuses — What a picture!"[32]

After the dispute with Bowen and his allies had subsided, Governor Prout turned his attention to the situation at Garroway. Acting Governor McGill had declared war against Nifou in 1854, but more than a year later nothing had been done, despite treaty obligations, to defend the Pedees. Trade dwindled, and Maryland's failure to intervene sent a message that any of her liege states might defy the government if they chose. In August, Prout persuaded the General Assembly to appropriate seventy-five dollars to assist the Pedees. The legislators knew that the amount was merely a token and that a military campaign might be necessary one day, but they could afford no more.[33]

The governor consulted with experienced citizens and concluded that the only effectual course was to take Nifou hostages and force a palaver, a tactic with long precedent in the country. The law fully backed him: as chief executive he was responsible for all palavers. Moreover, the legislature authorized action against Nifou. Prout patiently waited for an opportunity. Late in the afternoon of December 5, a delegation from Nifou arrived at Harper. They led a bullock, a peace offering according to the country custom. The governor questioned them, but they refused to reveal their intentions. He had three of the men arrested. As it was time for supper, Prout went home for the evening.[34]

That night news of what had transpired spread through the settlement. Prout's enemies, ever ready for opportunity to take issue with him, seized upon it. They pretended that Prout had endangered the lives and property of Marylanders in Nifou Country, though in fact they had almost no interest there. "The people was in a perfect state of indignation, bordering on frenzy," Boston Drayton later wrote. A group met early the next morning to compose a petition for the release of the hostages. A committee delivered it to Prout as he settled down to his day's work. They insinuated that citizens would break open the jail if he failed to comply. The governor called in what cabinet officers he could, and they advised him to resist the threats. Prout agreed at first but then thought more seriously of the potential for violence. Reluctantly, he ordered the jailer to free the prisoners.[35]

Prout's enemies sensed their advantage. They met again on the evening of December 6 and drew up a petition that called on Prout to resign. They handed it to him at nine the following morning. Prout was confounded. He sat for a while to consider how to proceed. He had faced opposition before, and he had watched both Russwurm and McGill resist challenges to their authority. The present situation was far more serious, since there was the clear threat of an assault. Within a half hour he was stirred from his contemplation by the sound of fife and drum. From his office window he saw a gang of young men, boisterously drunk, armed with pitchforks, bush knives, clubs, and flintlocks, marching toward the Government House. A few citizens had come onto their porches to see what was happening, and Prout watched fearfully as the mob beat some of them. He was alone. Resistance on his part would only result in violence, and perhaps his murder.

The governor tried to stall his opponents. Rashly, he sent word to the ruffians that he was sick and that he would place government in charge of Lieutenant Governor Drayton. He hoped that his capitulation would cause the mob to disperse and that they would come to their senses soon enough. The U.S.S. *Jamestown* was in the offing, and he believed that his friend Lieutenant Armstrong would help restore order. These rationalizations were vain, however, for he had blundered by handing authority to Drayton, who was in fact a principal mover of the rebellion. Only later did Prout learn that Drayton, Cassell, J. T. Gibson, Jackson, and Rock McGill had liquored and incited the mob before they marched on the Government House.[36]

Drayton and the other conspirators quickly consolidated their power. Within a few hours, nothing short of civil war could restore the rightful governor. Drayton scheduled a referendum for December 17, and two-thirds of those who voted chose to impeach Prout. William Cassell, Roszell McGill, Joseph Gibson, James Dennis, and Charles Harmon were named to take charge of the state's property and swear in Drayton as acting governor.[37] "It was a revolution of moral suasion," Drayton later declared, changing the truth to suit his own purposes. "It was a common thing to see Mr Prout whilst at the head of the Government drunk in the streets — Native towns — and laying prostrate on the ground; an absolute captive of the 'Hydra Monster.'"[38]

XXI.

"The Diabolical Plot"

RAYTON AND HIS COTERIE HAD LITTLE CONTACT WITH THE OUT-
side world for months after their insurrection, and when they
did they avoided the subject. Joseph Gibson sent a detailed
report of his activities as agent to Baltimore at the end of December,
but he did not so much as hint at what had happened.[1] Then in March,
he and others began to communicate, somewhat sheepishly, with the
society. "You have no doubt heard before this of our political disturbances," Gibson observed at the conclusion of a tedious business letter
to Dr. Hall. "Mr prout was deposed by a large majority of the citizens
in December last, and since then Rev B J. Drayton has discharged the
duties of Chief Executive. . . . Mr Prout's constant drunkenness and
other things had rendered him quite unpopular among a people who
not very many months previous had almost worshipped him." When
"in one of his drunken modes" Prout had seized and imprisoned "a
number of men from poor River" sent by their king with a bullock as a
dash to "talk some palaver" he "so exasperated the people that they
declared he should no longer govern them and after some three or four
days in which there was every indication of the swift approach of a civil
war, he finally agreed to have no more to do with the executive affairs."[2]
Gibson neglected to mention his role in the coup d'etat or that he assumed the office of lieutenant governor as a result of it.

Though most citizens supported the revolution, a sizable number sympathized with Prout, if for no other reason than to uphold the constitution. Major Anthony Wood discussed the incident in a March letter to Hall, in which he lamented the events of December 7. "The Minority contending for the Constitution, while the majority gloried in its violation." "How it mortifies me," he continued, "to think that as mutch intrest as many of us has taken, in forming this little State to see a Baptist minister who is paid by the Baptist Board to Preach Gospel, being one of the Characters in Encouraging of an rebellion in this enlightened day, and to usurp that which does not belong to him and I from necessity in a great many instances compelled to obey him." Once optimistic about Maryland's prospects, to Wood everything now seemed dismal.[3]

William Prout retired from public life and began to trade in a small way. In June he informed Hall of his plans and asked for help getting started. He had some idea of entering the palm oil trade but considered it risky, since he had only limited capital with which to work. To do the thing well, he would need a small schooner. The surf was dangerous, and during the previous week he had witnessed McGill, Brothers lose just such a boat when its anchor cable broke. They were large enough to withstand the loss, but it would have ruined him. He asked for a consignment of muslins, silk, and tawdries to start with. "It is an astonishing fact," he wrote, "that persons who hesitate, except when pressed by dire disease, to purchase a little sweetening, and who are never able to pay a cent for medical aid, can for such baubles at almost any time fork down the ready money." He hoped that Hall or someone else in America could ship him a steady supply of merchandise. Prout observed the new government quietly. "I stay at home and attend to my small business," he remarked in the same letter, "and as it is generally known that I give no encouragement to fawners, I am not pestered by them."[4]

Boston J. Drayton wrote to Hall for the first time as governor on April 24, 1856, nearly five months after seizing power, as if nothing out of the ordinary had happened. He related the sad news that William

Cassell had died the same evening of liver disease. "This event is distressing to all our fellow citizens, and who among us that doth not mourn! The sable-pall seem to be hanging over all alike. To loose such a man as he was, at this crisis, is no ordinary calamity to our State; knowing as we do, the want of intelligent men. The Almighty Disposer of human events has taken him from us, hence it becomes us to submit with reverence to him 'who maketh darkness his pavilion.'" With this exception, life in Maryland proceeded uneventfully, he wrote. He was proud to say that the palaver at Garroway was ended and that the State of Maryland had acquired the Wedibo country, up to the borders of Grand Cesters.[5] Six weeks later, he informed Hall of a plan to foster trade in the bush far up the Cavally River "by peacefull and friendly mediations" and insistence upon the terms of old treaties.[6] Drayton's self-congratulation over his diplomatic successes was only half true. Although he had suppressed one or two fights, others had taken their place.

In January 1856, Rocktown and Gbenelu argued over the ownership of a tract on their common border. Cape Palmas farmers cleared several acres, ignoring Rocktown's protests. The dispute grew so heated that war seemed likely. Drayton intervened, calling the headmen of both towns to a palaver at Harper. After hearing each side, he ordered them to cease preparing for war. He would appoint commissioners to survey the boundary, and they would clearly mark the line in the presence of witnesses from each town. The Rocktown headmen agreed to the solution, but when they went home their countrymen repudiated it, against the governor's expectations. Gbenelu continued to cut and plant on the disputed land, defying threats of war. Drayton offered once again to mediate, but Rocktown would have nothing of it. Soon after, Rocktown soldiers ambushed a Gbenewe work party on the newly cleared fields. They killed two and wounded two more. The rest fled home in terror. "They returned to the Cape in the greatest confusion in their inglorious retreat," Drayton reported. "Many swam across palms river — amidst the Volley of the Palmas women abused."[7]

Gbenelu pulled back from the contested land. Farmers prepared fields closer to home. The governor even granted permission for them to use some vacant settler plots. Skirmishes and ambushes continued for several days, with more psychological effect than physical loss.

On February 22, while Maryland celebrated its second anniversary as a free state, the *sedibo* of each town met on the beach near their mutual border. Cape Palmas soldiers formed a regular battle line, copying Maryland militia tactics, and advanced under heavy fire, fearlessly driving their enemy off the field. Gbenelu troops killed thirteen and wounded many more. They lost one man killed and had some sixty others wounded, according to Drayton. The war threatened to spread, for other Kudemowe and Nyomowe towns were likely to join the fight after planting season was done.[8]

Drayton realized the importance of preventing the war but his mediation had proven ineffectual. In May the U.S. Brig *Dolphin* hove-to off Harper. Captain Thomson agreed to help set the palaver, so Drayton and Joseph Gibson cruised up to Rocktown. The warship stood offshore, and the captain demanded that the headmen talk the palaver, but the messenger brought back a defiant refusal. The warship made menacing gestures, and the messenger went ashore a second time. Once again, he was rebuffed with threats. Upon his return, the *Dolphin* opened a steady fire, the shells at first sailing over the town into the bush, then landing closer until one house was blown up. A white flag went up immediately, and a messenger came from shore with word that the people of Rocktown would accept any terms the governor would state. The day was waning, so they set a meeting for the next morning.

Headmen and dignitaries of Gbenelu and Rocktown met aboard ship as scheduled. Drayton told them that they must put down their arms and make peace. He ordered each side to release its hostages. The disputed lands should be left alone until they could be properly surveyed. Each party then embraced and spewed water according to the country fashion.[9]

It is ironic that Drayton, who deposed Prout on the pretext that the governor was drawing the country into war, should have adopted so warlike a policy. "It behooves us," he wrote Hall on May 30, "on just and equitable principles, to struggle manfully to maintain our authority over the territory we own, for the purpose in one sence; of realizing a sufficient trade to give a stronger impetus to foreign commerce, wherefrom, we can only hope; for some time to come, to receive sufficient revenue to sustain the Government, and it is encouraging to know that from this source [i.e., the U.S. Navy], the State has received invaluable assistance." He satisfied himself that the peace he had imposed with the aid of a man-o'-war would be permanent.[10]

The first election since independence was held early in June. Prout's allies had formed a "Constitution Party." They selected Thomas Fuller to stand for governor, though he did not have the property qualification stipulated by the constitution. Even Prout would not vote for his friend. "If elected," the former governor wrote Hall soon after, Fuller could not take office without being sworn in by Drayton, "and the man who had usurped the office would not give place to another, unless he was prepared by all the Constitutional prerequisites to take his post." That being the case, Drayton would continue administering the government from year to year "without any lawful guarantee for his position; and unless placed under the wing of some other government, the present one here would eventuate in a dictatorship or something of the kind." As a consequence, the vote confirmed Drayton in the office of governor. The Constitution Party did not field a candidate for lieutenant governor, and Joseph T. Gibson, agent of the Maryland State Colonization Society, continued in the office unopposed. Moreover, Drayton placed all legislative seats in jeopardy, though the constitution clearly stated that only half should be. Prout marveled that the incumbents should have offered no objections to the proceedings, which were obviously illegal, but he said nothing publicly. He commented sourly on the youthfulness of the new legislators, some of whom were the very ruffians who had turned him out of office. "They know so much, that they never open a book, or take up a newspaper to find out the progress and movement of matters in the christian world."[11]

The former governor believed that nothing short of civil war could restore the constitutional government of Maryland. In that event, Greboes would certainly go to war as well, to put the Americans under their control. "If they ever move under such circumstances, every thing both little and big will be put to the sword," Prout observed. Indeed, he learned soon after his overthrow that the Grebo *sedibo* had taken up arms on December 7. Grebo military tactics had changed, as demonstrated in the recent war with Rocktown. "Some of their young men take aim at their object as we do," he noted, and valor now characterized their battles. To defeat such forces, Maryland must improve weapons and discipline.[12]

Monday, August 3, 1856, witnessed the inauguration of Boston J. Drayton. "The ceremony took place in front of the Government House, Cape Palmas, where a stage had been erected and appropriately decorated," an anonymous correspondent reported. The militia formed in a semi-circle in front of the stage, on which a number of citizens and government officers were seated. Ladies were confined to the piazza behind the militia. At precisely noon, the Drayton arose and delivered "an appropriate and well written address." Lieutenant Governor Joseph T. Gibson administered the oath of office, at the conclusion of which the militia fired a cannon salute and Drayton accepted congratulations. At three that afternoon, the governor, his officers, and about 150 citizens took a formal repast in the rear of Government House. "The weather was favorable, and everything was harmoniously and with propriety conducted."[13] The minister's illegal seizure of power was now consecrated by the constitution he had flouted.

About this time, Drayton received a letter from Rev. James B. Taylor, written on May 23 on behalf of his sponsors, the Southern Baptist missionary society. His failure to communicate first disappointed, then alarmed them, when they learned that he had taken public office, though his duty was evangelization. The missionary protested that his letters must have gone astray. "You alluded to my 'elevation in official influence,'" Drayton began by way of explanation. "It is as you have learned. The Government came into my hands in December last" when as lieutenant governor he had served out Prout's unexpired term. In

June, at the regular election, he was elected "almost unanimously" to a two-year term beginning in August. "It appeared to me, after due consultation and prayer, that I would be pursuing the path of duty," he insisted, ". . . to accept the office; and I feel that an All-Wise Creator intends me for special reasons, and for the accomplishment of certain ends, to move for a season in a two fold relation among my heathen brethren." The "will of the people . . . and my best friends, would not take any denial," hence he "submitted with a sense of my weakness and inability, and place myself under the care of the Lord." He admitted having "much to learn" about his new office, "but my country, my degraded and less favored brethren, have compelled the measure." Drayton believed that God had selected him to fulfill a divine plan. Taylor suggested that Drayton should resign his missionary duties, but he flatly refused. He assured Taylor that he had not for a moment lost interest in the great work, "as an instrument in His hands to assist in the establishment and spread of his lovely Gospel in this dark and benighted country." He admitted, though, that an assistant would be of benefit.[14]

All of the adulation and celebration seems to have blinded Governor Drayton to the feelings of his African constituents, so much so that he undertook a bold, even reckless, initiative with Gbenelu. He drew up a "Liberal Compact" designed to bring the Greboes of Cape Palmas under Maryland's direct control. In June, Thomas Mason, the secretary of state, presented the idea to a few of the Grebo headmen at a private palaver held in Gbenelu. They agreed to consider the matter and to present it to a more general meeting, which was duly scheduled. On the appointed day, Mason addressed the assembled people of Gbenelu on the subject of union. As he read the articles of the proposed treaty there arose a great murmur and objection. "They at once peremtorily declared that they wished no Treaty nor did they desire to be a unite with the American people." They had their own laws, after all, and saw no reason to submit to another government. Drayton had to withdraw the proposal.[15]

Such ill-considered diplomacy had an unsettling effect. The armistice between Cape Palmas and Rocktown was untenable. Cape Palmas

Greboes were indignant at Maryland's continuing trade with their enemies. The government of course had to buy rice and produce wherever it could find it, and it had no animosity toward Rocktown. The
bombardment earlier in the year was merely a tool of diplomacy in a
violent environment. The citizens of Gbenelu were of the opinion that
they were entitled to preference at all times because they were Harper's
closest neighbors. From their point of view, the new governor was proving himself an irrational and dangerous opponent. Clearly, he was
determined to put Gbenelu under his thumb. Governor Drayton's trade
with their enemies, his neutral stance in the war, and his attempt to
force a treaty of union upon them, were all signs of bad faith. They
feared that he might somehow betray them to their enemies, and there
was no telling what he might do next.

In consequence the *gnekbade,* or council of elders, decreed that all
traders coming to Harper by canoe must land their goods on the Agency
Wharf. They intended to post their own inspector there to keep track
of what was landed, and most probably collect a duty. Governor
Drayton vigorously protested this imposition to the headmen. They
assured him that they would repeal it. Even so, Yellow Will's inspectors
remained on the wharf, and several traders lost merchandise trying to
get over the bar. The governor continued to protest, but to no avail.[16]

About the same time, war erupted between Half Beriby and her
neighbors in the bush. A delegation of Half Beriby dignitaries traveled
up the beach to enlist support for their campaign. Grahway welcomed
them with fair promises to send soldiers and supplies. The Half Beriby
ambassadors came to Gbenelu next, accompanied by Grahway headmen, to make the same request. Yellow Will and his headmen were also
inclined to help, but they decided that it would be politic, given the
tense relations then existing between themselves and the Maryland government, to consult with the governor first. Drayton listened to Half
Beriby's presentation, then heard the opinions of Grahway and Gbenelu
on the matter. He then flatly rejected the undertaking as it conflicted
with his stated policy of maintaining peace among all of his liege peoples.
He told the Half Beriby men that they had every right to defend them-

selves if they were attacked, but they must not mount any offensive. The palaver seemed to end amicably, all parties agreeing with the governor's dictate.[17]

Their assurances were false. Soon after the palaver, Grahway hired an ocean-going canoe from McGill Brothers (for one bullock) to carry soldiers and supplies to Half Beriby. There they took part in an engagement, in which several of their young men were killed or wounded. They returned to Grahway, and news of their misfortune circulated widely.

The duplicity infuriated Drayton. Other recent incidents, most notably the robbery and beating of a boy belonging to the Episcopal Mission at Half Cavally, increased his anger. He summoned the headmen to answer for them. Drayton fined them for their transgressions, which they accepted without argument, but afterward they refused to pay. After so many broken promises, the governor was confirmed in his anger and mistrust of Gbenelu.[18]

Several months passed before the Maryland State Colonization Society received news of the coup d'etat in their former colony, and then it arrived in an offhanded way. Prout was embarrassed and humiliated by the events and glad to disappear from public view. The leaders of the coup had no interest in having the society involved. Whenever Gibson and others had to write home, they said as little as possible about the situation. The board was angry at the turn of events, but really there was little that they could do. Charles Howard, who had recently replaced John Latrobe as president, addressed a stern lecture to Drayton and a public address to the citizens of Maryland on the importance of respecting laws in a free society. Not knowing the details of the case, he wrote, he would withhold judgment whether citizens had been truly provoked to such an extreme course, but he warned them that their actions had a broader significance. "To the civilized communities which have been (in some degree through our instrumentality, and by your co-operation) established on the Western Shores of Africa, is entrusted, under Providence, the solution of the great question of the capacity of the African race to rise from the condition in which they have for so many centuries been placed." He continued: "We believe you to be capable of Self-Government, and that if you are true to yourselves and to your higher vocation, as you increase in Numbers, you might in like degree advance in Knowledge, Wealth, and Power, until you shall have elevated your State to a position commanding the respect of the world, and shall have accomplished the glorious mission of civilizing and converting to Christianity millions of the Native African tribes."[19]

Drayton wrote a reply on October 21 that presented a self-serving version of the coup. He noted that his administration had been an energetic one. He had sent emissaries to Monrovia and gotten diplomatic recognition. He had also investigated the potential for getting the same from Great Britain and France. Drayton politely asked for the society's continued good will, advice, and material assistance for such things as dashes, a state library, and a revenue cutter. He entertained great plans for expanding American settlement to Garroway and the bush. "We have peace with the surrounding tribes," he concluded, "the Palmas tribe living directly amongst are now observing the Lords day, our streets that day is quiet — the Law went forth from the Government in February last and instantly obeyed — and continued. Agriculture is receiving attention. We are using our best endeavors to settle all differences with our interior natives and open the roads to admit free the trade — and it requires much means."[20] Such enthusiastic statements once again belied a volatile and tense situation.

The Kudemowe towns were well aware of the government's disaffection with Gbenelu and Grahway, and they determined to increase the animosity, to serve their own interests. At the end of October, all of the Kudemowe towns—Rocktown, Half Cavally, Fishtown, Middletown and Crebo—invited Governor Drayton to visit Rocktown for a grand palaver. Whether Drayton recognized their opportunism is unclear. He did not attend himself but sent his secretary of state, Thomas Mason, in his place. The headmen informed Mason that they wished to unite more firmly with Maryland, asking with feigned innocence whether Gbenelu had been offered the same opportunity, as was rumored. The secretary told them it was so, and they expressed considerable surprise that Gbenelu had not been eager for union. In any event, they would be happy to join Maryland under the terms offered to Gbenelu, noting the benefit to trade and contribution to their security, since Gbenelu and Grahway had recently shown great belligerence toward them. The secretary returned to Harper with very good news.[21]

Soon after, Governor Drayton sailed to Rocktown with a copy of the Liberal Compact. Rocktown agreed to the terms with hardly any negotiation, and the document was returned triumphantly to the State Archives in Harper. The maneuver outraged Gbenelu and her Nyomowe allies, for it substantially altered the balance of power among the Grebo states. Drayton brushed off their protests, unaware of how seriously they regarded the matter. The course of "resentment" that followed caught him off guard. First, Gbenelu withdrew all of its citizens who worked in the settlement. The strike lasted a day or two, but they soon adopted a more subtle plan. The governor heard a growing number of rumors and insinuations against his new allies at Rocktown. Yellow Will and his headmen made much of the fact that Rocktown had not dashed the government an axe, the customary token of submission, and therefore, their profession of union was insincere.[22]

Gbenelu's tactic had an effect opposite what was intended. Rather than leading the governor to question and doubt the good faith of the Kudemowe towns, it raised his suspicions concerning his close neighbors even more. Drayton felt sure that some evil scheme was in the offing. Late in the afternoon of Sunday, December 12, an informant passed word to the governor that the Gbenelu *sedibo* was under arms and had plans to attack the settlement that night. Drayton took no time to investigate before declaring martial law. Civilians gathered in safe houses, the militia mustered, and soldiers hauled out the cannons for possible action.[23]

Gbenelu's *sedibo* immediately fell to arms. "Early part of the night the Three Towns was a perfect Ballroom," Drayton wrote soon after.

The steady bombing of drums, accompanied by singing and dancing, the traditional preparation for battle, confirmed settlers' worst fears. The *sedibo,* knowing that the Americans were braced for a fight, made no immediate offensive gesture.[24]

On Monday morning, Governor Drayton called in Yellow Will and his headmen to explain. They met him as ordered, at ten in the Executive Chambers, the former Agency House. The windows and doors were opened to make the proceedings public. The situation was dramatic, and Drayton, a natural showman, admirably played the role of prosecutor. "The Conference Opened without much respect to Formalities by the government," he reported:

> The Interrogatory put first by the Governer to Yellow will did your people arm themselves to Massacre my people! Will! To this he answered No: The question was put to each of the Delegation. A seeming triumph at the negative response was significantly enjoyed by them. At this moment the Governer Interrogated "Gee Palm" the Governer put his eyes in "Palms." he reiterated the question to Palm. Did you not know, that your people had prepared themselves to make an Secret Attack on the American people last night! Do you not know "Palm" that your people had passed inspection on Sunday afternoon, also the Distribution of powder, and you Palm sharpened your knife to cut my throat, was not fines imposed and collected from your Soldiers for not arming pursuant to your Headmen orders. To these leading questions, the king and principal headmen hid their faces in their hands. Yellow Will said Governer we are much ashamed for this palaver set it to day. The Governer questioned Palm whom did he tell, or was the other Head-men ignorant of this matter. He said he told them all, they all were acquainted, and approved of the step.

Having admitted that they were prepared for war, Greboes said that they had done so only because they feared an American attack. As the governor pressed them, their tale became more florid.

Lieutenant Governor Gibson also took a turn at questioning but failed to prove anything. Yellow Will asserted that Gibson himself had hinted to them that the government might be preparing for war. Gibson reproved them, reminding them of all the good things Americans had done for Gbenelu and how many transgressions they had let pass. Yellow Will had no answer. Clearly, the palaver was not leading to an amicable settlement. The governor therefore adjourned the meeting until tempers had a chance to cool and the truth be better understood.

As soon as the palaver ended, the militia redoubled preparations for war. Officers inventoried and inspected arms. Specialists prepared and handed out cartridges. The men shored up the fortifications. Drayton was careful to order settlers to leave their Grebo neighbors alone.[25] War hung in the balance, but it might be avoided with tact and forbearance.

During the next week, the government tested other Nyomowe towns. Drayton sent emissaries to Grahway to discuss their expedition to Half Beriby, as well as other robberies and assaults that had lately transpired without redress. Grahway's citizens treated the Americans insolently. "They would pay those claims, when all the Sand on the Beach was burnt up," they taunted. They then threatened the Americans with beatings or death if they ever dared to appear at Grahway again. Their territory was not part of Maryland, they boldly asserted, any treaties made years ago with Dr. Hall notwithstanding, and they would obey only their own leaders. The delegation returned to Harper in great excitement. "The report created quite a popular Out-burst of the Citezens," Drayton wrote, "indignation, not that mobid excitement which is the result of animal ebullition, but an inward apprehension of [danger] And that very Justly too, that a combination had entered into having for its object the consumation of the discovered insurrection. The treatment tendered our Commissioners was the effect of that Consolidated Scheme, which lead us to infer it was not over, further that the Government had not yet ferrited all the meanderings of this Diabolical plot." It now seemed obvious to Drayton that the Greboes intended war and that the only way to settle their differences was by violence.[26]

At dawn on Monday, December 22, 1856, Governor Drayton conferred with the lieutenant governor and secretary of state to confirm a plan of action. The militia was ready, and Rocktown had volunteered whatever assistance Harper might need. War canoes laden with troops rode just offshore, waiting only for the signal to join in. At seven, the governor demanded that Yellow Will and his headmen talk a palaver. They obeyed Drayton's call, but as they started for the Government House, someone spied the war canoes. There was no question they were Rocktown's, and the king and headmen returned to Gbenelu. The governor sent a messenger to ask why they had not come to the table. They responded that Drayton must call off the Rocktown forces. Drayton was reported to have said, "My plans are discovered."[27] Nevertheless, he refused to do so. The messenger went to Gbenelu three times to repeat the demand, but each time Yellow Will answered that he was too fearful of attack to risk himself in Harper.

The governor and his advisors now believed that they had done everything in their power to avoid a fight. Their duty was clear, according to Drayton:

> Every indication seemed pregnant with favorable Omen. The time. The season. All pointed to this epoch to Vindicate the down trodden rights, and uphold the strong arms of the majesty of Law and Order. The Palmas people had abused their Oppertunities the Government and people had lost their confidence in that people. The wonted forbearance of the Government had been exhausted — their was no more claims on the charity of the Government to be extended. The chain had Been severed asunder. The fact of the premeditated Massacre was too Obvious. Their was no passing this point without affixing to that Act the Government most Solemn disapprobation. Yet withal tempering the means so as to ride ourselves of all the inflamatous materials from our immediate Vicinage by peaceful method.[28]

A passion to annihilate the people he was commissioned to help had now taken full control of the minister.

At eleven, Drayton ordered the easternmost battery on the Cape to open fire. Major Anthony Wood could not believe his instructions, and he asked to have them repeated. The old brass field pieces, relics of James Hall's tenure, thundered, and the gunners corrected their aim as the shells landed on the town. The cannonade caught Gbenelu by surprise. Most of the townspeople were still at home, unsuspecting of the Americans' intentions. In times past, when war had threatened, they had cleared off their possessions to safe spots in the bush. This day, however, most of their belongings went up with their houses. A headman came out of Gbenelu waving a white flag, but he was forced to flee under heavy fire, and he later died from his wounds. "Less than 20 minutes after the first cannon was discharged the town presented one sheet of flame," Gibson reported. An hour later, Gbenelu was a heap of smoldering ashes.[29]

When the firing began, some two or three hundred Rocktown soldiers emerged from hiding places on the opposite bank of Hoffman's River. They kept up a regular fire on the Cape Palmas people as they fled, increasing the fear and panic. No one recorded Gbenelu's casualties, though their losses must have been considerable. One American was killed. Some refugees boated down Sheppard's Lake to Grahway. Many others ran across the low-lying area called Joe Wah's Field. They offered little resistance except to burn the new Baptist church and other buildings along their course. Once they had gotten safely out of cannon range some of them rallied. They approached one of the outposts along Maryland Avenue, but the militia put up a sharp fire from their stronghold and forced them to retreat. As they did so they ransacked and burned several empty houses. At the end of the day, settlers had scarcely twenty rounds of ammunition left. Roszell McGill had to supply them with more. Had he not done so, and had the Greboes fought back, they would have wiped out the state.[30]

William Allen Prout died on the night of December 22, his passing overlooked in the excitement of war. Only Joseph Gibson bothered to mention it, and then only in an off-handed manner. He stated that it was the result of a sudden illness, which lasted only one or two days, but the nature of the malady was unrecorded. Circumstance suggests that he was a suicide, but there is no evidence to prove it.[31]

On Christmas day, sixty militiamen under Captain J. W. Cooper, aided by one hundred or more of the Rocktown and Fishtown *sedibo*, attacked and burned Grahway, fulfilling their prophesy of burning up all the sand on the beach. There was really no contest, as the Americans' weapons and tactics were far superior. They marched on to Half Cavally, now their warm friend, and delivered weapons and ammunition. The soldiers returned to Harper on December 28 amidst great rejoicing. Success had intoxicated Governor Drayton. He exulted in the executive journal, "Not one man killed, or Badly wounded in that Engagement, which have so justly entitled the Commander to the Gallant Epentet of Chivalric. And the men 'the immortal Sixty.'"[32]

The same night, Grebo raiders burned Mt. Vaughan to the ground. After a week of fighting, the Americans had lost one man killed and another wounded. Joseph Gibson observed on the thirtieth, "While . . . we have many reasons to be thankful to the great arbiter of human affairs for the many manifestations of his goodness and mercy, we are not without cause for humiliation and regret. Many of our neighbors and friends who but a week ago appeared to be getting along prosperously are now bereft of all their earthly possession, and are thrown naked upon the mercy of a merciless world."[33]

After the burning of Gbenelu and Grahway, the Nyomowe towns were ready to capitulate. Drayton was determined to have nothing less than complete subjection of his enemies. On December 29 the defeated Greboes sent a neutral messenger to Harper with a request for a palaver. The governor consented and the man returned to the Nyomowe encampment, which had formed on the north shore of Lake Sheppard, about four miles east of the settlement. On January 2, as appointed, six of the principal headmen of Gbenelu and Grahway came to Harper, with the governor's guarantee of safety. When the meeting had come to order, the governor informed them that he would make peace on three conditions: first, the entire population of Grahway must migrate to Beriby, sixty miles to leeward; second, the Greboes of Cape Palmas must join their cousins at Grand Cavally, the smallest and poorest of the Grebo states; third, both moves must be done within one week or fighting would resume. The terms were absurdly harsh, and compliance was impossible. Even so, the headmen listened calmly, because the governor had the upper hand. When he finished, they got up to leave, but Drayton had two of the headmen seized in violation of his promise of safe passage. The rest promised to return in three days with an answer. In the event, they did not return, since they could not trust Drayton. Instead, they sent word by neutral parties that they had no means of transportation or food to take with them to their new homes. Moreover, the Beriby people would in all probability refuse to give them room to settle. They therefore begged Drayton to give them more lenient terms. He would yield nothing, however, for he was intent upon expulsion or extermination, if necessary. As the victor, he would dictate whatever terms pleased him.[34]

On January 5, 1857, McGill, Brothers' new ship, *Moses Sheppard*, called at Harper on a coasting voyage from Monrovia. Captain Urias McGill and his crew had no idea of the disturbance on shore until the collector of customs and some militiamen boarded and arrested fourteen of his passengers, Greboes from Cape Palmas whose labor contracts had expired. The captain protested vigorously, as they were noncombatants and he could easily return them to Monrovia, where they could cause no harm. Drayton, though, would do things his own way.[35]

Word did not reach Monrovia that hostilities had commenced at Cape Palmas until January 6. No one heard the news with more interest than Samuel Ford McGill, who had lived so much of his life there. He had left Harper in disgust two and a half years before, but time had healed some of the bad feelings, and he was at once prepared to lend his assistance. The next day found him on board the *George R. McGill*, one of the firm's smaller vessels, on his way to leeward. He landed at Harper on the tenth, and because of his force of character and history in the community he assumed a measure of authority.[36]

McGill took stock of the settlement's defenses. The militia included some 140 men, of whom 125 were fit for service. Each of them had a musket, but only three out of four guns were in good order. The artillery company had six cannon, with only thirty cannister shells and no round shot. The entire militia had only seventy pounds of powder, fifteen hundred pounds of lead, and some three thousand prepared cartridges: a paltry war chest by any reckoning. The Americans had no stockades, because building them was prohibitively expensive and there was little suitable timber available. The soldiers occupied five lightly fortified stations: Tubman Town, with twenty militiamen; Jackson's Corner, with forty; the jail, with eighteen; Latrobe, or East Harper, with forty; and Cape Palmas, with twenty-two. Except for the two posts closest to the Cape, the surrounding country was dangerous. Many settler farmsteads (approximately forty-two by the end of January) were burned in night raids by Grebo skirmishers. McGill loaned the state ten barrels of gunpowder.[37]

To make matters even worse, trade was entirely cut off, with no stores of food on hand or even "a single dollar in the treasury for its purchase." McGill reported to the president of the Maryland Colonization Society soon after, "With the commencement of the war, depredations by Americans on the farms of the more industrious and thrifty commenced, the impracticability of checking these, has resulted in the rapid consumption or destruction of products that might have served the entire community two or three months. All stock without regard to ownership, has been recklessly slaughtered by the Soldiery, or if any remains 'tis only a few head of Cattle that the owners are compelled to keep confined." McGill found parties of women and children venturing into the bush under armed guard to dig cassava from Grebo fields. The practice was acknowledged to be risky, but the people were desperate. McGill estimated that the supply of cassava might last two months, if Grebo ambushers did not prevent them from getting it. He sent four hundred bushels of rice ashore, all he had, and prospects for getting more were discouraging.[38]

The former governor regarded Drayton's intransigent stance as folly. He pressed for moderation, but the preacher was obsessed with a vision of a holy war against the heathen. About January 15, Governor Drayton resolved to attack the encampment on the north shore of Lake Sheppard, where the people of Grahway and Gbenelu had gathered. They numbered some 850 fighting men, and from their positions they launched nightly raids into the settlement. Even so, they were destitute, with only the clothing on their backs and barely any food to eat. They were ruined and sick of fighting. At last, Drayton consented to talk with his enemies once again. The result of this was an ultimatum: the Grebo headmen must come in to set the palaver by 10 A.M. on Monday, January 19, or face attack. One of the hostage headmen was released to carry the message.

Early on the morning set for the palaver, Yellow Will and his people sent an envoy to announce their decision to capitulate to Drayton's demands. Their defeat was nothing short of abject. Yet, as the messenger made his way to Harper, well before Drayton's deadline, he discovered a force of sixty militiamen on its way down Lake Sheppard in two large war canoes accompanied by several smaller boats. He ran back to his people, giving them fair warning of the double-dealing. The Gbenelu and Grahway *sedibo* ordered themselves among the mangroves to resist a landing. Each of the American war canoes had a cannon mounted in the bow and was burdened with soldiers and ammunition, amounting to almost the entire arsenal. Two hundred Rocktown soldiers paralleled them on the strand. Soon they approached the Nyomowe camp, which lay inside a cove formed by a rivulet entering the Lake on the north. They would scarcely have been able to see the camp, which was obstructed by dense mangrove thickets, except for the smoke of cooking fires. The canoes moved in quickly, expecting to catch the Nyomowe soldiers by surprise. As they glided into the cove they encountered a sharp musket fire, well aimed from hiding places among the bushes. The cannons were already primed and the canoes each fired cannister rounds at unseen targets. At each blast, the canoe would stagger, and hard paddling was necessary to regain momentum. The fire from shore continued, causing confusion at first, then panic on the water. An order was given to pull back. The gunners attempted to return fire as they went, but the ammunition had become damp, and they had difficulty maintaining their weapons within the confines of the dugout. A charge in the cannon on the larger canoe then failed to ignite properly. All twenty-four men aboard knew that the gun might explode. They rushed at once toward the stern just as it did, killing a number instantly and splitting the boat in two. The defenders on shore aimed their shots at those floundering in the water, and not one made it to safety. Four others on the strand were also killed. The other canoes fled to the ocean side of the lake under covering fire from the Rocktown *sedibo,* who were too far away from the action to make any more significant contribution. The Americans leaped from their boats and took only what they could carry, leaving behind a field piece and most of their ammunition. They ran as fast as they could back to Harper. "Had the Enemy followed them in the retreat into the settlement," McGill commented, "such was the panic produced by the disaster that . . . it would have resulted in the entire destruction of the once flourishing Colony of Maryland in Liberia."[39]

The *Moses Sheppard* sailed for Monrovia about a week after the defeat on Lake Sheppard. The defiant mood at Harper had been transformed, and the Marylanders looked desperately to the republic for assistance. Governor Drayton wrote President Stephen Allen Benson an account of what had happened and the current situation on January 26. He noted the victories and the defeat. "This catastrophe has in a measure dispirited some of my fellow citizens," he declared, "especially the gallant survivors of that expedition for their chivalric comrades who have met a watery grave. Composed as that expedition was of a number of the flower of our citizen soldiery, have cast the mantle of gloom over our community, and prudence dictates strict defensive character for the present; albeit not a station has been abandoned." The militia could defend the country against any immediate attack, but they must have a reinforcement of men and ammunition to win the war decisively, which he believed was essential. Greboes must be driven from the vicinity of the settlement. He asked for assistance under whatever terms the republic might name.[40]

On January 27, while the *Sheppard* was still sailing toward Monrovia, McGill wrote to Charles Howard, president of the Maryland Colonization Society. McGill, well-informed on such things, knew that the republic had no money to give to Harper, let alone the logistical difficulties of reconvening the legislature, collecting volunteers, and transporting them to Cape Palmas before the Americans faced an onslaught.

Still, he thought that President Benson, who was himself a native of the State of Maryland and whose father had volunteered to join the *Ann's* company, might be persuaded to act if he could find the money on good terms and get the legislature to agree. He suggested that the Marylanders might unilaterally renounce their sovereignty and declare themselves part of Liberia. Then, Benson would have no choice but to act. He repeated his assertion of years past that annexation to Liberia as a county was the only hope for Maryland's survival, as recent events had demonstrated. "These people now simply apply to our Republic for Aid," the doctor concluded, "men, arms, subsistence, money — All of the influence I can use shall be exerted in their behalf — and I feel sure that if once our flag is unfurled at Cape Palmas its salvation as well as its annexation will be effected. The Society have been hitherto ever confident of the ability of the people in Maryland in Liberia to sustain themselves — 'twas simply a mistake — the material, the men for the work have not emigrated from Maryland."[41]

Maryland in Liberia was spared an assault following the defeat on Lake Sheppard, which was fortunate, for citizens' morale had evaporated. The Nyomowe *sedibo* continued its campaign of harassment, burning property and picking off stragglers, but their leaders were also devastated by the losses they had suffered. On January 28, Grebo soldiers ambushed a party of settlers while they dug cassava. They killed one of the guards and wounded another seriously, but the women and children came home safely.[42]

Remarkably, Dr. James Hall was on his way to Africa when the war at Cape Palmas erupted. He was supercargo on the *Mary Caroline Stevens*, a fine clipper ship, 713 tons burthen, whose construction he had overseen on behalf of the American Colonization Society. This was her maiden voyage and his first visit to Africa since 1840. Business concerns had a role in his decision to sail to Liberia. Since the Maryland State Colonization Society was winding down active operations, he and his son George had gone into business together, in effect assuming control of the old Chesapeake and Liberia Trading Company. Hall intended to firm up a relationship with McGill Brothers at Monrovia. The memory of old times was of no less importance in his decision to sail. As the shipwrights applied finishing touches to the vessel in November 1856, exactly twenty-five years had elapsed since he, "a living skeleton," had boarded the *Orion*. Now approaching old age, he wished to visit the scene of his former labors and the people who were the object of his life's work. His daughter Catherine came with him to see where he had adventured when she was but a small girl.[43]

The voyage was an exciting one, the *Stevens* exhibiting great speed and agility on the water. James Hall shared the exhilaration of the emigrants, numbering some two hundred, most of them Virginians, who would make a new home in Africa. The first stop was Cape Mount, where a new settlement was gaining a foothold. Dr. Hall remembered seeing the wild mountain from the *Ann's* longboat early in 1834; in contrast now, from a great clipper ship, busy Robertsport was reminiscent of the first days at Cape Palmas. His romantic reveries were shattered by the news that met him when the kroomen clambered on board: "War lib for Cape Palmas!" What was worse, he could learn no details at all. He hurried the landing of passengers and stores, and the vessel was soon under way again.[44]

When Hall reached Mesurado Roads, all sorts of rumors were current, most quite lurid or gloomy. Since Liberians were not especially fond of the Marylanders, there was no telling how bad things really were. John Russwurm's widow, Sarah, was his best source. She had been visiting her brother, Roszell McGill, when the war broke out and had returned to Monrovia by the *G. R. McGill*, which carried her brother Ford to Harper. Mrs. Russwurm informed Hall of the series of blunders that had resulted in war.[45]

On February 3, James Hall waited at Monrovia to hear further details. Settlers would need supplies and ammunition, so he busied himself gathering whatever might come in handy, spending some $1,500 of his own money. He had some trouble getting rice, and imported goods were almost impossible to obtain. Who was to pay all these expenses was unclear, but Hall felt he must do whatever he could to help his old friends. On the night of the third, he wrote President Howard, "I need not say how painfull all this is to me. I am truly sick at heart and had rather die than visit Cape Palmas." The next day, Ford McGill returned from Harper with the news of the terrible defeat on Lake Sheppard and the complete demoralization of citizens. "The Shade of Drayton's folly and madness only being deepened," Hall wrote.[46]

Drayton had sent letters to the English and American consuls at Monrovia, and also to President Benson, each appealing for aid. The consuls could do very little since their warships were all away on cruises. The Liberian government was also in a difficult position, having depleted its treasury in the previous year in a settlement project at Cape Mount and a war at Sinoe. Hall considered sailing to Sierra Leone on the *Stevens* to seek an English man-o'-war, but he decided that this would involve too much delay. He also considered going directly to Cape Palmas to deliver what supplies he could and try to mediate a peaceful settlement of the war. Yet it was clear from Sarah Russwurm and her brother Ford that Governor Drayton was intent upon prosecuting the war no matter the cost. Without outside force, Hall might not be able to bring either Drayton or Greboes to the table to negotiate. He concluded that he must involve the Liberian government in the conflict.[47]

On February 4 he offered President Benson a loan of eight thousand dollars on behalf of the Maryland State Colonization Society to raise an expeditionary force. He stipulated that the Liberian government could not request annexation of Maryland in return for rescuing the citizens there. "Could this government, consistently with the claims of humanity, refrain from any participation in the matter, she would most gladly do so," Benson replied two days later. There was "no pecuniary nor territorial consideration . . . sufficiently strong to induce this government to persuade her citizens away from their fields and other peaceful and profitable avocations for the purpose of prosecuting warfare in a foreign State." He reassured Hall that whatever action his government took "is simply a response to their appeals to and claims upon our humanity." Even if Liberia wanted to annex Maryland, "she would disdain the idea and the act of taking advantage of the unfortunate difficulties and distresses of a sister State to secure this object." Maryland would not be annexed "otherwise than by the voluntary action of that government, or a majority of the people."[48]

The Liberian legislature convened for an extraordinary session to consider the matter. By February 6 both houses had authorized the state to intervene at Cape Palmas with a volunteer force of up to 225 men, to be governed by the militia statutes of the republic, headed by officers with a presidential commission. Volunteers were to receive two months' pay in advance, and upon completion of service, one town lot and one hundred acres of land in the bush. The president was authorized to borrow up to ten thousand dollars for the benefit of Maryland in Liberia, which money was to be regarded as a loan to the Free State of Maryland, which must be repaid. A supply of arms and ammunition should be sent to support the Maryland militia. A minister should be appointed to conduct diplomatic relations with Maryland. Postal arrangements should be established and an armed vessel assigned to visit Maryland on a regular basis.[49]

President Benson signed the bill on February 7. The same day, the militia had its quarterly parade at Monrovia, an extraordinarily festive day because the best companies would receive "Zouaive" uniforms donated by Napoleon III, Emperor of the French. Citizens of fighting age appeared on the field for their drills. Hall stood and watched. "Many of the 'Troops' . . . were *entirely* Liberians," he commented afterwards, "born and bred in Liberia, sons of old settlers, whom we knew twenty years since, and most of them had been there long enough to be thoroughly nationalized. A few, however, were new comers, who turned out merely for rations, a nondescript class undergoing the process of incubation or hatching from slavery to freedom, whom it was not difficult to distinguish at a glance." After their marching and inspection, President Benson stood before the men and read them the resolutions that the legislature had passed the previous day, noting the uniforms and bounties as well as the moral reasons for coming to the aid of Maryland. Not one man volunteered. "Then commenced the rounds of the sergeant or corporal and music, 'Roll went the drum and the fife played sweetly;' but few stragglers fell in: something was wrong, and we began to feel a failure," Hall recounted. Some questions were asked of the men, and the cause of their refusal was evident. Only when President Benson announced that former president Roberts would have command of them and that they would not be subject to the authority of Maryland did any number volunteer.[50]

The next morning approximately 115 men assembled on the field. "Many were young men or boys," according to Hall, "unbridled colts, who had never suffered even the curb of parental discipline; many had been in country factories, and accustomed to command and dictate to native subordinates, acquiring that pleasant habit of control, which our Southern friends consider so essential in the gentleman." These volunteers were attired in "fatigue dress." The doctor wrote with some humor,

> Had not every motley association of the kind, for the past two hundred years, been compared to Fallstaff's ragged regiment, we should certainly claim the privilege here, for we venture to assert that the word "troops" was never before applied to such a line of scaramouches. In cut, color and material of garments, not even Swedenbourg himself could discover a correspondence, if we except the blue "dungaree" inexpressables, which redeemed most of them from the charge of Sans Culottesism.

February 9 presented great contrast, as the volunteers were given uniforms to replace their fatigues. These costumes were nothing less than spectacular, modeled on Middle Eastern dress. "Nothing could be more picturesque or striking than a marching regiment in this Arab or African costume," Hall wrote. "It requires, however, the wild music of horns, cymbals, bagpipes and the like to correspond with the sight." The new uniforms consisted of a white turban, a light blue waistcoat with a red stripe down the front center, a gray jacket trimmed with red across the breast and buttoned to the throat, red "Turkish" trousers, gathered just below the calf, thick leather russet gaiters covering the shoes, and a blue sash around the waist. Late the next afternoon, the tenth, brilliantly dressed, muskets brightly polished, they marched to the cadence of a martial band to boats that would carry them to the *Stevens*. The vessel was underway at the first land breeze the next morning. The recruits drilled the whole way down, so that by the time the *Stevens* came in sight of Cape Palmas, they presented a truly ferocious appearance. Fighting contrary winds and tornadoes, the vessel arrived off Harper at about two in the afternoon, February 16, 1857.[51]

As soon as a launch could get off, James Hall sent a note to Drayton to offer his services. The governor did not respond personally. Instead, J. B. Phillips, who was acting as secretary, wrote on the governor's behalf to thank Hall for his efforts, adding that Drayton would hold the offer "in abeyance." Drayton vainly hoped to maintain his dignity and authority and naturally remained aloof from Hall and the Liberian authorities, who could only humiliate him for his shameful maladministration.[52]

Reverend C. C. Hoffman, who ran the Girl's Orphan Asylum at the western tip of the Cape, was much more enthusiastic. "Welcome, Welcome," he wrote, almost as soon as he was told of the ship, "Can it be true that *You* have really arrived at Cape Palmas and your daughter!! At such a time as *this*, that you should be here, is remarkable. I trust you may be the means of tranquilizing the unsettled elements now disturbing our little community and the Country Around." He noted that creditable reports had passed the previous day that the Nyomowe towns were preparing to attack Half Cavally. No smoke had been seen from the Cape, however, so things must be all right.[53]

Joseph Roberts had decided, with Hall's counsel (the doctor would assume no more authority than this), to take military authority out of Drayton's hands as soon as possible. They decided that the best way to accomplish this, short of actually deposing him, was to appoint an emergency government consisting of Roberts and three others of his choosing and Drayton, with two of his choice, making seven in all, the majority Monrovians. As soon as Roberts came ashore, he began to negotiate terms under which Liberia would assist Maryland.[54]

Governor Drayton ignored Hall for a full day after his arrival. On February 17, finding a "moment of some leisure" (but in reality at the insistence of Commissioner Roberts), he penned a brief letter thanking him for his assistance. Drayton informed Hall that he regarded the arrival of the ship with troops, through the efforts of the very man who had founded Maryland twenty-three years before, nothing less than "providential." He would welcome whatever suggestions the first governor might offer, and in consideration of this Drayton requested Hall to visit him at noon for a private discussion. He further asked the doctor and his daughter to have dinner with him the following day. "You may consider yourself the Guest of the State of Maryland in Liberia, hoping that during your stay among us nothing might arise to mar any of your expected plans," he concluded ludicrously.[55] Hall finally met with Governor Drayton on the third day, as appointed. He was polite and formal, and clearly uncomfortable with the situation. Hall came away with the impression that the governor was not completely truthful. He was also disappointed that Drayton did not ask for any advice.[56]

While ashore, Hall walked from Harper to the old Public Farm, across the burned site of Gbenelu, now nothing but ashes and raised circles that had been house floors, which the rains were already beginning to disintegrate. "We designated the old Palaver Place," he wrote later, "where under a broad spreading tree, we effected the purchase of territory, and where we have often met the old chiefs to settle other palavers of a less pleasing nature, and where too, we have sometimes met them to partake of the brimmers of the sweet palm wine, in their holiday season, when for nights and days together the women danced to the rapidly beaten drum. The visit brought all these scenes and the principal actors in them fresh to our mind, and keenly did we feel the change which a foolish, rash act had produced." His worst fears confirmed, he wanted only to leave. He returned to the *Stevens* and busied himself with unloading her cargo.[57]

By the end of the day on February 19, Joseph Roberts and Joseph Gibson had worked out terms of cooperation. Briefly, they agreed that the Liberian forces would act in whatever way was necessary to achieve "just and amicable terms of peace" between Maryland and the Nyomowe Greboes. Liberian officers would have command of their own troops, but the commander in the field would be the senior officer, whether a Marylander or Liberian. All Liberian volunteers would be responsible to local authorities for civil offences, but each force would retain its own military code and courts-martial. Executive authority was transferred to a committee including Drayton, Roberts, James Hall, and four other men to be named alternately by Drayton and Roberts. Maryland agreed to reimburse the Republic of Liberia for any expenses up to twenty thousand dollars. Other clauses concerned the resolution of disputes between the two governments. The next day, the parties to the treaty signed it, whereupon the legislature voted its approval. Drayton delivered a bond for his government to repay the debt at 6 percent interest in installments of three thousand a year in hard currency.[58]

Governor Drayton did not sign this treaty willingly, for he objected to the pacific interference of Hall and the Liberian forces. Depredations by Greboes continued—even on February 19 two more houses were burned—and he was eager to go to battle once again. On February 20 he asked Hall to give him control of the expeditionary force, or at least the munitions and provisions so that he could prepare a company of militia for an offensive. This was only delusional talk, for the matter was safely out of his hands.[59]

Though some, like Drayton, were for exterminating the Africans, the majority of Marylanders wanted to end the war. They knew that Greboes had suffered tremendously and were eager to have peace on any dignified terms. Greboes refused to talk with Drayton since he had repeatedly shown malicious duplicity. Hall and Roberts labored with Drayton and won the release of two headmen and a son of Yellow Will, who had been arrested despite promises of safe passage. They carried a note and a handsome dash from Roberts assuring his good faith and requesting a grand palaver. Roberts emphasized that Yellow Will and his colleagues would be able speak with perfect freedom. The booming of the captured cannon at their encampment evidenced favorable reception of the message. A messenger returned with word that Greboes were only too eager to have the truth brought out. They would come to Harper on the following Monday, the twenty-third.[60]

James Hall might have stayed to hear the palaver talked and to celebrate the colony's anniversary, on February 22, but he could not bear to do so under such gloomy circumstances. He left Cape Palmas on February 21, 1857. The day was quite rainy, which made the work of getting off rather uncomfortable. Hall was so eager to go that he repeatedly crossed the surf to expedite things. "We bade him a reluctant good bye on the wharf in front of the Store this evening about sunset," Joseph T. Gibson wrote Hall's son George, "and while he with his lovely daughter were gradually dwindling out of sight in the distance, every countenance seemed to say, God speed to him whom we cannot but regard with a sort of paternal affection."[61]

As appointed, Governor Roberts, state officials, and Grebo dignitaries met at noon on Monday in an assembly room of the Orphan Asylum, a neutral space. Yellow Will opened the palaver, angrily demanding to know why the governor had opened fire on his towns and then burned Grahway. He recalled the terms of the original treaty of 1834 and the promises made to Simleh Ballah in 1837, that the people of Gbenelu would always be able to keep their towns. Drayton answered that Yellow Will and his people had plotted a war against the Marylanders. The king vehemently denied the assertion, stating that his people had only prepared to defend themselves from what seemed an impending American attack. Drayton retorted that Will and his colleagues had admitted their warlike intentions at the conference on the Monday before the outbreak. At that palaver, Palm had confessed the fact and the others had been forced to admit it also. Yellow Will responded that the governor had completely twisted the story. Palm had in fact stated that Greboes were prepared for war, but in self-defense. Yellow Will related that Palm "had heard from his daughter . . . the wife of a Rock-town man, that the Governor had agreed with the Rock-town people to fight the Cape palmas people — and drive them from the country." The governor denied having made any such agreement with the Rocktown chiefs. The Grebo headmen diplomatically expressed their regrets at not having mentioned their fears and suspicions instead of preparing to defend themselves.[62] When he had finished, the king turned to Joseph Gibson, who admitted that the king's version of the palaver before the war was true. Amazingly, Gibson and others allowed Drayton to persist in his delusion through the reckless course of war. "How it was the Governor entertained the impression that they confessed a secret conspiracy — remains a mystery!" Roberts remarked to Hall shortly afterward. "The Governor seems to have imbibed the impression . . . that the Cape Palmas and Graway people did not respect him as they had done his predecessors" but held him in contempt, he elaborated. "This . . . annoyed the Governor." Rocktown, "inveterate enemies of the Cape Palmas and Graway people" discovered that fact and took advantage of it to mislead the Drayton. "By indirect means" they let Cape Palmas Greboes think "the Americans premeditated an attack on their towns to drive them out of the country — which they, the Rock-town people, earnestly desired." They also told Drayton "many stories about the Cape Palmas people. Many of which doubtless they induced the Governor to believe."[63] Drayton's complaints against Grahway turned out to be old palavers of minor importance, certainly not enough to justify the violent course he had taken.

Blundering, paranoid policy exposed, Roberts was able to impose a treaty of peace between the two communities during the next few days. This was signed on February 26. Its terms were rather straightforward. From the date of signing, Maryland in Liberia was to be at peace with its African neighbors. Grahway and Gbenelu affirmed the sovereignty ("protection and exclusive jurisdiction") of the Maryland government. Maryland in Liberia agreed to pay the value of a thousand dollars in tobacco, muskets, cloth, and other useful items to Gbenelu in installments to purchase the town site. In return, Yellow Will's people were to cross Hoffman's River to a site where factions from the town had earlier settled, where the convert teacher Harris had established an active school. They were also permitted a small town on the beach, from which they could follow their traditional maritime habits. Cape Palmas and Grahway were to pay two hundred kroos of rice for the burned buildings at Mount Vaughan, a token sum for the loss. They were also to return all items lost or stolen in the war or make restitution. Grahway had permission to rebuild on its old town site. Neither people was to interfere with Maryland's trade with other towns or with foreigners, nor were Marylanders to interfere with Grebo reconstruction or rob their farms any more. Shipwrecks were no longer to be plundered, and the ban on the slave trade was reaffirmed. Finally, Gbenelu and Grahway were to desist from exposing corpses on Russwurm's Island. Yellow Will (Pedah Neh), Simleh Ballah (Bill Williams), and King Palm (Peh Gikpameo) signed the treaty on behalf of Gbenelu. King Saba, Black Will, and two other headmen signed for Grahway. Boston J. Drayton, J. B. Phillips, and Anthony Wood signed for Maryland. Former president Joseph J. Roberts, chief negotiator, signed for the Republic of Liberia, and J. W. Livingston, in command of the U.S.S. *St. Louis*, Joseph T. Gibson, and H. W. Erskine affixed their names as witnesses. With that, the treaty was complete.[64]

Simultaneously with the peace negotiations, Marylanders reconsidered their political status. Independence had brought them nothing but worry and tribulation, culminating in a destructive war. Now with the fortuitous arrival of James Hall and Liberian troops, obtained at great expense for which Maryland was liable, most considered their sovereignty forfeit. The old plan of union, once the object of so much controversy, now seemed the best course. Just after James Hall sailed away, a public meeting of settlers petitioned the General Assembly to take action on the subject. They willingly obliged, and with the governor's approval the question of county annexation was put to a vote on February 24. The results were unanimous in favor of union. Citizens elected Drayton, Gibson, and Fuller commissioners to arrange matters. They immediately approached Roberts, who was inclined to approve the plan, but he had specific instructions not to initiate such discussions and by implication had no authority to conduct them once broached. He therefore informed them unofficially that Liberia would probably admit Maryland as a county.[65]

This did not satisfy the commissioners, and they determined to force the issue. On March 3, Governor Drayton read aloud a proclamation with the headline, "Union Is Strength." He reviewed recent events and the current impasse. "While the undersigned would be glad to settle definitely one or two points, which might be thought desirable, before annexation," the commissioners continued,

> still they deem it more desirable, nay important, in view of pressing circumstances, which threaten the tranquility of the State, and also involve the safety and happiness of the people — that annexation should not be delayed for these preliminaries.
>
> But having full faith in the justice and magnanimity of the Government of the Republic, and of the people of that Commonwealth, we at once dissolve the Government of the State of Maryland in Liberia, and throw ourselves into the arms of the Republic.
>
> The undersigned being sustained in this impression by the mass of the people of this State, prepare to surrender into the hands of the Commissioner of the Republic, all and every thing pertaining to the sovereignty of the State.

They added a few reservations and observations. Maryland in Liberia should be known as "Cape Palmas County." In addition to the two senators guaranteed by the republic's constitution, she should have three representatives. None of the agreements made with the Maryland State Colonization Society should be affected by the change, and all contracts and legal proceedings begun under the state government must be completed according to the old code. They noted the size, population and revenues of the State of Maryland and concluded:

> Now therefore, We, the undersigned Commissioners as aforesaid, acting on authority vested in us by the people of the State of Maryland in Liberia, do, in their name, and in their behalf, hereby dissolve the Government of the said State of Maryland in Liberia, and the same is henceforward dissolved, and by these presents we, the undersigned Commissioners as aforesaid, do cede to the Government of the Republic of Liberia, with all her bars, bays, rivers, creeks, lakes, and Atlantic waters thereunto appertaining, including the jurisdiction and sovereignty of the same, also all public buildings, forts, arsenals, guns and munitions of war of every kind and description

whatever, which we the undersigned Commissioners, acting as aforesaid, are prepared and will deliver to the Commissioner of the Republic of Liberia now present, in Harper, or to any one whom he
may designate as the Superintendant of the County of Cape Palmas
for the time being, and the said Commissioner of the Republic of
Liberia is requested to assume immediately, in the name of his government, the public affairs of the said County of Cape Palmas, and
establish here the authority of his government, by unfurling the Flag
of the Republic of Liberia.[66]

By this act, Maryland was thrown into limbo.

Roberts appointed Joseph T. Gibson superintendent of Cape Palmas
for the time being. A day or two later, the British war steamer *Heckla*
carried him and the volunteer soldiers back to Monrovia. Roberts conferred with James Hall on his return. The doctor was extremely disappointed to learn that the citizens of Maryland in Liberia had decided to
annex themselves to the republic. Even more wounding was the abandonment of the name "Maryland in Liberia" for the nondescript "Cape
Palmas County," which slighted the community's distinct heritage. Roberts had also wondered at the change but agreed to it at Drayton's
insistence. With Roberts's and President Benson's support, Hall in a
stern letter ordered Drayton to change the name to "Maryland County."
He also scolded Joseph Gibson for his spinelessness and complicity in
the demise of the State of Maryland.[67]

The Liberian legislature met in extraordinary session in the first
week of April. President Benson addressed the gentlemen at length on
the proceedings at Cape Palmas, reading to them all of the relevant
documents concerning the activities of Roberts's relief force and the
dissolution of the Free State of Maryland. He asked them to admit
Maryland as a county, as the citizens of Harper had requested. "No
matter what may have been the peculiar distinctive title of the government under which they lived," the president said,

the fact remains incontrovertible, that we have been, are, and will
continue to be one people with them! We are of the same race, and
have a common destiny. We were actuated by similar motives in
fleeing from the same land of oppression to this our common land

of refuge; here to build up and maintain a respectable home for ourselves and posterity. We are unquestionably identified in every possible conceivable interest.

Maryland was deserving of the most charitable feelings the legislature could muster, he told them, and trusted that they would receive a welcome into the republic. Moreover, Maryland would contribute greatly to the cultural and economic wealth of the country. He concluded:

> Gentlemen, the limit of our national destiny is unknown to us; and though by the aid of reason and contemplation we oft-time imagine, and are most sanguine, that we discover through the vista of our future, the glorious halo by which the national destiny of our race is to be circumscribed through the instrumentality of this Republic; especially, when through the instrumentality of this gradually spreading christian State, the vast multitudes of aborigines of this land shall have become as stones from the quarry, polished by art, and fully identified with us, yet the knowledge of our wisest men in that respect is limited, and must continue somewhat veiled in uncertainty, until the consummation of our great work — the mission with which we are charged by the God of nations.
>
> As a nation, small and impotent as we are, we have before us as great, as responsible, and as interesting a geographical field for moral and intellectual labor as any nation on earth. It is our duty, and therefore should be our policy to persevere in that course that will characterize us as an industrious, frugal, intelligent and moral people, meanwhile trusting in Divine Providence, and vigorously availing ourselves of every opening by His Providence to our national welfare. In this way we shall grow and spread beyond our own calculation; and christianity and civilization will soon be co-extensive on this continent with our geographical borders, which we both trust and believe will not be restrained, until our great mission as a christian nation on this continent is consummated, and our Fatherland is redeemed.

The two houses of the legislature voted to annex Maryland as a county with very little debate. Maryland quickly amalgamated with the republic. The work of rebuilding commenced immediately, and Governor Drayton's war became a sad memory for the peace-loving citizens—African and American—of Maryland.[68]

Annotated Roll of Settlers in Maryland in Liberia, 1820–1854

INDIVIDUALS SENT BY THE MARYLAND STATE COLONIZATION SOCIETY TO MONROVIA, SOME OF WHOM MIGRATED TO CAPE PALMAS

ORION, left Baltimore, November, 1831, and arrived at Monrovia, December, 1831:

1. Banks, Daniel: Freeborn resident of Baltimore, stated to be 19 at departure. Settled at Caldwell, Liberia, and subsequently moved to Cape Palmas. Worked in the colony as a rough carpenter. Signed open letter, Oct. 11, 1834. Married Caroline Scott, Feb. 2, 1837. Signed petition against Thomson, Dec. 2, 1837. Died of unknown cause, before 1843.

2. Banks, John: Freeborn resident of Baltimore, stated to be 16 at departure. Settled at Caldwell, Liberia. Moved to Cape Palmas, 1836, where he worked as a teacher in the ABCFM Mission. After 1842, he was a farmer and later a laborer. In ABCFM household, early 1837. Married Lucia Toliver, Mar. 9, 1837. Signed petition, Jan. 14, 1850. Does not appear in the record afterward.

3. Brown*, Elijah: Freeborn resident of Baltimore, a barber, stated to be 19 at departure. Settled at Caldwell, Liberia, and died of fever there, 1831.

4. Chase*, Joshua (brother of Henry Chase): Freed by a Mrs. Wallace of Baltimore, stated to be 18 at departure. Settled at Caldwell, Liberia, and died of diseased brain there, 1839.

5. Chase*, Henry (brother of Joshua Chase): Freed by a Mrs. Wallace of Baltimore, stated to be 13 at departure. Settled at Caldwell, Liberia, and living there, 1843.

6. Dansbury*, Emma (mother of John W. Dansbury): Freed resident of Baltimore, stated to be 24 at departure. Settled at Caldwell, Liberia, and living there, 1843.

7. Dansbury*, John W. (son of Emma Dansbury): Freed resident of Baltimore, stated to be 2 at departure. Settled at Caldwell, Liberia, and died of fever there, 1831.

8. Dunning*, Isaac: Freed by Comfort Tiffany of Baltimore, stated to be 13 at departure. Settled at Caldwell, Liberia, and living there, 1843.

9. Henson*, Henry (husband of Susan Henson): Freeborn resident of Baltimore, stated to be 21 at departure. Settled at Caldwell, Liberia, and died of anasarca there, 1838.

10. Henson*, Susan (wife of Henry Henson): Freeborn resident of Baltimore, stated to be 20 at departure. Settled at Caldwell, Liberia, and living there, 1843.

* These individuals never resided in Maryland in Liberia.

11. Jose*, Cassandra Anthony (mother of Manuel and sister[?] of Hannah): Freeborn resident of Baltimore, stated to be 50 at departure. Settled at Caldwell, Liberia, and died of anasarca there, 1838.

12. Jose*, Manuel Anthony (son of Cassandra Jose): Freeborn resident of Baltimore, stated to be 25 at departure. Settled at Caldwell, Liberia. Left Liberia at unknown date.

13. Jose*, Hannah Anthony (sister[?] of Cassandra): Freeborn resident of Baltimore, stated to be 40 at departure. Settled at Caldwell, Liberia, and living there in 1843.

14. Merricks*, Mary (single): Freeborn resident of Baltimore, stated to be 18 at departure. Settled at Caldwell, Liberia, and living there, 1843.

15. Nichols*, John (husband of Jane): Freeborn resident of Baltimore, a barber, stated to be 60 at departure. Settled at Caldwell, Liberia. Moved to Sierra Leone, 1836.

16. Nichols*, Jane (wife of John Nichols): Freeborn resident of Baltimore, stated to be 45 at departure. Settled at Caldwell, Liberia. Moved to Sierra Leone, 1836.

17. Nichols*, James (son of John): Freeborn resident of Baltimore, a barber, stated to be 18 at departure. Settled at Caldwell, Liberia. Moved to Sierra Leone, 1836.

18. Nichols*, Minta (grandmother of John Nichols): Freeborn resident of Baltimore, stated to be 110 at departure. Settled at Caldwell, Liberia, and died of old age there, 1831.

19. Nichols*, Joseph (son of John): Freeborn resident of Baltimore, stated to be 13 at departure. Settled at Caldwell, Liberia. Moved to Sierra Leone, 1836.

20. Nichols*, Sally Ann (daughter of John Nichols; also called Sarah Nichols): Freeborn resident of Baltimore, stated to be 12 at departure. Settled at Caldwell, Liberia. Moved to Sierra Leone, 1836.

21. Nichols*, Washington (son of John Nichols): Freeborn resident of Baltimore, stated to be 8 at departure. Settled at Caldwell, Liberia, and died of fever there, 1831.

22. Ridgway*, Caroline (single): Freeborn resident of Baltimore, a cook, stated to be 40 at departure. Settled at Caldwell, Liberia, and living there, 1843.

23. Stephens*, Joseph (husband of Catherine Stephens; also called John Stephens): Freeborn resident of Baltimore, a bricklayer, stated to be 47, at departure. Settled at Caldwell, Liberia, and died of diseased lungs there, 1836.

24. Stephens, Catherine (wife of Joseph Stephens; later called Catherine Scotland): Freeborn resident of Baltimore, stated to be 45 at departure. Settled at Caldwell, Liberia. Moved to Cape Palmas in 1836. Married Charles Scotland, about 1848. Does not appear in the record afterward.

25. Stephens*, James H. (son of Joseph Stephens): Freeborn resident of Baltimore, stated to be 19 at departure. Settled at Caldwell, Liberia, and living there, 1843.

26. Stephens, Mary Ann (daughter of Joseph Stephens; later called Mary Gutridge): Freeborn resident of Baltimore, stated to be 14 at departure. Settled at Caldwell, Liberia. Moved to Cape Palmas, 1836. Married Henry Gutridge, May 31, 1837. Died of unrecorded cause, Feb. 28, 1839.

27. Stephens*, Francis (possibly the son of Joseph Stephens; also called Francis Nichols): Freeborn resident of Baltimore, stated to be 10 at departure. Settled at Caldwell, Liberia, and died of fever there, 1831.

28. Stephens*, Joseph (son of Joseph Stephens): Freeborn resident of Baltimore, stated to be 9 at departure. Settled at Caldwell, Liberia, and died of fever there, 1832.

29. Stephens, George W. (son of Joseph Stephens): Freeborn resident of Baltimore, stated to be 8 at departure. Settled at Caldwell, Liberia. Moved to Cape Palmas, 1836. (Senate Document 150 erroneously says he died of fever at Caldwell, 1832.) Does not appear in the record after 1838.

30. Stephens, Alexander Boyer (son of Joseph Stephens): Freeborn resident of Balti-

more, stated to be 4 at departure. Settled at Caldwell, Liberia. Moved to Cape Palmas, 1836. Living with Catherine Stephens, 1843. (Senate Document 150 erroneously says he died of fever at Caldwell, 1831.) Signed petition, December, 1849. Married to Letitia A. Simpson, Census 1852, employed as a seaman.

31. Weignwright*, Lewis (single): Probably freeborn, resident of Dorchester Co., stated to be 26 at departure. Settled at Caldwell, Liberia, and living there in 1843.

LAFAYETTE, left Baltimore, December 9, 1832, arrived at Monrovia, February 7, 1833:
1. Allen*, Comfort Ann (daughter of Ann A. Fountain): Freeborn resident of Somerset Co., stated to be 17 at departure. Settled at Caldwell, Liberia, and died there of anasarca, 1838.

2. Allen*, Charlotte (daughter of Ann A. Fountain): Freeborn resident of Somerset Co., stated to be 15 at departure. Settled at Caldwell, Liberia, and living there in 1843.

3. Allen*, Samuel (also called Samuel A. Littleton; son of Ann A. Fountain): Freeborn resident of Somerset Co., stated to be 10 at departure. Settled at Caldwell, Liberia, and living there in 1843.

4. Barker*, Calvert (husband of Lydia Barker): Freed by Daniel Hughes, Executor of J. Lee Potts of Frederick Co., a farmer, stated to be 23 at departure. Settled at Caldwell, Liberia, died of diseased lungs there, 1840.

5. Barker*, Lydia (wife of Calvert Barker): Freed by Dr. Thomas W. Johnson to emigrate, resident of Frederick Co., a seamstress, stated to be 23 at departure. Settled at Caldwell, Liberia, died of diseased lungs there, 1835.

6. Bond*, William (single): Freeborn resident of Pennsylvania, a sailor, stated to be 23 at departure. Settled at Monrovia, and died by drowning, 1837.

7. Bowen, Lucy (single; attached to Calvert Barker family): Term slave manumitted early by Martha Graham of Frederick Co, to emigrate with the Barkers; a houseworker, stated to be 17 at departure. Settled at Caldwell, Liberia. Moved to Cape Palmas, 1835. Married Robert Scotland before 1843, listed as a widow in 1849. Resident of the colony, November, 1852.

8. Brown*, Louisa (single): Freeborn resident of Somerset Co., stated to be 22 at departure. Settled at Caldwell, Liberia, and living there in 1843.

9. Bryant*, James Henry (single): Freed by Wm. George Read of Baltimore Co., to emigrate, a farmer, stated to be 14 at departure. Settled at Monrovia, and living there in 1843.

10. Buley*, Ralph (husband of Nelly): Freeborn resident of Somerset Co., a farmer and seaman, stated to be 48 at departure. Settled at Caldwell, Liberia, and died of diseased lungs there, 1836.

11. Buley*, Nelly (wife of Ralph Buley; also called Ellen Buley): Freeborn resident of Somerset Co., stated to be 40 at departure. Settled at Caldwell, Liberia, and died of unknown cause there, 1837.

12. Buley*, Charlotte (daughter of Ralph and Nelly Buley): Freeborn resident of Somerset Co., stated to be 22 at departure. Settled at Caldwell, Liberia, and died of "decline" there, 1840.

13. Buley*, Ann (daughter of Ralph and Nelly Buley): Freeborn resident of Somerset Co., stated to be 14 at departure. Settled at Caldwell, Liberia, and living there, 1843.

14. Buley*, Polly Ellen (daughter of Ralph and Nelly Buley): Freeborn resident of Somerset Co., stated to be 10 at departure. Settled at Caldwell, Liberia, and died of fever there, 1833.

15. Buley*, Isaac James (son of Ralph and Nelly Buley): Freeborn resident of Somerset

Co., stated to be 6 at departure. Settled at Caldwell, Liberia. Moved to Accra, 1838.

16. Buley*, John Thomas (son of Ralph and Nelly Buley): Freeborn resident of Somerset Co., stated to be 1 at departure. Settled at Caldwell, Liberia, died of unknown cause there, 1835.

17. Burrows*, William Cathel (husband of Amelia): Freed by Arthur Dennis of Somerset Co., resident of Somerset Co., a carpenter, stated to be 40 at departure. Settled at Caldwell, Liberia, and living there in 1843.

18. Burrows*, Amelia C. (wife of William Burrows): Freeborn resident of Somerset Co., stated to be 29 at departure. Settled at Caldwell, Liberia, and living there in 1843.

19. Burrows*, Henry C. (son of William and Amelia Burrows): Freeborn resident of Somerset Co., stated to be 10 at departure. Settled at Caldwell, Liberia, and living there in 1843.

20. Burrows*, Rhoda C. (daughter of William and Amelia Burrows): Freeborn resident of Somerset Co., stated to be 8 at departure. Settled at Caldwell, Liberia, and living there in 1843.

21. Burrows*, Elizabeth C. (daughter of William and Amelia Burrows): Freeborn resident of Somerset Co., stated to be 6 at departure. Settled at Caldwell, Liberia, and living there in 1843.

22. Burrows*, George C. (son of William and Amelia Burrows): Freeborn resident of Somerset Co., stated to be 4 at departure. Settled at Caldwell, Liberia, and living there in 1843.

23. Burrows*, Rufus C. (son of William and Amelia Burrows): Freeborn resident of Somerset Co., stated to be 2 at departure. Settled at Caldwell, Liberia, and living there in 1843.

24. Craven*, Isaac (husband of Abigail Craven): Freed by Sarah E. Craven of Somerset Co., 1831; a house servant, stated to be 35 at departure. Settled at Caldwell, Liberia, and died there of unknown cause, 1842.

25. Craven*, Abigail (wife of Isaac Craven): Freed by the estate of Robert Patterson of Somerset Co., 1831; stated to be 35 at departure. Settled at Caldwell, Liberia, and living there in 1843.

26. Craven*, Margaretta (daughter of Isaac and Abigail Craven): Freed by the estate of Robert Patterson of Somerset Co., 1831; stated to be 13 at departure. Settled at Caldwell, Liberia, and living there in 1843.

27. Craven*, Owens (son of Isaac and Abigail Craven): Freed by the estate of Robert Patterson of Somerset Co., 1831; stated to be 8 at departure. Settled at Caldwell, Liberia, and living there in 1843.

28. Craven*, Peter B. (son of Isaac and Abigail Craven): Freed by the estate of Robert Patterson of Somerset Co., 1831, resident of Somerset Co., stated to be 5 at departure. Settled at Caldwell, Liberia, and living there in 1843.

29. Dashield*, Mary: Freed by S. H. White of Somerset Co., 1831; a house servant, stated to be 20 at departure. Settled at Caldwell, Liberia. Moved to Sierra Leone, 1835.

30. Dashield*, Fender Elizabeth (daughter of Mary Dashield): Freed by S. H. White of Somerset Co., 1831; stated to be 9 at departure. Settled at Caldwell, Liberia. Moved to Sierra Leone, 1835.

31. Dashield*, Augustus Ann (daughter of Mary Dashield): Freed by S. H. White of Somerset Co., 1831; stated to be 4 at departure. Settled at Caldwell, Liberia. Moved to Sierra Leone, 1835.

32. Dashield*, William (son of Mary Dashield): Freed by S. H. White of Somerset Co., 1831; stated to be 4 months at departure. Settled at Caldwell, Liberia, and died there of fever, 1833.

33. Dennis, Henry (husband of Mary Ann Dennis): Freed by H. Wallace Bleakely of Worcester Co.; a farmer, stated to be 47 at departure. Settled at Caldwell, Liberia. Moved to Cape Palmas on the *Ann,* 1834. Signed open letter, Oct. 11, 1834. Letter writer: July 23, 1835; May 30, and June 12, 1836. Died April 28, 1837, of "nervous fever."

34. Dennis, Mary Ann (wife of Henry Dennis): Freeborn resident of Worcester Co., stated to be 40 at departure. Settled at Caldwell, Liberia. Moved to Cape Palmas, 1834, and died there of unrecorded cause before July 1835.

35. Dennis, James B. (son of Henry and Mary Dennis): Freeborn resident of Worcester Co., stated to be 14 at departure. Settled at Caldwell, Liberia. Moved to Cape Palmas, 1834. Worked in the colony as a carpenter. Lived with Rev. Francis Burns in 1838; with A. Wood, 1840. Left Methodist Church to join Episcopal Church, 1847. Signed petition, April, 1849. Resident of the colony, November, 1852

36. Dennis, Julia (daughter of Henry and Mary Dennis): Freeborn resident of Worcester Co., stated to be 13 at departure. Settled at Caldwell, Liberia. Moved to Cape Palmas, 1834. Lived with Rev. Francis Burns in 1838; with A. Wood, 1839–40. Died Sept. 16, 1842.

37. Dennis*, Leah C. H. (daughter of Henry and Mary Dennis): Freeborn resident of Worcester Co., stated to be 13 at departure. Settled at Caldwell, Liberia, and died of fever there in 1833.

38. Dennis, Henry Worley (son of Henry and Mary Dennis): Freeborn resident of Worcester Co., stated to be 8 at departure. Settled at Caldwell, Liberia. Moved to Cape Palmas, 1834. Lived with Jacob Gross's family in 1838–9, then disappears from the record.

39. Dennis, Mary Ann (daughter of Henry Dennis): Freeborn resident of Worcester Co., stated to be 7 at departure. Settled at Caldwell, Liberia. Moved to Cape Palmas, 1834. Living in John Revey household, 1839–40. Later married Thomas Brown. Resident of the colony, November, 1852

40. Dennis, Martha (daughter of Henry and Mary Dennis): Freeborn resident of Worcester Co., stated to be 6 at departure. Settled at Caldwell, Liberia. Moved to Cape Palmas, 1834. Lived with J. Stewart family in 1838–43; then disappears from the record.

41. Dennis, Josiah Asbury (son of Henry and Mary Dennis; also called John): Freeborn resident of Worcester Co., stated to be 4 at departure. Settled at Caldwell, Liberia. Moved to Cape Palmas, 1834. In 1838, lived with William Hawkins family, then disappears from the record.

42. Dennis, John (son of Henry and Mary Dennis): Freeborn resident of Worcester Co., stated to be 2 at departure. Settled at Caldwell, Liberia. Moved to Cape Palmas, 1834. Living with Wm. Hawkins family, 1838–43; then disappears from the record.

43. Dixon, Mary (Single; later m. Burwell Minor): Freeborn resident of Somerset Co., stated to be 24 at departure. Settled at Caldwell, Liberia. Moved to Cape Palmas, 1835. Letter writer, Sept. 23, 1851. Resident of the colony, November, 1852, listed as a soapmaker.

44. Dixon, Unice (daughter of Mary; also called Vicey Ann Passon and Unice Minor): Freeborn resident of Somerset Co., stated to be 6 at departure. Settled at Caldwell, Liberia. Moved to Cape Palmas with her mother, 1833. Living with Burwell Minor family, 1837 and 1840. Resident of the colony, November, 1852, listed as a laundress

45. Dixon, Mariah (daughter of Mary; also called Mariah Ann Passon and Mariah Minor): Freeborn resident of Somerset Co., stated to be 3 at departure. Settled at Caldwell, Liberia. Moved to Cape Palmas with her mother, 1835. Living with Burwell Minor family, 1837 and 1839. Senate Document 150 states she died at Caldwell of fever, 1833. Actually, died at Cape Palmas, Dec. 16, 1852.

46. Dixon, Margaret (daughter of Mary Dixon; also called Margaret Ann Passon;

later Minor, then Harman): Freeborn resident of Somerset Co., stated to be 8 at departure. Settled at Caldwell, Liberia. Moved to Cape Palmas, 1835. Living with Burwell Minor family, 1837 and 1839. Appears as Henry Harman's wife, 1843. Does not appear in the record afterward.

47. Fountain*, Ann Allen (single): Freed by Thomas Fountain of Somerset Co. in 1815; resident of Somerset Co., stated to be 49 at departure. Settled at Caldwell, Liberia, and died there of fever, 1833.

48. Game*, George (uncertain relation of Spencer Game): Freeborn resident of Somerset Co., a farmer, stated to be 25 at departure. Settled at Caldwell, Liberia, and died by drowning there, 1836.

49. Game*, Spencer, Sr. (uncertain relation of George Game): Freeborn resident of Somerset Co., a farmer, stated to be 25 at departure. Settled at Caldwell, Liberia, and died there by drowning, 1836.

50. Harman, Nathan Greene (husband of Comfort Harman): Freeborn resident of Somerset Co., a farmer, stated to be 40 at departure. Settled at Caldwell, Liberia. Moved to Cape Palmas on the *Ann*, 1834. Worked in the colony as a farmer and laborer. Signed open letter, Oct. 11, 1834. Married Rachel Thomas, July 28, 1836. Supporter of Snetter, Sept. 12, 1838. Does not appear in the record after 1843.

51. Harman, Comfort (wife of Nathan): Freeborn resident of Somerset Co., stated to be 35 at departure. Settled at Caldwell, Liberia. Moved to Cape Palmas, 1834. Died of unrecorded cause before March 1836.

52. Harman, Joshua (son of Nathan and Comfort Greene): Freeborn resident of Somerset Co., stated to be 13 at departure. Settled at Caldwell, Liberia. Moved to Cape Palmas, 1834. Does not appear in the record.

53. Harman, George Thomas (son of Nathan and Comfort Greene): Freeborn resident of Somerset Co., stated to be 12 at departure. Settled at Caldwell, Liberia. Moved to Cape Palmas, 1834. Agricultural Census, 1839: 1.5 acres. Died of phthisis pulmonalis, 1840.

54. Harman, Henry (son of Nathan and Comfort Greene; also known as Charles): Freeborn resident of Somerset Co., stated to be 11 at departure. Settled at Caldwell, Liberia. Moved to Cape Palmas, 1834. Worked variously as a house carpenter, then teacher in the Episcopal Missions, and as a clerk in 1852. Supporter of Snetter, Sept. 12, 1838. Living in Burwell Minor household, 1840. Appointed justice of the peace, 1845. Signed petition, Jan. 14, 1850. Signed pro-annexation petition, 1851. Living with Elizabeth Becraft, Census 1852. Married Nelly Wilson, Dec. 2, 1852.

55. Harman, John Farmer (son of Nathan and Comfort Greene; also known as James Harman): Freeborn resident of Somerset Co., stated to be 10 at departure. Settled at Caldwell, Liberia. Moved to Cape Palmas, 1834. Living in J. Bowen household, 1839–43. Sent to canvas for the society, NovemBER, 1848. Died in the summer of 1850.

56. Harman, Major (son of Nathan and Comfort Greene; also known as "Curnel" Harman, 1852): Freeborn resident of Somerset Co., stated to be 9 at departure. Settled at Caldwell, Liberia, and reportedly died there of fever, 1833. Appears at Cape Palmas as Curnel Harmon, who drowned, July 24, 1852.

57. Harman, William (son of Nathan and Comfort Greene): Freeborn resident of Somerset Co., stated to be 6 at departure. Settled at Caldwell, Liberia, and reportedly died there of fever, 1833 (Senate Document 150), but later appears at Cape Palmas: Signed petition, Jan. 14, 1850. Died July 5, 1852.

58. Harman*, Nathaniel (son of Nathan and Comfort Greene): Freeborn resident of Somerset Co., stated to be 8 at departure. Settled at Caldwell, Liberia, and died there of fever, 1833.

59. Harman*, Samuel (son of Nathan and Comfort Greene): Freeborn resident of Somerset Co., stated to be 4 at departure. Not on register of arrivals at Monrovia, apparently died at sea.

60. Harman*, Elizabeth (mother of Nathan Greene): Freeborn resident of Somerset Co., stated to be 60 at departure. Settled at Caldwell, Liberia, and died there of old age, 1833.

61. Harper*, Stepney (husband of Ann Harper): Purchased himself from Wm. Franklin Harper, of Caroline Co.; resident of Caroline Co., a blacksmith, stated to be 50 at departure. Settled at Caldwell, Liberia, died of anasarca there, 1838.

62. Harper*, Ann (wife of Stepney Harper): Bought by her husband from George Read; resident of Caroline Co., stated to be 45 at departure. Settled at Caldwell, Liberia, died of consumption there, 1842.

63. Harper*, Lafayette (son of Stepney Harper): Freeborn resident of Caroline Co., stated to be 8 at departure. Settled at Caldwell, Liberia, and living there, 1843.

64. Harper*, Julia Ann (daughter of Stepney Harper): Freeborn resident of Caroline Co., stated to be 6 months at departure. Settled at Caldwell, Liberia, and died of fever there, 1833.

65. Hayes*, John (single): Freeborn resident of Baltimore Co., a gardener, stated to be 22 at departure. Settled at Caldwell, Liberia. Moved away from Liberia at uncertain date.

66. Jackson, Thomas (husband of Milly; later married Ann Mariah): Freed by William Ritchie of Frederick Co., resident of Baltimore, a brickmaker, stated to be 40 at departure. Settled at Caldwell, Liberia. Moved to Cape Palmas, 1834. Worked in the colony as a mason, then a farmer. Signed open letter, Oct. 11, 1834. Elected vice agent, 1835. Frequent letter writer. Appointed magistrate, 1837–48, and auctioneer, 1837. Signed petition, June 15, 1836. Visited U.S., 1838. Manager of the Public Farm, 1839. Left the Methodist Church to join the Episcopal, 1847. Cultivated 3 acres, 1848. Signed petition, December, 1849. Supporter of Annexation Club, 1851. Died of unrecorded cause, June 14 or 15, 1852.

67. Jackson*, Milly (wife of Thomas Jackson): Freed by John P. Thomson, of Frederick Co., resident of Baltimore, a seamstress, age at departure unstated. Settled at Caldwell, Liberia, and died there of unknown cause, 1834.

68. Johnson*, William (single): Freed by Wm. George Read of Baltimore Co., 1832, to emigrate resident of Baltimore Co., a farmer, stated to be 16 at departure. Settled at Monrovia, and died there of unknown cause, 1839.

69. Jones*, Jonathan Morris (single; also called George Jones): Freed by Lucretia Jones of Somerset Co.; resident of Somerset Co., a farmer, stated to be 23 at departure. Settled at Caldwell, Liberia, and died there of fever, 1833.

70. Jones*, Violet (single, mother of several children): Freed by Sarah Landreth of Somerset Co., 1831; resident of Somerset Co., stated to be 40 at departure. Settled at Caldwell, Liberia, and died there of fever, 1833.

71. Jones*, Ann (daughter of Violet Jones): Freed by Sarah Landreth of Somerset Co., 1831; resident of Somerset Co., stated to be 18 at departure. Settled at Caldwell, Liberia, and died there of consumption, 1840.

72. Jones*, William Henry (son of Violet Jones): Freed by Sarah Landreth of Somerset Co., 1831; resident of Somerset Co., stated to be 15 at departure. Settled at Caldwell, Liberia, and living there in 1843.

73. Jones*, Stephen W. (son of Violet Jones): Freed by Sarah Landreth of Somerset Co., 1831; resident of Somerset Co., stated to be 9 at departure. Settled at Caldwell, Liberia, and living there in 1843.

74. Jones*, Lucretia E. (daughter of Violet Jones): Freed by Sarah Landreth of Somerset Co., 1831; resident of Somerset Co., stated to be 10 at departure. Settled at Caldwell, Liberia, and living there in 1843.

75. Jones, Elijah R. C. (son of Violet Jones): Freed by Sarah Landreth of Somerset Co., 1831; resident of Somerset Co., stated to be 3 at departure. Settled at Caldwell, Liberia, and reportedly died there of fever, 1833.

76. Jones*, Spencer (husband of Lucy Jones): Freed by Col. William Jones of Somerset Co., 1832, to emigrate; resident of Somerset Co., a farmer, stated to be 45 at departure. Settled at Caldwell, Liberia, and died there of "decline," 1841.

77. Jones*, Lucy (wife of Spencer Jones; also called Lucretia Jones): Freed by Col. William Jones of Somerset Co., 1832, to emigrate; resident of Somerset Co., stated to be 40 at departure. Settled at Caldwell, Liberia, and died there of "decline," 1842.

78. Jones*, Sally (daughter of Spencer Jones; also called Sarah Jones): Freed by Col. William Jones of Somerset Co., 1832, to emigrate; resident of Somerset Co., stated to be 25 at departure. Settled at Caldwell, Liberia, and living there in 1843.

79. Jones*, Leah (daughter of Spencer Jones): Freed by Col. William Jones of Somerset Co., 1832, to emigrate; resident of Somerset Co., stated to be 25 at departure. Settled at Caldwell, Liberia, and died there of "decline," 1838.

80. Jones*, Mariah (daughter of Spencer Jones): Freed by Col. William Jones of Somerset Co., 1832, to emigrate; resident of Somerset Co., stated to be 20 at departure. Settled at Caldwell, Liberia, and living there in 1843.

81. Jones*, Tanner (son of Spencer Jones): Freed by Col. William Jones of Somerset Co., 1832, to emigrate; resident of Somerset Co., stated to be 16 at departure. Settled at Caldwell, Liberia, and living there in 1843.

82. Jones*, Eliza Jane (daughter of Spencer Jones): Freed by Col. William Jones of Somerset Co., 1832, to emigrate; resident of Somerset Co., stated to be 11 at departure. Settled at Caldwell, Liberia, and living there in 1843.

83. Jones*, Charles (son of Spencer Jones): Freed by Col. William Jones of Somerset Co., 1832, to emigrate; resident of Somerset Co., stated to be 9 at departure. Settled at Caldwell, Liberia, and died there of fever, 1833.

84. Jones*, William (son of Spencer Jones): Freed by Col. William Jones of Somerset Co., 1832, to emigrate; resident of Somerset Co., stated to be 9 at departure. Settled at Caldwell, Liberia, and died there of fever, 1833.

85. Jones*, Edward (son of Spencer Jones): Freed by Col. William Jones of Somerset Co., 1832, to emigrate; resident of Somerset Co., stated to be 7 at departure. Settled at Caldwell, Liberia, and died there of fever, 1833.

86. Jones*, Washington (son of Spencer Jones): Freed by Col. William Jones of Somerset Co., 1832, to emigrate; resident of Somerset Co., stated to be 4 at departure. Settled at Caldwell, Liberia, and died there of fever, 1833.

87. Jones*, Robert (son of Spencer Jones): Freed by Col. William Jones of Somerset Co., 1832, to emigrate; resident of Somerset Co., stated to be 4 at departure. Settled at Caldwell, Liberia, and died there of fever, 1833.

88. Jones*, Margaret (daughter of Spencer Jones): Freed by Col. William Jones of Somerset Co., 1832, to emigrate; resident of Somerset Co., stated to be 2 at departure. Settled at Caldwell, Liberia, and died there of fever, 1833.

89. Kiah*, James (husband of Charlotte Kiah): Freeborn resident of Baltimore, a sawyer, stated to be 26 at departure. Settled at Caldwell, Liberia, and died there by drowning, 1837.

90. Kiah*, Charlotte (wife of James Kiah): Freeborn resident of Baltimore, stated to

be 19 at departure. Settled at Caldwell, Liberia. Moved to Sierra Leone to marry, 1836.

91. Lee, Nathan (husband of Delia Lee): Freed by James Sewell of Elkton to emigrate; resident of Cecil Co., a farmer, stated to be 32 at departure. Settled at Caldwell, Liberia. Moved to Cape Palmas, 1834. Signed open letter, Oct. 11, 1834. Married Julia Ann Holland, June 1, 1835. Elected Counselor, 1835 and 1840. Letter writer: July 5, 1838. Agricultural Census, 1839: .5 acre. Died of consumption, April 16, 1842.

92. Lee*, Delia (wife of Nathan Lee): Freed by James Sewell of Elkton to emigrate; resident of Elkton, Cecil Co., a houseworker, stated to be 29 at departure. Settled at Caldwell, Liberia, and died of fever there, 1833.

93. Lee, James (son of Nathan Lee; deaf and dumb): Freed by James Sewell of Elkton to emigrate; resident of Elkton, Cecil Co., stated to be 13 at departure. Settled at Caldwell, Liberia. Moved to Cape Palmas, 1834.

94. Lee, Sylvia (daughter of Nathan Lee; later called Sylvia Tubman): Freed by Jas. Sewell, of Elkton, Cecil Co., to emigrate; resident of Cecil Co., stated to be 11 at departure. Settled at Caldwell, Liberia. Moved to Cape Palmas, 1834. In 1838, living with J. Stewart family. Married Steven Tubman, Nov. 17, 1842. Died before November, 1852.

95. Lee, Charles A. (son of Nathan Lee): Freed by James Sewell of Elkton to emigrate; resident of Elkton, Cecil Co., stated to be 9 at departure. Settled at Caldwell, Liberia. Moved to Cape Palmas, 1834. Living in Francis Burns household, 1839. Living in John Harris household, 1843. Agricultural Census 1848: 2 acres. Census 1849, listed as a seaman. Signed petition, Jan. 14, 1850. Does not appear in the record afterward.

96. Lee*, William Jefferson (son of Nathan Lee): Freed by James Sewell of Elkton to emigrate; resident of Elkton, Cecil Co., stated to be 5 at departure. Settled at Caldwell, Liberia, died of fever there, 1833.

97. Littleton*, Leah (daughter of Ann A. Fountain): Freed by Thomas Fountain of Somerset Co. in 1815; resident of Somerset Co., stated to be 25 at departure. Settled at Caldwell, Liberia, and died there of diseased lungs, 1837.

98. McBride*, William Thomas (associated with Winder family): Freeborn resident of Somerset Co. a farmer, stated to be 20 at departure. Settled at Caldwell, Liberia, and died there of fever, 1833.

99. McBride*, Azariah (adopted son of Elizabeth Winder, the child of a black father and white mother; also called Zachariah): Freeborn resident of Somerset Co., stated to be 3 at departure. Settled at Caldwell, Liberia.

100. Middleton*, Bill (husband of Rachel Middleton): Freed by Truss. Poor, of Chester Co. Penna., after period of term slavery beginning in 1812; resident of Elkton, Cecil Co., a farmer, stated to be 24 at departure. Settled at Caldwell, Liberia, died of unknown cause there, 1834.

101. Middleton*, Rachel (wife of Bill Middleton): Bought by her father from Samuel Phillips, of Elkton, Cecil Co., stated to be 18 at departure. Settled at Caldwell, Liberia, died of "decline" there, 1838.

102. Minor, Burwell (husband of Mary Minor; later married Mary Dixon): Status uncertain, resident of Virginia, a farmer, stated to be 26 at departure. Settled at Monrovia. Moved to Cape Palmas on the *Ann*, 1834. Signed open letter, Oct. 11, 1834. In 1838, married to Mary Dixon. Signed petition against Thomson, Dec. 2, 1837. Elected Treasurer, 1839. Letter writer: Jan. 20, 1846. Worked mainly as a rough carpenter, then as a laborer by 1849. Does not appear in the record afterward.

103. Minor*, Mary (wife of Burwell Minor): Status uncertain, resident of Virginia. Settled at Monrovia and died there before 1834.

104. Nutter*, Dover (husband of Sarah): Freed by Samuel Parker of Somerset Co., a

carpenter, stated to be 62 at departure. Settled at Caldwell, Liberia, died of "decline" there, 1836.

105. Nutter*, Sarah (wife of Dover Nutter): Freed by Matthias Cosden of Somerset Co. Settled at Caldwell, Liberia, died of "decline" there, 1837.

106. Nutter*, Charlotte (daughter of Dover Nutter): Freeborn resident of Somerset Co., stated to be 17 at departure. Settled at Caldwell, Liberia, and living there, 1843.

107. Nutter*, Noah (son of Dover Nutter): Freeborn resident of Somerset Co., stated to be 14 at departure. Settled at Caldwell, Liberia, and died of pleurisy there, 1840.

108. Nutter*, Margaretta (daughter of Dover Nutter): Freeborn resident of Somerset Co., stated to be 12 at departure. Settled at Caldwell, Liberia, and died of unknown cause there, 1835.

109. Nutter*, Handy (son of Dover Nutter): Freeborn resident of Somerset Co., stated to be 6 at departure. Settled at Caldwell, Liberia, and died of pleurisy there, 1839.

110. Nutter*, Emanuel (husband of Leah Nutter): Freeborn resident of Somerset Co., a shoemaker, stated to be 34 at departure. Settled at Caldwell, Liberia, and living there in 1843.

111. Nutter*, Leah (wife of Emanuel Nutter): Freeborn resident of Somerset Co., stated to be 30 at departure. Settled at Caldwell, Liberia, and died there of unknown cause, 1838.

112. Nutter*, Rhoda (daughter of Emanuel Nutter): Freeborn resident of Somerset Co., stated to be 13 at departure. Settled at Caldwell, Liberia, and living there in 1843.

113. Nutter*, Ann (daughter of Emanuel Nutter): Freeborn resident of Somerset Co., stated to be 8 at departure. Settled at Caldwell, Liberia, and living there in 1843.

114. Nutter*, Zedekiah (son of Emanuel Nutter): Freeborn resident of Somerset Co., stated to be 5 at departure. Settled at Caldwell, Liberia, and living there in 1843.

115. Nutter*, Mary (daughter of Emanuel Nutter): Freeborn resident of Somerset Co., stated to be 2 at departure. Settled at Caldwell, Liberia, and living there in 1843.

116. Pembleton*, Edmund (single): Freed by Mary Gordon of Talbot Co., resident of Caroline Co., a farmer, stated to be 27 at departure. Sent to Liberia to observe and make a report after a stay of six months. Returned to U.S. in 1833.

117. Polk*, Amie (mother of William Polk and others; sister of Dover Nutter): Purchased by her father in 1815; resident of Salisbury, Somerset Co., Md. Widowed before emigration; stated to be 40 at departure. Settled at Caldwell, Liberia.

118. Polk, William Townsend (son of Amie Polk; husband of Maria): Purchased by his grandfather, resident of Somerset Co., a farmer, stated to be 20 at departure. Moved to Cape Palmas on the *Ann*, 1834. Signed open letter, Oct. 11, 1834. Elected Register, Mar. 2, 1835. Married Maria White, Nov. 22, 1835. Letter writer: Nov. 29, 1835; Feb. 5, July 8, and Aug. 30, 1836. Signed petition, June 15, 1836. Died from an ulcer, May 27, 1837.

119. Polk, Mary (daughter of Amie): Purchased by her grandfather; resident of Somerset Co., stated to be 18 at departure. Settled at Caldwell, Liberia. Moved to Cape Palmas in 1834. Died of "female disease" in 1836.

120. Polk, Nancy (daughter of Amie): Freeborn resident of Somerset Co., stated to be 14 at departure. Settled at Caldwell, Liberia. Moved to Cape Palmas in 1834. Died of unrecorded cause in 1840.

121. Polk, Matilda (daughter of Amie): Freeborn resident of Somerset Co., stated to be 12 at departure. Settled at Caldwell, Liberia. Reportedly moved to Cape Palmas in 1834, but does not appear in the record.

122. Price*, James (single): Freeborn resident of Somerset Co., a clergyman, of uncertain age at departure. Sailed to visit Liberia and make a report back home (which was apparently not positive.)

123. Prout, Thomas (Single, brother of Jacob W. Prout): Freeborn resident of Baltimore, stated to be 13 at departure. Settled at Monrovia. Reportedly moved to Cape Palmas, 1840, but does not appear in the record.

124. Prout*, Jane (Single, sister of Jacob W. Prout): Freeborn resident of Baltimore, stated to be 15 at departure. Settled at Monrovia, and died there of fever, 1833.

125. Reese*, James (single): Freeborn resident of Somerset Co., a boot and shoe maker, stated to be 22 at departure. Settled at Monrovia. Returned to U.S., 1834.

126. Savage*, George Waters (single): Freed by Susan Waters of Somerset Co., 1831, resident of Somerset Co., a farmer, stated to be 24 at departure. Settled at Caldwell, Liberia, and died there of unknown cause, 1835.

127. Schockley*, Isaiah (single): Freeborn resident of Somerset Co., a farmer, stated to be 27 at departure. Settled at Caldwell, Liberia, and living there in 1843.

128. Sharpe*, Laura Jane (associated with Stepney Harper family): Freeborn resident of Caroline Co., a housekeeper, stated to be 16 at departure. Settled at Caldwell, Liberia, and living there, 1843.

129. Smith*, Ibby (mother of Jonathan S. Smith): Freed by Sarah Landreth of Somerset Co., 1831; resident of Somerset Co., stated to be 28 at departure. Settled at Caldwell, Liberia, and living there in 1843.

130. Smith*, Jonathan S. (son of Ibby Smith): Freed by Sarah Landreth of Somerset Co., 1831; resident of Somerset Co., stated to be 7 at departure. Settled at Caldwell, Liberia, and died there of fever, 1833.

131. Stratton*, Lucinda K. (mother of unnamed infant): Freed by Rev. Wm. B. Stratton of Worcester Co., 1832, to emigrate; resident of Worcester Co., stated to be 16 at departure. Settled at Caldwell, Liberia, and died there of unknown cause, 1836.

132. Stratton*, Unnamed infant (child of Lucinda Stratton): Freed by Rev. Wm. B. Stratton of Worcester Co., 1832, to emigrate; resident of Worcester Co., stated to be 5 months at departure. Settled at Caldwell, Liberia, and died there of fever, 1833.

133. Sturges*, Shadriack (single): Freed by John Sturges of Worcester Co., 1832, to emigrate; resident of Worcester Co., a farmer, stated to be 45 at departure. Settled at Caldwell, Liberia, and died there of decline, 1837.

134. Tippett*, Stephen (single): Freed by Lucretia Tippett of St. Mary's Co.; resident of St. Mary's Co., a farmer, stated to be 19 at departure. Settled at Caldwell, Liberia, and died of unknown cause there, 1837.

135. Welsh, Isaac (husband of Martha): Freed by George W. Ford of Baltimore, to emigrate; resident of Elkton, Cecil Co., a farmer, stated to be 33 at departure. Settled at Caldwell, Liberia. Moved to Cape Palmas on the *Ann,* 1834. Elected Treasurer, Mar. 2, 1835. Died about April, 1835.

136. Welsh, Martha (wife of Isaac Welsh; also called Patty): Freed by George W. Ford of Baltimore to emigrate; resident of Elkton, Cecil Co., a houseworker, stated to be 37 at departure. Settled at Caldwell, Liberia. Moved to Cape Palmas, 1834. Living with Scotland family, 1837; N. Edmondson family, 1838; C. Scotland family, 1839. Died Mar. 14, 1842.

137. White, Willoughby (husband of Sarah White): Freeborn resident of Somerset Co., a farmer, stated to be 46 at departure. Settled at Caldwell, Liberia. Moved to Cape Palmas on the *Ann,* 1834. Elected Sheriff, Mar. 2, 1835. Died of unrecorded cause, about April, 1835.

138. White, Sarah (wife of Willoughby White): Freeborn resident of Somerset Co., a housekeeper, stated age at departure unrecorded. Settled at Caldwell, Liberia. Reportedly moved to Cape Palmas, 1834, but does not appear in the record.

139. White, Mary A. (daughter of Willoughby; mother of Ann; later known as Mary Ann Fletcher): Freeborn, stated to be 12 at departure. Settled at Caldwell, Liberia. Moved to Cape Palmas, 1834. Living with Wm. Polk family, 1837, 1839 and 1843. Married Dempsey R. Fletcher, 1843. Left Methodist Church to join Episcopal Church, 1847. Resident of the colony, November, 1852.

140. White, Maria (daughter of Willoughby White): Freeborn resident of Somerset Co., a housekeeper, stated to be 14 at departure. Settled at Caldwell, Liberia. Moved to Cape Palmas, 1834. Married William Polk, Nov. 22, 1835. A widow by 1838, living with Mary White. Does not appear in the record afterward.

141. White, Amy (daughter of Willoughby White): Freeborn resident of Somerset Co., stated to be 10 at departure. Settled at Caldwell, Liberia. Reportedly moved to Cape Palmas, 1834, but does not appear in the record.

142. White, Catherine (daughter of Willoughby White): Freeborn resident of Somerset Co., stated to be 6 at departure. Settled at Caldwell, Liberia. Moved to Cape Palmas, 1834. Living with Maria Polk, 1840 and 1843. Married Jonathan W. Cooper, April 27, 1852.

143. White, Eleanor (daughter of Willoughby White; possibly also called Eleanor Murray): Freeborn resident of Somerset Co., stated to be 4 at departure. Settled at Caldwell, Liberia. Moved to Cape Palmas, 1834. Living with William Reynolds family as Eleanor Murray in 1838. Does not appear in the record afterward.

144. White*, Hester (daughter of Willoughby White): Freeborn resident of Somerset Co., stated to be 8 at departure. Settled at Caldwell, Liberia, and died of fever there, 1833.

145. Whittington*, James (single): Status uncertain; resident of Worcester Co., a farmer, age unstated at departure. Settled at Monrovia. Returned to the U.S., 1833.

146. Winder*, Leah (widow; mother of Elizabeth & John Winder): Freed by H. Gale, Somerset Co., in 1812; resident of Somerset Co., stated to be 45 at departure. Settled at Caldwell, Liberia, and died there of unknown cause, 1839.

147. Winder*, Elizabeth (daughter of Leah Winder): Freed by H. Gale, Somerset Co., in 1812; resident of Somerset Co., stated to be 25 at departure. Settled at Caldwell, Liberia, and died there of diseased lungs, 1837.

148. Winder*, John H. (son of Leah Winder): Freeborn resident of Somerset Co., a farmer, stated to be 20 at departure. Settled at Caldwell, Liberia, and died there by drowning, 1835.

149. Wright*, Edward (single): Freed by William George Read of Baltimore Co. to emigrate, a farmer, stated to be 16 at departure. Settled at Monrovia. Died there of anasarca, 1834.

INDIVIDUALS SENT BY THE MARYLAND STATE COLONIZATION SOCIETY
TO CAPE PALMAS

Brig ANN, left Baltimore, November 27, 1833, arrived at Cape Palmas, February 11, 1834:
1. Cassell, William (husband of Frances Cassell): Freeborn, resident of Baltimore, a barber and saddler, stated to be 25 at departure. Signed open letter, Oct. 11, 1834 (but expressed desire to return to U.S.) Returned to America on the *Bourne*, January, 1835. Subsequently studied law in Baltimore in the office of Hugh Davey Evans. Moved back to Cape Palmas again on Brig *Amazon*, February, 1848, with a commission as Chief Justice. Letter writer: Nov. 23, 1848. Signed petition, April, 1849. Visited U.S. in 1850. Appointed Gidu magistrate, 1852. Elected to committee to frame the constitution, February, 1852. Went to Baltimore with William Prout to negotiate independence, 1853–4.

Participated in deposing William Prout, December, 1855. Died of liver disease, April 24, 1856.

2. Cassell, Frances (wife of William Cassell): Freeborn, resident of Baltimore, a housewife, stated to be 31 at departure. Returned to America on the *Bourne,* January, 1835. Died in Baltimore.

3. Cassell, Charles H. (son of William and Frances Cassell): Freeborn, resident of Baltimore, stated to be 2 at departure. Returned to America on the *Bourne,* January, 1835. Came to Cape Palmas a second time: 1847, *Packet,* Voyage B. Worked for McGill, Bros., 1847. Living with his father in Josh Stewart's household, 1849. Resident of the colony, November, 1852.

4. Dellanot, Amelia (sister of Louisa Stewart; also called Amelia or Pamela Burns): Freeborn resident of Baltimore, a seamstress, stated to be 15 at departure. Married Francis Burns at Harper, Nov. 1, 1836. Moved to Monrovia with him, then returned several years later to Cape Palmas. Does not appear in the record after 1849.

5. Gross, Jacob (husband of Rossanna): Freed by John Walker of Frederick Co. to emigrate, resident of Frederick Co., a farmer, age at departure unknown. Signed open letter, Oct. 11, 1834. Elected selectman, Mar. 2, 1835; vice agent, 1837 and 1839. Signed petition, June 15, 1836. Agricultural Census, 1839: 1 acre; 1848: 3.25 acres. Signed petition, April, 1849; Jan. 14, 1850. Died in summer of 1850.

6. Gross, Rossanna (wife of Jacob Gross; also called Rosetta Gross): Freed by John Walker of Frederick Co. to emigrate, resident of Frederick Co., a farm wife, stated to be 33 at departure. Freed by John Walker of Frederick Co. to emigrate. Resident of the colony, November, 1852.

7. Gross, Clarissa (daughter of Jacob Gross): Freed by John Walker of Frederick Co. to emigrate, resident of Frederick Co., stated to be 10 at departure. Married Leonard Sprigg/Gant, May 4, 1842. Living in mother's household, 1852.

8. Gross, Margaretta (daughter of Jacob Gross): Freed by John Walker of Frederick Co. to emigrate, resident of Frederick Co., stated to be 8 at departure. Does not appear in the record after 1848.

9. Gross, Nancy (daughter of Jacob and Rosanna Gross): Freed by John Walker of Frederick Co. to emigrate, resident of Frederick Co., stated to be 5 at departure. Living in mother's household, 1852.

10. Gross, Caroline (daughter of Jacob and Rosanna Gross): Freed by John Walker of Frederick Co. to emigrate, resident of Frederick Co., stated to be 3 at departure. Married Wesley Harland, May 18, 1848.

11. Gross, Rossanna (daughter of Jacob and Rosanna Gross): Freed by John Walker of Frederick Co. to emigrate, resident of Frederick Co., stated to be 8 months old at departure. Does not appear in the record.

12. Jones, Jonathan (single): Freed, resident of Washington, D.C., a boatman, stated to be 35 at departure. Does not appear in the record.

13. Nelson, Eden (single; also called Eden Harding): Freeborn, resident of Baltimore, a rough house carpenter, stated to be 19 at departure. Signed open letter, Oct. 11, 1834. Does not appear in the record afterward.

14. Stewart, Joshua H. (husband of Louisa Stewart): Freeborn, resident of Baltimore, a barber, tailor, and cooper, stated to be 24 at departure. Signed open letter, Oct. 11, 1834. Appointed auctioneer, March 1832; magistrate, March 1837. Signed petition, June 15, 1836. Visited U.S. in 1838. Elected Register, 1839. Appointed collector of customs, 1846. Frequent letter writer: July 8, 1847; June 12, 1848; April 28, 1849. Signed petition, April, 1849. Appointed Gidu Magistrate, 1852. Elected vice agent, 1852.

15. Stewart, Louisa (wife of Joshua Stewart; also called Mary Louise Stewart): Freeborn, resident of Baltimore, stated to be 23 at departure. Worked in the colony as a seamstress. Resident of the colony, November, 1852.

16. Stewart, Joseph (son of Joshua and Louisa Stewart): Freeborn, resident of Baltimore, stated to be 1 at departure. Died of dysentery, June 10, 1834, the first American settler to die at Cape Palmas.

17. Stewart, James (single, brother of Joshua; later husband of Lydia): Freeborn, resident of Baltimore, stated to be 19 at departure. Signed open letter, Oct. 11, 1834. Married Lydia Fletcher at Cape Palmas, about 1836. Signed petition against Thomson, Dec. 2, 1837. Supporter of Snetter, Sept. 12, 1838. Died of phthisis pulmonalis, 1841.

18. Thompson, Nicholas (single): Freed by W. W. Ritchie to emigrate, a farmer, stated to be 40 at departure. Signed open letter, Oct. 11, 1834 (but expressed desire to return to U.S.) Does not appear in the record after 1834.

Brig BOURNE, left Baltimore, December 14, 1834, arrived at Cape Palmas, January 24, 1835:

1. Blake, Rachel (single; later married John Ross; also called Rachel or Mary Ross): Freeborn resident of Anne Arundel Co., stated to be 21 at departure. Listed as the wife of John Ross, Census 1848. Resident of the colony, November, 1852.

2. Chew, Caesar (husband of Patience Chew): Freed by John Wood, of Calvert Co.; resident of Anne Arundel Co., a farmer, stated to be 52 at departure. Letter writer: Sept. 2, 1835. Supported Snetter, Sept. 12, 1838. Worked variously as a farmer and laborer. Agricultural Census, 1839: .5 acre; 1848, 1.25 acres. Living in Benjamin Brown household, 1849. Not in the record afterwards.

3. Chew, Patience (wife of Caesar Chew): Freeborn resident of Anne Arundel Co., stated to be 31 at departure. Not in the record after 1843.

4. Chew, Henrietta (daughter of Caesar Chew; also called Henrietta Taylor): Freeborn resident of Anne Arundel Co., stated to be 11 at departure. Not in the record after 1843.

5. Chew, William (son of Caesar Chew): Freeborn resident of Anne Arundel Co., stated to be 8 at departure. Not in the record after 1840.

6. Coates, Job (husband of Fanny Coates): Free resident of Anne Arundel Co., stated to be 33 at departure. Elected to Committee on New Emigrants, March, 1837. Signed petition against Thomson, Dec. 2, 1837. Supporter of Snetter, Sept. 12, 1838. Worked variously as a sawyer and farmer. Refused appointment as Roadmaster, 1839. Agricultural Census, 1839: 3.75 acres. Signed petition, April, 1849. Listed in 1852 Census as a farmer.

7. Coates, Fanny (wife of Job Coates): Freed by Dr. Lawrence of Anne Arundel Co.; resident of Anne Arundel Co., stated to be 30 at departure. Living in the colony, November, 1852.

8. Dentley, Sally (single; also called Sarah Dentley): Freeborn resident of Calvert Co., stated to be 16 at departure. Living with Thomas Brown, 1837; with James Stewart family, 1838–9; with Maria Polk household, 1840. Died of hysteria, 1840.

9. Hall, William (son of Mary Watkins?; also called William Watkins): Freed by John Wood, of Calvert Co.; resident of Calvert Co., stated to be 12 at departure. Worked in the colony as a laborer, then a seaman. Living with Jeremiah Hardy, 1839; in George Hardy household, 1843. Not in the record after 1849.

10. Hance, Alexander (husband of Julia Hance): Freeborn resident of Calvert Co., a farmer, stated to be 40 at departure. Worked in the colony as a rough carpenter and farmer. Elected selectman, Mar. 2, 1835; councilor, 1837–8–9. Appointed justice of the peace, 1845. Letter writer: Mar. 14 and Aug. 30, 1835; Feb. 10, 1836; April 7 (twice), July 6

and 10, 1838. Visited U.S. in 1837–8, returned on *Niobe*. Agricultural Census, 1839: 2.25 acres. Left Methodist Church to join Episcopal Church, 1847. Sent to U.S. to recruit emigrants, 1848, but died in Baltimore.

11. Hance, Julia (wife of Alexander Hance): Freeborn resident of Calvert Co., stated to be 32 at departure. Left Methodist Church to join Episcopal Church, 1847. Resident of the colony, November, 1852.

12. Hance, William (son of Alexander Hance): Freeborn resident of Calvert Co., stated to be 1 at departure. Resident of the colony, November, 1852, listed as a carpenter.

13. Hance, John (son of Alexander Hance): Freeborn resident of Calvert Co., stated to be 2 months old at departure. Died during acclimation.

14. Hardy, George (husband of Dianah Hardy): Freed by Cosmo Sunderland, of Calvert Co.; a farmer, stated to be 26 at departure. Worked in the colony as a carpenter and farmer. Elected to Committee on New Emigrants, 1837–8. Supporter of Snetter, Sept. 12, 1838. Agricultural Census, 1839: 1.25 acres. Appointed Inspector of Shingles, 1845. Signed petition, April, 1849. Signed petition, Jan. 14, 1850. Died before November, 1852.

15. Hardy, Dianah (wife of George Hardy): Freed by Cosmo Sunderland, of Calvert Co.; stated to be 24 at departure. Letter writer: Sept. 4, 1837. Died before November, 1852

16. Hardy, David (son of George Hardy; also called James Hardy): Freed by Cosmo Sunderland, of Calvert Co.; stated to be 5 at departure. Does not appear in the record after 1849.

17. Hardy, Sophia J. (daughter of George Hardy; also called Sophia Davis): Freed by Cosmo Sunderland, of Calvert Co.; stated to be 4 at departure. Appears to have married John H. Davis, 1848 or 1849. Resident of the colony, November, 1852

18. Hardy, Mary Ann (daughter of George Hardy): Freed by Cosmo Sunderland, of Calvert Co.; stated to be 8 months old at departure. Died before September 1836 of unrecorded cause.

19. Hardy, Jeremiah (husband of Juliet Hardy, then Louisa Hall, then Mary Watkins): Freed by Cosmo Sunderland, of Calvert Co.; stated to be 26 at departure. Worked in the colony as a laborer, farmer, and shinglemaker. Married Louisa Hull ("Lucinda Hall") May 11, 1835; then married Mary Watkins, May 31, 1837. Supporter of Snetter, Sept. 12, 1838. Letter writer: Feb. 14, 1843. Signed petition, April, 1849. Listed in 1852 Census as a farmer.

20. Hardy*, Juliet (wife of Jeremiah Hardy): Freeborn resident of Calvert Co., stated to be 25 at departure. Died at sea, along with a newborn infant.

21. Hardy, Ellen Mary (daughter of Jeremiah Hardy; also called Ellen Murray): Freeborn resident of Calvert Co., stated to be 9 at departure. Living with William Reynolds family, under new name, 1837 and 1839–43. Living alone, 1848. Does not appear in the record afterwards.

22. Hardy, Mary Jane (daughter of Jeremiah Hardy): Freeborn, resident of Calvert Co., stated to be 7 at departure. Living with George Hardy family, 1837. Does not appear in the record afterwards.

23. Hardy, William (son of Jeremiah Hardy): Freeborn resident of Calvert Co., stated to be 5 at departure. Does not appear in the record.

24. Hardy, Juliet (daughter of Jeremiah Hardy): Freeborn resident of Calvert Co., stated to be 3 at departure. Does not appear in the record.

25. Hardy*, unnamed infant (child of Jeremiah and Juliet Hardy): Born and died at sea, along with mother.

26. Harris, John (husband of Jane Harris; later married Mary J. Scotland; also called Alexander Harris): Freed by Capt. John Wood, of Anne Arundel Co.; resident of Calvert Co., a farmer, stated to be 31 at departure. Worked in the colony as a house carpenter.

Married Mary Jane Scotland, Nov. 14, 1836, after his first wife's death. Letter writer: Mar. 2 and 11, 1835; Sept. 3, 1836; July 5, 1838. Signed petition against Thomson, Dec. 2, 1837. Supporter of Snetter, Sept. 12, 1838. Died of heart disease, Jan. 15, 1848.

27. Harris, Jane (wife of John Harris): Freed by Benjamin Sheppard, of Anne Arundel Co.; resident of Calvert Co., stated to be 25 at departure. Died April 15, 1836, of complications from childbirth.

28. Harris, Robert (son of John Harris): Freed by Benjamin Sheppard, of Anne Arundel Co.; resident of Calvert Co., stated to be 4 at departure. Died before September, 1836.

29. Harris, Fielder (son of John Harris): Freed by Benjamin Sheppard, of Anne Arundel Co.; resident of Calvert Co., stated to be 2 at departure. Died before September, 1836.

30. Harris, Maria (possibly sister of John Harris; also appears to have been called Maria Brown): Freed by Alfred Weeks, of Anne Arundel Co.; resident of Calvert Co., stated to be 12 at departure. Living with George Hardy's family in SeptemBER 1836, and September 1837. Died of the effects of an ulcer, Nov. 28, 1837.

31. Harris, Mordecai (possibly brother of John Harris): Freed by John Wood, of Calvert Co.; a farmer, stated to be 28 at departure. Worked in the colony as a sawyer and laborer. Signed petition against Thomson, Dec. 2, 1837. Elected selectman, 1838. Signed petition against Thomson, Dec. 2, 1837. Agricultural Census, 1839: .75 acre. Not in record after 1843.

32. Harvey, Nancy (related to Mary Watkins; also called Ellen Harvey, 1852): Freed by John Wood, of Calvert Co.; resident of Calvert Co., stated to be 16 at departure. Living with Asbury Wilson, 1838; with Jeremiah Hardy family, 1839 and 1843. Married to Isaac Bowen, Census 1848. Died Aug. 14, 1852.

33. Harvey, George H. (son of Mary Watkins): Freed by John Wood, of Calvert Co.; resident of Calvert Co., a farmer, stated to be 15 at departure. Worked in the colony as a laborer, then seaman. Signed petition against Thomson, Dec. 2, 1837. Supported Snetter, Sept. 12, 1838. Living with Henry Duncan family, 1838; with James Stewart family, 1839. Married Sarah Howard, Oct. 22, 1840. Visited U.S. in 1843. Letter writer: Jan. 15, 1844. Signed petition, December, 1849. Died before November, 1852.

34. Hawkins, William H. (single; later married Ann Scotland): Freeborn resident of Anne Arundel Co., a sawyer and farmer, stated to be 35 at departure. Worked in the colony as a carpenter, then specialized as a cooper. Married Ann Scotland , Feb. 16, 1837. Elected High Sheriff, 1837–8. Signed petition against Thomson, Dec. 2, 1837. Letter writer: Mar. 15, 1835; April 27, 1838. Appointed auctioneer, 1838–9. Signed petitions, Jan. 14, 1850, and August 1851. Listed in 1852 Census as a cooper.

35. Hull, Louisa (mother of Maria; also called Louisa or Lucinda Hardy): Freeborn resident of Allegany Co., a housekeeper, stated to be 25 at departure. Married Jeremiah Hardy at Cape Palmas, May 11, 1835. Died before 1837.

36. Hull, Maria (daughter of Louisa Hull; also called Coates and Hardy): Freeborn resident of Allegany Co., stated to be 2 at departure. Living with Job Coates's family, 1837–49 (as Hull again). Does not appear in the record after 1849.

37. Ireland, Jesse (single; later married Hannah Garns or Duncan): Freed by Dr. Lawrence of Anne Arundel Co.; resident of Anne Arundel Co., a farmer, stated to be 21 at departure. Married Hannah Garns or Duncan, April 9, 1837. Signed petition against Thomson, Dec. 2, 1837. Supporter of Snetter, Sept. 12, 1838. Agricultural Census, 1839: .5 acre. Died before 1849.

38. Moulton, Samuel (husband of Mary Moulton; also called Samuel Morton):

Freeborn resident of Cumberland, Allegany Co., a farmer, stated to be 60 at departure. Worked in the colony as a laborer and farmer. Signed petition against Thomson, Dec. 2, 1837. Died before 1839.

39. Moulton, Mary (wife of Samuel Moulton; also called Mary Morton and Mary Pratt): Freeborn resident of Cumberland, Allegany Co., a housekeeper, stated to be 45 at departure. Married Allen Pratt, March 1840. Died of puerperal peritonitis, 1840.

40. Moulton, Henson (son of Samuel Moulton; also called Henson Morton): Freeborn resident of Cumberland, Allegany Co., a farmer, stated to be 19 at departure. Worked in the colony as a sawyer. Appointed Measurer of Lumber and constable, 1845. Elected councilor, 1848. Signed petition, December, 1849. In 1852 Census, listed as a teacher. Elected to constitution committee, February 1853.

41. Moulton, John Elijah (son of Samuel Moulton; husband of Rachel Moulton; also called John E. Morton): Freeborn resident of Cumberland, Allegany Co., a farmer, stated to be 17 at departure. Appointed teacher of Free School #1, 1845. Letter writer: Nov. 19, 1848. Colonial Register, 1848. Signed petitions, April and December, 1849. Letter writer, April 25, 1849; Sept. 21 and 22, 1851. Listed in 1852 Census as a carpenter.

42. Moulton, James Washington (son of Samuel Moulton; also called James W. Morton): Freeborn resident of Cumberland, Allegany Co., a farmer, stated to be 14 at departure. Signed petition, April, 1849. Listed in 1852 Census as a sawyer.

43. Moulton, Priscilla Ellen (daughter of Samuel Moulton; also called Priscilla E. Morton): Freeborn resident of Cumberland, Allegany Co., stated to be 12 at departure. Died during acclimation.

44. Moulton, Mary Jane (daughter of Samuel Moulton; also called Mary Jane Morton): Freeborn resident of Cumberland, Allegany Co., stated to be 10 at departure. Died during acclimation.

45. Moulton, Susan Ann (daughter of Samuel Moulton; also called Susan Ann Morton): Freeborn resident of Cumberland, Allegany Co., stated to be 6 at departure. Died June, 1842.

46. Moulton, Diana Mariana (daughter of Samuel Moulton; also called Diana M. Morton): Freeborn resident of Cumberland, Allegany Co., stated to be 1 at departure. Died during acclimation.

47. Norris, Levi (husband of Milly Norris): Freeborn resident of Calvert Co., a farmer, stated to be 35 at departure. Letter writer: July 10, 1837. Supporter of Snetter, Sept. 12, 1838. Injured in a cannon blast, about July, 1846, losing one arm. Letter writer: May 3, 1848; July 13 and Oct. 14, 1849. Signed petition, April, 1849; Jan. 14, 1850. Not in record afterwards.

48. Norris, Milly (wife of Levi Norris; also called Amelia Norris): Freed by Cornelia Tauney to emigrate with her free husband; resident of Calvert Co., stated to be 25 at departure. Disabled, with only one arm. Letter writer, late 1835. Not in record after 1849.

49. Norris, Nelson (son of Levi Norris): Freed by Cornelia Tauney to emigrate with his parents; resident of Calvert Co., stated to be 7 at departure. Resident of the colony, November, 1852, listed as a seaman.

50. Norris, Filbert (son of Levi Norris): Freed by Cornelia Tauney to emigrate with his parents; resident of Calvert Co., stated to be 4 at departure. Does not appear in the record after 1843.

51. Norris, Mary Ann (daughter of Levi Norris; also called Sally Norris, 1849): Freed by Cornelia Tauney to emigrate with her parents; resident of Calvert Co., stated to be 9 months old at departure. Living with her brother Nelson, 1852.

52. Quary, Samuel (single): Freed by Cosmo Sunderland of Calvert Co.; resident of Calvert Co., a farmer, stated to be 28 at departure.

53. Ross, John (single): Freed by James Mills of Calvert Co.; resident of Calvert Co., a farmer, stated to be 30 at departure. Worked successively as a farmer, laborer, and ditcher. Signed petition against Thomson, Dec. 2, 1837. Supporter of Snetter, Sept. 12, 1838. Resident of the colony, November, 1852.

54. Scrivener, James (husband of Rachel Scrivener; also called James Scribner): Freeborn resident of Anne Arundel Co., a sawyer and farmer, stated to be 36 at departure. Worked in the colony as a sawyer and farmer at Cape Palmas. Elected vice agent, March 1836; councilor, March 1837. Supporter of Snetter, Sept. 12, 1838. Letter writer: Mar. 4, 1835. Died before Jan. 30, 1839.

55. Scrivener, Rachel (wife of James; m. Isaac Johnson by 1838): Freeborn resident of Anne Arundel Co., stated to be 26 at departure. Agricultural Census, 1839: 1 acre. Resident of the colony, November, 1852.

56. Scrivener, Susan (daughter of James Scrivener): Freeborn resident of Anne Arundel Co., stated to be 3 at departure. Died of fever, Feb. 20, 1835.

57. Scrivener, William (son of James Scrivener): Freeborn resident of Anne Arundel Co., stated to be 11 months old at departure. Died during acclimation.

58. Watkins, Mary (single; also called Mary Hardy): Freed by John Wood, of Calvert Co.; stated to be 33 at departure. Letter writer: Aug. 26, 1835. Married Jeremiah Hardy at Cape Palmas, May 31, 1837. Resident of the colony, November, 1852.

59. Watkins, Richard (related to Mary Watkins): Freed by John Wood, of Calvert Co.; stated to be 15 at departure. Living with J. Hardy, 1839; in George Hardy household, 1843. Mentioned by McGill, Dec. 17, 1847. Married Monica Buchanan, Jan. 11, 1848. Signed petition, April, 1849. Not in record after 1849.

The total number of emigrants sent to Cape Palmas thus far: 77.

Schooner HARMONY, left Baltimore, June 28, 1835, arrived at Cape Palmas August 23, 1835:

1. Buchanan, Monica (single, niece of Mary Ann Simpson): Freed by George D. Parnham of Charles Co.; stated to be 16 at departure. Living with Daniel Banks family, 1838; with Rebecca Gibson family, 1839; with Josh Stewart, 1840; alone, 1843. Married Richard Watkins, Jan. 11, 1848. Not in record after 1849.

2. Contee, Richard (single): Freed by Henry B. Goodwin of Charles Co.; stated to be 26 at departure. Signed petition against Thomson, Dec. 2, 1837. Supporter of Snetter, Sept. 12, 1838. Married Mariah Tubman, 1839. Living with Ambrose Simpson family, alone, 1840. Not in the record after 1843.

3. Gibson, Jacob (husband of Rebecca Gibson): Free resident of Talbot Co., stated to be 45 at departure. Known to have left children in slavery in Maryland. Letter writer: Aug. 31, 1835. Died before March, 1836, of unrecorded cause.

4. Gibson, Rebecca (wife of Jacob Gibson; also called Rebecca Dulany): Free resident of Talbot Co., stated to be 43 at departure. Letter writer, Aug. 31, 1836. Married Wm. Dulaney on Jan. 19, 1837. Letter writer, July 7, 1838; Feb. 1, 1846. Agricultural Census, 1839: .75 acre. Died of unrecorded cause, 1847.

5. Gibson, Joseph T. (son of Jacob Gibson): Free resident of Talbot Co., stated to be 12 at departure. Living with Asbury Wilson, 1838. Lay preacher at Mt. Vaughan, 1847. Principal of the High School there, 1848. Elected councilor, 1851. Letter writer: Feb. 4, 1853. Elected to constitution committee, February 1853. Participated in Boston Drayton's coup, December, 1855, and became lieutenant governor in the new regime. Appointed first superintendent of Maryland County, 1857.

6. Gibson, Mary Ann (daughter of Jacob Gibson; also called Mary Delaney): Free resident of Talbot Co., stated to be 10 at departure. Living with stepfather, Wm. Dulany family, 1838. Does not appear in the record after 1840.

7. Gibson, Samuel (son of Jacob Gibson; also called Samuel Gypson): Free resident of Talbot Co., stated to be 8 at departure. Living with stepfather, Wm. Dulany family, 1838. Died Dec. 6, 1842, by drowning.

8. Gibson, James Henry (son of Jacob Gibson): Free resident of Talbot Co., stated to be 7 at departure. Reported to have died of a head wound, Mar. 25, 1837 (age recorded as 12 years,) but reappears in Census 1848, living with his brother Joseph, and again in Census 1849, employed as an Episcopal mission teacher.

9. Gibson, Garretson (son of Jacob Gibson): Free resident of Talbot Co., stated to be 5 at departure. Living with stepfather, Wm. Dulany family, 1838; with Joseph T. Gibson, 1848–9; with brother R. H. Gibson, Census 1852.

10. Gibson, Louisa (daughter of Jacob Gibson): Free resident of Talbot Co., stated to be 4 at departure. Living with stepfather, Wm. Dulany family, 1838; with Joseph T. Gibson, 1848–9. Living in household of Orphans with Elizabeth Thomson, 1852.

11. Gibson, Ellen (niece of Jacob Gibson): Free resident of Talbot Co., stated to be 8 at departure. Living with Daniel Banks family, 1838; with Caroline Banks, 1839–40. Does not appear in the record after 1843.

12. Hanson, Cecilia Ann (single, related to Ambrose Simpson family): Freed by Henry B. Goodwin of Charles Co.; resident of Charles Co., stated to be 13 at departure. Living with Ambrose Simpson's family in 1837 and 1839. Does not appear in the record after 1839.

13. Scott, William (husband of Caroline C. Scott): Freed by the will of Dr. Hammond of Talbot Co. to emigrate or be sold; resident of Talbot Co., stated to be 21 at departure. Died of unknown cause shortly after arrival.

14. Scott, Caroline Chambers (wife of William Scott; also called Caroline Chambers, then Banks, then Pinkett): Freeborn resident of Talbot Co., age at departure not stated. Married Daniel Banks Feb. 2, 1837. Bore a daughter, Georgiann, April 29, 1837 (conceived out of wedlock). Later married Henry Pinkett. Resident of the colony, November, 1852.

15. Simpson, Ambrose (husband of Mary Ann; also called Lambert Simpson): Freed by George D. Parnham of Charles Co.; stated to be 26 at departure. Worked in the colony as a sawyer and rough carpenter. Letter writer: Sept. 1, 1835. Signed petitions, June 15, 1836, and Dec. 2, 1837. Supporter of Snetter, Sept. 12, 1838. Elected councilor in special election, 1846; re-elected, 1848. Left Methodist Church to join Episcopal Church, 1847. Expelled from the Episcopal Church, 1848, for affair with Jesse Ireland's widow, with whom he had a child. Signed petitions, April and December, 1849, August 1851. Listed in 1852 Census as a laborer. Elected to constitution framing committee, February, 1853.

16. Simpson, Mary Ann (wife of Ambrose Simpson): Freed by Henry B. Goodwin of Charles Co.; stated to be 25 at departure. Resident of the colony, November, 1852.

17. Simpson, Edward (son of Ambrose): Freed by Henry B. Goodwin of Charles Co.; stated to be 6 at departure. Resident of the colony, November, 1852.

18. Simpson, Letty Ann (daughter of Ambrose): Freed by Henry B. Goodwin of Charles Co.; stated to be 4 at departure. Later married Alexander Stephens. Resident of the colony, November, 1852.

19. Smith, Shadrack (husband of Mary Ann Smith): Free resident of Prince George's Co., stated to be 46 at departure. Worked variously as a farmer, laborer, shinglemaker, and sawyer. Elected selectman, March 1837. Letter writer: July 8, 1837. Signed petition against Thomson, Dec. 2, 1837. Supporter of Snetter, Sept. 12, 1838. Signed petitions,

April, 1849, and Jan. 14, 1850. Letter writer: Sept. 14, 1850. Listed in 1852 Census as a lumberer.

20. Smith, Mary Ann (wife of Shadrack Smith): Freed by Benjamin Lowndes of Prince George's County; stated to be 31 at departure. Resident of the colony, November, 1852.

21. Smith, Sarah (daughter of Shadrack Smith): Freed by Benjamin Lowndes of Prince George's County; stated to be 13 at departure. Resident of the colony, November, 1852.

22. Smith, Elias (son of Shadrack Smith): Freed by Benjamin Lowndes of Prince George's County; stated to be 11 at departure. Resident of the colony, November, 1852, listed as a laborer.

23. Smith, Mentor (son of Shadrack Smith; also called Netter Smith): Freed by Benjamin Lowndes of Prince George's County; stated to be 8 at departure. Signed petition, Jan. 14, 1850. Resident of the colony, November, 1852.

24. Smith, Mary (daughter of Shadrack Smith): Freed by Benjamin Lowndes of Prince George's County; stated to be 6 at departure. Died Feb. 12, 1852.

25. Smith, Henry (son of Shadrack Smith): Freed by Benjamin Lowndes of Prince George's County; stated to be 2 at departure. Died shortly after arrival.

26. Smith, Benjamin R. (son of Shadrack Smith): Freeborn resident of Prince George's Co., stated to be 1 month old at departure. Died shortly after arrival.

27. [Without surname], Anna Maria (single; also called Mary Jackson): Freed resident of Baltimore Co., stated to be 18 at departure. Married Thomas Jackson before February, 1837. Letter writer: July 20, 1836; Oct. 19, 1849; Mar. 30 and Sept. 16, 1850. Resident of the colony, November, 1852.

The total number of emigrants sent to Cape Palmas thus far: 104.

Brig FORTUNE, left Baltimore December 24, 1835, arrived at Cape Palmas, February 4, 1836:

1. Brown, Thomas (single): Freeborn resident of Queen Anne's Co., a farmer, stated to be 21 at departure. Living with S. Dentley, 1837. Letter writer: Sept. 13, 1836. Signed petition against Thomson, Dec. 2, 1837. Supporter of Snetter, Sept. 12, 1838. Signed petition, April, 1849; Jan. 14, 1850. Letter writer, April 25, 1849; April 1, 1851. Returned to Maryland in 1850 for a recruiting tour. Listed in 1852 Census as a sawyer.

2. Croney, Charles (husband of Lilly Croney): Freed by George Beall of Prince George's Co. to emigrate; a farmer, stated to be 35 at departure. Died of intemperance, April 20, 1836.

3. Croney, Lilly (wife of Charles Croney): Freed by Mrs. George Beall of Prince George's Co. to emigrate; stated to be 22 at departure. Died of intemperance and fever, May 9, 1836.

4. Croney, Maria (daughter of Charles Croney; also called Maria Howard): Freed by Mrs. George Beall of Prince George's Co. to emigrate; stated to be 2 at departure. Living with Henry Duncan's family in 1837 and 1839–40. In Nancy Johnson (Duncan's widow's) household, 1843; in Henry Duncan's household, 1849. Married Simon Howard, Feb. 19, 1852.

5. Dodson, Bazel (single): Freed by George Beall of Prince George's Co. to emigrate; a shoemaker and rough carpenter, stated to be 50 at departure. Does not appear in the record.

6. Dulany, William (husband of Maria Dulany; also known as William Delany):

Freeborn resident of Caroline Co., a farmer, stated to be 24 at departure. Letter writer: Sept. 4, 1836. Married Rebecca Gibson, Jan. 19, 1837. Elected selectman, 1837–8. Signed petition against Thomson, Dec. 2, 1837. Does not appear in the record after 1838.

7. Dulany, Maria (wife of William Dulany): Freed by Mary M. Thorndike, of Caroline Co.; stated to be 22 at departure. Died of diarrhea, April 7, 1836.

8. Dulany, William (also called William Henry Gibson): Freed by Mary M. Thorndike, of Caroline Co.; stated to be 1 at departure. Living in Thomas Brown household, 1849. Living in household of orphans with Elizabeth Thomson, 1852.

9. Gutridge, Henry (single): Freed by George Beall of Prince George's Co. to emigrate; a farmer and shoemaker, stated to be 25 at departure. Worked in the colony as a shoemaker. Elected selectman, March, 1837; councilor, 1840. Married Mary Stephens, May 31, 1837. Signed petition against Thomson, Dec. 2, 1837. Supporter of Snetter, Sept. 12, 1838. Agricultural Census, 1839: .5 acre. Living with David Whitfield, 1840. Married Amelia Fuller, March 1840. Not in record after 1843, deceased by 1852.

10. Harper, Harriet (mother of John Harper): Freed by E. C. Harper, of Queen Anne's Co.; stated to be 30 at departure. Moved to Monrovia in 1836 to care for her aged father there.

11. Harper, John (son of Harriet Harper): Freed by E. C. Harper, of Queen Anne's Co.; stated to be 3 at departure. Moved to Monrovia in 1836 with his mother.

12. Parker, Eben (husband of Charlotte Parker): Freed by Thomas Brown of Queen Anne's Co.; a farmer, stated to be 42 at departure. Killed by Barrawe soldiers, July 26, 1838.

13. Parker, Charlotte (wife of Eben Parker; also called Charlotte Hobbs): Free resident of Queen Anne's Co., stated to be 38 at departure. Married Moses Hobbs, July 30, 1840. Does not appear in the record afterward.

14. Parker, Amie (daughter of Eben Parker): Freeborn resident of Queen Anne's Co., stated to be 8 at departure. Killed by Barrawe soldiers, July 26, 1838.

15. Parker, Kittie (daughter of Eben Parker): Freeborn resident of Queen Anne's Co., stated to be 7 at departure. Killed by Barrawe soldiers, July 26, 1838.

16. Parker, Charlotte Ann (daughter of Eben Parker): Freeborn resident of Queen Anne's Co., stated to be 4 at departure. Died before July 1836, of fever.

17. Parker, Elizabeth (daughter of Eben Parker, also called Mary Elizabeth Parker or Elizabeth Watkins): Freeborn resident of Queen Anne's Co., stated to be 6 at departure. Appears to be attached to Henry Hannon household, 1843; in J. B. Dennis household, 1848; on her own, 1849.

18. Parker, Caroline (daughter of Eben Parker): Freeborn resident of Queen Anne's Co., stated to be 3 months old at departure. Killed by Barrawe soldiers, July 26, 1838.

19. Smith, John (grandson of Luke Walker): Freeborn resident of Caroline Co., stated to be 1 at departure. Returned to the United States on the *Niobe*, June, 1837.

20. Snoden, Isaac (single): Freed by George Beall of Prince George's Co. to emigrate; a farmer, stated to be 35 at departure. Does not appear in the record afterward.

21. Sprigg, James (single): Freed by George Beall of Prince George's Co. to emigrate; a farmer, stated to be 25 at departure. Died of fever, Mar. 24, 1836.

22. Walker, Luke (husband of Ann Walker): Freed by a man named Purnell of Caroline Co.; a sawyer, stated to be 50 at departure. Letter writer: Sept. 6, 1836. Appointed Measurer of Lumber and Inspector of Shingles, March 1837. Returned to the United States on the *Niobe*, June, 1837.

23. Walker, Ann (wife of Luke Walker): Purchased by her husband; resident of Caroline Co., stated to be 35 at departure. Returned to the United States on the *Niobe*, June, 1837.

24. Walker, Laura Ann (daughter of Luke Walker): Purchased by her father; resident

of Caroline Co., stated to be 15 at departure. Returned to the United States on the *Niobe*, June, 1837.

25. Walker, Thomas (son of Luke Walker): Purchased by his father; resident of Caroline Co., stated to be 13 at departure. Returned to the United States on the *Niobe*, June, 1837.

26. Walker, George (son of Luke Walker): Freeborn resident of Caroline Co., stated to be 11 at departure. Returned to the United States on the *Niobe*, June, 1837.

27. Walker, Mahala (daughter of Luke Walker): Freeborn resident of Caroline Co., stated to be 9 at departure. Returned to the United States on the *Niobe*, June, 1837.

28. Walker, William (son of Luke Walker): Freeborn resident of Caroline Co., stated to be 6 at departure. Returned to the United States on the *Niobe*, June, 1837.

29. Walker, Mary Adeline (daughter of Luke Walker): Freeborn resident of Caroline Co., stated to be 5 at departure. Returned to the United States on the *Niobe*, June, 1837.

30. Walker, Joseph (son of Luke Walker): Freeborn resident of Caroline Co., stated to be 4 at departure. Returned to the United States on the *Niobe*, June, 1837.

31. Walker, Elizabeth (daughter of Luke Walker): Freeborn resident of Caroline Co., stated to be 3 at departure. Returned to the United States on the *Niobe*, June, 1837.

32. Walker, Allen (son of Luke Walker): Freeborn resident of Caroline Co., stated to be 9 months old at departure. Returned to the United States on the *Niobe*, June, 1837.

33. Wilson, David (husband of Jane Wilson): Freeborn? resident of Queen Anne's Co., a farmer and shoemaker, stated to be 49 at departure. Letter writer, July 20 and Sept. 4, 1836; May 28 and 31, July 9, 1837. Appointed magistrate, March, 1837. Supported Snetter, Sept. 12, 1838. Returned to U.S. for a visit, January, 1847. Signed petition, April, 1849. Not in record after 1849.

34. Wilson, Jane (wife of David Wilson; also called Eliza Jane Wilson): Freeborn resident of Queen Anne's Co., stated to be 18 at departure. Letter writer: July 7, 1837; July 5, 1838. Died of pleuro-splenitis, 1841.

35. Wilson, Asbury (son of David Wilson): Freeborn resident of Queen Anne's Co., stated to be 21 at departure. Letter writer: Sept. 4, 1836; July 11, 1837; July 7, 1838. Married Jane Henson, 1839. Died Aug. 14, 1839, of phthisis.

36. Wilson, Arthur (son of David Wilson): Freeborn resident of Queen Anne's Co., stated to be 20 at departure. Letter writer, Sept. 3, 1836. Signed petition against Thomson, Dec. 2, 1837. Supporter of Snetter, Sept. 12, 1838. Died of consumption, Dec. 4, 1848.

37. Wilson, James H. (son of David Wilson): Freeborn resident of Queen Anne's Co., stated to be 9 at departure. Living in Thomas Clark household, 1849; in Susan Bradley household, 1852, working as a seaman.

38. Wilson, Rachel (daughter of David Wilson): Freeborn resident of Queen Anne's Co., stated to be 12 at departure. Does not appear in the record after 1843.

39. Wilson, John (son of David Wilson): Freeborn resident of Queen Anne's Co., stated to be 10 months old at departure. Died before July, 1836, of fever.

The total number of emigrants sent to Cape Palmas thus far: 143.

Brig FINANCIER, left Baltimore, July 5, 1836, arrived at Cape Palmas August 30, 1836:
1. Davenport, Thomas (husband of Frances Davenport): Freed by Adam Wever of Frederick Co. to emigrate, a farmer, stated to be 46 at departure. Worked in the colony as a farmer, laborer, and carpenter. Signed petition against Thomson, Dec. 2, 1837. Died Jan. 11, 1843, of dropsy.

2. Davenport, Frances (wife of Thomas Davenport; also called Fanny Davenport): Freed by Adam Wever of Frederick Co. to emigrate, stated to be 44 at departure. Letter

writer: Jan. 15, 1844; Nov. 21, 1848; April 26, 1849. Resident of the colony, November, 1852.

3. Davenport, Angelina (daughter of Thomas Davenport): Freed by Adam Wever of Frederick Co. to emigrate, stated to be 27 at departure. Died of debility, Oct. 18, 1836.

4. Davenport, John Randolph (son of Thomas Davenport): Freed by Elizabeth Balch of Frederick Co. to emigrate; a farmer, stated to be 25 at departure. Worked in the colony as a farmer and laborer. Married Ann Paine, Sept. 3, 1836 (three days after landing.) Signed petition against Thomson, Dec. 2, 1837. Supporter of Snetter, Sept. 12, 1838. Letter writer: Jan. 17, 1839. Signed petition, April, 1849. Died before 1852 Census.

5. Davenport, Emanuel (son of Thomas Davenport): Freed by Elizabeth Balch of Frederick Co. to emigrate; a farmer, stated to be 21 at departure. Worked in the colony as a laborer, then a sawyer. Signed petition against Thomson, Dec. 2, 1837. Supporter of Snetter, Sept. 12, 1838. Married Jane Hobbs, Oct. 22, 1840; divorced from her, 1846. Left Cape Palmas in November, 1844, to visit British Guiana, with the intention of resettling there with other Maryland settlers. Returned in September, 1845, disappointed. Signed petition, April, 1849. In 1852 Census, married to Lydia Edgefield(?) and working as a sawyer.

6. Davenport, Joseph (son of Thomas Davenport): Freed by Elizabeth Balch of Frederick Co. to emigrate; a farmer, stated to be 18 at departure. Death recorded as of "swelling," Feb. 26, 1837 and as "Chronic effection in the Head," Feb. 5, 1837.

7. Davenport, Adam (son of Thomas Davenport): Freed by Elizabeth Balch of Frederick Co. to emigrate; a farmer, stated to be 16 at departure. Married to Ellen ——, of uncertain origin, 1848. Signed petition, Jan. 14, 1850. Listed as a laborer in 1852 Census.

8. Davenport, Dinah (daughter of Thomas Davenport; also called Dianah Davenport): Freed by Elizabeth Balch of Frederick Co. to emigrate, stated to be 14 at departure. Married Nicholas Jackson, Jr., May 1, 1842. Resident of the colony, November, 1852.

9. Davenport, Lewis B. (son of Thomas Davenport; also called John L. Davenport): Freed by Elizabeth Balch of Frederick Co. to emigrate; a farmer, stated to be 12 at departure. Listed as a laborer in 1852 Census.

10. Davenport, Esther (daughter of Thomas Davenport): Freed by Elizabeth Balch of Frederick Co. to emigrate, stated to be 11 at departure. Resident of the colony, November, 1852.

11. Davenport, Louisa (daughter of Thomas Davenport): Freed by Elizabeth Balch of Frederick Co. to emigrate, stated to be 9 at departure. Living in John R. Davenport household, 1848. Does not appear in the record after 1848.

12. Davenport, Caspar Wever (son of Thomas Davenport also called Charles Davenport): Freed by Elizabeth Balch of Frederick Co. to emigrate, stated to be 5 at departure. Resident of the colony, November, 1852.

13. Davenport, Frances B. (daughter of Thomas Davenport): Freed by Elizabeth Balch of Frederick Co. to emigrate, stated to be 5 at departure. Does not appear in the record after 1838.

14. Davenport, Eliza (granddaughter of Thomas Davenport): Freed by Elizabeth Balch of Frederick Co. to emigrate, stated to be 8 at departure. Resident of the colony, November, 1852.

15. Davenport, George (grandson of Thomas Davenport): Freed by Elizabeth Balch of Frederick Co. to emigrate, stated to be 1 at departure. Died of fever or dropsy, Mar. 15, 1837.

16. Paine, Mary Ann (single; also called Mary A. Rock, then Davenport): Freed by Rev. Abram Rock of Frederick Co., stated to be 18 at departure. Married John Randolph Davenport at Harper, Sept. 3, 1836. Letter writer, Jan. 17, 1838. Resident of the colony, November, 1852.

17. Young, Steven (single): Freed by George Parnham of Charles Co. to emigrate, stated to be 36 at departure. Signed petition against Thomson, Dec. 2, 1837. Dissatisfied with Cape Palmas, walked away towards Sinoe with David James, about March 1838.

The total number of emigrants sent to Cape Palmas thus far: 160.

Brig NIOBE, first expedition, left Baltimore, November, 1836, arrived at Cape Palmas December 25, 1836:

1. Allen, Henry (single): Freeborn resident of Cecil Co., a farmer, stated to be 45 at departure. Worked principally as a farmer. Later married Rachel Greene. Assistant to D. James in unsuccessful AME Church, 1837–8. Appointed justice of the peace, 1839. Agricultural Census, 1839: .5 acre. Elected councilor, March, 1846. Not in the record after 1846.

2. Chambers, Oliver (single): Freeborn resident of Anne Arundel Co., a farmer, stated to be 26 at departure. Elected Register, 1837–8. Letter writer: July 10, 1838. Died of tuberculosis, 1838.

3. Dorsey, Josiah (single; also called John or Henry Dorsey, in 1848): Freed by a Mrs. Archer of Harford Co., stated to be 23 at departure. Employed as teacher by ABCFM, 1837–8. Married Mary Stevenson, June 10, 1848. Not in record after 1848.

4. Edmunds, Peter (single; also called Peter Redmond): Freed by Rev. Abram Rock of Frederick Co.; resident of Prince George's Co., a tanner, stated to be 38 at departure. Died during acclimation, Jan. 17, 1837.

5. Hall, Stephen A. (single): Purchased himself; resident of Harford Co., stated to be 30 at departure. Worked in the colony as a laborer, then a farmer. Letter writer: April 16, 1837; May 21, 1839; June 10 (twice), 1840; April, 1842. Married Mary Hobbs, June 9, 1840. Left Cape Palmas in November, 1844, to visit British Guiana, with the intention of resettling there with other Maryland settlers. Returned in September, 1845, disappointed. Elected councilor, March, 1846, but died before May 14.

6. Harrington, Ezekiel (husband of Henrietta Harrington): Freeborn resident of Cecil Co., a farmer, stated to be 37 at departure. Worked in the colony as a farmer. Letter writer: June 4, 1837; April 20 and 25, 1838. Agricultural Census, 1839: 2.5 acres. Died of chronic phrenitis, May 1841.

7. Harrington, Henrietta (wife of Ezekiel Harrington): Freeborn resident of Cecil Co., stated to be 35 at departure. Later married Frederick Lewis. Letter writer: Mar. 22, 1842. Resident of the colony, November, 1852.

8. Harrington, Eliza Ann (daughter of Ezekiel Harrington): Freeborn resident of Cecil Co., stated to be 7 at departure. Appears as R. H. Gibson's wife, Census 1852.

9. Harrington, Mary E. (daughter of Ezekiel Harrington also called Mary Cornelia Harrington): Freeborn resident of Cecil Co., stated to be 6 at departure. Living with mother in Frederick Lewis household, 1852.

10. Harrington, Thomas Henry (son of Ezekiel Harrington): Freeborn resident of Cecil Co., stated to be 5 at departure. Does not appear in the record after 1849.

11. Harrington, Joseph (son of Ezekiel Harrington): Freeborn resident of Cecil Co., stated to be 2 at departure. Died of fever complicated by worms, Feb. 16, 1837.

12. Harvey, James (also called James Johnson): Freeborn resident of Cecil Co., stated to be 11 at departure. Living with Alexander Hance family, 1837. Does not appear in the record afterward.

13. James, David (husband of Harriet James): Freeborn resident of Cecil Co., a farmer, stated to be 30 at departure. Attempted to establish an AME church at Cape Palmas, unsuccessfully. Had a history of fighting with Greboes and his wife, for which he

was convicted in court. About March 1838, he walked off towards Sinoe, abandoning his family.

14. James, Harriet (wife of David James; also called Hannah James): Freeborn resident of Cecil Co., stated to be 33 at departure. Living with Nathan Lee, 1839. Letter writer: May 19, 1839. Married Robert Hutchens, Aug. 15, 1848. Living as a widow, 1849. Not in record afterward.

15. James, David Jr. (son of David James): Freeborn resident of Cecil Co., stated to be 8 at departure. Living with Ezekiel Harrington's family, 1839. Died of dropsy, 1841.

16. James, Henry (son of David James): Freeborn resident of Cecil Co., stated to be 8 at departure. Living with Allen Pratt, 1839; in Henry Gutridge household, 1843; with Hannah James, 1849; and with Nancy MacFarland, 1852.

17. James, Lavinia (daughter of David James; also called Susannah, Louisa ['52]): Freeborn resident of Cecil Co., stated to be 4 at departure. Living in Nancy MacFarland household, Census 1852.

18. James, Samuel (son of David James): Freeborn resident of Cecil Co., stated to be 2 at departure. Does not appear in the record after 1843.

19. Pratt, Allen (single): Freeborn resident of Cecil Co., a farmer, stated to be 31 at departure. Worked in the colony as a farmer at Cape Palmas. Signed petition against Thomson, Dec. 2, 1837. Supporter of Snetter, Sept. 12, 1838. Married Mary Moulton, March, 1840. Does not appear in the record after 1843.

20. Smith, Benjamin (husband of Elizabeth Smith): Freeborn resident of Cecil Co., a farmer, stated to be 25 at departure. Worked variously as a farmer, laborer, and sawyer. Signed petition against Thomson, Dec. 2, 1837. Supported Snetter, Sept. 12, 1838. Agricultural Census, 1839: 30 perches. Signed petitions, April and December, 1849. Listed as a sawyer in 1852 Census.

21. Smith, Elizabeth (wife of Benjamin Smith): Free born resident of Cecil Co., stated to be 27 at departure. Listed twice, Census 1840, the other time as living alone, aged 31.

22. Sprigg, Thomas (husband of Grace Sprigg): Freed by Dr. A. M. Marbury of Prince George's Co.; stated to be 50 at departure. Died of dropsy, Aug. 8, 1837.

23. Sprigg, Grace (wife of Thomas Sprigg): Freed by Dr. A. M. Marbury of Prince George's Co.; stated to be 51 at departure. Married John Tubman, 1839, but by 1847 Census had resumed single life and resumed the name Sprigg. Does not appear in the record afterward.

24. Sprigg, Sophia (relative of Thomas Sprigg): Freed by Dr. A. M. Marbury of Prince George's Co.; stated to be 22 at departure. Does not appear in the record after 1840.

25. Sprigg, Leonard (relative of Thomas Sprigg; also called Leonard Gant): Freed by Dr. A. M. Marbury of Prince George's Co.; stated to be 15 at departure. Worked in the colony as a farmer and laborer. Married Clarissa Gross, May 4, 1842. Signed petitions, April, 1849 and Jan. 14, 1850. Died before 1852 Census.

26. Sprigg, Minta (relative of Thomas Sprigg): Freed by Dr. A. M. Marbury of Prince George's Co.; stated to be 11 at departure. Does not appear in the record after 1840.

27. Sprigg, Charles (relative of Thomas Sprigg): Freed by Dr. A. M. Marbury of Prince George's Co.; stated to be 15 at departure. Worked in the colony as a laborer, then a sawyer. Living with Grace Sprigg, 1843. Married to a woman named Hester, with a son, 1848. Signed petition, December, 1849. Married to Rachel, Census 1852, a sawyer.

28. Sprigg, Augustus (relative of Thomas Sprigg): Freed by Dr. A. M. Marbury of Prince George's Co.; stated to be 10 at departure. Living with Grace Sprigg, 1843. Does not appear in the record afterward.

29. Sprigg, William (relative of Thomas Sprigg): Freed by Dr. A. M. Marbury of Prince George's Co.; stated to be 9 at departure. Does not appear in the record after 1840.

30. Sprigg, Celia (relative of Thomas Sprigg): Freed by Dr. A. M. Marbury of Prince George's Co.; stated to be 11 at departure. Does not appear in the record after 1837.

31. Sprigg, Rachel (relative of Thomas Sprigg): Freed by Dr. A. M. Marbury of Prince George's Co.; stated to be 9 at departure. Living in John Ross household, 1839. Living with Grace Sprigg, 1843. Does not appear in the record afterward.

32. Sprigg, Samuel (possibly a son of Grace Sprigg; also called Samuel Tubman): Freed by Dr. A. M. Marbury of Prince George's Co.; stated to be 11 at departure. Living with Tubman family, 1840–43; in Henry Brown household, 1849. Resident of the colony, November, 1852, a sailor.

The total number of emigrants sent to Cape Palmas thus far: 192.

Brig BALTIMORE, left Baltimore, May 17, 1837, arrived at Cape Palmas July 4, 1837:

1. Cummings, Maria (single, mother of John Cummings; also called Maria Contee and Maria Brown): Freed by Mrs. Elizabeth H. Tubman of Augusta, Ga., age and relations unstated at departure. Living with Samuel and Madeira Tubman, 1838. Married Richard Contee, 1839; married Henry Brown May 22, 1848. Resident of the colony, November, 1852.

2. Cummings, John (son of Maria Cummings): Freed by Mrs. Elizabeth H. Tubman of Augusta, Ga., age and relations unstated at departure. Signed petition against Thomson, Dec. 2, 1837. Does not appear in the record after 1848.

3. Cummings, Rachel (mother of Jacob Cummings and others): Freed by Mrs. Elizabeth H. Tubman of Augusta, Ga., age and relations unstated at departure. Signed receipt for inheritance, Feb. 15, 1843. Living with Lydia Tubman, 1848; with Osborn Tubman, 1849. Does not appear in the record afterward.

4. Cummings, Jacob (probably son of Rachel Cummings): Freed by Mrs. Elizabeth H. Tubman of Augusta, Ga., age and relations unstated at departure. Signed petition against Thomson, Dec. 2, 1837. Supporter of Snetter, Sept. 12, 1838. Married J. Porter, 1839. Signed receipt for inheritance, Feb. 15, 1843. Married to Sophia Tubman, 1843. Signed petition, December, 1849. In Census 1852, a sawyer.

5. Cummings, Shadrack (probably son of Rachel Cummings; also called Tubman): Freed by Mrs. Elizabeth H. Tubman of Augusta, Ga., age and relations unstated at departure. Signed petition against Thomson, Dec. 2, 1837. Supporter of Snetter, Sept. 12, 1838. Married Sylvia Tubman, March 1840. Did not sign receipt for inheritance, 1843. Signed petitions, April and December, 1849. Living at Cape Palmas, 1852.

6. Cummings, Steven (probably son of Rachel Cummings; also called Tubman): Freed by Mrs. Elizabeth H. Tubman of Augusta, Ga., age and relations unstated at departure. Worked in the colony as a farmer, laborer, then sawyer. Signed petition against Thomson, Dec. 2, 1837. Supporter of Snetter, Sept. 12, 1838. Married Sylvia Lee, Nov. 17, 1842. Signed receipt for inheritance, Feb. 15, 1843. Appointed constable, 1845. Signed petition, December, 1849. Supporter of the Annexation Club, 1851. Resident of the colony, November, 1852.

7. Cummings, Osborn Jr. (probably son of Rachel Cummings): Freed by Mrs. Elizabeth H. Tubman of Augusta, Ga., age and relations unstated at departure. Worked in the colony as a farmer, then a sawyer. Living with Rachel Cummings/Tubman, 1839 and 1843. Signed receipt for inheritance, Feb. 15, 1843. Signed petitions, April and December, 1849. Married to Rosanna Smith, 1852.

8. Cummings, Meeky (daughter of Rachel Cummings, mother of Anthony Cummings; also called Maria or Michele): Freed by Mrs. Elizabeth H. Tubman of Augusta, Ga., age and relations unstated at departure. Living with Rachel Cummings/Tubman, 1839 and 1843. Signed receipt for inheritance, Feb. 15, 1843. Later married Alfred Dent. Living at Cape Palmas, 1852.

9. Cummings, Anthony (son of Meeky Cummings; also called Anthony Tubman, then Anthony Dent): Freed by Mrs. Elizabeth H. Tubman of Augusta, Ga., age and relations unstated at departure. Living with Rachel Cummings/Tubman, 1839 and 1843. Listed as a seaman in 1852 Census.

10. Cummings, Acquilla (husband of Peggy Cummings): Freed by Mrs. Elizabeth H. Tubman of Augusta, Ga., age and relations unstated at departure. Signed petition against Thomson, Dec. 2, 1837. Supporter of Snetter, Sept. 12, 1838.

11. Cummings, Peggy (wife of Acquilla Cummings; also called Margaret): Freed by Mrs. Elizabeth H. Tubman of Augusta, Ga., age and relations unstated at departure.

12. Cummings, Minty (daughter of Acquilla Cummings): Freed by Mrs. Elizabeth H. Tubman of Augusta, Ga., age and relations unstated at departure. Agricultural Census, 1839: 1.25 acres, with Letty Tubman.

13. Cummings, Eliza (daughter of Acquilla Cummings; also called Elizabeth Tubman): Freed by Mrs. Elizabeth H. Tubman of Augusta, Ga., to emigrate; age and relations unstated at departure. Later married Moses Ashton.

14. Cummings, Margaret (daughter of Acquila Cummings; also called Margaret Tubman): Freed by Mrs. Elizabeth H. Tubman of Augusta, Ga., age and relations unstated at departure. Living in Acquilla Tubman household, 1849. Married to John Davenport, Census 1852.

15. Cummings, Mary (daughter of Acquilla Cummings; also called Polly): Freed by Mrs. Elizabeth H. Tubman of Augusta, Ga., age and relations unstated at departure.

16. Cummings, Judith (daughter of Acquilla Cummings; also called Juda): Freed by Mrs. Elizabeth H. Tubman of Augusta, Ga., age and relations unstated at departure.

17. Cummings, Sylvia (daughter of Acquilla Cummings): Freed by Mrs. Elizabeth H. Tubman of Augusta, Ga., age and relations unstated at departure.

18. Cummings, Demba (husband of Liddy Cummings): Freed by Mrs. Elizabeth H. Tubman of Augusta, Ga., age and relations unstated at departure. A blind man. Agricultural Census, 1839: 1.25 acres.

19. Cummings, Liddy (wife of Dembo Cummings): Freed by Mrs. Elizabeth H. Tubman of Augusta, Ga., age and relations unstated at departure.

20. Cummings, Steven (age and relations unstated at departure; also called Stephen Tubman): Freed by Mrs. Elizabeth H. Tubman of Augusta, Ga. Age and relations unstated at departure. Worked in the colony as a farmer. Died of consumption, Dec. 25, 1848.

21. Cummings, Benjamin (single; also called Ben. Tubman): Freed by Mrs. Elizabeth H. Tubman of Augusta, Ga., age and relations unstated at departure. Agricultural Census, 1839: 1.5 acres, with Steven Tubman. Signed petition against Thomson, Dec. 2, 1837. Living in Osborn Tubman household, 1839. Signed petition, April, 1849. Does not appear in the record afterward.

22. Cummings*, Caesar (single): Freed by Mrs. Elizabeth H. Tubman of Augusta, Ga., age and relations unstated at departure. Died at sea.

23. Cummings, Nelly (possibly the daughter of Marina Cummings; also called Nelly or Ellen Tubman): Freed by Mrs. Elizabeth H. Tubman of Augusta, Ga., age and relations unstated at departure. Signed receipt for inheritance, Feb. 15, 1843. Married to

Asbury Wilson, 1843. Left Methodist Church to join Episcopal Church, 1847. Listed as wife of Arthur Wilson, Census 1848; widow in 1849. Married Charles Henry Harmon, Dec. 2, 1852.

24. Harris, Benjamin (single): Freed by a Mr. Wilmer Alexandria, Va., a turner, age stated to be 21 at departure. Worked in the colony as a turner and blacksmith. Signed petition against Thomson, Dec. 2, 1837. Married Adelia Adams, 1839. Does not appear in the record after 1848.

25. Jones, George (husband of Etheldra Jones): Freed by Elizabeth Chapman of Port Tobacco, Charles Co., a farmer, stated to be 35 at departure. Worked in the colony as a farmer and sawyer. Signed petition against Thomson, Dec. 2, 1837. Letter writer: April 28, 1838. Supporter of Snetter, Sept. 12, 1838. Agricultural Census, 1839: 1.25 acres; 1 acre in 1848.

26. Jones, Etheldra (wife of George Jones): Freed by Elizabeth Chapman of Port Tobacco, Charles Co., stated to be 27 at departure. Resident of the colony, November, 1852.

27. Jones, Amelia (daughter of George Jones): Freed by Elizabeth Chapman of Port Tobacco, Charles Co., stated to be 7 at departure. Resident of the colony, November, 1852.

28. Jones, William (son of George Jones): Freed by Elizabeth Chapman of Port Tobacco, Charles Co., stated to be 5 at departure. Died of fever, Sept. 25, 1837.

29. Jones, Samuel (son of George Jones): Freed by Elizabeth Chapman of Port Tobacco, Charles Co., stated to be 3 at departure. Died of worms during acclimation, Nov. 13, 1837.

30. Jones, Matilda (daughter of George Jones): Freed by Elizabeth Chapman of Port Tobacco, Charles Co., stated to be 1 at departure. Died of worms during acclimation, Nov. 15, 1837.

31. Minor, Elisha (single): Freed by a Mr. Minor of Fredericksburg, a farmer, stated to be 26 at departure. Living with Chas. Scotland family, 1838–40. Listed twice in Census 1839, with Scotlands and with Burwell Minor. In 1848, married to Ellen, cultivating .75 acre. Died before Census of 1849.

32. Smith, Stephen (single): Purchased himself; resident of St. Mary's Co., a blacksmith, stated to be 30 at departure. Worked in the colony as a blacksmith. Frequent letter writer. Supported Snetter, Sept. 12, 1838. Returned to St. Mary's in 1842 and purchased his wife Selitia and three children, coming back to Africa on the *Globe* at the end of the year. Appointed justice of the peace, 1845. Signed petition, Jan. 14, 1850. Returned to Maryland again in 1850 to recruit emigrants.

33. Tubman, Samuel: Freed by Mrs. Elizabeth H. Tubman of Augusta, Ga., age and relations unstated at departure. Worked variously as a farmer, laborer, and sawyer. Living with Madeira Tubman and others, 1838–9. Agricultural Census, 1839: 2.75 acres, with Dashwood Tubman. Signed receipt for inheritance, Feb. 15, 1843. Not in the record after 1843.

34. Tubman, Dashwood: Freed by Mrs. Elizabeth H. Tubman of Augusta, Ga., age and relations unstated at departure. Worked in the colony as a farmer and laborer. Signed petition against Thomson, Dec. 2, 1837. Living in Samuel Tubman household, 1838. Supporter of Snetter, Sept. 12, 1838. Married Maria or "Minty" Tubman, 1839. Agricultural Census, 1839: 2.75 acres, with Samuel Tubman. Died of phrenitis, in 1840.

35. Tubman, Fanny (also called Fanny Hobbs and Fanny Minor): Freed by Mrs. Elizabeth H. Tubman of Augusta, Ga., age and relations unstated at departure. Living with N. G. Harman in 1838; with Osmand Tubman, 1839. Signed receipt for inheritance, Feb. 15, 1843. Married Moses Hobbs, before 1843.

36. Tubman, Calfrey (husband of Lydia Tubman): Freed by Mrs. Elizabeth H. Tubman of Augusta, Ga., age and relations unstated at departure (appears to have been 23). Worked in the colony as a farmer, laborer, and principally as a sawyer. Letter writer: April 23, 1838. Supporter of Snetter, Sept. 12, 1838. Agricultural Census, 1839: .25 acre; 1.75 acres in 1848. Signed receipt for inheritance, Feb. 15, 1843. Died before 1852 Census.

37. Tubman, Lydia (wife of Calfrey Tubman): Freed by Mrs. Elizabeth H. Tubman of Augusta, Ga., age and relations unstated at departure. Signed receipt for inheritance, Feb. 15, 1843. Resident of the colony, November 1852.

38. Tubman, Riner: Freed by Mrs. Elizabeth H. Tubman of Augusta, Ga., age and relations unstated at departure. Signed receipt for inheritance, Feb. 15, 1843. Living in Asbury Wilson household, 1843. Living in Arthur Wilson household, 1848. Died June 30, 1852.

39. Tubman, Madura (also called Madeira Tubman): Freed by Mrs. Elizabeth H. Tubman of Augusta, Ga., age and relations unstated at departure (but appears to have been 47.) Living with Samuel Tubman and others, 1838–9. Signed receipt for inheritance, Feb. 15, 1843. Living in Shadrack Tubman household, 1849. Described as a widow, Census 1852.

40. Tubman, Sylvia: Freed by Mrs. Elizabeth H. Tubman of Augusta, Ga., age and relations unstated at departure. Married Shadrack Tubman, March, 1840. Signed receipt for inheritance, Feb. 15, 1843. Resident of the colony, November, 1852.

41. Tubman, Samuel (son of Judith Tubman): Freed by Mrs. Elizabeth H. Tubman of Augusta, Ga., age and relations unstated at departure. Living with Samuel and Madeira Tubman, 1838; with Dashwood Tubman, 1839. Living in Richard Contee household, 1843; in Osborn Tubman Sr. household, 1849. Resident of the colony, November, 1852.

42. Tubman, Johnson: Freed by Mrs. Elizabeth H. Tubman of Augusta, Ga., age and relations unstated at departure. Living with Madeira and Samuel Tubman, 1838; with Dashwood Tubman, 1839. Living in Richard Contee household, 1843; in Henry Brown household, 1849. Resident of the colony, November, 1852, a sailor.

43. Tubman, Major: Freed by Mrs. Elizabeth H. Tubman of Augusta, Ga., age and relations unstated at departure. Living with Samuel and Madeira Tubman, 1838; with Dashwood Tubman, 1839. Living in Richard Tubman household, 1843; in Henry Brown household, 1849. Resident of the colony, November, 1852, a sailor.

44. Tubman, Cyrus: Freed by Mrs. Elizabeth H. Tubman of Augusta, Ga., age and relations unstated at departure. Worked principally as a farmer. Later married Ann Mitchell. Letter writer: July 10, 1837. Signed petition against Thomson, Dec. 2, 1837. Elected councilor, 1839. Living with William and Richard Tubman, 1839. Agricultural Census, 1839: 3.75 acres; 1848: 2 acres. Visited United States, 1842. Signed receipt for inheritance, Feb. 15, 1843. Listed in 1852 Census as a storekeeper.

45. Tubman, Jeremiah: Freed by Mrs. Elizabeth H. Tubman of Augusta, Ga., age and relations unstated at departure. Died of old age, Nov. 15, 1837.

46. Tubman, William: Freed by Mrs. Elizabeth H. Tubman of Augusta, Ga., age and relations unstated at departure. Signed petition against Thomson, Dec. 2, 1837. Appointed Roadmaster, 1839. Living with Richard and Cyrus Tubman, 1839. Agricultural Census, 1839: .5 acre. Signed receipt for inheritance, Feb. 15, 1843. Not in the record after 1843.

47. Tubman, Richard: Freed by Mrs. Elizabeth H. Tubman of Augusta, Ga., age and relations unstated at departure. Signed petition against Thomson, Dec. 2, 1837. Supporter of Snetter, Sept. 12, 1838. Living with William and Cyrus Tubman in 1839. Signed receipt for inheritance, Feb. 15, 1843. Not in record after 1843.

48. Tubman, Susan (also called Susan Gayner): Freed by Mrs. Elizabeth H. Tubman of Augusta, Ga., age and relations unstated at departure. In 1839, living in Osmand Tubman household. Signed receipt for inheritance, Feb. 15, 1843. Living in Moses Hobbs household, 1843. Possibly the wife of Nelson Jackson, Census 1848. Not in record after 1848.

49. Tubman, Frederick: Freed by Mrs. Elizabeth H. Tubman of Augusta, Ga., age and relations unstated at departure. Worked in the colony as a carpenter. Signed petition against Thomson, Dec. 2, 1837. Living with Osmand Tubman, 1839. Signed receipt for inheritance, Feb. 15, 1843. Married to Priscilla Tubman, 1843. Signed petition, April, 1849. Listed as a carpenter, 1852 Census.

50. Tubman, Dennis: Freed by Mrs. Elizabeth H. Tubman of Augusta, Ga., age and relations unstated at departure. Does not appear in the record after 1838.

51. Tubman, Jack (also called John Tubman): Freed by Mrs. Elizabeth H. Tubman of Augusta, Ga., age and relations unstated at departure. Died Aug. 17, 1837: "Vexingly imprudent in the fever."

52. Tubman, Letty: Freed by Mrs. Elizabeth H. Tubman of Augusta, Ga., age and relations unstated at departure. Agricultural Census, 1839: 1.25 acres, with Minta Tubman. Signed receipt for inheritance, Feb. 15, 1843. Does not appear in the record afterward.

53. Tubman, Benjamin Sr.: Freed by Mrs. Elizabeth H. Tubman of Augusta, Ga., age and relations unstated at departure. Worked in the colony as a farmer and carpenter. Letter writer: July 10 and Dec. 1, 1837; April 28, 1838; May, 1839; July 15, 1842. Listed in agricultural Census 1839 with 2.75 acres, and in 1848 with 3 acres. Signed receipt for inheritance, Feb. 15, 1843. Letter writer, April 27 and Oct. 16, 1849. Does not appear in the record afterward.

54. Tubman, Monty (also called Monteith Tubman): Freed by Mrs. Elizabeth H. Tubman of Augusta, Ga., age and relations unstated at departure (but appears to have been 42.) Worked in the colony as a farmer. Signed petition against Thomson, Dec. 2, 1837. Supporter of Snetter, Sept. 12, 1838. Signed receipt for inheritance, Feb. 15, 1843. Does not appear in the record afterward.

55. Tubman, Osborn (also called Osmand Tubman): Freed by Mrs. Elizabeth H. Tubman of Augusta, Ga., age and relations unstated at departure. Worked in the colony as a farmer and laborer. Signed petition against Thomson, Dec. 2, 1837. Elected selectman, 1838–9. Married to Judith, 1848 Census. Agricultural Census, 1839: 2 acres; 1848: .75 acre. Did not sign inheritance receipt. Signed petition, April, 1849. Died before 1852 Census.

The total number of emigrants sent to Cape Palmas thus far: 247.

Brig NIOBE, second voyage, left Baltimore, November 27, 1837, and arrived at Cape Palmas, January 12, 1838:

1. Alleyne, Benjamin (husband of Sophia Alleyne): Freeborn resident of Baltimore, a schoolmaster, age at departure unstated. Died of hepatitis, Feb. 12, 1839.

2. Alleyne, Sophia (wife of Benjamin): Freeborn resident of Baltimore, a schoolmistress, age unstated at departure. Married Major Hicks, Jan. 3, 1841. Does not appear in the record afterward.

3. Ballard, Araminta (single, possibly the mother of James Robertson; possibly also called Araminta Robertson): Free resident of Dorchester Co., age at departure unstated. Appears to have lived with Priscilla Ireland and other single women in a household, 1838. Does not appear in the record afterward.

4. Barnes, Francis (single): Freed by Roger Brooks, Esq., of Calvert Co., stated to be 60 at departure. Worked in the colony as a laborer and farmer, cultivating 32 perches in 1839. Died of erysipilas gangrenosum, 1841.

5. Boone, Caroline (single woman; mother of James): Free resident of Calvert Co., stated to be 35 at departure. Died before 1848.

6. Boone, James (son of Caroline): Free resident of Calvert Co., stated to be 2 at departure. Living in David Boone household, 1843. Living in Elizabeth Hall household, 1848; in Daniel Wilson household, 1849; in Julia Hance household, 1852.

7. Bowen, Isaac (single): Free resident of Calvert Co., stated to be 15 at departure. Living with Charles Gross family, 1838–9. Married to one Nancy, of uncertain origin, 1848. Does not appear in the record afterward.

8. Briscoe, James (brother of Peter Briscoe): Freed by Dr. A. Ritchie of Frederick Co., stated to be 22 at departure. Worked in the colony as a laborer, farmer, and sawyer. Living in Thomas Jackson household, 1838. Supporter of Snetter, Sept. 12, 1838. Married Emiline Johnson, Oct. 22, 1840. Agricultural Census, 1848: 1.5 acres. Died before 1852.

9. Briscoe, Peter (brother of James Briscoe): Freed by Dr. A. Ritchie of Frederick Co., stated to be 22 at departure. Worked mainly as a laborer, then as a gardener. Living in Thomas Jackson household, 1838. Supporter of Snetter, Sept. 12, 1838. Living with Henry Duncan family, 1840. Married Eliza Duncan, July 30, 1840. Appointed constable, 1845. Signed petition, April, 1849. Listed as a gardener in 1852 Census.

10. Brooks, Jacob (brother of John; husband of Amelia): Free resident of Calvert Co., stated to be 37 at departure. Worked in the colony as a farmer and laborer. Letter writer: July 7, 1838. Supporter of Snetter, Sept. 12, 1838. Agricultural Census, 1839: .25 acre. Died before 1843 Census.

11. Brooks, Amelia (wife of Jacob Brooks; also called Cornelia): Free resident of Calvert Co., stated to be 24 at departure. Living with Philip Dorsey, 1848. Resident of the colony, November, 1852.

12. Brooks, John Thomas (son of Jacob Brooks): Free resident of Calvert Co., stated to be 10 at departure. Resident of the colony, November, 1852.

13. Brooks, William (son of Jacob Brooks): Free resident of Calvert Co., stated to be 10 at departure. Worked in the colony as a sawyer. Married Mary E. Edwards, Sept. 9, 1852.

14. Brooks, Mary (daughter of Jacob Brooks): Free resident of Calvert Co., stated to be 8 at departure. Resident of the colony, November, 1852.

15. Brooks, Benjamin (son of Jacob Brooks): Free resident of Calvert Co., stated to be 3 at departure. Does not appear in the record.

16. Brooks, Jacob Jr. (son of Jacob Brooks): Free resident of Calvert Co., stated to be 3 at departure. Does not appear in the record after 1838.

17. Brooks, Dinah (single): Freed by Roger Brooks, Esq., of Calvert Co., stated to be 49 at departure. Living with Phillip Dorsey family, 1838. Does not appear in the record afterward.

18. Brooks, Araminta (single; mother of George Brooks): Freed by Roger Brooks, Esq., of Calvert Co., stated to be 20 at departure. Does not appear in the record after 1838.

19. Brooks, George (son of Araminta Brooks; also called John Brooks): Freed by Roger Brooks, Esq., of Calvert Co., stated to be 1 at departure. Resident of the colony, November, 1852.

20. Burley, Edward (single; also called Thomas E. Burley): Freed by Jonathan Sellman of Anne Arundel Co., stated to be 18 at departure. Worked in the colony as a laborer. Does not appear in the record after 1840.

21. Cornish, Joshua (husband of Mary Cornish): Freed by Major William Newton of Dorchester Co., age at departure unstated. Worked in the colony as a farmer. Letter writer: April 20 and 28, 1838. Supported Snetter, Sept. 12, 1838. In agricultural Census, 1839, had 3 acres in cultivation, in 1848, 3.25 acres. In 1840 Census, listed a second time as a single man, 51, attached to Tubmans. Visited United States, 1842. Listed as a farmer, 1852 Census.

22. Cornish, Mary (wife of Joshua Cornish): Free resident of Dorchester Co., age at departure unstated. Letter writer: April 27, 1838. Does not appear in the record after 1843.

23. Cornish, Jane (daughter of Joshua Cornish; also called Sarah Jane): Free resident of Dorchester Co., age at departure unstated. Does not appear in the record after 1843.

24. Cornish, Antoinette (daughter of Joshua Cornish): Free resident of Dorchester Co., age at departure unstated. Does not appear in the record after 1843.

25. Cornish, Araminta (daughter of Joshua Cornish; also called Margaretta and Mary Ellen): Free resident of Dorchester Co., age at departure unstated. Living with her father, 1849. Resident of the colony, November, 1852.

26. Cornish, Arabella (daughter of Joshua Cornish): Free resident of Dorchester Co., age at departure unstated. Resident of the colony, November, 1852.

27. Dorsey, Philip (husband of Araminta Dorsey): Free resident of Calvert Co, a farmer, stated to be 40 at departure. Worked in the colony as a laborer, farmer, and sawyer. Supporter of Snetter, Sept. 12, 1838. Agricultural Census, 1839: 1 acre. Living with Amelia Brooks and her children, 1848. Signed petition, December 1849. Resident of the colony, November, 1852, a sawyer.

28. Dorsey, Araminta (wife of Philip Dorsey): Free resident of Calvert Co., a farmer, stated to be 45 at departure. Died about 1848, of unrecorded cause.

29. Greenfield, James (husband of Julia Greenfield): Free resident of Calvert Co., stated to be 28 at departure. Worked in the colony as a farmer, shinglemaker, and sawyer. Letter writer: April 25, 1838. Supporter of Snetter, Sept. 12, 1838. Agricultural Census, 1839: 1.5 acre; in 1848, 3 acres. Signed petition, Jan. 14, 1850. Resident of the colony, November, 1852, a sawyer.

30. Greenfield, Julia A. (wife of James Greenfield): Free resident of Calvert Co., stated to be 22 at departure. Resident of the colony, November, 1852.

31. Greenfield, Dinah (daughter of James Greenfield): Free resident of Calvert Co., stated to be 7 at departure. Died Dec. 13, 1852, aged 18.

32. Greenfield, Barbara Jane (daughter of James Greenfield; also called Mary [1848]): Free resident of Calvert Co., stated to be 5 at departure. Resident of the colony, November, 1852.

33. Greenfield, John Richard (son of James Greenfield): Free resident of Calvert Co., stated to be 2 at departure. Resident of the colony, November, 1852.

34. Gross, Thomas (husband of Albitha Gross): Once the slave of Robert B. Wilkinson; resident of Calvert Co., a farmer, stated to be 37 at departure. Worked in the colony as a farmer, sawyer, shinglemaker, and laborer. Letter writer: April 28, July 9, 1838. Supporter of Snetter, Sept. 12, 1838. Letter writer: Oct. 17, 1849. Resident of the colony, November, 1852, a laborer.

35. Gross, Albitha (wife of Thomas Gross; also called Alethia): Free resident of Calvert Co., stated to be 25 at departure. Resident of the colony, November, 1852.

36. Gross, William (son of Thomas Gross): Free resident of Calvert Co., stated to be 6 at departure. Does not appear in the record after 1849.

37. Gross, Richard (son of Thomas Gross): Free resident of Calvert Co., stated to be 4 at departure. Living in father's household, 1852, a laborer.

38. Gross, Thomas Hersey (son of Thomas Gross): Free resident of Calvert Co., stated to be 2 at departure. Living in father's household, 1852, a laborer.

39. Gross, Charles (husband of Charlotte Gross): Free resident of Calvert Co., stated to be 31 at departure. Worked in the colony as a farmer and carpenter. Letter writer: April 27, 1838. Agricultural Census, 1839: 2 acres; 1848: 2.5 acres. Reportedly died Sept. 12, 1842, of consumption, but continues in the record until 1848.

40. Gross, Charlotte (wife of Charles Gross): Free resident of Calvert Co., stated to be 23 at departure. Died before November, 1852.

41. Gross, Jane (daughter of Charles Gross; also called Sarah Jane): Free resident of Calvert Co., stated to be 6 at departure. Resident of the colony, November, 1852.

42. Gross, Henry (son of Charles Gross): Free resident of Calvert Co., stated to be 4 at departure. Resident of the colony, November, 1852.

43. Gross, Jacob (son of Charles Gross): Free resident of Calvert Co., stated to be 3 at departure. Resident of the colony, November, 1852.

44 . Gross, Susan (daughter of Charles Gross; also called Susannah or Dolly Ann): Free resident of Calvert Co., stated to be 1 at departure. Resident of the colony, November, 1852.

45. Hall, Charles (single; father of Elizabeth and Araminta Hall): Free resident of Calvert Co., stated to be 26 at departure. Worked in the colony as a farmer and laborer. Supported Snetter, Sept. 12, 1838. Elected selectman, 1839. Does not appear in the record after 1840.

46. Hall, Elizabeth (daughter of Charles Hall; also called Betsy): Free resident of Calvert Co., stated to be 4 at departure. Living in Joseph Odley household, 1843. Does not appear in the record after 1843.

47. Hall, Araminta (daughter of Charles Hall): Free resident of Calvert Co., stated to be 2 at departure. Does not appear in the record after 1840.

48. Hammond, Charles (husband of Sophia Hammond; also called Harmon): Free resident of Calvert Co., stated to be 36 at departure. Worked in the colony as a farmer, laborer, shoemaker, sawyer, boardmaker, and lumberer. Appointed Roadmaster, 1839. Resident of the colony, November, 1852, a lumberer.

49. Hammond, Sophia (wife of Charles Hammond): Free resident of Calvert Co., stated to be 33 at departure. Died before November, 1852.

50. Hammond, Dinah (daughter of Charles Hammond): Free resident of Calvert Co., stated to be 12 at departure. Does not appear in the record after 1838.

51. Hammond, William (son of Charles Hammond): Free resident of Calvert Co., stated to be 10 at departure. Does not appear in the record after 1849.

52. Hammond, Charles Jr. (son of Charles Hammond): Free resident of Calvert Co., stated to be 8 at departure. Does not appear in the record after 1849.

53. Hammond, Joseph (son of Charles Hammond): Free resident of Calvert Co., age at departure unstated. Resident of the colony, November, 1852.

54. Hammond, Clarissa (daughter of Charles Hammond): Free resident of Calvert Co., stated to be 11 months old at departure. Resident of the colony, November, 1852.

55. Hance, Nancy (daughter of Alexander Hance): Bought by her father during his visit to the United States from James Somerville of Prince George's Co., 1837, stated to be 14 at departure. Does not appear in the record after 1840.

56. Hance, Maria (daughter of Alexander): Bought by her father during his visit to the United States from James Somerville of Prince George's Co., 1837, age unstated at departure. Married Daniel Wilson, May 2, 1848. Resident of the colony, November, 1852.

57. Hance, Charlotte (daughter of Alexander Hance; also called Maria): Bought by

her father during his visit to the United States from James Somerville of Prince George's Co., 1837, age at departure unstated. Does not appear in the record after 1848.

58. Hannon, Henry (single): Freed by Richard Dorsey of Baltimore; formerly property of Larkin Dorsey of Anne Arundel Co.; resident of Anne Arundel Co., stated to be 36 at departure. Appointed teacher of Free School #1, 1839; Mt. Tubman storekeeper, justice of the peace, and Measurer, 1845. Letter writer: Sept. 17, 1841; Jan. 23, 1846; April 26 and Oct. 16, 1849. Married Jane Wilson, April 8, 1841. Agricultural Census 1848: 1 acre cultivated. Signed petition, April, 1849; Jan. 14, 1850, August 1851. Compiled Census, November, 1852. Listed as a surveyor in 1852 Census.

59. Harrod, Clement (single): Free resident of Calvert Co., stated to be 39 at departure. Worked in the colony as a laborer and rough carpenter. Living with Daniel Banks family, 1838. Supporter of Snetter, Sept. 12, 1838. Does not appear in the record after 1840.

60. Hooper, John (single): Free resident of Dorchester Co., age unstated at departure. Worked in the colony as a laborer. Living with Joshua Cornish family, 1838; with Caroline Boone family, 1839. Supporter of Snetter, Sept. 12, 1838. Does not appear in the record after 1843.

61. Ireland, Priscilla (single): Free resident of Baltimore, stated to be 23 at departure. Living in non-nuclear household with P. Young and others, 1838; in Caroline Banks household, 1839; with Jesse Ireland, 1843. Does not appear in the record afterward.

62. Jackson, Nicholas (single, brother of Nicholas Jackson Jr.): Freed by Larkin Dorsey of Anne Arundel Co., stated to be 26 at departure. Supporter of Snetter, Sept. 12, 1838. Elected to New Emigrant Committee, 1839. Married Phoebe Wheeler, 1839. Returned for a recruiting tour in his old neighborhood in 1847. Farmed 3.5 acres in 1848. Signed petitions, April and December, 1849; Jan. 14, 1850. Resident of the colony, November, 1852.

63. Jackson, Nicholas Jr. (single, brother of Nicholas Jackson): Freed by Larkin Dorsey of Anne Arundel Co., stated to be 22 at departure. Worked variously as a farmer, teacher, and civil officer. Supporter of Snetter, Sept. 12, 1838. Appointed teacher of Free School #2, 1839. Agricultural Census, 1839: 1 acre; 1848: 3.5 acres. Married Dianah Davenport, May 1, 1842. councilor, 1846; vice agent, 1848. Signed petition, December, 1849. Listed in 1852 Census as a storekeeper. Letter writer: April 4, 1848; and Feb. 4, 1853.

64. Jackson, John (single, brother of Nicholas Jackson): Freed by Larkin Dorsey of Anne Arundel Co., stated to be 18 at departure. Worked in the colony as a laborer. Supporter of Snetter, Sept. 12, 1838. Living with Nicholas Jackson, 1839. Died of consumption, June 13, 1848.

65. Jackson, Samuel (single, brother of Nicholas Jackson): Freed by Larkin Dorsey of Anne Arundel Co., stated to be 16 at departure. Worked in the colony as a carpenter. Living in Henry Duncan household, 1839; with Tubman/Cummings extended family, 1840. Not in the record after 1840.

66. Jackson, William (single, brother of Nicholas Jackson): Freed by Larkin Dorsey of Anne Arundel Co., stated to be 14 at departure. Does not appear in the record after 1838.

67. Jackson, Cornelius (single, brother of Nicholas Jackson): Freed by Larkin Dorsey of Anne Arundel Co., stated to be 28 at departure. Living with Charles Scotland family, 1838; with Nicholas Jackson, 1839. Died by drowning, May 5, 1842.

68. Jackson, Richard (single, brother of Nicholas Jackson; also called Richard Donaldson): Freed by Larkin Dorsey of Anne Arundel Co., stated to be 17 at departure. Worked in the colony as a laborer. Does not appear in the record after 1838.

69. Johnson, Benjamin (husband of Alletha Johnson): Freed by J. W. Richardson of

Calvert Co., stated to be 28 at departure. Worked in the colony as a farmer, laborer, carpenter, and sawyer. Supporter of Snetter, Sept. 12, 1838. Appointed constable, 1839. Signed petition, April, 1849. Died before November, 1852.

70. Johnson, Alletha (wife of Benjamin Johnson): Freed by J. W. Richardson of Calvert Co., stated to be 22 at departure. Died of "cachucia Africanus," Jan. 20, 1848, aged 33.

71. Johnson, Rachel Ann (daughter of Benjamin Johnson; also called Rachel A. Brown ['52]): Freed by J. W. Richardson of Calvert Co., stated to be 3 at departure. Resident of the colony, November, 1852.

72. Johnson, Jane (single, mother of Martha Johnson): Freed by J. W. Richardson of Calvert Co., stated to be 23 at departure. Living with Benjamin Johnson family, 1838. Does not appear in the record after 1840.

73. Johnson, Martha Ann (daughter of Martha Johnson): Freed by J. W. Richardson of Calvert Co., stated to be 1 at departure. Living with Benjamin Johnson family, 1838. Does not appear in the record after 1843.

74. Sprigg, Elizabeth (single): Freed by Roger Brooks, Esq., of Calvert Co., stated to be 50 at departure. Living with James Martin family, 1838–9. Agricultural Census, 1839: 1.25 acres. Died of dysentery, 1841.

75. Williamson, Amelia (single, mother of Abuta): Freed by Robert Griffith, Esq. of Anne Arundel Co., stated to be 24 at departure. Does not appear in the record after 1840.

76. Williamson, Abuta (daughter of Amelia Williamson): Freed by Robert Griffith, Esq. of Anne Arundel Co., stated to be 7 at departure. Does not appear in the record.

77. Williamson, Ariel (daughter of Amelia Williamson): Freed by Robert Griffith, Esq. of Anne Arundel Co., stated to be 5 at departure. Does not appear in the record.

78. Williamson, Eliza (daughter of Amelia Williamson): Freed by Robert Griffith, Esq. of Anne Arundel Co., stated to be 4 at departure. Does not appear in the record after 1840.

79. Williamson, Charles W. (son of Amelia Williamson): Freed by Robert Griffith, Esq. of Anne Arundel Co., stated to be 3 at departure. Does not appear in the record.

80. Young, Jane (single): Freeborn resident of Calvert Co., a farmer, stated to be 28 at departure. Living in mixed household, Census 1839, with C. McIntosh and others. Married J. Odley, April 12, 1839. Visited the United States 1852, returned on Ralph Cross, but died Sept. 18, 1852.

81. Young, Lavinia (single; sister of Priscilla Young): Free resident of Calvert Co., stated to be 30 at departure. Does not appear in the record after 1838.

82. Young, Priscilla (single; sister of Lavinia Young): Free resident of Calvert Co., stated to be 24 at departure. Living with Allen Pratt, 1843. Does not appear in the record afterward.

83. Young, James (son of Priscilla Young): Free resident of Calvert Co., stated to be 1 at departure. Died July 25, 1839, of dropsy.

The total number of emigrants sent to Cape Palmas thus far: 330.

Schooner COLUMBIA, left Savannah, Georgia, May 15, 1838, arrived at Cape Palmas July 2, 1838:

1. Adams, Delia (relations unclear in emigrant list; also called Amelia Harris): Freed by Nicholas Bayard of Savannah and Mrs. J. L. Wilson, stated to be 20 at departure. Does not appear in the record after 1843

2. Adams, Alexander (relations unclear in emigrant list): Freed by Nicholas Bayard of

Savannah and Mrs. J. L. Wilson, stated to be 15 at departure. Worked in the colony as a laborer. Living in Anthony Wood household, 1840, as an apprentice blacksmith; with F. Baxter and B. Bostic, 1843; living in Samuel Scotland household, 1848. Does not appear in the record afterward.

3. Adams, Adam (relations unclear in emigrant list): Freed by Nicholas Bayard of Savannah and Mrs. J. L. Wilson, stated to be 1 at departure. Does not appear in the record.

4. Biggers, Henry (husband of Catherine Biggers): Free resident of Frederick Co., stated to be 46 at departure. Worked in the colony as a laborer. Supporter of Snetter, Sept. 12, 1838. Died of ulcerated bowel, 1839.

5. Biggers, Catherine (wife of Henry Biggers; also called Bighurst): Free resident of Frederick Co., stated to be 46 at departure. Agricultural Census, 1839: 1.25 acres. In 1848, adopted name of Simms, living with her two sons. Name reverted to Biggers, 1849. Resident of the colony, November, 1852.

6. Biggers, Upton (son of Henry Biggers): Free resident of Frederick Co., stated to be 4 at departure. Died of ulceration of the collar, 1839.

7. Biggers, Ephraim (son of Henry Biggers; also called Bighurst): Free resident of Frederick Co., stated to be 7 at departure. Resident of the colony, November, 1852.

8. Biggers, John H. (son of Henry Biggers; also called Bighurst): Free resident of Frederick Co., stated to be 2 at departure. Resident of the colony, November, 1852.

9. Jackson, Jeremiah (son of Rhina Johnson; also called Jeremiah Johnson): Freed by Nicholas Bayard of Savannah and Mrs. J. L. Wilson, stated to be 3 at departure. Relations unclear in emigrant list. Living in John Johnson household, 1848, "His Boy." Does not appear in the record afterward.

10. Jenkins, William (single): Freed by Nicholas Bayard of Savannah and Mrs. J. L. Wilson, stated to be 32 at departure. Worked in the colony as a farmer, sawyer, and laborer. Supporter of Snetter, Sept. 12, 1838. Married Catherine Ross, 1839. Agricultural Census, 1839: .5 acre. Married Elizabeth Diggs, Jan. 13, 1848. Signed petition, December, 1849. Does not appear in the record afterward.

11. Jenkins, Jane (daughter of Wm. Jenkins): Freed by Nicholas Bayard of Savannah and Mrs. J. L. Wilson, stated to be 4 at departure. Worked in the colony as a spinster. Living in Benj. Harris household, 1843; in W. Jenkins household, 1848. Does not appear in the record after 1849.

12. Johnson, John (husband of Catherine Johnson): Freed by Nicholas Bayard of Savannah and Mrs. J. L. Wilson, stated to be 35 at departure. Supported Snetter, Sept. 12, 1838. Cultivated 1.75 acres in 1839. Does not appear in the record after 1848.

13. Johnson, Catherine (wife if John Johnson; also called Catherine Jacobs): Freed by Nicholas Bayard of Savannah and Mrs. J. L. Wilson, stated to be 40 at departure. Does not appear in the record after 1848.

14. Johnson, Rhina (mother of Jeremiah Jackson): Freed by Nicholas Bayard of Savannah and Mrs. J. L. Wilson, stated to be 21 at departure. Worked in the colony as a spinster. Does not appear in the record after 1849.

15. Jones, James (single): Free resident of Frederick Co.; stated to be 30 at departure. Does not appear in the record.

16. McIntosh, Belinda (relations unclear on emigrant list): Freed by Nicholas Bayard of Savannah and Mrs. J. L. Wilson, stated to be 30 at departure. Does not appear in the record.

17. McIntosh, Mary (relations unclear on emigrant list): Freed by Nicholas Bayard of Savannah and Mrs. J. L. Wilson, stated to be 50 at departure. Worked in the colony as a

spinster. Living with Belinda Mumford, 1839. Does not appear in the record after 1849.

18. McIntosh, Charles (relations unclear on emigrant list): Freed by Nicholas Bayard of Savannah and Mrs. J. L. Wilson, stated to be 18 at departure. Worked in the colony as a laborer. Supported Snetter, Sept. 12, 1838. Living with Jane Odley/Young, 1839. Married a woman named Georgianna, 1840, but living by himself, 1843. Agricultural Census, 1839: .25 acre. Appointed constable, 1845. Living with two other storekeepers, 1848. Signed petition, Jan. 14, 1850. Married to Nancy, 1852, working as a laborer.

19. McIntosh, Juba (relations unclear on emigrant list; also called Inda Potter): Freed by Nicholas Bayard of Savannah and Mrs. J. L. Wilson, stated to be 26 at departure. Living with Charles and Mary McIntosh, 1839. Does not appear in the record afterward.

20. McIntosh, Diana (relations unclear on emigrant list): Freed by Nicholas Bayard of Savannah and Mrs. J. L. Wilson, stated to be 17 at departure. Does not appear in the record.

21. McIntosh, Mary (relations unclear on emigrant list): Freed by Nicholas Bayard of Savannah and Mrs. J. L. Wilson, stated to be 11 at departure. Living in Tubman/Cummings extended family, 1840. Does not appear in the record afterward.

22. McIntosh, Grace (relations unclear on emigrant list; also called Grace Potter): Freed by Nicholas Bayard of Savannah and Mrs. J. L. Wilson, stated to be 6 at departure. Living in Caroline Boone household, 1839, as Gracy Potter; in Hester Mumford household, 1840, as Grace McIntosh. Does not appear in the record afterward.

23. McIntosh, Hosa (relations unclear on emigrant list, son of Grace McIntosh): Freed by Nicholas Bayard of Savannah and Mrs. J. L. Wilson, stated to be 1 at departure. Does not appear in the record after 1840.

24. McIntosh, Samuel (relations unclear on emigrant list, son of Grace McIntosh; also called Samuel Potter and Charles McIntosh): Freed by Nicholas Bayard of Savannah and Mrs. J. L. Wilson, stated to be 1 at departure. Living with Charles and Mary McIntosh, 1839. Does not appear in the record after 1848.

25. Mumford, Belinda (relations unclear on emigrant list): Freed by Nicholas Bayard of Savannah and Mrs. J. L. Wilson, stated to be 69 at departure. Does not appear in the record after 1839.

26. Mumford, Isaac (relations unclear on emigrant list): Freed by Nicholas Bayard of Savannah and Mrs. J. L. Wilson, stated to be 31 at departure. Worked in the colony as a laborer. Supporter of Snetter, Sept. 12, 1838. Agricultural Census, 1839: .5 acre. Married Fanny Jarrett, Nov. 24, 1842. Died before 1852 Census.

27. Mumford, Hester (relations unclear on emigrant list): Freed by Nicholas Bayard of Savannah and Mrs. J. L. Wilson, stated to be 26 at departure. Relations unclear in emigrant list. Married Benjamin Tubman Jr. before 1843. Later married Thomas Brown. Resident of the colony, November, 1852.

28. Odley, Joseph (relations unclear on emigrant list): Freed by Nicholas Bayard of Savannah and Mrs. J. L. Wilson, stated to be 30 at departure. Worked in the colony as a laborer and farmer. Supporter of Snetter, Sept. 12, 1838. Letter writer: Jan. 20, 1839. Living with Tasker and Belinda Wiley, Census 1839. Married Jane Young, April 12, 1839. Appointed Manager of Public Farm, 1845. Signed petitions, April and December, 1849. Died in summer of 1850.

29. Sansey, Charles (husband of Mary Sansey): Freed by Nicholas Bayard of Savannah and Mrs. J. L. Wilson, stated to be 69 at departure. Worked in the colony as a farmer, listed in agricultural Census, 1839 with 1 acre, with his brother Paul Sansey. Died before the 1843 Census.

30. Sansey, Mary (wife of Charles Sansey; also called Josephine Sansey): Freed by

Nicholas Bayard of Savannah and Mrs. J. L. Wilson, stated to be 66 at departure. Living with her daughter Charlotte, 1848. Does not appear in the record after 1849.

31. Sansey, Charlotte (daughter of Charles Sansey): Freed by Nicholas Bayard of Savannah and Mrs. J. L. Wilson, a housemaid, stated to be 25 at departure. In 1848, mother of Martha and Elizabeth Brooks. Married to Richard Donaldson, 1852. Visited United States in 1852, returned on Ralph Cross. Living at Cape Palmas 1852.

32. Sansey, Paul F. (son of Charles Sansey): Freed by Nicholas Bayard of Savannah and Mrs. J. L. Wilson, stated to be 31 at departure. Worked in the colony as a carpenter. Letter writer: Jan. 16, 1839. Agricultural Census, 1839: 1 acre, with Charles Sansey. Appointed Measurer of Lumber and Buildings, 1845. Cultivated 3.5 acres in 1848. Signed petition, April, 1849. Signed petition, Jan. 14, 1850. Living at Cape Palmas, 1852, a carpenter.

33. Smith, William (single): Free resident of Frederick Co., stated to be 28 at departure. In 1848, married to one Margaret, of uncertain origin, with .5 acre cultivated. Does not appear in the record afterward.

34. Ward, Clarissa (single, mother of Susana and Clarissa): Freed by Nicholas Bayard of Savannah and Mrs. J. L. Wilson, stated to be 50 at departure. Worked for the Episcopal mission, 1839; listed as a spinster, 1849. Does not appear in the record afterward.

35. Ward, Susana (daughter of Clarissa Ward): Freed by Nicholas Bayard of Savannah and Mrs. J. L. Wilson, stated to be 13 at departure. Died Jan. 5, 1843, of a wound.

36. Ward, Clarissa (daughter of Clarissa Ward; also called Clarissa James [1848]): Freed by Nicholas Bayard of Savannah and Mrs. J. L. Wilson, stated to be 11 at departure. Does not appear in the record after 1848.

The total number of emigrants sent to Cape Palmas thus far: 366.

Brig OBERON, left Baltimore, November 22, 1838, arrived at Cape Palmas January 13, 1839:

1. Barnes, John (husband of Amelia Barnes): Freed by Thomas Oliver; resident of Frederick Co.; stated to be 50 at departure. Worked in the colony as a farmer. Later married one Melinda, of untraced origin. Letter writer: Jan. 17, 1839. Agricultural Census, 1839: 2 acres; in 1848: 4.5 acres. Signed petition, April, 1849. Died before 1849 Census.

2. Barnes, Amelia (wife of John Barnes): Freed by Thomas Oliver; resident of Frederick Co.; stated to be 50 at departure. Died of fever complicated by gastritis, before April, 1839.

3. Barnes, Charlotte (daughter of John Barnes): Freed by Thomas Oliver; resident of Frederick Co.; stated to be 14 at departure. Living in Jane Revey household, 1843. Does not appear in the record afterward.

4. Barnes, Maria (daughter of John Barnes): Freed by Thomas Oliver; resident of Frederick Co.; stated to be 12 at departure. Does not appear in the record after 1843.

5. Barnes, Augustus (son of John Barnes): Freed by Thomas Oliver; resident of Frederick Co.; stated to be 10 at departure. Worked in the colony as a laborer. Signed petition, April, 1849. Living in Linda Barnes household, Census 1849–52. Signed petition, Jan. 14, 1850. Died Nov. 17, 1852.

6. Barnes, Harriet (daughter of John Barnes): Freed by Thomas Oliver; resident of Frederick Co.; stated to be 9 at departure. Does not appear in the record after 1843.

7. Barnes, Thomas (son of John Barnes): Freed by Thomas Oliver; resident of Frederick Co.; stated to be 8 at departure. Living in Henry Duncan household, 1849. Resident of the colony, November, 1852.

8. Barnes, Laura (daughter of John Barnes): Freed by Thomas Oliver; resident of Frederick Co.; stated to be 6 at departure. Died of fever, complicated by worms, before April, 1839.

9. Barnes, Margaret (daughter of John Barnes): Freed by Thomas Oliver; resident of Frederick Co.; stated to be 4 at departure. Does not appear in the record after 1843.

10. Boardley, John (husband of Mary Boardley): Freed resident of Anne Arundel Co.; stated to be 55 at departure. Worked in the colony as a farmer. Appointed Roadmaster, 1839. Letter writer: April 22, 1838; Sept. 23, 1841; and June 17, 1848. Visited United States, 1842. Cultivated 2.5 acres in 1848. Signed petition, December 1849. Resident of the colony, November, 1852.

11. Boardley, Mary (wife of John Boardley): Resident of Anne Arundel Co.; stated to be 47 at departure. Worked in the colony as a midwife. Resident of the colony, November, 1852.

12. Boardley, Mary (daughter of John Boardley; also called Rachel Boardley): Resident of Anne Arundel Co.; aged about 7 at departure. Died of "ileus," July 11, 1848.

13. Boardley, Charles Wesley (son of John Boardley): Resident of Anne Arundel Co.; aged 10 at departure. Worked in the colony as a seaman. Resident of the colony, November, 1852.

14. Bowen, John (single): Status unrecorded; resident of Frederick Co.; stated to be 27 at departure. Worked in the colony as a farmer, sawyer, and shinglemaker. Living in Allen Pratt household, 1843. Cultivated 1.25 acres in 1848. Signed petitions, April and December, 1849. Married Ellen Harris, May 6, 1852.

15. Johnson, Emiline (daughter of Samuel Johnson): Status unrecorded; resident of Calvert Co.; stated to be 16 at departure. Married James Briscoe, Oct. 22, 1840. Resident of the colony, November, 1852.

16. Hammond, James (husband of Rebecca Hammond): Status unrecorded; resident of Calvert Co.; stated to be 31 at departure. Worked in the colony as a shinglemaker and sawyer. Visited the United States, 1849. Died before November, 1852.

17. Hammond, Rebecca (wife of James Hammond): Status unrecorded; resident of Calvert Co.; stated to be 28 at departure. Resident of the colony, November, 1852.

18. Hammond, Colonel (son of James Hammond): Status unrecorded; resident of Calvert Co.; stated to be 10 at departure. Does not appear in the record after 1849.

19. Hammond, Mary (daughter of James Hammond): Status unrecorded; resident of Calvert Co.; stated to be 8 at departure. Resident of the colony, November, 1852.

20. Hammond, Nelly (daughter of James Hammond; also called Ellen or Eleanor): Status unrecorded; resident of Calvert Co.; stated to be 6 at departure. Resident of the colony, November, 1852.

21. Hammond, Eliza (daughter of James Hammond): Status unrecorded; resident of Calvert Co.; stated to be 4 at departure. Resident of the colony, November, 1852.

22. Hammond, Rebecca A. (daughter of James Hammond): Status unrecorded; resident of Calvert Co.; stated to be 2 at departure. Resident of the colony, November, 1852.

23. Hammond, Sophia (daughter of James Hammond): Status unrecorded; resident of Calvert Co.; stated to be 1 at departure. Resident of the colony, November, 1852.

24. Hanson, John (husband of Fanny Hanson): Status unrecorded; resident of Harford Co.; stated to be 30 at departure. Worked in the colony as a farmer, carpenter, and laborer. Cultivated .75 acre in 1839, and one acre in 1848. Died before November, 1852.

25. Hanson, Fanny (wife of John Hanson; also called Ann F. Hanson): Status unrecorded; resident of Harford Co.; stated to be 40 at departure. Resident of the colony, November, 1852.

26. Hanson, Eliza (daughter of John Hanson): Status unrecorded; resident of Harford Co.; stated to be 14 at departure. Living in George Harvey household, 1849. Living with her mother Fanny, 1852.

27. Hanson, Margaret (daughter of John Hanson): Status unrecorded; resident of Harford Co.; stated to be 5 at departure. Resident of the colony, November, 1852.

28. Hanson, Mary Jane (daughter of John Hanson): Status unrecorded; resident of Harford Co.; stated to be 2 at departure. Resident of the colony, November, 1852.

29. Jackson, John (husband of Rachel Jackson): Status unrecorded; resident of Calvert Co.; stated to be 28 at departure. Worked in the colony as a laborer and farmer. Living without his wife in N. Jackson household, 1840. Died before the 1849 Census.

30. Jackson, Rachel (wife of John Jackson): Status unrecorded; resident of Calvert Co.; stated to be 23 at departure. Cultivated .75 acre in 1848. Died before November, 1852.

31. Jackson, Mary Ann (daughter of John Jackson): Status unrecorded; resident of Calvert Co.; stated to be 10 months old at departure. Living in Philip Gross household, 1852.

32. Johnson, Samuel (husband of Priscilla Johnson): Status unrecorded; resident of Calvert Co.; stated to be 50 at departure. Worked in the colony as a sawyer, farmer, and laborer. Cultivated 1.25 acres in 1839, 2.5 acres in 1848. Died April 19, 1852.

33. Johnson, Priscilla (wife of Samuel Johnson): Status unrecorded; resident of Calvert Co.; stated to be 45 at departure. Resident of the colony, November, 1852.

34. Johnson, Henry (son of Samuel Johnson): Status unrecorded; resident of Calvert Co.; stated to be 21 at departure. Died of hydrothorax, before April, 1839.

35. Johnson, Rebecca (daughter of Samuel Johnson): Status unrecorded; resident of Calvert Co.; stated to be 15 at departure. Does not appear in the record after 1840.

36. Johnson, Augustus (son of Samuel Johnson; also called Gusty): Status unrecorded; resident of Calvert Co.; stated to be 14 at departure. Resident of the colony, November, 1852.

37. Johnson, Letty (daughter of Samuel Johnson; also called Siney or Celia): Status unrecorded; resident of Calvert Co.; stated to be 15 at departure. Does not appear in the record after 1849.

38. Johnson, Priscilla (daughter of Samuel Johnson): Status unrecorded; resident of Calvert Co.; stated to be 10 at departure. Resident of the colony, November, 1852.

39. Johnson, Samuel (son of Samuel Johnson): Status unrecorded; resident of Calvert Co.; stated to be 9 at departure. Died of African fever, 1839.

40. Johnson, Julia E. (daughter of Samuel Johnson): Status unrecorded; resident of Calvert Co.; stated to be 7 at departure. Resident of the colony, November, 1852.

41. Johnson, Thomas (son of Samuel Johnson): Status unrecorded; resident of Calvert Co.; stated to be 4 months old at departure. Resident of the colony, November, 1852.

42. Johnson, Charlotte E. (uncertain relation of Samuel Johnson): Status unrecorded; resident of Calvert Co.; stated to be 2 months old at departure. Does not appear in the record after 1840.

43. Johnson, Henry (husband of Amie Johnson): Status unrecorded; resident of Calvert Co.; stated to be 47 at departure. Agricultural Census, 1839: .5 acre. Died of epistaxis, 1841.

44. Johnson, Amie (wife of Henry Johnson): Status unrecorded; resident of Calvert Co.; stated to be 47 at departure. Does not appear in the record.

45. Johnson, John (single): Status unrecorded; resident of Frederick Co.; stated to be 26 at departure. Does not appear in the record.

46. Ross, Catherine (single, mother of Mary and others; also called Catherine Jenkins): Freed resident of Calvert Co.; stated to be 45 at departure. Letter writer: May 21, 1839.

Married William Jenkins, 1839. Living single with children as C. Ross, 1843. Resident of the colony, November, 1852.

47. Ross, Mary (daughter of Catherine Ross): Freed by George Dorsey to emigrate; resident of Calvert Co.; stated to be 20 at departure. Does not appear in the record after 1843.

48. Ross, Ellen (daughter of Catherine Ross): Freeborn resident of Calvert Co.; stated to be 10 at departure. Does not appear in the record after 1843.

49. Ross, Margaret (daughter of Catherine Ross): Freeborn resident of Calvert Co.; stated to be 7 at departure. Bore illegitimate twins, Sept. 13, 1852.

50. Ross, Frances (daughter of Catherine Ross): Freeborn resident of Calvert Co.; stated to be 6 at departure. Resident of the colony, November, 1852.

51. Scotland, Robert (single, related to Charles Scotland): Status uncertain, resident of Virginia; stated to be 25 at departure. Worked in the colony as a rough carpenter and laborer. Living in Charles Scotland household, 1840. Married Lucy Bowen, 1842. Died before the 1849 Census.

53. Snowden, Darius (single; also called James Snowden): Freed by his master to visit Cape Palmas and return with a report of the country; resident of Frederick Co.; stated to be 21 at departure. Letter writer: Jan. 15, 1839. Does not appear in the record afterward.

54. Sprigg, Allen (single): Status unrecorded; resident of Baltimore Co.; stated to be 24 at departure. Does not appear in the record.

55. Trellis, Alexander (single): Not on the register of emigrants, origin and status unrecorded; stated to be 22 at departure. Died of fever, before April, 1839.

The total number of emigrants sent to Cape Palmas thus far: 421.

Brig BOXER, left Baltimore, December 12, 1839, arrived at Cape Palmas about January 18, 1840:

1. Baxter, Fitney (single): Status uncertain; resident of Queen Ann Co.; stated to be 24 at departure. Living with B. Bostick and Alex. Adams, 1843; with Rachel Harman, 1849; on her own, 1852.

2. Bostic, Benjamin (single): Status uncertain; resident of Frederick Co.; stated to be 68 at departure. Letter writer: September, 1841. Living with Fitney Baxter and Alex. Adams, 1843. Died before Jan. 17, 1846.

3. Browne, Willis (single): Status uncertain; resident of Washington Co.; stated to be 21 at departure. Living with Susan and Henson Dent, 1843. Signed petition, December, 1849. Resident of the colony, November, 1852, a seaman.

4. Davis, Stephen (husband of Mary Davis): Status uncertain; resident of Anne Arundel Co.; stated to be 44 at departure. Worked in the colony as a farmer. Died before 1848 Census.

5. Davis, Mary (wife of Stephen Davis): Status uncertain; resident of Anne Arundel Co.; stated to be 40 at departure. Cultivated .5 acre, 1848. Resident of the colony, November, 1852.

6. Davis, Thomas (son of Stephen Davis): Status uncertain; resident of Anne Arundel Co.; stated to be 10 at departure. Worked in the colony as a seaman. Married Grace Jackson, Feb. 9, 1852.

7. Davis, Maria (daughter of Stephen Davis): Status uncertain; resident of Anne Arundel Co.; stated to be 8 at departure. Bore illegitimate daughter, Mar. 4, 1852.

8. Davis, Priscilla (daughter of Stephen Davis): Status uncertain; resident of Anne Arundel Co.; stated to be 4 at departure. Resident of the colony, November, 1852.

9. Dent, Hanson (brother of Susan Dent): Status uncertain; resident of Washington Co.; stated to be 22 at departure. Signed petition, Jan. 14, 1850. Living in Louisa Dade household, 1852, a seaman.

10. Dent, Susan (sister of Hanson Dent): Status uncertain; resident of Washington Co.; stated to be 19 at departure. Married to Nelson Jackson, 1849. Resident of the colony, November, 1852.

11. Gibson, Jacob (husband of Eliza Gibson): Status uncertain; resident of Queen Ann Co.; stated to be 38 at departure. Worked in the colony as a farmer. Died of pulmonary disease, December, 1843.

12. Gibson, Eliza (wife of Jacob Gibson; also called Sarah Ann Gibson): Status uncertain; resident of Queen Ann Co.; stated to be 33 at departure. Later married Charles Scotland. Letter writer: Jan. 19, 1844. Resident of the colony, November, 1852.

13. Gibson, George (son of Jacob Gibson): Status uncertain; resident of Queen Ann Co.; stated to be 13 at departure. Later married Lavinia Ashton. Resident of the colony, November, 1852, a seaman.

14. Gibson, William (son of Jacob Gibson): Status uncertain; resident of Queen Ann Co.; stated to be 10 at departure. Worked in the colony as a seaman. Signed petition, Jan. 14, 1850. Died June 17, 1852.

15. Gibson, Martha (daughter of Jacob Gibson): Status uncertain; resident of Queen Ann Co.; stated to be 8 at departure. Living in Charles Scotland household, 1852.

16. Gibson, Sarah A. (daughter of Jacob Gibson): Status uncertain; resident of Queen Ann Co.; stated to be 6 at departure. Does not appear in the record after 1849.

17. Gibson, Mary E. (daughter of Jacob Gibson): Status uncertain; resident of Queen Ann Co.; stated to be 4 at departure. Living in Charles Scotland household, 1852.

18. Gibson, Jacob (son of Jacob Gibson): Status uncertain; resident of Queen Ann Co.; stated to be 5 months old at departure. Does not appear in the record.

19. Gross, Henry (single): Status uncertain; resident of Frederick Co.; stated to be 22 at departure. Does not appear in the record.

20. Hobbs, Moses (single, father of Mary Hobbs): Status uncertain; resident of Anne Arundel Co.; stated to be 50 at departure. Worked in the colony as a sawyer. Married Charlotte Parker, July 30, 1840; later married Fanny Tubman. Does not appear in the record after 1843.

21. Hobbs, Mary (daughter of Moses Hobbs, mother of John C. Hobbs; also called Mary Davis): Status uncertain; resident of Anne Arundel Co.; stated to be 23 at departure. Married Stephen Hall, June 9, 1840. Reportedly died of chronic phrenitis, 1841, but continues in the record as late as 1848.

22. Hobbs, John C. (son of Mary Hobbs): Status uncertain; resident of Anne Arundel Co.; stated to be 1 at departure. Does not appear in the record.

23. Hobbs, Jane (daughter of Moses Hobbs): Status uncertain; resident of Anne Arundel Co.; stated to be 18 at departure. Married Emanuel Davenport, Oct. 22, 1840; tried to get divorce from him, 1846. Remained married to him, 1848, but divorced by 1852.

24. Hobbs, Henry (son of Moses Hobbs): Status uncertain; resident of Anne Arundel Co.; stated to be 15 at departure. Living in Jacob Gross household, 1843. Lived with two other storekeepers, 1848. Does not appear in the record afterward.

25. Johnson, Henry (single): Status uncertain; resident of Frederick Co.; stated to be 25 at departure. Later married Nancy Johnson. Died before the 1849 Census.

26. Jarrett, Fanny (single, related to the Tippetts, mother of Robert Tippett; also called Fanny Johnson): Status uncertain; resident of Anne Arundel Co.; stated to be 19

at departure. Married Isaac Mumford, Nov. 24, 1842. Resident of the colony, November, 1852.

27. Tippett, Robert (son of Fanny Jarrett): Status uncertain; resident of St. Mary's Co.; stated to be 6 months old at departure. Died during acclimation, before June 8, 1840.

28. Tippett, William H. (husband of Matilda Tippett, father of Mary Tippett; also called William H. Neal): Status uncertain; resident of St. Mary's Co.; stated to be 24 at departure. Worked in the colony as a sawyer. Resident of the colony, November, 1852.

29. Tippett, Matilda (wife of William Tippett; also called Jane Neal): Status uncertain; resident of St. Mary's Co.; stated to be 20 at departure. Died April 12, 1852.

30. Tippett, Jane Catherine (single, mother of Rebecca Tippett; also called Kitty Tippett): Status uncertain; resident of St. Mary's Co.; stated to be 19 at departure. Living in William Neal household, 1843. Resident of the colony, November, 1852.

31. Tippett, Rebecca (daughter of Jane Tippett): Status uncertain; resident of St. Mary's Co.; stated to be 4 months old at departure. Died during acclimation, before June 8, 1840.

32. Tippett, William (uncertain relation to other Tippetts): Status uncertain; resident of St. Mary's Co.; stated to be at departure. Living in Paul Sansey household, 1843. Does not appear in the record afterward.

The total number of emigrants sent to Cape Palmas thus far: 453.

Brig HARRIET left Baltimore, December, 1841, arrived at Cape Palmas January 30, 1842:

1. Greene, Rachel (single, mother of several children; also called Rachel Allen): Status uncertain; resident of Calvert Co.; stated to be 40 at departure. Last name changed to Allen in 1848 Census. Cultivated 1.5 acres in 1848. Resident of the colony, November, 1852.

2. Greene, Clarissa (daughter of Rachel Greene): Status uncertain; resident of Calvert Co.; stated to be 16 at departure. Wife of James Martin, 1848 Census. Does not appear in the record afterward.

3. Greene, Sarah (daughter of Rachel Greene): Status uncertain; resident of Calvert Co.; stated to be 14 at departure. Died Sept. 19, 1842.

4. Greene, Emiline (daughter of Rachel Greene): Status uncertain; resident of Calvert Co.; stated to be 13 at departure. Resident of the colony, November, 1852.

5. Greene, Ann (daughter of Rachel Greene; also called Greene, Harriet): Status uncertain; resident of Calvert Co.; stated to be 10 at departure. Does not appear in the record after 1848.

6. Greene, Amelia (daughter of Rachel Greene): Status uncertain; resident of Calvert Co.; stated to be 10 at departure. Does not appear in the record after 1849.

7. Greene, John (son of Rachel Greene): Status uncertain; resident of Calvert Co.; stated to be 6 at departure. Resident of the colony, November, 1852.

8. Greene, Mahala (daughter of Rachel Greene): Status uncertain; resident of Calvert Co.; stated to be 3 at departure. Resident of the colony, November, 1852.

9. Greene, William (son of Rachel Greene; also called Henry H. Greene): Status uncertain; resident of Calvert Co.; stated to be 5 months old at departure. Does not appear in the record after 1843.

10. Greene, Eliza Ann (daughter of Emiline Greene): Status uncertain; resident of Calvert Co.; stated to be 4 months old at departure. Resident of the colony, November, 1852.

11. Lee, Harriet (single, mother of Frederick Lee; also called Harriet Toliver): Freed by a Mr. Calvert of Prince George's Co.; stated to be 25 at departure. Later appears married to Stern Toliver, with additional children by him. Does not appear in the record after 1849.

12. Lee, Frederick (son of Harriet Lee): Freed by a Mr. Calvert of Prince George's Co.; stated to be 8 at departure. Appears in Stephen Smith household, 1848, as his child (but unlikely so.) Does not appear in the record after 1849.

13. Lee, Edmund (son of Harriet Lee): Freed by a Mr. Calvert of Prince George's Co.; stated to be 6 at departure. Does not appear in the record after 1843.

14. Lee, Jessie Ann (daughter of Harriet Lee): Freed by a Mr. Calvert of Prince George's Co.; stated to be 3 at departure.

15. McFarland, Thomas (husband of Phebe McFarland): Status uncertain; resident of Petersburg, Va.; stated to be 50 at departure. Worked in the colony as a farmer; cultivated 2.5 acres in 1848. Later married Nancy Hutchins. Signed petition April, 1849. Died before 1852 Census.

16. McFarland, Phebe (wife of Thomas McFarland): Status uncertain; resident of Petersburg, Va.; stated to be 40 at departure. Died shortly after arrival in Africa.

17. McFarland, Eliza (daughter of Thomas McFarland; also called Eliza Coleman): Status uncertain; resident of Petersburg, Va.; stated to be 15 at departure. Worked in the colony as a spinster. Does not appear in the record after 1849.

18. McFarland, James (son of Thomas McFarland): Status uncertain; resident of Petersburg, Va.; stated to be 17 at departure. Died June 23, 1842.

19. McFarland, Sandy (son of Thomas McFarland): Status uncertain; resident of Petersburg, Va.; stated to be 15 at departure. Does not appear in the record after 1848.

20. Mills, Thomas F. (single): Status uncertain; resident of Baltimore Co.; stated to be 35 at departure. Worked in the colony as a carpenter. Resident of the colony, November, 1852.

21. Wilder, Nathaniel (brother of Alfred Wilder): Status uncertain; resident of St. Mary's Co.; stated to be 35 at departure. Does not appear in the record.

22. Wilder, Alfred (brother of Nathaniel Wilder): Status uncertain; resident of St. Mary's Co.; stated to be 24 at departure. Does not appear in the record.

23. Wilder, Thomas (brother of Nathaniel Wilder): Status uncertain; resident of St. Mary's Co.; stated to be 22 at departure. Does not appear in the record.

24. Wilder, Henry (brother of Nathaniel Wilder): Status uncertain; resident of St. Mary's Co.; stated to be 20 at departure. Does not appear in the record.

The total number of emigrants sent to Cape Palmas thus far: 477.

Brig GLOBE, left Baltimore, December 23, 1842, arrived at Cape Palmas, February 11, 1843:

1. Allen, Sarah A. (single; mother of Mary): Status uncertain; resident of St. Mary's Co.; stated to be 30 at departure. Does not appear in the record after 1843.

2. Allen, Mary A. (daughter of Sarah Allen): Status uncertain; resident of St. Mary's Co.; stated to be 10 at departure. Living in Cyrus Tubman household, Census 1852.

3. Allen, Alexander (son of Sarah Allen): Status uncertain; resident of St. Mary's Co.; stated to be 8 at departure. Does not appear in the record after 1843.

4. Allen, Matilda (daughter of Sarah Allen): Status uncertain; resident of St. Mary's Co.; stated to be 6 at departure. Does not appear in the record after 1843.

5. Ashton*, Moses (husband of Polly Ashton): Free resident of St. Mary's Co.; stated to be 44 at departure. Died of pleurisy, at sea.

6. Ashton, Polly (wife of Moses Ashton, daughter of James Lauder; also called Mary): Free resident of St. Mary's Co.; stated to be 38 at departure. Letter writer: Aug. 22, 1844. Married to Nicholas Jackson, Census 1848. Resident of the colony, November, 1852.

7. Ashton, James (son of Moses Ashton): Free resident of St. Mary's Co.; stated to be 16 at departure. Adopted son of N. Jackson, Sr., Census 1848. Signed petition, April, 1849 (as Ashton.) Resident of the colony, November, 1852.

8. Ashton, Thomas (son of Moses Ashton): Free resident of St. Mary's Co.; stated to be 14 at departure. Adopted son of N. Jackson, Sr., Census 1848. Signed petition, April, 1849, as Thomas Ashton. Surnamed Ashton, Census 1852, a laborer.

9. Ashton, Lavinia A. (daughter of Moses Ashton; also called Winnie A. Ashton ['49]): Free resident of St. Mary's Co.; stated to be 13 at departure. Living in Nicholas Jackson Sr. household, 1849. Married to George Gibson, Census 1852.

10. Ashton, Hannah (daughter of Moses Ashton): Free resident of St. Mary's Co.; stated to be 6 at departure. Adopted daughter of N. Jackson, Sr., Census 1848. Does not appear in the record after 1849.

11. Ashton, Sarah (daughter of Moses Ashton): Free resident of St. Mary's Co.; stated to be 4 at departure. Adopted daughter of N. Jackson, Sr., Census 1848. Resident of the colony, November, 1852.

12. Ashton, Polly (daughter of Moses Ashton): Free resident of St. Mary's Co.; stated to be 3 at departure. Adopted daughter of N. Jackson, Sr., Census 1848. Does not appear in the record after 1849.

13. Ashton, Moses (son of Moses Ashton): Free resident of St. Mary's Co.; stated to be 3 months old at departure. Reportedly died at sea, but recorded in 1843 Census, 3 months old. Does not appear in the record afterward.

14. Auther, Henry (brother of John Auther; also called James [pet. January, 1850]): Status uncertain; resident of St. Mary's Co.; stated to be 30 at departure. Signed petition, Jan. 14, 1850. Does not appear in the record afterward.

15. Auther, John (brother of Henry Auther, husband of Mary Auther): Status uncertain; resident of St. Mary's Co.; stated to be 32 at departure. Worked in the colony as a tailor, laborer, and farmer. Cultivated 2 acres in 1848. Signed petitions, April 1849, and January, 1850. Resident of the colony, November, 1852.

16. Auther, Mary (wife of John Auther): Status uncertain; resident of St. Mary's Co.; stated to be 30 at departure. Resident of the colony, November, 1852.

17. Auther, John (son of John Auther): Status uncertain; resident of St. Mary's Co.; stated to be 3 weeks old at departure. Died during acclimation, Mar. 12, 1843.

18. Banks, Lilly (single): Status uncertain; resident of Dorchester Co.; stated to be 55 at departure. Does not appear in the record after 1843.

19. Barnes, William A (husband of Mary Barnes): Free resident of St. Mary's Co.; stated to be 31 at departure. Worked in the colony as a sawyer and farmer. Cultivated 2 acres in 1848. Signed petition, Jan. 14, 1850. Died before November, 1852.

20. Barnes, Mary (wife of William Barnes): Free resident of St. Mary's Co.; stated to be 38 at departure. Resident of the colony, November, 1852.

21. Barnes, William A., Jr. (son of William Barnes): Free resident of St. Mary's Co.; stated to be 7 at departure. Reportedly died of fever complicated by worms, Mar. 6, 1843. Reappears in Census 1852, living in his mother's household.

22. Barnes, James (son of William Barnes): Free resident of St. Mary's Co.; stated to be 2 at departure. Died of fever complicated by worms, Mar. 25, 1843.

23. Barnes, Sarah (sister of William Barnes; also called S. Mills ['48]): Free resident of St. Mary's Co.; stated to be 36 at departure. Does not appear in the record after 1849.

24. Barnes, Martha (daughter of Sarah Barnes): Free resident of St. Mary's Co.; stated to be 15 at departure. Does not appear in the record after 1843.

25. Barnes, Moses L. (son of Sarah Barnes): Free resident of St. Mary's Co.; stated to be 10 at departure. Living with his mother, Census 1848–9; in Medley Scotland household, 1852.

26. Barnes, Sarah E. (daughter of Sarah Barnes): Free resident of St. Mary's Co.; stated to be 8 at departure. Does not appear in the record after 1843.

27. Barnes, George R. (son of Sarah Barnes): Free resident of St. Mary's Co.; stated to be 2 at departure. Does not appear in the record after 1843.

28. Brooks, Philip (husband of Sally Brooks): Status uncertain; resident of St. Mary's Co.; stated to be 59 at departure. Does not appear in the record after 1843.

29. Brooks, Sally (wife of Philip Brooks): Status uncertain; resident of St. Mary's Co.; stated to be 38 at departure. Died of fever and complications of childbirth, Mar. 10, 1843.

30. Brooks, John (son of Philip Brooks): Free resident of St. Mary's Co.; stated to be 14 at departure. Does not appear in the record after 1843.

31. Brooks, Philip (son of Philip Brooks): Status uncertain; resident of St. Mary's Co.; stated to be 10 at departure. Died during acclimation, Mar. 7, 1843.

32. Brooks, Martha (daughter of Philip Brooks): Status uncertain; resident of St. Mary's Co.; stated to be 7 at departure. Does not appear in the record after 1843.

33. Brooks, Ralph (son of Philip Brooks): Status uncertain; resident of St. Mary's Co.; stated to be 5 at departure. Living in Josh Stewart household, 1849. Does not appear in the record afterward.

34. Brooks, Mary E. (daughter of Philip Brooks): Status uncertain; resident of St. Mary's Co.; stated to be 2 at departure. Does not appear in the record after 1843.

35. Coleman, Ann M. (single): Status uncertain; resident of Dorchester Co.; stated to be 19 at departure. Does not appear in the record after 1843.

36. Coleman, Leah (single): Status uncertain; resident of Dorchester Co.; stated to be 32 at departure. Worked in the colony as a spinster. Married Samuel Scotland, about 1850. Resident of the colony, November, 1852.

37. Cornish, Harrison (husband of Mary Cornish): Status uncertain; resident of Dorchester Co.; stated to be 30 at departure. Worked in the colony as a laborer and sawyer. Cultivated one acre in 1848. Signed petition, Jan. 14, 1850. Does not appear in the record after 1850.

38. Cornish, Mary (wife of Harrison Cornish): Status uncertain; resident of Dorchester Co.; stated to be 27 at departure. Does not appear in the record after 1848.

39. Cornish, David M. (son of Harrison Cornish; also called Matthias ['49]): Status uncertain; resident of Dorchester Co.; stated to be 4 at departure. Does not appear in the record after 1849.

40. Cornish, John H. (son of Harrison Cornish): Status uncertain; resident of Dorchester Co.; stated to be 2 at departure. Died of fever, Mar. 25, 1843.

41. Cornish, Caroline (single; mother of Arabella Cornish): Status uncertain; resident of Dorchester Co.; stated to be 23 at departure. Does not appear in the record after 1843.

42. Cornish, Arabella A. (daughter of Caroline Cornish): Status uncertain; resident of Dorchester Co.; stated to be 1 at departure. Lived in Harrison Cornish household, 1849; in Joshua Cornish household, 1852.

43. Cornish, Eliza (single): Status uncertain; resident of Dorchester Co.; stated to be 22 at departure. Does not appear in the record after 1843.

44. Curtis, Julia (sister of Margaret Lauder): Free resident of St. Mary's Co.; stated to be 20 at departure. Fell on board the ship, suffering a brain injury that left her helpless.

Living in Lavinia Jones household, 1843; in Stephen Smith household, 1848, described as his child. Does not appear in the record after 1848.

45. Dawson, James (son of Sarah Morris): Free resident of St. Mary's Co.; stated to be 18 at departure. Does not appear in the record after 1843.

46. Dawson, Sally Ann (daughter of Sarah Morris): Free resident of St. Mary's Co.; stated to be 16 at departure. Does not appear in the record after 1843.

47. Dennard, John (single): Status uncertain; resident of Dorchester Co.; stated to be 29 at departure. Does not appear in the record after 1843.

48. Denton, Henry (husband of Cornelia Denton): Status uncertain; resident of St. Mary's Co.; stated to be 19 at departure. Does not appear in the record after 1843.

49. Denton, Cornelia (wife of Henry Denton): Status uncertain; resident of St. Mary's Co.; stated to be 17 at departure. Died during acclimation, Mar. 6, 1843.

50. Denton, David M. (son of Henry Denton): Status uncertain; resident of St. Mary's Co.; stated to be 10 months old at departure. Died during acclimation, Mar. 13, 1843.

51. Enalls, Greenbury (single): Status uncertain; resident of Dorchester Co.; stated to be 25 at departure. Worked in the colony as a laborer. Signed petition, April, 1849. Does not appear in the record afterward.

52. Gibson, Polly (single): Status uncertain; resident of Dorchester Co.; stated to be 50 at departure. Does not appear in the record after 1843.

53. Gibson, James (son of Polly Gibson): Status uncertain; resident of Baltimore; stated to be 29 at departure. Does not appear in the record after 1843.

54. Green, Benson (husband of Dinah Green): Status uncertain; resident of St. Mary's Co.; stated to be 30 at departure. Worked in the colony as a sawyer and farmer. Cultivated two acres, 1848. Signed petitions, April and December, 1849. Died before November, 1852.

55. Green, Dinah (wife of Benson Green): Status uncertain; resident of St. Mary's Co.; stated to be 30 at departure. Resident of the colony, November, 1852.

56. Green, Sarah A. (daughter of Benson Green): Status uncertain; resident of St. Mary's Co.; stated to be 13 at departure. Resident of the colony, November, 1852.

57. Green, Caroline (daughter of Benson Green): Status uncertain; resident of St. Mary's Co.; stated to be 6 at departure. Reportedly died of unrecorded cause, Sept. 19, 1842, but entered in Census 1843 as age 6. Does not appear in the record afterward.

58. Green, George H. (son of Benson Green): Status uncertain; resident of St. Mary's Co.; stated to be 5 at departure. Resident of the colony, November, 1852.

59. Green, Esther (daughter of Benson Green): Status uncertain; resident of St. Mary's Co.; stated to be 4 at departure. Resident of the colony, November, 1852.

60. Green, Julia A. (daughter of Benson Green): Status uncertain; resident of St. Mary's Co.; stated to be 2 at departure. Resident of the colony, November, 1852.

61. Green, Benson James (son of Benson Green): Status uncertain; resident of St. Mary's Co.; stated to be 1 at departure. Resident of the colony, November, 1852.

62. Harris, Joshua (single; also called James): Status uncertain; resident of Dorchester Co.; stated to be 32 at departure. Worked in the colony as a cooper. Later married a woman named Ann, of uncertain origin. Signed petition, April, 1849. Died shortly afterward.

63. Jenkins, Susan (single; mother of Elizabeth Jenkins): Status uncertain; resident of Dorchester Co.; stated to be 24 at departure. Living with Samuel Lilly and others, 1852.

64. Jenkins, Elizabeth (daughter of Susan Jenkins): Status uncertain; resident of Dorchester Co.; stated to be 2 at departure. Does not appear in the record after 1843.

65. Lauder*, James (husband of Margaret Lauder): Free resident of St. Mary's Co., a

farmer and ferry operator; stated to be 62 at departure. Died of gangrene, at sea.

66. Lauder*, Margaret (wife of James Lauder): Free resident of St. Mary's Co.; stated to be 40 at departure. Died of complications from pregnancy, at sea.

67. Lauder, Thomas (son of James Lauder, husband of Catherine Lauder): Free resident of St. Mary's Co.; stated to be 34 at departure. Worked in the colony as a farmer. Cultivated 2 acres in 1848. Letter writer: Aug. 22, 1844; Jan. 2, 1846; Jan. 25, 1847. Died in December, 1847.

68. Lauder, Catherine (wife of Thomas Lauder; also called Kitty Lauder): Free resident of St. Mary's Co.; stated to be 35 at departure. Died before January, 1847.

69. Lauder, James (son of Thomas Lauder): Free resident of St. Mary's Co.; stated to be 7 at departure. Living with Mary Lauder, 1849. Does not appear in the record afterward.

70. Lauder, Polly (daughter of Thomas Lauder; also called Mary): Free resident of St. Mary's Co.; stated to be 5 at departure. Living as child of Mary Lauder, Census 1848. Does not appear in the record afterward.

71. Lauder, Rebecca (daughter of Thomas Lauder): Free resident of St. Mary's Co.; stated to be 2 at departure. Living as child of Mary Lauder, Census 1848. Does not appear in the record afterward.

72. McGill, Lydia (wife of Samuel F. McGill): Free resident of Baltimore; stated to be 20 at departure. Died of fever, late 1843.

73. Minskie, William (single): Status uncertain; resident of St. Mary's Co.; stated to be 30 at departure. Does not appear in the record after 1843.

74. Mitchell, Thomas (son of Ann Mitchell): Status uncertain; resident of Dorchester Co.; stated to be 1 at departure. Resident of the colony, November, 1852.

75. Morris, Sarah (single, mother of John T. Morris, related to James Lauder): Free resident of St. Mary's Co.; stated to be 39 at departure. Letter writer: Aug. 22, 1844. Does not appear in the record afterward.

76. Morris, John T. (son of Sarah Morris): Free resident of St. Mary's Co.; stated to be 13 at departure. Living alone with younger brother and sister, Census 1848. Living in N. Jackson Sr. household, 1849. Resident of the colony, November, 1852.

77. Morris, Job R. (son of Sarah Morris): Free resident of St. Mary's Co.; stated to be 11 at departure. Living in N. Jackson Sr. household, 1849. Resident of the colony, November, 1852, a seaman.

78. Morris, Fanny (daughter of Sarah Morris): Free resident of St. Mary's Co.; stated to be 8 at departure. Living with brother John, Census 1848. Living in N. Jackson Sr. household, 1849 and 1852.

79. Morris, Battle (son of Sarah Morris): Free resident of St. Mary's Co.; stated to be 5 at departure. Living with brother John, Census 1848. Living in N. Jackson Sr. household, 1849 and 1852.

80. Pinkett, Henry (husband of Harriet Pinkett): Status uncertain; resident of Dorchester Co.; stated to be 32 at departure. Worked in the colony as a ship carpenter and farmer. Cultivated 2.5 acres in 1848. Signed petition, Jan. 14, 1850. Elected councilor, 1851. Resident of the colony, November, 1852.

81. Pinkett, Harriet (wife of Henry Pinkett): Status uncertain; resident of Dorchester Co.; stated to be 28 at departure. Appears to have died before 1848.

82. Pinkett, Mary (daughter of Henry Pinkett): Status uncertain; resident of Dorchester Co.; stated to be 11 at departure. Does not appear in the record after 1848.

83. Pinkett, William H. (son of Henry Pinkett): Status uncertain; resident of Dorchester Co.; stated to be 10 at departure. Resident of the colony, November, 1852.

84. Pinkett, Harriet A. (daughter of Henry Pinkett; also called Georgeanna): Status uncertain; resident of Dorchester Co.; stated to be 4 at departure. Resident of the colony, November, 1852.

85. Pinkett, Thomas D. (son of Henry Pinkett): Status uncertain; resident of Dorchester Co.; stated to be 2 at departure. Resident of the colony, November, 1852.

86. Smith, Selitia (wife of Stephen Smith; also called Cecilia): Purchased by her husband, 1842; resident of St. Mary's Co.; stated to be 48 at departure. Letter writer: Oct. 20, 1849. Resident of the colony, November, 1852.

87. Smith, John H. (son of Stephen Smith): Purchased by his father, 1842; resident of St. Mary's Co.; stated to be 14 at departure. Resident of the colony, November, 1852.

88. Smith, Ellen (daughter of Stephen Smith): Purchased by her father, 1842; resident of St. Mary's Co.; stated to be 11 at departure. Resident of the colony, November, 1852.

89. Smith, Eliza D. (daughter of Stephen Smith): Purchased by her father, 1842; resident of St. Mary's Co.; stated to be 2 at departure. Resident of the colony, November, 1852.

90. Smith, Paul (single): Free resident of St. Mary's Co.; stated to be 27 at departure. Worked in the colony as a blacksmith and lighthouse keeper. Signed petition, December, 1849. Returned to Maryland in 1850 for a recruiting tour. Resident of the colony, November, 1852.

91. Thompson, John (son of Mary Barnes): Free resident of St. Mary's Co.; stated to be 8 at departure. Does not appear in the record after 1843.

92. Thompson, Joseph C. (husband of Mary Thompson): Status uncertain; resident of Dorchester Co.; stated to be 38 at departure. Worked in the colony as a sawyer and farmer. Appointed Measurer of Lumber, 1845. Letter writer: Dec. 16, 1847; June 16, 1848. Cultivated 1.25 acres in 1848. Administrator of Thomas Lauder's estate. Signed pro-annexation petition, 1851. Died before November 1852.

93. Thompson, Mary (wife of Joseph C. Thompson): Status uncertain; resident of Dorchester Co.; stated to be 32 at departure. Resident of the colony, November, 1852.

94. Thompson, Rachel (daughter of Joseph C. Thompson): Status uncertain; resident of Dorchester Co.; stated to be 12 at departure. Does not appear in the record after 1849.

95. Thompson, Jeffrey (son of Joseph C. Thompson): Status uncertain; resident of Dorchester Co.; stated to be 10 at departure. Worked in the colony as a sawyer. Resident of the colony, November, 1852.

96. Thompson, Sarah J. (daughter of Joseph C. Thompson): Status uncertain; resident of Dorchester Co.; stated to be 8 at departure. Resident of the colony, November, 1852.

97. Thompson, Thomas J. (son of Joseph C. Thompson): Status uncertain; resident of Dorchester Co.; stated to be 5 at departure. Does not appear in the record after 1849.

98. Thompson, Joseph (son of Joseph C. Thompson): Status uncertain; resident of Dorchester Co.; stated to be 3 at departure. Does not appear in the record after 1848.

99. Thompson, James (son of Joseph C. Thompson): Status uncertain; resident of Dorchester Co.; stated to be 1 at departure. Resident of the colony, November, 1852.

100. Tippett, Maria (single; mother of John Tippett): Status uncertain; resident of St. Mary's Co.; stated to be 26 at departure. Worked in the colony as a seamstress. Married to Thomas Dent by 1848. Resident of the colony, November, 1852.

101. Tippett, John (son of Maria Tippett): Status uncertain; resident of St. Mary's Co.; stated to be 7 at departure. Living in Thomas Dent household, 1849. Does not appear in the record afterward.

102. Tippett, George (son of Maria Tippett): Status uncertain; resident of St. Mary's Co.; stated to be 2 at departure. Does not appear in the record after 1843.

103. Tippett, Sylvester (son of Maria Tippett): Status uncertain; resident of St. Mary's Co.; stated to be 1 at departure. Does not appear in the record after 1843.

104. Mitchell, Ann (single, mother of Jane Mitchell): Status uncertain; resident of Dorchester Co.; stated to be 23 at departure. Later married Cyrus Tubman. Resident of the colony, November, 1852.

105. Watts, John (brother of James and Cornelius Watts): Free resident of St. Mary's Co.; stated to be 21 at departure. Worked in the colony as a sawyer and farmer. Letter writer: Aug. 22, 1844; June 16, 1848. Cultivated 2 acres in 1848. Does not appear in the record afterward.

106. Watts, James (brother of John and Cornelius): Free resident of St. Mary's Co.; stated to be 19 at departure. Struck by lightning, shortly after arrival at Cape Palmas.

107. Watts, Cornelius (brother of James and John): Free resident of St. Mary's Co.; stated to be 17 at departure. Mentioned in letter, June 16, 1848. Living in Hannah James household, 1849; living alone, 1852.

108. Watts, Sarah (sister of John Watts): Free resident of St. Mary's Co.; stated to be 16 at departure. Does not appear in the record after 1843.

109. Willson, Daniel (single): Status uncertain; resident of St. Mary's Co.; stated to be 15 at departure. Living in Sarah Allen household, 1843. Returned for a recruiting tour in his old neighborhood, 1847. Does not appear in the record afterward.

The total number of emigrants sent to Cape Palmas thus far: 587.

LATROBE, left Baltimore, early November, 1843, arrived at Cape Palmas, January 12, 1844:

1. Barnett, Rachel (single; mother of Samuel Barnett; also called R. Barnard): Status uncertain; resident of Calvert Co.; stated to be 26 at departure. Worked in the colony as a spinster. Resident of the colony, November, 1852.

2. Barnett, Samuel (son of Rachel Barnett; also called Barnard): Status uncertain; resident of Calvert Co.; stated to be 7 at departure. Does not appear in the record after 1849.

3. Barnett, James (son of Rachel Barnett; also called Barnard): Status uncertain; resident of Calvert Co.; stated to be 4 at departure. Resident of the colony, November, 1852.

4. Barnett, Julia Ann (daughter of Rachel Barnett; also called Barnard): Status uncertain; resident of Calvert Co.; stated to be 3 at departure. Resident of the colony, November, 1852.

5. Buchanan, Delia (single; also called Delilah): Status uncertain; resident of Charles Co.; stated to be 15 at departure. Worked in the colony as a spinster. Living in Willis Brown household, 1852.

6. Buchanan, Milly (single): Status uncertain; resident of Charles Co.; stated to be 19 at departure. Living in Rachel Hughes household, 1852.

7. Buchanan, Ann (relations unclear; also called Maria A. Buchanan ['52]): Status uncertain; resident of Charles Co.; stated to be 10 at departure. Living in J. B. Dennis household, 1848; with sisters Delia and Milly, 1849. Resident of the colony, November, 1852.

8. Buchanan, Harriet (mother of Cecilia Buchanan): Status uncertain; resident of Charles Co.; stated to be 18 at departure. Does not appear in the record.

9. Buchanan, Cecilia (daughter of Harriet Buchanan): Status uncertain; resident of Charles Co.; stated to be 3 months old at departure. Does not appear in the record.

10. Carpenter, Eve (single; mother of Henry Carpenter): Status uncertain; resident of Charles Co.; stated to be 38 at departure. Worked in the colony as a spinster. Died Feb. 19, 1852.

11. Carpenter, Henry (son of Eve Carpenter; also called Charles Henry Carpenter ['52]): Status uncertain; resident of Charles Co.; stated to be 14 at departure. Resident of the colony, November, 1852.

12. Carpenter, Minty (daughter of Eve Carpenter): Status uncertain; resident of Charles Co.; stated to be 12 at departure. Resident of the colony, November, 1852.

13. Carpenter, Marshall (son of Eve Carpenter): Status uncertain; resident of Charles Co.; stated to be 9 at departure. Resident of the colony, November, 1852.

14. Carpenter, Spencer (son of Eve Carpenter): Status uncertain; resident of Charles Co.; stated to be 7 at departure. Living in Calfrey Tubman household, 1848. Does not appear in the record afterward.

15. Carpenter, Cornelius (son of Eve Carpenter): Status uncertain; resident of Charles Co.; stated to be 4 at departure. Resident of the colony, November, 1852.

16. Carpenter, Richard (son of Eve Carpenter): Status uncertain; resident of Charles Co.; stated to be 2 at departure. Resident of the colony, November, 1852.

17. Carpenter, Julia (daughter of Eve Carpenter; also called Juliet A. Carpenter): Status uncertain; resident of Charles Co.; stated to be 5 months old at departure. Resident of the colony, November, 1852.

18. Contee, Abednego (husband of Ann Contee): Status uncertain; resident of Charles Co.; stated to be 56 at departure. Died before 1848 Census.

19. Contee, Ann (wife of Abednego Contee; also called Nancy): Status uncertain; resident of Charles Co.; stated to be 51 at departure. Worked in the colony as a laundress. Cultivated .5 acre in 1848. Resident of the colony, November, 1852.

20. Contee, Susan Ann (daughter of Abednego Contee): Status uncertain; resident of Charles Co.; stated to be 11 at departure. Does not appear in the record after 1848.

21. Contee, Letty (daughter of Abednego Contee): Status uncertain; resident of Charles Co.; stated to be 4 at departure. Living in Ann Contee household, 1852.

22. Contee, Meeckey(?) (unknown relation to Abednego Contee): Status uncertain; resident of Charles Co.; stated to be 32 at departure. Does not appear in the record.

23. Contee, Nancy (unknown relation to Abednego Contee): Status uncertain; resident of Charles Co.; stated to be 7 at departure. Does not appear in the record after 1848.

24. Contee, Lewellen H. (grandson of Abednego Contee): Status uncertain; resident of Charles Co.; stated to be 4 at departure. Does not appear in the record after 1849.

25. Contee, Rezin (unknown relation to Abednego Contee): Status uncertain; resident of Charles Co.; stated to be 3 at departure. Does not appear in the record.

26. Covington, John (unknown relation to other Covingtons; also called Covender): Status uncertain; resident of Calvert Co.; stated to be 35 at departure. Cultivated .75 acre in 1848. Does not appear in the record afterward.

27. Covington, Nicholas (uncertain family relations; also called Carpenter, Covender): Status uncertain; resident of Calvert Co.; stated to be 25 at departure. Worked in the colony as a sawyer and farmer. Married one Amelia, of uncertain origin. Cultivated 1.25 acres in 1848. Signed petition, Jan. 14, 1850. Died before November, 1852.

28. Covington, Charles (uncertain family relations; also called Covender and Carpenter [from 1849]): Status uncertain; resident of Calvert Co.; stated to be 24 at departure. Worked in the colony as a farmer, laborer, and sawyer. Cultivated 1 acre in 1848. Signed petition, Jan. 14, 1850. Resident of the colony, November, 1852.

29. Covington, Mary (mother of Matilda Covington; also called Stevenson, then Dorsey): Status uncertain; resident of Calvert Co.; stated to be 25 at departure. Married Phillip Dorsey, June 10, 1848. Resident of the colony, November, 1852.

30. Covington, Matilda (daughter of Mary Covington; also called Matilda Stevenson): Status uncertain; resident of Calvert Co.; stated to be 9 at departure. Resident of the colony, November, 1852.

31. Covington, John (son of Mary Covington; also called John Stevenson): Status uncertain; resident of Calvert Co.; stated to be 8 at departure. Resident of the colony, November, 1852.

32. Covington, William (of Mary Covington; also called William Stevenson): Status uncertain; resident of Calvert Co.; stated to be 4 at departure. Resident of the colony, November, 1852.

33. Covington, Ann Maria (daughter of Mary Covington; also called Ame Stevenson ['49]): Status uncertain; resident of Calvert Co.; stated to be 5 at departure. Resident of the colony, November, 1852.

34. Covington, Anthony (son of Mary Covington; also called Anthony Stevenson): Status uncertain; resident of Calvert Co.; stated to be 1 at departure. Resident of the colony, November, 1852.

35. Covington, Harriet (daughter of Ellen Harris; also called Henrietta Harris [after '52]): Status uncertain; resident of Calvert Co.; stated to be 5 at departure. (Surname changed at 1848 Census.) Living as an orphan in the house of Rachel Barnet, 1852.

36. Covington, Isabel (daughter of Ellen Harris; also called Eliza Harris): Status uncertain; resident of Calvert Co.; stated to be 3 at departure. (Surname and Christian name changed at 1848 Census.) Living as an orphan in the house of Rachel Barnet, 1852.

37. Covington, Hillary (daughter of Ellen Harris; also called Hillary Harris): Status uncertain; resident of Calvert Co.; stated to be 7 months old at departure.(Surname changed at 1848 Census.) Living as an orphan in the house of Rachel Barnet, 1852.

38. Dade, Louisa (single woman; mother of Mary Ann or Jane Speakes): Status uncertain; resident of Charles Co.; stated to be 39 at departure. Living with James B. Dennis family, 1849. Head of household, 1852.

39. Dorsey, Peggy (single; mother of Eliza Jane): Status uncertain; resident of Charles Co.; stated to be 26 at departure. Does not appear in the record.

40. Dorsey, Eliza Jane (daughter of Peggy Dorsey): Status uncertain; resident of Charles Co.; stated to be 9 at departure. Does not appear in the record.

41. Dorsey, Josias (son of Peggy Dorsey): Status uncertain; resident of Charles Co.; stated to be 3 at departure. Does not appear in the record.

42. Dorsey, John Lewis (son of Peggy Dorsey): Status uncertain; resident of Charles Co.; stated to be 18 months old at departure. Does not appear in the record.

43. Dorsey, Mary (daughter of Peggy Dorsey): Status uncertain; resident of Charles Co.; stated to be 3 months old at departure. Does not appear in the record.

44. Hall, Andrew (husband of Eliza Hall): Status uncertain; resident of Anne Arundel Co.; stated to be 33 at departure. Worked in the colony as a farmer. Letter writer: Jan. 24, 1847. Cultivated 2.5 acres in 1848. Died of dropsy, Jan. 16, 1848.

45. Hall, Eliza (wife of Andrew Hall): Status uncertain; resident of Anne Arundel Co.; stated to be 30 at departure. Resident of the colony, November, 1852.

46. Hall, John T. (son of Andrew Hall): Status uncertain; resident of Anne Arundel Co.; stated to be 14 at departure. Worked in the colony as a laborer. Resident of the colony, November, 1852.

47. Hall, Joseph (uncertain relation to Andrew Hall): Status uncertain; resident of Anne Arundel Co.; stated to be 13 at departure. Does not appear in the record.

48. Hanson, James (single): Status uncertain; resident of Charles Co.; stated to be 24 at departure. Worked in the colony as a laborer. Later married Mary A. Bowyer. Returned for a recruiting tour of his old neighborhood in 1847. Signed petition, Jan. 14, 1850. Resident of the colony, November, 1852.

49. Harris, Ellen (single; mother of Harriet, Hillary, and Isabel Covington): Status uncertain; resident of Calvert Co.; stated to be 25 at departure. Worked in the colony as a spinster. Cultivated 1.5 acres in 1848. Died before November, 1852.

50. Hutchins, Robert (single): Status uncertain; resident of Charles Co.; stated to be 30 at departure. Worked in the colony as a farmer and rough carpenter. Cultivated 2.5 acres in 1848. Married Harriet Jarvis, Aug. 15, 1848. Signed petition, Jan. 14, 1850. Died before November, 1852.

51. Smith, Sophia (single, unclear relation to Charles, and Margaret Smith): Status uncertain; resident of Calvert Co.; stated to be 50 at departure. Does not appear in the record.

52. Smith, Rosina (uncertain relation of Cornelius Smith): Status uncertain; resident of Calvert Co.; stated to be 20 at departure. Appears as the wife of Osborn Tubman, 1848 and after. Resident of the colony, November, 1852.

53. Smith, Charles (son of Rosina Smith): Status uncertain; resident of Calvert Co.; stated to be 7 at departure. Resident of the colony, November, 1852.

54. Smith, Margaret (daughter of Rosina Smith): Status uncertain; resident of Calvert Co.; stated to be 4 at departure. Resident of the colony, November, 1852.

55. Smith, Cornelia (single; mother of Esther Ann Smith and other children): Status uncertain; resident of Calvert Co.; stated to be 25 at departure. Married John Henry Thomas, Nov. 23, 1848. Appears to have visited the United States, 1849. Resident of the colony, November, 1852.

56. Smith, Esther Ann (daughter of Cornelia Smith; also called "Lethey" and with surname Thomas): Status uncertain; resident of Calvert Co.; stated to be 8 at departure. Resident of the colony, November, 1852.

57. Smith, Martha Ann (daughter of Cornelia Smith; also called Thomas): Status uncertain; resident of Calvert Co.; stated to be 6 at departure. Resident of the colony, November, 1852.

58. Smith, Louisa (daughter of Cornelia Smith; also called Jessie): Status uncertain; resident of Calvert Co.; stated to be 5 at departure. Does not appear in the record after 1848.

59. Smith, Caroline (daughter of Cornelia Smith; also called Thomas): Status uncertain; resident of Calvert Co.; stated to be 2 at departure. Resident of the colony, November, 1852.

60. Smith, James (son of Cornelia Smith; also called Thomas): Status uncertain; resident of Calvert Co.; stated to be 1 month old at departure. Resident of the colony, November, 1852.

61. Speaks, Jane (single; also called Mary Ann Speakes or Dent): Status uncertain; resident of Charles Co.; stated to be 19 at departure. Married Henson Dent about 1847. Living in Louisa Dade household, 1852.

62. Stewart, Ruthy (single; grandmother(?) of John Wesley Stewart): Status uncertain; resident of Calvert Co.; stated to be 75 at departure. Does not appear in the record.

63. Stewart, John Wesley (grandson of Ruthy Stewart): Status uncertain; resident of

Calvert Co.; stated to be 1 month old at departure. Possibly the same as "James Stewart," apprentice, aged 8, in household of Henry Duncan, 1849, and again in Lydia Howard's house, 1852, aged 14.

64. Turner, Cecilia (single): Status uncertain; resident of Charles Co.; stated to be 39 at departure. Does not appear in the record.

65. Young, Sarah Ann (single): Status uncertain; resident of Charles Co.; stated to be 14 at departure. Does not appear in the record.

The total number of emigrants sent to Cape Palmas thus far: 652.

CHIPOLA, left Baltimore mid-November, 1844, arrived at Cape Palmas January 10, 1845:

1. [Without Surname], William (family relations unspecified): Freed to emigrate by a master in Matthews Co., Va., who paid for their passage to Africa; stated to be 23 at departure. Does not appear in the record.

2. [Without Surname], James (family relations unspecified): Freed to emigrate by a master in Matthews Co., Va., who paid for their passage to Africa; stated to be 24 at departure. Does not appear in the record.

3. [Without Surname], Thomas (family relations unspecified): Freed to emigrate by a master in Matthews Co., Va., who paid for their passage to Africa; stated to be 27 at departure. Does not appear in the record.

4. [Without Surname], Fanny (family relations unspecified): Freed to emigrate by a master in Matthews Co., Va., who paid for their passage to Africa; stated to be 24 at departure. Does not appear in the record.

5. [Without Surname], Mary Ann (family relations unspecified): Freed to emigrate by a master in Matthews Co., Va., who paid for their passage to Africa; stated to be 21 at departure. Does not appear in the record.

6. [Without Surname], Samson (family relations unspecified): Freed to emigrate by a master in Matthews Co., Va., who paid for their passage to Africa; stated to be 11 at departure. Does not appear in the record.

7. [Without Surname], Betsy (family relations unspecified): Freed to emigrate by a master in Matthews Co., Va., who paid for their passage to Africa; stated to be 19 at departure. Does not appear in the record.

8. [Without Surname], Harriet (family relations unspecified): Freed to emigrate by a master in Matthews Co., Va., who paid for their passage to Africa; stated to be 17 at departure. Does not appear in the record.

9. [Without Surname], Frank (family relations unspecified): Freed to emigrate by a master in Matthews Co., Va., who paid for their passage to Africa; stated to be 2 at departure. Does not appear in the record.

10. [Without Surname], John William (family relations unspecified): Freed to emigrate by a master in Matthews Co., Va., who paid for their passage to Africa; stated to be 2 at departure. Does not appear in the record.

11. [Bond], Samuel (husband of Mary Bond; surname adopted in Liberia): Freed to emigrate by a master in Matthews Co., Va., who paid for their passage to Africa; stated to be 17 at departure. Worked in the colony as a laborer. Does not appear in the record after 1848.

12. [Bond], Mary (wife of Samuel Bond; surname adopted in Liberia): Freed to emigrate by a master in Matthews Co., Va., who paid for their passage to Africa; stated to be 18 at departure. Does not appear in the record after 1848.

13. [Diggs], Judy (family relations uncertain; surname adopted in Liberia; also called India or Julia Diggs): Freed to emigrate by a master in Matthews Co., Va., who paid for their passage to Africa; stated to be 35 at departure. Worked in the colony as a spinster. Cultivated .5 acre in 1848. Resident of the colony, November, 1852.

14. [Diggs], Nancy (family relations uncertain; surname adopted in Liberia): Freed to emigrate by a master in Matthews Co., Va., who paid for their passage to Africa; stated to be 13 at departure. Does not appear in the record after 1848.

15. [Diggs], Caroline (family relations uncertain; surname adopted in Liberia): Freed to emigrate by a master in Matthews Co., Va., who paid for their passage to Africa; stated to be 12 at departure. Resident of the colony, November, 1852.

16. [Diggs], Richard (family relations uncertain; surname adopted in Liberia): Freed to emigrate by a master in Matthews Co., Va., who paid for their passage to Africa; stated to be 11 at departure. Resident of the colony, November, 1852.

17. [Diggs], Henry (family relations uncertain; surname adopted in Liberia): Freed to emigrate by a master in Matthews Co., Va., who paid for their passage to Africa; stated to be 7 at departure. Resident of the colony, November, 1852.

18. [Diggs], Nelly (family relations uncertain; surname adopted in Liberia; also called Louisa Diggs): Freed to emigrate by a master in Matthews Co., Va., who paid for their passage to Africa; stated to be 7 at departure. Does not appear in the record after 1848.

19. [Diggs], Edward (family relations uncertain; surname adopted in Liberia): Freed to emigrate by a master in Matthews Co., Va., who paid for their passage to Africa; stated to be 3 at departure. Resident of the colony, November, 1852.

20. [Diggs], Ralph (family relations uncertain; surname adopted in Liberia): Freed to emigrate by a master in Matthews Co., Va., who paid for their passage to Africa; stated to be 3 months old at departure. Resident of the colony, November, 1852.

21. Flanagan, Jesse (single): Freed by Henry Goodwin of Charles County, to emigrate; resident of Charles Co.; stated to be 70 at departure. Died during acclimation.

22. Gross, Philip (husband of Mary Gross): Free resident of Frederick Co.; stated to be 26 at departure. Appointed Schoolteacher for Ladies' Academy, 1845. Letter writer: Jan. 17 and 22, 1846; Nov. 20, 1848; and April 26, 1849. Missionary to Denah in 1848. Signed petition, April, 1849. Resident of the colony, November, 1852, listed as "Teacher of Natives."

23. Gross, Mary G. (wife of Philip Gross; also called Amelia [1851]): Free resident of Frederick Co.; stated to be 26 at departure. Letter writer: Mar. 30, 1851. Resident of the colony, November, 1852.

24. Gross, Philip T. (son of Philip Gross): Free resident of Frederick Co.; stated to be 3 at departure. Resident of the colony, November, 1852.

25. Gross, Francis A. (son of Philip Gross): Free resident of Frederick Co.; stated to be 3 months old at departure. Resident of the colony, November, 1852.

26. Gross, Jeremiah (husband of Mary Gross; father of Philip Gross): Free resident of Frederick Co.; stated to be 48 at departure. Died of dropsy, Jan. 14, 1848.

27. Gross, Mary Amelia (wife of Jeremiah Gross): Free resident of Frederick Co.; stated to be 47 at departure. Living with her son Philip, Census 1848–52.

28. [Hutchins], John (family relations uncertain; surname adopted in Liberia): Freed to emigrate by a master in Matthews Co., Va., who paid for their passage to Africa; stated to be 11 at departure. Resident of the colony, November, 1852, a seaman.

29. [Hutchins], William (family relations uncertain; surname adopted in Liberia): Freed to emigrate by a master in Matthews Co., Va., who paid for their passage to Africa; stated to be 10 at departure. Resident of the colony, November, 1852, a laborer.

30. [Hutchins], Cesar (family relations uncertain; surname adopted in Liberia): Freed to emigrate by a master in Matthews Co., Va., who paid for their passage to Africa; stated to be 6 at departure. Resident of the colony, November, 1852.

31. [Hutchins], Delia (family relations uncertain; surname adopted in Liberia): Freed to emigrate by a master in Matthews Co., Va., who paid for their passage to Africa; stated to be 4 at departure. Resident of the colony, November, 1852.

32. [Hutchins], Peter (family relations uncertain; surname adopted in Liberia): Freed to emigrate by a master in Matthews Co., Va., who paid for their passage to Africa; stated to be 2 at departure. Resident of the colony, November, 1852.

33. [Hutchins], Nancy (family relations uncertain; surname adopted in Liberia): Freed to emigrate by a master in Matthews Co., Va., who paid for their passage to Africa; stated to be 30 at departure. Married Thomas McFarland. Cultivated 1 acre in 1848. Married William Carroll, Dec. 7, 1852. Resident of the colony, November, 1852, a nurse.

34. Simpson, Peggy (single): Freed by Henry Goodwin of Charles County, to emigrate; stated to be 75 at departure. Does not appear in the record.

The total number of emigrants sent to Cape Palmas thus far: 686.

Brigantine KENT, left Baltimore, mid-November, 1845, arrived at Cape Palmas, January 18, 1846:

1. Bolon, Major (husband of Mary Bolon): Free resident of Baltimore, a shipwright; stated to be 40 at departure. Sent to Cape Palmas under contract to build two ships for the Colonial Agency. Letter writer: Jan. 20 and 21, May 25, July 11, 1846. Returned to Baltimore on the *Liberia Packet*, January, 1847.

2. Bolon, Mary (wife of Major Bolon): Free resident of Baltimore; stated to be 38 at departure. Went to Cape Palmas with her husband, who was under contract to build two ships for the Colonial Agency. Returned to Baltimore on the *Liberia Packet*, January, 1847.

3. Clark, Thomas (brother of Hannibal Clark): Free resident of Baltimore; stated to be 25 at departure. Worked in the colony as a laborer. Jailed for unknown reason, 1849. Resident of the colony, November, 1852.

4. Clark, Cordelia (wife of Thomas Clark; also called Adelia ['52]): Free resident of Baltimore; stated to be 23 at departure. Living with James Wilson, 1849 (husband in jail.) Resident of the colony, November, 1852.

5. Clark, Hannibal (brother of Thomas Clark; husband of Susan Clark): Free resident of Baltimore; stated to be 24 at departure. Worked in the colony as a carpenter. Signed petition, April, 1849. Signed petition, Jan. 14, 1850. Resident of the colony, November, 1852.

6. Clark, Susan (wife of Hannibal Clark): Free resident of Baltimore; stated to be 23 at departure. Does not appear in the record after 1849.

7. Clark, William T. (son of Hannibal Clark): Free resident of Baltimore; stated to be 4 at departure. Does not appear in the record after 1849.

8. Clark, Mary Ann (daughter of Hannibal Clark): Free resident of Baltimore; stated to be 6 months old at departure. Died May 7, 1852.

9. Dent, Charlotte (single; mother of Benjamin Dent and of the earlier emigrant Hanson Dent): Freed by a Mr. Crane; resident of Baltimore; stated to be 45 at departure. Died of fever shortly after arrival in Africa.

10. Dent, Benjamin (son of Charlotte Dent): Freed by a Mr. Crane; resident of

Baltimore; stated to be 16 at departure. Worked in the colony as a seaman. Does not appear in the record after 1849.

11. Dent, Charlotte (daughter of Charlotte Dent): Freed by a Mr. Crane; resident of Baltimore; stated to be 14 at departure. Does not appear in the record.

12. Lewis, John (single, family left in Baltimore): Free resident of Baltimore; stated to be 40 at departure. Worked in the colony as a caulker in Baltimore. Went to Cape Palmas to assist Major Bolon in shipbuilding. Returned to Baltimore on the *Liberia Packet*, January, 1847.

13. Payne, Mary Jane (single): Inherited by Rev. John Payne from a relative in Port Conway, King George Co., Va., and sent to Africa to be freed; stated to be 8 at departure. Living with Martha Dennis, Census 1848. Does not appear in the record afterward.

The total number of emigrants sent to Cape Palmas thus far: 699.

LIBERIA PACKET, Voyage A, left Baltimore about December 1, 1846, arrived at Cape Palmas, January 23, 1847:

1. [Without surname], Knacky (single): Status uncertain; resident of Frederick Co.; stated to be 55 at departure. Does not appear in the record.

2. Brown, Henry (single, brother of Austin Brown): Status uncertain; resident of Baltimore Co.; stated to be 22 at departure. Worked in the colony as a sawyer, then sailor. Employee of the Agency, 1848. Married Mariah Contee, May 22, 1848. Signed petition, April, 1849. Signed petition, Jan. 14, 1850. Resident of the colony, November, 1852.

3. Brown, Austin (single, brother of Henry Brown; also called "Oster," Oscar ['52]): Status uncertain; resident of Baltimore Co.; stated to be 17 at departure. Worked in the colony as a laborer. Living with Harriet Jarvis, Census 1848; in Josh Stewart household, 1849. Signed petition, Jan. 14, 1850. Living in Rachel Barnett household, 1852.

4. Clemments, Thomas (husband of Charity Clemments; also called Clemmons): Free resident of Williamsport, Washington Co.; stated to be 35 at departure. Worked in the colony as a farmer, jailkeeper, and laborer. Visited United States in 1851–2, returning to Africa on the *Liberia Packet*, Voyage K. Resident of the colony, November, 1852.

5. Clemments, Charity (wife of Thomas Clemments): Status uncertain; resident of Williamsport, Washington Co.; stated to be 36 at departure. Resident of the colony, November, 1852.

6. Clemments, Charles (son of Thomas Clemments): Status uncertain; resident of Williamsport, Washington Co.; stated to be 10 at departure. Resident of the colony, November, 1852.

7. Clemments, Mary J. (daughter of Thomas Clemments): Status uncertain; resident of Williamsport, Washington Co.; stated to be 8 at departure. Resident of the colony, November, 1852.

8. Clemments, Eliza F. (daughter of Thomas Clemments): Status uncertain; resident of Williamsport, Washington Co.; stated to be 5 at departure. Resident of the colony, November, 1852.

9. Clemments, George H. (son of Thomas Clemments): Status uncertain; resident of Williamsport, Washington Co.; stated to be 3 at departure. Resident of the colony, November, 1852.

10. Clemments, Susan E. R. (daughter of Thomas Clemments): Status uncertain; resident of Williamsport, Washington Co.; stated to be 2 at departure. Resident of the colony, November, 1852.

11. Scotland, Medley (husband of Elizabeth Scotland): Status uncertain; resident of Fauquier Co., Va.; stated to be 24 at departure. Worked in the colony as a farmer, laborer, and lumberer. Cultivated .75 acre in 1848. Signed petition, April, 1849; Jan. 14, 1850. Resident of the colony, November, 1852.

12. Scotland, Elizabeth (wife of Medley Scotland; also called Ann E. Scotland): Status uncertain; resident of Fauquier Co., Va.; stated to be 25 at departure. Resident of the colony, November, 1852.

13. Scotland, John S. (son of Medley Scotland): Status uncertain; resident of Fauquier Co., Va.; stated to be 6 months old at departure. Resident of the colony, November, 1852.

14. Thompson, Joseph (single): Status uncertain; resident of Fauquier Co., Va.; stated to be 50 at departure. Died of pneumonia, Sept. 19, 1848.

The total number of emigrants sent to Cape Palmas thus far: 713.

LIBERIA PACKET, Voyage B, left Baltimore August 29, 1847, arrived at Cape Palmas, December 15, 1847:

1. Blackston, Samuel (Husband of Mary Blackston): Status uncertain; resident of Annapolis, Anne Arundel Co.; stated to be 30 at departure. Worked in the colony as a farmer. Signed petition, April, 1849. Letter writer, April 26, 1849. Does not appear in the record afterward.

2. Blackston, Mary (wife of Samuel Blackston): Status uncertain; resident of Annapolis, Anne Arundel Co.; stated to be 25 at departure. Does not appear in the record after 1849.

3. Blackston, Prudence (daughter of Samuel Blackston): Status uncertain; resident of Annapolis, Anne Arundel Co.; stated to be 1 at departure. Does not appear in the record after 1848.

4. Brown, Enid A. (single; mother of Ann Maria Brown; also called Ann): Status uncertain; resident of Baltimore; stated to be 26 at departure. Worked in the colony as a spinster. Resident of the colony, November, 1852.

5. Brown, Ann Maria (daughter of Enid A. Brown): Status uncertain; resident of Baltimore; stated to be 6 at departure. Resident of the colony, November, 1852.

6. Brown, Martha C. (daughter of Enid A. Brown): Status uncertain; resident of Baltimore; stated to be 3 at departure. Resident of the colony, November, 1852.

7. Chambers, Charles (single): Freed resident of Baltimore, trained in the shop of his master, a tinker; stated to be 22 at departure. In 1848, Russwurm attempted to get him tools and materials to make toleware (tin) for the settlement. Does not appear in the record afterward.

8. Cook, Samuel (husband of Mary Cook): Status uncertain; resident of Baltimore; stated to be 35 at departure. Worked in the colony as a farmer. Abandoned wife and children about Sept. 1, 1848, and left colony by foot with Charles Spencer.

9. Cook, Mary (wife of Samuel Cook): Status uncertain; resident of Baltimore; stated to be 25 at departure. Living in household of Christina Edmondson, 1852.

10. Cook, Ann Mariah (daughter of Samuel Cook): Status uncertain; resident of Baltimore; stated to be 8 at departure. Resident of the colony, November, 1852.

11. Cook, Sarah Elizabeth (daughter of Samuel Cook): Status uncertain; resident of Baltimore; stated to be 7 at departure. Resident of the colony, November, 1852.

12. Cook, Samuel Jr. (son of Samuel Cook): Status uncertain; resident of Baltimore; stated to be 3 at departure. Living with his mother in Christina Edmondson household, 1852.

13. Cook, Nicholas (son of Samuel Cook): Status uncertain; resident of Baltimore; stated to be 5 months old at departure. Resident of the colony, November, 1852.

14. Cooper, James (single): Status uncertain; resident of Baltimore; stated to be 30 at departure. Worked in the colony as a laborer. Married Frances Cook, Feb. 3, 1848. Signed petition, Jan. 14, 1850. Resident of the colony, November, 1852.

15. Goodwin, Daniel (son of Malinda Parks; also called David Parks or Sparks ['49]): Status uncertain; resident of Elkridge Landing, Baltimore Co.; stated to be 13 at departure. Resident of the colony, November, 1852.

16. Goodwin, Mary I. (daughter of Malindah Parks; also called Parks): Status uncertain; resident of Elkridge Landing, Baltimore Co.; stated to be 11 at departure. Resident of the colony, November, 1852.

17. Goodwin, Phebe A. (daughter of Malindah Parks; also called Parks): Status uncertain; resident of Elkridge Landing, Baltimore Co.; stated to be 8 at departure. Resident of the colony, November, 1852.

18. Goodwin, Almira A. (daughter of Malindah Parks; also called Amelia or Emiline Parks): Status uncertain; resident of Elkridge Landing, Baltimore Co.; stated to be 5 at departure. Resident of the colony, November, 1852.

19. Hughes, Henry (husband of Rachel Hughes): Status uncertain; resident of resident of Charles Co.; stated to be 60 at departure. Worked in the colony as a farmer. Died of fever, June 23, 1848.

20. Hughes, Rachel (wife of Henry Hughes): Freeborn resident of Charles Co.; stated to be 43 at departure. Worked in the colony as a spinster. Living in Elizabeth Jones household, 1849. Returned to Maryland in 1850 to get her daughter Mary. Resident of the colony, November, 1852.

21. Hughes, Ann Eliza (daughter of Henry Hughes): Status uncertain; resident of Charles Co.; stated to be 18 at departure. Living in Elizabeth Jones household, 1849. Does not appear in the record afterward.

22. Hughes, Lucinda (single woman; daughter of Henry Hughes; also called Lucinda Hanson): Status uncertain; resident of Charles Co.; stated to be 17 at departure. Married Charles Wesley Bordely, about 1850. Resident of the colony, November, 1852.

23. Hughes, Caroline R. (daughter of Henry Hughes): Status uncertain; resident of Charles Co.; stated to be 6 at departure. Living in Daniel Wilson household, 1849; with mother Rachel, 1852.

24. Hughes, Rosetta S. (daughter of Henry Hughes): Status uncertain; resident of Charles Co.; stated to be 3 at departure. Living in Elizabeth Jones household, 1849; counted both with her mother Rachel and Charles H. B. Scotland, 1852.

25. Jackson, Phoebe Ann (single; sister of Eliza Jackson): Status uncertain; resident of Baltimore; stated to be 16 at departure. Living with Charles Ridgely, Census 1848; married to him, Census 1849, and 1852.

26. Jackson, Eliza (single, sister of Phebe; also called Elizabeth Jackson): Status uncertain; resident of Baltimore; stated to be 12 at departure. Living with Charles Ridgely, Census 1848. Living in N. Jackson Sr. household, 1849 and 1852, listed as his daughter.

27. Joyce, Margaret (single): Status uncertain; resident of Baltimore; stated to be 28 at departure. Died during acclimation, Jan. 27, 1848.

28. Lomax, Lemuel (husband of Sarah Lomax; also called Samuel Lomax): Status uncertain; resident of Anne Arundel Co.; stated to be 23 at departure. Worked in the colony as a farmer and laborer. Signed petition, April, 1849. Signed petition, Jan. 14, 1850. Died Feb. 5, 1852.

29. Lomax, Sarah (wife of Lemuel Lomax): Status uncertain; resident of Anne Arundel Co.; stated to be 32 at departure. Does not appear in the record after 1849.

30. Nichols, Fanny (single): Status uncertain; resident of Baltimore; stated to be 16 at departure. Does not appear in the record.

31. Parks, Malindah (single woman; mother of Daniel Goodwin; also called Belinda; Sparks): Status uncertain; resident of Elkridge Landing, Baltimore Co.; stated to be 30 at departure. Worked in the colony as a spinster. Resident of the colony, November, 1852.

32. Ridgely, Charles (single): Status uncertain; resident of Baltimore; stated to be 20 at departure. Worked in the colony as a farmer, laborer, and seaman. Living with Elizabeth and Phoebe Jackson, Census 1848. Married to Phoebe Jackson, Census 1849. Resident of the colony, November, 1852.

33. Siscoe, Peter (husband of Margaret Siscoe): Status uncertain; resident of Annapolis, Anne Arundel Co.; stated to be 41 at departure. Worked in the colony as a gunsmith and blacksmith. Signed petitions, April and December, 1849. Resident of the colony, November, 1852. Letter writer, Feb. 6, 1853.

34. Siscoe, Margaret (wife of Peter Siscoe): Status uncertain; resident of Annapolis, Anne Arundel Co.; stated to be 23 at departure. Resident of the colony, November, 1852.

35. Siscoe, Richard (son of Peter Siscoe; also called Lewis Siscoe ['49]): Status uncertain; resident of Annapolis, Anne Arundel Co.; stated to be 8 months old at departure. Resident of the colony, November, 1852.

36. Spencer, Alfred (single): Status uncertain; resident of Baltimore; stated to be 22 at departure. Worked in the colony as a farmer. Married a woman named Amanda, of untraced origin, soon after arrival. Left Maryland on foot with Samuel Cook, about Sept. 1, 1848.

37. Thompson, Mary J. (single): Status uncertain; resident of Baltimore; stated to be 21 at departure. Does not appear in the record.

The total number of emigrants sent to Cape Palmas thus far: 750.

Brig AMAZON, arrived at Cape Palmas March 31, 1848:
1. Lee, Charles H. (single): Status uncertain; resident of Baltimore; stated to be 25 at departure. Reportedly abandoned the expedition at Monrovia to return to U.S., but listed as a resident of Dr. Fletcher's household, 1852.

2. Ransom, Acre (single): Status uncertain; resident of Jefferson Co., Va.; stated to be 35 at departure. Worked in the colony as a laborer. Signed petitions, April 1849, and Jan. 14, 1850. Resident of the colony, November, 1852.

The total number of emigrants sent to Cape Palmas thus far: 752.

LIBERIA PACKET, Voyage C, left Baltimore April 11, 1848, arrived at Cape Palmas June 11, 1848:
1. Saunders, Martha (single, mother of Mary Saunders; also called Mary Saunders): Freed by a Mr. Murdock; resident of Baltimore; age at departure unstated. Died during acclimation, one month after arrival.

2. Saunders, Mary (): Freed by a Mr. Murdock; resident of Baltimore; stated to be 3 at departure. Does not appear in the record.

3. Thomas, John Henry (single): Status uncertain; resident of Baltimore; stated to be 40 at departure. Married Cornelia Smith, Nov. 23, 1848. Signed petition, April, 1849. Does not appear in the record afterward.

The total number of emigrants sent to Cape Palmas thus far: 755.

LIBERIA PACKET, Voyage D, left Baltimore early September, 1848, arrived at Cape Palmas, November 17, 1848:
    1. Bowser, Henry (single): Status uncertain; resident of Baltimore; stated to be 12 at departure. Does not appear in the record.
    2. Howard, William (single): Freed by Mrs. Cyril Harper to emigrate; resident of Anne Arundel Co.; stated to be 34 at departure. Worked in the colony as a laborer. Living in John Auther household, 1849. Letter writer: Oct. 17, 1849; Sept. 22, 1851. Signed petition, Jan. 14, 1850. Letter writer, July 14, 1852. Living with Catherine Martin, 1852.
    3. Tomkins, Lewis (possibly the brother of William Tomkins): Status uncertain; resident of Baltimore, stated to be 35 at departure. Does not appear in the record.
    4. Tomkins, William (possibly the brother of Lewis Tomkins): Status uncertain; resident of Baltimore; stated to be 18 at departure. Does not appear in the record.

The total number of emigrants sent to Cape Palmas thus far: 759.

Schooner GEORGE R. MCGILL, left Baltimore late, 1848, arrived at Cape Palmas, February, 1849:
    1. Thomas, Charles (single): Status uncertain; resident of Baltimore; stated to be 19 at departure. Worked in the colony as a laborer. Associated with J. Odley household, 1849. Does not appear in the record afterward.

The total number of emigrants sent to Cape Palmas thus far: 760.

LIBERIA PACKET, Voyage E, arrived at Cape Palmas April 25, 1849:
    1. Gross, Charles (son of Jacob Gross): Status uncertain; resident of Frederick, Md.; stated to be 26 at departure. Does not appear in the record.
    2. Gross, Wesley (son of Jacob Gross): Status uncertain; resident of Frederick, Md.; stated to be 24 at departure. Does not appear in the record.

The total number of emigrants sent to Cape Palmas thus far: 762.

LIBERIA PACKET, Voyage G, left Baltimore August 1, 1849, arrived at Cape Palmas about October 16, 1849:
    1. Gross, Thomas (husband of Mary Gross): Status uncertain; resident of Howard District, Anne Arundel Co., prior to its county incorporation.; stated to be 29 at departure. Worked in the colony as a teacher. Letter writer: Mar. 30, 1851; April 9, 1851; Feb. 4, 1853. Resident of the colony, November, 1852.
    2. Gross, Mary A. (wife of Thomas Gross): Status uncertain; resident of Howard District, Anne Arundel Co., prior to its county incorporation.; stated to be 27 at departure. Resident of the colony, November, 1852.
    3. Gross, Harriet (daughter of Thomas Gross): Status uncertain; resident of Howard District, Anne Arundel Co., prior to its county incorporation.; stated to be 1 at departure. Resident of the colony, November, 1852.
    4. Gross, Unnamed child (child of Thomas Gross): Status uncertain; resident of Howard District, Anne Arundel Co., prior to its county incorporation.; stated to be 4 at departure. Does not appear in the record.
    5. Gross, John W. (son of Thomas Gross): Status uncertain; resident of Howard

District, Anne Arundel Co., prior to its county incorporation.; stated to be 2 at departure. Resident of the colony, November, 1852.

The total number of emigrants sent to Cape Palmas thus far: 767.

LIBERIA PACKET, Voyage H, left Baltimore about December 20, 1850, arrived at Cape Palmas March 30, 1851:

1. Anderson, Henry (single): Freed by Julia Done of Baltimore; stated to be 19 at departure. Does not appear in the record.

2. Barnes, George F. (single): Freeborn resident of Leonardtown, Calvert Co.; stated to be 22 at departure. Does not appear in the record.

3. Becraft, Elizabeth (single): Freeborn resident of Washington, D.C.; stated to be 28 at departure. Apparently living with Charles Harmon, 1852.

4. Butler, Peter (husband of Elizabeth Butler): Freed by the will of John Davis of St. Mary's Co.; stated to be 40 at departure. Worked in the colony as a laborer. Resident of the colony, November, 1852.

5. Butler, Elizabeth (wife of Peter Butler): Freed by Rebecca Hayden of St. Mary's Co.; stated to be 41 at departure. Resident of the colony, November, 1852.

6. Butler, John Lewis (uncertain relation to Peter Butler): Freed by the will of John Davis of St. Mary's Co.; stated to be 28 at departure. Does not appear in the record.

7. Butler, Benedict (uncertain relation to Peter Butler; also called Thomas): Freed by William Briscoe of St. Mary's Co.; stated to be 20 at departure. Does not appear in the record.

8. Cassell, Mary Ann (second wife of William Cassell): Freeborn resident of Washington, D.C.; stated to be 35 at departure. Resident of the colony, November, 1852.

9. Cox, James (single): Freed by William M. Merrick of Frederick, Md.; stated to be 22 at departure. Worked in the colony as factory clerk at Mt. Tubman. Living with Stephen and other members of the Tubman family, Census 1852.

10. Dayson, Sally (single; mother of James R. Dayson): Freed by Rebecca Hayden of St. Mary's Co.; stated to be 35 at departure. Died Mar. 6, 1852.

11. Dayson, James Richard (son of Sally Dayson; also called Dyson): Freeborn resident of St. Mary's Co.; stated to be 11 at departure. Listed as an orphan, Census 1852.

12. Dayson, John Henry (son of Sally Dayson): Freeborn resident of St. Mary's Co.; stated to be 9 at departure. Resident of the colony, November, 1852.

13. Dayson, Sarah Ann O. (daughter of Sally Dayson): Freeborn resident of St. Mary's Co.; stated to be 6 at departure. Resident of the colony, November, 1852.

14. Dayson, George Washington (son of Sally Dayson): Freeborn resident of St. Mary's Co.; stated to be 4 at departure. Died of complications from worms, before April 10, 1851.

15. Fasker, Jacob (single; also called Jacob Tasco): Freed by James Marquiss of Calvert Co.; stated to be 25 at departure. Resident of the colony, November, 1852.

16. Harden, Joseph M. (husband of Henrietta Harden): Free resident of Baltimore; stated to be 22 at departure. Does not appear in the record.

17. Harden, Henrietta (wife of Joseph M. Harden): Free resident of Baltimore; stated to be 23 at departure. Does not appear in the record.

18. Harris, Edward (single): Freed by a Mrs. Gibson of Baltimore; stated to be 10 at departure. Living in Thomas Dent household, 1852.

19. Hughes, Mary (daughter of Rachel Hughes): Freed by Rev. Henry Goodwin of Charles Co.; stated to be 12 at departure. Resident of the colony, November, 1852.

20. Hutchins, James Henry (single, probably related to Robert Hutchins): Freeborn resident of St. Mary's Co.; stated to be 22 at departure. Worked in the colony as a sawyer. Living with Harriet Hutchins, Census 1852.

21. Johnson, William (single): Freeborn resident of Baltimore; stated to be 23 at departure. Living in James Cooper household, 1852.

22. Lane, Jesse (single; also called James ['52]): Freed by the will of a Col. Harrison of Anne Arundel Co.; stated to be 30 at departure. Worked in the colony as a porter in McGill, Bros. store. Living in the McGill household, 1852.

23. Neale, Lydia Ann (daughter of Peter Butler, sister of Sally Ann Neale): Freeborn resident of St. Mary's Co.; stated to be 16 at departure. Resident of the colony, November, 1852.

24. Neale, Sally Ann (daughter of Peter Butler; also called Sarah): Freeborn resident of St. Mary's Co.; stated to be 14 at departure. Resident of the colony, November, 1852.

25. Neale, Jane Rebecca (daughter of Peter Butler): Freeborn resident of St. Mary's Co.; stated to be 11 at departure. Resident of the colony, November, 1852.

26. Neale, James Judson (son of Peter Butler): Freeborn resident of St. Mary's Co.; stated to be 8 at departure. Resident of the colony, November, 1852.

27. Neale, John Henry (son of Peter Butler): Freeborn resident of St. Mary's Co.; stated to be 6 at departure. Resident of the colony, November, 1852.

28. Neale, Stephen Robert (son of Peter Butler): Freeborn resident of St. Mary's Co.; stated to be 4 at departure. Resident of the colony, November, 1852.

29. Neale, Ambrose Gilbert (son of Peter Butler): Freeborn resident of St. Mary's Co.; stated to be 1 at departure. Resident of the colony, November, 1852.

30. Young, Sarah Ann (single): Freeborn resident of St. Mary's Co.; stated to be 18 at departure. Does not appear in the record.

The total number of emigrants sent to Cape Palmas thus far: 797.

LIBERIA PACKET, Voyage I, left Baltimore end of July, 1851, arrived at Cape Palmas September 24, 1851:

1. Beems, David (husband of Ann Beems): Free resident of Virginia; stated to be 30 at departure. Does not appear in the record.

2. Beems, Ann (wife of David Beems): Free resident of Virginia; stated to be 30 at departure. Does not appear in the record.

3. Beems, W. F. (son of David Beems): Free resident of Virginia; stated to be 13 at departure. Does not appear in the record.

4. Beems, Anne E. (daughter of David Beems): Free resident of Virginia; stated to be 9 at departure. Does not appear in the record.

5. Beems, Susannah (daughter of David Beems): Free resident of Virginia; stated to be 3 at departure. Does not appear in the record.

6. Bowie, John M. (husband of Eliza Bowie): Free resident of Virginia; stated to be 45 at departure. Does not appear in the record.

7. Bowie, Eliza (wife of John Bowie): Free resident of Virginia; stated to be 32 at departure. Does not appear in the record.

8. Bowie, Charles (son of John Bowie): Free resident of Virginia; stated to be 11 at departure. Does not appear in the record.

9. Bowie, John (son of John Bowie): Free resident of Virginia; stated to be 6 at departure. Does not appear in the record.

10. Decoursey, Major T. (husband of Caroline Decoursey): Free resident of Baltimore; stated to be32 at departure. Does not appear in the record.

11. Decoursey, Caroline (wife of Major T. Decoursey): Free resident of Baltimore; stated to be 22 at departure. Does not appear in the record.

12. Dennis, Henry (husband of Caroline Dennis): Free resident of Worcester Co.; stated to be 34 at departure. Does not appear in the record.

13. Dennis, Caroline P. (wife of Henry Dennis): Free resident of Worcester Co.; stated to be 30 at departure. Does not appear in the record.

14. Dennis, James W. (son of Henry Dennis): Free resident of Worcester Co.; stated to be 6 at departure. Does not appear in the record.

15. Field, Eleanor (single): Free resident of Virginia; stated to be 52 at departure. Does not appear in the record.

16. Fisher, John H. (husband of Margaret Fisher): Free resident of Baltimore; stated to be 37 at departure. Does not appear in the record.

17. Fisher, Margaret (wife of John Fisher): Free resident of Baltimore; stated to be 32 at departure. Does not appear in the record.

18. Fuller, Thomas (single): Free resident of Cambridge, Dorchester Co., a Methodist Minister; stated to be 33 at departure. Sent to Africa to make a report on the state of the American settlements in Liberia. (Would later return to Cape Palmas with his family on the *Banshee*, April, 1853.)

19. Hammond, Richard (single): Free resident of Virginia; stated to be 24 at departure. Does not appear in the record.

20. Harrison, George H. (single): Free resident of Virginia; stated to be 11 at departure. Does not appear in the record.

21. Jennifer, Benjamin (single): Free resident of Cambridge, Dorchester Co., a Methodist minister; stated to be 40 at departure. Sent to Africa to make a report on the state of the American settlements in Liberia. Does not appear in the record.

22. Lockman, Thomas (husband of Jane Lockman): Free resident of Virginia; stated to be 46 at departure. Does not appear in the record.

23. Lockman, Jane (wife of Thomas Lockman): Free resident of Virginia; stated to be 40 at departure. Does not appear in the record.

24. Lockman, Mary Jane (daughter of Thomas Lockman): Free resident of Virginia; stated to be 11 at departure. Does not appear in the record.

25. Lockman, Susan (daughter of Thomas Lockman): Free resident of Virginia; stated to be 6 at departure. Does not appear in the record.

26. Lockman, Robert (son of Thomas Lockman): Free resident of Virginia; stated to be 3 at departure. Does not appear in the record.

27. Miles, Charity (single, mother of three children): Free resident of Virginia; stated to be 36 at departure. Does not appear in the record.

28. Miles, Frances Ann (daughter of Charity Miles): Free resident of Virginia; stated to be 15 at departure. Does not appear in the record.

29. Miles, Malachi (son of Charity Miles): Free resident of Virginia; stated to be 14 at departure. Does not appear in the record.

30. Miles, Martha (daughter of Charity Miles): Free resident of Virginia; stated to be 2 at departure. Does not appear in the record.

31. Moore, Jacob M. (husband of Comfort Moore): Free resident of Baltimore, a Methodist Minister; stated to be 39 at departure. Does not appear in the record.

32. Moore, Comfort (wife of Jacob Moore): Free resident of Baltimore; stated to be 40 at departure. Does not appear in the record.

33. Moore, Mathias (son of Jacob Moore): Free resident of Baltimore; stated to be 18 at departure. Does not appear in the record.

34. Moore, Jacob M. Jr. (son of Jacob Moore): Free resident of Baltimore; stated to be 16 at departure. Does not appear in the record.

35. Moore, James (son of Jacob Moore) Free resident of Baltimore; stated to be 11 at departure. Does not appear in the record.

36. Moore, Daniel (son of Jacob Moore): Free resident of Baltimore; stated to be 8 at departure. Does not appear in the record.

37. Nugent, Nicholas (husband of Eliza Nugent): Free resident of Baltimore; stated to be 49 at departure. Does not appear in the record.

38. Nugent, Eliza (wife of Nicholas Nugent): Free resident of Baltimore; stated to be 38 at departure. Does not appear in the record.

39. Nugent, Rachel (daughter of Nicholas Nugent): Free resident of Baltimore; stated to be 14 at departure. Does not appear in the record.

40. Nugent, Arabella (daughter of Nicholas Nugent): Free resident of Baltimore; stated to be 12 at departure. Does not appear in the record.

41. Nugent, Frances (daughter of Nicholas Nugent): Free resident of Baltimore; stated to be 10 at departure. Does not appear in the record.

42. Nugent, Jacob (son of Nicholas Nugent): Free resident of Baltimore; stated to be 6 at departure. Does not appear in the record.

43. Nugent, Bazil (son of Nicholas Nugent): Free resident of Baltimore; stated to be 4 at departure. Does not appear in the record.

The total number of emigrants sent to Cape Palmas thus far: 840.

MORGAN DIX, left Baltimore November, 1851, arrived at Cape Palmas January 3, 1852:
1. Tilghman, Thomas (single): Freeborn resident of Hagerstown, Washington Co.; stated to be 22 at departure. Does not appear in the record.

The total number of emigrants sent to Cape Palmas thus far: 841.

LIBERIA PACKET, Voyage K, left Baltimore January, 1852, arrived at Cape Palmas April 12, 1852:
1. Anderson, Henrietta (single, mother of two children): Free resident of Baltimore; stated to be 35 at departure. Does not appear in the record.

2. Anderson, Benjamin (son of Henrietta Anderson): Free resident of Baltimore; stated to be 16 at departure. Does not appear in the record.

3. Anderson, July (daughter of Henrietta Anderson): Free resident of Baltimore; stated to be 19 at departure. Does not appear in the record.

4. Bowie, Levi (husband of Eliza Bowie; also called Bowyer): Free resident of Weverton, Charles Co.; stated to be 39 at departure. Resident of the colony, November, 1852, a stonemason.

5. Bowie, Eliza (wife of Levi Bowie): Free resident of Weverton, Charles Co.; stated to be 31 at departure. Resident of the colony, November, 1852.

6. Bowie, Alfred (son of Levi Bowie): Free resident of Weverton, Charles Co.; stated to be 14 at departure. Resident of the colony, November, 1852.

7. Bowie, Harriet (daughter of Levi Bowie): Free resident of Weverton, Charles Co.; stated to be 9 at departure. Died June 23, 1852.

8. Bowie, Amelia (daughter of Levi Bowie): Free resident of Weverton, Charles Co.; stated to be 6 at departure. Resident of the colony, November, 1852.

9. Bowie, Rebecca (daughter of Levi Bowie): Free resident of Weverton, Charles Co.; stated to be 4 at departure. Resident of the colony, November, 1852.

10. Bowie, Margaret (daughter of Levi Bowie): Free resident of Weverton, Charles Co.; stated to be 2 at departure. Resident of the colony, November, 1852.

11. Burley, Samuel H. (single): Freed by Alvin Dorsey, of Elkridge, Howard District of Anne Arundel Co.; stated to be 3 at departure. Does not appear in the record.

12. Butler, Samuel (husband of Martha Butler): Freed by Alvin Dorsey, of Elkridge, Howard District of Anne Arundel Co.; stated to be 33 at departure. Does not appear in the record.

13. Butler, Martha (wife of Samuel Butler): Freed by Alvin Dorsey, of Elkridge, Howard District of Anne Arundel Co.; stated to be 20 at departure. Does not appear in the record.

14. Carter, Jane (single, mother of three children): Freed by Alvin Dorsey, of Elkridge, Howard District of Anne Arundel Co.; stated to be 52 at departure. Does not appear in the record.

15. Carter, Charles (son of Jane Carter): Freed by Alvin Dorsey, of Elkridge, Howard District of Anne Arundel Co.; stated to be 25 at departure. Does not appear in the record.

16. Carter, Henry (son of Jane Carter): Freed by Alvin Dorsey, of Elkridge, Howard District of Anne Arundel Co.; stated to be 27 at departure. Does not appear in the record.

17. Carter, Daniel (son of Jane Carter): Freed by Alvin Dorsey, of Elkridge, Howard District of Anne Arundel Co.; stated to be 23 at departure. Does not appear in the record.

18. Chase, Nathaniel (single): Free resident of Cumberland, Alleghany Co.; stated to be 30 at departure. Living with James Stark, 1852. Does not appear in the record.

19. Collins, Stephen (uncertain relation to Barbara Collins): Freed by Alvin Dorsey, of Elkridge, Howard District of Anne Arundel Co.; stated to be 30 at departure. Does not appear in the record.

20. Collins, Barbara (uncertain relation to Stephen Collins): Freed by Alvin Dorsey, of Elkridge, Howard District of Anne Arundel Co.; stated to be 17 at departure. Does not appear in the record.

21. Deter, Charles (single, father of two): Free resident of Baltimore; stated to be 42 at departure. Does not appear in the record.

22. Deter, Lewis (son of Charles Deter): Free resident of Baltimore; stated to be 19 at departure. Does not appear in the record.

23. Deter, George Alexander (son of Charles Deter): Free resident of Baltimore; stated to be 11 at departure. Does not appear in the record.

24. Hill, Pippin (husband of Nancy Hill): Free resident of Baltimore; stated to be 65 at departure. Does not appear in the record.

25. Hill, Nancy (wife of Pippin Hill): Free resident of Baltimore; stated to be 67 at departure. Does not appear in the record.

26. Johns, Asbury (single): Free resident of Baltimore; stated to be 32 at departure. Does not appear in the record.

27. Pinkney, Henrietta (single, mother of Dennis H. B. Pinkney): Free resident of Cumberland, Allegheny Co.; stated to be 32 at departure. Resident of the colony, November, 1852.

28. Pinkney, Dennis H. B. (son of Henrietta Pinkney): Free resident of Cumberland, Allegheny Co.; stated to be 3 at departure. Resident of the colony, November, 1852.

29. Smith, Thomas Henry (single): Free resident of Baltimore; stated to be 24 at departure. Does not appear in the record.

The total number of emigrants sent to Cape Palmas thus far: 870.

Brig *RALPH CROSS,* arrived at Cape Palmas about July 15, 1852 (wrecked off Cape Palmas, July 19):

1. Allen, Nelson (single): Status uncertain, origin unrecorded; age at departure unstated (about 30.) Worked in the colony as a bricklayer. Returned to U.S. for a visit on the *Shirley*'s second voyage, September, 1853.

2. Bowie, Mary Ann (single; also called Bowyer): Status uncertain, resident of Baltimore; stated to be 31 at departure. Living in William Taylor household, 1852.

3. Brown, Samuel (husband of Nancy Brown): Status uncertain, origin unrecorded; age at departure unstated (about 39.) Resident of the colony, November, 1852.

4. Brown, Nancy (wife of Samuel Brown): Status uncertain, origin unrecorded; age at departure unstated (about 33.) Resident of the colony, November, 1852.

5. Brown, Charles (son of Samuel Brown): Status uncertain, origin unrecorded; age at departure unstated (about 2.) Resident of the colony, November, 1852.

6. Brown, Unnamed Child (child of Samuel Brown): Status uncertain, origin unrecorded; age at departure unstated. Died during acclimation.

7. Dominis, Henry (single, father of two): Status uncertain, origin unrecorded; age at departure unstated (about 48.) Worked in the colony as a tobacconist. Resident of the colony, November, 1852.

8. Dominis, Lewis A. (son of Henry Dominis): Status uncertain, origin unrecorded; age at departure unstated.

9. Dominis, John H. L. (son of Henry Dominis): Status uncertain, origin unrecorded; age at departure unstated (about 16.) Resident of the colony, November, 1852.

10. Hammond, Cyrus (single; also called Silas): Freed resident of Caroline Co.; stated to be 29 at departure. Worked in the colony as a carpenter. Resident of the colony, November, 1852. Returned to U.S. on the *Banshee,* 1853, to try and get his family.

11. Massey, Luke (single): Status uncertain, resident of Worcester Co.; stated to be 41 at departure. Resident of the colony, November, 1852.

12. Stark, James (single): Slave from Virginia whose mistress sent him to see Africa with view of resettling others there; his age at departure unstated (about 30.) McGill persuaded him to assert his freedom and remain at Cape Palmas, partly by refusing to give him a free passage back to United States. Resident of the colony, November, 1852, living with Nathaniel Chase.

The total number of emigrants sent to Cape Palmas thus far: 882.

Brig SHIRLEY, left Baltimore late November, 1852, arrived at Cape Palmas January 25, 1853:

1. Adams, Peter (single): Status uncertain, origin unrecorded; age at departure unstated. Does not appear in the record.

2. Bowen, Diana (single; uncertain relation to William Bowen): Freeborn resident of Worcester Co.; stated to be 65 at departure. Died before June 27, 1853, during acclimation.

3. Bowen, William (husband of Comfort Bowen, uncertain relation to Diana Bowen):

Freeborn resident of Worcester Co.; stated to be 26 at departure. Does not appear in the record.

4. Bowen, Comfort (wife of William Bowen): Freeborn resident of Worcester Co.; stated to be 26 at departure. Does not appear in the record.

5. Bowen, Mary Frances (daughter of William Bowen): Freeborn resident of Worcester Co.; stated to be 3 at departure. Does not appear in the record.

6. Bowen, Sally Matilda (daughter of William Bowen): Freeborn resident of Worcester Co.; stated to be 1 at departure. Does not appear in the record.

7. Dorsey, Solomon (single; father of Henry Dorsey): Free resident of Baltimore Co.; stated to be 60 at departure. Died before June 27, 1853, during acclimation.

8. Dorsey, Henry C. (husband of Maria Dorsey): Freeborn resident of Baltimore Co.; stated to be 40 at departure. Worked in the Powhatan Mill Store near Baltimore for 27 years before emigrating. Died before June 27, 1853, during acclimation, complicated by abuse of Brandreth's Pills, which he believed would cure malaria.

9. Dorsey, Maria (wife of Henry C. Dorsey): Free resident of Baltimore Co.; stated to be 30 at departure. Does not appear in the record.

10. Dorsey, Mary Ann (daughter of Henry C. Dorsey): Free resident of Baltimore Co.; stated to be 10 at departure. Does not appear in the record.

11. Dorsey, Henry (son of Henry C. Dorsey): Free resident of Baltimore Co.; stated to be 8 at departure. Does not appear in the record.

12. Dorsey, Martha (daughter of Henry C. Dorsey): Free resident of Baltimore Co.; stated to be 5 at departure. Died before June 27, 1853, during acclimation.

13. Dorsey, Ellen (daughter of Henry C. Dorsey): Free resident of Baltimore Co.; stated to be 1 at departure. Does not appear in the record.

14. Elzy, John (single): Freeborn resident of Worcester Co.; stated to be 20 at departure. Does not appear in the record.

15. Fookes, Isaac (husband of Leah Fookes): Freeborn resident of Worcester Co.; stated to be 50 at departure. Does not appear in the record.

16. Fookes, Leah (wife of Isaac Fookes): Freeborn resident of Worcester Co.; stated to be 52 at departure. Does not appear in the record.

17. Fookes, Eve (daughter of Isaac Fookes): Freeborn resident of Worcester Co.; stated to be 28 at departure. Does not appear in the record.

18. Fookes, Ellen Louisa (daughter of Isaac Fookes): Freeborn resident of Worcester Co.; stated to be 16 at departure. Does not appear in the record.

19. Fookes, Samuel (son of Isaac Fookes): Freeborn resident of Worcester Co.; stated to be 14 at departure. Does not appear in the record.

20. Fookes, Isaac (son of Isaac Fookes): Freeborn resident of Worcester Co.; stated to be 11 at departure. Does not appear in the record.

21. Fookes, Esther (daughter of Isaac Fookes): Freeborn resident of Worcester Co.; stated to be 8 at departure. Does not appear in the record.

22. Fookes, Mary (daughter of Isaac Fookes): Freeborn resident of Worcester Co.; stated to be 6 at departure. Does not appear in the record.

23. Fookes, William (son of Isaac Fookes): Freeborn resident of Worcester Co.; stated to be 4 at departure. Does not appear in the record.

24. Gray, Isaac H. (husband of Rachel Gray): Freeborn resident of Worcester Co.; stated to be 72 at departure. Does not appear in the record.

25. Gray, Rachel (wife of Isaac Gray): Freeborn resident of Worcester Co.; stated to be 55 at departure. Does not appear in the record.

26. Gray, Benjamin (son of Isaac Gray): Freeborn resident of Worcester Co.; stated to be 26 at departure. Does not appear in the record.

27. Gray, Mary Jane (uncertain relation to Isaac Gray): Freeborn resident of Worcester Co.; stated to be 9 at departure. Does not appear in the record.

28. Gray, George (uncertain relation to Isaac Gray; also called George W. Gaitor): Freeborn resident of Worcester Co.; stated to be 8 at departure. Living in Benjamin Tubman household, Census 1852.

29. Gray, Charles H. (uncertain relation to Isaac Gray): Freeborn resident of Worcester Co.; stated to be 4 at departure. Does not appear in the record.

30. Hanson, Walter (single): Freed by Rev. W. Goodwin of Charles Co.; stated to be 19 at departure. Does not appear in the record.

31. Hughes, Martha Ann (single): Freed by Rev. W. Goodwin of Charles Co.; stated to be 18 at departure. Does not appear in the record.

32. Neal, Hanson (uncertain relation to Laudy Neal): Freed by Rev. W. Goodwin of Charles Co.; stated to be 20 at departure. Does not appear in the record.

33. Neal, Laudy (uncertain relation to Hanson Neal): Freed by Rev. W. Goodwin of Charles Co.; stated to be 23 at departure. Does not appear in the record.

34. Stevenson, Sarah Ann (single): Freeborn resident of Worcester Co.; stated to be 22 at departure. Does not appear in the record.

35. Thomas, Martha (single): Freeborn resident of Baltimore; stated to be 35 at departure. Does not appear in the record.

36. Webster, [no first name recorded] (single): Free resident of Indiana; stated to be 28 at departure. Originally slated to land at Monrovia, but opted to settle at Cape Palmas. Does not appear in the record.

The total number of emigrants sent to Cape Palmas thus far: 918.

Brig BANSHEE, first voyage, arrived at Cape Palmas June 27, 1853:

1. Campbell, Cornelius (husband of Mary Campbell): Status uncertain; resident of Frederick, Frederick Co.; stated to be 24 at departure.

2. Campbell, Mary (wife of Cornelius Campbell): Status uncertain; resident of Frederick, Frederick Co.; stated to be 24 at departure.

3. Campbell, Charlotte E. (daughter of Cornelius Campbell): Status uncertain; resident of Frederick, Frederick Co.; stated to be 3 at departure.

4. Campbell, Catherine M. (daughter of Cornelius Campbell): Status uncertain; resident of Frederick, Frederick Co.; stated to be 1 at departure.

5. Dent, James (single): Free resident of Weverton, Charles Co.; stated to be 78 at departure.

6. Fisher, W. H. (single): Status uncertain; resident of Frederick Co.; stated to be 23 at departure.

7. Ford, Thomas (single): Status uncertain; resident of Frederick Co.; stated to be 25 at departure.

8. Fuller, Mary (wife of Thomas Fuller): Free resident of Dorchester Co.; stated to be 27 at departure.

9. Fuller, Unnamed infant (child of Thomas Fuller): Free resident of Dorchester Co.; stated to be 6 months old at departure.

10. Jackson, Joseph (husband of Mary Jane Jackson): Status uncertain; resident of Frederick Co.; stated to be 25 at departure.

11. Jackson, Mary Jane (wife of Joseph Jackson): Status uncertain; resident of Frederick Co.; stated to be 21 at departure.

12. Mathews, Dennis (single): Status uncertain; resident of Frederick Co.; stated to be 23 at departure.

13. Nelson, Samuel (husband of Harriet Nelson): Status uncertain; resident of Frederick Co.; stated to be 45 at departure.

14. Nelson, Harriet (wife of Samuel Nelson): Status uncertain; resident of Frederick Co.; stated to be 33 at departure.

15. Nelson, Samuel (son of Samuel Nelson): Status uncertain; resident of Frederick Co.; stated to be 13 at departure.

16. Nelson, Benjamin (son of Samuel Nelson): Status uncertain; resident of Frederick Co.; stated to be 11 at departure.

17. Nelson, Margaret A. (daughter of Samuel Nelson): Status uncertain; resident of Frederick Co.; stated to be 9 at departure.

18. Nelson, Caroline M. (daughter of Samuel Nelson): Status uncertain; resident of Frederick Co.; stated to be 6 at departure.

19. Nelson, H. Timothy (son of Samuel Nelson): Status uncertain; resident of Frederick Co.; stated to be 4 at departure. Died before Jan. 10, 1854.

20. Owens, Samuel (husband of Henrietta Owens): Status uncertain; resident of Frederick Co.; stated to be 58 at departure.

21. Owens, Henrietta (wife of Samuel Owens): Status uncertain; resident of Frederick Co.; stated to be 44 at departure. Died before Jan. 10, 1854.

22. Owens, Eliza Jane (daughter of Samuel Owens): Status uncertain; resident of Frederick Co.; stated to be 20 at departure.

23. Owens, Charles H. (son of Samuel Owens): Status uncertain; resident of Frederick Co.; stated to be 18 at departure.

24. Owens, Rachael A. (daughter of Samuel Owens): Status uncertain; resident of Frederick Co.; stated to be 16 at departure.

25. Owens, Martha E. (daughter of Samuel Owens): Status uncertain; resident of Frederick Co.; stated to be 14 at departure.

26. Owens, Elizabeth (daughter of Samuel Owens): Status uncertain; resident of Frederick Co.; stated to be 12 at departure.

27. Smith, Solomon (husband of Diana): Status uncertain; resident of Harford Co.; stated to be 37 at departure.

28. Smith, Diana (wife of Solomon Smith): Status uncertain; resident of Harford Co.; stated to be 30 at departure.

29. Smith, William T. (son of Solomon Smith): Status uncertain; resident of Harford Co.; stated to be 9 at departure.

30. Smith, Susan (daughter of Solomon Smith): Status uncertain; resident of Harford Co.; stated to be 4 at departure.

31. Smith, Milcha (daughter of Solomon Smith): Status uncertain; resident of Harford Co.; stated to be 3 at departure.

32. Smith, Solomon (son of Solomon Smith): Status uncertain; resident of Harford Co.; stated to be 2 at departure.

33. Smith, Hannah (daughter of Solomon Smith): Status uncertain; resident of Harford Co.; stated to be 1 at departure.

34. Smith, Henry (husband of Susan Smith): Status uncertain; resident of Harford Co; stated to be 38 at departure.

35. Smith, Susan (wife of Henry Smith): Status uncertain; resident of Harford Co.; stated to be 32 at departure.

36. Smith, Hanson Thomas (single): Status uncertain; resident of Frederick, Frederick Co.; stated to be 32 at departure. Returned to United States, 1854.

37. Snowden, David (single): Status uncertain; resident of Frederick, Frederick Co.; stated to be 10 at departure.

38. Thompson, Lewis (single): Status uncertain; resident of Frederick, Frederick Co.; stated to be 45 at departure. Died before Jan. 10, 1854.

The total number of emigrants sent to Cape Palmas thus far: 956.

Brig BANSHEE, second voyage, arrived at Cape Palmas January 8, 1854:

1. Jackson, Isaac (single): Status uncertain; resident of Frederick Co.; stated to be 28 at departure.

2. Smith, Moses (single, father of seven children): Status uncertain; resident of Baltimore; stated to be 42 at departure. Died before May 17, 1854.

3. Smith, Moses Jr. (son of Moses Smith): Status uncertain; resident of Baltimore; stated to be 20 at departure.

4. Smith, Joshua (son of Moses Smith): Status uncertain; resident of Baltimore; stated to be 15 at departure.

5. Smith, Rachael (daughter of Moses Smith): Status uncertain; resident of Baltimore; stated to be 14 at departure.

6. Smith, Israel (son of Moses Smith): Status uncertain; resident of Baltimore; stated to be 11 at departure.

7. Smith, Henrietta (daughter of Moses Smith): Status uncertain; resident of Baltimore; stated to be 9 at departure.

8. Smith, John (son of Moses Smith): Status uncertain; resident of Baltimore; stated to be 6 at departure.

9. Smith, Catherine (daughter of Moses Smith): Status uncertain; resident of Baltimore; stated to be 18 months old at departure.

10. Smith, Rachael (uncertain relation to Moses Smith): Status uncertain; resident of Baltimore; stated to be 29 at departure.

11. Smith, Israel (husband of Elizabeth Smith, uncertain relation to Moses Smith): Status uncertain; resident of Frederick, Frederick Co.; stated to be 37 at departure. Returned to the United States, 1854.

12. Smith, Elizabeth (wife of Israel Smith): Status uncertain; resident of Frederick, Frederick Co.; stated to be 38 at departure. Returned to the United States, 1854.

13. Smith, Mary E. (daughter of Israel Smith): Status uncertain; resident of Frederick, Frederick Co.; stated to be 5 at departure. Died before May 17, 1854.

14. Smith, Ariana (daughter of Israel Smith): Status uncertain; resident of Frederick, Frederick Co.; stated to be 2 at departure. Died before May 17, 1854.

The total number of emigrants sent to Cape Palmas thus far: 970.

Brig LINDA STEWART, arrived at Cape Palmas May 7, 1854:

1. Smith, Charles (single): Status uncertain; resident of St. Mary's Co.; stated to be 17 at departure.

2. Williams, Georgianna (single): Status uncertain; resident of Baltimore; stated to be 32 at departure.

The total number of emigrants sent to Cape Palmas thus far: 972.

Brig EUPHRASIA, arrived at Cape Palmas late February, 1855:
1. Carroll, Robert (husband of Sally Carroll): Status uncertain; resident of Alexandria, Va.; stated to be 48 at departure.
2. Carroll, Sally (wife of Robert Carroll): Status uncertain; resident of Alexandria, Va.; stated to be 49 at departure.
3. Carroll, Rosa (daughter of Robert Carroll): Status uncertain; resident of Alexandria, Va.; stated to be 8 at departure.
4. Carroll, Kesiah (daughter of Robert Carroll): Status uncertain; resident of Alexandria, Va.; stated to be 4 at departure.
5. Carroll, Sally (daughter of Robert Carroll): Status uncertain; resident of Alexandria, Va.; stated to be 2 at departure.
6. Carroll, Aaron (single, possibly the brother of Robert Carroll): Status uncertain; resident of Alexandria, Va.; stated to be 25 at departure.
7. Curry, Ralph (single): Status uncertain; resident of Shepherdstown, (West) Virginia; stated to be 30 at departure.

The total number of emigrants sent to Cape Palmas thus far: 979.

Brig GENERAL PIERCE, arrived at Cape Palmas about March 6, 1855:
1. Anderson, William (single): Status uncertain; resident of Hinesville, Ga.; stated to be 30 at departure.
2. Andrews, Ephraim (husband of Eliza Andrews): Status uncertain; resident of Riceboro, Ga.; stated to be 30 at departure.
3. Andrews, Eliza (wife of Ephraim Andrews): Status uncertain; resident of Riceboro, Ga.; stated to be 26 at departure.
4. Andrews, Benjamin (son of Ephraim Andrews): Status uncertain; resident of Riceboro, Ga.; stated to be 8 at departure.
5. Bacon, Harry (husband of Eliza Bacon): Status uncertain; resident of Hinesville, Ga.; stated to be 40 at departure.
6. Bacon, Eliza (wife of Harry Bacon): Status uncertain; resident of Hinesville, Ga.; stated to be 30 at departure.
7. Bacon, Henry (son of Harry Bacon): Status uncertain; resident of Hinesville, Ga.; stated to be 15 at departure.
8. Bacon, Phebe A. (daughter of Harry Bacon): Status uncertain; resident of Hinesville, Ga.; stated to be 12 at departure.
9. Bacon, Edward (son of Harry Bacon): Status uncertain; resident of Hinesville, Ga.; stated to be 10 at departure.
10. Bacon, Richard (son of Harry Bacon): Status uncertain; resident of Hinesville, Ga.; stated to be 8 at departure.
11. Bacon, R. Ann (daughter of Harry Bacon): Status uncertain; resident of Hinesville, Ga.; stated to be 6 at departure.
12. Bacon, Mary A. (daughter of Harry Bacon): Status uncertain; resident of Hinesville, Ga.; stated to be 4 at departure.
13. Bacon, Daniel (son of Harry Bacon): Status uncertain; resident of Hinesville, Ga.; stated to be 2 at departure.
14. Bacon, Pompey (uncertain relation to Harry Bacon): Status uncertain; resident of Hinesville, Ga.; stated to be 31 at departure.

15. Bacon, Phebe (uncertain relation to Harry Bacon): Status uncertain; resident of Hinesville, Ga.; stated to be 40 at departure.

16. Bacon, Mary Ann (single, mother of four, uncertain relation to Harry Bacon): Status uncertain; resident of Hinesville, Ga.; stated to be 25 at departure.

17. Bacon, Martha (daughter of Mary Ann Bacon): Status uncertain; resident of Hinesville, Ga.; stated to be 8 at departure.

18. Bacon, Louisa (daughter of Mary Ann Bacon): Status uncertain; resident of Hinesville, Ga.; stated to be 6 at departure.

19. Bacon, William L. (son of Mary Ann Bacon): Status uncertain; resident of Hinesville, Ga.; stated to be 4 at departure.

20. Bacon, Joseph (son of Mary Ann Bacon): Status uncertain; resident of Hinesville, Ga.; stated to be 2 at departure.

21. Bacon, Nancy (single, mother of two, uncertain relation to Harry Bacon): Status uncertain; resident of Hinesville, Ga.; stated to be 19 at departure.

22. Bacon, Fillmore (son of Nancy Bacon): Status uncertain; resident of Hinesville, Ga.; stated to be 2 at departure.

23. Bacon, Unnamed infant (child of Nancy Bacon): Status uncertain; resident of Hinesville, Ga.; stated to be 3 months old at departure.

The total number of emigrants sent to Cape Palmas thus far: 1002.

INDIVIDUALS SENT TO AFRICA BY THE AMERICAN COLONIZATION SOCIETY OR BY OTHERS, WHO LATER SETTLED AT CAPE PALMAS

Ship ELIZABETH, arrived at Sierra Leone, March 9, 1820:
1. Revey, John (single): Freeborn resident of New York; stated to be 19 at departure. Settled at Sherbro. Refugee at Sierra Leone, 1821; a founder of Monrovia, later superintendent of Junk River settlement. Moved to Cape Palmas, 1837, and immediately took office of colonial secretary. Helped establish the Baptist Church at Cape Palmas. Died Mar. 14, 1842, of unrecorded cause.

OSWEGO, arrived at Monrovia, May 24, 1823:
1. Alter, Juliet (single): Freeborn resident of Maryland; stated to be 16 at departure. Settled at Monrovia. Reportedly moved to Cape Palmas, 1835, but does not appear in the record.

2. Johnson, Benjamin (single): Freeborn resident of Maryland; stated to be 45 at departure. Settled at Monrovia. Moved to Cape Palmas on the *Ann*, 1834. Appointed collector of customs, March, 1835 and 1837; justice of the peace and member of Committee on New Emigrants, 1838. Signed petition against Thomson, 1837. Died of consumption, Mar. 1, 1842.

3. Williams, A. D. (single): Freeborn resident of Maryland, a shoemaker; stated to be 24 at departure. Settled at Monrovia. Moved to Cape Palmas, 1840. Performed marriages at Cape Palmas, March 1840, as a Methodist minister. Living in Monrovia, 1847.

Brig HUNTER, arrived at Monrovia, March 13, 1825:
1. Jones, Jane (mother of Alexander Jones): Freeborn resident of Virginia; stated to be 34 at departure. Settled at Monrovia with husband and three children, all but one of whom died. Married John Revey at Monrovia. Moved to Cape Palmas, 1837. Resident of the colony, November, 1852.

2. Jones, Alexander L. (son of Jane Jones): Freeborn resident of Virginia; stated to be 9 at departure. Settled at Monrovia with parents and two siblings, all but mother died. Moved to Cape Palmas, 1837. Lived in John Revey household, 1840–43. Elected vice agent, 1846. Died about Oct. 20, 1846, of unrecorded cause.

Ship INDIAN CHIEF, arrived at Monrovia, March 22, 1826:
1. Wheeler, Samuel (single): Freeborn resident of Maryland; stated to be 25 at departure. Settled at Caldwell. Moved to Cape Palmas, 1834. Signed open letter, Oct. 11, 1834. Does not appear in the record afterward.

Brig DORIS, first voyage, arrived at Monrovia, August 11, 1827:
1. Wheeler, Phaiby (single; also called Emily Jackson): Freed resident of North Carolina; stated to be 23 at departure. Settled at Monrovia. Went to Cape Palmas at uncertain date. Married Nicholas Jackson, 1839. Died of puerpural peritonitis, 1841.

2. McGill, George R. (single, father of Samuel Ford McGill and others): Born a slave on the Eastern Shore of Maryland; purchased himself and family and moved to Baltimore; a teacher, preacher, and entrepreneur; stated to be 40 at departure. Settled at Monrovia, where he served in various capacities, including vice agent. Went to Cape Palmas on the *Ann*, 1834. After a brief return to Monrovia, moved permanently to Cape Palmas, 1837, taking post of assistant agent. Frequent letter writer. Took charge of the factory at Mt. Tubman and also ran the Public Farm there, 1839. Instructor of the Ladies' Academy, 1843. Married Lucinda Jones secretly, Jan. 15, 1843, and had a child with her early in 1844. Died in 1845.

3. McGill, Samuel Ford (son of George R. McGill): Freeborn resident of Baltimore; stated to be 12 at departure. Settled at Monrovia. Went to Cape Palmas, 1836, for a brief stay, then went to New England for medical school at Vermont College and Dartmouth, where he earned a degree in 1838. Returned to Cape Palmas on *Oberon*, January 1839. Letter writer: Jan. 17, April 16, 1839. Visited the United States in 1842 to recruit emigrants and court a Baltimore woman, Lydia (last name untraced), whom he married and brought back to Africa. After his first wife's death in 1843, he married Elizabeth Devaney, a young woman born in Africa, late in 1844. She died in mid-1846, after bearing a daughter. Visited U.S. in 1847. Married Louisa K. Coke, of untraced origin, May 9, 1848. On Russwurm's death in 1852, he succeeded to office of governor, which he held until independence, July, 1854. He then moved to Monrovia with his family.

Brig DORIS, second voyage, arrived at Monrovia, January 15, 1828:
1. Wood, Anthony: Born a slave in the West Indies and imported illegally to Maryland after 1807. Freed by legal action of Elisha Tyson. Resided in Baltimore, a blacksmith; stated to be 30 at departure. Settled at Monrovia, where his wife and son died in 1828. Went to Cape Palmas on the *Ann*, 1834. Worked in the colony as a blacksmith. Signed open letter, Oct. 11, 1834. Appointed justice of the peace, March, 1835. Signed petitions, June 15, 1836; Dec. 2, 1837; and April, 1849. Elected vice agent, 1838. Visited the United States to recruit emigrants, 1844–5. Appointed justice of the peace, 1845. Frequent letter writer. Married a woman named Mariah, of untraced origin, at Cape Palmas. Elected councilor, 1852. Elected to committee to frame the constitution, February, 1853. As senior military officer, led the bombardment of Gbenelu in 1856.

Brig NAUTILUS, arrived at Monrovia, February 19, 1828:
1. Brown, John (single): Freeborn resident of Maryland; stated to be 37 at departure.

Placed at Caldwell. Moved to Cape Palmas, 1836, but does not appear in the record.

2. Prout, William Allen (brother of Susan Prout): Purchased by his father; resident of Baltimore; stated to be 8 at departure. Placed at Caldwell, where his father died in 1828. Moved to Cape Palmas in 1834. Appointed acting storekeeper, 1838–9; colonial secretary and justice of the peace, 1845 and following. Frequent letter writer. Wrote petition, Jan. 14, 1850. Head of a mixed household, 1852. The architect of the independent State of Maryland in Liberia. Went to Baltimore in 1853–4 to negotiate terms of independence, then elected governor of the Free State of Maryland in Liberia. Deposed by Boston Drayton, December, 1855. Died Dec. 22, 1856.

3. Prout, Susan (sister of William A. Prout): Purchased by her father; resident of Baltimore; stated to be 10 at departure. Placed at Caldwell, where her father died in 1828. Moved to Cape Palmas before 1837, but does not appear in the record.

4. Fletcher, Dempsey Rollo (brother of Lydia Fletcher): Freed by a Mr. Fletcher of North Carolina to emigrate; stated to be 5. Placed at Monrovia. Moved to Cape Palmas at uncertain date, before 1838. Trained by Dr. S. F. McGill in medicine. Sent to Dr. Phelps at Dartmouth for further training in 1845. Returned to Cape Palmas on the *Packet's* first voyage, 1847. Frequent letter writer. Signed petition, December 1849. Appointed Gidu Magistrate, 1852. Continued to practice medicine in Maryland at least until 1856.

5. Fletcher, Lydia (sister of Dempsey R. Fletcher; also called Lydia Stewart): Freed by a Mr. Fletcher of North Carolina to emigrate; stated to be 12 at departure. Placed at Monrovia. Moved to Cape Palmas at uncertain date. Married James Stewart about 1836. Does not appear in the record after 1843.

Schooner RANDOLPH, arrived at Monrovia, July 17, 1828:

1. McDermit, Rachel (single): Freed by a Mr. McDermit of Georgia to emigrate; stated to be 57 at departure. Placed at Millsburg with the rest of the McDermit slaves, most of whom were dead by 1840. Moved to Cape Palmas 1837 and married Nathan Greene Harman. Does not appear in the record after 1838.

Ship HARRIET, arrived at Monrovia, March 24, 1829:

1. Jennings, Sykey (single, mother of several children; also called Sykey Martin): Freed by Margaret Mercer, of Maryland, to emigrate; stated to be 26 at departure. Placed at Monrovia and married James Martin there. Moved to Cape Palmas, 1834. Died of dysentery, 1841.

2. Jennings, Julia (daughter of Sykey Jennings; also called Julia Bowen): Freed by Margaret Mercer, of Maryland, to emigrate; stated to be 13 at departure. Placed at Monrovia. Moved to Cape Palmas, 1834. Married John B. Bowen, Sept. 4, 1836. Resident of the colony, November, 1852.

3. Jennings, James (son of Sykey Jennings): Freed by Margaret Mercer, of Maryland, to emigrate; stated to be 14 at departure. Placed at Monrovia. Reportedly moved to Cape Palmas, 1834, but does not appear in the record.

4. Jennings, Charles (son of Sykey Jennings): Freed by Margaret Mercer, of Maryland, to emigrate; stated to be 9 at departure. Placed at Monrovia. Moved to Cape Palmas, 1834. Living in James Martin household, 1839–40. Died of dysentery, 1841.

5. Jennings, Peter (son of Sykey Jennings): Freed by Margaret Mercer, of Maryland, to emigrate; stated to be 1 at departure. Placed at Monrovia. Reportedly moved to Cape Palmas, 1834, but does not appear in the record.

6. Martin, James (father of Catherine Martin): Freeborn resident of Maryland;

stated to be 30 at departure. Placed at Monrovia. Second marriage to Sykey Jennings. Moved to Cape Palmas, 1834. Worked in the colony as a sawyer. Signed open letter, Oct. 11, 1834. Signed petition against Thomson, Dec. 2, 1837. Died of hydrothorax, 1840.

7. Martin, Catherine (daughter of James Martin): Freeborn resident of Maryland; stated to be 2 at departure. Placed at Monrovia. Moved to Cape Palmas with her father, 1834. Living in Nancy Johnson household, 1843. Resident of the colony, November, 1852, living in William Howard household.

Ship CAROLINIAN, arrived at Monrovia, December 4, 1830:
1. Small, Lewis (single): Freeborn resident of Virginia, a farmer; stated to be 42 at departure. Placed at Monrovia, Liberia. Reportedly moved to Cape Palmas, 1837, but does not appear in the record.

Brig LIBERIA, arrived at Monrovia, February 17, 1830:
1. Denison, Martha (sister of Frances Denison): Freeborn resident of Virginia; stated to be 7 at departure. Placed at Monrovia, Liberia. Moved to Cape Palmas, 1837, where she went to live with J. M. Thomson's family. Does not appear in the record after 1838.

2. Denison, Frances Ann (sister of Martha Denison; also called Frances Moore or Thomson): Freeborn resident of Virginia; stated to be 5 at departure. Placed at Monrovia, Liberia. Moved to Cape Palmas, 1837, where she went to live with J. M. Thomson's family. Still in Thomson household, 1839. Appears to have married John D. Moore by 1843, then moved back to Monrovia.

3. Erskins, Hopkins: Free resident of Tennessee; stated to be 10 at departure. Placed at Caldwell, Liberia. Reportedly moved to Cape Palmas, 1843, but does not appear in the record.

4. Lucas, Hannah (single): Free resident of Virginia; stated to be 45 at departure. Placed at Caldwell, Liberia. Moved to Cape Palmas, 1834, and died there of debility and complications of an ulcer, Jan. 26, 1837.

Brig SUSAN, a private merchant ship, arrived at Monrovia, 1830:
1. Russwurm, John Browne (single): Freeborn octoroon, originally from Port Antonio, Jamaica. Graduate of Bowdoin College and founder of first black newspaper in the United States. Resident of New York City, a newspaper editor; stated to be 35 at departure. Settled at Monrovia, where he held office of colonial secretary and was publisher of the *Liberia Herald*. Later married Sarah E. McGill (the daughter of George R. McGill). Appointed governor of Maryland in Liberia, 1836, which office he held until his death, June 10, 1851.

Schooner REAPER, arrived at Monrovia, February 18, 1831:
1. McGill, Roszell (son of George R. McGill): Freeborn resident of Baltimore; stated to be 16 at departure. Placed at Monrovia, Liberia. Moved to Cape Palmas, 1840, but apparently divided his time between Harper and Monrovia, working in the family business. Appointed Gidu Magistrate, 1852.

2. McGill, Cleopatra (daughter of George R. McGill): Freeborn resident of Baltimore; stated to be 7 at departure. Placed at Monrovia, Liberia. Moved to Cape Palmas, 1836. Died of phthisis pulmonalis, 1841.

3. McGill, Urias (son of George R. McGill): Freeborn resident of Baltimore; stated to be 6 at departure. Placed at Monrovia, Liberia. Moved to Cape Palmas, 1836. Living in

George McGill household, 1843. Later moved back to Monrovia, where he helped manage the family merchant house.

4. McGill, James S. (son of George R. McGill): Freeborn resident of Baltimore; age at departure unstated. Placed at Monrovia, Liberia. Apparently lived at Cape Palmas temporarily in 1848. Letter writer: Sept. 15, 1850.

5. McGill, Sarah E. (daughter of George R. McGill; also called Sarah E. Russwurm): Freeborn resident of Baltimore; stated to be 16 at departure. Placed at Monrovia, Liberia. Married John Russwurm there in 1835. Moved to Cape Palmas, 1836. Visited U.S. in 1847. After John Russwurm's death, moved to Monrovia.

Brig AMERICAN, arrived at Monrovia, September 16, 1832:

1. Duncan, Henry (husband of Mary Duncan): Freeborn resident of North Carolina, a stonemason; stated to be 22 at departure. Placed at Monrovia. Moved to Cape Palmas, 1834. Worked in the colony as a stonemason. Signed open letter, Oct. 11, 1834. Elected selectman, Mar. 2, 1835. Caused scandal in 1848 by keeping a mistress. Signed petition, April, 1849. Resident of the colony, November, 1852.

2. Duncan, Mary A (wife of Henry Duncan): Freeborn resident of North Carolina; stated to be 31 at departure. Placed at Monrovia. Moved to Cape Palmas, 1836. Letter writer, Jan. 25. 1847. Died Dec. 14, 1852.

3. Duncan, Mary (mother of Henry Duncan): Freeborn resident of North Carolina; stated to be 48 at departure. Placed at Monrovia. Moved to Cape Palmas, 1836. In 1838, living with her daughter Hannah at Jesse Ireland's. Does not appear in the record afterward.

4. Duncan, William (son of Henry Duncan): Freeborn resident of North Carolina; stated to be 13 at departure. Placed at Monrovia. Moved to Cape Palmas, 1836. Killed in a cannon explosion at Russwurm's arrival, Nov. 12, 1836.

5. Duncan, Hannah (daughter of Henry Duncan; also called Hannah Garns): Freeborn resident of North Carolina; stated to be 10 at departure. Placed at Monrovia. Moved to Cape Palmas, 1835. Married Jesse Ireland April 9, 1837. Bore illegitimate child of A. Simpson, October, 1848. Listed as a widow, 1849. Resident of the colony, November, 1852.

6. Duncan, Mary (daughter of Henry Duncan): Freeborn resident of North Carolina; stated to be 5 at departure. Placed at Monrovia. Moved to Cape Palmas, 1835. Living with Jesse Ireland family, 1838; with Rachel Barnett household, 1848. Does not appear in the record afterward.

7. Duncan, Esther (daughter of Henry Duncan): Freeborn resident of North Carolina; stated to be 11 at departure. Placed at Monrovia. Moved to Cape Palmas, 1835, and died there of unknown cause, Sept. 18, 1836.

8. Howard, Anthony (husband of Eliza Howard): Freeborn resident of North Carolina, a seaman; stated to be 34 at departure. Placed at Monrovia. Signed open letter, Oct. 11, 1834. Moved to Cape Palmas, 1834. Worked variously as sawyer, mason, and farmer. Elected to Committee on New Emigrants, 1837–8. Married a woman named Lydia of uncertain origin. Signed petition against Thomson, Dec. 2, 1837. Appointed collector of customs, 1838–9; Roadmaster, 1839. Supported Snetter, Sept. 12, 1838. Letter writer: May 20, 1839. Cultivated 3.75 acres in 1839; 3 acres in 1848. Died of pneumonia, July 12, 1848.

9. Howard, Eliza (wife of Anthony Howard; also called Elizabeth Howard): Freeborn resident of North Carolina; stated to be 29 at departure. Placed at Monrovia. Moved to Cape Palmas, 1837. Died of tuberculosis, Jan. 20, 1842.

10. Howard, Sarah (daughter of Anthony Howard, mother of John R. Williams): Freeborn resident of North Carolina; stated to be 9 at departure. Placed at Monrovia. Moved to Cape Palmas, 1837. Married George Harvey, Oct. 22, 1840. Living as a single woman, surnamed Dawson, 1852.

11. Howard, Simon (son of Anthony Howard): Freeborn resident of North Carolina; stated to be 7 at departure. Placed at Monrovia. Moved to Cape Palmas, 1837. Worked in the colony as a seaman. Married Maria Croney, Feb. 19, 1852, and before year's end had an infant daughter.

12. Howard, John (son of Anthony Howard): Freeborn resident of North Carolina; stated to be 5 at departure. Placed at Monrovia. Moved to Cape Palmas, 1837. Resident of the colony, November, 1852.

13. Howard, Elizabeth (daughter of Anthony Howard, mother of William Hawkins, Jr., illegitimate; also called Betty Howard): Freeborn resident of North Carolina; stated to be 3 at departure. Placed at Monrovia. Moved to Cape Palmas, 1837. Resident of the colony, November, 1852.

14. Wilkerson, Gabriel (possibly the son of Henry Duncan; also called Johnson and Duncan): Freeborn resident of North Carolina; stated to be 4 at departure. Placed at Monrovia. Moved to Cape Palmas, 1835. In 1838, living with his mother and sister at Jesse Ireland's. Living with Randolph Davenport family, 1839. Living with Mary Johnson as "Gabriel Johnson," 1843. Resumed name of Wilkerson and living alone, 1852, working as a stonemason.

Schooner CRAWFORD, arrived at Monrovia, February, 1832:

1. Allen, Mary (single): Freed resident of Louisiana; stated to be 18 at departure. Placed at Millsburg, Liberia. Reportedly moved to Cape Palmas, 1837, but does not appear in the record.

2. Jackson, Martha (mother of Delilah; also called Martha Snetter): Freed resident of Louisiana; stated to be 18 at departure. Placed at Millsburg, Liberia. Married Charles Snetter in Liberia. Moved to Cape Palmas, 1836; moved back to Monrovia, 1838.

3. Jackson, Delilah (daughter of Martha Jackson): Freed resident of Louisiana; stated to be 2 at departure. Placed at Millsburg, Liberia. Moved to Cape Palmas with her mother, 1836, then presumably moved back to Monrovia with her mother, 1838.

4. McFagen, Rachel (single, mother of two): Freed resident of Louisiana; stated to be 28 at departure. Placed at Millsburg, Liberia. Reportedly moved to Cape Palmas, 1842, but does not appear in the record.

5. McFagen, Rosetta (daughter of Rachel McFagen): Freed resident of Louisiana; stated to be 28 at departure. Placed at Millsburg, Liberia. Reportedly moved to Cape Palmas, 1842, but does not appear in the record.

6. McFagen, Juliet (daughter of Rachel McFagen): Freed resident of Louisiana; stated to be 1 at departure. Placed at Millsburg, Liberia. Reportedly moved to Cape Palmas with her mother, 1842. Possibly the same Julia, aged 17, apprentice in Francis Burns household, 1849.

Ship JAMES PERKINS, arrived at Monrovia, January 14, 1832:

1. Brown, Rebecca (single): Freeborn resident of Virginia; stated to be 18 at departure. Placed at Caldwell, Liberia. Reportedly moved to Cape Palmas, 1836, but does not appear in the record.

2. Butler, Stephen (single): Freeborn resident of Virginia; stated to be 10 at departure. Placed at Caldwell, Liberia. Reportedly moved to Cape Palmas, 1840, but does not appear in the record.

3. Cooper, Ann (single): Freeborn resident of North Carolina; stated to be 5 at departure. Placed at Caldwell, Liberia. Reportedly moved to Cape Palmas, 1835, but does not appear in the record.

4. Ferrin, Emily (orphan): Freeborn resident of North Carolina; stated to be 4 at departure. Placed at Caldwell, Liberia. Reportedly moved to Cape Palmas, 1837, but does not appear in the record.

5. Jones, Sophia (single, mother of two; also called Lavinia and Elizabeth [1849]): Freeborn resident of Virginia; stated to be 29 at departure. Placed at Monrovia, Liberia. Moved to Cape Palmas, 1837. Living in Lucinda McGill household, 1848. Does not appear in the record after 1849.

6. Jones, Lavinia (daughter of Sophia Jones): Freeborn resident of Virginia; stated to be 5 at departure. Placed at Monrovia, Liberia. Moved to Cape Palmas, 1837. Living in Lucinda McGill household, 1848; with her mother, 1849; in Rachel Barnett household, 1852, described as "Idiot."

7. Jones, Lucinda (daughter of Sophia Jones): Freeborn resident of Virginia; stated to be 10 at departure. Placed at Monrovia, Liberia. Moved to Cape Palmas, 1837. Living in McGill household, 1843. Married George McGill, Jan. 15, 1843. Supported by S. F. McGill for some time after George McGill's death. Associated with Joseph Odley household, 1849. Does not appear in the record afterward.

8. Richardson, Mary (single): Freeborn resident of North Carolina; stated to be 6 at departure. Placed at New Georgia, Liberia. Reportedly moved to Cape Palmas, 1837, but does not appear in the record.

Ship JUPITER, arrived at Monrovia, June 29, 1832:
1. Bradley, Lewis (brother of Stern Bradley): Freed by Dr. James Bradley of Georgia to emigrate; a farmer; stated to be 22 at departure. Placed at Caldwell, Liberia. Reportedly moved to Cape Palmas, 1840, but does not appear in the record.

2. Bradley, Stern (husband of Harriet Bradley, brother of Lewis Bradley; also called Toliver or Taliaferro): Freed by Dr. James Bradley of Georgia to emigrate; a farmer; stated to be 28 at departure. Placed at Caldwell, Liberia. Moved to Cape Palmas, 1842. Worked in the colony as a sawyer and farmer. Signed petition, Jan. 14, 1850. Does not appear in the record afterward.

3. Bradley, Harriet (wife of Stern Bradley; also called Toliver or Taliaferro): Freed by Dr. James Bradley of Georgia to emigrate; stated to be 14 at departure. Placed at Caldwell, Liberia. Moved to Cape Palmas, 1842. Does not appear in the record after 1848.

4. Bradley, Eleanor (sister of Harriet Bradley): Freed by Dr. James Bradley of Georgia to emigrate, a barber; stated to be 9 at departure. Placed at Caldwell, Liberia. Moved to Cape Palmas, 1842. Does not appear in the record after 1848.

5. Harvey, James Green (brother of Stern Bradley): Freed by Dr. James Bradley of Georgia to emigrate; stated to be 6 at departure. Placed at Caldwell, Liberia. Moved to Cape Palmas before 1837. Worked in the colony as a laborer, then seaman. Living with Ezekiel Harrington's family in 1837. Signed petition, Jan. 14, 1850. Does not appear in the record afterward.

6. Scotland, Charles (husband of Dorcas Scotland): Freed resident of Virginia, a farmer; stated to be 49 at departure. Placed at Caldwell, Liberia. Moved to Cape Palmas, 1834. Worked as a house carpenter and farmer. Signed open letter, Oct. 11, 1834. Elected counselor, Mar. 2, 1835. Appointed commissary, Dec. 4, 1836. Signed petition, June 15, 1836; Dec. 2, 1837. Visited U.S., 1846, then returned to Africa with family on *Packet*, Voyage A. Signed petition, April, 1849; Jan. 14, 1850. In 1852, married to Sarah Gibson.

7. Scotland, Dorcas (wife of Charles Scotland): Freed resident of Virginia; stated to be 49 at departure. Placed at Caldwell, Liberia. Moved to Cape Palmas, 1834. Died before 1848.

8. Scotland, Mary A. (daughter of Charles Scotland): Freed resident of Virginia; stated to be 23 at departure. Placed at Caldwell, Liberia. Moved to Cape Palmas with her parents, 1834. Worked in the colony as a laundress. Married John Harris at Harper, Nov. 14, 1836. Resident of the colony, November, 1852.

9. Scotland, Julia Ann (daughter of Charles Scotland): Freed resident of Virginia; stated to be 16 at departure. Placed at Caldwell, Liberia. Moved to Cape Palmas with her parents, 1834. Married William Hawkins at Harper, Feb. 16, 1837. Died between 1849 and 1852.

10. Scotland, Alexander (son of Charles Scotland; also called "Sandy" or Amos): Freed resident of Virginia; stated to be 8 at departure. Placed at Caldwell, Liberia. Moved to Cape Palmas with his parents, 1834. Died of ileus, Nov. 11, 1848.

11. Scotland, Henry (son of Charles Scotland): Freed resident of Virginia; stated to be 3 at departure. Placed at Caldwell, Liberia. Moved to Cape Palmas with his family, 1834. Living with stepfather John Harris in 1837 and 1839. Signed petition, Jan. 14, 1850. Does not appear in the record afterward.

12. Snetter, Charles (father of Charles Snetter, Jr.): Freeborn resident of Charleston, S.C.; stated to be 30 at departure. Placed at Monrovia. Moved to Cape Palmas, 1836. Letter writer: July 7 and 9, 1837. Elected councilor, 1838. Court-martialled and banished from the colony. Moved back to Monrovia, early 1839.

13. Snetter, Charles, Jr. (son of Charles Snetter): Freeborn resident of Charleston, S.C.; stated to be 2 at departure. Placed at Monrovia, Liberia. Moved to Cape Palmas with his father, 1836. Moved back to Monrovia, early 1839.

14. Thomson, James M.: Born in British Guiana; moved to England as a boy and received a liberal education; settled in New York, where he was a teacher in the Free School. Sailed with wife and two children; stated to be 25 at departure. Settled at Monrovia, where his family died. Later married Elizabeth M. Johnson (Margaret Mercer, 1833). Went to Cape Palmas on the *Ann*, 1834, as James Hall's secretary. Served as colonial secretary and storekeeper. In 1836, appointed first missionary of the Episcopal Church in Africa, but resigned in disgrace in 1838. Died before Jan. 30, 1839, of unrecorded cause.

15. Whitfield, Reddach (single; also called Robert Whitfield): Freed resident of Virginia; stated to be 29 at departure. Placed at Grand Bassa. Married a woman named Matilda, whose maiden name is not recorded. Moved to Cape Palmas, 1834. Signed open letter, Oct. 11, 1834. Disabled in cannon blast at Russwurm's arrival, Nov. 12, 1836. Signed petition against Thomson, Dec. 2, 1837. Supporter of Snetter, Sept. 12, 1838. Letter writer: April 24, 1838. Elected to New Emigrant Committee, 1839. Does not appear in the record after 1840.

Brig AJAX, arrived at Monrovia, July 11, 1833:

1. Bibb, Lavina (sister of Phillis Bibb): Freed by R. Bibb of Kentucky, to emigrate; stated to be 15 at departure. Placed at Caldwell, Liberia. Reportedly moved to Cape Palmas, 1837, but does not appear in the record.

2. Bibb, Phillis (sister of Lavina Bibb): Freed by R. Bibb of Kentucky, to emigrate; stated to be 28 at departure. Placed at Caldwell, Liberia. Reportedly moved to Cape Palmas, 1837, but does not appear in the record.

Ship HERCULES, arrived at Monrovia, January 16, 1833:

1. Clark, Mary (mother of Elizabeth Clark): Freeborn resident of South Carolina, a mantua maker; stated to be 23 at departure. Placed at Monrovia; widowed in 1833. Reportedly moved to Cape Palmas, 1836, to marry, but does not appear in the record.

2. Clark, Elizabeth (daughter of Mary Clark): Freeborn resident of South Carolina; stated to be 4 at departure. Placed at Monrovia. Moved to Cape Palmas with mother, 1836. Living in McGill household, 1843, 1848–9. Does not appear in the record afterward.

3. Clark, James (son of Mary Clark; also called Weston Clark): Freeborn resident of South Carolina; stated to be 1 at departure. Placed at Monrovia. Moved to Cape Palmas with mother, 1836. Living in McGill household, 1843, 1848; in Elizabeth Thomson household, 1849. Does not appear in the record afterward. Associated with McGill household, 1852, working as a clerk. Died Dec. 15, 1852.

4. Eden, Samuel (orphan): Freeborn resident of South Carolina; stated to be 11 at departure. Placed at Monrovia. Moved to Cape Palmas, 1836. Living at Fair Hope in 1837. Died of typhoid fever, Oct. 29, 1837.

5. Mathews, Eliza A. (orphan): Freeborn resident of South Carolina; stated to be 11 at departure. Placed at Monrovia. Reportedly moved to Cape Palmas, 1843, to marry, but does not appear in the record.

Ship JUPITER, arrived at Monrovia, March 8, 1833:

1. Bowen, John B. (single): Freed resident of Virginia; stated to be 21 at departure. Placed at Caldwell, Liberia. Moved to Cape Palmas, 1834. Signed open letter, Oct. 11, 1834. Married Julia Jennings, Sept. 4, 1836. Appointed justice of the peace and Measurer, 1838–9. Agricultural Census, 1839: .75 acre. Letter writer: Jan. 26, 1847; Sept. 24, 1851. Signed petition, April, 1849. Elected vice agent, 1851. Elected to constitution drafting committee, February 1853.

Schooner MARGARET MERCER, arrived at Monrovia, 1833:

1. Johnson, Elizabeth M. (single): Freed resident of Connecticut; stated to be 29 at departure. Placed at Monrovia. Apparently married James M. Thomson soon after arrival in Monrovia. Moved to Cape Palmas 1834. Resumed name Johnson in 1839; and then later reverted to Thomson. Letter writer Oct. 6, 1849. Worked in the colony as a teacher in the Episcopal Mission. Resident of the colony, November, 1852.

Brig ROANOKE, arrived at Monrovia, February 17, 1833:

1. Reynolds, William (husband of Maria Reynolds): Freeborn resident of New York; stated to be 43 at departure. Placed at Caldwell, Liberia. Moved to Cape Palmas, 1834. Worked in the colony as a rough carpenter. Signed open letter, Oct. 11, 1834 (but expressed desire to return to U.S.). Appointed constable, March, 1837–8. Elected sheriff, 1839. Agricultural Census, 1839: 1.75 acres. Died of dropsy, 1841.

2. Reynolds, Maria (wife of William Reynolds): Freeborn resident of New York; stated to be 29 at departure. Placed at Caldwell, Liberia. Moved to Cape Palmas, 1834. Does not appear in the record after 1843.

3. Reynolds, William (son of William Reynolds): Freeborn resident of New York; stated to be 8 at departure. Placed at Caldwell, Liberia. Moved to Cape Palmas, 1834. Died of effects of an ulcer, Dec. 24, 1837.

4. Reynolds, Charlotte (daughter of William Reynolds): Freeborn resident of New York; stated to be 2 at departure. Placed at Caldwell, Liberia. Moved to Cape Palmas, 1834. Does not appear in the record after 1843.

Brig ARGUS, arrived at Monrovia, April, 1834:
1. MacFarland, Daniel C. (husband of Matilda MacFarland): Freed by J. MacFarland of Alexandria, D.C. to emigrate; a teacher; stated to be 18 at departure. Placed at Monrovia, where his wife died. Moved to Cape Palmas, 1843. Became agency storekeeper, Feb. 20, 1843; reappointed, March 1845. Fired as collector of customs, February, 1846. Disappears from the record after this, probably returned to Monrovia.

JUPITER, arrived at Monrovia, January 1,1834:
1. Gray, Phoebe (single): Freed by William Atkins of Virginia to emigrate; stated to be at departure. Placed at Monrovia. Reportedly moved to Cape Palmas, 1835, but does not appear in the record.
2. Wilson, Henry (single; also called Jameson, Henry [possibly]): Freed by William Atkins of Virginia to emigrate; stated to be at departure. Placed at Monrovia. Moved to Cape Palmas, 1835. (Possibly In ABCFM household, early 1837, as Henry Jameson.) Died of typhoid fever, Sept. 18, 1837.

Ship NINUS, arrived at Monrovia, December 9, 1834:
1. Lilly, Harvey (single): Freed resident of Virginia; stated to be 68 at departure. Placed at Bassa Cove. Reportedly moved to Cape Palmas, 1839, but does not appear in the record.
2. Smith, William (single): Freed resident of Virginia; stated to be 42 at departure. Placed at Bassa Cove. Reportedly moved to Cape Palmas, 1839, but does not appear in the record.

Brig SUSAN ELIZABETH, a merchant vessel, arrived at Monrovia, 1834:
1. Burns, Francis (single): Free resident of New York, a schoolteacher; stated to be 30 at departure. Paid for his own passage from New York; settled at Monrovia. Moved to Cape Palmas about 1836 where he served as Methodist minister. Married Amelia Dellanot, Nov. 1, 1836. Moved to Monrovia about 1839, then returned to his old post at Cape Palmas, 1846. Signed pro-annexation petition, 1851. Does not appear in the record afterward.

Brig ROVER, arrived at Monrovia, April, 1835:
1. Moore, John D. (single; also called David Moore): Purchased his own freedom in Mississippi; stated to be 14 at departure. Placed at Monrovia. Moved to Cape Palmas, 1837. Where he worked for the Episcopal mission as clerk and teacher. Appointed Measurer of Buildings, 1845. Elected councilor, 1846, after which he disappears from the record.

Brig LUNA, arrived at Monrovia, April, 1836:
1. Long, Judith (single; also called Judith Myers): Freed resident of Virginia, stated to be 25 at departure. Placed at Bassa Cove, Liberia. Married Samuel Myers there. Reportedly moved to Cape Palmas, 1837, but does not appear in the record.
2. Myers, Samuel (single): Freed resident of Virginia, stated to be 28 at departure. Placed at Bassa Cove, Liberia. Married Judith Long there. Reportedly moved to Cape Palmas, 1837, but does not appear in the record.

Schooner SWIFT, arrived at Monrovia, July, 1836:
1. Foster, William Thomas (orphan): Freed by William Foster of Mississippi to emi-

grate; stated to be 10 at departure. Placed at Millsburg, Liberia. Reportedly moved to Cape Palmas, 1836, but does not appear in the record until 1848 Census, listed as a seaman.

Brig ROUNDOUT, arrived at Monrovia, February 4, 1837:
1. Schumann, Susanna (single): Freed by Shadrack Schumann of North Carolina; age at departure unstated. Placed at Millsburg, Liberia. Reportedly moved to Cape Palmas, 1839, but does not appear in the record.

Ship EMPEROR, arrived at Monrovia, February 12, 1838:
1. Smith, Temple (single): Freed by John Smith, Sr., of Virginia to emigrate; stated to be 18 at departure. Placed at Millsburg, Liberia. Reportedly moved to Cape Palmas, 1840, but does not appear in the record.

Barque MARINE, arrived at Bassa Cove, February, 1838:
1. Buley, Isaac (single): Freed resident of North Carolina; stated to be 12 at departure. Placed at Edina, then Bexley, Liberia. Reportedly moved to Cape Palmas, 1839, but does not appear in the record.
2. Leaper, Matilda (single): Freeborn resident of Mississippi; stated to be 19 at departure. Placed at Sinoe, Liberia. Reportedly moved to Cape Palmas to marry, 1842, but does not appear in the record.
3. Smith, Harriet (single): Freed resident of North Carolina; stated to be 20 at departure. Placed at Edina, then Bexley, Liberia. Reportedly moved to Cape Palmas, 1839, but does not appear in the record.

Ship SALUDA, first voyage, arrived at Monrovia, April 1, 1839:
1. Jenks, Munday (single): Status and residence uncertain; stated to be 23 at departure. Placed at Caldwell, Liberia. Reportedly moved to Cape Palmas, 1840, but does not appear in the record.

Ship SALUDA, second voyage, arrived at Bassa Cove, March 30, 1840:
1. Winkie, Solomon (orphan, brother of Martha Winkie): Status uncertain; resident of Kentucky; stated to be 10 at departure. Placed at Bassa Cove, Liberia. Reportedly moved to Cape Palmas, 1841, but does not appear in the record.
2. Winkie, Martha (orphan, sister of Solomon Winkie): Status uncertain; resident of Kentucky; stated to be 8 at departure. Placed at Bassa Cove, Liberia. Reportedly moved to Cape Palmas, 1841, but does not appear in the record.

Barque UNION, arrived at Monrovia, July 1, 1841:
1. Curd, William (single): Freed by a Mr. Curd of Kentucky to emigrate; a farmer; stated to be 13 at departure. Placed at Monrovia, Liberia. Reportedly moved to Cape Palmas, 1841, but does not appear in the record.
2. White, Robert, Jr. (brother of Euphemia White): Freed by Lee White of Kentucky to emigrate; a cook; stated to be 22 at departure. Placed at Monrovia, Liberia. Reportedly moved to Cape Palmas, 1841, but does not appear in the record.
3. White, Euphemia (sister of Robert White Jr.): Freed by Lee White of Kentucky to emigrate; a cook; stated to be 14 at departure. Placed at Monrovia, Liberia. Reportedly moved to Cape Palmas, 1841, but does not appear in the record.

Ship MARIPOSE, arrived at Monrovia, August 21, 1842:

1. ——, Phillis (single): Status uncertain; resident of Missouri; stated to be 13 at departure. Placed at Monrovia, Liberia. Reportedly moved to Cape Palmas, 1843, but does not appear in the record.

2. Dickson, Martha (sister of George Dickson): Freedom purchased by her family in East Tennessee; stated to be 12 at departure. Placed at Caldwell, Liberia. Reportedly moved to Cape Palmas, 1843, but does not appear in the record.

3. Dickson, George (brother of Martha Dickson): Freedom purchased by his family in East Tennessee; stated to be 8 at departure. Placed at Caldwell, Liberia. Reportedly moved to Cape Palmas, 1843, but does not appear in the record.

4. Dorothy, Rhody (sister of William C. Dorothy, related to the Dicksons): Freedom purchased by her family in East Tennessee; stated to be 12 at departure. Placed at Caldwell, Liberia. Reportedly moved to Cape Palmas, 1843, but does not appear in the record.

5. Dorothy, William C. (brother of Rhody Dorothy, related to the Dicksons): Freedom purchased by his family in East Tennessee; stated to be 10 at departure. Placed at Caldwell, Liberia. Reportedly moved to Cape Palmas, 1843, but does not appear in the record.

6. Wright, George B. (single): Freeborn resident of Alabama; stated to be 15 at departure. Placed at Monrovia, Liberia. Reportedly moved to Cape Palmas, 1843, but does not appear in the record.

Barque GLOBE, arrived at Monrovia, December 31, 1843:

1. Lynch, Elmira (single; also called Mary Brown): Freed by a Mr. Lynch of Lynchburg, Va., to emigrate; stated to be 13 at departure. Placed at Monrovia, Liberia. Moved to Cape Palmas, 1843. Married Washington Brown, Aug. 22, 1848. Does not appear in the record afterward.

References

Introduction: "Two Warring Ideals"

[1] Symbolic meaning of Africa: Philip D. Curtin, *The Image of Africa: British Ideals & Action, 1780–1850* (Madison: University of Wisconsin Press, 1964) includes considerable relevant material and analysis.

[2] Maryland County today: Mary H. Moran, *Civilized Women: Gender and Prestige in Southeastern Liberia* (Ithaca: Cornell University Press, 1980); Andreas Massing; *The Economic Anthropology of the Kru (West Africa)* (Wiesbaden: Franz Steiner Verlag GMBH, 1980).

[3] Ethiopianism in colonization ideology: John H. B. Latrobe; *Maryland in Liberia: A History of the Colony Planted by the Maryland State Colonization Society Under the Auspices of the State of Maryland, U.S. at Cape Palmas on the South-West Coast of Africa, 1833–1853. A Paper Read Before the Maryland Historical Society, March 9, 1885. Fund Publication No. 21* (Baltimore: Maryland Historical Society, 1885); Blyden, Edward Wilmot; *Christianity, Islam, and the Negro Race* (London, 1887) notably the essay "African Colonisation"; Eugene Genovese; *A Consuming Fire: The Fall of the Confederacy in the White Christian South* (Athens: University of Georgia Press, 1998). For further reference, see Chapter 1, note 17, below.

[4] David Walker, *Appeal in Four Articles; Together With a Preamble to the Colored Citizens of the World, but in Particular, and Very Expressly, to Those of the United States of America* (Boston, 1829, and many subsequent editions) the work includes a chapter, "Our Wretchedness in Consequence of the Colonizing Plan."

William Watkins of Baltimore had letters published in *The Genius of Universal Emancipation* during Garrison's tenure there which condemned Africa as a land where black Americans would surely perish. See Christopher Phillips, *Freedom's Port: The African American Community of Baltimore, 1790–1860* (Urbana: University of Illinois Press, 1997), pp. 220–23; Leroy Graham, *Baltimore: The Nineteenth Century Black Capital* (Lanham: University Press of America, 1982), pp. 96–99.

[5] John Kennard to Rev. Ira Easter; Kent Island, Md., June 15, 1836: p. 2, in Maryland State Colonization Society Papers, Maryland Historical Society, Baltimore (hereinafter MSCS).

[6] See the Annotated Roll of Settlers for a summary of the backgrounds of emigrants.

[7] W. E. B. Dubois, *The Souls of Black Folk: Essays and Sketches*, 4th ed. (Chicago: A. C. McClurg, 1904), pp. 3–4.

[8] Robert Farris Thompson; *Flash of the Spirit: African and Afro-american Art and Philosophy* (New York: Vintage Books, 1984).

[9] Osagie, Iyonolu Folayan; *The Amistad Revolt: Memory, Slavery, and the Politics of Identity in the United States and Sierra Leone* (Athens: University of Georgia Press,

2000) provides a thorough and interesting examination of these issues in the context of the mutiny, trial, and subsequent return of a group of African captives to Africa.

[10] Kru ethnic identity: Andreas Massing provides the best analysis in his forgotten book, *The Economic Anthropology of the Kru* (Wiesbaden: Steiner, 1980). George Brooks; *The Kru Mariner in the Nineteenth Century: A Historical Compendium* (Newark, Del.: Liberian Studies Monograph Series, No. 1, 1972) is also useful.

A series of articles appeared in *Africa* and other journals, developing the idea that ethnic identities were applied by outsiders and then taken up by Southeastern Liberian peoples as they were convenient or useful, varying over time. Notable among them: Frederick D. McEvoy; "Understanding Ethnic Realities Among the Grebo and Kru Peoples of West Africa," in *Africa*, 47:62–79, which defies almost the entire historical record of the area in the nineteenth century in favor of a theoretical hypothesis of cultural homogeneity; and L. B. Breitborde, "City, Countryside and Kru Ethnicity," 61:186–201, which states more clearly the point that "Kru" is an ethnic identity created by outsiders, originally to define a socio-economic niche, but which took on a life of its own among the heterodox peoples to whom it was applied. It is important to understand that "Kru" or "Fishmen" identity could sometimes expand to include elements of Grebo society.

[11] This archive is the principal source for this history. All references to follow refer to the society's annual letterbooks unless otherwise noted.

1. *"They Foundation Stone of a Nation"*

Latrobe, John H. B.; *Maryland in Liberia: A History of the Colony Planted by the Maryland State Colonization Society Under the Auspices of the State of Maryland, U.S. at Cape Palmas on the South-west Coast of Africa, 1833–1853. A Paper Read Before the Maryland Historical Society, March 9, 1885. Fund Publication No. 21* (Baltimore: Maryland Historical Society, 1885). For the flag, p. 134; for the hymn, which Latrobe composed for the occasion, see pp. 133–34; the *Ann*'s departure, p. 37; some details of the voyage, pp. 37–38. The middle two verses of the hymn are as follows:

> For Africa, For Africa, our flag is floating fair
> We have taken Freedom's banner, though its stars are wanting there
> But in their stead the holy sign is on the azure field
> And cross and stripes have now become our standard and our shield
> And yet, where Afric's palm-trees wave, where sweeps the dread simoon
> May mark, where pilgrims, wending home, may loose their sandal shoon.
>
> For Africa, For Africa, — we bear the glorious light
> Which, gushing from revealed truth is, like the sunbeam bright
> Where hearts of wandering thousands no softening thoughts have known
> Where prayer has never yet gone up to Heaven's Eternal throne
> We'll plant the cross, — the idol break — we'll teach the sacred word
> Until through Heathen Africa, our God shall be adored.

[2] Accounts of the first voyage published in *The African Repository* include: James

Hall, "Cape Palmas, Liberia," 60, no. 4 (Oct., 1884): 97–108; J. H. B. Latrobe, "Cape Palmas, Liberia," 61, no. 1 (Jan., 1885): 1–8; J. H. B. Latrobe; "Dr. James Hall," Vol. 65, no. 4 (Oct., 1889): 117–19.

³ Hall, "Cape Palmas," p. 101. John Hersey was rather a remarkable character. In the early years of the nineteenth century, he was a prosperous merchant in Georgetown, D.C. Financial reverses and the betrayal of a partner left him bankrupt, sometime about 1815. Deserted by his fiancée, and with scarcely a possession in the world, he began a vagrant life. Formerly irreligious, he was converted to Methodism and began preaching. Under Monroe's administration, about 1817, he was appointed clerk of the General Government Depot in the Choctaw Nation, where he resided for several years, known as "the man who talks to the clouds." A visitor in 1820 remembered Hersey as "a small, cadaverous looking man, thin breasted, slightly stooping in the shoulders, with features clean cut, somewhat wrinkled, and strikingly expressive of earnestness and tenderness." He dressed in Quaker fashion, shunning buttons in favor of hooks and eyes. The same visitor related a story illustrative of his fearless morality:

> While surrounded by his staff officers, the chiefs of the nations and a crowd of braves, who had been his allies in many battles, [General Andrew Jackson] in the excitement of the moment, uttered an oath, "by the eternal!" The little clerk, placing himself in front of the great Chieftain, and looking up respectfully and earnestly into his face, reminded him that he had not only offended God, but had set a bad example to the Indians, thus counterworking the efforts of their friends to instruct and save them. The General was taken aback, and looking down upon the diminutive hero, who had pub-licly and decisively dared to rebuke him, after a pause, and calling to mind that the speaker was a brave and conscientious minister of the gospel, accepted the reproof with characteristic candor, publicly con-fessing his sin and asking pardon.

Hersey continued to travel and preach with the same courage until his death in 1862. In 1833 he published a slim pamphlet in Baltimore: *An Appeal to Christians, on the Subject of Slavery,* which advocated African colonization. See James E. Armstrong, *History of the Old Baltimore Conference, From the Planting of Methodism in 1773 to the Division of the Conference in 1857* (Baltimore, 1907), pp. 186–98. There is also a tract, "Sketches of John Hersey," by F. E. Marine, which I have not seen.

⁴ Latrobe, *Maryland in Liberia,* p. 37; see also, the Emigrant Roll in Maryland State Colonization Society Papers, Maryland Historical Society [hereinafter MSCS].

⁵ Hall, "Cape Palmas," p. 102.

⁶ James Hall to J. H. B. Latrobe, Brig *Ann,* near Cape Henry, Dec. 2, 1833, pp. 1–2, MSCS.

⁷ Rev. John Hersey to William McKenney; At sea, Jan. 14, 1834, p. 2, MSCS.

⁸ Ibid., p. 1.

⁹ Ibid., pp. 2–3.

¹⁰ Hall, "Cape Palmas," p. 102.

¹¹ Any number of books on Liberia detail the origins of the colonization movement, and it would be redundant and beside my purpose to recount them here, except in brief. Those interested in the subject might consult the following works: Alexander, Archibald,

A History of Colonization on the Western Coast of Africa, 2nd ed. (1849; repr., Freeport, N.Y.: Books for Libraries Press, 1971); P. J. Staudenraus, *The American Colonization Movement, 1816–1865.* (New York: Columbia University Press, 1961); J. Gus Liebenow, *Liberia: The Evolution of Privilege* (Ithaca: Cornell University Press, 1969); Liebenow, *Liberia: The Quest for Democracy* (Bloomington: University of Indiana Press; 1987); Amos Sawyer, *The Emergence of Autocracy in Liberia: Tragedy and Challenge* (San Francisco: Institute for Contemporary Studies, 1992); C. Abayomi Cassell, *Liberia: History of the First African Republic* (New York: Fountainhead Publishers, 1970).

[12] At that time, there was a widespread belief that mankind could be neatly divided into categories based upon inherited physical and mental characteristics. With ethnocentric pride, Western scientists thought that some races were inherently superior to others, Caucasians being better than all the rest. One may wonder that educated men could have entertained such illogical and prejudiced opinions, yet they were accepted almost without question by many of the most intelligent men of the age, acquiring the authority of custom, religion, and science.

The most impressive of the many works of anthropological pseudo-science was J. C. Nott and George R. Gliddon's, *Types of Mankind; Or, Ethnological Researches Based Upon the Ancient Monuments, Paintings, Sculptures, and Crania of Races; And Upon Their Natural, Geographical, Philological, and Biblical History* (Philadelphia, 1854). Embellished with numerous fine cuts and maps, with all the scholarly trappings, the work persuasively demonstrated to its nineteenth-century readers the physical and mental constancy of the races throughout history. The authors posited,

> history affords no evidence that education, or any influence of civilization that may be brought to bear on races of inferior organization, can radically change their physical, nor, consequently, their moral characters. That the brain, for example, which is the organ of intellect, cannot be expanded or altered in form, is now admitted by every anatomist. (p. 185)

Few could challenge the seeming weight of evidence they brought to bear in favor of the proposition that the nature of man was unchangeable because of his physiognomy. As for the African race, the "cursed sons of Ham," they grandly pronounced,

> In a word, the whole of Africa, south of 10 [degrees] N. lat., shows a succession of human beings with intellects as dark as their skins, and with a cephalic conformation that renders all expectance of their melioration an Utopian dream, philanthropical, but somewhat senile.
>
> The truth of these observations is sustained by all past history, backed by every movement. Much as the success of the infant colony at Liberia is to be desired by every true philanthropist, it is with regret that, whilst wishing well to the Negroes, we cannot divest our minds of melancholy forebodings. Dr. Morton . . . has proven that the Negro races possess about nine cubic inches less of brain than the Teuton. (pp. 189)

See Stephen J. Gould's *The Mismeasure of Man* (New York: W. W. Norton & Co., 1981) for a fine account of the biological determinists of the last century.

[13] The British anti-slavery movement had a clear impact on the American attitude toward slavery, and the ideologies of the abolition and colonization movements of the United States ought to be understood in an international context. In Great Britain, emancipation and colonization were kindred ideas. The English promoters of colonization were religious and political radicals. Many were Quakers, Methodists, and even Swedenborgians, motivated by a spiritual conviction to seek justice. The iniquities of the slave trade left them with a profound sense of personal anguish, both for those enslaved and for the resulting destruction of Africa. They believed that their repatriate colonies would serve the dual purpose of rescuing enslaved Africans and regenerating African civilization.

Among the most influential of the English works on the subject was *An Essay Upon Colonization, Particularly Applied to the Western Coast of Africa, with Some Free Thoughts on Cultivation and Commerce, . . .*, by C. B. Wadstrom, which was published in two parts in London, 1794 and 1795. The author pointed to the relative backwardness and barbarism of Africa and laid the blame squarely on "the *Slave-Trade*, that scourge of the human race, which has kept down a great part of the Africans in a state of anarchy and blood, and which, while its nefarious existence is tolerated, will prove *the* grand obstacle to their improvement and civilization" (p. 4). He believed that accidental circumstances had played some part in the exploitation of Africa as a source of slaves for the American colonies, yet Europe was responsible for the "villainy" and ought to set things straight. He thought that, "the most likely way to promote the civilizations of mankind, would be to lead their activity into the cultivation of their country, as the best exercise for their affections, and to diffuse among them a spirit of *liberal* commerce, to exercise their understanding. Thus cultivation and commerce established on right principles, rendering the mind active, would early dispose it for the reception of pure moral instruction: commodities in this case would not fail to become the vehicles of ideas and inventions" (pp. iii–iv). Wadstrom termed this ideal trade "commission-commerce," and he contrasted it with "speculation-commerce," which was a corrupter of social order and appeared whenever agriculture was held in low esteem (pp. 65–66, 102).

Wadstrom asserted that the best way to bring about a redirection of Africans' minds toward the land was the establishment of enclaves in barbarous areas to provide an example, which the less civilized would naturally follow:

> Let us form agricultural colonies on its coast, which present a variety of situations, where we shall be little, or not at all, disturbed in our operations. Let us kindly mix well with the inhabitants, and assist them in cultivating their fertile soil, with the view of inviting them to participate with us in its inexhaustible stores, and in the concomitant blessings of improving reason and progressive civilization. Let us give them a manly and generous education, which will make them feel the nobility of their origin, and show them of what great things they are capable (p. 3, also see p. 6).

On Paul Cuffe, see George Arnold Salvador, *Paul Cuffe: The Black Yankee, 1759–1817* (New Bedford: Reynolds-De Walt Printing, 1969); Sheldon H. Harris, *Paul Cuffe: Black America and the African Return* (New York: Simon and Schuster, 1972).

[14] The literature on the paradoxical status of free black people in United States society

is extensive, forming a subject of debate even in the seventeenth century. As it relates to Maryland, the reader might consult Christopher Phillips, *Freedom's Port: The African-American Community of Baltimore, 1790–1860* (Urbana: University of Illinois Press, 1997); T. Stephen Whitman, *The Price of Freedom: Slavery and Manumission in Baltimore and Early National Maryland* (New York & London: Routledge, 2000); Leroy Graham, *Baltimore: The Nineteenth-Century Black Capital* (Lanham, Md.: University Press of America, 1982); or go back further to James M. Wright, *The Free Negro in Maryland, 1634–1860* (New York: Columbia University Press, 1921)

[15] The principal promoters of colonization had a clear desire to establish a new, Christian, agrarian civilization, which one day would overspread the African continent. The physiocratic ideals of the French Enlightenment, best expressed in the writings of De Quesnay, in turn derived from Renaissance political theorists, notably Machiavelli, found a home, in modified form, in the young United States through the writings and politics of such men as Thomas Jefferson. In his only published book, *Notes on the State of Virginia*, Jefferson outlined this ideal:

> Those who labor in the earth are the chosen people of God, if ever he had a chosen people, whose breasts he has made his peculiar deposit for substantial and genuine virtue. It is the focus in which he keeps alive that sacred fire which otherwise might escape from the face of the earth. Corruption of morals in the mass of cultivators is a phaenomenon of which no age nor nation has furnished an example. It is the mark set on those, who not looking up to heaven, to their own soil and industry, as does the husbandman for their existence, depend for it upon the casualties and caprice of customers. Dependence begets subservience and venality, suffocates the germ of virtue, and prepares fit tools, for the designs of ambition. (original edition, pp. 165–66)

The ideal of a republic of virtuous husbandmen had an extensive currency in the United States. Its symbols occurred constantly in American art, literature, and politics. The American promoters of colonization, to whom Jefferson was sympathetic, consistently applied these agrarian ideals to their colonies. Among the most common metaphors for the regeneration of Africa was cultivation: men would be cultivated in the fertile soils of the African colonies. In fact, their intense faith in the civilizing influence of agriculture probably hindered the development of a viable economy when American-style agriculture proved impractical.

[16] Advocates of black repatriation in Africa were imbued with a sense of their ability to engineer a new civilization in Africa. "Civilization" is a concept pregnant with meaning, of particular significance in American history. As Americans used the term, civilization consisted of the higher technological and cultural advancements of their society, including agriculture, industry, commerce, the arts, education, and Christianity. Each of these elements was a means to, and at the same time the goal of, civilization. Thus, technological advancement, by which the overall state of civilization could be improved, was at the same time the object of raising the level of civilization. Moreover, civilization could refer to the passive fact of society or to the ongoing process by which that fact was achieved.

[17] It should be noted that many Americans of the time believed that Africa's degrada-

tion was a direct result of Noah's curse upon his son, Ham, the supposed progenitor of the African race, who exposed and mocked his naked and drunken father. This curse extended even to the land itself. An address printed in the *Tenth Annual Report of the American Colonization Society* (Washington: 1827), for example:

> To many, the very name of Africa conveys an idea of indistinct horror; in the imagination, that word is often associated with all that is fearful in nature. It implies endless forests, into which man never penetrated; vast deserts, whose sands are eternally tossed by the whirlwind; sweeping torrents, spreading devastation; poisonous serpents, darting upon the adventurous traveller; furious beasts, and every wild and formidable terror. (p. 7)

This antipathy toward wilderness, or nature beyond the control of man, is distinctly American. Jefferson held the ordered, cultivated countryside as the ideal, not the partially cleared frontier.

Others looked to ancient Egypt and the old Roman Empire and perceived a fallen African civilization, which might be revived. Like the British colonizationists, American supporters argued that Africa was the cradle of civilization but had fallen from its former glory, in large measure because of the slave trade. They and their countrymen had profited by the ruin of Africa and therefore bore a tremendous obligation. A speaker at the society's fifteenth annual meeting, early in 1832, exclaimed,

> Happy for America, if she shall take an honorable lead in this great and beneficial work! Happy, if having presented to the world on her own soil a great model of popular institutions, she could now become an efficient agent, in their diffusion over the ancient abodes of civilization, now relapsed into barbarity. Happy, if she shall be forward to acquit her share of the mighty debt, which is due to injured Africa from the civilized nations of the world.... Who can dwell on this spectacle [the slave trade], and not turn with a throbbing heart to the sight of a company of emigrants, the children of Africa, wafted over the oceans to the land of their fathers, bound toward the great and genial home of their race, commissioners to trample the slave trade into the dust, returning from a civilized land, to scatter the seeds of civilization over the mighty extent of western Africa. (p. xx)

Similarly, another orator at the society's tenth annual meeting, in 1827, expressed a hope shared by many:

> He, who two centuries hence, shall look abroad upon reclaimed and rejuvenated Africa, behold her cultivated fields and smiling harvests; her well-built cities, and rivers white with the sails of commerce: her schools and churches; and see elevated high above her civilized and joyful population, the ensign of freedom and the banner of the Cross, will more justly estimate and feel the importance of the efforts of this society. (p. 18)

Those who supported colonization for evangelical reasons had a vision of a distinctive future African civilization. One such was Alexander Kinmont, who devoted a chapter to the subject in *Twelve Lectures on the Natural History of Man* (Cincinnati, 1839). He believed that "man, of all living beings, is the most versatile and the least fixed in his ways and genius; he is not made perfect, but intended to be perfected by the influence of the arts and education, which he is himself to evolve" (pp. 173–74). He asserted that the white and black races had fundamentally different natures, and that each must develop along its own path. He also believed that a rekindled African civilization would one day surpass white American civilization. "It will be — indeed it must be — a civilization of a peculiar stamp," he wrote,

> perhaps we might venture to conjecture, not so much distinguished by art as a certain beautiful nature, not so much marked or adorned by science as exalted and refined by a certain new and lovely theology; — a reflection of the light of heaven more perfect and endearing than that which the intellectuals of the Caucasian race have yet exhibited. (p. 190)

Such ideas were taken up a generation later by such black intellectuals as Alexander Crummell, a Cambridge-educated Episcopal minister, who resided some years in Maryland in Liberia. Later, from a pulpit in Washington, D.C., he exercised great influence on black American thought. Crummell shared the vision of a spiritual, specifically Christian, African civilization. In his opinion, the whole history of Africa manifested a divine plan by which Africa would be carried to unmatched achievements. "Divine Providence designs a FUTURE for this people," he told a Monrovian audience in the late 1850s. "This particular section of the human species is not doomed to destruction, . . . the elevation, the civilization, the evangelization of the Negro are determined purposes of the Divine mind for the future. Ethiopia SHALL stretch forth her hands unto God." (As published in *The Future of Africa*; New York: C. Scribner, 1862; p. 320.)

Other books which deal with a millenarian Africa include David Christy, *Ethiopia: Her Gloom and Glory* (1859; repr. New York: Negro Universities Press, 1969); Rev. Hollis Reade, *The Negro Problem Solved; Or, Africa as She Was, as She Is, and as She Shall Be, Her Curse and Her Cure* (New York, 1864).

[18] *U.S. Senate, 28th Congress, 2nd Session, Public Document #150: "Information Relative To the Operations of the United States Squadron on the West Coast of Africa, the Condition of the American Colonies There, And the Commerce of the United States Therewith"* (Washington, 1845), pp. 152–93. [This important work will hereafter be cited as *Senate Document #150*.]

[19] John Hanson to John H. B. Latrobe, Monrovia, March 19, 1830, p. 2, MSCS.

[20] Garrison vilified a prominent New England merchant in an issue of the *Genius of Universal Emancipation* published on November 13, 1829. The merchant brought a lawsuit for libel and won his point in court. Garrison refused to pay the fine levied against him and was thrown into jail for several months in 1830. When freed, he made his way to Boston, where he published the first number of *The Liberator* on January 1, 1831. See Letter 33 in Walter M. Merrill, ed.; *The Letters of William Lloyd Garrison. Vol. I: "I Will Be Heard!"* (Cambridge: Belknap Press, 1971), pp. 91–93. Also, Walter M. Merrill; *Against Wind and Tide: A Biography of William Lloyd Garrison* (Cambridge: Harvard University Press, 1963), pp. 26–39; and Oliver Johnson; *William Lloyd Garrison And His Times; Or,*

Sketches of the Anti-slavery Movement in America, and of the Man Who Was Its Founder and Moral Leader (Boston, 1880), pp. 25–49.

[21] *Senate Document 150*, pp. 209–40, lists seven ships arriving at Monrovia between December 1831, and the end of January, 1833, carrying 1,037 emigrants.

[22] For Baltimore's African-American population, see Graham, *Baltimore: The Nineteenth-Century Black Capital*; Phillips, *Freedom's Port*; and Whitman, *The Price of Freedom*.

[23] Biographies of early colonizationists: "Robert Goodloe Harper," in *Appleton's Cyclopedia*; Phillips, *Freedom's Port*; Graham, *Baltimore*; John E. Semmes; *John H. B. Latrobe and His Times, 1803–1891* (Baltimore: Norman, Remington, 1919), pp. 139ff.

[24] Anonymous, "Maryland in Liberia," in *The African Repository*, 62, no. 4 (October, 1886): 111; John H. B. Latrobe; "Dr. James Hall," in *The African Repository*, 65, no. 4 (Oct., 1889): 117; Semmes; *John H. B. Latrobe*.

[25] George McGill: Graham, *Baltimore*, pp. 77–79, 103–4, and 125–26; Baltimore City Directories of the period.

[26] *Eleventh Annual Report of the American Colonization Society* (Washington, 1828).

[27] George McGill to John H. B. Latrobe, Monrovia, September 2, 1831, p. 2, MSCS.

[28] James Hall gave an autobiographical account of himself in "My First Visit to Liberia" in *The African Repository*, 62, no. 4 (October, 1886): 97–107.

[29] Hall, "My First Visit," pp. 97–98.

[30] Ibid., p. 99.

[31] Ibid., p. 103.

[32] The cabin boy: Hall; "My First Visit," pp. 101–2; James Hall, in *Maryland Colonization Journal*, 9:84: "We found near half a pint of black ants, with which the ship was filled, embedded in his flesh."

[33] Hall, "My First Visit," pp. 106–7. Other accounts of Liberia at this period include: "The Colony of Liberia," a series of articles published in *The Friend*, Vol. II (1829); F. H. Rankin; *The White Man's Grave* (London, 1836); Charles Rockwell; *Sketches of Foreign Travel . . .* (Boston, 1842).

[34] Remus Harvey to John H. B. Latrobe, Monrovia, May 26, 1829, p. 1, MSCS.

[35] This has been discussed at length in Phillips, *Freedom's Port*, Graham, *Baltimore: The Nineteenth-Century Black Capital*, and a number of other works.

[36] There is an extensive reference of the importance of churches in the free black community, but some more recent references relevant to Maryland are: Phillips; *Freedom's Port*, pp. 117–44; Graham; *Baltimore*; Lawrence W. Levine; *Black Culture and Black Consciousness: Afro-American Folk Thought from Slavery to Freedom* (Oxford, London, New York: Oxford University Press, 1977).

[37] Settler extravagance: Captain William Hardie, "Statement in regard to Emigrants per Ship Lafayette," April 11, 1833, MSCS; Hall, "My First Visit," second part, pp. 6–7.

[38] Hall, "My First Visit," second part, p. 6.

[39] George R. McGill to John H. B. Latrobe, Monrovia, July 12, 1832, PP. 1–2, MSCS.

[40] James Hall to Dr. Eli Ayres, Monrovia, July, 1832, extracted in "Minutes of the Maryland State Colonization Society," 1:101–2, MSCS; also printed in *Maryland Colonization Journal*, n.s., 5:132. Dr. Ayres had left Baltimore in the meantime. See John H. B. Latrobe, "Dr. James Hall" in *The African Repository*, 65:117–19; and Semmes, *John H. B. Latrobe*, p. 145.

[41] The Act of 1831 (actually dated March 12, 1832) : *Laws of Maryland, 1831,* chapters 281 and 323 (Annapolis, Md., 1832), reprinted in *Maryland Colonization Journal,* n.s., 9:183ff.; John H. B. Latrobe, *Maryland in Liberia,* pp. 14–16.

[42] John H. B. Latrobe, Diary, August 2, 1833–May 1, 1839, entry for September 6, 1833 (p. 16), MS 1677, Maryland Historical Society.

[43] The *Orion* expedition: Emigrant Roll, MSCS; Latrobe, *Maryland in Liberia,* p. 17; *Senate Document 150,* pp. 209–10.

[44] *Orion* settlers' experiences: "Extracts from Sundry letters addressed to the Board of Managers dated Caldwell; Liberia in Africa 3 Feby 1833." (Contemporary transcript of the original letters, not located); Gov. Joseph Mechlin, Jr. to Charles C. Harper, Liberia, February 10, 1833; Henry Dennis to George Hudson, Caldwell, April 10, 1833 (as transcribed by the recipient); Captain William Hardie, Statement, April 11, 1833; Remus Harvey to Charles C. Harper and Moses Sheppard, Liberia, July 29, 1833, all in MSCS.

[45] John H. B. Latrobe to Cortland Van Rensellaer, Baltimore, July 10, 1833, Corresponding Secretary's Letterbook, MS, No. 1, pp. 10–16, in MSCS.

[46] John H. B. Latrobe, Diary, Aug. 2, 1833–May 1, 1839, entry for Nov. 27, 1833, MS 1677, Maryland Historical Society.

[47] Minute Book of the Maryland State Colonization Society, 1:64–66, MSCS.

[48] Planning new colony: John H. B. Latrobe, Diary, Aug. 2, 1833–May 1, 1839, entry for Sept. 9, 1833, MS 1677, MdHS; Minute Book of the Maryland State Colonization Society, 1:68–70 (the resolutions are also summarized in the Record Book of the Board of Managers, 2:33), all in MSCS.

[49] Anonymous editorial in *Maryland Colonization Journal,* 1, no. 1 (May, 1835): 1.

[50] Anonymous editorial in ibid., 1, no. 22 (Nov., 1838): 90.

[51] Land allocation: [Hugh Davey Evans and John H. B. Latrobe], *Laws of Maryland in Liberia.* 2nd ed. (Baltimore, 1847). Tropical exuberance: Philip D. Curtin, *The Image of Africa: British Ideas and Action, 1780–1850* (Madison: University of Wisconsin Press, 1964), pp. 60–65, 434–35.

[52] Latrobe, *Maryland in Liberia,* pp. 22, 33.

[53] James Hall, "Cape Palmas, Liberia," in *The African Repository,* 60 (Oct., 1884): 100.

[54] John H. B. Latrobe, "Dr. James Hall," in *The African Repository,* 65, no. 4 (Oct., 1889): 118. Latrobe received a letter from Hall formally accepting his appointment as agent on September 27, 1833. On the twenty-ninth the doctor arrived in Baltimore. At a meeting on September 30, the Board of Managers fixed Hall's salary at $2,000 per annum, a substantial sum, with an allowance for personal expenses. Latrobe commented in his diary that Hall appeared a good choice. Many years later, Latrobe reminisced, "His heart was in the cause, not exactly of Colonization, but of Liberia." "The Cape Palmas plan is getting nearer and nearer to an issue," he wrote in his diary early in November. "It is four years since I first urged it at Washington; and most devoutly do I now pray to almighty God, that it may be for the benefit of the cause of freedom and religion, — that I may not have to reproach myself with the loss of lives or any unhappy results attending it to one human being. His mercy, may it guard it."

[55] These and the following details are gleaned from Latrobe's diary and from the Minute Book of the Maryland State Colonization Society, 1:83–173, MSCS.

[56] Latrobe, *Maryland in Liberia,* pp. 30–36.

[57] The rum question: Latrobe, *Maryland in Liberia*, p. 36; Minute Book of the Maryland State Colonization Society, 1:118–19.

2. *"Close on the Promised Land"*

[1] For the passage of the longboat, see James Hall to John H. B. Latrobe, Monrovia, Jan. 29, 1834, pp. 1–2, MSCS; James Hall, "Cape Palmas, Liberia," in *The African Repository*, 60, no. 4 (Oct., 1884): 102–3.

[2] James Hall to John H. B. Latrobe, Monrovia, Jan. 29, 1834, pp. 2–3, MSCS.

[3] John B. Russwurm to John H. B. Latrobe, Monrovia, Feb. 23, 1834, pp. 1–2, MSCS.

[4] James Hall to John H. B. Latrobe, Monrovia, Jan. 29, 1834, p. 3, MSCS.

[5] John Hersey to William McKenney, At Sea, Jan. 14, 1834 (continued at later dates), p. 3, MSCS. See also, Hersey to John H. B. Latrobe, Monrovia, Feb. 3, 1834, MSCS.

[6] James Hall to John H. B. Latrobe, Brig *Ann*, off Drou, Feb. 9, 1834, p. 1, MSCS.

[7] Ibid., Monrovia, Jan. 29, 1834, p. 4, MSCS.

[8] Stephen R. Wynkoop and John L. Wilson, "Western Africa. Extracts from the Journals of Messrs. Wilson and Wynkoop," *The Missionary Herald*, 30:288.

[9] James Hall to John H. B. Latrobe, Brig *Ann*, off Drou, Feb. 9, 1834, p. 1, MSCS.

[10] Hersey's trials: John Hersey to the Board of Managers, Baltimore, July 1, 1834, p. 1; Hall's illness: James Hall to John H. B. Latrobe, Brig *Ann*, off Drou, Feb. 9, 1834, p. 1, MSCS.

[11] Wynkoop and Wilson, "Western Africa," in *The Missionary Herald*, 30:289. See also, James Hall to John H. B. Latrobe, Brig *Ann*, off Drou, Feb. 9, 1834, p. 2, MSCS.

[12] Wynkoop and Wilson, "Western Africa," *The Missionary Herald*, 30:337.

[13] James Hall, "Fishtown," *Maryland Colonization Journal*, n.s. 2:51.

[14] The Maryland Historical Society has a painting of Cape Palmas, attributed to Latrobe, but which could also be the work of an officer aboard an American warship (as mentioned by Captain Mayo in a letter to Latrobe, Porto Praya, February 18, 1855, published in *Maryland Colonization Journal*, n.s., 7:354: "I have had a handsome painting taken of Harper, Maryland in Liberia, which I will send you on my return home.") Semmes, *Latrobe and His Times* (Baltimore: Norman Remington, 1917), pp. 426–27, notes that Latrobe worked mainly in pencil and watercolor, though he also painted some copies of famous paintings and some portraits, principally of himself as gifts to his children.

Other pictorial evidence may be found in a variety of published sources, including: *Report of the Secretary of State, Communicating the Report of Rev. R.. R.. Gurley, Who Was Recently Sent Out by the Government to Obtain Information in Respect to Liberia* (31st Congress, 1st Session, Senate Ex. Doc. 75, Washington, 1850), pp. 106–7 and illustration, "Cape Palmas"; J. Buttikofer, *Reisebilder Aus Liberia* (Leiden, 1890), Vol. II, Plate 18, facing p. 435, "Cape Palmas," a photograph depicting the south shore of the Cape, looking toward the west; Dr. James Hall, *An Address to the Free People of Color of the State of Maryland* (Baltimore, 1859), frontispiece: "View of Cape Palmas, from the Beach opposite, taken in 1850"; William F. Lynch, *Report to the U.S. Navy Department in relation to his mission to the Coast of Africa* (Washington, 1853), p. 49, gives a vivid verbal description; Harriet Brittan, *Scenes and Incidents of Every-day Life in Africa* (New York, 1860; repr. Negro Universities Press, 1969), p. 40; Anna Maria Scott, *Day Dawn in Africa* (New York, 1858), p. 195, illustration, "Female Orphan Asylum at Cape Palmas, W.A."

[15] Gbenelu is pronounced with the "G" nearly silent. James Hall to John H. B. Latrobe, Brig *Ann*, off Drou, Feb. 9, 1834, p. 2, MSCS.

[16] John L. Wilson, *Western Africa: Its History, Condition, and Prospects* (New York, 1856), p. 105. See also Ira Berlin, *Many Thousands Gone: The First Two Centuries of Slavery in North America* (Cambridge: The Belknap Press of Harvard University Press, 1998) for a discussion of the transcultural "Atlantic Creole" society and its central role in the development of seventeenth-century American society. The Grebo and Kru peoples carried on the same traditions into the twentieth Century.

[17] MacGregor Laird and R. A. K. Oldfield, *Narrative of an Expedition into the Interior of Africa, by the River Niger, in the Steam-vessels Quorrah and Alburkah, in 1832, 1833, and 1834,* 2 vols. (London, 1837), 1:46.

[18] Wilson and Wynkoop, "Western Africa," *The Missionary Herald,* 30:215.

[19] Oliver Holmes, Jr. to John H. B. Latrobe, July 13, 1836, p. 7, MSCS.

[20] He came close, however, in a letter written at sea, May 1, 1836, pp. 5–11, MSCS.

[21] Wilson and Wynkoop, "Western Africa," *The Missionary Herald,* 30:337.

[22] James Hall to John H. B. Latrobe, Brig *Ann* off Drou, Feb. 9, 1834, p. 2, MSCS.

[23] This and the preceding quotation may be found in, Wilson and Wynkoop, "Western Africa," *The Missionary Herald,* 30:337.

[24] This palaver is described in James Hall to John H. B. Latrobe, Brig *Ann* off Drou, Feb. 9, 1834, pp. 2–4, MSCS; Wilson and Wynkoop, "Western Africa," *The Missionary Herald,* 30:290; John H. B. Latrobe, *Maryland in Liberia,* pp. 39–41; and James Hall, "Cape Palmas, Liberia," *The African Repository,* 60, no. 4 (Oct. 1884): 104–6.

[25] John L. Wilson, *Western Africa* (New York, 1856), pp. 131–33. See also, *Traditional History and Folklore of the Glebo Tribe* (Monrovia: Bureau of Folkways, 1957), p. 51.

[26] James Hall, "Cape Palmas, Liberia," *The African Repository,* 60, no. 4 (Oct. 1884): 105.

[27] Language differences complicated the palaver of February 13. Negotiations were carried on through an interpreter, though at least some of the Africans present understood English. Baphro, for instance, spoke the language fairly well, but he sat silently through the proceedings. Hall spoke as simply as possible to his interpreter, Joe Wilson, whose English was the distinctive pidgin in common use all along the West African coast, which was born of the need to communicate in the course of foreign trade. This language had its origins in medieval Portuguese contacts, but by the nineteenth century, its basis was English. John Wilson later estimated that "three-fourths of the male population of the Kru country [referring to the Eastern Liberian coastline] speak imperfect, but intelligible English" (*Western Africa,* New York, 1856, p. 103, continuing, "They have more knowledge of the customs and habits of civilized man than any other people in Western Africa"). West Africans used pidgin chiefly with seamen and merchants. Vocabulary was therefore trade-oriented, and some things difficult to describe. For instance, Simleh Ballah, who visited Baltimore in 1836, was given a neoclassical pedestal table, which he described thus: "He have no more but one leg in middle but he got sum feet live him Bottom." (Simleh Ballah to John H. B. Latrobe, April 27, 1838, MSCS.) Similarly, the use of pidgin as a language of political discourse posed peculiar problems.

[28] James Hall, "Cape Palmas, Liberia," *The African Repository,* 60, no. 4 (Oct. 1884): 105.

[29] Ibid. John L. Wilson, *Western Africa* (New York: 1856), p. 469: "The Grebo counts

up to five, and then there is a reduplication up to ten, and then another up to twenty; after which they count by twenties up to ten twenties, which is *huba* or two hundred."

[30] James Hall to John H. B. Latrobe, Brig *Ann* off Drou, Feb. 9, 1834, p. 4, MSCS.

[31] James Hall, "Cape Palmas, Liberia," *The African Repository*, 60, no. 4 (Oct. 1884): 105.

[32] Ibid.

[33] As enumerated in the deed.

[34] James Hall, "Cape Palmas, Liberia," *The African Repository*, 60, no. 4 (Oct. 1884): 106.

[35] James Hall to John H. B. Latrobe, Brig *Ann* off Drou, Feb. 9, 1834, p. 3, MSCS.

[36] "Deed No. 1. From King Freeman and King Will, of Cape Palmas," MSCS. (also reprinted with corrections in John H. B. Latrobe, *Maryland in Liberia*, pp. 95–97) reads as follows:

> Know all men by these presents that for considerations hereinafter mentioned, we King Freeman alias Parmah of Cape Palmas, King Will alias Weah Bolio of Grahway, and King Joe Holland alias Pahfleur of Grand Cavally, have granted and sold, and do by these presents, grant and sell to the Maryland State Colonization Society in Maryland in the United States of North America the following tract of land of which we are at this time lawfully seized by right of possession and descent, viz. commencing on the Sea beach about three miles to the North West of Cape Palmas at a cocoa nut tree known as the large cocoa nut, separating this territory from that of the King of Rock Town; thence running in about an east north east direction, one days journey, until it shall reach the territory of Kava King of the interior; from thence running east south east, six hours walk, until it shall reach the town of King Tom on the Cavally river; from thence down the Cavally River to its mouth; then running along the beach passing the town of Cavalley, Grahway and Cape Palmas to the point of starting viz the large cocoa nut tree, including all the rivers, bays, creeks, anchorages, timber and mines on the same, excepting as follows; a tract of land deeded and given some time since, by the above–named King Will, alias Weah Bolio of Grahway, to King Yellow Will of Little Cavally. Also excepting so much of the said territory as is now under cultivation by the inhabitants thereof, or such places as are occupied by us or our dependents as towns and villages; reserving also the right of passing and repassing up and down all rivers and creeks and of traversing all sections of the country not inhabited by the Colonists of the said Society; the said society to have and to hold the same for its own special benefit and behoof forever; and we do agree to warrant and defend the same against the claims of all persons whatever; and it (the said Society) shall have power by its factors or agents to exercise all authority in the above named territory, reserving to ourselves and our descendants the right of governing and setting all palavers among our own people, so long as we shall see fit to occupy any part of said territory. And we do hereby acknowledge ourselves as members of the Colony

of Maryland in Liberia, so far as to unite in common defence in case
of War or foreign aggression.

We do also acknowledge the receipt of the following articles of
Merchandize of James Hall Esq agent of the said society and Governor of said territory as a full and ample compensation therefor. Viz.
4 Cases Muskets, 20 Kegs Powder 110 pieces of Cloth, 10 Neptunes,
10 Brass Kettles 20 Hats 100 Cutlasses 200 lbs Beads 1500 lbs of Iron
Pots, 6 doz looking Glasses, 4 framed ditto, 24 Iron bars, 100 trade
knives 100 wash basins, 3 Hogds. Tobacco 10 Boxes pipes, 2 Kegs
Flints 6 doz locks 24 Decanters, 50 Tumblers, 50 Wine Glasses, 24
Stone Jugs 10 Demijohns 3 Suits of Cloths, 3 cocked hats, 25 Razors
in Cases, 50 Pitchers, 50 Mugs, 50 Bowls, 3 pr Brass barreled pistols
1000 Fish hooks 50 pr Scissors, 50 Spanish dollars. And I the said
Hall, do in the name of the said society, hereby guarantee the said
Kings and their dependents the above reserved rights and further
that neither themselves or property shall be trespassed upon or molested in any manner whatever, and no lands under cultivation, or
towns or Villages shall be taken from them, except by special contract; paying the desired remuneration Therefor. And I do further
agree for and in the name of the said Society, that free schools shall
be established for the benefit of the Children in each of the following Towns, in one year from the date hereof, viz. one at Cape
Palmas, one at Garraway, and one at Grand Cavally.

[37] See C. K. Meek, *Land Law and Custom in the Colonies*, 2nd ed. (London: Frank
Cass, 1968); and Kenneth Parsons, "Land Reform and Agricultural Development," in
Parsons, R. J. Penn, and P. M. Raup, eds., *Land Tenure* (Madison: University of Wisconsin Press, 1956). Parsons makes the important observation, "In a very deep sense, land
tenure problems are power problems, problems of disparity in economic, social, and
political power."

[38] For examples of these treaties, see, U.S. Commissioner of Indian Affairs, *Treaties
Between the United States of America, and the Several Indian Tribes, From 1778 to 1837*
(1837; repr. Millwood, N.Y.: Kraus Reprint Co., 1975). An interesting account of the
purchase of Cape Mesurado (the site of Monrovia) may be found in Archibald Alexander's
History of Colonization, pp. 167–74. See also, *The Life and Speeches of Robert Field
Stockton* (New York, 1856).

[39] James Hall admitted as much in his letter to John H. B. Latrobe that night, which
is quoted below. See also, James Hall to John H. B. Latrobe, Sept. 10, 1835, MSCS, which
is also quoted below.

[40] See Philip D. Curtin, *The Image of Africa*, pp. 60–65 and 434–35 for a relevant
discussion of Western ideas of tropical exuberance. James Hall to John H. B. Latrobe,
April 24, 1834, pp. 6–13, clearly reflects this attitude.

[41] "If a man reclaims a piece of land from its primitive woods, it is considered his and
his descendents' as long as they choose to use it, but it can not be transferred like other
property. The people, by common consent, may sell any portion of it to a stranger, for
the purpose of erecting a trading factory, for a garden, or a farm; but in their minds this
transaction, even when subjected to the formality of a written contract, amounts to

little more than a general consent to the stranger living among them and enjoying all the rights of citizenship; and with the expectation that the land will revert to themselves, as a matter of course, should he die or leave their country." J. L. Wilson, *Western Africa*, p. 138.

[42] Ibid.

[43] Ibid., p. 380.

[44] A transcription from the original made by James Hall is included among the deeds in the MSCS. Christopher Fyfe, *A History of Sierra Leone* (London: Oxford University Press, 1963), pp. 133, 636, identifies George Robertson as a Liverpool trader who published a book, *Notes on Africa*, in 1819. He urged British annexation of the whole West African coast. Fyfe adds that Robertson bargained for land in the name of the Crown, without sanction, at Cape Palmas and Fernando Poo.

[45] Oliver Holmes, Jr. to John H. B. Latrobe, July 13, 1836, as transcribed in Foreign Letterbook I, p. 219, MSCS.

[46] James Hall to John H. B. Latrobe, At Sea, May 1, 1836, pp. 5–6, MSCS.

[47] As reported in *Maryland Colonization Journal*, 1, no. 5, p. 23.

[48] See Petition of Settlers to James Hall, June 24, 1835, MSCS; also, the Board of Managers to James Hall, Baltimore, Nov. 25, 1833, transcribed in Corresponding Secretary's Letterbook No. I, pp. 90–107.

[49] James Hall to John H. B. Latrobe, Brig *Ann* off Drou, Feb. 9, 1834, p. 5, MSCS: "No local bounds are set to our particular territory," he wrote Latrobe two days after the purchase, "this I thought advisable for various reasons, but more particularly as I Know little of the resources of this country, or what tract would be most desirable for cultivation, and time would admit of no delay as two or three English vessels are on the way down from Cape Mesurada, and self interest prompts them to use all measures to prevent our purchase. – Another reason why I wished to consider the whole territory as common rather than to separate to ourselves our part, was to prevent any factories from being established by the Cape Mesurada speculators near us and not exactly under our jurisdiction."

[50] James Hall to John H. B. Latrobe, Nov, 3, 1835, MSCS. See *Traditional History and Folklore of the Glebo Tribe*, for more information on these changes. Also, Massing, *Economic Anthropology of the Kru (West Africa)*.

Modern ethnographers classify the people of Southeastern Liberia as Kru or Grebo, basing the classification on linguistic and broad cultural similarities. This masks the genuine differences in culture between coastal inhabitants and those further inland as they existed in the nineteenth century. A band of refugees arriving with little besides what they could put in stolen canoes would very likely have appropriated whatever they could of their neighbors goods, including husbands and wives, and still retained a sense of ethnic distinctiveness. The momentum for linguistic assimilation between the bush and the beach must have been great: both were dependent upon one another economically. Further, the concentration of different tongues in so small a region made language a fluid thing, and it is easy to imagine a convergence taking place over a generation or two. This line was steadily blurred as settlers and missions extended their influence in the first half of the century. Later, the Liberian government continued the process, making travel easier. The development of the immense Firestone Rubber plantations a few miles north of Cape Palmas in the 1930s, which drew laborers from across the region, broke down these barriers even further, providing economic opportunities that previously had been available only on the beach. Moreover, the disappearance of the old maritime way of life has made the peoples of the area seem more homogeneous.

Witness the debate in the journal, *Africa*, which was carried on over several years. (See Introduction, note 10.) Distinctions which were quite clear in the mid-nineteenth century have become muddled in the twenty-first, and the geographical focus of the culture has shifted two hundred and fifty miles. Moreover, some ethnic classifications have simply evaporated: for instance, Fishmen, once a powerful ethnic entity have disappeared from the scene.

Modern Greboes distinguish the same two *pano* groupings on the beach as did their ancestors in the first half of the nineteenth century: *Nyomowe* and *Kuniwe* (shortened from the older pronunciation). See Moran, *Civilized Women*, p. 20.

[51] There are two distinct versions of Grebo history: the one, oral and current in the mid-nineteenth century; the other, written by ethnologists and more modern in origin. The Episcopal missionary, John Payne, recorded the oral history in Grebo and published excerpts in *The Cavalla Messenger*, the mission's journal. The complete version in the Grebo language was published by Edward D. Jenkins in New York in 1860, with the title, *Grebo Konah Ah Te; Or, History of the Greboes*. English extracts appeared in *The Spirit of Missions* and were reprinted in such works as Anna Maria Scott's *Day Dawn in Africa*, pp. 54–55. Payne's account, based upon nearly twenty years' study is corroborated in Wilson's *Western Africa*, p. 98, and in *Traditional History and Folklore of the Glebo Tribe*, a government-sponsored oral history project published in 1957. This oral history is one of migration and internal schisms, with some admixture of heroic legend. The ethnological history, exemplified in Jane Jackson Martin, "The Dual Legacy: Government Authority and Mission Influence Among the Glebo of Eastern Liberia, 1834–1910" (Ph.D. diss., Boston University, 1968); and Massing, *Economic Anthropology of the Kru (West Africa)*, ties Greboes more strongly to their neighbors in the bush, primarily on linguistic evidence.

There are good reasons to credit the older story in its broader outlines. First, the oral history records events extending barely a century and a quarter before, the bulk of which must have been almost within living memory: the stories grandparent-participants could have told the young. Second, foreign accounts before about 1700 do not mention any people resembling Greboes living at Cape Palmas. Third, the oral history goes so far in explaining the political and social divisions among Greboes in the early nineteenth century.

[52] Payne recounted the story: "The name *Grebo* is composed of *Gre* and *bo*. The latter designates a class, (for example, degu, a doctor; degu-bo, doctors.) The former, 'Gre,' is the name of a species of monkey which leaps with remarkable agility. In getting off from the shore at the time of emigration, it appears that many canoes were capsized. The Grebo word for capsize is *wore*, and hence those who capsized and remained were called *Worebo*. Those who were successful in embarking, leaping over the waves like the 'Gre,' were styled *Grebo*."

3. "A Field for the Farmer"

[1] G. R. McGill to J. H. B. Latrobe, Feb. 15, 1834, p. 1, MSCS.

[2] G. R. McGill to J. H. B. Latrobe, Monrovia, March 8, 1834, p. 2, MSCS.

[3] James Hall, "Cape Palmas, Liberia," *The African Repository*, 60, no. 4 (Oct. 1884): 106–7.

[4] Choice of Cape for settlement: James Hall to J. H. B. Latrobe, Brig *Ann* off Drou, Feb. 9, 1834, p. 5; J. H. B. Latrobe, "Cape Palmas, Liberia," *The African Repository*, 61, no. 1, pp. 1–2.

[5] James Hall to J. H. B. Latrobe, Brig *Ann* off Drou, Feb. 9, 1834, pp. 6–7, MSCS.

[6] James Hall, "Cape Palmas, Liberia," The *African Repository*, 60, no. 4 (Oct. 1884): 107.

[7] Oliver Holmes to J. H. B. Latrobe, July 13, 1836, p. 19, MSCS:

> The natives will not place the Thatch on as they would for themselves, they cannot be hired or persuaded to take the necessary pains. The Thatch is destroyed in a great degree whilst it is yet green, by hundreds of Bugs, Lizards etc. that afterwards have their nests in it and are continually shakeing down the dust and dirt, all which evils render one of these Thatched houses absolutely untenable during the rainy season. The reasons for thatched houses leaking does not apply to the native houses as the smoke of their fires which is generally in the center or a little to one side has a tendency to keep Bugs etc. away and it is not every person among them by a long ways who undertakes to cover his owne house although very few of them do not feel themselves competent to cover a house for a Colonist.

George W. McDaniel has idealized the thatching skills of old Maryland slaves in his interesting study, *Hearth and Home: Preserving a People's Culture* (Philadelphia: Temple University Press, 1982), pp. 85–90, but data from Cape Palmas contradicts the argument. Interestingly, the author draws his information from interviews with descendants of the Tubman family in Maryland, who informed him that some of their ancestors had returned to Africa, rightly claiming kinship with Liberia's President Tubman. The author was not told, however, that the Tubman family was Georgian until about 1837. When their master died, they were freed. About half went to Cape Palmas, and the rest settled in Maryland. Their traditions of house thatching may therefore have come from the deep South.

[8] References to deforestation: James Hall to J. H. B. Latrobe, Brig *Ann* off Drou, Feb. 9, 1834, continued at later dates, p. 5, MSCS; James Hall to J. H. B. Latrobe, February 23, 1834, p. 2, MSCS; J. V. Thirgood, "Land-Use Problems of the Liberian Coastal Savannah," *Commonwealth Forestry Review*, 44 (1965): 46–47.

[9] Grebo hostages: James Hall to J. H. B. Latrobe, April 24, 1834, pp. 2–3; James Hall to J. H. B. Latrobe, Brig *Ann* off Drou, Feb. 9, 1834, p. 6, MSCS.

[10] James Hall to J. H. B. Latrobe, Feb. 23, 1834, p. 1, MSCS.

[11] Ibid.

[12] Departure of the *Ann*: ibid.; Wynkoop and Wilson's report was published in *The Missionary Herald*, 30:212–19; J. L. Wilson to J. H. B. Latrobe, Monrovia, March 6, 1834, p. 1, MSCS, sends a bill for the hostages' passage to Baltimore.

[13] James Hall to J. H. B. Latrobe, Feb. 23, 1834, p. 1, MSCS.

[14] J. Hersey to the Board of Managers, Baltimore, July 21, 1834, pp. 1–2, MSCS.

[15] Tom W. Shick, *Behold the Promised Land: A History of Afro-american Settler Society*

in Nineteenth-century Liberia (Baltimore: Johns Hopkins University Press, 1980), pp. 26–28 and 50, discusses the high mortality suffered by emigrants to Liberia (averaging 22 percent in the first year for the period before the Civil War), noting that for emigrants who survived for more than two years, death rates were never more than 3 percent per annum.

[16] James Hall to J. H. B. Latrobe, April 24, 1834, cntd. on June 10, p. 14, MSCS.

[17] See James Hall to J. H. B. Latrobe, Brig *Ann*, Feb. 9, 1834, cntd. on Feb. 13, p. 6, MSCS Archive, for a list of medicines he needed.

[18] Joshua Stewart to Dr. Macauley, n.d., but probably March, 1834, MSCS.

[19] Stewart's disaffection: Joshua Stewart to Charlotte Stewart, May 5, 1834; James Hall to J. H. B. Latrobe, April 24, 1834, cntd. on June 10, p. 14, both MSCS.

[20] James Hall to J. H. B. Latrobe, April 16, 1834, p. 1, MSCS.

[21] John Hersey to the Board of Managers, Baltimore, July 21, 1834, p. 3, MSCS.

[22] James Hall to J. H. B. Latrobe, April 24, 1834, pp. 15–16, MSCS.

[23] Ibid., April 24, 1834, p. 1, MSCS.

[24] These accounts, scrawled out on oversize sheets of paper, are preserved MSCS. The society had great trouble reconciling them, and it was not until 1836 that a regular system of accounting was introduced.

[25] James Hall to J. H. B. Latrobe, April 16, 1834, pp. 1–2, MSCS.

[26] Ibid., April 24, 1834, p. 1, MSCS.

[27] Ibid., April 24, 1834, cntd. on May 15, p. 3, MSCS.

[28] Ibid., April 24, 1834, cntd. on May 15, pp. 3–4, MSCS. See the "Thirteenth Annual Report of the Maryland State Colonization Society," as written in *Minutebook of the Executive Committee of the Maryland State Colonization Society No. 4* in March 1845, (p. 245) which gives an interesting variant version of the story:

> Soon after Dr. Hall landed at the Cape, and when the whole force of the settlement did not exceed thirty men capable of bearing arms, King Freeman attempted to attack the colonial boat on its way to obtain provisions from the nearest tribe to windward at Rocktown. Dr. Hall sent for the King; told him that the Americans preferred death by fighting to starvation; called his attention to the fact that the only available piece of cannon was loaded to the muzzle with grape and pointed, at point blank range, at the King's palaver house, and that it would be discharged again and again, while an American remained alive to load it, if but a single canoe left the beach in pursuit of the boat about to be dispatched to Rocktown.

[29] A few days earlier, on April 16, James Hall had written J. H. B. Latrobe: "From our first landing I have endeavoured to convince them of the numerous advantages that would accrue to the country from our coming hither, and they appeared to be fully sensible of it. They appeared to wish that we should sit down with them and become one people, possess one country and have one national flag in common. . . . They were fully sensible of the total change that would ultimately take place in their National character in almost every point of view, from living in contact with our Americo-Africans. Yet with all this they are so fickle and capricious that we are obliged to be ever upon the look out." He noted that despite threats of violence, "They appear rather to wish to intimidate

us that in affairs of trade we may come to their terms, than to commence actual hostilities: for as I before observed the more intelligent of them are sensible that the country will ultimately be much benefited by our settling in it" (pp. 1–2).

[30] Settlers arrived without much food and found rice very hard to obtain. See, James Hall to J. H. B. Latrobe, Brig *Ann*, Feb. 9, 1834, cntd. on Feb. 13, p. 7; James Hall to J. H. B. Latrobe, Feb. 23, 1834, p. 2; James Hall to J. H. B. Latrobe, April 16, 1834, pp. 1–2, MSCS.

[31] Physical geography: Sir Richard F. Burton, *Wanderings in West Africa, from Liverpool to Fernando Po* (London, Tinsley Bros., 1863), 1:289; Rev. Alexander M. Cowan, *Liberia as I Found It, in 1858* (Frankfort, Ky., 1858), p. 113; Reginald C. F. Maugham, *The Republic of Liberia* (New York: C. Scribner's Sons, 1920), pp. 127–28: "For a distance of twenty miles or so from the coast, one finds dark red laterite (disintegrated gneiss), diorite, and iron-stone. This gradually gives place to metamorphic rocks, probably granite since it is intermingled with quartz crystals, to aplite, an admixture of orthoclase and quartz, which shows itself in the boulders of the mountain ranges, and here and there to pegmatite and porphyritic felspar."

[32] Useful examples include, W. Reed, *Reconnaissance Soil Survey of Liberia,* Agriculture Information Bulletin No. 66 (Washington: USDA Office of Foreign Agricultural Relations and U.S. Dept. of State Technical Co-operation Administration, 1951), p. 10; B. W. Andah, "Processes of Coastal Evolution in West Africa During the Quaternary," in B. K. Schwartz, Jr., and R. E. Dumett, eds., *West African Culture Dynamics: Archaeological and Historical Perspectives* (The Hague: Mouton Publishers, 1980), p. 18; A. Van Wambeke, *Management Properties of Ferralsols* (Rome: Food and Agriculture Organization of the U.N., 1974), pp. 2–7, 10, 16–17, 86–88.

[33] Relatively speaking, the youngest and lowest land borders the Atlantic Ocean, and this results in fundamental differences in drainage patterns, soils, and ecology with distance inland. In West Africa, few hills reach elevations exceeding 2,000 feet. The land surface and its underlying rocks are quite old: most of the region is an ancient uplifted plateau whose Precambrian metamorphic rocks have been weathered and eroded over time. To the north of this plateau is a sandy depression of Quaternary age, through which flow the Niger, Senegal, and Gambia Rivers. South of the plateau are younger land surfaces that meet the Atlantic coast with a network of marshes, lagoons, and barrier islands. According to Reginald Maugham, "Near the coast a light, friable, sandy soil is fairly general; organic matter is here scanty, but it would be impossible to imagine a more admirable producer of coconut-palms, cassava, and other food-stuffs." (Maugham, *Republic of Liberia*, p. 108).

N. C. Pollock writes in his *Regional Geography of Africa* (London: University of London, 1968) that, "The coastline consists of narrow strips of alluvium and recent marine sediments. . . . Behind the coastline is the dissected edge of the interior plateau, possibly downwarped toward the coast in Nigeria. Pre-Cambrian and Archaean rocks are exposed over wide areas. The landscape, developed under humid conditions, is surprisingly rounded considering the general lack of altitude, and steep forested slopes are common. Inselbergs and bare rocky domes rear up from the floor of the forest and, if climbable, provide far-reaching views" (pp. 243–44).

The most specific description of the countryside around Cape Palmas comes from the Rev. Alexander Cowan, who visited Maryland in Liberia in January, 1858. He published his observations a few months later at Frankfort, Kentucky, for an audience of farmers who wanted specific information about Liberia and its potential. Walking inland along the settlement's main road, in the midst of the angle formed by Hoffman's River to the north and west and Lake Sheppard on the south, he noted, "The land widens in breadth as you proceed east, embracing wet ground, that has to be ditched to have a dry road through it — then land that is very sandy — then land that is clay, and then land that is black loam, with gravel some eighteen to twenty inches deep." He also mentioned that the soils at Harper, Gbenelu town, and Latrobe, all of which are hilltops, are covered with clay (*Liberia as I Found It, in 1858*, pp. 115–18, 222). William Allen and T. R. H. Thomson, who visited the colony in 1841, also describe this hilltop soil as a "stiff iron-clay, having its origin, . . . in the *debris* of granite veins piercing through the rock" which they identified cryptically as "hornblende-slate or mica-slate" (*A Narrative of the Expedition . . . to the River Niger, in 1841* [London, 1848], 1:109). The report of Capt. William Lynch, a U.S. Navy officer, gives similar details in *Report to the U.S. Navy Department,* pp. 48–58. Cowan's and the other travelers' reports seem to indicate that sandy soils covered the lower slopes of the hills, which were capped with heavy red clay. Stream beds and swamps had soils higher in organic matter, his "black loam."

In the terminology of the world soil classification of the Food and Agriculture Organization of the United Nations (FAO-UN), ferralsols would be expected to dominate the area in the form of red clays. Ferralsols (which correspond to the latosols or Oxisols of rival American classifications) are very thick soils with indistinct definition of horizons. They are formed in tropical forests subject to high annual rainfall. Hence, leaching, but not erosion, is a significant factor in soil formation. Moreover, they are associated with level land surfaces that have been subject to weathering for very long periods of time: often, 50,000 years or more. As a result, there are almost no rocks remaining within reach of plant roots, and mineral nutrients have eluviated, leaving high concentrations of kaolin clay and sesquioxides of iron and aluminum. Kaolin is a poor retainer of nutrient cations. The fertility of the soil consequently depends upon the amount and quality of the organic matter at or near the soil's surface, a fragile factor. When such soils are farmed, organic matter is reduced, and long periods of fallow are needed to maintain productivity.

The soils covering the hilltops around Cape Palmas and the rice-growing lands further inland probably belong to the family of Rhodic Ferralsols of the FAO classification. These are dark reddish-brown soils that are formed on basic rocks, such as basalt or diorite, which compose the hills in the area. They are considered the most productive of the ferralsols: neither weathered so deeply or so well drained as other types. This means that they have a greater supply of weatherable minerals near the surface and that leaching does not remove nutrients so quickly. They also contain relatively high amounts of calcium and phosphorus, two essential nutrients, which also help to preserve organic matter. The Rhodic Ferralsols are generally confined to the level land of hilltops and plateaux, and thus would be more common inland, where the land is more elevated, than around Cape Palmas. On the hillsides Xanthic or Orthic Ferralsols would be found. These are related in structure to the Rhodic Ferralsol, but not quite as fertile. Their color is lighter, and perhaps this is what led Cowan to describe the hillside east of Latrobe township as "sandy."

Ferralsols are notorious for their tendency to form rock (laterite) under certain conditions. When such soils are subjected to a fluctuating water table or direct, unprotected exposure to rainfall, alternating with sun baking, aluminum and iron oxides in the soil concrete. Improper care of the soil, usually associated with overintensive use, can lead to laterization, which is irreversible. This is not a necessary result, for if ferralsols are carefully maintained, they can keep their agricultural value indefinitely.

[34] Weather patterns: *Report on the Agro-ecological Zones Project. Vol. I: Methodology and Results for Africa* (Rome: FAO-UN, 1978), p. 40; James Hall to J. H. B. Latrobe, July 12, 1835, provides a detailed account of the weather at Cape Palmas during the course of a year.

[35] For a detailed discussion of the coastal terrain, see, G. H. H. Tate, "The Lower Cavally River, West Africa," *Geographical Review*, 32 (1965): 574–76; and B. W. Andah, "Processes of Coastal Evolution," already cited.

[36] James Hall to J. H. B. Latrobe, April 24, 1834 (cntd. on May 20), p. 8, MSCS.

[37] Ibid.

[38] A good discussion of local flora is J. V. Thirgood, "Land-Use Problems of the Liberian Coastal Savannah," *Commonwealth Forestry Review*, 44 (1965), no. 1.

[39] James Hall to J. H. B. Latrobe, April 24, 1834 (cntd. at later dates), pp. 4–8, MSCS.

[40] Edward Pembleton and others to the Board of Managers, Caldwell, Feb. 3, 1833, p. 1, MSCS.

[41] Dr. Thomas Savage, *The Spirit of Missions*, 2:312.

[42] The Episcopal missionaries also relied heavily on quinine. See, *The Spirit of Missions*, 4:362. See also Lynch, *Report to the U.S. Navy Department*, p. 57, for more on the use of quinine.

[43] James Hall to J. H. B. Latrobe, April 24, 1834 (cntd. at later dates), p. 6, MSCS.

[44] Thirgood, "Land-Use Problems of the Liberian Coastal Savannah," 43–44.

[45] James Hall to J. H. B. Latrobe, April 24, 1834 (cntd. at later dates), p. 5, MSCS.

[46] James Hall, "My First Visit to Liberia," *The African Repository*, 42, no. 4, pp. 104–5.

[47] James Hall to J. H. B. Latrobe, April 24, 1834 (cntd. at later dates), p. 6, MSCS.

[48] Ibid.

[49] Ibid., p. 7.

[50] J. Payne The *Spirit of Missions*, 6:17.

[51] James Hall to J. H. B. Latrobe, April 24, 1834 (cntd. at later dates), pp. 7–8, MSCS.

[52] Ibid., p. 14.

[53] Ibid., pp. 19–20.

[54] James Hall to J. H. B. Latrobe, April 24, 1834 (cntd. on June 27), p. 18, MSCS.

[55] Ibid., p. 19.

[56] James Hall, "Proclamation to the Inhabitants of Maryland in Liberia," June 20, 1834, MSCS.

[57] James Hall to J. H. B. Latrobe, August 17, 1834, p. 1, MSCS.

[58] Ibid., p. 2ff, and October 15, 1834, pp. 1–3, both MSCS.

[59] James Hall to J. H. B. Latrobe, April 24, 1834, p. 2, MSCS.

[60] Samuel F. McGill to James Hall, Dec. 15, 1851, pp. 1–2, MSCS.

[61] James Hall to J. H. B. Latrobe, August 17, 1834, p. 2, MSCS.

[62] Ibid., p. 3.

[63] Ibid.

[64] James Hall to J. H. B. Latrobe, October 15, 1834, p. 2, MSCS.

[65] Ibid., p. 3.

[66] Ibid.

4. *"Oborigences"*

[1] "Memorial of Colonists to the Board of Managers," June 15, 1836, p. 2, MSCS.

[2] This is evident in the detailed requests for trade goods sent by Hall and his successors as agent, for instance, to the beginning of 1836: James Hall to J. H. B. Latrobe, Feb. 9, 1834 (cntd. on Feb. 13), p. 6; Hall to Solomon Etting, Feb. 22, 1834, p. 1; John Hersey to the Board of Managers, Baltimore, July 31, 1834 (critical of the manner of trade); Hall to J. H. B. Latrobe, Jan. 27, 1835, p. 2; Hall to J. H. B. Latrobe, March 1, 1835, pp. 6–7; Hall to J. H. B. Latrobe, Aug. 26, 1835, p. 4; and Hall to J. H. B. Latrobe, Nov. 3, 1835 (cntd. on Nov. 29), pp. 38–39, all in MSCS.

[3] Thomas Fuller, a free black man from the Eastern Shore, visited Cape Palmas in 1850 and soon after emigrated there with his family. His account, *Journal of a Voyage to Liberia* (Baltimore, 1851) included a description of Gbenelu's populace:

> [Of] the inhabitants, we could say many things, together with their manners and customs and vulgar appearance; but for fear we will say too much, we will say nothing; but hope and pray that the powers that be, will, for the sake of Maryland in Liberia, for the colonists' sake, for the sake of their children; for morality's sake, for the sake of modesty, for the sake of all that is beneficial to the well being of a civilized community, have those disgusting things covered or removed to some point where the demoralizing influences and customs will not be a poisonous vapour hung thick and fearful around the colony. (pp. 17–18)

[4] His instructions from the MSCS, dated November 25, 1833, were quite specific about dividing territory into townships, with evenly spaced parallel avenues and cross streets, intersecting wherever possible at right angles.

[5] For instance, "Harper," "Latrobe," "Jackson's Corner," and "Tubman Town" would soon make their appearance in the local geography.

[6] J. L. Wilson, *Western Africa* (New York, 1856), p. 112.

[7] Lynch, *Report to the U.S. Navy Department*, pp. 49–50.

[8] The "palaver house" or *takae*: Scott, *Day-dawn*, pp. 46–47; J. L. Wilson, *Western Africa*, p. 131; *Traditional History and Folklore of the Glebo Tribe*, pp. 48–50; Brittan, *Scenes and Incidents of Every-day Life in Africa*, illustration, p. 49, "The Devil-House, Cape Palmas, W. Af.," p. 49; *The Spirit of Missions*, 2:273, 313.

[9] Dr. Thomas Ramsay Steele to his mother, March 14, 1854 (cntd. on March 18), in Ramsay-Steele Family Papers, MS 1769, Maryland Historical Society, Baltimore.

[10] Exemplary descriptions of Grebo houses may be found in, J. L. Wilson, *Western Africa*, pp. 112ff; Scott, *Day-dawn*, pp. 145ff; Lynch, *Report to the U.S. Navy Department*, pp. 49–50; *The Spirit of Missions*, 2:273.

[11] Most slaves and poor black people in Maryland ate humbly. Frederick Douglass gave vivid descriptions of his diet of ash cakes in his autobiographies, and other examples may be found in the fugitive slave narratives. A useful work on slave diet is Sam Bowers Hilliard, *Hog Meat and Hoecake: Food Supply in the Old South, 1840–1860* (Carbondale: Southern Illinois University Press, 1972).

[12] On Grebo diet: J. L. Wilson, *Western Africa,* pp. 122–24, in which he comments in part, "The food of the Kru people consists of but few articles, and these are prepared in the most simple manner. Rice and cassava are the vegetables most used. Beef, mutton, fowls, fish, shell-fish, and game of almost every kind, from the leopard to the wood-rat, is used, but in comparatively small quantities. Any man who can have a bowl of rice and palm-oil placed before him twice in the day, would be called a good liver." *Traditional History and Folklore of the Glebo Tribe,* pp. 58–71, describes Grebo food habits at length.

[13] Grebo land ownership: Brittan, *Every-day Life,* p. 147; Scott, *Day-dawn,* pp. 56–63, 145; *The Spirit of Missions,* Vol. II, pp. 273, 339, Vol. VI, p. 271, Vol. X, pp. 331, 339.

[14] Livestock: Brittan, *Every-day Life,* p. 43; Sir Harry Hamilton Johnston, *Liberia* (New York: Dodd, Mead and Co., 1906; repr. Negro Universities Press, 1969), 2:906–20; Joshua A. Carnes, *Journal of a Voyage from Boston to the West Coast of Africa* (New York, 1852; repr. Negro Universities Press, 1969), p. 139. Concerning paper money, see Latrobe, *Maryland in Liberia,* which describes the money and reproduces the notes.

[15] Draining of Lake Sheppard: James Hall to J. H. B. Latrobe, April 24, 1834 (cntd. on May 20) pp. 4–5, MSCS; T. S. Savage, in *The Spirit of Missions,* Vol. II, p. 311.

[16] Wilson, *Western Africa,* p. 109.

[17] Cassava: Scott, *Day-dawn,* p. 268; P. W. Porter, "Liberia," in *World Atlas of Agriculture* (Novara, Italy: Istituto Geographico de Agostini, 1976), 4:293. Some evidence suggests that the Americans introduced a sweet variety of cassava at Cape Palmas in 1834. If so, its adoption by Greboes was rapid.

[18] Grebo rice: R. Schnell, *Plantes Alimentaires Et Vie Agricole De L'afrique Noire: Essai De Phytogeographie Alimentaire* (Paris: Editions Larose, 1957); W. Allen, *The African Husbandman* (New York: Barnes and Noble, 1965).

[19] Wilson, *Western Africa,* p. 109.

[20] Quoted in E. F. Hening, *History of the African Mission* (New York, 1850), pp. 56–57.

[21] Wilson, *Western Africa,* pp. 109–10.

[22] Grebo age-grades and political organization: Scott, *Day-dawn,* pp. 51–63; Wilson, *Western Africa,* pp. 129–31; Lynch, *Report,* pp. 52–55; *Traditional History and Folklore of the Glebo Tribe,* pp. 52–53.

These social categories exist to the present day, though their roles in the community have necessarily evolved over generations. Modern scholars have changed the spelling of some of these terms, perhaps reflecting changes of pronunciation. Mary Moran's *Civilized Women,* for instance, identifies the nineteenth-century *chiehnbo* as *kyinibo.* The *kinibo* retains its former spelling, but *sedibo* becomes *sidibo,* and *gnekbade* becomes *nyekbade.* I have chosen to retain the older spellings for the sake of consistency with the documentary sources, and also to make clear that the age grades of today are not identical to those 150 years ago.

[23] Wilson, *Western Africa,* p. 130.

[24] Grebo political organization: Wilson, *Western Africa,* pp. 128–29:

> The ostensible form of government among them is monarchy. Hence every village or cluster of small villages has its king, its prince, its governor, dukes, etc. But these terms have undoubtedly been borrowed from European nations, and are not the proper indices of any corresponding offices among themselves. The prevailing form of government, if this term may properly be used, is a much nearer

approximation to true democracy than any other type of government of which we have any knowledge.

See also, p. 139. *Traditional History and Folklore of the Glebo Tribe*, pp. 42–51, describes
the principal dignitaries in good detail.

[25] Dr. Thomas R. Steele to his mother, March 14, 1854, MS 1769, Maryland Historical
Society. See also, Scott, *Day-dawn*, p. 49; *The Spirit of Missions*, 2:278–79, and 3:82–83;
Wilson, *Western Africa*, pp. 112–16.

[26] An accurate description of Grebo religious beliefs and institutions at the time of
American settlement is made the more difficult for two reasons. First, settlers and other
foreign observers almost always regarded Africans scornfully as savage pagans. Their
Christian culture, which held that all those outside the faith were destined for Hell, left
no room for sympathetic understanding. Moreover, difficulties in communication ob-
scured the picture. A comical, sinister example: Greboes learned from foreigners to call
their *kwi*, or guardian spirits, "devils," not knowing the connotations of the word in
standard English. American settlers and missionaries were quite willing to take Greboes
at their word when they explained their religion as "devil worship." Second, Greboes were
in the habit of concealing their customs and beliefs when outsiders questioned them.
Only close observation over long periods, combined with the trust of informants, could
lead to any genuine understanding of Grebo culture. Paradoxically, missionaries, whose
intent was to overthrow Grebo animist beliefs, were simultaneously their most avid
students and recorders. James Hall credited John Payne, an Episcopal missionary who
first came to Cape Palmas in 1838 and lived nearby for twenty-five years after, with
having the most extensive and accurate knowledge of Grebo culture. See, *Maryland
Colonization Journal*, n.s. 5:313.

[27] The oracle of Bulyemah: James Hall to J. H. B. Latrobe, Nov. 3, 1835, MSCS; Scott,
Day-dawn, pp. 68–70, gives the Grebo name as *Bidi Nyima*; *The Spirit of Missions*, 4:145.
Traditional History and Folklore of the Glebo Tribe, pp. 83–95, describes in detail the most
important rocks and other sites sacred to Greboes, with associated legends. Interestingly,
the Bulyemah oracle is not mentioned at all.

[28] Scott, *Day-dawn*, pp. 60–63, and 75–76. The *kwi iru* is analogous to the Dan *poro*
society. Their masks are rather similar, with the exception that the face is typically a little
more realistic, the forehead more rounded, and a raised vertical line continuing the
bridge of the nose. Examples collected about the turn of the century are illustrated in
Kurt Krieger, *Westafrikanische Plastik I* (Berlin: Museum Fur Volkerkunde, 1965).

[29] The *deyabo*: Scott, *Day-dawn*, pp. 56–63; *The Spirit of Missions*, 2:313; Wilson,
Western Africa, pp. 129–31 and 133–35; S. F. McGill to M. Sheppard, Sept. 15, 1841, as
quoted in *Maryland Colonization Journal*, n.s. 1:57–59.

[30] Rev. J. L. Wilson, as quoted in *The Missionary Herald*, 30:336.

[31] The education of a *deya*: Scott, *Day-dawn*, pp. 63–64; *The Spirit of Missions*,
3:304–5.

[32] Initiation of a *deya*: Wilson, *Western Africa*, pp. 133–5; S. F. McGill to M. Sheppard,
quoted in *Maryland Colonization Journal*, n.s. 1:57.

[33] Personal "greegrees": Wilson, *Western Africa*, p. 135; Lynch, *Report*, p. 50; *The Spirit
of Missions*, 2:274 and 3:422; Hening, *History of the African Mission*, p. 166.

[34] Protective charms: E. F. Hening, *History of the African Mission*, p. 25; *The Spirit of
Missions*, 4:185, a beach-sand shrine at Barrakah; Scott, *Day-Dawn*, p. 73.

[35] Dr. T. S. Savage, journal entry, January 17, 1837, quoted in *The Spirit of Missions*, 2:274.

[36] Dr. T. S. Savage, journal entry, January 17, 1837, quoted in ibid., 2:313.

[37] Rev. John Payne, journal entry, May 28, 1839, quoted in ibid., 4:359.

[38] Grebo beliefs about death: Lynch, *Report*, pp. 51–52; *The Spirit of Missions*, 2:338, 4:17–21, and 8:198; Brittan, *Every-day Life*, illustration, "African Cemetery, Russwurm I.," facing p. 233.

[39] S. F. McGill, "Mode of Conducting a Native Funeral Ceremony at Cape Palmas," in *Maryland Colonization Journal*, n.s. 1:88.

[40] S. F. McGill, "Mode of Conducting a Native Funeral Ceremony at Cape Palmas," in *Maryland Colonization Journal*, n.s. 1:88.

[41] Grebo Cemetery: S. F. McGill, "Mode of Conducting a Native Funeral Ceremony at Cape Palmas," in *Maryland Colonization Journal*, n.s. 1:89; Rev. R. R. Gurley, *Report*, p. 107.

[42] Necromancy: Scott, *Day-dawn*, pp. 61–62 and 308–9.

[43] S. F. McGill to M. Sheppard, Oct. 6, 1839 (cntd. on Jan. 3, 1840), as quoted in *Maryland Colonization Journal*, n.s. 2:76.

[44] Ibid., 2:73.

[45] Ibid., 2:74–76, relates a particularly violent episode, which ended with the murder of the accused woman. "The whole scene was enacted in Cape Palmas," the doctor commented, "the colonists, and even the children were eye-witnesses — even in sight of two missionary establishments, and yet we must calmly look on and say nothing. Humanity shrinks on the representation of such barbarities. I ardently look forward to the period when we shall be allowed by force of arms, (since persuasions effect nothing) to abolish this system of murder, in our immediate neighborhood."

[46] James Hall, "Notes on Africa. No. 2," in *Maryland Colonization Journal*, 1:160.

Another illustration of the resistance to change and its relation to sorcery may be found in W. Allen and T. R. H. Thomson, *Narrative of the Expedition . . . to the River Niger*, 1:110. In their account of Cape Palmas, the authors reported that they had observed coconut palms near Harper, but only a few, because of the steadfast Grebo belief that whoever planted one would certainly die before it bore fruit. Russwurm had conversed at length with the King on the subject: "[Freeman] was fully sensible of the great uses of the tree, and desirous of possessing some; therefore, in order to avoid the fatal consequences supposed to attach to those who are directly instrumental in sowing them, [Russwurm] devised an ingenious method of providing a subterfuge. Having placed some nuts at the brink of holes previously drilled, he caused cattle to be driven about over the ground thus prepared, untill all the nuts were thrown into the spaces and covered over by the hoofs of the beasts."

[47] Frequency of deaths by gidu: James Hall to J. H. B. Latrobe, October 15, 1834, p. 6, MSCS. See also Scott, *Day-dawn*, p. 256, which quotes Rev. John Payne's statement that Greboes suffer twelve to twenty deaths per year, per 10,000 of population.

[48] James Hall to J. H. B. Latrobe, Oct. 15, 1834, pp. 6–8, MSCS.

5. *"Better Than Mere Eating"*

[1] See *The Missionary Herald*, 30:212–19.

[2] As extracted from Vol. 31 of the *Missionary Herald* and published in *Maryland Colonization Journal*, 1:5.

[3] Ibid.

[4] See the Emigrant List for the names and backgrounds of this company. Some biographical details of R. B. F. Gould are recorded in *Maryland Colonization Journal*, 1:6–8.

James Hall managed to avert a palaver over Charles's death without much difficulty: see R. B. F. Gould to William McKenney, Jan. 28, 1835, p. 1; and James Hall to J. H. B. Latrobe, Jan. 28, 1835, p. 2, both MSCS.

[5] James Scribner to William McKenney, March 4, 1835, p. 1, MSCS.

[6] R. B. F. Gould to William McKenney, Monrovia, Jan. 20, 1835, pp. 1–3, MSCS.

[7] Ibid., Jan. 28, 1835, pp. 1–3, MSCS.

[8] Hall's poor health: James Hall to J. H. B. Latrobe, Jan. 27, 1835, p. 1; James Hall to J. H. B. Latrobe, March 1, 1835, p. 1; R. B. F. Gould to William McKenney, Jan. 28, 1835, p. 1, MSCS. Charles Snetter: James Hall to J. H. B. Latrobe, March 1, 1835, pp. 1–2, MSCS.

[9] James Hall to J. H. B. Latrobe, March 1, 1835 (cntd. on March 16), p. 3, MSCS.

[10] James Hall to J. H. B. Latrobe, April 1, 1835, p. 2, MSCS. For further criticisms, see, James Hall to J. H. B. Latrobe, June 1, 1835 (cntd. on June 14), p. 9, MSCS. Hall closed the letter with a full measure of spleen: "It is really discouraging to see how little tact and management the majority of them have and how much they need their overseer." Speaking of the deaths among the *Bourne*'s children, he continued, "The fact is the parents are in most cases totally unfit to manage their children. They lack the judgement of Human beings and the instinct of Brutes."

[11] John Harris to William McKenney, March 2 and March 11, 1835, both in MSCS.

[12] James Scribner to William McKenney, March 4, 1835, MSCS.

[13] Alexander Hance to William McKenney, March 14, 1835, MSCS.

[14] William Hawkins to William McKenney, March 15, 1835, MSCS.

[15] James Hall to J. H. B. Latrobe, June 1, 1835, pp. 1–3, MSCS.

[16] Citizens of Harper to James Hall, June 24, 1835, MSCS. On June 15, 1836, many of the same settlers met again to address another remonstrance to the board, elaborating on their complaints of the previous year. They were in a delicate position, for they recognized Hall's achievements in the face of serious impediments. He had established and preserved the colony, and they were afraid to be called ungrateful. The doctor, they wrote, "will live long in our memories as the pioneer of our Colony and Experienced and Skillful physician, as the Companion of our suffering, and the father of our people." They praised his Grebo policy, which had kept the settlement at peace. Even so, they went on, Hall's administration was marred by certain circumstances, of which the board must be unaware.

They knew that Hall had reported to the board that settlers were self-sufficient, and that their debts to the store could be paid off quickly. The petitioners vehemently denied this. In fact, they countered, James Hall left his successor to deal with the problem with nothing more than hopeful words. "We are compelled to Contradict these assersions," they wrote, "if maney of our Colonist were Cut of from the store (thare is but one) without the intervention of some foreign aid, thay would not subsist." The colony was still in its infancy, and settlers labored simply to survive. Everyone was indebted to the agency, which paid low wages and charged high prices in the store. Moreover, since they had no currency to pay their debts, settlers must work for the agency rather than earn an independent living. The grievance against the agency broadened into a general complaint about the scarcity and high price of building materials and other necessities. They pleaded for enough cloth to dress decently for church. Sugar was unavailable, except to the sick, and then only grudgingly. Palm oil, rice, and salt meat, staples of diet, were only occasionally for sale, although large amounts were reportedly hoarded in the store. They concluded with a note that the housing for new emigrants was leaky and uncomfortable and that the militia was inadequate for the threat the colony faced.

[17] Henry Dennis to Dr. John Martin, July 23, 1835, MSCS.

[18] James Hall to J. H. B. Latrobe, July 12, 1835 (cntd. at later dates), in Foreign Letterbook, Vol. I, pp. 108–22 (as transcribed).

[19] James Hall to J. H. B. Latrobe, Brig *Luna*, at sea, May 1, 1836, pp. 8–10, MSCS.

[20] See the Emigrant List, MSCS.

[21] James Hall to J. H. B. Latrobe, August 25, 1835, pp. 1–2, MSCS.

[22] Jacob Gibson to J. H. B. Latrobe and William McKenney, Aug. 31, 1835, MSCS.

[23] Ambrose Simpson to William McKenney, Sept. 1, 1835, MSCS. (The individual who penned the letter for Simpson evidently had trouble spelling his first name, making it "Lambert.")

[24] James Hall to J. H. B. Latrobe, Nov. 3, 1835 (cntd. at later dates), pp. 1–35, MSCS.

[25] Hall's trip up Cavally River: James Hall to J. H. B. Latrobe, Nov. 3, 1835 (cntd. on Nov. 26), pp. 35–36; Deed of Bulyemah to the Maryland State Colonization Society, October 16, 1835; Deed of Half Cavally to the Maryland State Colonization Society, Nov. 25, 1835, all in MSCS.

6. *"Infirmities of Our Comon Nature"*

[1] James Hall to J. H. B. Latrobe, Dec. 10, 1835, MSCS.

[2] William Polk to Capt. Thomas Hooper, Nov. 29, 1835, MSCS.

According to the Emigrant Roll, William Polk went to Africa aboard the *Lafayette* in 1831, at the age of twenty, accompanied by his widowed mother and three sisters. At Caldwell, the family suffered many privations, including the mother's death. He and his sisters moved to Cape Palmas in 1834 (see Senate Document 150).

See also William Polk to William McKenney, Feb. 5, 1836, MSCS. McKenney was instrumental in persuading the Polks to emigrate. As he wrote to Hooper, Polk told McKenney that he was eager to see more people settle at Cape Palmas. He expressed regret that McKenney had not gone back to Somerset County to solicit emigrants. "I hope you have Not give them up yet," he continued, "because I want to See them on the Shores of africa whare thay con be free and Not Molested by No nation whatever." He asked McKenney to tell the black residents of Somerset that he was in Africa, where he would live out his days in freedom, and invite them to join him:

> I Con heare of thair Conditions and Circumstances, and I would not be in thair places, no; not for all the Luxuries in the United States could afford. what is the Colered Man in that Country? I will answer the Question My Self. He is No More than a Dog or a beast of burden. Let him be free or slave he Must labour fer the white man, and after all he can only obtain a good nam and hardly that, fer If he once obtains it he must Look out If he do not lose it again.

He apologized for the negative reports of two *Lafayette* emigrants who returned to

America after terrible suffering in Liberia, where, "thay could see nothing but an Ill Conducted government and a parcel of Disatisfied people." He had been unhappy himself at first, but had resolved stoically to bear the worst rather than "return to a place that Could not give me a home altho it give me birth." Closing, he expressed disappointment at the slow pace of emigration, admitting that he had nearly given up on his obstinate old neighbors.

[3] James Hall, "Proclamation," Jan. 21, 1836, pp. 1–2, MSCS.

[4] Thomson's appointment: James Hall to J. H. B. Latrobe, Brig *Luna* at sea, May 1, 1836, pp. 1–3; Oliver Holmes, Jr. to J. H. B. Latrobe, July 13, 1836, pp. 5, 10, MSCS.

[5] The *Fortune* expedition: Oliver Holmes, Jr. to J. H. B. Latrobe, Feb. 10, 1836, pp. 1–3; Oliver Holmes, Jr. to J. H. B. Latrobe, July 13, 1836, pp. 21–3; Arthur Wilson to J. H. B. Latrobe, Sept. 3, 1836; Asbury Wilson to William McKenney, Sept. 4, 1836; David Wilson to William McKenney, Sept. 4, 1836: all MSCS.

[6] Luke Walker to J. H. B. Latrobe, Sept. 6, 1836, pp. 1–2, MSCS.

[7] Hall prepares to depart: James Hall to Oliver Holmes, Jr., March 19, 1836, pp. 3–4; James Hall to J. H. B. Latrobe, Brig *Luna* at sea, May 1, 1836, pp. 2–3; Oliver Holmes, Jr. to J. H. B. Latrobe, July 13, 1836, pp. 24, 30–1, all MSCS.

[8] Holmes's dispute with Perry: Oliver Holmes, Jr. to J. H. B. Latrobe, July 13, 1836, pp. 23–24; Oliver Holmes, Jr. to J. H. B. Latrobe, Feb. 10, 1836, pp. 3–4, MSCS.

[9] Oliver Holmes, Jr. to J. H. B. Latrobe, July 13, 1836, p. 1, MSCS.

[10] Ibid., p. 18, MSCS.

[11] Ibid., March 24, 1836, MSCS.

[12] James Hall to J. H. B. Latrobe, Brig *Luna* at sea, May 1, 1836, pp. 2–3, MSCS.

[13] Oliver Holmes, Jr. to J. H. B. Latrobe, July 13, 1836, pp. 1–2, MSCS.

[14] Ibid., pp. 24–28, MSCS.

[15] Ibid., p. 29, MSCS.

[16] Hall's final instructions: James Hall to Oliver Holmes, Jr., March 19, 1836; Oliver Holmes, Jr. to J. H. B. Latrobe, July 13, 1836, p. 31, MSCS.

[17] Appointment of Charles Snetter: James Hall to J. H. B. Latrobe, Brig *Luna* at sea, May 1, 1836, pp. 3–4; James Hall to J. H. B. Latrobe, March 1, 1835, pp. 1–2, MSCS:

> I know Snetter to be a capable, enterprising popular fellow . . . [I] feel that I could entrust the Colony with him in case of accident with more confidence than any other Coloured man in Liberia, especially when connected with Mr Thomson. He is much better calculated to keep the troublesome ones *in cow*, than Thomson, possesses more energy of character, and in fact I think he will one day be a man of consequence in *this* Liberia.

Charles Snetter was born free in 1802, probably in Charleston, South Carolina. The only clue as to his family, is the mention of an African aunt living in Savannah, Georgia, and the consequence that one of his parents was also African. Whether he had white ancestors as well (many of Charleston's free black people did) is uncertain. The experiences of his youth on the streets of Charleston are also uncertain. It is on record, however, that he learned to read and write, that he married and had two children, and that he came under the influence of a prominent dissident against slavery. See Senate Document 150, p.226; J. L. Wilson to J. H. B. Latrobe, Sept. 6, 1836, p. 2, MSCS.

Experiences that shaped Snetter's early life can only be inferred from South Carolina's social and political history.

The environment in which Snetter grew, and the sweeping economic changes he must have witnessed, left their mark on the adult who sailed to Africa. In 1802, the year of his birth, Charleston was the largest port in the South, fourth-largest city in the nation. The city's fortunes were intimately connected with the slave-based production of cotton and rice. Therefore, the city was subject to intense social and political struggle as the old plantation regime was transformed in the early nineteenth century.

Briefly, rice and indigo had made South Carolina the richest of the English colonies on the North American mainland. In those days, Charleston was the principal debarking point for African captives. A white minority, fabulously rich by colonial standards, subsisted in Charleston on income generated by estates in the surrounding low country. These plantations were worked by slaves who lived in squalor. The economic disruption and destruction attending the Revolution, which was followed by persistent economic weakness, ruined many of the old planters. Others barely held on to their estates. Near the turn of the century, however, Eli Whitney invented a machine that could separate cotton fiber from the seeds. Charleston's fortunes reversed as cotton production increased geometrically. The demand for labor increased almost as sharply, and slaves were imported in huge numbers from the depressed farms of the Chesapeake Tidewater, from the West Indies, and from Africa. The best book on slavery in early South Carolina is Peter H. Wood, *Black Majority: Negroes in Colonial South Carolina from 1670 Through the Stono Rebellion* (New York: W. W. Norton and Co., 1975)

With the influx of new slaves was an increase in the number of free black people. In 1790, Charleston's population of free black people was a little less than six hundred. By 1830 the number had increased to something more than two thousand, still a tiny fraction of the total population. See John Lofton, *Denmark Vesey's Revolt: The Slave Plot that Lit a Fuse to Fort Sumter* (Kent, Ohio: Kent State University Press, 1983), p. 80. Slaves obtained their freedom in various ways. Occasionally masters manumitted their mulatto offspring in their wills. Other slaves worked and saved their money over years and eventually purchased freedom from their masters. Still others got free by luck, or as a reward for outstanding services. Thus Denmark Vesey, sometime property of a West Indian slave dealer, won a lottery in Charleston and purchased his freedom. In 1822 the slave who betrayed a revolt that Vesey plotted was freed in gratitude, with an annuity from the state of $1,000. See E. Horace Fitchett, "The Traditions of the Free Negro in Charleston, South Carolina," in *Journal of Negro History*, 25 (1940): 142, 147.

Snetter was part of a distinct cultural enclave of free black people who congregated in Charleston. The city provided opportunities to landless laborers for employment. Charleston's free black population was composed chiefly of artisans, who were extremely conscious of their precarious niche in society. Churches of several denominations, especially the African Methodist Episcopal Church, were active. In addition, there were several mutual aid societies to which members contributed small sums. The oldest and most prestigious of these was the Brown Fellowship Society, founded in 1790 by a group of free mulattoes. Such institutions were exclusive and demanded certain standards of behavior from members. In an aristocracy of complexion, lighter skins added to social status. Quite a few free black people prospered. Many were slaveholders themselves: those who chose to live in the South often aspired to the ideals and way of life of the white elites. Yet, the free black caste was vulnerable despite its social institutions and imitation of upper-class values. Attitudes of the white ruling class and the law stood against meaningful political expression on their part.

An economy based upon coerced labor was a principal cause of this. Economic and social changes brought on by the cotton boom caused anxiety among the powerful class of planters, who looked fearfully upon their captive work force. They regarded free black people as a serious threat, for they contradicted the notion that Africans were naturally subservient and therefore deserved to be enslaved. On a more practical level, free blacks could move among the slave population to plant dangerous ideas of liberty.

In 1822, when Snetter was twenty, plans for a slave revolt were revealed, realizing the worst fears of the white community. Denmark Vesey, an ex-slave from St. Croix, had drawn a conjectured six thousand slaves into a plot to kill their masters and sail to Haiti. Charleston's reaction was swift and harsh. Thirty-five men, including Vesey, were hanged, and many others were banished. Soon after, South Carolina's legislature passed several acts to restrict the free black community. The most severe was the Negro Seaman's Act, which forbade black sailors from calling at Charleston. Any who did so could be taken off their ships and thrown in jail until the vessel was ready to depart. Detainees who could not pay expenses for their lodging would be sold. The law raised a storm of national protest, but white South Carolinians were afraid of the ideas that free northern black people might bring ashore with them. In response to continuing federal opposition to the Negro Seaman's Act, South Carolinians asserted more adamantly their right to impose laws as they saw fit. The legitimacy of slavery, and their right to use slaves, became a keystone of their ideology. Vesey's revolt marked the beginning of a fierce sectional conflict that prepared the nation for civil war. See David D. Wallace, *South Carolina: A Short History, 1520–1948* (Chapel Hill: University of North Carolina Press, 1951), pp. 384–86; and Lofton, *Denmark Vesey's Revolt*, chapter 12 and pp. 197–210.

Though most white South Carolinians were increasingly jealous of their black property, a few disagreed. The most prominent dissidents were children of Judge John Faucheraud Grimké. The Grimkés were descendants of Huguenot refugees who came to South Carolina in the late seventeenth century. Over several generations, they accumulated extensive landholdings and numerous slaves. Judge Grimké was an important figure in the formation of the United States. His two daughters, Sarah and Angelina, were vocal critics of slavery. They scandalized Charleston by uniting with the Society of Friends, and soon after Vesey's plot was suppressed, they were forced to leave the city. (In Philadelphia, the two sisters were influential advocates of abolition and women's rights.)

Charles Snetter was a friend and confidant of Thomas H. Grimké, their older, more conservative brother. Thomas remained in Charleston after his sisters left, constantly voicing his opposition to slavery. In 1832, during the Nullification crisis, when South Carolina defied the authority of the federal government and militias mustered to fight, he was a leading voice for moderation. He was also South Carolina's most ardent colonizationist, believing that emigration to Liberia was the best hope for black people. (In 1833, Grimké joined the American Peace Society, a pacifist organization. His life was cut short by cholera, which he contracted in Cincinnati while on a lecture tour in October 1834.) See, David D. Wallace, *South Carolina: A Short History*, p. 435; Gerda Lerner, *The Grimké Sisters from South Carolina: Rebels Against Slavery* (Boston: Houghton Mifflin, 1967), pp. 12–7, 56–58, and 108; Adrienne Koch, "Two Charlestonians in Search of Truth: The Grimké Brothers," in the *South Carolina Historical Magazine*, 69 (1968): 159–70.

Nat Turner's uprising in 1831 reminded South Carolina's planters of their vulnerability and threw them into an uproar. Snetter, like many other free blacks, considered emigration, perhaps at Grimké's urging. Whatever the case, he was among a small group which met on December 6, 1831, to discuss the matter. They gathered at the house of one Titus Gregoire, whose name suggests he may have been Haitian, maybe a veteran of the only successful slave revolution in the New World. After a brief opening statement, Charles Henry stood and expressed a millenarian view of Africa and linked the destiny of his audience with their ancestral home:

> Africa, the land of our fathers, although surrounded with clouds of darkness, seems to me to be extending her arms towards us as her only hope of relief, and calling on us loudly for help, saying, "I struggle for light and for liberty, and call upon you by the *names* of your ancestors to come to MY *help* and YOUR *rightful possession.* Tarry thou not, but come over and help dispel the darkness from your benighted land. Come, and inspire us by your example with sentiments of virtue, and with a love of the duties taught by the meek and lowly Jesus. Come and erect altars, and light them with the pure fire of devotion to the only living and true God. Come and enforce the empire of reason, truth, and christianity over our benighted minds. Be no longer as a sentinel asleep at your post; desert not your own people and the country of your ancestors.

Henry then offered a series of resolutions strongly tinctured with the same sort of religious allusions: that they all should accept the American Colonization Society's offer to carry them to Africa; that the Bible should be their map on the journey; that they would come to Liberia as "Harbingers of Peace in the fulness of the blessing of the Gospel of Christ"; and that in Africa they should live as one family, bound to care for each other. A final resolution reflected the tense political atmosphere, and the risk of their meeting: "we will not harbor or encourage any designs that may tend to disturb the peace and harmony of this state, or by any means alienate the affections of our brethren who are held as property, from their subordinate channel."

Individuals then rose to offer their opinions. Charles Snetter concurred wholeheartedly with the resolutions and pledged to leave for Africa with his family. He produced a letter from his African aunt in Savannah, stating her willingness to return to the place of her birth. An African at the meeting, Pharaoh Moses, then said, "If you, who are natives of this country, and have never seen Africa, speak so highly of her, what must I say who have trod the soil — the soil which gave me birth, and where yet live my relations and kindred, from whom by the hand of violence I was torn away and deprived of freedom, which, thanks be to God, I have again obtained, also the liberty of the companion of my life, and that of two children. I go with you, my brethren. It is a good land." The meeting approved Henry's resolutions without amendment. The chairman urged everyone to sell his belongings and make ready to leave. Snetter moved that a copy of the proceedings be sent to American Colonization Society, which in fact published them. See *The African Repository*, 8:74–77.

A few months later, "a respectable free coloured man" of Charleston directed a copy of an open letter to the black people of America to the editor of *The African Repository*. It is tempting to suppose that Snetter wrote it or had a hand in its composition, but this cannot be determined. Certainly, it parallels Snetter's thinking, for all of his later actions in Liberia are expressions of these sentiments. The writer first noted the deteriorating legal and economic standing of free black people in Charleston and the nation: "Our children are likely to be much worse situated than we are — as we ourselves are not as well situated in many respects as our parents were." The only real hope for black people, he asserted, was emigration to Liberia. There, black Americans could create their own democratic republic. He did not expect settlers to mix with native Africans. On the contrary, he recognized that many of his peers objected to "emigrating to a country whose inhabitants are shrouded in deep ignorance — whom long and deep-rooted custom forbids us to have social intercourse with in the various relations of civilized life upon fair and equal terms of husband and wife, and whose complexion is darker than many of ours." He countered with the over-riding benefit of emigration, "to a country more adapted to promote your interests, because a very plain reason presents itself for such removal — and that is, in Liberia you will enjoy moral and political liberty." He scolded black people for standing idly by while white missionaries went fearlessly, at great personal hazard. Liberia called black Americans to a great civilizing mission, and nothing should stand in their way. He wrote,

> In Liberia, you can erect a temple of worship to God, in the beauty of holiness; without fear you can set up, and protect your sacred altars, and pour out the orisons of the devout and pious heart before them, in praise and thanksgiving to God. In Liberia, you can establish Academies and Colleges, to instruct youth in Theology, in Physic, and in Law. You will there know no superiors but virtue, and the laws of your country — no religion but the revealed revelation of God — and recollect all of this is for you yourselves. "Opinions of a Free South Carolinian," in *The African Repository*, 8:239–43.

Charles Snetter took his wife and two young sons to Norfolk, Virginia, where they boarded the ship *Jupiter*, in May, 1832. The vessel carried 169 emigrants in all, including sixty-eight Virginians, thirty-nine Georgians, and thirty-four South Carolinians. The great majority were slaves freed to go to Africa, and few had Snetter's advantages. A notable exception was James M. Thomson, who had been born in Demerara, British Guiana, twenty-five years before. As a young man, he went to England, where he received a classical education. Later, he moved to New York, where he married and had two children. Like Snetter, he looked to Africa as a place to enjoy the dignity and freedom denied him in America. He and Snetter both found work in Monrovia, but politics there did not agree with Thomson as well as Snetter. When the *Ann* called early in 1834, Thomson readily agreed to join his old friend, James Hall, as Secretary. See, Senate Document 150, p. 226; James Hall to J. H. B. Latrobe, April 24, 1834, p. 16, MSCS.

[18] Oliver Holmes, Jr. to J. H. B. Latrobe, July 13, 1836, pp. 2–17, MSCS.

[19] Henry Dennis to Dr. John Martin, May 30, 1836, MSCS. Dennis directed a letter with similar content to William McKenney and Moses Sheppard on June 12, 1836, also in MSCS.

[20] Acclimation of *Fortune* company: Oliver Holmes, Jr. to J. H. B. Latrobe, March 24,

1836; Oliver Holmes, Jr. to J. H. B. Latrobe, July 21, 1836, p. 1; Oliver Holmes, Jr. to J. H. B. Latrobe, July 13, 1836, pp. 19–20; J. L. Wilson to Ira Easter, June 2, 1836; "Memorial of Colonists to the Board of Managers," June 15, 1836, pp. 4–5; Arthur Wilson to J. H. B. Latrobe, Sept. 3, 1836; Luke Walker to J. H. B. Latrobe, Sept. 6, 1836, pp. 2–3, all in MSCS.

[21] Oliver Holmes, Jr. to J. H. B. Latrobe, July 13, 1836, pp. 28, 38–39, MSCS.

[22] Henry Dennis gave the first indication of trouble in a letter of May 30, 1836, MSCS.

[23] James M. Thomson to J. H. B. Latrobe, Sept. 6, 1836, p. 1, MSCS.

[24] Charles Snetter to J. H. B. Latrobe, July 7, 1837, MSCS.

[25] Feud between Holmes and Snetter: J. L. Wilson to J. H. B. Latrobe, Sept. 6, 1836, pp. 1–2; Charles Snetter to J. H. B. Latrobe, July 7, 1837, both in MSCS.

[26] Rev. John L. Wilson to J. H. B. Latrobe, June 25, 1836, pp. 3–4, MSCS.

[27] Concerning missions paying bride-price for girls: *The Spirit of Missions*, 2:278–79, and 3:82–83 and 146; James M. Thomson to Oliver Holmes, Jr., Dec. 28, 1837, pp. 3–4, MSCS.

[28] Rev. John L. Wilson to J. H. B. Latrobe, July 22, 1837, p. 2, MSCS.

[29] Oliver Holmes, Jr. to J. H. B. Latrobe, July 21, 1836, MSCS.

[30] William Woodward (president of the Young Men's Colonization Society) and others to Dr. Samuel K. Jennings (Dean of Faculty, Washington Medical College), Baltimore, Nov. 10, 1836, MSCS Letterbook, 1836B. Incidentally, forty-five individuals, many of them prominent citizens, attached their names to the letter.

[31] Dr. S. K. Jennings to the Young Men's Colonization Society, n.p., n.d., appended to the letter addressed to him on Nov. 10, MSCS.

[32] Correspondence between James Hall and Dr. Phelps: Hall to Phelps, Baltimore, Oct. 30, 1836; Phelps to Hall, Windsor, Vt., Nov. 4, 1836, both in MSCS.

[33] Moses Sheppard to Samuel Ford McGill, Baltimore, Jan. 12, 1836, MSCS, Letterbook 1836A, also quoted in Penelope Campbell, "Medical Education," p. 131.

[34] Genevieve Miller, "A Nineteenth-Century Medical School: Washington University of Baltimore," in *Bulletin of the History of Medicine*, 14 (1943): 14–17. The owners of the school purchased an association with Washington College in Pennsylvania. The school's hospital building, subsequently the Church Home (now closed), stands very close to Johns Hopkins Hospital. Edgar Allan Poe died in the Washington College Infirmary in 1848.

[35] Dr. E. E. Phelps to Rev. Ira Easter, Windsor, Vt., Jan. 9, 1837, MSCS.

[36] [Students of Washington Medical College], "Resolutions of a meeting held, Monday, December 12th, 1836 in the lecture room," MSCS.

[37] Students of Washington Medical College to Dr. S. K. Jennings, Baltimore, n.d. (about Dec. 12, 1836), MSCS.

[38] Attempt to readmit McGill: Resolutions of the Young Men's Colonization Society, Dec. 15, 1836; Rev. Ira Easter to the Students of Washington Medical College, Baltimore, Dec. 17, 1836, both in MSCS.

[39] H. D. McCulloch and other students to Rev. Ira Easter, Baltimore, Dec. 26, 1836, MSCS.

[40] Thomas Jackson to Charles Howard, Sept. 6, 1836, MSCS.

[41] Charles Snetter to J. H. B. Latrobe, July 7, 1837, MSCS.

[42] J. M. Thomson to J. H. B. Latrobe, Sept. 6, 1836, p. 1, MSCS.

[43] Rev. John L. Wilson to J. H. B. Latrobe, Sept. 6, 1836, pp. 1–3, MSCS. Here was a

hypocritical point, for Wilson, like Holmes, was dependent on laudanum or opium as well as calomel. Those who had access to medicine used it freely, and consequently often suffered periods of irrationality or impairment.

⁴⁴ Thomas Jackson to Charles Howard, Sept. 6, 1836, MSCS.

⁴⁵ Holmes addressed letters to each of his assistants, formally granting them authority to enforce the constitution and statutes of Maryland in Liberia. The colony was therefore completely under control of settlers for the first time in its history. See J. M. Thomson to J. H. B. Latrobe, Sept. 6, 1836, p. 2, MSCS.

7. *"Liberty and Equality"*

¹ Edward Long, *The History of Jamaica* (London, 1774; repr. London: Frank Cass and Co., 1970), p. 174.

² John Stewart, *An Account of Jamaica* (London, 1808; repr. Freeport, New York: Books for Libraries Press, 1971), p. 195.

³ Gad J. Heuman, *Between Black and White: Race, Politics, and the Free Coloreds in Jamaica, 1792–1865* (Westport, Conn.: Greenwood Press, 1981), pp. 4, 10–13.

⁴ The most authoritative source for the early life of Russwurm is an article which appeared in *Maryland Colonization Journal*, n.s., 6:350–52, which contains James Hall's personal reminiscences and long extracts from a letter written by Russwurm's stepmother.

⁵ Anonymous, "Documents: Letters to the American Colonization Society," in *Journal of Negro History*, 10 (1925): 156.

⁶ Russwurm as schoolteacher: Bella Gross, "Freedom's Journal and the Rights of All," in *Journal of Negro History*, 17 (1932): 278; Philip S. Foner, *History of Black Americans*, 3 vols. (Westport, Conn.: Greenwood Press, 1983), 2:218.

⁷ Russwurm at Bowdoin: Nehemiah Cleaveland and Alphaeus S. Packard, *History of Bowdoin College* (Boston: James R. Osgood and Co., 1892), pp. 281–360; Horatio Bridge, *Personal Recollections of Nathaniel Hawthorne* (New York: Harper and Bros., 1893), pp. 16–31.

Russwurm graduated just eleven days after Edward Jones, who earned his degree from Amherst College after six years' study. Jones later became a missionary in Sierra Leone. See J. P. Davis, ed., *The American Negro Reference Book* (Englewood Cliffs, N.J.: Prentice-Hall, 1967), p. 550, which cites in turn H. Hawkins in *School and Society*, 89, pp. 375–76.

⁸ James Hall, "John Browne Russwurm," in *Maryland Colonization Journal*, n.s. 6:352.

⁹ H. Bridge, *Recollections of Hawthorne*, p. 30.

¹⁰ Russwurm's valedictory: L. H. Fishel and Benjamin Quarles, *The Negro American: A Documentary History* (Atlanta: Scott, Foresman and Co., 1967), p. 158; Foner, *History of Black Americans*, 2:227.

¹¹ Russwurm and *Freedom's Journal*: Anonymous, "Documents: Letters to the American Colonization Society," p. 156; Gross, "Freedom's Journal and the Rights of All," p. 248. This paper was organized in meetings at the home of Boston Crummell, whose youthful son, Alexander, would one day find his fortunes connected with Maryland in Liberia, and who would eventually become one of the most influential exponents of black nationalism.

¹² Russwurm's advocacy of colonization: Gross, "Freedom's Journal and the Rights of All," p. 248; Foner, *History of Black Americans*, 2:256, 259. Russwurm's defection brought

down the enduring wrath of abolitionists. Years later, Garrison's *Liberator*, for example, published a letter full of malice towards him: "After he subverted the pledge he made to his colored brethren, he left, to our satisfaction, his country — suffused with shame — and branded with the stigma of disgrace — to dwell in that land for which the temptor MONEY caused him to avow his preferment." (Quoted in Carter G. Woodson, *The Mind of the Negro* [New York: Negro Universities Press, 1969), p. 161.)

[13] Philip Foner, who does not cite the source, writes that Russwurm returned to Bowdoin, where he earned a master's degree. The published Bowdoin histories do not mention it, however.

[14] Anonymous reporter in the *Thirteenth Annual Report of the American Colonization Society* (Washington, 1830), p. 11, states that Russwurm had sailed for Liberia "a few months before" the annual meeting, held in January. See also, *Fourteenth Annual Report* (Washington, 1831)

[15] Russwurm to Latrobe, Monrovia, February 5, 1833, pp. 1–2, MSCS.

[16] Ezekiel Skinner to Ralph R. Gurley, Monrovia, August 15, 1835, p. 2, ACS, Letters Received, Library of Congress.

[17] John B. Russwurm to Ralph R. Gurley, Monrovia, Oct. 5, 1835, ACS, Letters Received, Library of Congress.

[18] Partisanship at Monrovia: John B. Russwurm to R. R. Gurley, Monrovia, May 5, 1834, p. 3; J. W. Prout to R. R. Gurley, Monrovia, May 13, 1835, both in ACS, Letters Received, Library of Congress.

[19] Hilary Teague, Colin's son, informed Ralph Gurley in Washington:

> Messrs Daily and Russwurm are known to be commission merchants in this place. They have had for two or three years, a small Vessel of forty to fifty tons burthen, employed in trading on the Coast. This Vessel Mr. Daily has lately taken to the Gallinas, since when she has not returned to this place. She is now in the possession of *Pedro Blancho* the most notorious slaver on the Windward coast, and is employed as we learn, in carrying provisions, and no doubt slaves, to and from the different factories and Vessels. I do not pretend to say that Messrs D and R have now any interest in the Vessel, or are in any way concerned in her. I know nothing of the contract. They may have made a final sale of her; — all that I will say, is that she is in the *slave trade*.

Hilary Teague to Ralph R. Gurley, Monrovia, July 1, 1835, p. 3, ACS, Letters Received, Library of Congress.

[20] John B. Russwurm to Ralph R. Gurley, Monrovia, Oct. 5, 1835, ACS, Letters Received, Library of Congress.

[21] Holmes's movements to and from Monrovia: John B. Russwurm to J. H. B. Latrobe, Monrovia, Sept. 28, 1836, pp. 2–3; and Harper, Dec. 16, 1836, p. 1, both in MSCS.

[22] John B. Russwurm to J. H. B. Latrobe, Dec. 16, 1836, p. 1, MSCS.

[23] Russwurm's arrival at Harper: John B. Russwurm to J. H. B. Latrobe, Feb. 12, 1837, p. 1; Robert Whitfield to J. H. B. Latrobe, April 24, 1838: both in MSCS.

[24] The accounts were sent to Baltimore semi-annually and provide a valuable window on African trade during that period.

[25] Change of colonial personnel: John B. Russwurm to J. H. B. Latrobe, Monrovia,

Sept. 28, 1836, pp. 2–3; Harper, Dec. 16, 1836, p. 4, both in MSCS.

[26] John L. Wilson to J. H. B. Latrobe, July 6, 1837, p. 3, MSCS.

[27] John B. Russwurm to J. H. B. Latrobe, Dec. 16, 1836, p. 4, MSCS.

[28] Visit of the *Potomac*: John B. Russwurm to the Secretary of the Navy, Dec. 17, 1836, in American Naval Records, Squadron Letters, National Archives; John B. Russwurm to J. H. B. Latrobe, Dec. 16, 1836, pp. 2–3, MSCS.

[29] G. R. McGill to the Board of Managers, May 13, 1837, pp. 2, 4–5, MSCS.

[30] Effects of *Potomac*'s visit: John B. Russwurm to J. H. B. Latrobe, Dec. 16, 1836, pp. 2–4; Capt. J. J. Nicholson to John B. Russwurm, no date (about Dec. 15, 1836); Capt. J. J. Nicholson to J. H. B. Latrobe, Aboard U.S.S. *Potomac*, Hampton Roads, March 3, 1837, all three in MSCS.

[31] John B. Russwurm to J. H. B. Latrobe, Feb. 12, 1837, pp. 1–6, MSCS.

[32] An explicit statement of this may be found in Simleh Ballah and John L. Wilson to J. H. B. Latrobe, June 6, 1837, MSCS, in which Wilson writes for Simleh: "he says that his people only wanted to frighten the Americans because the magistrates had wofully abused their power and they thought those abuses ought to be rectified in season; and they knew of no other plan that could be adopted to effect the end. He likewise thinks that these occasionaly irruptions are inseparable from any state of society and asks if the people in Baltimore did not pull down each others houses just before he went to America."

[33] John B. Russwurm to J. H. B. Latrobe, Feb. 10, 1837, p. 1, MSCS.

[34] Thomas S. Savage, Dec. 28, 1837, quoted in *The Spirit of Missions*, 2:153–55.

[35] George R. McGill to the Board of Managers, May 13, 1837, pp. 3–4, MSCS.

[36] See entry in *Appleton's Cyclopedia* for biography of Squire Chase. John Revey, "Celebration of the third anniversary of the Colony of Maryland in Liberia," MSCS.

According to a biography by Samuel McGill printed in *Maryland Colonization Journal*, n.s. Vol. I, p. 204, John Revey went to Africa at the age of seventeen, having left his native New York for no other reason than "a disposition to roam." He was one of the *Elizabeth*'s company and a survivor of the disastrous first attempt to settle Sherbro Island. He settled at Sierra Leone, where he learned to read and write. There he soon won a position as a clerk in a merchant house, making periodic trips in the bush on business. In 1828 he migrated to Monrovia, where he was a leader in intellectual and social life. McGill noted that he worked in turn as a missionary in the Vey Country, High Sheriff of Liberia, public surveyor, and superintendent of schools. In 1836 he became a Baptist minister. Shortly after, he moved to Cape Palmas to work for Russwurm.

[37] Recorded in "Proceedings of the Agent and Council," transcribed by John Revey, MSCS.

[38] John Bowen: *Senate Document 150*, p. 244; Census of Maryland in Liberia, 1837.

[39] "Proceedings of the Agent and Council," May 6, 1837, p. 1, MSCS.

[40] John B. Russwurm to J. H. B. Latrobe, Feb. 12, 1837 (cntd. at later dates), p. 16, MSCS.

[41] Jose de Amorio to Russwurm, April 17, 1837, MSCS.

> "El Capitan de la Goleta portuguesa Constanza a el S. Gobernador de Cabo Palma la parte de haber fondeado en su pte con el objeto de reponer algunas Averias Ocasionadas en el tiempo que ha esta do en esta Costa haciendo en Negocio de Arroz Y.S.
>
> Cabo Palmas 17. Abl. 1837, Joao Joze de Amorio

[42] The instructions of the board of managers to James Hall and his successors, dated November 25, 1833, in Corresponding Secretary's Letterbook, No. 1, p. 103, MSCS, were explicit:

> In your intercourse with the persons who visit the coast be always conciliating. The slave traders will doubtless call on you often. Avoid them as much as practicable — but make no war upon them. They are powerful to do mischief to the few Emigrants who will form the first settlement. Wait until you get force and strength enough before you interfere with them. A Quixotic act might read well in print, but it might result in the destruction of the settlement.
>   Avoid interference with the slave trader therefore, until you have strength to interfere with effect.

[43] John L. Wilson to J. H. B. Latrobe, March 18, 1837 (cntd. on April 21), pp. 4–10, MSCS.

[44] Complaints of the missions engaging too much in trade and taking advantage of poor settlers would become more frequent. See John L. Wilson to J. H. B. Latrobe, March 18, 1837, p. 11; George R. McGill to J. H. B. Latrobe, Dec. 25, 1837, p. 2; John B. Russwurm to J. H. B. Latrobe, April 28, 1838, p. 1; John B. Russwurm to J. H. B. Latrobe, July 7, 1838, p. 4, all of which are in MSCS.

[45] "Proceedings of the Agent and Council," Dec. 4, 1836 and March 18, 1837; John L. Wilson to J. H. B. Latrobe, March 18, 1837 (cntd. on April 21), p. 11; John B. Russwurm to J. H. B. Latrobe, Monrovia, June 22, 1837, p. 2; John L. Wilson to J. H. B. Latrobe, July 6, 1837, pp. 1–3, all of which are in MSCS.

[46] John B. Russwurm to J. H. B. Latrobe, May 12, 1837, p. 1; John B. Russwurm to J. H. B. Latrobe, Monrovia, June 22, 1837, p. 1; John B. Russwurm to Ira Easter, June 2, 1837, p. 3, MSCS.

8. *"The Dismal Fountain of Vice"*

[1] Thomas S. Savage, journal entry for April 8, 1837, quoted in *The Spirit of Missions*, 2:309.

[2] Thomas S. Savage to Charles Snetter and others, Sept. 15, 1837, as quoted in a remonstrance of August 9, 1837, p. 7, MSCS.

[3] John L. Wilson to J. H. B. Latrobe, July 27, 1836 and July 6, 1837 (p. 2), MSCS.

[4] Thomson's rumored crimes: Thomas S. Savage to Charles Snetter and others, Sept. 15, 1837, as quoted in a remonstrance of August 9, 1837, p. 7; George McGill to J. H. B. Latrobe, Dec. 25, 1837, p. 3; John B. Russwurm to J. H. B. Latrobe, Dec. 27, 1837, p. 1; James M. Thomson to Oliver Holmes, Dec. 28, 1837, pp. 1–2, MSCS.

[5] James M. Thomson to Oliver Holmes, Dec. 28, 1837, pp. 2–3, MSCS.

[6] Thomas S. Savage to James M. Thomson, n.d., as quoted in Thomson to Holmes, Dec. 28, 1837, p. 8. The same is also quoted in the settler remonstrance, p. 13, with variations of spelling and punctuation.

[7] Thomas S. Savage to James M. Thomson, n.d., as quoted in Thomson to Holmes, Dec. 28, 1837, p. 9. Also paraphrased in the settler remonstrance, pp. 10–11.

[8] James M. Thomson to Oliver Holmes, Dec. 28, 1837, pp. 2–3, MSCS. Thomson referred to his confession a few lines further on as his "calamity — *cursed* folly — unguarded conscience."

[9] Thomas S. Savage to James M. Thomson, quoted in Thomson to Holmes, Dec. 27, 1837, p. 10, MSCS.

[10] Thomson to Holmes, Dec. 28, 1837, pp. 5–6, MSCS.

[11] Thomson brought before the court: George McGill to J. H. B. Latrobe, Dec. 25, 1837, p. 3; John B. Russwurm to J. H. B. Latrobe, Dec. 27, 1837, p. 2; Thomas Jackson, fragment of a letter, Dec. 27, 1837, all three in MSCS.

[12] Thomas Jackson, fragment of a letter, Dec. 27, 1837, MSCS.

[13] The Tubmans: Emigrant List; *Maryland Colonization Journal*, n.s. 1:57–58 (reprinted in the society's *Sixth Annual Report*); Record Book of the Board of Managers, 2:248–50, MSCS.

[14] Thomas Jackson to Franklin Anderson, July 6, 1837, p. 5, MSCS.

[15] Charles Snetter to J. H. B. Latrobe, July 9, 1837, p. 3, MSCS.

[16] John L. Wilson to J. H. B. Latrobe, July 6, 1837, p. 4, MSCS.

[17] James M. Thomson to Oliver Holmes, Dec. 28, 1837, p. 5, MSCS.

[18] Thomas S. Savage to James M. Thomson, about July 15, 1837, quoted in Thomson to Holmes, Dec. 28, 1837, pp. 10–11, MSCS.

[19] Remarkably, Russwurm was still trying to disentangle himself from Daily at the end of 1847. On November 8, that year, he authorized Hall to increase an offer to one of Daily's creditors to $1,000, hoping that that would end the matter. "Daily is a pretty fellow," he commented, "after spending so much and running our late concern in debt without even consulting me, to say, that he has been defrauded of one penny is infamous." At last report, Daily was in business at Sierra Leone, selling English goods, though he was unsure whether the scoundrel was still living, as "black vomit" was then epidemic there. (John B. Russwurm to James Hall, November 8, 1847 [first letter], pp. 2–3, MSCS.)

[20] Russwurm to Latrobe, Dec. 27, 1837, p. 2; Russwurm to Oliver Holmes, Dec. 27, 1837, MSCS.

[21] Accounts of the trial: George McGill to J. H. B. Latrobe, Dec. 25, 1837, pp. 3–4; John B. Russwurm to J. H. B. Latrobe, Dec. 27, 1837, pp. 2–3; Thomas Jackson, Fragment of a letter, Dec. 27, 1837; James M. Thomson to Oliver Holmes, Dec. 28, 1837, pp. 5–6, all in MSCS.

[22] George McGill to J. H. B. Latrobe, Dec. 25, 1837, p. 4, MSCS.

[23] "They are the weakest and most suspicious of all testimony; ever liable to be obtained by artifice, false hopes, promises of favor, or menaces; seldom remembered accurately, or reported with due precision; and incapable in their nature of being disproved by other negative evidence." Blackstone, *Commentaries*, Book IV, Section iv.

[24] Thomson takes back his evidence: George McGill to J. H. B. Latrobe, Dec. 25, 1837, pp. 4–5; John B. Russwurm to J. H. B. Latrobe, Dec. 27, 1837, pp. 2–3, both in MSCS.

[25] The court's decision: John B. Russwurm to J. H. B. Latrobe, Dec. 27, 1837, p. 3; George McGill to J. H. B. Latrobe, Dec. 25, 1837, p. 5; James M. Thomson to Oliver Holmes, Dec. 28, 1837, pp. 5–6, all in MSCS.

[26] The proceedings of the committee, with transcripts of some of Savage's letters, are preserved in a remonstrance drafted between August 9, and December 2, 1837, MSCS.

9. *"A Prey Unto Themselves"*

[1] John B. Russwurm to J. H. B. Latrobe, Feb. 12, 1837 (cntd. on April 10), p. 16, MSCS: "This scarcity will I hope, be a lesson to our colonists not to depend so much on the natives for rice in the future."

[2] John B. Russwurm to J. H. B. Latrobe, Nov. 14, 1837, pp. 1–3, MSCS. Henceforth, the prices were fixed at: "3 Romaul Handkerchiefs or 2 yds Satin Stripe or Blue Baft or 3 yds Cloth or 2 bars Iron or crockery for one croo Rice, and 3 bars of every description of goods for one croo palm oil."

[3] *Niobe* expedition: Emigrant List; John B. Russwurm to J. H. B. Latrobe, Jan. 18, 1838; Benjamin Alleyne to J. H. B. Latrobe, Jan. 18, 1838; Mathias Appleby to Ira Easter, Jan. 18, 1838, all in MSCS. Problems caused by *Niobe*: Alexander Hance to J. H. B. Latrobe, April 7, 1838; Alexander Hance to John Kennard, April 7, 1838; John B. Russwurm to J. H. B. Latrobe, April 26, 1838, pp. 1–2; "Annual Election at Cape Palmas," March 6, 1838, MSCS.

[4] Alexander Hance to John Kennard, April 7, 1838, p. 2, MSCS.

[5] John B. Russwurm to J. H. B. Latrobe, April 26, 1838, p. 18 (describes anniversary celebration), pp. 6–10 (recounts the trip to the Cavally River), MSCS.

[6] King Freeman to J. H. B. Latrobe, April 27, 1838, MSCS. The king asked for boats to attack the Cavally River towns.

[7] Tentative peace between agency and Episcopal mission: John B. Russwurm to J. H. B. Latrobe, April 28, 1838, p. 2; John B. Russwurm to Oliver Holmes, April 28, 1838, p. 2, MSCS.

[8] John L. Wilson to J. H. B. Latrobe, Jan. 16, 1838, pp. 1–2, MSCS.

[9] Case of John Banks: John L. Wilson to J. H. B. Latrobe, July 6, 1837, pp. 1–2; John L. Wilson to J. H. B. Latrobe, Jan. 16, 1838, p. 2; George McGill to J. H. B. Latrobe, Dec. 25, 1837, p. 2; John B. Russwurm to Oliver Holmes, April 28, 1838, p. 2, all in MSCS.

[10] These were copied and sent home with John B. Russwurm's despatch to J. H. B. Latrobe, April 28, 1838, MSCS.

[11] References to hard times: John B. Russwurm to J. H. B. Latrobe, April 26, 1838, pp. 3–6, 13, 15; John B. Russwurm to J. H. B. Latrobe, April 28, 1838, p. 3; John B. Russwurm to Oliver Holmes, April 28, 1838, pp. 1, 3, MSCS.

[12] John L. Wilson to N. L. Bayard, April 26, 1838, as quoted by Bayard in a letter to J. H. B. Latrobe, Savannah, July 10, 1838, p. 2, MSCS.

[13] George McGill to J. H. B. Latrobe, Dec. 25, 1837, p. 2, MSCS.

[14] O. A. Chambers to Ira Easter, July 10, 1838, MSCS.

[15] John B. Russwurm's reports are filled with accounts of activities on the Public Farms, including attempts to introduce new crops, to use draft animals, and to plow the soil. Settlers constantly asked for garden seeds and tools in their letters home, often noting their frustration at not being able to farm the way they had in America. The agent urged settlers to follow the Grebo lead in planting and harvesting times, but many resisted any change. See A. G. Hopkins, *An Economic History of West Africa* (New York: Columbia University Press, 1973), chapter 2, especially pp. 27–43 for a good discussion of the political economy of pre-colonial agricultural production.

[16] Launcelot B. Minor to J. H. B. Latrobe and Ira Easter, n.d. but probably April 1838. In a similar vein, Stephen Smith wrote Zachariah Tippett, his old master, on July 6, 1838, that he was "not pleased with the arrangement of the co[l]oney and the reason is that wee are all among the natives and thear is a nuf of them heare to tend evry foot of land that is heare and tha heave as much rite to the land as wee heve and as thea become inlightened theare would requier more room and wheare is it to come from." MSCS.

[17] Land degradation is the key to understanding the relative concept of overpopulation.

[18] See for example, Hopkins, *Economic History of West Africa.*

[19] Opportunities for estimating critical densities of population in an historical context are scarce. Africa poses particular problems, because its agricultural systems are relatively unfamiliar to Westerners, and specific facts about production in the past are hard to find, as are reliable demographic data. Maryland in Liberia's records are exceptionally detailed, however, and the circumstances they indicate encourage the researcher to consider the problem of chronic systemic food shortage. The analysis of such a situation in Grebo country is based on simple premises which are discussed at length in William Allen's, *The African Husbandman*, and other works, including numerous FAO-UN publications.

[20] Estimates of Grebo population: John Payne, quoted in Scott, *Day-dawn in Africa*, p. 55: 25,000; Lynch, *Report*, p. 52: 20,000 in 1853; T. Savage, in *The Spirit of Missions*, 3:148: 60,000 to 70,000 within a fifty-mile radius of Cape Palmas in 1838.

[21] James Hall to J. H. B. Latrobe, Feb. 9–16, 1834, pp. 4–5. A large manuscript map, "Maryland in Liberia," dated 1839, is in MSCS. Another useful document, "Map of the Grebo Country, Cape Palmas West Africa. 1841," appeared in *The Spirit of Missions*, vol. 3.

[22] Lowland varieties of rice were probably unknown to Grebo cultivators, never having been developed locally, though the lowland crops typically yield much more (forty or fifty bushels for every two planted). Horatio Bridge, *Journal of an African Cruiser* (repr. London: Dawsons, 1968), pp. 46–47. This is supported by Charles Rockwell, *Sketches of Foreign Travel* (Boston, 1842), 2:265. See also, Schnell, *Plantes Alimentaires*, p. 78; and V. A. Oyenga, *Agriculture in Nigeria, An Introduction* (Rome: FAO-UN, 1967), p. 194.

[23] P. W. Porter, "Liberia," in *The World Atlas of Agriculture* (Novara, Italy: Istituto Geographico de Agostini, 1976), 4:291–92, gives detailed figures on the subject.

[24] P. W. Porter, "Liberia," p. 292, reports that the rate observed in Maryland County in the 1970s was sixteen years.

[25] John Payne, quoted in *The Spirit of Missions*, 6:17. Early commentators indicate that the rice trade with the interior was voluminous and jealously guarded. "Unlike the natives of Cape Palmas," John Payne wrote of Grand Cavally, "this people, having no American settlement amongst them — having a poor, exhausted soil to cultivate, situated at the mouth of the river on the seacoast, are in every respect interested in maintaining an extensive and uninterrupted intercourse with the interior natives; while the latter depending upon them for salt, as well as all foreign manufactures, are equally interested in cultivating it."

[26] John B. Russwurm to J. H. B. Latrobe, April 28, 1838, p. 1, MSCS.

[27] John L. Wilson to Ira Easter, July 5, 1838, p. 4, MSCS. In a letter to J. H. B. Latrobe, dated July 5, 1838, Nathan Lee complained bitterly about the contempt with which Greboes treated settlers: "it is Sir much as ever we can do to pass without being terribly abused. it is the cry of the Natives Most Special these young lads [i.e. mission scholars] calling us Slaves" (p. 2, MSCS).

[28] Eben Parker: Emigrant List; Census of 1837, both in MSCS.

[29] The most detailed account of Parker's troubles, from which this narrative is drawn is a remonstrance to the Board of Managers, January 8, 1839, pp. 2–3, MSCS. See also, John B. Russwurm to J. H. B. Latrobe, August 21, 1838, pp. 2–3, MSCS, for a more critical account of Parker.

[30] Poor relations between colony and Greboes: Minutes of the Agent and Council, June 16, 1838; Benjamin Alleyne to Ira Easter, July 10, 1838, p. 4, MSCS.

[31] N. J. Bayard to Ira Easter, Savannah, Ga., March 4, 1837, reports reasons for delaying the emigration of his slaves.

[32] John L. Wilson to Ira Easter, July 5, 1838, MSCS. Other references to the difficult times may be found in: E. Byron to Ira Easter, July 4, 1838; Alexander Hance to Ira Easter, July 5, 1838; Jane Wilson to Oliver Holmes, July 5, 1838; John B. Russwurm to J. H. B. Latrobe, July 7, 1838; B. Alleyne to Ira Easter, July 10, 1838; John B. Russwurm to J. H. B. Latrobe, Nov. 1, 1838, pp. 3–4, all in MSCS.

[33] John B. Russwurm to J. H. B. Latrobe, Aug. 21, 1838, pp. 2–3; Snetter, et al. to the Board of Managers, Jan. 8, 1839, pp. 2–3, MSCS.

[34] Attack on Eben Parker's homestead: "Extract from John Wilson's Diary," August 13, 1838; John B. Russwurm to J. H. B. Latrobe, August 6, 1838; "Proceedings of a Court of Inquiry," August 18 and 20, 1838; John B. Russwurm to J. H. B. Latrobe, August 21, 1838, pp. 2–3, all in MSCS.

[35] *Joshua*, Chapter VIII, v. 26–8: "For Joshua drew not his hand back, wherewith he stretched out the spear, until he had utterly destroyed all the inhabitants of Ai. Only the cattle and the spoil of that city Israel took for a prey unto themselves, according unto the word of the Lord which he commanded Joshua. And Joshua burnt Ai, and made it an heap for ever, *even* a desolation unto this day." For the aftermath of Parker's murder: John B. Russwurm to J. H. B. Latrobe, August 21, 1838, p. 2; John B. Russwurm to J. H. B. Latrobe, Nov. 1, 1838, pp. 8–10; John B. Russwurm to Oliver Holmes, May 24, 1839, p. 2; Snetter et al. to the Board of Managers, Jan. 8, 1839, p. 5, all in MSCS.

[36] John B. Russwurm to J. H. B. Latrobe, Nov. 1, 1838, p. 9, MSCS.

[37] Proceedings of the Agent and Council, August 8, 1838, MSCS.

[38] "Proceedings of a Court of Inquiry," August 18 and 20, 1838, p. 7, also transcribed in "Minutes of a Public Meeting," Sept. 5, 1838, both in MSCS.

[39] "Minutes of a Public Meeting," Sept. 5, 1838, MSCS.

[40] "Remonstrance of Citizens of Maryland in Liberia," Sept. 12, 1838, MSCS.

[41] John B. Russwurm to J. H. B. Latrobe, August 21, 1838, p. 3, MSCS.

[42] For comments on Snetter's activities after his conviction, see: John B. Russwurm to J. H. B. Latrobe, Nov. 1, 1838, pp. 8–9; Snetter et al. to the Board of Managers, Jan. 8, 1839, pp. 8–9; John B. Russwurm to Oliver Holmes, May 24, 1839, pp. 1–3, all in MSCS.

[43] Snetter boarded a ship bound for Monrovia in late January or February, 1839. He rejoined his wife and son, but he would find no peace. As captain commanding the Rifle Corps, he would soon lead a campaign against an African state.

In 1836, Sao Boso, a powerful king in the hinterland of Monrovia, who was friendly to the Liberians, died. Afterwards, rival chiefs fought for control of the old king's territories and valuable trade routes into the interior. One of these men, Getumbe, a supplier of slaves, came to the fore because of his outstanding ferocity. In 1838 he nearly wiped out the Dei, who in 1820 had sold the first tract of land to the American settlers. The survivors of Getumbe's attack fled to a spot near the settlement of Millsburg, and the colonial authorities promised to protect them. Getumbe, scornful of Liberia's power, attacked the Dei settlement late in 1839. Millsburg's militia turned out to defend their African neighbors and prevented a general massacre. Even so, Getumbe's forces wounded four and took away twelve captives. Settlers urgently called Governor Buchanan for aid. He sent cannons and troops, and followed soon after to try and make a peaceful end to the palaver. His negotiations failed.

On March 8, 1840, a detachment of three or four hundred of Getumbe's soldiers, under command of one Getorah, attacked the Methodist mission at Heddington, a few miles upriver from Millsburg. Mr. Brown, the minister in charge, and his staff put up a fierce resistance. Getorah was reported to have "brought his pot for the purpose of cooking his breakfast of Mr. Brown," but no such thing occurred. On the contrary, he and fifty of his men were killed, and an untold number wounded.

Since it was now evident that conciliation would not work, Buchanan prepared massive retaliation. On March 23 he assembled an expedition of some two hundred militiamen. Snetter had command of the Rifle Corps. At first light on the twenty-seventh, the troops struck north from Millsburg, through the forest toward Suehn, Getumbe's fortified town. A heavy downpour impeded their progress across the trackless forest, and six miles along, the army laid aside its cannons. They halted at two in the afternoon at a town recently destroyed by Getumbe and camped there for the night. Before dawn the next day they were on their feet again. "The path was so narrow that we had to follow each other in single file," Governor Buchanan reported soon after. Rains during the preceding two days had flooded the swamps and streams, so that "the chief alternations of the route were mud to the knees and water to the waist." At ten in the morning, they paused for breakfast, aware that their goal was near, but unsure just where it was or what they would find. Three hours later, the column, still single file, with Snetter and his son in the lead, advanced up a long slope, having just scrambled up from a muddy gully. A force of Getumbe's soldiers lay in wait and opened fire. Snetter and his son both fell, mortally wounded. The Liberian soldiers did not falter, however, and went quickly about their work, destroying Getumbe's town with little more loss of life. Charles Snetter was carried back to Millsburg, where he died the following morning in great pain.

For details of the expedition against Getumbe: *The African Repository*, 16 (1841): 118, 177–80, and 17 (1842): 41; Svend Holsoe, "A Study of Relations Between Settlers and Indigenous Peoples in Western Liberia, 1821–1847," in *African Historical Studies*, 4 (1971): 346–52.

10. *"Suitable Locations for Man"*

[1] See Colonial Accounts for the period. Also: John B. Russwurm to J. H. B. Latrobe, Jan. 30, 1839, pp. 1–2; John B. Russwurm to J. H. B. Latrobe, Dec. 8, 1839, p. 6; King Freeman and Simleh Ballah to J. H. B. Latrobe, June 9, 1840: all in MSCS.

[2] References to draft animals and agriculture: Benjamin Tubman, Sr. to J. H. B. Latrobe, April 28, 1838: description of his farm; Launcelot B. Minor to the Board of Managers, April 28, 1838: on soil quality and introduction of tropical crops; John L. Wilson to Ira Easter, July 5, 1838, p. 3, criticism of settlers for attention to lumber rather than farming, leaving them dependent on Grebo farmers; John Payne to Ira Easter, July 6, 1838, pp. 1–2, on his unsuccessful experiments with corn and the potential of tropical crops; John B. Russwurm to J. H. B. Latrobe, July 7, 1838, pp. 6–7, on need for draft animals; Asbury Wilson to Ira Easter, July 7, 1838: disappointment with soil quality, description of his farm; B. Alleyne to Ira Easter, July 10, 1838, p. 4, on settler improvidence and neglect of farms; O. A. Chambers to Ira Easter, July, 1838: hopes that hard times would encourage settlers to raise more food; John B. Russwurm to J. H. B. Latrobe, Nov. 1, 1838, p. 1, favorable prospects for farming, p. 2, destitution of Gbenelu, p. 4,

increase of land under cultivation, experiments on Public Farm, need for draft animals, difficulty persuading settlers of nobility of agriculture, p. 5, comments on choice between wage labor and farming, pp. 5–7, more on crop introduction; Paul Sansay to Ira Easter, Jan. 16, 1839: description of his farm, with agrarian ideal; George R. McGill to J. H. B. Latrobe, Jan. 17, 1839: growing sugar at new Mt. Tubman farm; Joseph Orderly to Capt. Mason: Jan. 20, 1839: description of his farm, growing peanuts, rice, and cotton; John B. Russwurm to J. H. B. Latrobe, Jan. 30, 1839, pp. 2–3, on sugar cane; Robert MacDowell to Latrobe, April 9, 1839, pp. 1–2, soils and climate at Cape Palmas, vegetable gardens, lack of exportable crops, settler impatience with slow return of farming, prizes for best farms, example of the Public farms; S. F. McGill to Ira Easter, April 16, 1839: on agricultural progress of colony during his absence; Thomas Jackson to Ira Easter, April 21, 1839: on progress of agriculture; R. MacDowell to J. H. B. Latrobe, April 21, 1839: on agriculture and need for draft animals; John B. Russwurm to J. H. B. Latrobe, April 23, 1839, pp. 1–2, the Mt. Tubman farm, abundance of produce, especially potatoes, pp. 2–3, need for draft animals; Anthony Howard to Oliver Holmes, May 20, 1839: state of his farm; Catherine Ross to Ira Easter and John Kennard, May 21, 1839: state of her farm, problems starting with nothing; John B. Russwurm to Oliver Holmes, May 24, 1839, p. 4, notes on crop introduction; John B. Russwurm to J. H. B. Latrobe, June 24, 1839: the yam and cassava crops; Benjamin Tubman to J. H. B. Latrobe, June, 1839: the plowing of his land; John B. Russwurm to J. H. B. Latrobe, Dec. 8, 1839, pp. 1–3, progress of agriculture, the Grebo harvest, p. 7, the beach's dependence on interior for rice; Agricultural Survey of Maryland in Liberia, end of 1839, all in MSCS.

[3] References to the palaver include: King Freeman to J. H. B. Latrobe, April 27, 1838: the King asks for boats to attack Ploroh; John B. Russwurm to J. H. B. Latrobe, April 28, 1838, p. 3, contemplates a military campaign; John B. Russwurm to Oliver Holmes, April 28, 1838, p. 2, on Baphro's treachery, poverty of the river towns; Russwurm to Latrobe, July 7, 1838: p. 5, Toureh in open rebellion against Robookah; John B. Russwurm to J. H. B. Latrobe, Nov. 1, 1838 (cntd. at later dates), pp. 1–3, the grand palaver; John B. Russwurm to J. H. B. Latrobe, April 7, 1839: discusses resolution of the palaver, all in MSCS.

[4] Fortification of Mt. Tubman: George R. McGill to J. H. B. Latrobe, April 26, 1838, p. 1; John B. Russwurm to J. H. B. Latrobe, Nov. 1, 1838 (cntd. at later dates), pp. 6–7, both MSCS.

[5] George McGill: George R. McGill to J. H. B. Latrobe, April 26, 1838, p. 2; John B. Russwurm to J. H. B. Latrobe, April 26, 1838, p. 17; George R. McGill to J. H. B. Latrobe, Jan. 17, 1839; John B. Russwurm to J. H. B. Latrobe, Jan. 30, 1839, pp. 2–3, all in MSCS.

[6] Dr. E. E. Phelps to Ira Easter, Windsor, Vt., Jan. 9, 1837, MSCS.

[7] Ira Easter to Samuel Ford McGill, Baltimore, Jan. 17, 1837, MSCS.

[8] Dr. E. E. Phelps to Ira Easter, Windsor, Vt., Feb. 27, 1837, MSCS. One might interpret Dr. Phelps's decision to have McGill have his meals with a black family as a sign of prejudice, however that would conflict with the clear generosity he was showing in other respects. It is more likely that he wished to maintain a more formal hierarchy of teacher and student and moreover to provide the young man with some sociability he might not otherwise have had.

[9] McGill's correspondence with Moses Sheppard is among the Sheppard Papers in the Friends' Historical Library at Swarthmore College. Samuel Ford McGill to Ira Easter, Windsor, Vt., June 29, 1837, MSCS.

[10] Decision to send McGill to Dartmouth: Dr. E. E. Phelps to Ira Easter, Windsor, Vt., July 17, 1837; Samuel Ford McGill to Ira Easter, Windsor, Vt. July 17, 1837: both in MSCS.

[11] Samuel Ford McGill to Ira Easter, Hanover, N.H., Aug. 17, 1837, MSCS.

[12] Samuel Ford McGill to Ira Easter, Windsor, Vt., Jan 29, 1838, MSCS.

[13] Later references to McGill's education: Samuel Ford McGill to Ira Easter, Hanover, Aug. 11, 1838; Samuel Ford McGill to Ira Easter, Hanover, Oct. 16, 1838: both in MSCS.

[14] See the Emigrant List.

[15] Samuel Ford McGill to Ira Easter, April 16, 1839, MSCS.

[16] Wilson's cruise to leeward: R. MacDowell, "Essay on the Effects of Western Colonies in suppressing the Slave Trade," April, 1839, p. 3; John B. Russwurm to J. H. B. Latrobe, April 23, 1839, p. 2, MSCS.

[17] John B. Russwurm to J. H. B. Latrobe, Dec. 8, 1839, p. 1, MSCS.

[18] Catherine Ross to Ira Easter and John Kennard, May 21, 1839, MSCS.

[19] Morality and jails: John B. Russwurm to J. H. B. Latrobe, Dec. 8, 1839, pp. 3–4, 5; R. MacDowell to Latrobe, April 9, 1839, p. 2, MSCS.

[20] John B. Russwurm to J. H. B. Latrobe, Dec. 8, 1839, p. 1, on the rice harvest, pp. 6–7, on relations with Greboes, MSCS.

[21] John B. Russwurm to J. H. B. Latrobe, Dec. 8, 1839, pp. 7–8, MSCS.

[22] John B. Russwurm to J. H. B. Latrobe, Jan. 18, 1840, p. 1, MSCS.

[23] McGill assumes medical practice: Samuel Ford McGill to J. H. B. Latrobe, Jan. 20, 1840; Samuel Ford McGill to J. H. B. Latrobe, June 8, 1840; John B. Russwurm to J. H. B. Latrobe, June 10, 1840, p. 4, all in MSCS.

[24] Settler attempts at farming, 1840: John B. Russwurm to J. H. B. Latrobe, Jan. 18, 1840, pp. 1–3; John B. Russwurm to J. H. B. Latrobe, April 7, 1840; Samuel Ford McGill to J. H. B. Latrobe, June 8, 1840; L. B. Minor to J. H. B. Latrobe, June 8, 1840; John B. Russwurm to J. H. B. Latrobe, June 10, 1840; John B. Russwurm to J. H. B. Latrobe, July 27, 1840, p. 1; John B. Russwurm to J. H. B. Latrobe, Sept. 27, 1840, pp. 1–3, all in MSCS.

[25] Condition of settlement, late 1840: Samuel Ford McGill to J. H. B. Latrobe, Sept. 26, 1840; John B. Russwurm to J. H. B. Latrobe, Sept. 27, 1840; John B. Russwurm to J. H. B. Latrobe, Jan. 27, 1841, all in MSCS.

[26] Purchase of a boat: John B. Russwurm to J. H. B. Latrobe, June 10, 1840, pp. 3–4, MSCS; Christopher Fyfe, *A History of Sierra Leone* (London: Oxford University Press, 1963) p. 133, identifies Spence as an Englishman who set up a factory near the River Cestos in 1820. He says that Spence died at Sierra Leone in 1839.

[27] Agency trade: John B. Russwurm to J. H. B. Latrobe, July 27, 1840, p. 1; John B. Russwurm to J. H. B. Latrobe, Sept. 27, 1840, pp. 1–3; Samuel Ford McGill to J. H. B. Latrobe, Sept. 26, 1840, p. 1, all in MSCS.

[28] The oil trade: James Hall to J. H. B. Latrobe, Sierra Leone, Aug. 28, 1840; John B. Russwurm to J. H. B. Latrobe, June 10, 1840, pp. 3–4; John B. Russwurm to J. H. B. Latrobe, July 27, 1840, p. 2, all in MSCS. James Hall's letter is misfiled in the letterbook for 1839.

[29] Trade at beginning of 1841: John B. Russwurm to J. H. B. Latrobe, Jan. 27, 1841: comments on protested drafts; John B. Russwurm to J. H. B. Latrobe, May 31, 1841, pp. 4–5, increasing English participation in oil trade; John B. Russwurm to J. H. B. Latrobe, May 31, 1841, pp. 4–5, on Agency trade and another protested draft, p. 7, the ruinous nature of the oil trade this season, warning against investing too much in it, all in MSCS.

[30] John B. Russwurm to J. H. B. Latrobe, May 31, 1841, p. 1, MSCS.

[31] Ibid., pp. 1, 6, MSCS.

[32] Russwurm's desire to purchase Fishtown: John B. Russwurm to J. H. B. Latrobe, March 12, 1841, p. 2; John B. Russwurm to J. H. B. Latrobe, Sept. 27, 1840, pp. 2–3, both in MSCS.

[33] Purchase of another boat: John B. Russwurm to J. H. B. Latrobe, March 12, 1841, pp. 1, 3; John Revey to J. H. B. Latrobe, April 8, 1841, p. 1, both in MSCS.

[34] The *Latrobe*: John B. Russwurm to J. H. B. Latrobe, March 12, 1841, pp. 1,3; J. Revey to J. H. B. Latrobe, April 8, 1841; Samuel Ford McGill to J. H. B. Latrobe, April 9, 1841, p. 1; John B. Russwurm to J. H. B. Latrobe, May 31, 1841, pp. 1–2, 5–6, all in MSCS.

[35] John B. Russwurm to J. H. B. Latrobe, May 31, 1841, p. 2, MSCS.

[36] Ibid., pp. 2–4, MSCS.

[37] Russwurm's wish to resign, his fight with Wilson: John B. Russwurm to J. H. B. Latrobe, June 24, 1841, pp. 1–2; "Correspondence concerning Missionary Trade," July – August, 1841, pp. 1–3; John B. Russwurm to J. H. B. Latrobe, Sept. 22, 1841, pp. 1–3; George McGill to the Board of Managers, Sept. 24, 1841, p. 2, all in MSCS.

[38] Henry Hannon to the Board of Managers, Sept. 17, 1841, pp. 1–2, MSCS.

[39] John B. Russwurm to J. H. B. Latrobe, Sept. 22, 1841, pp. 1–2, MSCS.

[40] "Correspondence concerning Missionary Trade," July–August, 1841: MSCS.

[41] Settler attitude toward African education: John B. Russwurm to J. H. B. Latrobe, Dec. 8, 1839, p. 8; B. V. R. James to J. Kennard, May 21, 1839, p. 3; R. MacDowell to Easter, May 21, 1839: all in MSCS.

[42] Samuel Ford McGill to J. H. B. Latrobe, June 8, 1839, pp. 2–3, MSCS.

[43] John B. Russwurm to J. H. B. Latrobe, Sept. 22, 1841, p. 2, MSCS.

[44] As quoted in *Maryland Colonization Journal*, n.s. Vol. I, pp. 275–77.

[45] John B. Russwurm to J. H. B. Latrobe, Sept. 22, 1841, p. 2, MSCS.

[46] Benjamin Bostick to John Kennard, n.d. (August or September, 1841), MSCS.

[47] John B. Russwurm to J. H. B. Latrobe, Sept. 22, 1841 (cntd. on Oct. 10), pp. 5–6, MSCS.

[48] John B. Russwurm to J. H. B. Latrobe, Sept. 22, 1841, pp. 4–5, MSCS.

[49] George R. McGill to the Board of Managers, Sept. 24, 1841, p. 2, MSCS.

11. *"Muskets Are Too Light"*

[1] The Roman Catholic Mission: Minute Book of the Executive Committee of the Maryland State Colonization Society, Number 3," entry for September 27, 1841, MS, MSCS; "The Mission to Liberia: Diary of the Rev. John Kelly," in *Historical Records and Studies*, 14 (1920): 120–53; "Journal of John Kelly, Catholic Mission Ss. Peter and Paul, Cape Palmas, W. Africa, 1842," in *Notes et Documents Relatifs a la Vie et a l'Oeuvre du Ven. F.-M.-P. Liebermann*, 5 (1936): 145–80; *Maryland Colonization Journal*, n.s., 1:85–87; MacMaster, "Bishop Barron and the West African Missions, 1841–1845," in *Historical Records and Studies*, 6 (1910): 83–129.

[2] First acts of the Catholics: Kelly, "The Mission to Liberia," pp. 123–25; John Russwurm to J. H. B. Latrobe, Feb. 12, 1842, p. 5, MSCS; Russwurm to Latrobe, April 7, 1842, p. 3, MSCS.

[3] Catholics' relations with other missions: Kelly, "The Mission to Liberia," *passim*, esp. p. 123.

[4] Subsequent Catholic activities: Kelly, "The Mission to Liberia," pp. 133–53.

[5] John Russwurm to J. H. B. Latrobe, Feb. 12, 1842, pp. 1, 4, MSCS.

[6] Ibid., pp. 1–3, MSCS.

[7] French at Garroway: John Russwurm to J. H. B. Latrobe, Feb. 12, 1842, p. 3; Russwurm to Latrobe, April 7, 1842, pp. 1–2, both in MSCS.

The Maryland State Colonization Society received news of the French purchase of Garroway with mixed feelings. James Hall wondered in an editorial for *Maryland Colonization Journal* why European powers had not taken control of the entire West African coast a long time since, "for the cost of one ship of the line," to enforce sovereignty. The United States was missing an opportunity, he asserted. Legitimate trade was growing tremendously, and items in demand on the coast were either American products or ones that American industry could supply more cheaply than Europeans. If the British and French decided to occupy the coast, they would exclude American merchants. The doctor wrote with considerable irony, though, that if America would ignore Africa, he was thankful at least for the civilizing agency of the European powers. Even if the French made Roman Catholics of the inhabitants of Garroway, that was better than to leave them as they were. Black Americans could do better, though, because they would settle among the African community, providing an example of civilized life. Moreover, they would introduce a more tolerant religion, he thought. "No matter however good may be the intentions of the French government towards the natives in establishing her colonies," he wrote,

> still the character of the agents which they must of necessity employ, will essentially change the character of the operations from the intent of the government. 'Tis the management of an affair at arms length at second and third hands through the agents of agencies, and therefore to great disadvantages. But we have no guarantee that benefit to the African, forms any part of the plan of the French government, and doubtless any good that can result to them must be incidental and entirely a secondary consideration. The extending of their empire and increasing their commerce are of course their main objects, and the influence of colonies established for such motives on savage nations is already but too well known.

Hall also worried that a French colony at Garroway might attract settlers from Cape Palmas in search of better employment, yet he consoled himself with the thought that settlers would not have crossed the ocean and suffered to make a new life for themselves, "merely to exchange one white master for another!" (*Maryland Colonization Journal*, n.s., 2:37–39.)

[8] Fishtown and A.B.C.F.M.: John Russwurm to J. H. B. Latrobe, April 7, 1842, p. 2; Russwurm to Latrobe, June 26, 1843; Russwurm to Latrobe, July 31, 1843, all in MSCS.

[9] Launcelot Byrd Minor was born September 9, 1813, at "Topping Castle" in Caroline County, Virginia, an heir to a gentry family of the first rank. His father was General John Minor, of Fredericksburg. His mother, Lucy, was the daughter of Landon Carter, an heir of Robert "King" Carter, the grandest of the old Virginia planters. The boy developed an adventurous, wandering, introverted personality, living with various relatives during his youth, used to long wilderness tramps, painfully self-conscious in society. He was raised

to follow the moral values of the Roman Stoics, influenced by one uncle in particular, who also provided him with the works of Mungo Park and other explorers. At the age of sixteen, he enrolled in Kenyon College, in Ontario, where his education was considerably broadened. Three times, he walked from school to Fredericksburg, each time arriving home penniless because he could not resist calls for charity. These journeys accustomed him to hunger, exposure, and other hardships, but they also damaged his health, and he struggled with bouts of illness. His mother was extremely religious, and she pushed her son, by nature a pious person, to devote his life to the church. He had resisted her to some extent, but at the age of nineteen he nearly died as a result of his third trek. He experienced a conversion, and in the fall of 1833 he entered the Virginia Theological Seminary at Alexandria. There, with John Payne and Dr. Thomas Savage, he resolved to devote his life to the evangelization of Africa. (See *Maryland Colonization Journal* and *The Spirit of Missions* for biographical details.)

Concerning African competition to control the coast, see M. C. Perry to David Henshaw, Aboard U.S.F. *Macedonian*, Sierra Leone, Jan. 15, 1844, quoted in Senate Document 150, pp. 55–56:

> It is considered, by all those tribes living within one or two hundred miles of the seacoast, a great advantage to have possession of the immediate coast or "beach," as they term it; and, to gain this advantage, wars are frequent among them, and the coveted territory invariably falls to the most warlike and powerful.
>
> In this manner the Cracow tribe, originally occupying a territory about two days' journey in the interior, fought their way to the sea side, and seized from the Bassa and Berriby people about ten miles of coast, upon which they erected . . . five towns.

[10] Launcelot B. Minor to Hon. Abel P. Upshur, Secretary of the Navy, Tabou, April 25, 1842, as quoted in E. F. Hening, *History of the African Mission of the Protestant Episcopal Church in the United States, with Memoirs of Deceased Missionaries, and Notices of Native Customs* (New York, 1850), pp. 183–84.

Other accounts of the attack on *Mary Carver*: John Russwurm to Matthew C. Perry, July 10, 1843: as quoted in Senate Document 150, pp. 40–41, with specific details of who was responsible; John Russwurm to J. H. B. Latrobe, May 24, 1842, p. 2, MSCS.

[11] Benjamin Griswold to Prof. Goodrich, Feb. 5, 1842, p. 3, in Ford Collection, New York Public Library.

[12] John Russwurm to J. H. B. Latrobe, May 24, 1842, pp. 1–2, MSCS.

[13] McGill and Alexander Crummell: Moses, Wilson J., *Alexander Crummell: A Study of Civilization and Discontent* (New York: Oxford University Press, 1989), p. 166; Rigsby, Gregory U., *Alexander Crummell: Pioneer in Nineteenth-century Pan-African Thought; Contributions in Afro-American and African Studies, No. 101* (New York: Greenwood Press, 1987).

McGill was among the first backers of Liberia College, at which E. W. Blyden was a professor. The two must have been well acquainted with each other.

McGill and Martin Delany: Ulman, Victor, *Martin R. Delany: The Beginnings of Black Nationalism* (Boston: Beacon Press, 1971), pp. 228–32. When Martin Delany, who is commonly described as the first African American to earn a medical degree in the

United States, sojourned at Monrovia during July and August, 1859, he stayed with Dr. McGill. Their conversations were not recorded, but they must indeed have been fascinating. Subsequently, he stayed for a month at Mt. Vaughan, the guest of Alexander Crummell.

[14] *Maryland Colonization Journal*, n.s., 1:257–59.

[15] *Maryland Colonization Journal*, n.s., 1:260–63. Americans at home and in Liberia debated whether settlers would ever effect substantial cultural change among Africans, or, as they put it, "civilize," Africa. I have already discussed this notion of civilization in note 16, chapter 1. See John Russwurm to J. H. B. Latrobe, July 31, 1843, p. 2, MSCS, for the following passage:

> Giving all due credit to other influences, at work among the natives, I question, if all united, are doing as much for the civilization of Africa, as the location of a colony of people civilized, of a like complexion, in their midst. If this is a continent ever to be civilized, God has decreed, that the work is to be accomplished by Colored men, who are to be the pioneers in planting colonies and schools in all quarters — and doing all of the efficient labor towards carrying forward this great end. The mere teaching of letters, without a knowledge of some mechanical art, will never civilize a savage — he must also be taught to support himself as a civilized Being — in which state, he has a hundred more wants, for all of which he must be able to provide.

The rhetoric laid aside, settlers did have tremendous influence on their neighbors. Greboes held American technology and industrial products in high esteem. The magical power of the written word awed them. Most settlers took in African children to work around the house or on the farms in return for room and board. African parents were often eager to place their children in such situations so they could learn English and other skills. Most such "apprentices" were afraid or disapproving of many American customs. They loyally maintained their own, and in the colony's first few years, only a handful wholeheartedly adopted American culture. Those who did were sheltered by the missions or in settler homes.

In February 1843, Ford McGill, returning to Africa on the *Globe*, came ashore at Monrovia to visit his brothers. He prevailed on brother Roszell, who had charge of G. McGill and Sons' interests there, to give him the use of a young African as a house-servant for his new wife. On the run to Cape Palmas, McGill had argued with Rev. Samuel Hazlehurst, a new Episcopal missionary, that he, a man without religion, could still bring about the "civilization" and conversion of his new servant. They made a light-hearted bet, and in honor of the occasion, McGill dubbed the boy "Chancellor Walworth," to mock the author of the American board's critique of Maryland.

The desired effects were not long in coming. On reaching Harper, McGill had Walworth clothed in American fashion and sent him to church each Sunday. At first, the change of circumstance did not rest easily, and Walworth often fought with other boys, ducking work when he could. After a few weeks, he became friendly with African servants in Russwurm's household and began to attend Methodist meetings with them. In April or May, the Methodists held one of their periodic revivals, which included emotional night meetings. McGill told Walworth to attend, and the experience brought on a crisis, the classic overwhelming sense of sin and ensuing acceptance of the Christian promise of salvation. In an essay on the subject, McGill quoted what Walworth told him: "Long time my heart no lay down, plenty! plenty trouble!!! I beg God, I no sleep, I no eat, I cry all time, Debbil trouble me plenty, he go catch me, but I pray hard for God, him done hear my word, and he make my heart lay down." Walworth joined a Sunday school class and with newfound energy learned the intricacies of his adoptive culture. By the end of June, he was generally recognized as a changed man. See S. F. McGill, "Chancellor Walworth," MSCS Letterbook 1843, reprinted in *Maryland Colonization Journal*, n.s., 2:33–35.

Thus Ford McGill won his bet: settlers had influence, just as missionaries, in transforming the lives of Africans. Yet this process of *civilization* was full of contradictions, for the individuals who made the change found themselves cut off from their families and community, but still unaccepted by Americans. Having given up the culture of his childhood, aspiring to a new way of life shown by settlers and their ministers, Walworth could never return to his old life. For all this, he remained an African, with all the negative associations the term held for Americans. His was now a lonely life, where employment was assured, but opportunities for social advancement limited, analogous to the situation of free black people in the South.

In fact, Walworth's position was probably somewhat better than that of the converts of the Protestant missionaries, who segregated them in private villages, away from both settlers and unconverted Africans. Descriptions of such enclaves: Hening, *History*, p. 156; Scott, *Day-dawn*, pp. 45, 86–89; Brittan, *Every-day Life*, p. 55. Mary Moran's *Civilized Women* describes the descendants of such people as they live today in Harper.

[16] The *Globe* expedition: Emigrant List; *Maryland Colonization Journal*, n.s., 1:289–90. During the summer of 1842, Joshua Cornish was especially successful at persuading old friends in Dorchester County, on Maryland's Eastern Shore, to return with him to Africa. He had originally emigrated to Africa early in 1838 aboard the *Niobe*, on her second voyage, with his wife and four young children. James Hall later wrote of meeting Cornish on his farm on Holmes Road, near the edge of the settlement about 1840. "The whole lot was under cultivation," he wrote,

> well secured by a light yet sufficient fence; the house was a neat little twelve-footer, weather-boarded and shingled, flanked by a snug little piggery and fowl-house: the whole surrounded and overshadowed by the beautiful broad-leaved plantain and banana, swaying to and fro under the heavy masses of its golden fruit. The rich perennial lima and butter beans formed a beautiful arbor, which screened the labourer from the mid-day sun and furnished an important item for the dinner table. In the back ground was a large field of the sweet potato, whose broad ridges were cracked into large veins, indicating the heavy growth beneath. This was the homestead — the domain of the free man Joshua Cornish.

The East New Market Colonization Society had corresponded with Cornish since his departure. They urged him to come visit them, to demonstrate the opportunities presented by colonization. Early in 1842 he provided for his family and reluctantly returned to America aboard the schooner *Herald* of Boston.

James Hall seems to have liked Cornish and took time to get to know him. He recorded the settler's oral autobiography for *Maryland Colonization Journal* in language that rings true and offers interesting detail:

> I dont know sir 'zactly where I was born, nor how old I be, but I reckon I is well nigh sixty, and I believe I was born near Cambridge, in Dorchester County, and was owned by Mr. David Parker, who sold me to Mr. Samuel Elsby when I was right smart of a boy, near about twelve year old. When he died I fell to his wife and then to Major Newton of New Market, whose slave I always was till I went to Cape Palmas. I had two wives both free women, but was not properly married to any one till I went to Africa. Major Newton said a good many years ago that I might have my freedom if I would go to Africa, but I would not, all the coloured folks believed we was only to go to Georgia, and did not believe a word of all the talk about Africa. But one time I heard Mr. Hersey preach at a camp-meeting, and he told about Africa, said he had been there and knew all about it, I did not believe he would lie, so I began to think I should like to go and be free rather than to live a slave all my life, and I knew I never could be free here. But all the coloured people again persuaded me not to go. After a while Mr. Hance came over from Africa and I heard him tell all about it, and I determined to go if one-half he said was true. After I made up my mind to go I would not go near the coloured people till I got ready, for I knew they would persuade me out ont, I remember when I was going down to the boat with master, that a coloured blacksmith, named Josiah Bowley, asked me where I was going, I told him to Africa, you fool you, said he, you are going to Georgia, for tis the only way your master can sell you. Well I though I'd run the risk and went on. Well we got aboard the boat at last, all on us, and we was glad enough to get away from the coloured people of Baltimore, who kept telling us we was fools, and should all be sold to Georgia, or die with fever or be eat up by snakes.

As a matter of fact, the society lost many potential emigrants because of the concerted opposition of the black community. Africa held no romance for them, and it was an easy matter to persuade simple country people that they would either die in the African wilds or be offered for sale in the Deep South. Most black people believed that white colonizationists, who would never have to risk their lives there, could invent all the myth they wanted about "Ethiopia" and the black man's Promised Land, but America, however bad, was home, where they felt that black people had a duty to struggle for equal rights. See *Maryland Colonization Journal*, n.s., 1:220–22.

[17] Voyage of the *Globe*: S. F. McGill to James Hall, Feb. 17, 1843, pp. 1–2; John Russwurm to J. H. B. Latrobe, Feb. 20, 1843, p. 1, both in MSCS.

On February 25, twenty-four adults who had been slaves of Richard and Elizabeth Tubman gathered to divide $2,659.36, the balance of a bequest from their former master. A cash box was brought out, and each one signed a receipt as the shares of $110.80 were handed out, first to twelve men, then to twelve women. Each share represented as much as most of them might earn in a year, and all had grand plans for their windfalls. See,

Receipt of the Tubman Family, Feb. 15, 1843; S. F. McGill to James Hall, Feb. 17, 1843, p. 2; John Russwurm to J. H. B. Latrobe, Feb. 20, 1843, p. 1, all in MSCS.

By contrast, the Lauders would have a rough time getting adjusted to their new life. The old Captain had held them together. As he lay on his deathbed, Lauder named as his executors S. F. McGill and John Russwurm (whom he had never met). After his death, the rest were at a loss how to proceed. Russwurm described them, "two widows with 6 and 7 children and Tom with five, with a head as thick and hard as a brickbat." They were not so great in spirit as the old man had been. Margaret, James's wife, who died in mid-passage, left her estate, which included a house in Washington and $200 in other assets, to her niece, Julia Curtis, who had fallen on the *Globe* and was now senseless, "helpless as an infant." Russwurm asked the society to make sure that the estate was settled properly so that the girl would have some support. In the meantime, she was living with Stephen Smith's family. Just before leaving America, James Lauder had lent Smith money to buy one of his children, fulfilling in part his dream of bringing his whole family to freedom. Smith planned to pay Lauder back from the proceeds of property to be sold for him in southern Maryland, but this would take some months. Lauder's heirs wanted their father's money back, and they pressed Smith for it within a few days of landing at Harper. See, S. F. McGill to James Hall, Feb. 17, 1843, pp. 1–2; S. Smith to James Hall, Feb. 14, 1843; John Russwurm to James Hall, June 28, 1843, p. 1, all in MSCS.

[18] *Globe* company's care: John Russwurm to J. H. B. Latrobe, Feb. 20, 1843, p. 1; S. F. McGill to J. H. B. Latrobe, April 16, 1843, pp. 1–2 and enclosure; S. F. McGill to J. H. B. Latrobe, June 24, 1843, p. 1; John Russwurm to J. H. B. Latrobe, June 26, 1843, p. 1; John Russwurm to J. H. B. Latrobe, July 31, 1843, pp. 2–3, all in MSCS.

[19] Pattern of settlement: John Russwurm to J. H. B. Latrobe, June 26, 1843, pp. 1–2, MSCS.

[20] George McGill to James Hall, Jan. 15, 1844, MSCS. George McGill ceased to teach the Ladies' Academy in the second half of 1843, several months before his contract was up. He felt his abilities declining, and with a pregnant wife, he turned his energies to trade once again. The school had some forty children in attendance and needed a teacher of great energy and competence. The ladies were disappointed with George McGill, not least because his reports were scarcely legible, because of his creative spelling and arthritic handwriting. Unaware that he had already quit, they fired him. The *Latrobe* carried out a letter of dismissal which deeply hurt the old man's feelings. "More was said then was ever said to me by any one calling themselves Ladyes or gentlemen before," he wrote Hall in January, 1844. He offered to pay back his salary if asked. The ladies appealed to Hall for help to find a new teacher, but he had no ideas. Unfortunately, the Ladies' Society faced a crisis of funding, and they considered dissolving their operation altogether. John Russwurm responded to the news sorrowfully in a letter of January 15, 1844. Their cause was too important to give up, he wrote James Hall.

[21] Lydia McGill's death: *Maryland Colonization Journal*, n.s., 2:64; S. F. McGill to J. H. B. Latrobe, Jan. 13, 1844, p. 2, MSCS.

[22] Aftermath of *Vandalia* incident: John Russwurm to J. H. B. Latrobe, Feb. 20, 1843, pp. 1–2 and June 26, 1843, p. 1, both MSCS.

[23] Withdrawal of A.B.C.F.M.: S. F. McGill to J. H. B. Latrobe, June 24, 1843, pp. 1–2; John Russwurm to J. H. B. Latrobe, June 26, 1843, pp. 1–3, both in MSCS.

12. *"Powder and Ball Diplomacy"*

[1] Colonial influence: J. B. Russwurm to J. H. B. Latrobe, July 31, 1843, p. 2, MSCS. The chapter title is from the biography of Matthew C. Perry included in *Appleton's Cyclopaedia of American Biography.*

[2] The grand palaver was scarcely noticed by colonial authorities at the time: S. F. McGill to J. H. B. Latrobe, Dec. 17, 1843, p. 1; J. B. Russwurm to J. H. B. Latrobe, Dec. 23, 1843, p. 1, both in MSCS.

[3] Motives for second Grebo congress: S. F. McGill to J. H. B. Latrobe, Dec. 17, 1843, pp. 1–2; J. B. Russwurm to J. H. B. Latrobe, Dec. 23, 1843, pp. 1–2, both in MSCS.

[4] Background and movements of the African Squadron: U.S. Senate (28th Congress, 2nd Session), *Public Document 150: "Information Relative to the Operations of the United States Squadron on the West Coast of Africa . . ."* (Washington, 1845), pp. 1–61, containing an accurate transcription of most of the correspondence preserved in American Naval Archives, Squadron Letters, in the National Archives, Washington; Samuel Eliot Morison, *"Old Bruin" Commodore Matthew C. Perry 1794–1858 . . .* (Boston: Little, Brown, and Co., 1967), pp. 163–78; Alan R. Booth, "The United States African Squadron 1843–1861," in Jeffrey Butler, ed., *Boston University Papers in African History*, Vol. I (Boston: Boston U. Press, 1964), pp. 77–118; "Marposo," "Battle of Grand Berribe," in *The United Service* for Sept. 1882, pp. 294–97; Horatio Bridge (N. Hawthorne, ed.), *Journal of an African Cruiser* (New York, 1845); [Horatio Bridge to Mary Stewart Minor], U.S.S. *Saratoga* at sea, Jan. 10, 1844, in *The African Repository*, 20, no. 4 (1844): 117–24; Joseph J. Roberts to R. R. Gurley, Monrovia, Dec. 28, 1843, in *The African Repository*, 20, no. 5 (1844): 133–44.

[5] The African Squadron: Matthew C. Perry to Abel Upshur, U.S.S. *Saratoga* at Sta. Cruz, Tenerife, June 29, 1843, in Senate Document 150, p. 4.; Matthew C. Perry to Abel Upshur, U.S.S. *Saratoga* at Porto Praya, July 18, 1843, in Senate Document 150, pp. 6–7; Matthew C. Perry to Abel Upshur, U.S.S. *Saratoga* at Porto Praya July 21, 1843, in Senate Document 150, p. 8; Matthew C. Perry to Abel Upshur, U.S.S. *Saratoga* at Porto Praya, July 22, 1843, in Senate Document 150, p. 9.

[6] In 1843, Liberia and the colony of Maryland had title to nearly the whole stretch of coast from Sierra Leone a hundred or more miles into the Ivory Coast. Even so, their authority was minimal in most places, and foreigners traded at will. Some of them, violating local customs or cheating those on shore, ran afoul, sometimes with violent results. One such incident occurred near Sinoe in April, 1843. The *Edward Burley*, skippered by one Burke, had for some time past been buying rice. Governor Roberts reported that the vessel's "movements on the coast have been very strange, and by some held suspicious," suggesting she was buying supplies for the slave factories. Differing versions of what happened were told, but it seems Burke had called at Blue Barra, a Fishmen town, to recruit kroomen. He hired three, advancing to each ten or fifteen pounds of tobacco. One, Jack Dandy, jumped ship almost immediately, however. In a rage, the captain threatened to withhold pay from the other two unless they paid their comrade's debt. They escaped also, and took a couple of canoes with them. Burke's mate went ashore to retrieve the boats, but he and a seaman were detained. Colonial authorities interceded on their behalf and they were freed the next day. The incident whipped the captain and his men into a fury. They tried to capture one or two of the townsmen on the water. At length, they spied a Fishman in a canoe and sent a man after him, but

the pursuit went awry. The sailor was himself captured and taken ashore. Seeing this disaster, the mate, cook, and a couple of seamen from the Gold Coast then made for shore in a boat. A war canoe came out from shore, and the foreigners were easily captured. The Fishmen harpooned the cook, then stripped the mate of his clothes and threw him in the water. They tormented him for a time then harpooned him also. The African sailors were wounded but carried ashore. Burke stood out to sea while the mate was still struggling and was gone as quickly as the wind would carry him. Soon after, the vessel called at Monrovia on her way to Gallinas, the notorious slave port. Burke said he would sell her there and take passage for the United States. See J. J. Roberts to R. R. Gurley, Monrovia, Dec. 28, 1843, in *The African Repository*, 20 (1844): 133.

[7] Movements of the African Squadron: J. B. Russwurm to J. H. B. Latrobe, July 31, 1843 (cntd. at later dates), p. 3, MSCS; Matthew C. Perry to Abel Upshur, U.S.S. *Saratoga* at Mesurado Roads, Aug. 3, 1843, in Senate Document 150, pp. 9–10.

[8] Movements of the Squadron: Matthew C. Perry to Abel Upshur, U.S.S. *Saratoga* at Porto Grande, St. Vincent, Sept. 4, 1843, in Senate Document 150, pp. 12–13; Matthew C. Perry to David Henshaw, U.S.S. *Saratoga* at Porto Grande, Sept. 10, 1843, in Senate Document 150, pp. 13–14.

[9] Beginning of punitive expedition: Matthew C. Perry to David Henshaw, U.S.F. *Macedonian* at Porto Praya, Oct. 12, 1843, in Senate Document 150, p. 18; Matthew C. Perry to David Henshaw, U.S.F. *Macedonian* at Mesurado Roads, Nov. 22, 1843, in Senate Document 150, p. 20; Joseph J. Roberts to Ralph R. Gurley, Monrovia, Dec. 28, 1843, in *The African Repository*, 20 (1844): 133.

[10] Joseph J. Roberts to Ralph R. Gurley, Monrovia, Dec. 28, 1843, in *The African Repository*, 20 (1844): 134.

[11] Matthew C. Perry to Abel Upshur, U.S.S. *Saratoga* at Porto Grande, Sept. 5, 1843. This is not published in Senate Document 150, but is in American Naval Records, Squadron Letters, at the National Archives.

[12] Response to *Edward Burley* incident: "Notes of the Proceedings of a council held on board the United States frigate Macedonian, in the harbor of Sinoe, west coast of Africa, November 29, 1843," in Senate Document 150, pp. 23–27; Joseph J. Roberts to Ralph R. Gurley, Monrovia Dec. 28, 1843, in *The African Repository*, 20 (1844): 133.

[13] Events on shore at Sinoe: [Horatio Bridge to Mary Stewart Minor], U.S.S. *Saratoga*, at sea, Jan. 10, 1844, in *The African Repository*, 20 (1844): 117–18; S. E. Morison, "*old Bruin*," pp. 171–73; "Notes of a palaver, held at Sinoe, on Wednesday, the 29th of November, 1843," in Senate Document 150, pp. 27–29.

[14] Palaver at Sinoe: "Notes of a palaver, held at Sinoe" . . . "Second Day" and "Third Day," Senate Document 150, pp. 29–30; Joseph J. Roberts to Ralph R. Gurley, Monrovia, Dec. 28, 1843, in *The African Repository*, 20 (1844): 136.

[15] Squadron at Settra Kroo: Bridge to Minor, U.S.S. *Saratoga*, at sea, Jan. 10, 1844, in *The African Repository*, 20 (1844): 118; Joseph J. Roberts to Ralph R. Gurley, Monrovia, dec. 28, 1843, in *The African Repository*, 20 (1844): 136–37.

[16] Palaver at Settra Kroo: "Notes of a palaver held, on Monday the 4th of December, 1843," in Senate Document 150, pp. 30–31; Joseph J. Roberts to Ralph R. Gurley, Monrovia, Dec. 28, 1843, in *The African Repository*, 20 (1844): 137–38.

[17] Squadron arrives at Cape Palmas: "Notes of events which transpired at Cape Palmas . . . ," in Senate Document 150, pp. 31–32; J. B. Russwurm to Matthew C. Perry,

Dec. 6, 1843, in Senate Document 150, p. 32; Joseph J. Roberts to Ralph R. Gurley, Monrovia, Dec. 28, 1843, in *The African Repository*, 20 (1844): 138.

[18] The development of the palaver at Half Cavally is vividly recorded in the Journals of John Payne, which are in the Episcopal Church Archive in Austin, Texas. They were reprinted at length in *The Spirit of Missions*, 9 (1844): 112–22, 143–53, and 253–60.

[19] S. F. McGill to J. H. B. Latrobe, Dec. 17, 1843, p. 2, MSCS.

[20] S. F. McGill noted the irony of this in a letter to J. H. B. Latrobe, Dec. 17, 1843, p. 3.

See also, J. B. Russwurm to J. H. B. Latrobe, Dec. 23, 1843, p. 3, MSCS; Joel Abbot to Matthew C. Perry, U.S.S. *Decatur*, off Half Cavally, Dec. 7, 1843, in Senate Document 150, pp. 34–35.

[21] Events of December 7 at Cape Palmas: S. F. McGill to J. H. B. Latrobe, Dec. 17, 1843, pp. 2–3, MSCS; J. B. Russwurm to J. H. B. Latrobe, Dec. 23, 1843, p. 2, MSCS; "Notes of a palaver held at Cape Palmas on the 8th of December 1843 and proceedings preliminary thereto," in Senate Document 150, pp. 33–34; Joseph J. Roberts to Ralph R. Gurley, Monrovia, Dec. 28, 1843, in *The African Repository*, 20 (1844): 138–39; S. E. Morison, *"old Bruin,"* p. 173. Perry's instructions to Lt. Poor, dated December 6, and Poor's report the next morning are printed in Senate Document 150, p. 33.

[22] Rescue of the condemned man: "Note Z" in Senate Document 150, pp. 60–61; [Bridge to Minor], Jan. 10, 1844, in *The African Repository*, 20 (1844): 118–19; Joseph J. Roberts to Ralph R. Gurley, Monrovia, Dec. 28, 1843, in *The African Repository*, 20 (1844): 138–39.

[23] [Bridge to Minor], Jan. 10, 1844, in *The African Repository*, 20 (1844): 119.

[24] Palaver at Cape Palmas: Senate Document 150, p. 36: Perry recorded the palaver at length. An example of Freeman's twisting the truth for his own advantage: during the talks, Russwurm asserted that Freeman had repeatedly broken his word, and that Americans and Greboes could no longer live together. "King Freeman acknowledged having assented to the law complained of," Perry wrote,

> but denied having broken his promises, and said the settlers must answer for the first breach of faith. King Freeman said there was an article in the deed of sale of the Cape, which made it obligatory on each party to punish with death any of its members who might murder a member of the other; that Mr. Parker, a trader, having shot two Bushmen, was not punished with death according to the compact, and, in consequence, his (Freeman's) town was set on fire in the night by a party of Bushmen, who, at the same time, proceeded to the house of Mr. Parker, and, in revenge, murdered him and his family

[Bridge to Minor], Jan. 10, 1844, in *The African Repository*, 20 (1844): 120, described the African dignitaries at the palaver:

> A palaver was held with King Freeman and the other kings and headmen of the tribes in the vicinity, numbering twenty-four. Among these were several men of striking appearance, and there were few who did not bear the stamp of native talent and greatness. One of them was very like Henry Clay, . . . Yellow Will was the interpreter

> on this occasion, and was clothed in a damask silk mantel of crim-
> son, trimmed with broad gold lace.

Joseph J. Roberts to Ralph R. Gurley, Monrovia, Dec. 28, 1843, in *The African Repository*, 20 (1844): 139–40.

[25] Perry sets palaver: S. F. McGill to J. H. B. Latrobe, Dec. 17, 1843, p. 3, MSCS; J. B. Russwurm to J. H. B. Latrobe, Dec. 23, 1843, p. 2, MSCS; "Notes of a palaver held at Cape Palmas on the 8th of December, 1843," in Senate Document 150, pp. 35–38.

[26] S. F. McGill to J. H. B. Latrobe, Dec. 17, 1843, pp. 3–4, MSCS.

[27] J. B. Russwurm to Matthew C. Perry, August 11, 1843, in Senate Document 150, pp. 41–43.

[28] Strategy against Half Beriby: "Minutes of a council held on . . . the 9th of December 1843," and "Minutes of a council held on . . . December 10, 1843," in Senate Document 150, pp. 38–40; Joseph J. Roberts to Ralph R. Gurley, Monrovia, Dec. 28, 1843, in *The African Repository*, 20 (1844): 140.

[29] Landing at Robookah: Senate Document 150, pp. 43–44; [Bridge to Minor], Jan. 10, 1844, in *The African Repository*, 20 (1844): 120; Joseph J. Roberts to Ralph R. Gurley, Monrovia, Dec. 28, 1843, in *The African Repository*, 20 (1844): 140–41.

[30] Preparations for palaver at Robookah: Senate Document 150, p. 44; Joseph J. Roberts to Ralph R. Gurley, Monrovia, Dec. 28, 1843, in *The African Repository*, 20 (1844): 141.

[31] Palaver at Robookah: "Notes of a council held . . . on the morning of the 13th of December, 1843" in Senate Document 150, pp. 44–45; S. E. Morison, *"old Bruin,"* pp. 173–75, gives an account cast inappropriately in a humorous light, with several casual inaccuracies; "Marposo," "Battle of Grand Berribe" in *The United Service*, pp. 294–97; Commodore Andrew H. Foote, *Africa and the American Flag* (New York, 1854), pp. 235ff. gives some details of the incident and important commentary on its significance.

[32] Joseph J. Roberts to Ralph R. Gurley, Monrovia, Dec. 28, 1843, in *The African Repository*, 20 (1844): 141.

[33] Palaver at Half Beriby: "Notes of a palaver held at Little Berriby" in Senate Document 150, p. 45; [Bridge to Minor], Jan. 10, 1844, in *The African Repository*, 20 (1844): 121; Joseph J. Roberts to Ralph R. Gurley, Monrovia, Dec. 28, 1843, in ibid., 141–42.

[34] Battle at Half Beriby: "Notes of a palaver held at Little Berriby" in Senate Document 150, p. 45; Joseph J. Roberts to Ralph R. Gurley, Monrovia, Dec. 28, 1843, in *The African Repository*, 20 (1844): 142–43.

[35] [Bridge to Minor], Jan. 10, 1844, in *The African Repository*, 20 (1844): 121, relates that the town was abandoned:

> within ten minutes, the palisades were cut through, and the houses
> all in flames. Not a native remained in the town; even an old man
> apparently ninety years of age, had been carried out into the woods
> behind. A party of Saratogas had passed through the town, and one
> of the men seeing the poor old creature move, fired at him and
> fortunately missed. On approaching the miserable object, he held
> up his hands in supplication. They brought him food, placed him in
> a more sheltered spot, and left him.

[36] [Bridge to Minor], Jan. 10, 1844, in *The African Repository*, 20 (1844): 122, states that,

"in a writing desk found at one of the towns, was a love-letter, addressed to Captain Robert MacFarland, jr., postmarked Castine, Me., February 18, 1838, and written in a beautiful hand. The contents may not be told. . . ."

[37] With regard to the scuffle, and more particularly the circumstances of Krakow's death, I have relied most heavily on "Marposo"'s essay, "Battle of Grand Berribe." He is the only witness who seems to have given a candid account, perhaps emboldened by the passage of forty years. He told of the bombardment of the bush, which all the others left out, and in general gave details of a clumsy operation that succeeded despite itself. Without question, the palaver was handled very poorly. McGill quoted Roberts as saying, "There was more confusion in the ranks of the Americans, than he had ever witnessed in one of our colonial engagements." Perry and his colleagues preferred to call attention to the results of the palaver rather than its conduct. The commodore mentioned the brawl only tersely and stated simply that Krakow died in the incident. Roberts gave more details of the fight, but asserted that Mayo caught Krakow reaching for a gun, that this was the cause of their wrestling, rather than an intention to execute him. Bridge made many additions to the story, but left out Krakow's death.

[38] "Compact" in Senate Document 150, pp. 46–47.

[39] Attack on other Krakow towns: [Bridge to Minor], Jan. 10, 1844, in *The African Repository*, 20 (1844): 121–22, comments:

> It was the Commodore's orders to destroy property, but spare life. And it is said, that only four were killed of the enemy, while two of our men were wounded, one mortally. Many cattle were killed and several canoes were taken or cut to pieces; to say nothing of the numerous curiosities taken, which will surfeit the United States on our return.

Joseph J. Roberts to Ralph R. Gurley, Monrovia, Dec. 28, 1843, in *The African Repository*, 20 (1844): 143.

[40] Senate Document 150, pp. 149–50.

[41] Restoration of peace: S. F. McGill to J. H. B. Latrobe, Dec. 17, 1843, p. 4; J. B. Russwurm to J. H. B. Latrobe, Dec. 23, 1843, pp. 2–3, both in MSCS.

13. *"Liberty Without Bread"*

[1] King Freeman to the Board of Managers, [March, 1844], MSCS.

[2] See *Maryland Colonization Journal*, n.s., 2:65ff., for complete text of the ordinance with commentary.

[3] Russwurm to Latrobe, Feb. 13, 1844, p. 4, MSCS.

[4] Extract from Minutes of Agent and Council, Feb. 12, 1844, MSCS.

[5] Strategic importance of Fishtown: James Hall, "Fishtown," in *Maryland Colonization Journal*, n.s., 2:50–52; The map is preserved in American Naval Records, Cartographic Division, in the National Archives.

[6] Purchase of Fishtown: Russwurm to Latrobe, Jan. 12, 1844, p. 1; Russwurm to Latrobe, Feb. 13, 1844, pp. 1–3; Extract from Minutes of Agent and Council, February 12, 1844, all in MSCS.

[7] Catholic Mission dispute: Patrick Kelly to Russwurm, [Jan. 1844]; Russwurm to Hall, Jan. 12, 1844, pp. 1–3, both in MSCS.

[8] Edward Barron to Russwurm, Assinee, April 18, 1844, MSCS.

[9] This and the following narrative are drawn from an account in *Maryland Colonization Journal*, n.s., 2:260–62. See also, Russwurm to Latrobe, August 24, 1844, pp. 2–3, MSCS.

Seys had occasion to deal with the courts personally. An African servant he had brought with him from Monrovia was one day confronted by a young Grebo who hit him with a rock. A Grebo constable made quick work of finding and arresting the assailant. The matter was tried at the next sitting of the Court of Monthly Sessions. The Judge sat at 6 A.M. as stipulated in the Colonial Code, and each party stated his case, called witnesses, and proceeded as in an American court. The trial was finished by eight. The Grebo defendant was convicted and assessed a fine of one bullock.

[10] Movement of Greboes from Harper: Russwurm to Latrobe, August 24, 1844, pp. 2–3, MSCS; editorial in *Maryland Colonization Journal*, n.s., 2:161.

[11] S. F. McGill to James Hall, August 22, 1844, pp. 1–2, MSCS.

[12] Russwurm to Latrobe, August 24, 1844, pp. 1–2, MSCS.

[13] Russwurm to Hall, October 27, 1844, MSCS. See also, Phillips, *Freedom's Port*, pp. 215–20, which describes similar efforts to solicit emigration to Guiana from Baltimore.

[14] Petition of Citizens to Governor Russwurm, October 24, 1844, MSCS.

[15] Russwurm to Hall, October 27, 1844, MSCS.

[16] Ibid., Sept. 18, 1845, p. 1, MSCS.

[17] Arrival of *Chipola*: Russwurm to Latrobe, Jan. 16, 1845; Russwurm to Hall, Jan. 16, 1845, both in MSCS.

[18] Dempsey Fletcher: *Maryland Colonization Journal*, n.s., 2:327–28; Dempsey Rollo Fletcher to James Hall, Jan. 14, 1844, p. 1; D. R. Fletcher to Latrobe, Sep. 1, 1844, pp. 1–2; Russwurm to Hall, Jan. 16, 1845, p. 2, all in MSCS.

[19] Russwurm to Hall, Jan. 16, 1845, p. 2, MSCS, notes that the colony was then at peace with its neighbors, except for Half Cavally, which had tried to prevent the agent's visit to Denah. Russwurm to Latrobe, March 7, 1845, pp. 1–2, MSCS, gives details of the beginning of the conflict.

Sources in *Maryland Colonization Journal* include, John Payne to the Board of Managers, April 11, 1845, n.s., 2:369–70; S. F. McGill to unknown correspondent at Monrovia, published in *Africa's Luminary*, March 25, 1845, and reprinted in n.s., 2:377–79, Anonymous correspondent, published in *Africa's Luminary*, Feb. 26, 1845, and reprinted in n.s., 2:372; Anonymous correspondent, without date, n.s., 2:27–29.

Other sources of information on the war: J. Payne to Hall, Half Cavally, April 11, 1845, pp. 2–4; S. F. McGill to Hall, June 8, 1845, p. 1; Russwurm to Hall, June 9, 1845, p. 2, all in MSCS. See also, *The Spirit of Missions*.

[20] Continuation of Grebo war: John Payne to Hall, Half Cavally, April 11, 1845; S. F. McGill to Hall, June 8, 1845, p. 1, both in MSCS.

[21] Russwurm to Hall, June 9, 1845, p. 2, MSCS.

[22] End of Grebo war: Russwurm to Hall, June 9, 1845, p. 2; Russwurm to Hall, July 28, 1845, p. 2; Dr. S. F. McGill to Hall, June 8, 1845, p. 1, MSCS.

[23] During 1845 the total value of palm oil, camwood, and rice exported from Harper was $21,013. The colonial store accounted for a value of $8,600. McGill Brothers did something less than half as much, $4,160. Other traders, the principal of whom was John D. Moore, exported $2,953 in the same articles. At the same time, the colony's

imports amounted to a declared value of $19,850, which was probably somewhat under the true cost. Of this amount, American merchants carried $9,000, English $6,500, and the Colonization Society $3,450. Portuguese, German, and French vessels accounted for less than $1,000 together. Russwurm's responsibilities had doubled during the previous two years. He attributed this principally to the increase of trade with the bush. As agent, he personally conducted all trade palavers, making any advances to Grebo factors, and enforcing bargains. He opened his office at six or seven each morning and worked until dark, with only a few hours between for food and rest. See Statistics for 1845 MSCS, Letterbook 1845. Also, Russwurm to Latrobe, Dec. 30, 1845, p. 5, MSCS.

[24] Russwurm to Hall, Sept. 18, 1845, pp. 1–2, MSCS.

[25] Ibid., Oct. 25, 1845, p. 1, MSCS.

[26] The manuscript journal and map prepared by Banks and Stewart, catalogued in the archives of the MSCS, were misplaced at the time of my research. The account was published in form which appears true to the original in the pages of *Maryland Colonization Journal*, n.s., 3:163ff and 187ff.

[27] Russwurm to Latrobe, Dec. 30, 1845, p. 1, MSCS.

14. *"The True Yankee Enterprise"*

[1] An account of Anthony Wood's life and his visit to Baltimore was published by James Hall in *Maryland Colonization Journal*, n.s., 2:162–63, and 240.

[2] Notices of the Chesapeake and Liberia Trading Co. in *Maryland Colonization Journal* include, n.s., 2:337ff., 347.

[3] The Brig *Kent*: Russwurm to Hall, January 24, 1846, p. 1; Russwurm to Latrobe, January 24, 1846, p. 1; Major Bolon to Hall, January 21, 1846, p. 1, all in MSCS. The *Kent* stopped briefly at Monrovia, where she picked up five of the settler Charles Scotland's children.

[4] Agency activities: Russwurm to Hall, Jan. 24, 1846, pp. 1–2; Russwurm to Latrobe, March 16, 1846, pp. 1–2, both in MSCS.

[5] Maj. Anthony Wood to Hall, Jan. 23, 1846, MSCS.

[6] Major Bolon to Hall, Jan. 21, 1846, p. 1, MSCS.

[7] S. F. McGill to Moses Sheppard, May 7, 1844, in Sheppard Papers at Swarthmore College.

[8] Dr. S. F. McGill to Latrobe, Jan. 24, 1846, pp. 1–2, MSCS.

[9] Problems in the Customs House: "Minutes of the Agent and Council During 1846," entry for Feb. 15, p. 2; Russwurm to Hall, Jan. 10, 1846, p. 2; Russwurm to Latrobe, May 13, 1846, pp. 1–2, all in MSCS.

[10] Russwurm to Latrobe, May 13, 1846, MSCS.

[11] McGill's dispute with Russwurm: S. F. McGill to Latrobe, March 18, 1846, pp. 1–2; S. F. McGill to Latrobe, July 12, 1846, pp. 3–4; Anthony Wood to unknown correspondent, July 15, 1846, pp. 1–2; McGill to Latrobe, Sept. 6, 1846, pp. 2–4, all in MSCS.

[12] Russwurm to Latrobe, May 13, 1846, pp. 2–3, MSCS.

[13] "Minutes of the Agent and Council during 1846," May 14, 15, and 16, pp. 3–6, MSCS.

[14] S. F. McGill to Latrobe, July 12, 1846, pp. 3–4, MSCS.

[15] Dispute between Russwurm and McGill: McGill to Latrobe, July 12, 1846, p. 4; Russwurm to Latrobe, May 13, 1846, p. 3; Anthony Wood to unknown correspondent, July 15, 1846, p. 2, all in MSCS.

[16] Russwurm to Latrobe, Dec. 30, 1845, p. 6, MSCS.

[17] Russwurm to Hall, July 21, [1846], p. 2, misfiled in MSCS, Letterbook 1845.

[18] Russwurm, Proclamation, March 3, 1846, MSCS, Letterbook 1846. The Deed is in MSCS. It was also published as an appendix to Latrobe, *Maryland in Liberia*.

[19] Russwurm to Hall, July 21, [1846], p. 2, MSCS, misfiled in Letterbook 1845.

[20] John Payne to Hall, May 8, 1846, p. 2, MSCS.

[21] McGill to Latrobe, July 12, 1846, pp. 1–3, MSCS.

[22] Cannon explosion: Russwurm to Hall, March 17, 1846, p. 3; McGill to Latrobe, Sept. 6, 1846, p. 1; Russwurm to Hall, Oct. 27, 1846, p. 3, all in MSCS. Accidental shooting: McGill to Latrobe, Sept. 6, 1846, p. 1, MSCS. Improvement of health: McGill to Latrobe, Sept. 6, 1846, p. 1; Russwurm to Hall, Oct. 27, 1846, p. 3, both in MSCS.

[23] The shipwrights: Russwurm to Hall, March 17, 1846, pp. 1–2; Major Bolon to Hall, May 25, 1846; Major Bolon to Hall, July 11, 1846, all in MSCS.

[24] McGill's opinions: McGill to Latrobe, July 12, 1846, p. 5; McGill to Latrobe, Sept. 6, 1846, p. 4, both in MSCS.

[25] Russwurm to Latrobe, Jan. 23, 1847, pp. 2–3, MSCS.

[26] Launching the *Cavally*: Russwurm to Latrobe, Jan. 23, 1847, pp. 2–3; Russwurm to Hall, Jan. 24, 1847, p. 2, both in MSCS.

[27] Russwurm to Latrobe, Jan. 23, 1847, pp. 2–3, MSCS.

[28] Development of the Chesapeake and Liberia Trading Co.: *Maryland Colonization Journal*, n.s., 2:337ff and 347, 3:272ff and 368ff.

[29] James Hall, editorial in *Maryland Colonization Journal*, n.s., 3:274.

15. *"A Clap of Thunder"*

[1] Russwurm to Latrobe, Jan. 23, 1847, pp. 4–5, MSCS.

[2] Arrival of the *Liberia Packet*: Russwurm to Hall, Jan. 24, 1847, p. 1, MSCS; *Maryland Colonization Journal*, n.s., 3:272ff. Colonial legal system: Russwurm to Latrobe, Jan. 23, 1847, pp. 1, 5–6, 7, MSCS.

[3] The new medical policy: Fletcher to Hall, Jan. 25, 1847; Russwurm to Hall, March 1, 1847, p. 1; Fletcher to Hall, March 3, 1847, pp. 1–2, all in MSCS.

[4] Health of colony at end of 1847: Fletcher to unknown correspondent, Oct. 5, 1847, pp. 1–2; Russwurm to Latrobe, Sept. 29, 1847, p. 2; Russwurm to Latrobe, Nov. 8, 1847 (second letter), p. 1; Fletcher to Latrobe, Nov. 9, 1847, p. 2, all in MSCS.

[5] Fletcher begins practice: Fletcher to unknown correspondent, Oct. 5, 1847, pp. 1–2; Fletcher to Hall, Jan. 25, 1847, both in MSCS.

[6] *Maryland Colonization Journal*, n.s., 3:352.

[7] Russwurm's health: Russwurm to Latrobe, Sept. 29, 1847, pp. 1–2; Russwurm to Hall, Oct. 1, 1847, p. 2; Fletcher to unknown correspondent, Oct. 5, 1847, p. 1, all in MSCS.

[8] William A. Prout: Russwurm to Hall, Nov. 8, 1847 (first letter), p. 4; McGill to Hall, Dec. 17, 1847, p. 2, both in MSCS.

[9] Russwurm to Latrobe, Sept. 29. 1847, p. 1, MSCS.

[10] The wreck of the *Cavally*: Russwurm to Latrobe, Sep. 29, 1847, p. 1; Russwurm to Hall, Oct. 1, 1847, p. 1, both in MSCS.

[11] Aftermath of *Cavally*'s capsizing: Russwurm to Latrobe, Sept. 29, 1847, pp. 1–2; D. R. Fletcher to unknown correspondent, Oct. 5, 1847, p. 1; Russwurm to Hall, Nov. 8, 1847, p. 4, "As far as I am concerned in equipping etc. I feel no blame, but I am conscious

that I placed too much confidence in the master and mate who, though fully competent, yet prized not enough the fine vessel over which they were placed," all in MSCS.

[12] Health of Governor Russwurm: Russwurm to Latrobe, Sept. 29, 1847, pp. 1, 2; Russwurm to Hall, Oct. 1, 1847, p. 2; Fletcher to unknown correspondent, Oct. 5, 1847, p. 1, all in MSCS.

[13] Wreck of the small schooner: Russwurm to Hall, Nov. 8, 1847 (first letter), p. 4, MSCS.

[14] Russwurm to Hall, Nov. 8, 1847 (first letter), pp. 3, 4, MSCS.

[15] Ibid., Nov. 8, 1847 (first letter), pp. 1–3, MSCS.

[16] Ibid., Dec. 18, 1847, MSCS.

[17] Voyage of *Liberia Packet*: Emigrant List; McGill to Hall, Dec. 17, 1847, pp. 1–2, in MSCS.

[18] McGill to Hall, Dec. 17, 1847, pp. 2–3, MSCS.

[19] Information concerning McGill Brothers: McGill to Hall, Dec. 17, 1847, pp. 3–4; James Hall in *Maryland Colonization Journal*, n.s., 1:275, 4:68, 8:277.

[20] McGill to Hall, Dec. 17, 1847, p. 3, MSCS.

[21] Russwurm to Latrobe, May 5, 1848, pp. 1–2, MSCS.

[22] Russwurm takes vacation: McGill to Hall, March 28, 1848, p. 2; Prout to Hall, March 28, 1848, p. 1; Nicholas Jackson to Latrobe or Hall, April 4, 1848, all in MSCS.

[23] Resurgence of Grebo war: McGill to Hall, March 28, 1848, p. 2; Prout to Hall, March 28, 1848, p. 1; Nicholas Jackson, April 4, 1848, p. 1, all in MSCS.

[24] McGill to Moses Sheppard, March 31, 1848, in Sheppard Papers, Friends Historical Library, Swarthmore College.

[25] McGill to Sheppard, March 31, 1848: Sheppard Papers, Swarthmore. Other references to the scarcity of food: McGill to Hall, March 28, 1848, pp. 1–2; , Prout to Hall, March 28, 1848; Nicholas Jackson to Latrobe or Hall, April 4, 1848; Russwurm to Hall, May 4, 1848, pp. 2–3, all in MSCS.

[26] Arrival of *Amazon*: McGill to Hall, March 28, 1848, p. 1; Prout to Hall, March 28, 1848, both in MSCS.

[27] Russwurm's voyage: Russwurm to Hall, May 4, 1848, pp. 1–4; Russwurm to Hall, Jan. 18, 1849, pp. 1–3, both in MSCS.

[28] William Cassell: *Maryland Colonization Journal*, n.s., 5:292–98; Emigrant List, *Ann* Company. See also, *Maryland Colonization Journal*, n.s., 4:235ff. for Latrobe's letter of instructions to Cassell, and ibid., 4:299, for a letter of Cassell to Richard Watkins.

[29] Joshua H. Sewart to Hall, June 12, 1848, p. 2, MSCS. Cassell and his son were guests in Stewart's house until their own was completed.

[30] Cassell's employment: Russwurm to Latrobe, May 5, 1848, p. 2; Wm. Cassell to Hall, May 5, 1848, p. 3, both in MSCS.

[31] McGill to Hall, March 28, 1848, pp. 1–2, MSCS. The previous July, settlers had been roused almost to violence after Jackson refused to allow a defendant to answer his accusers then convicted him, imposing a high fine. Jackson lacked the proper education for a judge, Joshua Stewart wrote Latrobe immediately afterward. Moreover, he was too much of a tyrant, "grinding the faces of the Poor people." He levied fines for petty infractions where a reprimand was sufficient. Before Jackson had resumed his office, upon his return from the bush school, people had lived in harmony, but now they chafed under arbitrary judgement.

My fellow citizen say they are Slave in this Colony Not in flesh But in Mind Sentament they are Debared of there priveleg they feal that the Right of a freeman is Not Allowed them it is taken away I Sir did not Leave America for that purpose I left America, that I might injoy the Rights of a freeman in cappalmas on the Wester shors of Africa But if i cant injoy it here I dont whant to stay nether could i.

He warned that if there was ever a rebellion in the colony, Thomas Jackson would be a principal cause. Joshua H. Stewart to Latrobe, July 8, 1847, MSCS. Settlers continued to petition against him, and a suit was pending in the April session of the court. During Russwurm's absence to leeward, McGill promised to do what he could to keep down any mob, though he was probably Jackson's most powerful antagonist. McGill to Hall, March 28, 1848, p. 2, MSCS.

Jackson had written the board of managers in his own defense on December 17, 1847. "I am a supporter of religion and morality and therein our laws," he wrote. For this, he had suffered the malice of a small group of settlers, and three years before, left the colony to teach school for the Methodist mission in the bush. When he returned to the colony, the governor restored him in the office of justice of the peace, without his asking for the honor. He found the community sadly degraded in its morals, and vigorously set about correcting things with "the strong Arm of the law." He had enemies once again, but was resolved to persevere. Thomas Jackson to the Board of Managers, Dec. 17, 1847, pp. 1–2, MSCS.

[32] Russwurm's preparations to depart: Russwurm to Latrobe, May 5, 1848, pp. 1–2; McGill to Latrobe, June 1, 1848, p. 1; McGill to the Board of Managers, June 11, 1848, p. 1, all in MSCS.

[33] J. H. Stewart to Hall, June 12, 1848, pp. 1–2, MSCS.

[34] King Freeman to Latrobe, June 16, 1848, p. 1, MSCS.

[35] Russwurm to McGill, June 17, 1848, pp. 1–3, MSCS. McGill was to follow established protocol in his dealings with Greboes. Freeman was always invited to sit at palavers, whether or not Gbenelu or its citizens were involved. Prout should have a free hand in managing the agency's trade. He should be careful not to advance more goods for palm oil, since too much was already out, from the Cape all the way to Beriby. Most of the tobacco then on hand, landed by the *Amazon*, was of very poor quality. It should be traded away as soon as possible, mixed with the small stock of "Best." Prout should try to buy as much rice as he could, and keep it in the new Rock Store. The best trade goods, he noted, were in the attic of the agency house, and enough merchandise was on hand to last for three or four months. Russwurm had purchased a schooner from John Bowen, and the note would come due during his absence. McGill was to pay it. Other instructions concerned arrangements for building houses for new arrivals and other minor matters.

[36] McGill to Hall, June 17, 1848, p. 1, MSCS.

[37] The offer a college presidency was something of a secret. Russwurm mentioned it in a letter to Hall, September 16, 1850, p. 2, MSCS, only in relation to his having turned it down.

[38] Russwurm's brief visit to the United States was scarcely documented: proceedings of the board of managers contain some congratulatory resolutions; and *Maryland Colonization Journal*, n.s., 4:233, includes some brief comments by James Hall.

[39] McGill to Hall, August 1, 1848, p. 1, MSCS.

[40] Ibid., p. 2, MSCS.

[41] Ibid., pp. 1–2, MSCS.

[42] Ibid., August 1, 1848 (cntd. on Aug. 9), p. 3, MSCS.

[43] Continued hard times: McGill to Hall, August 1, 1848 (Cntd. on Aug. 9, and Nov. 6), p. 3; McGill to Latrobe, Nov. 6, 1848, pp. 1–2, both in MSCS.

[44] Fourth voyage of the *Packet*: Russwurm to Hall, Nov. 22, 1848; Russwurm to Latrobe, Nov. 22, 1848, both in MSCS.

[45] Russwurm and Prout: Russwurm to Hall, November 22, 1848, pp. 1 and 3, MSCS.

[46] Settlement of the war: Russwurm to Latrobe, Nov. 22, 1848, pp. 1–2; Russwurm to Hall, Jan. 20, 1849, p. 1, both in MSCS. See also, McGill to Latrobe, Nov. 6, 1848, pp. 1–2, for an account of the acting governor's failed attempt to win peace.

[47] "Journal of the Rev. John Payne," in *The Spirit of Missions*, extracted in *Maryland Colonization Journal*, n.s., 4:82–83.

16. *"A Threat at Nationality"*

[1] Dr. McGill initially shared Russwurm's opinion: "I once used to ridicule the idea of Liberian independence," he wrote Moses Sheppard on March 31, 1848, "it appeared to me a mere farce got up for effect." He understood the rationale, but he believed that Liberia had none of the resources or institutions to lay claim to nationality. Yet to his surprise, autonomy infused Liberian society with a new spirit. Men who had formerly been content to rely on whatever meager supplies their patrons might provide had now done for themselves. He was filled with admiration for patriotic Liberians, who believed that they were making history and that the future of the black race depended upon their actions. In the small community at Harper, he found very little companionship, for most settlers detested his arrogance. He could not help but think he was trapped in a backwater. "There are not enough well informed among us to leaven the mass of ignorance which predominates," he continued bluntly, "One is forced to turn away in hopelessness and despondency; the old ones are incorrigibly stupid, the young are not yet ready to take their places." Maryland needed more young men like himself, with education and capital, before the people could be waked from their stupor, he asserted. Moses Sheppard Papers, Friends' Historical Library, Swarthmore College.

[2] Russwurm to Latrobe, April 26, 1849, p. 2, MSCS.

[3] Minutes of Public Meetings, April, 1849, pp. 1–5, including a copy of the petition, MSCS. Joshua Stewart wrote James Hall on April 28, 1849, to elaborate on the issue of currency raised in the petition, then about to go home. The society's old shinplasters were accepted only at the agency store and at McGill's. Even at the agency, purchases with currency were restricted. With it, a settler could buy only a quart of palm oil, two pounds of meat, and two or three yards of cloth at a time. The situation left settlers depressed materially and spiritually. Their labor counted for nothing, and to hear the authorities tell them only to work harder at their farms was an insult.

> Our people are down, as low, as they poseble Can be. I dont Know
> What is to Raise them upe, they are Still Dependent on that Public
> Store, and What are they to do, to prevent their despondency? It
> Whant be, potatar and Cassava etc. etc. No, Never, they Cant procour

Suficient quantaty of Seed to Plant, So as to mak farming an object, What must be done, I Cant Say, our people ar; Without Jesting; Extremely poore they Realy do Sufer for the whant Suiteble Comfort of Life they work it is true, But the moneys they Receive in Returns is Worth nothing.

If the currency were backed up with something more substantial than the few items available at the store, settlers would be far happier. He also recommended a reduction of license fees to encourage settlers to go into business, increasing the prosperity of the entire community. Settlers were hard workers and eager for opportunities. All they needed was a clear path, he asserted. Joshua Stewart to Hall; April 28, 1849, pp. 1–2, MSCS.

The society's archive includes an anonymous fragment of a letter, written by some settler who had fair knowledge of the society in Baltimore and of the operations of the store. He wrote an anonymous friend that James Hall was much to blame for the current difficulties. Emigrants had only the poorest accommodation, with inadequate provisions and housing. "I cannot tell what the Doctor is doing," he observed. "It seems to me, that he is sitting down there in the office and feathering his nest in the eyes of all the society." Older settlers had a terrible time, as there was very little wage labor available, and the governor refused to hire them when new arrivals needed work. When an old settler could get a job for a short period, he was paid in currency, which was accepted only at the store, and then only for certain items. Common necessities, like flour and salt meat were never available. He recommended that the Agency make a plantation for cotton, coffee, and ginger. With an exportable crop, the agency would be able to employ the single women and old men who now had no way to support themselves. Two or three individuals were now getting rich, he believed, buying up the store's surplus and selling at a high profit. Everyone else suffered. Anonymous fragment of a letter, mid-1849, MSCS, Letterbook 1849. The only person with such knowledge must have been William Cassell.

[4] Russwurm's response to the petition: Russwurm to Latrobe, April 17, 1849, pp. 1–2; Russwurm to Latrobe, April 26, 1849, p. 2, both in MSCS.

[5] Russwurm to Latrobe, April 17, 1849, pp. 2–4, MSCS.

[6] Increased settler political activity: *Maryland Colonization Journal*, n.s., 5:143.

Many settlers also concerned themselves with their own future, concluding that some form of union with the Republic of Liberia was inevitable. Samuel Ford McGill was perhaps the most intellectual and outspoken commentator on the subject, as illustrated in a letter to his old mentor, Moses Sheppard, written at Harper on April 25, 1849. Sheppard had asked the doctor for his opinion of the question whether the money spent by the British government to suppress the slave trade had been used to best advantage. McGill responded with relish, employing the opportunity to expound upon the promise of a black republic. Estimates varied, he informed Sheppard, but at least £750,000 (then, $3,600,000) had been spent to keep Royal Navy cruisers on the coast during the previous twenty-five years. Though the captains of these vessels had made a valiant effort, the task was impossible. The length of coastline under surveillance was immense; the slavers were fast and clever, many of them flying American colors and therefore immune from search and seizure; and Africans on shore remained eager to engage in the business. "More is realized from the slave trade," he concluded succinctly, and with less labour than from legitimate traffick, and as long as this is the case the African like the white man will continue it. So long as there is a demand, there will be a constant supply, unless strings of colonies along the coast, by their contiguity and strength are enabled to inflict summary punishment on those who persist in selling their brethren.

He added that had the British put the same money into settlements on shore, like Liberia and their own Sierra Leone, the slave trade north of the Equator would long since have been quashed.

McGill championed the merits of black people from North America over West Indies for this great work, even suggesting that Britain ought to underwrite the emigration of free blacks from the United States. He saw in the recognition and generous assistance that Britain and France gave the new Republic of Liberia an acknowledgement of the contribution that the colony had made in expelling the traders. To his great disappointment, the United States government had not followed suit. The Monroe administration had helped pay for the first settlement of Liberia, and subsequent presidents had made the colonies' protection a matter of national policy. The sustained efforts of charities and a few dedicated individuals had proven that the scheme was workable, but the present government balked at recognizing its own offspring. "The subject of Negro Slavery, and the wrongs of the Coloured or African race, are now causes of great disorders in the U. States," he commented, continuing prophetically,

> there must be some ground of compromise between, the pro and anti-slavery states otherwise the union itself must be dissolved — no one can reasonably doubt the liability of this — colonization seems to me the only means whereby this danger can be averted, that is practicable — whether the black man remains in the U. States a slave or freeman, his presence there, and dissatisfaction whilst denied either social or political rights will ever make his removal necessary.

Mere expedience ought to lead the United States to foster Liberia, as a vent for future social unrest. The material benefits to whichever country supported Liberia, be it Britain or the United States, were clear: "The government to extend her power and greatness, the manufacturer to secure a market for his fabrics, the merchant to increase his gains, the philanthropist to abolish the horrible traffick in human flesh and the missionary to promulgate the Gospel of Christ to the barbarous millions of this benighted land."

As for Liberian independence, McGill confessed that he had initially scoffed at the idea, because the population was too small and lacked the social institutions and revenues necessary to support a government. Yet when the supervision and financial assistance of the American Colonization Society were withdrawn, the new government did not wither. "My heart bounded with joy," he wrote, "I regretted that I too was not among those who stood alone:— among a people, where every one was forced to consider, that to a certain amount the well fare of the whole depended upon his individual exertions." Here, at last, was Liberty, that soul-stirring state of existence that he had sought his whole life. "Liberians are engaged in a glorious struggle such indeed as the world has never before witnessed, and one in which if she triumphs will be considering the means etc.

unprecedented in the history of nations." Everything connected with Maryland in Liberia now seemed second-rate, and he longed to participate in the bold deeds at Monrovia. This was impossible, however, because of his obligations to the Maryland State Colonization Society and his mercantile interests. He therefore contented himself with speculation on the future union of Maryland with Liberia. He promised Sheppard that he would not assume the role of activist for such a movement, though when the time to make a decision should come, he would do what he felt was best for his country. McGill to Sheppard, April 25, 1849, pp. 1–7, in Sheppard Papers, Swarthmore College.

[7] Russwurm to Latrobe, April 26, 1849, pp. 1–5, MSCS. The *Packet* returned to Cape Palmas about the fifteenth of October. She carried dispatches from the board in response to Russwurm's bitter criticisms of the previous April. The governor replied on the eighteenth that he was hurt by the suggestion in the board's earlier communications that he was acting unfaithfully by issuing so many drafts. Settler dissatisfaction was then at a peak, and he was suffering terribly from loneliness because of the prolonged absence of his wife. "I was aware my action was right and my motives the purest: and to have them called into question was irritating," he wrote Hall. He asked for some consideration of his difficult circumstances. When the *Packet* arrived in July, he had gone to the Agency Wharf to welcome his wife back home. The disappointment left him terribly depressed. Then to return to his office to open letters critical of his actions and attitude was more than he could bear. Russwurm to Hall, Oct. 18, 1849, p. 1, MSCS.

In a second letter of October 19 to Hall, Russwurm went into still greater detail. Hall had rebuked him in his letter of February 17 for drawing so much on the society. Russwurm was deeply chagrined, for he had always acted in good faith. "Urgent necessity alone compelled me to draw for what I did in purchasing every barrel of breadstuffs," he explained, continuing,

> Our native trade has altered very much from what it was when you were on the coast. Then American Romauls and furniture check were in great demand for Rice or even Palm Oil, but the case is altered now: they demand the best English goods for Rice even, Gun Powder and good tobacco are always in demand however.

Even though he had written specifically and told Hall during his visit to Baltimore the previous year to stop sending out blue checks, every cargo contained them, to the exclusion of other items. When the *Packet* brought out even more, he was completely disgusted. In the belief that they would never sell, he shipped them back to Baltimore. "This was better than suffering them to rot in the Society's store." Hall of course was surprised to see the returns and responded angrily in his latest letter. "Do tell me seriously," Russwurm countered, "if you believe that these goods have been demanded by the colonists with *money in hand*, and been refused." Settlers wanted English trade goods to buy rice, and these he refused to sell, since they had been obtained on credit expressly for the oil trade. Russwurm to Hall, Oct. 19, 1849, pp. 1–3, MSCS.

[8] Purchase of Garroway: Russwurm to Latrobe, Oct. 23, 1849, p. 3; Russwurm to Latrobe, Jan. 4, 1850, p. 1, both in MSCS.

[9] Russwurm's health: McGill to Hall, Oct. 20, 1849, p. 2; Russwurm to Hall, Nov. 19, 1849, p. 1; Russwurm to Latrobe, Jan. 4, 1850, p. 1, all in MSCS.

[10] *Maryland Colonization Journal*, n.s., 5:17.

[11] "Minutes of a Meeting, July 9, 1849, in *Minutebook of the Board of Managers No. 3*, p. 315, MSCS.

[12] McGill to Hall, Oct. 20, 1849, p. 3. See also, Russwurm to Latrobe, Jan. 4, 1850, both in MSCS.

[13] Henry Hannon to James Hall, Oct. 16, 1849, MSCS.

[14] Thomas Jackson to Latrobe, October, 1849, p. 1, MSCS.

[15] W. Prout and others to the Board of Managers, Jan. 14, 1850, pp. 1–4, MSCS.

[16] Russwurm to Latrobe, Jan. 4, 1850, MSCS.

[17] Russwurm to Latrobe, March 29, 1850, MSCS.

17. *"A Microscope"*

[1] S. F. McGill to Hall, Sept. 18, 1851, p. 2, MSCS.

[2] The society's decision to encourage independence of Maryland: "Minutes of a Meeting, July 17, 1851," in *Minutebook of the Board of Managers of the Maryland State Colonization Society, No. 3*, pp. 322–25 and 329; "Twentieth Annual Report of the Maryland State Colonization Society," in *Minutebook of the Board of Managers of the Maryland State Colonization Society, No. 4*, p. 1ff. (esp. pp. 11–14); "Report of Charles Howard with regard to independence" at a meeting of the Board of Managers, Nov. 20, 1852, p. 44ff.; John H. B. Latrobe to S. F. McGill, Baltimore, Nov. 20, 1852, transcribed in *Minutebook of the Board of Managers of the Maryland State Colonization Society, No. 4*, pp. 50–59 and a second, private letter of the same date, pp.59–65.

Initial settler response: Prout to Latrobe, Jan. 6, 1852, pp. 1–2; McGill to Latrobe, Jan. 6, 1852; McGill to Latrobe, Jan. 9, 1852; J. Stewart to Latrobe, Jan. 7, 1852

[3] Russwurm to Hall, Sept. 16, 1850, pp. 1–2, MSCS.

President Roberts, one of Russwurm's oldest friends in Liberia, visited Cape Palmas in October, 1850. They talked at length about the possibility of Maryland uniting with the Republic. Both agreed that Maryland must eventually comprise part of Liberia proper, but obstacles, notably the relationship of the Maryland State Colonization Society with its colony, would prevent any such union in the next few years at least. A small but vocal party favored annexation, but they had confederation in mind. The Republic's constitution would allow the admission of counties, rather than sovereign states (as in the United States). All but the most ardent supporters of annexation found this unacceptable. (See also, D. R. Fletcher to Hall, March 29, 1850, MSCS.)

[4] Grebo Headmen to the Board of Managers, Half Cavally, Oct., 1850, pp. 1–2, MSCS. A schoolboy from the Episcopal mission wrote their message in faint pencil on a scrap of paper.

[5] The threat of war, early 1851: S. F. McGill to Hall, Sept. 18, 1851, p. 1; Thomas Gross to Hall, March 30, 1851, p. 3, MSCS.

[6] Russwurm's declining health, 1851: S. F. McGill to Latrobe, July 11, 1851, p. 1; Prout to Latrobe, July 16, 1851, pp. 1–3, MSCS.

[7] S. F. McGill to James Hall, Sept. 15, 1850, pp. 1–3, MSCS. "Fletcher is careless, and inefficient," he wrote, adding, "can't be stimulated to any thing brilliant. I'm in a measure to blame for this, I sought for a pupil who would never prove mutinous and refractory, never supposing that a different disposition might be desirable." As for William Cassell, "What a pity you had not induced him to pay some attention to the study of general principles of law previous to his residence among us." At least he was a good

citizen, and a benefit to the community. His brother Roszell, nicknamed Rock, whom he had nursed during extended periods of ill health, was now about to leave Maryland, and he was depressed at the departure of a close friend and jealous of his ability to move on.

[8] McGill informed his patron Moses Sheppard of his plans while he remained in Monrovia. The old man cannot very easily have approved of them, as Maryland was his special project, and great expense and care had been taken to prepare McGill for usefulness there. The doctor explained that he had long wanted to leave Maryland, but "a strong sense of duty and obligation" had prevented him. He had done what he could to improve society at Harper and make himself happy there, he wrote, but he could not overcome "the opposing current of ignorance and lack of energy, that characterized the emigrants from the low Counties of Maryland." The seeming vigor and luster of the republican capital made all else seem inferior. "I could perhaps be ruler there some day," he wrote presciently of Cape Palmas, "but it would have been over a spiritless and helpless people. I could have acquired wealth there beyond what is possible here, but wealth without social and political elevation, would be worthless." He would miss his sister, Sarah Russwurm, he wrote, but she was determined to stay with her husband, who refused to retire, although he was exhausted and unpopular. S. F. McGill to Moses Sheppard, Monrovia, April 23, 1851, in Sheppard Papers, Swarthmore College.

[9] The board had written instructions to Russwurm on this subject as early as his visit to Baltimore late in 1848 (see J. H. B. Latrobe to John Russwurm, Baltimore, Sept. 5, 1848, transcribed in *Minutebook of the Board of Managers of the Maryland State Colonization Society, No 3*). I have been unable to locate proclamation regarding the colony's future and instructions to Russwurm in the society's archive.

[10] Russwurm's inability to follow through: McGill to Hall, Dec. 15, 1851; Prout to Latrobe, Sept. 23, 1851; A. Wood to Latrobe, Sept. 24, 1851; J. Stewart to the Board of Managers, Sept. 25, 1851, all in MSCS.

[11] D. R. Fletcher to Latrobe, April 10, 1851, p.2, MSCS.

[12] Notices of Russwurm's death: Petition of Settlers to the Board, June, 1851; J. Rambo to Hall, June 16, 1851; J. J. Roberts to Hall, Monrovia, June 28, 1851; S. F. McGill to Latrobe, July 11, 1851; Prout to Latrobe, July 16, 1851; J. Stewart to the Board of Managers, Sept. 25, 1851, all in MSCS.

[13] B. J. Drayton to Latrobe, Sept. 25, 1851, p.1, MSCS.

[14] S. F. McGill to Latrobe, July 11, 1851, p.5, MSCS.

[15] Cassell's character: S. F. McGill to Latrobe, July 11, 1851, p. 5, MSCS; biography in *Maryland Colonization Journal*, n.s., 8:194, in which James Hall wrote, "having once tasted freedom in Africa, [he] found it difficult to remain in a country where he could not be recognized as a man — although as much respected by all classes, with whom he came in contact, as any one of his color could be."

Prout's unhappiness: Prout to Latrobe, July 16, 1851, MSCS.

[16] Settler opposition to McGill: J. H. Stewart to Latrobe, Jan. 7, 1852, pp.5–6, MSCS. Joshua Stewart and Anthony Wood to the Board of Managers, June 18, 1851, p. 1, MSCS. "As a people," they began, "in a Body, Haveing felt the Great loss of him Who have been our Chief Magistrat, and Agent for your Society for this last 14 years and upwards, and Whom we had considered A Statesman, a Patriot, and a Christian Brother, We are Left, to Lement, and to Simpathise with you Gentlemen on the death of So good a man." They asked the board to waste no time in appointing a successor, but to be careful to

choose an appropriate one. Moreover, the society should limit the term of office to four years. Samuel McGill had assumed the duties of governor, because he was assistant agent, but neither he nor settlers were happy with the arrangement. McGill was unpopular (to say the least), and before Russwurm's death, he had publicly announced his intention to leave Maryland. He had even gone so far, a day or two after Russwurm's death, to request settlers to petition the board for his dismissal, as they now did. Many settlers would have agreed with these sentiments, but the intended popular remonstrance instead went to Baltimore with only two signatures.

A public meeting of citizens, held on August 2 expressed a similar opinion. In the resulting letter home, they reiterated their sense of loss in the passing of their governor: "Pen cannot ascribe our fealing, no Sir, our lips cannot tell our fealing on hearing the Report." "But, *Sirs*," they continued,

> one thing is worst than all, who shall we have next, where is his Equals to be found, as a States man, a Philanthropist, and a christian, we fear it cannot be, no *Sirs*, not among the Colered Population. we only ask for one that will lookout for us, and for our best intrest, and we will not be a wate on his hands, no, we will hold them, oh, sir can you sympatise with and for us, that we do not Pine away and die in our youth, but let us grow.

(Letter from Citizens to the Board of Managers, August 1851, p. 1, MSCS.)

[17] S. F. McGill to Latrobe, July 11, 1851, p. 2, MSCS.

[18] Anthony Wood was a target of abuse: "He rarely works at his trade, or at any thing else, while his wife toils like a slave for the support of his family," Dr. McGill wrote scathingly at the end of April, 1852.

A few months before, Rev. Boston Drayton had criticized these settlers in a most ironic manner, considering subsequent events: "They wants to have a new governor so that, they might Carry war against the Natives. It is all folly. The time will come when they deem it necessary to remove, to keep sacred their own institution, provided, the gospel dont break in upon them before. We come here not to carry war and carnage, but the blessed peace of Righteousness." (Boston Jenkins Drayton to Latrobe, April 10, 1851, p.1, MSCS.)

S. F. McGill to Latrobe, Sept. 15, 1851, p. 4, MSCS, comments that there would be interruptions, simply because of the daily contact of the two communities, which remained so different in culture. McGill, who was no friend of Africa, but who hated Maryland settlers even more, was happy to blame settlers in advance for any disturbance that might arise. They treated Africans disrespectfully. He condemned the attitude for its hypocrisy, "inflicting upon them here that wrong and injustice, which we experienced in the United States, and escaped by seeking our home in this Country." He continued boldly, "I am disposed to give the Native African justice, to treat him as a man and a brother, by uniform Kindness to convince him of my disposition to benefit him, and then to permit not of his encroachment upon our right or liberties without an effort to inflict well deserved punishment."

[19] Publication of the Board's proclamation on independence: McGill to Hall, Dec. 15, 1851, pp. 2–3; Prout to Latrobe, Sept. 23, 1851, pp. 1–3, both in MSCS.

[20] Prout and McGill's meeting: McGill to Hall, Dec. 15, 1851, pp. 2–3; Prout to Latrobe, Sept. 23, 1851, pp. 1–3, both in MSCS.

McGill was well placed to know the politics current at Monrovia. His brother James was a senator, and the family had been active in politics there since the late 1820s. McGill wrote Latrobe not long after Russwurm's death concerning the prospects of union as a state. Maryland might join Liberia as a county, but never as a state, he wrote, as the Republic's constitution did not provide for states. Liberia certainly would not alter her constitution for such a purpose, for she had little to gain from Maryland's admission. Maryland was a poor backwater from their standpoint, and the expense of administering more territory would only burden her treasury. Union would bring Maryland innumerable advantages, however. Cape Palmas would receive a new influx of emigrants. The colony would have the benefit of Liberia's vigorously enforced revenue laws, which protected local traders from foreign competitors. Moreover, the Republic would have the military force to remove Gbenelu, "upon the very first offence."

[21] Prout to Latrobe, July 16, 1851, p. 2, MSCS.

[22] S. F. McGill to Latrobe, Jan. 6, 1852, p. 6, MSCS.

[23] Anthony Wood to Latrobe, Sept. 24, 1851, p. 1, MSCS.

[24] Proclamation, about July 20, 1851, in Letterbook, 1851, MSCS.

"The Love of Liberty brought us Here."

REPUBLICANISM AND ANNEXATION.

Whereas, we the undersigned on proper principles of national freedom regard ourselves identified in feeling to the people of the Republic of Liberia, do highly and enthusiastically approve of the Step which they have taken to be one of the nations of the Earth: And whereas, we believe that it was for this glorious end why the Colonization Society was founded, and that this result prompted us to forsake our homes; we do cordially, and in the fear of God who planted and sustained us here, Adopt the following Resolutions:

Resolved, That we beleive the time has come wherein we Should begin to think, speak, and Act upon the important and desirable subject of we being *Annexed* to the Republic of Liberia, and as freemen in common with them Shall use every honourable exertion, to be united to them with credit to ourselves and posterity. We hope to do nothing in the dark, but rather to advise and confer with the parent Society, that we may receive from them all possible aid and advice in such an event.

Resolved, That we will with due respect to our present situation Celebrate the 26 day of July 1851; it being the Anniversary of the Republic of Liberia, And all who feel themselves United by common ties to the Republic; are requested to give a small amount to have prepared a "Lunch" for the Occasion — Say $

Resolved: That we will from time to time advise and confer with the Agent, or Governor on all matters touching our relation with the Society, while in the prosecution of this our desirable Object.

ANNEXATION!

[25] McGill to Latrobe, Sept. 16, 1851, pp. 6–7, MSCS.

[26] Petition of Settlers to the Agent and Council, August, 1851, pp. 1–2, MSCS, Letterbook, 1851.

[27] S. F. McGill to Latrobe, Jan. 6, 1851, p. 3, MSCS.

[28] Joshua Stewart to Latrobe, n.d. [mid-1851], p. 1, MSCS. This change of feeling is manifested in many of the letters directed to the society at the time. John Moulton, for instance, wrote John Latrobe on September 21, a typical sort of letter, asking if he could visit home to persuade his old friends in Cumberland to move to Africa. He then discussed society and politics at the Cape, stating firmly that he did not want to be annexed to the Republic. His principal reason was that union would allow ardent spirits into the community. Settlers were now devoting more attention to farming, and if they had done so from the beginning, Maryland would be quite prosperous. Having closed his letter, Moulton realized that he had more to say. He picked up his pen again to ask, daringly, what the society's plans were for the colony, and further, what instructions the board might have for settlers. He observed that union with the Republic as a state was acceptable to most citizens, but it was clear that this was not acceptable to Liberia. "I wish to See these people a independant people to them Selves, or at least a State," he wrote. Agriculture found adherents as never before, settlers "adviseing with each-other which is the most profetable thing to attend to." William Cassell was active in creating an agricultural society. Many were planting coffee, and the future seemed promising. He longed for the day when the world would recognize Maryland's achievement, but perseverance would be necessary.

[29] All of this business frustrated the Acting Governor, as he styled himself. He had bought a house in Monrovia and ordered fine furniture from America, which would arrive in a few months. He had been close to fulfilling his "desire to be among those who are engaged in the noble effort of maintaining their independence," he told Latrobe on July 11, but now all had to be postponed. He had also looked forward to making more money in Monrovia, a pressing concern. "I am engaged in mercantile business," he wrote defiantly, "but it is at present transacted by my Brother Roszell. I do not even pretend to have withdrawn my interest in it, nor indeed shall I do so: this is contrary to the letter of the laws of the Colony I know, but as I was thus engaged ere being honoured by your appointment I cannot think that it is expected that it should be abandoned for the temporary advantages that may accrue from my present office." (S. F. McGill to Latrobe, July 11, 1851, p. 3, MSCS.)

[30] Prout's address, Nov. 10, 1851, MSCS.

[31] Prout's comments concerning the form of government are worthy of a lengthy quote:

> Having remarked that in my opinion this government in some particulars should take the form of some of the States in America, I would in continuation advise that the highest officer of our Commonwealth be denominated, governor. His duties, functions, power etc. of course to be determined by delegates in convention assembled. I would further advise that there be a deputy or lieutenant governor, whose duties to be defined in convention. I would further advise that you have an Assembly to consist of Senate and House of Representatives. The former to consist of two members, and the

latter four. And in order that the officers of these respective houses should be chosen out of the inhabitants of different parts of the Colony, I would advise, for the time being, that the Settlement be divided into two divisions to be denominated the districts of East Harper and West Harper, the respective limits and bearings of which to be defined by delegates in Convention; and I would further advise that said districts of East Harper and West Harper be, east, divided into two Sections and appropriate names and denominations given as may be judged suitable by said delegates in convention. The Senetors, to be nominated, one out of each district of West Harper and East Harper, and the Representatives, one out of each Section. The qualifications and duties of said officers to be determined by deligates in convention assembled on the drafting of a Constitution for the independent government to be erected. Provided, nevertheless, that nothing in this my advice is to be understood as confining the election of said officers to the polls of each and respectively the districts of West Harper and East Harper, or of the Sections to be named, but determining and confining the polling to one place to be provided, where the election of all officers should take place for the time being.

I further advise the appointment of a Secretary of the Treasury, whose duties to be defined in Convention. Besides such duties as are common to such officers, I would recommend that he conduct the financial transactions of the government on a plan of which I am to speak, for the raising of a fund to be contributed toward the support of Government, that he be invested with power (subject to such action in point of instructions as the Legislature may deem meet for his guidance and procedure from time to time) to enter into agreements, contracts local or foreign for the purpose of raising sum or sums of money, for and on account of government, for which he should be bound in sufficient security for the faithful discharge of so high a trust.

My further advice is, that there should be a Secretary of State; an Inspector of the armory, munitions of war etc., and one Notary public, whose duties, functions, obligations and compensation to be defined (or so much thereof as may be within their province) by the members in convention on the formation of a plan of government for the independence of this Colony.

I further recommend, that in the Judiciary, there be a Chief Justice, four associate Judges and four Justices of the Peace. The Chief Justice and two associates to preside in the Supreme Judicial Court to which an appeal will lie in cases of capital offence or high misdemeanor for final decision; and one associate and two Justices of the peace to preside in Court of Monthly Sessions. The Associate Judges etc. to take their terms in rotation. The Chief Justice to be appointed by the Executive with the advice and consent of the Senate and house of Representatives, to be allowed a fixed salary, and to be subject to removal on presentation for mal-administration in office by a majority of both houses. He should act as Judge of probate Court during the time being. The Associates in both Courts to be allowed compensation per diem. Their duties, powers, emoluments, qualifications, form of installment etc. to be regulated in convention.

Further, that the Register and Sheriff be elected, one of each being sufficient for the time being.

And further, I advise thJose de Amorio to Russwurm, April 17, 1837, MSCS.e election of four Selectmen, to be nominated, one out of every section of the Colony as aforesaid for the time being.

And lastly, I have thus hastily enumerated certain officers which you will find important to your government, but there are others necessary and incident to a well organized government, however small. They, I hope, will be regulated and provided for, by the Gentlemen whom you may depute to arrange a form of the government contemplated.

[32] W. Cassell and others to the Board of Managers, Nov. 15, 1851, pp. 5–6, MSCS: They noted that most settlers would like things to remain as before, with the colonization society at the head of government and supporting public works, but everyone realized that this must end. Citizens were now resolved to take charge of their own affairs.

> To have remained inactive under the gathering of a storm growing more and more dark and lowering until it broke full upon our heads, with the detriment consequent thereupon, would have been far from wise and prudent. The expedience therefore of making estimates of expenditure and the importance of attending to the subject of a providence to meet these expenditures consequent on a change of government, involved, among other considerations, a matter of great importance to us.

Most citizens favored union with Liberia as a state, they noted, since Cape Palmas was used to making its own laws. They pointedly criticized McGill for his partisan activities, which hindered Maryland's progress. The remainder of the letter consisted of a gloss of Prout's address, principally concerning the transfer of the society's property in Africa. The most troublesome issue was how to pay for the projected government. The committee judged that the revenue of the new state must be derived from trade. They asked the society to consider a loan to capitalize a government mercantile venture.

Prout's most controversial suggestion was to allow the trade of ardent spirits. The committee commented:

> The tolerance of liquor as an article of trade, will evidently have the object of developing the resources of the Country, by opening the avenues now closed to the inhabitants of the distant regions of the interior and cause an influx of trade to the Colony. It will afford the means of controlling the trade coastwise, and command that which has been heretofore engrossed by foreign merchantmen. The people wish the Board to be informed, that, no circumstances could have prompted them to the propriety of this measure (out of deference to the temperance code on which it was the pleasure of the Society that

the colony should be based) but the ends already suggested. They therefore hope for your concurrence on this head. (Ibid., p. 3.)

[33] McGill's criticism of Prout's motives: McGill to Hall, Dec. 15, 1851, p. 3, MSCS. McGill calls Prout a drunkard to foreigners, Prout's comments: Prout to Hall, May 18, 1854, MSCS.

[34] John Bowen to the Board of Managers, Sept. 24, 1851, MSCS.

[35] W. Prout to Latrobe, Jan. 6, 1852, p. 4, MSCS.

[36] Anthony Wood to Latrobe, Sept. 24, 1851, MSCS.

[37] W. Prout to Latrobe, Jan. 6, 1852, p. 4, MSCS. In another session of the legislature, at the end of 1851, McGill tried to have a similar measure passed, but the councilors refused to permit it.

[38] W. Prout to Latrobe, Jan. 6, 1852, p. 3, MSCS.

[39] S. F. McGill to Hall, Dec. 15, 1851, p. 2, MSCS.

[40] McGill's military activities, late 1851: McGill to Hall, Dec. 15, 1851, p. 1; McGill to Latrobe, Jan. 9, 1852, p. 4, both in MSCS.

[41] Joshua Stewart to Latrobe, Jan. 7, 1852, MSCS.

Even so, McGill succeeded in paying off the agency's principal debts by the end of 1851. In the middle of December he had 5,000 gallons of palm oil and five tons of camwood in stock. If trade goods arrived from the society soon, he would send the produce back to Baltimore for the society's benefit. Otherwise, he would have to use it to purchase tobacco and gunpowder from the first merchant who could supply it. McGill to Hall, Dec. 15, 1851, MSCS.

[42] Criticism of McGill's handling of agency trade: J. B. Bowen to the Board of Managers, Sept. 24, 1851; J. Stewart to the Board, Sept. 25, 1851; A. Wood to Latrobe, Sept. 24, 1851; Prout to Latrobe, Jan. 6, 1852, pp. 3–4; J. Stewart to Latrobe, Jan. 7, 1852, pp. 3–8, all in MSCS.

[43] McGill to Hall, Sept. 18, 1851, p. 2, MSCS.

[44] *Maryland Colonization Journal*, n.s., 6:161.

[45] Renewal of the Maryland State appropriation for colonization: S. F. McGill to Latrobe, Jan. 28, 1853, pp. 1–2; McGill to Latrobe, July 12, 1852, p. 4, both in MSCS.

18. *"Civilized Modes of Living"*

[1] William A. Prout to Latrobe, April 12, 1852, p. 3, MSCS.

[2] Joshua Stewart to Latrobe, Jan. 7, 1852, pp. 9–10, MSCS.

[3] Sources for the topographical description of the settlement: Burton, R., *Wanderings in West Africa . . .*; Alexander Cowan, *Liberia as I Found It, in 1858 . . .*; John Revey, "Map of Maryland in Liberia," MSCS.

[4] Housing: Colonial Accounts, filed semi-annually give precise details of building materials; Russwurm to McGill, June 11, 1848: mentions shingles and framing; McGill to Hall, Jan. 10, 1854: mentions that settlers construct their own house frames from materials supplied by the agency; McGill to Joseph Gibson, [about June 1, 1854]: gives list of materials composing a house frame; Phillip Gross to Hall, Feb. 17, 1845, p. 3, lists items wanted for his house, including glass window panes, putty, green paint, and white wash brushes; Phillip Gross to Frederick Mayor, D. Hughes, Jan. 17, 1846: reports his and father's houses measure 22 by 16 feet; Lemuel Herring to Hall, Jan. 25, 1846: asks for window sashes with twelve panes each, and two small hanging mirrors; J. W. Lugenbeel

to Hall, May 26, 1846, pp. 2–3, notes that the only thatched houses in the colony belonged to Africans.

⁵ S. F. McGill to Latrobe, Sept. 16, 1851, p. 2, MSCS.

⁶ Interestingly, Mary Moran, in her book on modern Maryland County, finds similar attitudes existing to this day. *Civilized Women,* pp. 5, 68–69, 135–36, 139–40.

⁷ Clothing of settlers: References from Colonial Accounts, passim; McGill to Joseph Gibson, [about June 1, 1854], p. 3; Christopher Phillips, *Freedom's Port,* pp. 147–50 discusses the importance of apparel in defining class and aspirations and as a means of self-expression among Baltimore's black community.

⁸ Used and home-made clothing: letter from McGill requesting used clothing; Fanny Davenport to Hall, Nov. 21, 1848: asks Hall to sell a pocket watch left behind in Baltimore, concluding, "out of the money of the watch Please send me one Shawl and som calico to make me a Dress." Census of 1852, MSCS, which lists only four female occupations, the others being Laundress (of which there were five), together with one teacher and one soap-maker. Most women, even among the fifty single heads of household had no listed occupation.

⁹ S. F. McGill, "Inventory of Goods, Wares, and Merchandise in the Agency Store, Cape Palmas," June 1, 1854, p. 1 [I have omitted the valuations from the extract.]

¹⁰ A good example of settler taste is provided in a letter of Phillip Gross to James Hall. He sent Hall a list of items he wanted for trade to his neighbors as well as his family's use. These included, "8 pare of Brogan shoes Number 4 4 pare of them fine 4 pare of women shoes morocco num 4 2 leghorn hats mens ware 1 fine Straw Bonnet and Box 1 Dozen paste Boards 3 peices Romal Cloth 20 yards of Striped Cotten mens ware 30 yards of calico Small prints for Shirts 10 yards in A peice and Differrent prints 20 yards of White Drillen for pants 20 yards of Brown Linen for coats 8 wescoat patners Differrent prints not over costly." He added, "I would like you without fail if you please to get My Wife two [Godey's] ladys Books at Mr taylors south Street as they will be very profitble to her Business to have the lates fashions in Dress Makeing the Numbers she wishes is Mays and Junes." (Phillip Gross to James Hall, Feb. 17, 1845, pp. 2–3, MSCS.)

Other letters mentioning settler fashion: Joshua Stewart to Hall, June 12, 1848, p. 2: "Send me out one or 2 Skins of moroker to mak Shoes for My Self and famel as I cant Git uper Lether in Africa particular at Monrovia But Sole Lether a plenty of it." Russwurm to Hall, March 1, 1847, p. 1, mentions current settler taste for blue stripe and blue drill material.

¹¹ McGill to Gibson, [about June 1, 1854], lists furniture and utensils given to each head of a family. The Emigrant Expenses lists in the Semi-Annual Colonial Accounts contain regular entries of payments for rough tables, stools, and bedsteads made on order by local carpenters.

Russwurm to Hall, Dec. 18, 1847, MSCS: complains, "I sent for a turning lathe complete — not for a part of one. Rev. Herring's was the model I had in view whether our turners are capable or not, none has offered to make the bench and wheel."

¹² Rations to new emigrants: Russwurm to McGill, June 11, 1848, instructs the doctor to buy all the rice he can during his absence, and further, "I have generally retailed on Saturday when to spare one Barrel Salt Fish or Meat." McGill to Gibson [about June 1, 1854], both in MSCS.

¹³ Settler diet: Colonial Accounts, passim; J. W. Lugenbeel to Hall, May 26, 1846, p. 3:

"There is a good garden attached to the government house, in which nearly all the vegetables are raised, which are used at the Governor's table. . . . On one occasion in company with a considerable number of invited guests, I perceived that every article on the table was of African production, except wheat bread and a ham; nor was there the least scarcity, or want of variety. The sweet potatoes were equal to any I ever saw; and the white and delicate cabbage heads reminded me of my native land." Catherine Ross to Ira Easter and John Kennard, May 21, 1839, MSCS, asking for meat while her crops mature; Dianah Hardy to Cosmo Sunderland and her parents (his slaves), Sept. 4, 1836, MSCS, speaking of her family's gardening and asking for various herbs and seeds; Russwurm to Latrobe, April 26, 1849: during a period of rice shortage, reports that settlers resort to cassava and sweet potatoes.

[14] Agency's role as middleman in trade: Russwurm to Latrobe, Oct. 23, 1849, p. 2, MSCS. "We have penetrated 250 miles (in a N. E. direction) into the interior where we found the *Pahs* very hospitable and friendly. They wish to bring their Camwood and Ivory directly to the Cape, but are prevented by intervening tribes, who want to act as brokers, and cheat them out of half their sales." Elsewhere in the same letter, "Our interior trade is capable of being extended as a great supply must be needed to meet their wants: they place the highest estimate upon all goods and wares of foreign manufacture; and [although] the *Pahs* manufacture good strong cloth of their own they prefer the foreign — thin and slazy as it often is."

[15] Designing trade goods for the African market: Russwurm to Hall, Nov. 8, 1847, pp. 1–2, MSCS.

Specific purchasing powers of trade goods: Russwurm to Latrobe, April 26, 1849, pp. 4–5; Russwurm to Hall, Oct. 19, 1849, p. 3; Colonial Accounts, *passim*.

[16] Formalization of terms of trade: Russwurm to Latrobe, Oct. 23, 1849, p. 2, MSCS. Speaking of the falling international price for camwood, he notes that trade has fallen off, "With the price once established, it is very hard to purchase for less from the natives." J. Russwurm to James Hall, Jan. 24, 1847, p. 2, MSCS.

[17] Changes of taste: Russwurm to Hall, Oct. 19, 1849, pp. 1–2, MSCS.

Difficulties from spoilage: Russwurm to Latrobe, April 25, 1849, p. 5; Russwurm to Hall, Nov. 19, 1849, MSCS. The reader will recall an instance in the late 1830s when the warehouse suffered structural damage as a result of the mass of materials stored in it.

[18] Manner of trade with African factors: See chapter 3, note 29.

[19] Sample statistics of palm oil trade in 1850: *Maryland Colonization Journal*, n.s., 6:21.

[20] Profit from the agency's African trade through 1849: *Maryland Colonization Journal*, n.s., 5:147.

[21] The situation in 1851: *Maryland Colonization Journal*, n.s., 6:132.

[22] On the society's international trade: "Yankee Traders, Old Coasters, and African Middlemen," Agent's letters, *passim*. J. B. Russwurm to S. F. McGill, June 11, 1848, MSCS. In a letter of instructions, the agent notes, "The Board expect the Agent in Africa to make all he can by trade in Palm Oil and other produce."

[23] *Maryland Colonization Journal*, n.s., 6:22.

[24] Shift of African trade toward big capital: Russwurm to Latrobe, Jan. 4, 1850, MSCS; James Hall, in an editorial in *Maryland Colonization Journal*, n.s., 1:24–25, wrote: "How provoking that we have not the means to avail ourselves of the most possible good from

our peculiar position and the superior capacity and talents of our officers in Africa!"
Speech of J. H. B. Latrobe to the Massachusetts Colonization Society on "Commerce
and Civilization," published in *Maryland Colonization Journal*, n.s., 7:57.

[25] Narrative of the formation of the C&L Trading Company: in *Maryland Colonization Journal*, n.s., 2:337–39, 365–66.

[26] Competition from Europeans: J. B. Russwurm to Latrobe, Oct. 23, 1849, p. 2,
MSCS. "We deal mostly with the English, as their vessels supply us with goods suitable for
our trade. We prefer dealing with American vessels if we can procure what we want (for
our native trade): American vessels frequently call, but many are unwilling to receive
produce in payment for their goods." James Hall, "Our 'African Squadrons'," editorial in
Maryland Colonization Journal, n.s., 6:81–88.

German traders: Russwurm to Hall, Oct. 1, 1847, p. 3; Russwurm to Hall, Nov. 8, 1847,
pp. 1–2, both in MSCS.

[27] *Maryland Colonization Journal*, n.s., 2:65–72

[28] Russwurm to Latrobe, April 26, 1849, p. 3, MSCS.

[29] McGill to Hall, Sept. 18, 1851, pp. 1–2, MSCS. See also J. B. Russwurm to James Hall,
March 1, 1847, MSCS, who condemns the resistance of settlers to having to pay for
medical treatment, "I laugh at them, though angry at their foolishness, and I hope the
Board will just return the petition. Our people have been made children of so long, that
they are really spoiled."

[30] Settlers sometimes used the society's shinplasters, first issued in the late 1830s and
then reissued late in Russwurm's tenure. There was not very much in circulation, however, probably less than $500. In June 1854, the agency held $126. Much of the rest was in
the hands of mutual aid societies as insurance funds. The limited purchasing power of
the currency frustrated settlers. In April 1849, they petitioned the board to base it on
African produce or remove it altogether. An anonymous correspondent at the time
commented, "We have a paper currency redeemable at the store, with goods: and they
never have any thing that is for anything that they will let you have for it, and in the other
stores they will not take it at all, and you cannot get that money but seldom. . . . As it
regards the paper money, I may say it is good for nothing for we can not get such things
as we need, with it in our hands." Anonymous fragment of a letter, about April, 1849, pp.
2–3, MSCS.

Russwurm was very jealous of the agency's trading interests and was quick to punish
any infraction. A case in point is his dispute with the elder Benjamin Tubman, early in
1845. Late the previous year, Tubman had contracted to build an American-style house at
Barrakah in exchange for three bullocks. When he finished, the purchasers refused to
give him more than one "woman-bullock" and a sheep for his troubles. He resorted to
the governor, who won the promise of ten croos of rice to make up the difference. Some
days passed before Barrawe trade men returned to the colony, and when they did, they
had no rice. They told Tubman and Russwurm that they could obtain none, but that they
might get a bullock if Tubman would accept that. The deal was struck, with the provision
that the rice or bullock must be delivered within ten days. If they failed, Russwurm
authorized Tubman to seize any Barrawe property he could lay hands on, to the value
due. The tenth day passed, the contract unfulfilled. Soon after, Tubman discovered some
Barrawe trademen carrying rice to the beach. He took ten croos from them and sent
word to the governor that he was satisfied. What was his surprise then to see the sheriff

appear at his gate and seize his jenny and her foal. It seems that Tubman seized rice already contracted by the agency. Russwurm was furious at the interference and reclaimed the animals in retribution. Tubman had to beg John Latrobe to intercede on his behalf, for he had gotten the animal near death and had nursed it very carefully, finally succeeding in breeding her. The outcome is not recorded. (Benjamin Tubman Sr. to Latrobe, March, 1845, MSCS.

[31] Public Farm statistics: Agricultural Census for 1848, p. 1, MSCS. Indigent labor on the farm: McGill to Latrobe, Sept. 16, 1851, pp. 2–3, MSCS. McGill added that most of the farm's produce was given away to the poor.

[32] Joshua Stewart to Hall, April 28, 1849, pp. 1–2, MSCS.

[33] Settler ideal of the agrarian life: Charles Scotland to Hall, Jan. 17, 1845, pp. 1–2, MSCS; Prout to Latrobe, Sept. 23, 1851, MSCS, mentions formation of an agricultural society and the settler concept of self-reliance.

[34] Oliver A. Chambers to Rev. Ira Easter, July 10, 1838, pp. 1–2, MSCS.

[35] J. E. Moulton to Latrobe, [Sept., 1851], pp. 1–2, MSCS.

[36] McGill to Gibson, [about June 1, 1854], p. 2, MSCS. In fact the shortage of necessary tools was almost desperate, as in the case of Rebecca Delany, who wrote Hall on Feb. 1, 1846: "When I came out to this place I had some hoes and you told me that the Colonist was poor and as I had not children big enough to use the hoes to let you have 2 for the colonist and when my children got big enough to work that you would let me have too more and now all my children big enough to work please to send them and pleese to send me a Sifter."

[37] Unfamiliar crops and seasons: see Nicholas Jackson to unknown correspondent, April 4, 1848, MSCS: "I have Encouraged and will endeavour to encourage agriculture, but i think the Colonys have attended their farmes more this year than usual, but as their is a grate failure in the Rice Crops and our crops failed in part by the excessive heat and but little Rain, Should their bin means for agriculture it would be a great plus, but not having means it is abstract to agriculture."

[38] Soil depletion: Petition of Citizens, Oct. 24, 1844, MSCS. Also, see the earlier discussion of soil types and ecological degradation in chapters 3 and 9.

[39] Problems with livestock: McGill to Latrobe, July 12, 1846, MSCS, describes an epidemic that swept the area, killing fourteen Americans and an unknown but larger number of Greboes. The disease had an even more devastating effect on livestock, killing cows and horses, "sheep, hogs, and even dogs." Russwurm to Latrobe, Nov. 28, 1848, p. 2, complains of the extreme shortage of riding animals; Russwurm to Latrobe, April 26, 1849, p. 3, criticizes settlers for wasting cattle by using them for hauling lumber from the swamps.

[40] Agricultural Census, 1848, MSCS. Settler letters mentioning their farming activities include: Phillip Gross to Mayor D. Hughes, Jan. 17, 1846: "The lots is eighty feet in front and two hundred back we have now growing in our lots cabbage tomatto lima beans and potatoes our Waster mellons and canter lope season are just over. . . . we have twenty chickens and one hog runing in the yard I have also twenty coffy trees comeing on and two orange trees which I hope I will have luck with if I Do I intend to plant out more." Joshua Stewart to Hall, Sept. 23, 1851, p. 2, "I have a garden a Large one, that I keep up thru much difficulty — planty of Vegitable a Hous that Shelter Me and My famela

from the Stormy Blast Day and Night with my Stock around me." Benjamin Tubman Jr. to Latrobe, Jan. 20, 1846; J. W. Lugenbeel to Hall, Frederick Co., Md., May 26, 1846, p. 2.

[41] Settler traders: Benjamin Tubman Jr. to Latrobe, Jan. 20, 1846, mentions that he trades as a supplement to his farming; Lemuel Herring to Hall, Jan. 25, 1846, offers to pay for 200 pounds of tobacco with camwood and palm oil upon receipt.

Women in business: Statute of 1845 imposing trading license fees, exempted for women with inventories less than $100; S. E. Russwurm to Hall, Oct. 15, 1849, indicates that she was engaged in trade. Rev. John Payne has purchased $178.54 in goods from her, and she instructed Hall to pay $64 for twelve bonnets and $70 for miscellaneous other goods. She also placed an order for

> 24 pairs thick souled Ladies shoes (retail $1)
> 36 do. black Kid slippers at 720 per dozen
> 36 do. Kid bronze slippers and ties
> 12 do. childrens bootes from 10 to 13 Nos.
> 1 Keg of Lard and 1 good Butter

to be purchased from Thorne's New York Shoe Store in downtown Baltimore. She apologized for troubling Dr. Hall, but a woman friend who would normally have done the favor was away.

Children in business: Rev. John Payne to Latrobe, Nov. 22, 1848, commenting on the anticipated opening of a manual labor school at Mount Vaughan, states, "many Colonist youth pass most of their time in trafficking amongst the natives at a time when the character is forming, and when under such circumstances, it is [poorly] forming, and *evil. . . .* Of one thing be assured, the evil sought to be remedied is a most serious and increasing one. There is far more licentiousness than in former years amongst the young in the Colony, and I attribute it in a great degree to the fact above alluded to." See also, Prout to Latrobe, April 12, 1852, p. 2, MSCS, concerning his youthful experiences as a trader at Little Bassa.

[42] Proceedings of Agent and Council, March 20, 1840, MSCS.

[43] History of McGill, Brothers: *Maryland Colonization Journal*, n.s., 1:274, 4:68, 8:273. Merchant capital at Cape Palmas: J. B. Russwurm to James Hall, Nov. 8, 1847, p. 4, MSCS; James Hall in *Maryland Colonization Journal* n.s., 1:161–72, concerning the advantages of local traders with small boats in the coastal trade; J. B. McGill to James Hall, Sept. 15, 1850, MSCS; J. B. McGill to James Hall, Oct. 1, 1850, MSCS concerning McGill, Bros. activities.

[44] Conflict over import duties: Russwurm to Latrobe, May 13, 1846, pp. 1–3; Anthony Wood to unidentified correspondent, July 15, 1846; McGill to Latrobe, Sept. 6, 1846, p. 3; J. B. Bowen to James Hall, Jan. 26, 1847, MSCS; D. R. Fletcher to unidentified Correspondent [probably James Hall], Oct. 5, 1847, p. 2, MSCS. Conflict over rum trade: Russwurm to Latrobe, May 13, 1846, p. 3; McGill to Latrobe, July 12, 1846, p. 4; D. R. Fletcher to James Hall, Jan. 26, 1847, MSCS.

[45] Anonymous fragment of a letter, [1849], pp. 1–2, MSCS.

[46] Occupations as listed in the Census of Maryland in Liberia, 1852.

[47] Concerning settler occupations: Stephen Smith to George Roberts, Jan. 7, 1845, orders leather to repair his bellows; Russwurm to Hall, Sept. 18, 1845, p. 2, comments on settler soap-making and self-sufficiency; Russwurm to Hall, Oct. 25, 1845, pp. 1–2, more

comments on self-sufficiency; J. H. Stewart to Hall, June 12, 1848, p. 2, complains of the shortage of leather. "If I was able to by Lether from the Stats I could mak More Money then What I do"; John Bordely to unidentified correspondent, June 17, 1848, p. 2, mentions his wife, who makes money as a midwife, a son who is a seaman, and a daughter who is a housekeeper; Russwurm to Hall, Nov. 22, 1848, p. 2: "There is a young man from Baltimore whose master was a tinman: he is called Chs. Chambers: he wants a box of tin and all of the tools which they use except the shears: he seems industrious"; L. G. Herring to Hall, [Dec.] 22, 1848: requests a water-driven sawmill, clamps and files, having prepared a site, and promises to pay for it immediately "in cash or oil."

[48] McGill to Latrobe, Sept. 16, 1851, p. 2, MSCS.

[49] Statistics of emigrants: Emigrant Roll; Senate Document #150; Semi-annual reports, Anecdotal material from letters, *passim*; Vital Statistics for 1837, in Letterbook, 1837, MSCS; "List of Deaths and Marriages by the Colonial Register" in Latterbook, 1839, MSCS; *Maryland Colonization Journal*, n.s., Vol. II, pp. 7–9; "Colonial Register for Jan., 1840 to Feb. 1843" in Letterbook 1843, MSCS; "Births, Deaths, and Marriages for 1845" Box 48, MSCS; *Maryland Colonization Journal*, n.s., Vol. III, p. 162 and Vol. IV, pp. 237–38; "Births, marriages and deaths in 1848" in Letterbook 1848, MSCS; *Maryland Colonization Journal*, n.s., Vol. V, pp. 2–3; Vol. V, pp. 281–83; Vol. VI, pp. 23–24; and "Births, Deaths and Marriages for 1852" in Letterbook 1852, MSCS .

The number of emigrants who went to Cape Palmas is not obvious from the rolls of the Maryland State Colonization Society. In its early days, the society sent settlers to Liberia proper (and even to Haiti, though I have left them off the list altogether), on the *Orion* and then on the *Lafayette*. Some of these subsequently moved to Cape Palmas. Others, sent out by the American Colonization Society, later moved down the coast. Records of individuals moving from Liberia to Cape Palmas have been published only through 1842. We may assume that others went to Cape Palmas after that date, but the numbers were probably not very high. It is also very likely that there was a reciprocal flow of settlers from Maryland to Liberia. James Hall indicated this in an editorial in *Maryland Colonization Journal* of July, 1847: "It may be remarked that there have been other acquisitions to the colony besides emigrants from Maryland. . . . But we think this number is fully equalled by those who have left the colony." He mentioned Luke Walker and his family, who returned to Maryland after only a brief stay in Africa, as well as three individuals living in Baltimore. "Some are also in other colonies along the coast, changing their residence, as might be expected in a free country. The conclusion is but fair, that independent of immigration, we have a regular increase, although a small one, over all deaths from acclimation, casualties and accidents, a remarkable circumstance in the settlement of any new country, and we believe unprecedented in the tropical world" (n.s., 2:7).

One would like to know much more about the demographic characteristics of the emigrant population, and the records would seem to offer a wonderful window on this. There are significant obstacles to research along these lines, however. It is clear that settlers left behind kin, but just how many, and under what circumstances is unrecorded in most instances. Thus, information about birthrates and family relationships is necessarily flawed. Moreover, settlers frequently did not know or keep track of their ages. Officers of the society seem usually to have guessed ages when they recorded the names and background of emigrants. The absence of seasonal patterns at Cape Palmas made it even harder to track age, a point abundantly clear as one follows the records of citizens in the annual census lists. This presents an interesting and valuable sociological fact, but it is a demographer's nightmare.

[50] The impact of leaving family members behind: Charles Scotland to James Hall, Jan. 17, 1845, pp. 1–2, expressing his desire to return to America himself or to send his son to gather up the rest of his family; S. F. McGill to H. B. Goodwin, March 15, 1845, p. 1, comments to the former master on the refusal of Jesse Flanagan's family to emigrate. "It is to be hoped that the wife and children of Flannegan may yet find it to their interest to accept of their freedom and join him. It is to me a matter strange and inexplicable that there should be individuals in this world so strangely constituted as to prefer slavery to freedom"; Andrew Hall to James Hall, Jan. 24, 1847, asks for help getting his son sent out to Africa; Thomas Brown to James Hall, April 25, 1849, asks for permission to visit the United States, "I have been here now about thirteen years and no one has come here from my part of the country since I came. I wish to come in and try if I can not bring out a brother and some other relatives of mine"; J. G. Moulton to James Hall, "I Should like very much to Come home, but I should not like to Come in the Cold weather: this would be the very time If I was ready, but I am not Got Sufficient Clothin at Present. I however assure You that it would only be for the Cause of the Poor Blacks that would ever Cause me to Put myself to any truble to Come to the States, My Relations Being Dear to me As well as all other men of Colour. I would feel it a duty to try to do all I Could, to better their Conditions"; Mary Jackson to James Hall, Oct. 19, 1849: "My Son Thomas has Grown to be quite a man and as I have a good many Kind folk in america that would come out to africa if they Could see any of my Children. . . . I have no doubt but what it will Be the means of a great many of the Coloured friends coming out of my neighbohood."

An extreme case was that of Stephen Smith, a blacksmith from St. Mary's County who had purchased his own freedom and acquired some real estate and personal property. Smith emigrated to Cape Palmas in 1837 on the brig *Baltimore*, leaving three or more children in bondage. He hoped that the sale of his property would pay to free them. In 1845 his property remained unsold and his children slaves. In the meantime he had remarried and started a new family, but his longing for lost family persisted. He received news that the master of one of his sons, held by a farmer near Chaptico in St. Mary's County, would sell at a discount if Smith came in person to buy him, and the settler resolved to go get him. The society sponsored his return to America, and Smith rode through southern Maryland with Rev. George Roberts, the society's traveling agent, to encourage emigration. Smith was instrumental in persuading his old friend James Lauder to move to Cape Palmas with his entire family. Lauder conducted a ferry across the Potomac River and owned several boats, land, and other property. Smith was unable to buy his son as promised, but a daughter was available, at the high price of $413. Lauder lent Smith the money, which he hoped to repay by selling his American holdings.

Soon after his return to Harper, the Lauder family pressed Smith for their money back. Smith had little property in Africa, and his income was hardly enough to pay the debt. At length, the Lauders sued and succeeded in depriving Smith of almost all his material possessions. Still, he pined for his family. In October, 1849, his wife wrote John Latrobe for help in recovering what little proceeds there had been from the sale of his property in St. Mary's County. She wrote, "I would like my husband to go on in the next trip the Packet makes and see about geting his sons, and the property left behind, and wish that you would make arrangements for him to come." She added, "I wish that you would make some inquiry about my two sons one I left with george Dorseys and one at Joseph Shamels St Marys."

The story of Steven Smith: S. Smith to George Roberts, Jan. 17, 1845; Thomas Lauder to James Hall, Jan. 23, 1846: sent a copy of Stephen Smith's note to James Lauder in the amount of $413 plus interest; Stephen Smith to John Niles, Jan. 23, 1846: reminded Niles of the circumstances of his debt and asked for help. Lauder's heirs had seized all of his property, and none of the money supposed to be forthcoming from the sale of his possessions in America had arrived; Stephen Smith to James Hall, Jan. 23, 1846, asked Hall to check the records of George Roberts to find whether he had in fact recovered any debts due him from individuals in St. Mary's County. He further asked that Hall use any such money to buy trade goods in Baltimore and send them to him at Cape Palmas; Stephen Smith to James Hall, Oct. 19, 1849: the matter of $150 left in the hands of Roberts was still unresolved, and he appealed again for help. The Lauder family had seized all of his possessions; Celia Ann Smith to John Latrobe, Oct. 20, 1849, appealed for help. Apparently the society had guaranteed James Lauder that he would be repaid for his assistance in buying Stephen Smith's young daughter; Celia Ann Smith to J. H. B. Latrobe, March 29, 1850, complained that Dr. Hall and Rev. George Roberts promised to buy her children and send them out to her. She begged for help, writing, "if you ever knew what it was to be seperated from you Children certainly you would Simpythise with me and Do all you can to Send them to me." *Maryland Colonization Journal*, n.s., 8:315–17.

[51] The remarriage of Hawkins: Thomas Jackson to J. H. B. Latrobe, Feb. 23, 1837; William Hawkins to J. H. B. Latrobe, April 27, 1838, reported that he has given up his American wife and remarried at Cape Palmas. He asked to come home to persuade his relatives to emigrate, without mentioning his first wife and child.

[52] Dr. S. F. McGill to James Hall, August 22, 1844, as published in *Maryland Colonization Journal*, n.s., 2:283.

[53] Census of 1852. The Census, completed on Nov. 1, 1852, appears very thorough on its face, but a careful examination reveals many points of uncertainty. I have used my best judgement in identifying household groupings, but Henry Hannon's entries were inconsistent. Moreover, the doubtful statements of age, already observed, make much demographic analysis suspect. My sense is that Hannon did not make a door-to-door canvass of the settlement. Rather settlers were ordered to make a return in person or through some neighborhood captain. Therefore, the actual population of the settlement was almost certainly considerably larger, but we have no way of knowing.

With this in mind, I have reluctantly included the available data concerning household composition, advising the reader that they are incomplete. I have also refrained from any questions involving age as it relates to the community's structure. The sample is small, and I find comparative statistical analysis of such numbers to be misleading in many instances, so I have left them out, save for the statement of mean household size.

[54] Census of 1852. Female household heads: Letters of female settlers describing their circumstances, including Rachel Harmon to James Hall, Jan. 24, 1846: her life in poverty, nearly blind, with a son too sick to work. She asked Hall to appeal to Baltimore Baptists to take up a collection for her.

Orphans and apprentices: J. W. Lugenbeel to James Hall, Frederick Co., Md., May 26, 1846, p. 3, noted that the Public Farm prefers to employ orphans and indigent children, providing them with schooling during part of the day.

The importance of marriage: Rachel Harmon to James Hall, Jan. 15, 1845, related that her husband had abandoned her, "Mr. Harmon does not live with me, or do any thing for me and I am getting so old I can do but little for myself." "Minutes of the Council during 1846," in Letterbook, 1846, MSCS, includes notes on the suit of Emanuel Davenport for divorce from his wife. Significantly, the case was heard by the council and not by the Court of Quarterly Sessions; J. B. Russwurm to James Hall, Nov. 22, 1849, commented disapprovingly on two current cases of infidelity, resulting in expulsion from church congregations and general shunning; John Russwurm to John Latrobe, April 26, 1849, p. 5, mentioned "increase of vice and immorality in the colony" which he attributed to "a great want of vital piety."

See also, Ezekiel Harrington to John Kennard, April 25, 1838, recounting disturbance in the Methodist church, when David James abused his wife then abandoned her. Hannah James to John Kennard, May 19, 1839: told the same story, adding that her husband was rumored to have returned to the United States, and commenting on her isolation and dependence on the charity of her neighbors.

[55] On the importance politeness, public morality and laws: J. B. Russwurm to Latrobe, Jan. 23, 1847, pp. 2–3 (Major Bolon fined twice for swearing in public), pp. 5–6, asked for spelling books, readers, and globes. "In a poor community like Cape Palmas every thing will depend. . . . the same path here in Africa." He added that settlers were clamoring to have the colonial laws printed, "for many can read print who can't read writing." The twenty-five copies issued years before were so highly prized that their owners would let no on else touch them. He stated that settlers would gladly pay to have a new edition; J. B. Bowen to James Hall, Jan. 26, 1847: "peple here fear Law in every shape and I do not know of but few instances where Law has been violated and they were thro ignorance, but now they are more enlightened and see *good* from *Evil.*" Dempsey Fletcher to James Hall, Nov. 8, 1847, p. 5; Thomas Jackson to the Board of Managers, Dec. 17, 1847: commented on his responsibility in exercising the "strong Arm of the law."; Petition of Citizens, April, 1849: An illustration of the institution of the public meeting and remonstrance, conducted repeatedly during the settlement's history. The petition in particular is couched in language that stresses the right and duty of citizens to make their feelings known for the benefit of the community. They began, "We whose names are underwritten, inhabitants of Maryland in Liberia, impressed with a deep sense of our duty, as Freemen, and aware that in a crisis of danger, no nerve should be left unexerted to promote and secure the public Weal. . . . In Petitioning to your Honerable Body, we are moved by natural, patriotic, and christian feelings, to pray for the removal of certain objects, which we earnestly beleive long since, have been, are now, impediments in rendering us comfortable. To set aside the sad and unpleasant feelings of despondency, which under existing circumstances nessarily arises, and according to the virtue of the priviledge; which the "*Law*" *guarantees* we as sufferers, are not timid to make known, emphatically, yet respectfully our need. *We* further remark, that a systematic arrangement of affairs, All, harmonizing in measures for the public good, and mutual confidence, is the ornament and strength of society, but when they disagrees the sky of prosperity is darkened; and the peace and happiness of the community interrupted. The

Laws and Regulations, ought to be in most respcts parallel with our circumstances; it should not demand no more of us, than we can honestly and honerably support. Good and wholesome laws, are the great and securable "Golden Band" around any country to enhance its interest, But when astringent though but a portion the whole are irksome. It is clear there fore, that what we now testify against, tends to destroy the sinews of government, nor is it difficult to discern its tendency, to sap the foundations of our hoped for comforts; which we expect in this our "Adopted Country" dear to us, because we Anticipate while being here, through the kind Providence of God, to enjoy "Sweet Liberty" in all its various branches, According to Law and Gospel." J. B. McGill to James Hall, Sept. 15, 1850, p. 3; Boston J. Drayton to J. H. B. Latrobe, April 10, 1851; Joshua H. Stewart to J. H. B. Latrobe, Jan. 7, 1854, pp. 5 and 7, wrote that although most settlers are illiterate, they were able to judge their leaders and vote responsibly.

[56] Civic organizations: Russwurm to Latrobe, Dec. 30, 1845, p. 2; William A. Prout to James Hall, April 24, 1848. *Maryland Colonization Journal*, n.s., 8:7, contains a description of the anniversary celebration of the "Russwurm Literary Association" with comments on the ideology of education. See also, William Prout to James Hall, April 24, 1848, MSCS, also published in *Maryland Colonization Journal*, n.s., 4:203.

[57] The agency's schools: S. F. McGill to J. H. B. Latrobe, Sept. 16, 1851, pp. 3–4, gives a succinct statement of the schools operating in the colony and the difficulties of finding competent teachers; Russwurm to James Hall, July 28, 1845: mentions the difficulties finding and keeping good teachers for the public schools. In 1845, Russwurm had hired a young settler to teach at the Ladies' School, but he was hardly competent, and so sick as to render him useless. The agent dismissed him after just a few months. At the same time, he experimented with new school formats, including a school for girls aged four to twelve; Russwurm to Latrobe, Dec. 30, 1845, pp. 1–2, mentions the brief employment of Phillip Gross and his subsequent efforts to open a girls' school in the Ladies' School. At the time there were two schools run by the agency, one each by the Methodists and Episcopalians. The Episcopal school was newly reopened, and Russwurm hoped that it would not be closed again at the first disagreement with the agency; Russwurm to James Hall, Oct. 25, 1845, p. 2, "For our schools, we need 12 dozen Gallaudets and Hooker's Spelling books and 12 dozen Testaments." Russwurm to Latrobe, Jan. 28, 1847, pp. 5–6; S. F. McGill to J. H. B. Latrobe, Nov. 6, 1848, p. 3; Russwurm to Latrobe, April 26, 1849, p. 5, "schools are under good discipline and the children are improving in all the elementary branches." "Summary of Schools in Maryland in Liberia," Oct. 17, 1849: Lists five day schools with a total of 120 students, and five Sunday schools, with 182 students.

[58] The importance of the church and ministers in everyday life should be evident to the reader. It parallels the importance of the churches in the settler community at Monrovia as well as back home in Maryland. See chapter 1, note 35.

[59] Methodist church: Dempsey Fletcher to James Hall, Nov. 8, 1847, p. 5, noted that two-thirds of settlers were Methodists; J. B. Russwurm, "Addenda for Report, Etc.," Oct. 23, 1849: Methodist Church had 210 communicants; operated two schools in the bush; had one formal mission station; Henry Hannon, "Report of the different School in the Colony . . . ," Oct. 17, 1849: found a day school run by Miss Johnson with twenty students, and Rev. Burns's Sunday school with seventy students.

[60] State of Methodist Church schools in 1852: Rev. A. F. Russell to Rev. John Seys, July 13, 1852: as printed in *Maryland Colonization Journal*, n.s., 6:297–98.

[61] John B. Russwurm to James Hall, Nov. 8, 1847, pp. 3–4, MSCS.

[62] Troubles with the Methodist school at Saurekah, 1846: J. B. Russwurm to J. H. B. Latrobe, Jan. 23, 1847, pp. 4–5, MSCS.

[63] Thomas Jackson restored to militia rank: "Minutes of the Council during 1846" (Session of May 14, 1846), in Letterbook 1846, MSCS.

[64] The Episcopal mission: J. B. Russwurm to James Hall, Oct. 1, 1847, pp. 2–3; J. B. Russwurm, "Addenda for Report, Etc.," Oct. 23, 1849; Henry Hannon, "Report of the different School in the Colony . . . ," Oct. 17, 1849: listed five schools — a day and Sunday school run by E. M. Thomson, a day and Sunday school run by Joseph to Gibson, and a Sunday school under charge of J. B. Dennis; R. H. Gibson to [James Hall], Sept. 10, 1850; S. F. McGill to James Hall, Sept. 15, 1850, pp. 2–3.

[65] Manual Labor High School at Mt. Vaughan: John Payne to Latrobe, Nov. 22, 1848; Russwurm to James Hall, Nov. 22, 1848, p. 2, MSCS.

[66] Controversies in the Episcopal Church: J. B. Russwurm to James Hall, Oct. 1, 1847, pp. 2–3; Randall Burkett, "Black Missionaries to Africa to 1865," typescript in Maryland Diocesan Archives, Baltimore, Maryland; Rev. Eli Stokes to Bishop W. R. Whittingham, March 21, 1850, MS in Maryland Diocesan Archives, Baltimore, Maryland; S. F. McGill to James Hall, Sept. 15 1850, pp. 2–3, MSCS.

[67] The Baptist Church: J. B. Russwurm, "Addenda for Report, etc.," Oct. 23, 1849; J. Drayton to J. H. B. Latrobe, April 10, 1851, p. 3, MSCS. Boston J. Drayton to J. H. B. Latrobe, April 10, 1851, p. 3, describes the Baptist church and school (*Maryland Colonization Journal*, 6:136).

[68] J. B. Russwurm, "Addenda for Report, Etc.," Oct. 23, 1849. William Howard to unidentified correspondent [probably James Hall], Sept. 22, 1851, MSCS.

[69] Henry Hannon to the Board of Managers, Oct. 21, 1844, MSCS.

[70] Thomas Gross to James Hall, March 30, 1851, pp. 1–2, MSCS.

[71] Distant government: W. A. Prout to J. H. B. Latrobe, Sept. 23, 1851, p. 3 and April 12, 1852, p. 1. For an example of settler suspiciousness of the distant government of Monrovia, see also p. 4 of the same letter.

[72] Rev. A. F. Russell to Rev. John Seys, July 13, 1852, as printed in *Maryland Colonization Journal*, n.s., 6:297–98.

[73] Samuel F. McGill to Henry B. Goodwin, March 15, 1845, pp. 1–3, MSCS.

[74] Opposition to colonization: Louis Filler, *Crusade Against Slavery: Friends, Foes, and Reforms, 1820–1860* (Algonac, Mich.: Reference Publications, Inc., 1986), pp. 36–40; Christopher Phillips, *Freedom's Port*, pp. 185–88, and 211–26; Whitman, *Price of Freedom*, pp. 143–45, 148–50.

Examples of the settler ideal of freedom, directed back at America: Mary Duncan to James Hall, Jan. 25, 1847; J. E. Moulton to Latrobe, Sept. 21, 1851, pp. 1–2, offered to come back to the United States to solicit emigrants around Cumberland, "should I Be Blessed to come in and Get a few poor Slaves from under their task masters I will then think I have done my part for the cause of freeing a part of my Race," MSCS.

[75] J. B. Russwurm to Latrobe, March 7, 1845, p. 2, MSCS. See Alexander Hance to John Kennard, July 6, 1838, for an expression of the ideal of freedom in biblical terms.

[76] Settler efforts to extend their culture among Africans: Russwurm, "Addenda for Report, Etc.," Oct. 23, 1849, pp. 1–2, stated that the colony and missions together have had a tremendous impact on Grebo culture. English has become the language of busi-

ness. Moreover, "in the vicinity of Cape Palmas and Half Cavally, the most casual observer can perceive something like the first steps in civilization. Many of the boys and young men can read and write. The education of young females is likely to effect great revolution in the course of years. As the rising sun dispels the mists and darkness of night, gladdens the heart of man and beast and instils new life into every tree and flower, so great is the change which civilization and Christianity are likely to effect on the pagan nations of this continent: through their influence nations now debased by the most bloody rites and superstitions are yet to be heralds in proclaiming these blessings by means of their Pauls, Cyprians and Tertullians, until the millions are redeemed and regenerated, and take their stand among the nations." Boston J. Drayton to J. H. B. Latrobe, April 10, 1851, p. 3, MSCS.

[77] Joshua Stewart to Moses Sheppard, March 14, 1844, MSCS.

[78] See chapter 9, which describes the behavior of the community in reaction to Parker's murder. See also, John Payne to J. H. B. Latrobe, Nov. 22, 1848, p. 2; S. F. McGill to J. H. B. Latrobe, Sept. 16, 1851, p. 4, MSCS.

19. *"The Invaluable Rights of Freemen"*

[1] S. F. McGill to Latrobe, April 12, 1852, p. 1, MSCS.

[2] S. F. McGill to Latrobe, July 12, 1852, p. 1, MSCS.

[3] S. F. McGill to Moses Sheppard, July, 1852: in Sheppard Papers, Swarthmore College.

[4] S. F. McGill to Latrobe, July 12, 1852, p. 1, MSCS.

[5] During their negotiations, McGill mentioned to Freeman that scientists had experimented with the poison on cats and found that it was lethal in all cases. "I asked the King if Cats were witches," he wrote wryly. "He expressed the greatest contempt for my ignorance, and declared that all Cats were witches and particularly Black Cats. 'Have you never heard them caterwauling at night,' enquired he imitating them admirably, 'then they are making witch strong.'"

[6] The agreement reads as follows:

> Articles of a treaty made and concluded in Harper, Cape Palmas the fifteenth day of June, in the year of our Lord one thousand, eight hundred and fifty-two, by Saml. F. McGill, Agent of the Maryland State Colonization Society and Governor of Maryland in Liberia, on the part of the American Colonists; and the King, and Headmen of the native towns and people of Cape Palmas, assembled in council, witnesseth:
>
> Whereas the native Africans of Cape Palmas have reason to apprehend serious and fatal affrays between themselves and the American Colonists, from the custom practised by the former of administering an infusion of the Bark of Sassy tree to individuals of their tribe accused of sorcery, and other crimes, whereby such as drink it, are frequently killed, and their bodies indecently exposed on the streets and roads of the American Colony: And whereas the American inhabitants of Cape Palmas, always express the greatest abhorrence to the custom, pronouncing it barbarous and inhuman, and often interfere to hinder and obstruct its operation, and have frequently rescued natives who were adjudged to trial by this ordeal;

and in one instance, recently, did rescue a native woman from which cause one of the colonists was seriously injured: and whereas the King and headmen of the Cape Palmas people are disposed to evince their disapprobation of this outrage on said colonist, to give satisfaction to the Governor for the same, and to guard against the possibility of similar complaints in future: And Whereas the Governor of Maryland in Liberia being anxious to promote the peace, prosperity and happiness of his native friends, and being determined to use every means in his power to suppress the heathenish and inhuman custom of forcing poison on persons charged with offences, which only exist and are originated by ignorance and superstition —

Therefore taking into consideration the foregoing premises, the following articles of treaty are entered into between the Agent of the Maryland State Colonization Society and Governor of Maryland in Liberia, and King Freeman and Headmen of the native towns of Cape Palmas:

Article 1. The King and headmen of Cape Palmas, the names of who are hereunto annexed, and their successors in office, in consideration of the premises above recited, and the covenants hereinafter contained to be performed on the part of the Governor of Maryland in Liberia, do hereby give to the Governor and to his successors in office, and to four other gentlemen of character and respectability to be named by him, the right to ask and demand the delivery of the persons of all or any native of their tribe living in Cape Palmas, who may hereafter be required to drink Sassy Bark infusion for sorcery and to demand and release from their hands any individual who may have been compelled to drink the same for sorcery at any moment before it proves fatal to life.

Article 2. It is agreed between the parties, that where natives are charged and proved guilty of Capital crimes, such as wilful murder, arson and the like, the penalty of which is death — the natives shall be permitted to administer "Sassy wood" without being interfered with, providing the criminal is not driven for execution along the streets and roads of the Colony.

Article 3. It is further agreed that no native, nor party of natives, shall never interfere to obstruct or hinder the rescue of any man or woman when it is being done by the authority of the Governor, or when it is being done by either of the four gentlemen who have been regularly appointed or by their successors, and that where the enmity or ill will of accusers may induce them to offer opposition to such rescue, the native Soldiers old and young bind themselves to aid and assist the Governor and his officers in their humane purposes.

Article 4. No American colonists other than those duly appointed, and whose appointment shall have been made known to the natives, shall ever attempt a rescue, without being called upon to aid and assist by one of the officers, who must be present.

In consideration of the above named privileges granted the Americans, we the King and Headmen hereby acknowledge the receipt of two pieces of Blue Baft, twenty bars Tobacco and two dozen wash Basins from the Governor of Maryland in Liberia.

IN TESTIMONY WHEREOF the Governor of Maryland in Liberia, and the King and Headmen whose names are hereunto annexed, being duly authorized, have hereunto set their hands and seals at the time and place above written.

King Pa Neemar X alias, King Freeman Dueh X
Baphro X Bodio of town Flabo Neh X
Toh X Bill Williams X
Simlah Ballah
Sabbar X
Saubo X Saml. F. McGill
Governor Md. Liberia

[7] S. F. McGill to the Gidu Commissioners, June 19, 1852, MSCS.

For present-day practice of gidu, see Moran, *Civilized Women,* pp. 38–40; also see United Nations Annual Reports of the Committee for Human Rights which regularly cites the practice in Maryland County and other parts of Liberia.

[8] King Freeman and Bill Williams to Latrobe and Hall, July 15, 1852, pp. 1–3, MSCS.

[9] S. F. McGill to Latrobe, July 12, 1852, p. 1, MSCS.

[10] *Maryland Colonization Journal,* n.s., 6:97, 161, 257, and 274ff. When the *Packet* returned in July, Hall sold her.

[11] *Maryland Colonization Journal,* n.s., 6:145, 161.

[12] Ibid., 6:276. James Hall did not learn of the loss of the *Ralph Cross* for several months. "Since our engagement in the business of fitting out expeditions to Liberia, we have never labored in so dense a fog as at the present time," he worried publicly in the October issue of the *Maryland Colonization Journal.* To fulfill contractual obligations, the company would have to pay to charter a vessel and then have to keep the *Ralph Cross* idle in port for several months before the next departure, scheduled for May, if in fact she was even afloat. Reluctantly, he contracted for the brig *Linda Stewart,* which sailed from Baltimore on November 20 with forty emigrants. At Norfolk, she picked up 175 more, bound for Monrovia.

When at last the directors of the company received news of the wreck of the *Ralph Cross,* they wondered whether the venture was worth continuing. Since *Liberia Packet's* first voyage in 1846, operations had been modestly successful. The stock yielded an average cash dividend of 10 percent per annum, but Hall and his associates were rather disappointed. They had undertaken the venture with the sanguine expectation that the Chesapeake and Liberia Trading Company would soon be wholly owned and operated by black people. Of $25,000 in capital stock, only $3,325 was in the hands of black investors, and about nine-tenths of that belonged to Liberians. Moreover, the company had never succeeded in hiring a black captain. The wreck of the *Ralph Cross* left the firm without any vessels. Hall commented in the *Journal,*

The present condition of the Company is therefore somewhat novel, it may be said to be out of business, and in a condition, if thought advisable, to wind up and discontinue operating. It is entirely solvent, able to pay all its liabilities of debts or stock, and have a small balance left, provided the insurance of the Ralph Cross is duly paid, which cannot be doubted. The question now occurs, what is to be done?

[13] S. F. McGill to Latrobe, July 12, 1852, p. 4, MSCS.

[14] S. F. McGill to Latrobe, April 12, 1852, MSCS.

[15] S. F. McGill to Moses Sheppard, April 13, 1852: in Sheppard Papers, Swarthmore College.

[16] When James Hall learned of the death of the old man later in the spring, he offered a eulogy in *Maryland Colonization Journal*, recalling their first meeting and the firm friendship they later developed. "Although he never changed his modes of life," Hall wrote, "yet he was gradually induced to appreciate the advantages of civilization, and became much interested in the affairs of the colony and died its fast friend."

[17] S. F. McGill to Latrobe, Jan. 28, 1853, pp. 4–5, MSCS.

[18] *Maryland Colonization Journal*, n.s., 6:374.

[19] S. F. McGill to Latrobe, Jan. 28, 1853, p. 5, MSCS.

[20] Report of an *ad hoc* committee, Nov. 11, 1852, and transcription of a letter from J. H. B. Latrobe to William Cassell and others of a committee, Baltimore, Nov. 20, 1852, in *Minutebook of the Executive Committee of the Maryland State Colonization Society, No. 4*, pp. 66–69. See also Latrobe's letter to W. A. Prout, Nov. 20, 1852, also in Minutebook No. 4, p. 76. Details of the Shirley's voyage: *Maryland Colonization Journal*, n.s., 6:273

[21] McGill to Latrobe, Jan. 28, 1853, pp. 1–2, MSCS.

[22] Nicholas Jackson to Latrobe, Feb. 4, 1853, MSCS.

[23] S. F. McGill to Hall, Jan. 30, 1853, pp. 1–2, MSCS.

[24] Election for constitutional convention: McGill to Latrobe, Feb. 9, 1853, pp. 1–2; McGill to Latrobe, Feb. 15, 1853, p. 1, MSCS.

[25] S. F. McGill to Latrobe, Feb. 15, 1853, p. 1, MSCS.

[26] Drafts of the Constitution and of the Declaration of Rights are preserved in the Letterbooks of the MSCS.

[27] S. F. McGill to Latrobe, Feb. 9, 1853, pp. 2–3, MSCS. See also, I. K. Sundiata, *Black Scandal: America and the Liberian Labor Crisis, 1929–1936* (Philadelphia: Institute for the Study of Human Issues, 1980).

[28] See I. K. Sundiata, *Black Scandal: America and the Liberian Labor Crisis, 1929–1936* (Philadelphia: Institute for the Study of Human Issues, 1980).

[29] Departure of the *Banshee*: *Maryland Colonization Journal*, n.s., 6:337.

[30] *Banshee* at Cape Palmas: McGill to Wm. F. Giles, June 27, 1853, p. 3; McGill to Hall, June 30, 1853, p. 1, MSCS.

[31] McGill to Hall, June 30, 1853, p. 4, MSCS.

[32] Departure of Prout and Cassell on *Shirley*: McGill to Hall, Aug. 30, 1853; McGill to whom it may concern, Sept. 2, 1853, both in MSCS.

[33] War at mouth of Cavally River: McGill to Hall, Aug. 30, 1853, p. 2; Treaty between the Grand Cavally and Barbo People, Sept. 1853; McGill to Hall, Sept. 10, 1853, all in MSCS.

[34] By way of explanation, the West African coast was occupied by an extremely complex matrix of ethnic groups, divided into tiny states. Within these states, there were often ethnic subdivisions. For instance, in a Grebo town there might well be enclaves of Fishmen, Kroomen, and bushmen, all of them more or less subject to the authority of their hosts. The Americans had much the same relationship with Gbenelu. The colonies of Fishmen who inhabited many towns had a reputation for aggressive behavior and maritime plunder. Like Greboes, they had a traditional history of migration to the ocean from some point in the bush about two centuries before the founding of Liberia. "They soon extended themselves up and down the coast," James Hall wrote of them,

> squatting down in the neighborhood of the beach towns of the different tribes, at first as dependents, getting their subsistence by supplying the native inhabitants with fish in exchange for grains, vegetables, and meat. Gradually they began to act as brokers between the trading vessels and their shore patrons, at the same time increasing their numbers until they equalled them, then suffering no traffic, except what should pass through their hands, retaining, of course, the lion's share, and ultimately making the rightful possessors of the soil their tributaries and dependents.

Fishmen had also actively assisted European slave traders in their dirty work, acting as factors on shore and assisting the transport of cargo across the surf. They bitterly opposed Liberia's efforts to thwart the business, which led to serious outbreaks of violence. See *Maryland Colonization Journal*, n.s., 6:146.

[35] Fishmen conquer Garroway, McGill's ineffectual response: McGill to Hall, Sept. 30, 1853; McGill to Hall, Jan. 10, 1854, both in MSCS.

[36] Treaty between the Grand Cavally and Barbo People, U.S.S. *Constitution,* off Cavally River, Sept. 6, 1853, MSCS.

[37] Traditionally, this ceremony of spewing water also included consumption of a morsel of human liver, which was dispensed with in this case.

[38] Second warship enforces peace at Cavally: *Maryland Colonization Journal*, n.s., 7:115ff, 185–86.

[39] Royal Navy attacks Tabou and other leeward towns: McGill to Hall, Aug. 30, 1853, p. 2; McGill to Hall, Sept. 10, 1853, p. 2; McGill to Hall, Jan. 10, 1854, p. 2, all in MSCS. See also an illustrated article in *London Illustrated News*, mid-1854.

20. *"The Poisenest Licquid"*

[1] The voyage of the *Shirley*: *Maryland Colonization Journal*, n.s., 7:97; Prout to Hall, Baltimore, Jan. 28, 1854, p. 2, MSCS.

[2] Negotiations for independence: McGill to Wm. F. Giles, June 27, 1853, p. 2, MSCS; McGill to the Constitutional Convention, with response, printed in *Maryland Colonization Journal*.

[3] W. A. Prout to Hall, Baltimore, Jan. 28, 1854, p. 2, MSCS.

[4] Return of Prout and Cassell to Harper: McGill to Charles Howard, May 13, 1854; D. R. Fletcher to Hall, May 17, 1854, MSCS.

[5] The constitutional convention convenes: McGill to C. Howard, May 13, 1854;

McGill to Hall, May 17, 1854, MSCS. McGill's comments on Prout's drunkeness: McGill to Hall, May 17, 1854, p. 2, MSCS.

[6] McGill strips Prout of office: McGill to Hall, May 17, 1854, p. 3, MSCS. Prout's defense of himself and McGill's slander to the Navy: Prout to Hall, May 18, 1854, MSCS.

[7] Simleh Ballah and others to the Board of Managers, May 12, 1854, p. 1, MSCS.

[8] S. F. McGill to Charles Howard, May 13, 1854, p. 2, MSCS.

[9] S. F. McGill to James Hall, May 17, 1854, p. 1, MSCS.

[10] Proceedings of the constitutional convention: McGill to Hall, May 17, 1854, pp. 2–3; Fletcher to Hall, May 17, 1854, both in MSCS. Prout stands for governor: Prout to Hall, June 12, 1854; McGill to Hall, Monrovia, June 17, 1854, p. 1, both in MSCS.

[11] Results of the election: Prout to Hall, June 12, 1854, p. 2; McGill to Hall, Monrovia, June 17, 1854, p. 1, both in MSCS.

[12] Prout's inaugural address, June 8, 1854, MSCS Letterbook.

[13] The independence day ceremonies: Prout to Hall, June 12, 1854; McGill to Hall, Monrovia, June 17, 1854, both in MSCS.

[14] S. F. McGill to Hall, Monrovia, June 17, 1854, p. 2, MSCS.

[15] W. Prout, Address to the Senate and House of Delegates, July 5, 1854, MSCS. The General Assembly's first act was to ratify independence, as Prout had advised them, though the language of the bill they approved differed in some minor points from the one he had offered, which hurt his feelings. Still, he signed the new law on July 12 without delay. They failed, however to appoint and send ambassadors to Monrovia.

[16] List of official appointments, July 11, 1854, MSCS Letterbook.

[17] William Prout to James Hall, July 13, 1854, MSCS.

[18] The society's archives are silent, and since letters seem usually to bring news of problems or misadventure, their absence is a sign of contentment.

[19] Prout to Hall, August 14, 1855, p. 1, MSCS.

[20] Fletcher to Hall, March 14, 1855, p. 2, MSCS.

[21] Prout to Hall, March 6, 1855, p. 2, MSCS.

[22] Wreck of the *Earl of Liverpool*: Prout to the Legislature, Aug. 7, 1855, pp. 2–3; Diplomatic Correspondence, Monrovia and Harper, June 18 to August 15, 1855, a transcript in MSCS.

[23] J. G. C. L. Newnham to Prout, Monrovia, June 18 1855: transcript in MSCS.

[24] Prout to Hall, Aug. 15, 1855, p. 2, MSCS.

[25] Misunderstanding following the decision: Newnham to Prout, July 14, 1855, transcript; Prout to Hall, Aug. 14, 1855, both in MSCS.

[26] Prout to Hall, July 6, 1855, p. 2, MSCS.

[27] Prout's opponents: Prout to Hall, Aug. 14, 1855, pp. 1–2; Prout to Hall, March 20, 1856, p. 2; Anthony Wood to Hall, March 24, 1856, p. 2, all in MSCS.

[28] Joshua H. Stewart to Hall, n.d. [probably Jan., 1855], p. 2, MSCS.

[29] Prout to Hall, Aug. 14, 1855, p. 2, MSCS.

[30] Thomas Fuller to John Seys, July 23, 1855, quoted in *Maryland Colonization Journal*, n.s., 8:106–7.

[31] W. A. Prout to the Legislature of Maryland in Liberia, August 7, 1855, MSCS.

[32] Prout to Hall, August 14, 1855, p. 2, MSCS.

[33] Ibid., March 20, 1856, pp. 4–5, MSCS.

[34] Ibid., p. 6, MSCS.

[35] Ibid., pp. 6–7, MSCS.

[36] The coup d'etat: Prout to Hall, March 20, 1856, pp. 8–10; Anthony Wood to Hall, March 24, 1856, pp. 1–2; J. T. Gibson to Hall, March 26, 1856, pp. 2–3, all in MSCS.

[37] Drayton consolidates his power: Prout to Hall, March 20, 1856, p. 10; Prout to Hall, June 24, 1856, pp. 1–2, both in MSCS.

[38] B. J. Drayton to Charles Howard, Oct. 21, 1856, pp. 1–2, MSCS.

21. *"The Diabolical Plot"*

[1] J. T. Gibson to James Hall, Dec. 27, 1855, MSCS.

[2] Ibid., March 26, 1856, p. 3, MSCS.

[3] Anthony Wood to James Hall, March 24, 1856, pp. 2–3, MSCS.

[4] William Prout to James Hall, June 24, 1856, MSCS.

[5] B. J. Drayton to Hall, April 24, 1856, pp. 1–2, MSCS.

[6] Ibid., May 30, 1856, pp. 1–2, MSCS.

[7] Origins of war: "Gov. Drayton's Statement, as to the Cause and history of the War between the Greboes and Colonists," Jan., 1857, pp. 1–2; B. J. Drayton to Hall, May 30, 1856, p. 1, both in MSCS.

[8] Outbreak of war: "Gov. Drayton's Statement," pp. 2–3; Wm. Prout to Hall, June 24, 1856, p. 3, both in MSCS.

[9] "Gov. Drayton's Statement", p. 3, MSCS.

[10] B. J. Drayton to Hall, May 30, 1856, pp. 1–2, MSCS.

[11] Election and results: W. Prout to James Hall, June 24, 1856, p. 2; Drayton to C. Howard, Oct. 21, 1856, p. 3, both in MSCS.

[12] Prout to Hall, June 24, 1856, p. 2, MSCS.

[13] *Maryland Colonization Journal*, n.s., 8:352.

[14] Ibid., 8:349.

[15] "Gov. Drayton's Statement," p. 4.

[16] Ibid.

[17] Ibid., pp. 4–5.

[18] Ibid., p. 6.

[19] The board's response to the coup d'etat: Address of President Charles Howard to the Citizens of Maryland in Liberia, July 29, 1856, in *Minutebook of the Executive Committee of the Maryland State Colonization Society, No. 4*, pp. 173–77.

There was no official action of the board of managers because of a lack of a quorum at the time of the news reaching Baltimore, until their meeting of Dec. 28, 1856. Then, Hall was about to sail for Africa on the *M.C. Stevens*. The board gave him full authority to sack any society employee who had participated in the coup d'etat (*Minutebook No. 4*, p. 172). See also, Charles Howard to Gov. Drayton, Baltimore, July 9, 1856, MSCS.

[20] B. J. Drayton to Charles Howard, Oct. 21, 1856, p. 4, MSCS.

[21] Rocktown accepts Liberal Compact: "Gov. Drayton's Statement," pp. 6–7; James Hall to C. Howard, Mesurado Roads, Feb. 3, 1857, p. 1, both in MSCS.

[22] "Gov. Drayton's Statement," p. 7.

[23] Ibid., pp. 7–8.

[24] Ibid., pp. 8–9.

[25] Ibid., pp. 9–10.

[26] Ibid., pp. 12–13.

[27] Morning of Dec. 22: "Gov. Drayton's Statement," pp. 13–14; J. Hall to C. Howard, Mesurado Roads, Feb. 3, 1857, p. 2; "Extracts from Letters of Bishop Payne, C. C. Hoffman, and R. Rambo, *Maryland Colonization Journal*, n.s., 8:338–39.

[28] "Gov. Drayton's Statement," p. 14.

[29] Outbreak of hostilities: "Gov. Drayton's Statement," p. 14; J. Hall to C. Howard, Mesurado Roads, Feb. 3, 1857, pp. 2–3, both in MSCS.

[30] Situation at end of first day: "Gov. Drayton's Statement," p. 14; J. Hall to C. Howard, Mesurado Roads, Feb. 3, 1857, p. 2; J. T. Gibson to J. Hall, Dec. 30, 1856, pp. 2–3, all in MSCS.

[31] J. T. Gibson to J. Hall, Dec. 30, 1856, p. 4, MSCS.

[32] Attack on Grahway: "Gov. Drayton's Statement," p. 15; J. T. Gibson to J. Hall, Dec. 30, 1856, p. 3; J. Hall to C. Howard, Mesurado Roads, Feb. 3, 1857, p. 2, all in MSCS.

[33] Destruction of Mt. Vaughan: J. T. Gibson to Hall, Dec. 30, 1856, p. 3; C. C. Hoffman to J. Hall, Jan. 8, 1857, p. 1, MSCS.

[34] S. F. McGill to C. Howard, Jan. 27, 1857, pp. 3–4, MSCS.

[35] Ibid., p. 4.

[36] Ibid., p. 1.

[37] Ibid., p. 3.

[38] Ibid., p. 2.

[39] Ibid., pp. 5–6.

[40] Drayton to Pres. Stephen A. Benson, Jan. 26, 1857, MSCS.

[41] S. F. McGill to C. Howard, Jan. 27 1857, MSCS.

[42] Ibid., p. 7.

[43] The *Stevens*: *Maryland Colonization Journal*, n.s., VIII, no. 19, Supplement. On Hall's reasons for visiting Africa, see especially, *Maryland Colonization Journal*, n.s., 9:82–85.

[44] *Maryland Colonization Journal*, n.s., 9:148.

[45] J. Hall to C. Howard, Mesurado Roads, Feb. 3, 1857, p. 1, MSCS.

[46] Ibid., p. 5.

[47] Ibid., pp. 7–9.

[48] Benson to Hall, Monrovia, Feb. 6, 1857, pp. 1–2, MSCS.
Related correspondence: Benson to the Legislature, Monrovia, Feb. 4, 1857; Hall to Benson, Feb. 4, 1857, both in MSCS.

[49] An Act of the Liberian Legislature, Feb. 7, 1857, copy enclosed with Benson to Hall, Feb. 8, 1857, MSCS.

[50] *Maryland Colonization Journal*, n.s., 9:161. Also, J. Hall to C. Howard, Mesurado Roads, Feb. 3, 1857, pp. 5–6, MSCS.

[51] *Maryland Colonization Journal*, n.s., 9:162–63.

[52] Hall's first contact with Drayton: J. B. Phillips to Hall, Feb. 16 1857; J. Hall to C. Howard, aboard *M.C. Stevens*, April 4, 1857, p. 2, both in MSCS.

[53] C. C. Hoffman to J. Hall, Feb. 16, 1857, MSCS.

[54] Drayton forced from power: J. Hall to C. Howard, Mesurado Roads, Feb. 3, 1857, pp. 7–9; J. J. Roberts to J. Hall, Monrovia, March 9, 1857, pp. 10–11; J. Hall to C. Howard, aboard *M.C. Stevens*, April 4, 1857, all in MSCS.

[55] Drayton to J. Hall, Feb. 17, 1857, MSCS.

[56] J. Hall to C. Howard, aboard *M.C. Stevens*, April 4, 1857, pp. 3–4, MSCS.

[57] *Maryland Colonization Journal*, n.s., 9:164.

[58] Agreement between Maryland and the Republic: J. J. Roberts to J. Hall, Monrovia, March 9, 1857; J. Hall to C. Howard, aboard *M.C. Stevens*, April 4, 1857, pp. 1–3, both in MSCS.

[59] B. J. Drayton to Hall, Feb. 20, 1857, MSCS.

[60] Roberts gets Greboes to table: J. Hall to C. Howard, aboard *M.C. Stevens*, April 4, 1857, pp. 4–5; J. J. Roberts to J. Hall, Monrovia, March 9, 1857, p. 2, both in MSCS.

[61] J. T. Gibson to G. W. S. Hall, Feb. 21, 1857, p. 2, MSCS.

[62] J. J. Roberts to J. Hall, Monrovia, March 9, 1857, pp. 3–4, MSCS.

[63] Ibid., pp. 9–10.
A special committee of the Board of Managers concluded likewise: "The conduct of Governor Drayton, in his relations with the native tribes, was, to say the least, rash and imprudent; and . . . the exercise on his part of a judicious discretion, would have saved his fellow-citizens from the calamities and dangers to which they have been exposed." *Maryland Colonization Journal*, n.s., 8:369.

[64] "Treaty between Greboes and the Government of Maryland in Liberia, Feb. 26, 1857," MSCS.

[65] Decision to unite with Liberia: J. T. Gibson to G. W. S. Hall, Feb. 21, 1857, p. 3; Drayton to C. Howard, March 8, 1857, pp. 1–2; J. J. Roberts to J. Hall, Monrovia, March 9, 1857, p. 11; J. Hall to C. Howard, aboard *M.C. Stevens*, April 4, 1857, pp. 5–6, all in MSCS.

[66] B. J. Drayton, "Proclamation," March 3, 1857, MSCS.

[67] "Maryland County": J. J. Roberts to J. Hall, Monrovia, March 9, 1857, pp. 11–12; J. Hall to C. Howard, aboard *M.C. Stevens*, April 4, 1857, pp. 6–7; S. A. Benson to J. Hall, April 18, 1857, p. 1, all in MSCS.

[68] *Maryland Colonization Journal*, n.s., 9:11–12.

Bibliography

MANUSCRIPT SOURCES

Records of the Maryland State Colonization Society, MS 571, Maryland Historical Society, Baltimore, Maryland.

Archives of the American Colonization Society, Library of Congress, Washington, D.C.

American Naval Records, Squadron Letters, National Archives, Washington, D.C.

Griswold, Benjamin. Letter to Prof. Goodrich, Feb. 5, 1842. Ford Collection, New York Public Library.

Latrobe, John H. B. Diary, Aug. 2, 1833–May 1, 1839, MS 1677, Maryland Historical Society.

McGill, Dr. Samuel F. Correspondence with Moses Sheppard. The Sheppard Papers, Friends' Historical Library, Swarthmore College.

Steele, Dr. Thomas Ramsay. Letters to his family in Ramsay-Steele Family Papers, MS 1769, Maryland Historical Society.

PRIMARY SOURCES (*firsthand accounts of Maryland, by participants*)

The African Repository. Washington, D.C.: American Colonization Society.

Africa's Luminary. Monrovia: John Seys, Methodist Mission.

Allen, William, and T. R. H. Thomson. *A Narrative of the Expedition . . . to the River Niger, in 1841.* 2 vols. London: R. Bentley, 1848.

Anonymous. "The Colony of Liberia," a series of articles published in *The Friend*, Vol. 2, 1829.

Anonymous. "Documents: Letters to the American Colonization Society." *Journal of Negro History*, 10 (1925): 156.

Anonymous. "Maryland in Liberia." *The African Repository*, 62, no. 4 (October, 1886): 111.

Armstrong, James E. *History of the Old Baltimore Conference, From the Planting of Methodism in 1773 to the Division of the Conference in 1857.* Baltimore: Privately printed, 1907.

Bridge, Horatio. *Personal Recollections of Nathaniel Hawthorne.* New York: Harper & Bros., 1893.

————. *Journal of an African Cruiser.* Repr. London: Dawsons, 1968.

Brittan, Harriet. *Scenes and Incidents of Every-day Life in Africa.* 1860; repr., Negro Universities Press, 1969.

Burton, Sir Richard F. *Wanderings in West Africa, From Liverpool to Fernando Po.* 2 vols. London: Tinsley Bros., 1863.

Buttikofer, J. *Reisebilder Aus Liberia.* 2 vols. Leyden: E. J. Brill, 1890.

Carnes, Joshua A. *Journal of a Voyage from Boston to the West Coast of Africa.* 1852; repr., Negro Universities Press, 1969.

Cowan, Rev. Alexander M. *Liberia as I Found It, in 1858.* Frankfort, Ky.: A. G. Hodges, 1858.

[Evans, Hugh Davey, and John H. B. Latrobe] *Laws of Maryland in Liberia.* 2nd ed. Baltimore: John D. Toy, 1847.

Fishel, L. H., and Benjamin Quarles, eds. *The Negro American: A Documentary History.* Atlanta: Scott, Foresman and Co., 1967.

Fuller, Thomas. *Journal of a Voyage to Liberia.* Baltimore: J. D. Toy, 1851.

Gurley, Ralph R. 31st Congress, 1st Session, Senate Ex. Doc. 75: *Report of the Secretary of State, Communicating the Report of Rev. R. R. Gurley, Who Was Recently Sent Out by the Government to Obtain Information in Respect to Liberia.* Washington, D.C.: Government Printing Office, 1850.

Hall, James. "Cape Palmas, Liberia." *The African Repository,* 60, no. 4 (October, 1884): 97–108.

————. "My First Visit to Liberia." *The African Repository,* 62, no. 4 (October, 1886): 97–107 and no. 5 (November, 1886): 6–7.

————. "Fishtown." *Maryland Colonization Journal,* n.s. 2:51.

————. *An Address to the Free People of Color of the State of Maryland.* Baltimore: John D. Toy, 1859.

Hening, E. F. *History of the African Mission of the Protestant Episcopal Church in the United States, with Memoirs of Deceased Missionaries, and Notices of Native Customs.* New York: Stanford and Swords, 1850.

Kelly, Rev. John. "The Mission to Liberia: Diary of the Rev. John Kelly." *Historical Records and Studies,* 14 (1920): 120–53.

Laird, MacGregor, and R. A. K. Oldfield. *Narrative of an Expedition into the Interior of Africa, by the River Niger, in the Steam-vessels Quorrah and Alburkah, in 1832, 1833, and 1834.* 2 vols. London: R. Bentley, 1837.

Latrobe, John H. B. *Maryland in Liberia: A History of the Colony Planted by the Maryland State Colonization Society Under the Auspices of the State of Mary-*

land, U.S. at Cape Palmas on the South-West Coast of Africa, 1833–1853. Baltimore: Maryland Historical Society, 1885.

————. "Cape Palmas, Liberia." *The African Repository*, 61, no. 1 (January 1885): 1–8.

————. "Dr. James Hall." *The African Repository*, 65, no. 4 (October 1889): 117–19.

Lynch, Capt. William F. *Report to the U.S. Navy Department in Relation to His Mission to the Coast of Africa*. Washington: Government Printing Office, 1853.

"Marposo." "Battle of Grand Berribe." *The United Service*, September 1882, pp. 294–97.

Maryland Colonization Journal. Baltimore: Maryland State Colonization Society.

The Missionary Herald: Containing the Proceedings at Large of the American Board of Commissioners for Foreign Missions, with a General View of Other Benevolent Operations. Boston: American Board of Commissioners for Foreign Missions.

Payne, Rev. John, ed. *The Cavalla Messenger*. Half Cavally, Maryland in Liberia: Episcopal Mission Press.

————. *Grebo Konah Ah Te; Or, History of the Greboes*. New York: Edward D. Jenkins, 1860.

Rockwell, Charles. *Sketches of Foreign Travel . . .* Boston: Tappan & Dennett, 1842.

Scott, Anna Maria. *Day-Dawn in Africa; or, Progress of the Prot. Epis. Mission at Cape Palmas, West Africa*. New York: Protestant Episcopal Society for the Promotion of Evangelical Knowledge, 1858.

The Spirit of Missions. New York: Protestant Episcopal Church of the United States of America.

State of Maryland, General Assembly. *Laws of Maryland, 1831*. Annapolis, Md.: n.p., 1832.

U.S. Senate. *28th Congress, 2nd Session, Public Document #150: "Information Relative to the Operations of the United States Squadron on the West Coast of Africa, the Condition of the American Colonies There, and the Commerce of the United States Therewith."* Washington, D.C.: Government Printing Office, 1845.

Wilson, Rev. John Leighton. *Western Africa: Its History, Condition, and Prospects*. New York: Harper and Bros., 1856.

Woodson, Carter G. *The Mind of the Negro as Reflected in Letters Written During the Crisis, 1800–1860.* 1926; repr. New York: Russell & Russell, 1969.

Wynkoop, Stephen R., and John L. Wilson. "Western Africa. Extracts from the Journals of Messrs. Wilson and Wynkoop." *The Missionary Herald*, vol. 30, pp. 212–19, 288ff., and 337ff.

SECONDARY SOURCES (about participants and events in Maryland in Liberia)

Anonymous. *Traditional History and Folklore of the Glebo Tribe.* Monrovia: Bureau of Folkways, 1957.

Alexander, Archibald. *A History of Colonization on the Western Coast of Africa.* 2nd Ed. Philadelphia: W. S. Martien, 1849.

Booth, Alan R. "The United States African Squadron 1843–1861." In Jeffrey Butler, ed., *Boston University Papers in African History, Vol. I.* Boston: Boston University Press, 1964.

Campbell, Penelope. *Maryland in Africa: The Maryland State Colonization Society, 1831–1857.* Urbana: University of Illinois Press, 1971.

———. "Medical Education for an African Colonist." *Maryland Historical Magazine*, 65 (1970): 130–37.

Cassell, Dr. C. Abayomi. *Liberia: History of the First African Republic.* New York: Fountainhead Publishers, 1970.

Cleaveland, Nehemiah, and Alphaeus S. Packard. *History of Bowdoin College.* Boston: James R. Osgood and Co., 1892.

Davis, J. P., ed. *The American Negro Reference Book.* Englewood Cliffs, N.J.: Prentice-Hall, 1967.

Foner, Philip S. *History of Black Americans.* Vol. II. Westport, Conn.: Greenwood Press, 1983.

Foote, Commodore Andrew H. *Africa and the American Flag.* New York: D. Appleton & Co., 1854.

Fyfe, Christopher. *A History of Sierra Leone.* London: Oxford University Press, 1963.

Graham, Leroy. *Baltimore: The Nineteenth Century Black Capital.* Lanham, Md.: University Press of America, 1982.

Gross, Bella. "Freedom's Journal and the Rights of All." *Journal of Negro History*, 17 (1932).

Holsoe, Svend. "A Study of Relations Between Settlers and Indigenous Peoples in Western Liberia, 1821–1847." *African Historical Studies*, Vol. IV, pp. 346–52.

Hopkins, A. G. *An Economic History of West Africa.* New York: Columbia University Press, 1973.

Liebenow, J. Gus. *Liberia: The Evolution of Privilege.* Ithaca: Cornell University Press, 1969.

―――. *Liberia: The Quest for Democracy.* Bloomington: Indiana University Press, 1987.

Lofton, John. *Denmark Vesey's Revolt: The Slave Plot That Lit a Fuse to Fort Sumter.* Kent, Oh.: Kent State University Press, 1983.

Martin, Jane Jackson. "The Dual Legacy: Government Authority and Mission Influence Among the Glebo of Eastern Liberia, 1834–1910." Unpublished Ph.D. diss., Boston University, 1968.

Maugham, Reginald C. F. *The Republic of Liberia.* New York: Charles Scribner's Sons, 1920.

McDaniel, George W. *Hearth and Home: Preserving a People's Culture.* Philadelphia: Temple University Press, 1982.

Morison, Samuel Eliot. *"Old Bruin": Commodore Matthew C. Perry, 1794–1858 . . .* Boston: Little, Brown, and Co., 1967.

Moses, Wilson J. *Alexander Crummell: A Study of Civilization and Discontent.* New York: Oxford University Press, 1989.

Phillips, Christopher. *Freedom's Port: The African-American Community of Baltimore, 1790–1860.* Urbana: University of Illinois Press, 1997.

Rigsby, Gregory U. *Alexander Crummell: Pioneer in Nineteenth-century Panafrican Thought; Contributions in Afro-american and African Studies, No. 101.* New York: Greenwood Press, 1987.

Robertson, George. *Notes on Africa.* London: 1819.

Sawyer, Amos. *The Emergence of Autocracy in Liberia: Tragedy and Challenge.* San Francisco: Institute for Contemporary Studies, 1992.

Semmes, John E. *John H. B. Latrobe and His Times, 1803–1891.* Baltimore: Norman, Remington, 1919.

Staudenraus, P. J. *The American Colonization Movement, 1816–1865.* New York: Columbia University Press, 1961.

Ulman, Victor. *Martin R. Delany: The Beginnings of Black Nationalism.* Boston: Beacon Press, 1971.

Wilson, James Grant, and John Fiske, eds. *Appleton's Cyclopaedia of American Biography.* Six Volumes. New York: D. Appleton & Co., 1888.

Tertiary Sources *(Mentioned in text or concerning issues explored in the work)*

Allen, W. *The African Husbandman.* New York: Barnes and Noble, 1965.

American Colonization Society. *Tenth Annual Report.* Washington: American Colonization Society, 1827.

———. *Thirteenth Annual Report* Washington: ACS, 1830.

———. *Fourteenth Annual Report* Washington: ACS, 1831.

Andah, B. W. "Processes of Coastal Evolution in West Africa During the Quaternary," in B. K. Schwartz, Jr. and R. E. Dumett, eds. *West African Culture Dynamics: Archaeological and Historical Perspectives.* The Hague: Mouton Publishers, 1980.

Berlin, Ira. *Many Thousands Gone: The First Two Centuries of Slavery in North America.* Cambridge: The Belknap Press of the Harvard University Press, 1998.

Beyan, Amos J. *The American Colonization Society and the Creation of the Liberian State: A Historical Perspective, 1822–1900.* Lanham, Md.: University Press of America, 1991.

The Holy Bible, Containing the Old and New Testaments . . . King James Edition., The Book of Joshua.

Blackstone, Samuel. *Commentaries Upon the Common Law of England,* Book IV.

Blyden, Edward Wilmot. *Christianity, Islam, and the Negro Race.* London: W. B. Whittingham & Co., 1887.

Breitborde, L. B. "City, Countryside, and Kru Ethnicity." *Africa,* Vol. 61, pp. 186–201.

Brooks, George. *The Kru Mariner in the Nineteenth Century: A Historical Compendium. Liberian Studies Monograph Series, No. 1.* Newark, Del.: Liberian Studies Association, 1972.

Christy, David. *Ethiopia: Her Gloom and Glory.* 1859; repr., New York: Negro Universities Press, 1969.

Crummell, Alexander. *The Future of Africa.* New York: C. Scribner, 1862.

Curtin, Philip D. *The Image of Africa: British Ideals and Action, 1780–1850.* Madison: University of Wisconsin Press, 1964.

Dubois, William E. B. *The Souls of Black Folk, Essays and Sketches.* 4th ed. Chicago: A. C. McClurg, 1904.

Filler, Louis. *Crusade Against Slavery: Friends, Foes, and Reforms, 1820–1860.* Algonac, Mich.: Reference Publications, Inc., 1986.

Fitchett, E. Horace. "The Traditions of the Free Negro in Charleston, South Carolina." *Journal of Negro History*, 25 (1940): 142, 147.

Garrison, William Lloyd, ed. *The Liberator.* Boston, Mass.

Genovese, Eugene. *A Consuming Fire: The Fall of the Confederacy in the White Christian South* Athens: University of Georgia Press, 1998.

Gould, Stephen J. *The Mismeasure of Man.* New York: W. W. Norton & Co., 1981.

Harris, Sheldon H. *Paul Cuffe: Black America and the African Return.* New York: Simon and Schuster, 1972.

Heuman, Gad J. *Between Black and White: Race, Politics, and the Free Coloreds in Jamaica, 1792–1865.* Westport, Conn.: Greenwood Press, 1981.

Hilliard, S. B. *Hog Meat and Hoe Cake: Food Supply in the Old South, 1840–1860.* Urbana: University of Illinois Press, 1972.

Jefferson, Thomas. *Notes on the State of Virginia.* Baltimore: W. Mechin, 1800.

Johnson, Charles S. *Bitter Canaan: The Story of the Negro Republic.* New Brunswick, N.J.: Transaction Books, 1987.

Johnson, Oliver. *William Lloyd Garrison and His Times; Or, Sketches of the Anti-slavery Movement in America, and of the Man Who Was Its Founder and Moral Leader.* Boston: B. B. Russell and Co., 1880.

Johnston, Sir Harry H. *Liberia.* 2 vols. New York: Dodd, Mead and Co, 1906. Repr. Negro Universities Press, 1969.

Kinmont, Alexander. *Twelve Lectures on the Natural History of Man.* Cincinnati: U. P. James, 1839.

Koch, Adrienne. "Two Charlestonians in Search of Truth: The Grimke Brothers." *South Carolina Historical Magazine*, 64 (1963): 159–70.

Krieger, Kurt. *Westafrikanische Plastik.* Band I. Berlin: Museum Fur Volkerkunde, 1965.

Lerner, Gerda. *The Grimke Sisters from South Carolina: Rebels Against Slavery.* Boston: Houghton Mifflin, 1967.

Long, Edward. *The History of Jamaica.* 1774; repr. London: Frank Cass & Co., 1970.

Lundy, Benjamin, ed. *The Genius of Universal Emancipation.* Baltimore: The Editor.

Massing, Andreas. *The Economic Anthropology of the Kru west Africa.* Wiesbaden: Franz Steiner Verlag, 1980.

McEvoy, Frederick D. "Understanding Ethnic Realities among the Grebo and Kru Peoples of West Africa." *Africa*, Vol. 47, pp. 62–79.

Meek, C. K. *Land Law and Custom in the Colonies*. 2nd ed. London: Frank Cass, 1968.

Merrill, Walter M., ed. *Against Wind and Tide: A Biography of William Lloyd Garrison*. Cambridge: Harvard University Press, 1963.

————., ed. *The Letters of William Lloyd Garrison. Vol. I: "I Will Be Heard!"* Cambridge: Belknap Division of Harvard University Press, 1971.

Miller, Genevieve. "A Nineteenth Century Medical School: Washington University of Baltimore." *Bulletin of the History of Medicine*, 14 (1940): 14–17.

Moran, Mary H. *Civilized Women: Gender and Prestige in Southeastern Liberia*. Ithaca: Cornell University Press, 1990.

Nott, J. C., and George R. Gliddon. *Types of Mankind; Or, Ethnological Researches Based Upon the Ancient Monuments, Paintings, Sculptures, and Crania of Races; And Upon Their Natural, Geographical, Philological, and Biblical History*. Philadelphia: Lippincott, Grambo, & Co., 1854.

Osagie, Iyonolu Folayan. *The Amistad Revolt: Memory, Slavery, and the Politics of Identity in the United States and Sierra Leone*. Athens: University of Georgia Press, 2000.

Oyenga, V. A. *Agriculture in Nigeria, An Introduction*. Rome: FAO-UN, 1967.

Parsons, Kenneth. "Land Reform and Agricultural Development," in Parsons, R. J. Penn, and P. M. Raup, eds. *Land Tenure*. Madison: University of Wisconsin Press, 1956.

Pollock, N. C. *Regional Geography of Africa*. London: University of London, 1968.

Porter, P. W. "Liberia." *World Atlas of Agriculture*. 4:293. Novara, Italy: Istituto Geographico de Agostini, 1976.

Rankin, F. H. *The White Man's Grave*. London: 1836.

Reade, Rev. Hollis. *The Negro Problem Solved; Or, Africa as She Was, as She Is, and as She Shall Be, Her Curse and Her Cure*. New York: A. A. Constantine, 1864.

Reed, W. *Reconnaissance Soil Survey of Liberia*. Agriculture Information Bulletin No. 66. Washington: U.S. Department of Agriculture, Office of Foreign Agricultural Relations and U.S. Dept. of State Technical Co-operation Administration, 1951.

Salvador, George Arnold. *Paul Cuffe, The Black Yankee, 1759–1817*. New Bedford: Reynolds-De Walt Printing, 1969.

Schick, Tom W. *Behold the Promised Land: A History of Afro-American Settler Society in Nineteenth-Century Liberia*. Baltimore: Johns Hopkins University Press, 1987.

Schnell, R. *Plantes Alimentaires Et Vie Agricole De L'afrique Noire: Essai De Phytogeographie Alimentaire.* Paris: Editions Larose, 1957.

Smith, James W. *Sojourners in Search of Freedom: The Settlement of Liberia by Black Americans.* Lanham, Md.: University Press of America, 1987.

Stewart, John. *An Account of Jamaica.* 1808, repr., Freeport, N.Y.: Books for Libraries Press, 1971.

Stockton, Robert Field. *The Life and Speeches of Robert Field Stockton.* New York: 1856.

Tate, G. H. H. "The Lower Cavally River, West Africa." *The Geographical Review,* 32 (1947): 574–76.

Thirgood, J. V. "Land-Use Problems of the Liberian Coastal Savannah." *The Commonwealth Forestry Review,* 44 no. 1.

Thompson, Robert Farris. *Flash of the Spirit: African and Afro-American Art and Philosophy* New York: Vintage Books Division of Random House, 1984.

U.S. Commissioner of Indian Affairs. *Treaties Between the United States of America, and the Several Indian Tribes, from 1778 to 1837.* 1837; repr., Millwood, N.Y.: Kraus Reprint Co., 1975.

United Nations, Food and Agriculture Organization. *Report on the Agro-ecological Zones Project. Vol. I: Methodology and Results for Africa.* Rome: FAO-UN, 1978.

Van Wambeke, A. *Management Properties of Ferralsols.* Rome: FAO-UN, 1974.

Wadstrom, C. B. *An Essay Upon Colonization, Particularly Applied to the Western Coast of Africa, With Some Free Thoughts on Cultivation and Commerce,* . . . Two Parts London: For Many, 1794–95.

Walker, David. *Appeal in Four Articles; Together with a Preamble to the Colored Citizens of the World, But in Particular, and Very Expressly, to Those of the United States of America.* Boston, 1829.

Wallace, David D. *South Carolina: A Short History, 1520–1948.* Chapel Hill: University of North Carolina Press, 1951.

West, Richard. *Back to Africa: A History of Sierra Leone and Liberia.* New York: Holt, Rhinehart & Winston, 1971.

Wood, Peter H. *Black Majority: Negroes in Colonial South Carolina from 1670 Through the Stono Rebellion.* New York: W. W. Norton and Co., 1975.

Wright, James M. *The Free Negro in Maryland, 1634–1860.* New York: Columbia University Press, 1921.

Index

Numbers followed by n indicate notes.